ArtScroll Mishnah Series®

A rabbinic commentary to the Six Orders of the Mishnah

Rabbis Nosson Scherman / Meir Zlotowitz

General Editors

the mishnah

ARTSCROLL MISHNAH SERIES / A NEW TRANSLATION WITH A COMMENTARY **YAD AVRAHAM** ANTHOLOGIZED FROM TALMUDIC SOURCES AND CLASSIC COMMENTATORS.

Published by

Mesorah Publications, ltd

THE COMMENTARY HAS BEEN NAMED **YAD AVRAHAM**
AS AN EVERLASTING MEMORIAL AND SOURCE OF MERIT
FOR THE *NESHAMAH* OF
אברהם יוסף ע״ה בן הר״ר אליעזר הכהן גליק נ״י
AVRAHAM YOSEF GLICK ע״ה
WHOSE LIFE WAS CUT SHORT ON 3 TEVES, 5735

Inaugural Volume
FIRST EDITION
First Impression . . . September 1979
SECOND EDITION
First Impression . . . May 1981
Second Impression . . . March 1987
Third Impression . . . November 1989
Fourth Impression . . . October 1993
Fifth Impression . . . April 1994
Sixth Impression . . . February 1996
Seventh Impression . . . April 1998

Published and Distributed by
MESORAH PUBLICATIONS, Ltd.
4401 Second Avenue
Brooklyn, New York 11232

Distributed in Europe by
J. LEHMANN HEBREW BOOKSELLERS
20 Cambridge Terrace
Gateshead, Tyne and Wear
England NE8 1RP

Distributed in Israel by
SIFRIATI / A. GITLER – BOOKS
10 Hashomer Street
Bnei Brak 51361

Distributed in Australia & New Zealand by
GOLDS BOOK & GIFT CO.
36 William Street
Balaclava 3183, Vic., Australia

Distributed in South Africa by
KOLLEL BOOKSHOP
Shop 8A Norwood Hypermarket
Norwood 2196, Johannesburg, South Africa

THE ARTSCROLL MISHNAH SERIES ®
SEDER MOED Vol. IV; *TAANIS / MEGILLAH / MOED KATAN / CHAGIGAH*

ISBN
0-89906-258-X (hard cover)
0-89906-259-8 (paperback)

Typography by Compuscribe at ArtScroll Studios, Ltd.
4401 Second Avenue / Brooklyn, NY 11232 / (718) 921-9000

Printed in the United States of America by Moriah Offset
Bound by Sefercraft, Quality Bookbinders, Ltd. Brooklyn, N.Y.

◆§ Seder Moed Vol. IV:

Taanis/תענית

Megillah/מגילה

Moed Katan/מועד קטן

Chagigah/חגיגה

The Publishers are grateful to
YESHIVA TORAH VODAATH AND MESIVTA
for their efforts in the publication of the
ARTSCROLL MISHNAH SERIES

מוקדש לזכר נשמת

מו״ר הרה״ג

ר׳ גדליה הלוי שארר זצ״ל

ראש ישיבת תורה ודעת

ובית מדרש עליון

נפטר לעולמו ז׳ תמוז תשל״ט

This inaugural volume of the ArtScroll Mishnah Series is dedicated to the memory of

Hagaon Harav
Gedalia Halevi Schorr זצ״ל

Rosh Hayeshivah of Mesivta Torah Vodaath and Beth Medrash Elyon

He breathed the soul of Torah into America, planting the seed of future greatness

ת נ צ ב״ה

הסכמה

RABBI MOSES FEINSTEIN
455 F. D. R. DRIVE
NEW YORK, N. Y. 10002

ORegon 7-1222

משה פיינשטיין
ר״מ תפארת ירושלים
בנוא יארק

בע״ה

הנה ידידי הרב הגאון ר׳ אברהם יוסף ראזענבערג שליט״א אשר היה מתלמידי החשובים ביותר וגם הרביץ תורה בכמה ישיבות ואצלינו בישיבתנו בסטעטן איילאנד, ובזמן האחרון הוא מתעסק בתרגום ספרי קודש ללשון אנגלית המדוברת ומובנת לבני מדינה זו, וכבר איתמחי גברא בענין תרגום לאנגלית וכעת תרגם משניות לשפת אנגלית וגם לקוטים מדברי רבותינו מפרשי משניות על כל משנה ומשנה בערך, והוא לתועלת גדול להרבה אינשי ממדינה זו שלא התרגלו מילדותם ללמוד המשנה וגם יש הרבה שבעזר השי״ת התקרבו לתורה ויראת שמים כשכבר נתגדלו ורוצים ללמוד שיוכלו ללמוד משניות בנקל בשפה המורגלת להם, שהוא ממזכי הרבים בלמוד משניות וזכותו גדול. ואני מברכו שיצליחהו השי״ת בחבורו זה. וגם אני מברך את חברת ארטסקרול אשר תחת הנהלת הרב הנכבד ידידי מוהר״ר מאיר יעקב בן ידידי הגאון ר׳ אהרן שליט״א זלאטאוויץ אשר הוציאו כבר הרבה חבורים חשובים לזכות את הרבים וכעת הם מוציאים לאור את המשניות הנ״ל.

ועל זה באתי על החתום בז׳ אדר תשל״ט בנוא יארק.

נאום משה פיינשטיין

מכתב ברכה

יעקב קמנצקי
RABBI J. KAMENECKI
38 SADDLE RIVER ROAD
MONSEY, NEW YORK 10952

בע"ה

יום ה׳ ערב חג השבועות תשל"ס, פה מאנסי.

כבוד הרבני איש החסד שוע ונדיב מוקיר רבנן מר אלעזר נ"י גליק שלו׳ וברכת כל טוב.

מה מאד שמחתי בהודעי כי כבודו רכש לעצמו הזכות שייקרא ע"ש בנו המנוח הפירוש מבואר על כל ששת סדרי משנה ע"י "ארטסקראל" והנה חברה זו יצאה לה מוניטין בפירושה על תנ"ך, והנה נקוה שכשם שהצליחה בתורה שבכתב כן תצליח בתורה שבע"פ. ובהיות שאותיות "משנה" הן כאותיות "נשמה" לפיכך טוב עשה בכוונתו לעשות זאת לעילוי נשמת בנו המנוח אברהם יוסף ע"ה, ומאד מתאים השם "יד אברהם" לזה הפירוש, כדמצינו במקרא (ש"ב י"ח) כי אמר אין לי בן בעבור הזכיר שמי וגו׳. ואין לך דבר גדול מזה להפיץ ידיעת תורה שבע"פ בקרב אחינו שאינם רגילים בלשון הקדש. וד׳ הטוב יהי׳ בעזרו ויוכל לברך על המוגמר. וירוה רוב נחת מכל אשר אתו כנפש מברכו.

יעקב קמנצקי

מכתב ברכה

ישיבת טלז
קרית טלז-סטון
ירושלים

YESHIVAT TELSHE
Kiryat Telshe Stone
Jerusalem, Israel

בע״ה — ד׳ בהעלותך — לבני א״י, תשל״ט — פה קרית טלז, באה״ק

מע״כ ידידי האהובים הרב ר׳ מאיר והרב ר׳ נתן, נר״ו, שלום וברכה נצח!

אחדשה״ט באהבה ויקר,

לשמחה רבה היא לי להודע שהרחבתם גדול עבודתכם בקודש לתורה שבע״פ, בהוצאת המשנה בתרגום וביאור באנגלית, וראשית עבודתכם במס׳ מגילה.

אני תקוה שתשימו לב שיצאו הדברים מתוקנים מנקודת ההלכה, וחזקה עליכם שתוציאו דבר נאה ומתוקן.

בפנותכם לתורה שבע״פ יפתח אופק חדש בתורת ה׳ לאלה שקשה עליהם ללמוד הדברים במקורם, ואלה שכבר נתעשרו מעבודתכם במגילת אסתר יכנסו עתה לטרקלין חדש וישמשו להם הדברים דחף ללימוד המשנה, וגדול יהי׳ שכרכם.

יהא ה׳ בעזרכם בהוספת טבעת חדשה באותה שלשלת זהב של הפצת תורת ה׳ להמוני עם לקרב לב ישראל לאבינו שבשמים בתורה ואמונה טהורה.

אוהבכם מלונ״ח,
מרדכי

מכתב ברכה

RABBI SHNEUR KOTLER
BETH MEDRASH GOVOHA
LAKEWOOD, N. J.

בע״ה

שניאור קוטלר
בית מדרש גבוה
לייקוואוד, נ. דז.

בשורת התרחבות עבודתם הגדולה של סגל חבורת ,,ארטסקרול״, המעתיקים ומפרשים, לתחומי התושבע״פ, לשים אלה המשפטים לפני הציבור כשלחן ערוך ומוכן לאכול לפני האדם [ל׳ רש״י], ולשימה בפיהם — לפתוח אוצרות בשנות בצורת ולהשמיעם בכל לשון שהם שומעים — מבשרת צבא רב לתורה ולימודה [ע׳ תהלים ס״ח י״ב בתרגום יונתן], והיא מאותות ההתעוררות ללימוד התורה, וזאת התעודה על התנוצצות קיום ההבטחה ,,כי לא תשכח מפי זרעו״. אשרי הזוכים להיות בין שלוחי ההשגחה לקיומה וביצועה.

יה״ר כי תצליח מלאכת שמים בידם, ויזכו ללמוד וללמד ולשמור מסורת הקבלה כי בהרקת המים החיים מכלי אל כלי תשתמר חיותם, יעמוד טעמם בם וריחם לא נמר. [וע׳ משאחז״ל בכ״מ ושמרתם זו משנה — וע׳ חי׳ מרן רי״ז הלוי עה״ת בפ׳ ואתחנן] ותהי׳ משנתם שלמה וברורה, ישמחו בעבודתם חברים ותלמידים, ,,ישוטטו רבים ותרבה הדעת״, עד יקויים ,,אז אהפוך אל העמים שפה ברורה וגו׳ ״ [צפני׳ ג׳ ט׳, עי׳ פי׳ אבן עזרא ומצודת דוד שם].

ונזכה כולנו לראות בהתכנסות הגליות בזכות המשניות כל׳ חז״ל עפ״י הכתוב ,,גם כי יתנו בגוים עתה אקבצם״, בגאולה השלמה• בב״א.

הכו״ח לכבוד התורה, יום ו׳ עש״ק לס׳ ,,ויוצא פרח ויצץ ציץ ויגמול שקדים״, ד׳ תמוז התשל״ט

יוסף חיים שניאור קוטלר
בלאאמו״ר הגר״א זצוק״ל

מכתב ברכה

ב״ה

ישיבה דפילאדעלפיא

ב״ה

לכבוד ידידי וידיד ישיבתנו, מהראשונים לכל דבר שבקדושה
הרבני הנדיב המפורסם ר׳ אליעזר הכהן גליק נ״י
אחדשה״ה באהבה,

בשורה טובה שמעתי שכב׳ מצא את המקום המתאים לעשות יד ושם להנציח זכרו של בנו **אברהם יוסף ע״ה** שנקטף בנעוריו. ,,ונתתי להם בביתי ובחומתי יד ושם״. אין לו להקב״ה אלא ד׳ אמות של הלכה בלבד. א״כ זהו בית ד׳ לימוד תורה שבע״פ וזהו המקום לעשות יד ושם לנשמת בנו ע״ה.

נר ד׳ נשמת אדם אמר הקב״ה נרי בידך ונרך בידי. נר מצוה ותורה אור, תורה זהו הנר של הקב״ה וכששומרים נר של הקב״ה שעל ידי הפירוש ,,**יד אברהם**״ בשפה הלעוזית יתרבה ויתפשט לימוד ושקיעת התורה בבתי ישראל. ד׳ ישמור נשמת אדם.

בנו אברהם יוסף ע״ה נתברך בהמדה שבו נכללות כל המדות, לב טוב והיה אהוב לחבריו. בלמדו בישיבתנו היה לו הרצון לעלות במעלות התורה וכשעלה לארצנו הקדושה היתה מבוקשו להמשיך בלמודיו. ביקוש זה ימצא מלואו על ידי הרבים המבקשים דרך ד׳, שהפירוש ,,**יד אברהם**״ יהא מפתח להם לים התלמוד.

התורה נקראת ,,אש דת״ ונמשלה לאש ויש לה הכח לפעפע ברזל לפצוץ כוחות האדם, הניצוץ שהאיר בך רבנו הרב שרגא פייוועל מנדלויץ זצ״ל שמרת עליו, ועשה חיל. עכשיו אתה מסייע להאיר נצוצות בנשמות בני ישראל שיעשה חיל ויהא לאור גדול.

תקותי עזה שכל התלמידי חכמים שנדבה רוחם להוציא לפועל מלאכה ענקית זו לפרש המשניות כולה, יצא עבודתם ברוח פאר והדר ויכוונו לאמיתה של תורה ויתקדש ויתרבה שם שמים על ידי מלאכה זו.

יתברך כב׳ וב״ב לראות ולרוות נחת רוח מצאצאיו.

הכו״ח לכבוד התורה ותומכיה עש״ק במדבר תשל״ט

אלי׳ שווי

מכתב ברכה

דוד קאהן

ביהמ״ד גבול יעבץ
ברוקלין, נוא יארק

בס״ד כ״ה למטמונים תשל״ט

כבוד רחימא דנפשאי, עושה ומעשה
ר׳ אלעזר הכהן גליק נטריה רחמנא ופרקיה

שמוע שמעתי שכבר תקעת כפיך לתמוך במפעל האדיר של חברת ארטסקרול — הידוע בכל קצווי תבל ע״י עבודתה הכבירה בהפצת תורה — לתרגם ולבאר ששה סדרי משנה באנגלית. כוונתך להנציח זכר בנך הנחמד אברהם יוסף ז״ל שנקטף באבו בזמן שעלה לארץ הקודש בתקופת התרוממות הנפש ושאיפה לקדושה, ולמטרה זו יכונה הפירוש בשם „**יד אברהם**״; וגם האיר ה׳ רוחך לגרום עילוי לנשמתו הטהורה שעי״ז יתרבה לימוד התורה שניתנה בשבעים לשון, על ידי כלי מפואר זה.

מכיוון שהנני מכיר היטיב שני הצדדים, אוכל לומר לדבק טוב, והנני תקוה שיצליח המפעל הלזה לתת יד ושם וזכות לנשמת אברהם יוסף ז״ל. חזקה על חברת ארטסקרול שתוציא דבר נאה מתוקן ומתקבל מתחת ידה להגדיל תורה ולהאדירה.

והנני מברך אותך שתמצא נוחם לנפשך, שהאבא זוכה לברא, ותשבע נחת — אתה עם רעיתך תחיה — מכל צאצאיכם היקרים אכי״ר

ידידך עז
דוד קאהן

Preface

אָמַר ר׳ יוֹחָנָן: לֹא כָּרַת הקב״ה בְּרִית עִם יִשְׂרָאֵל אֶלָּא עַל־תּוֹרָה שֶׁבְּעַל־פֶּה שֶׁנֶּאֱמַר ,,כִּי עַל־פִּי הַדְּבָרִים הָאֵלֶּה כָּרַתִּי אִתְּךָ בְּרִית...״
R' Yochanan said: The Holy One, Blessed be He, did not seal a covenant with Israel except because of the Oral Torah, as it is said (Exodus 34:27): For according to these words have I sealed a covenant with you... (Gittin 60b).

As this first volume of the ARTSCROLL MISHNAH SERIES *is presented to the Torah public, we turn to* HASHEM *Yisborach with a* בִּרְכַּת הוֹדָיָה, a blessing of thanksgiving, *for having granted us the privilege of becoming a vehicle to disseminate knowledge of the Mishnah. We pray that we may succeed in this new and unique venture at making the Oral Torah accessible to the Jewish public. Simultaneous with the ongoing work on Tanach and the* Siddur, *the new Mishnah Series will* אי״ה *be a major service to the English-speaking public which has echoed the words of David:* גַּל־עֵינַי וְאַבִּיטָה נִפְלָאוֹת מִתּוֹרָתֶךָ, *Uncover my eyes that I may see the wonders of Your Torah (Psalms 119:18).*

Heretofore, there has been a serious lack of an adequate English treatment of the Mishnah. In the view of roshei hayeshivah and Torah scholars, there exists a need for a work that will deal with the Mishnah with depth and scope. Like the ARTSCROLL TANACH SERIES, *it draws upon large cross-sections of Talmudic, rabbinic, and halachic sources. The purpose is to enable the reader to study each mishnah as though he were sitting in the study hall, participating in the give and take of Talmudic scholarship.*

Nevertheless, we must inject two words of caution. First: Although the Mishnah, by definition, is a compendium of laws, the final halachah does not necessarily follow the Mishnah. The development of the final halachah proceeds through the Gemara, commentators, codifiers, responsa, and the acknowledged Torah poskim. Even when our commentary cites the Shulchan Aruch, the intention is to sharpen the reader's understanding of the mishnah and never to serve as a basis for actual practice. In short, this work is meant as a study of the first step in our recorded Oral Law — no more.

Second: As we have stressed in our other books, an ArtScroll commentary is not meant as a substitute for study of the sources. While this commentary, like the others in the various series, will be immensely useful even to accomplished scholars and will often bring to light ideas and sources they may have overlooked, we strongly urge those who are able to study the classic seforim in the original to do so.

The pattern of the commentary and the style of transliteration follow those of the ARTSCROLL TANACH SERIES.

Hebrew terms connoting concepts for which there are no exact

English translations are defined the first time they appear and are transliterated thereafter.

For the reader's convenience, every word of the mishnah has been included in the commentary headings. Therefore, the reader may study the commentary continuously without constantly referring back to the text, should he so desire.

The translation attempts to follow the text faithfully. Variations have been made when dictated by the need for clarity or English usage and syntax. Any words that have been added for the sake of flow and clarity are bracketed.

The classical sources from which the commentary has been culled range [in part] from the **GEMARA** *(abbreviated Gem.) with its commentaries:* **RASHI** *(1040-1105);* **TOSAFOS** *(Tos.), [Talmudic glosses by the school of scholars known collectively as Tosafists who flourished in the generations following Rashi]; to the classical Mishnah commentators:* **RAMBAM** *(1135-1204);* **R' MENACHEM MEIRI** *(1249-1306);* **RITVA** *[R' Yom Tov Ishbili (1250-1330)];* **RAN** *[R' Nissim Gerondi (mid-14th cent.)];* **NIMUKEI YOSEF** *[R' Yosef Chaviva (early 15th cent.)];* **RAV** *[R' Ovadiah of Bertinoro (end of 15th cent.)];* **TOSEFOS YOM TOV** *(Tos. Yom Tov), [R' Yom Tov Lipmann Heller (1579-1659)]; to more recent commentators;* **R' AKIVA EIGER** *[1761-1837];* **TIFERES YISRAEL** *(Tif. Yis.), R' Yisrael Lipschutz (1782-1860)]; as well as to the contemporary* **MISHNAYOS MEVUAROS** *by R' Pinchas Kehati.*

No such work can serve the need for which it is intended unless the author is a talmid chochom of a very high caliber. We are particularly gratified, therefore, that we have engaged a group of authors of high scholarship and accomplishment. Although each commentary is anthologized from numerous sources, each is original in the sense that it reflects the author's own understanding, selection, and presentation.

For this inaugural volume of the Mishnah Series, we are privileged to present the commentary anthologized by RABBI AVROHOM YOSAIF ROSENBERG, *a distinguished talmid chochom and rosh yeshiva. The quality of the work attests to the caliber of the author, and Mesorah Publications is proud to be associated with a man of his stature.*

No work of such magnitude can be done single-handedly. Though the scholarship is that of Rabbi Rosenberg, many members of the editorial staff have contributed to a final product of the standard ArtScroll readers have come to expect. They are RABBIS DAVID LANDESMAN *of Jerusalem,* SHEAH BRANDER, *and* AVIE GOLD.

We express our thanks to RABBI DAVID FEINSTEIN *and* RABBI DAVID COHEN *whose constant concern and interest throughout the history of the ArtScroll Series have been in further evidence in the course of this work.*

MR. DAVID H. SCHWARTZ, *too, has lent encouragement and assistance at vital junctures; we are deeply grateful.*

ZUNDEL BERMAN, *distributor of this and of many previous* ARTSCROLL *Seforim, continues to serve as the source of Torah literature for major segments of the Torah public. His friendship and support from the outset of our work are deeply appreciated.*

We express our deep appreciation to MR. *and* MRS. LOUIS GLICK *who have dedicated the commentary. It bears the name* YAD AVRAHAM, *in memory of their son* AVRAHAM YOSEF ע״ה. *An appreciation of the niftar will appear in Tractate* Berachos. *May this dissemination of the Mishnah be a source of merit for his soul. And may his parents* יב״ל *be blessed for their generous dedication to Torah, of which this project is but one more instance.*

Rabbis Nosson Scherman / Meir Zlotowitz
General Editors

ט״ו מנחם אב תשל״ט/August 8, 1979
Brooklyn, New York

◆§ מסכת תענית

◆§ Tractate Taanis

Translation and anthologized commentary by
Rabbi Avrohom Yoseif Rosenberg

Mesorah Publications, ltd

◆§ Tractate Taanis

Sound the shofar *in Zion, sanctify a fast, summon an assembly. Gather the people, sanctify the congregation, assemble the elders, gather youngsters and suckling infants. Let the bridegroom leave his chamber and the bride her canopy... Let the* kohanim, *servants of* HASHEM, *weep, and let them say: 'Have mercy,* HASHEM, *on Your people. Do not deliver Your heritage to disgrace...'*

HASHEM *then avenged His land and showed mercy to His people. And* HASHEM *responded to His people saying: 'Behold, I send you the grain, the wine, and the oil, that they shall satiate you... And you shall know that I am among the Israelites. I am your God, and there is no other...' (Joel 2:15-27).*

The prophet tells the nation to fast and sound the *shofar,* indeed, to summon the entire populace to assemble, repent the evil of their ways, cry out to God to come to their salvation, and thus be saved from whatever catastrophe has befallen them. The Torah ordains: *When the adversary oppresses you, you shall blow with the trumpets (Num.* 10:9). Thus, regardless of the nature of the adversary — be it blight, drought, locusts, or any calamitous situation — the trumpets should be sounded in a call to repentance. If, at the time of national crisis, the people recognize that the predicament in which they find themselves has been imposed upon them by Heaven because of their iniquities, they will mend their ways and take to heart the words of *Jeremiah* (5:25): *Your sins have withheld goodness from you,* and God will forgive their past misdeeds.

However, if they do not cry out penitentially, if they do not issue a clarion call for all to turn to God's Torah, if they ascribe their desperate plight to the natural course of world events, if all is seen as mere coincidence, then they will reinforce and perpetuate the evil of their ways. As a result, they will aggravate their situation and bring increased Heavenly retribution upon themselves.

The prophets ordained fasting as a means of awakening the people to repentance in times of calamity. These fasts, along with the supplications and sounding of the trumpets, continue until the nation becomes deserving of Divine Mercy and its plight is relieved (*Rambam, Taaniyos* 1:1-4).

The need for an order of penance, through fasting and prayer, during periods of national distress form the frameword of tractate *Taanis* [lit. *Fast Day*]. Included is also an exposition of the attitudes to be engendered within each individual by means of prayer, supplication, and fasting.

These aspects are discussed in the following order: praises of God for sending the rains in their proper season, prayers for rain, and the ordering of public penitence through prayer and fast when He withholds them; the declaration of fast days, special prayer services, and sounding of the trumpets at times when other disasters — potential or actual — befall the nation; and rules of conduct on these specially decreed fast days and on public fast days decreed by the prophets in commemoration of national calamities which occurred on those days — *Tishah B'Av,* Seventeenth of *Tammuz,* Tenth of *Teves,* and *Tzom Gedaliah (Meiri).*

א
א

[א] **מֵאֵימָתַי** מַזְכִּירִין גְּבוּרוֹת גְּשָׁמִים? רַבִּי אֱלִיעֶזֶר אוֹמֵר: מִיּוֹם טוֹב הָרִאשׁוֹן שֶׁל חָג. רַבִּי יְהוֹשֻׁעַ אוֹמֵר: מִיּוֹם טוֹב הָאַחֲרוֹן שֶׁל חָג.

אָמַר לוֹ רַבִּי יְהוֹשֻׁעַ: הוֹאִיל וְאֵין הַגְּשָׁמִים אֶלָּא סִימַן קְלָלָה בֶּחָג, לָמָּה מַזְכִּיר?

יד אברהם *

Chapter 1

1.

⁂Power of Rain

Rain is mentioned twice in the *Shemoneh Esrei*. In the second blessing, God is praised as the One Who makes the wind blow and the rain descend. Later, in the ninth blessing of the weekday *Shemoneh Esrei*, we pray to Him to *give* us rain. The former expression of praise is known as גְּבוּרוֹת גְּשָׁמִים, *powers of rain* (see *comm.* below), while the latter prayer is known as שְׁאֵלַת גְּשָׁמִים, *request for rain.*

The mishnah states in *Berachos* 5:2: *We mention the power of rain in* [the second blessing of *Shemoneh Esrei* i.e.,] *the resurrection of the dead, and the request* [for rain] *in the* [ninth blessing of the *Shemoneh Esrei*, in which we pray for prosperity, i.e., the] *blessing of the years.* As the Talmud explains, the gift of rain is equivalent to the resurrection of the dead (*Berachos* 33a) because it gives life to the earth just as the resurrection will give life to the dead *(Yerushalmi Berachos* 5:2).

Since the need for rain is limited to יְמוֹת הַגְּשָׁמִים, *the rainy season*, neither the praise nor the request is recited at other times of the year. Chapter one deals with the dates on which the power of rain is inserted in the *Shemoneh Esrei*, and with the special fasts which are proclaimed in *Eretz Yisrael* if rain failed to fall in its proper time.

Our tractate should logically begin with the statement that, in season, the *Shemoneh Esrei* must contain praise of God as the Giver of rain, and then continue with a discussion of the date when the praise is inaugurated. Our mishnah, however, begins with the timing and omits mentioning the rule. The statement of the rule, however, is not necessary here because *Taanis* follows *Rosh HaShanah*, which taught that the extent of the world's rainfall is judged and determined on Succos *(Rosh HaShanah* 1:2). Thus, it is implicitly understood that the Judge and Giver should be praised; the only question is when. Our tractate, therefore, begins with the matter of when the prayers for rain are to be recited *(Rav; Tos. Yom Tov).*

מֵאֵימָתַי מַזְכִּירִין גְּבוּרוֹת גְּשָׁמִים? — *From when do we mention the powers of rain?*

I.e., from when do we begin to mention מַשִּׁיב הָרוּחַ וּמוֹרִיד הַגֶּשֶׁם, *He causes the wind to blow and the rain to descend*, in the second blessing of *Shemoneh Esrei?*

The expression *'powers'* in connection with rain is based on *Job*

* [The commentary has been named **Yad Avraham** as an everlasting memorial and source of merit for the *neshamah of* אברהם יוסף ע״ה בן הר״ר אלעזר הכהן גליק נ״י, **Avraham Yosef Glick** ע״ה, whose life was cut short on 3 Teves 5735. An appreciation of the *niftar* will appear in Tractate Berachos. תנצב״ה.]

1
1

1. From when do we mention the powers of rain? R' Eliezer says: From the first *Yom Tov* of the Festival. R' Yehoshua says: From the last *Yom Tov* of the Festival.

R' Yehoshua said to him: Since rain is but a symptom of curse during the Festival, why mention [it]?

5:9-10, which describes the gift of rain as a manifestation of God's strength *(Rav; Gem.* 2a).

Tiferes Yisrael (Berachos 5:2) cites rain as an expression of God's power because He causes rain to fall even when people do not deserve it. Thus, rain shows God's Attribute of Mercy *overpowering* His Attribute of Strict Justice.

רַבִּי אֱלִיעֶזֶר אוֹמֵר: מִיּוֹם טוֹב הָרִאשׁוֹן שֶׁל חָג. — *R' Eliezer says: From the first Yom Tov of the festival.*

[Scripture identifies each of the three pilgrimage festivals with the word חַג, *festival:* בְּחַג הַמַּצּוֹת וּבְחַג הַשָּׁבֻעוֹת וּבְחַג הַסֻּכּוֹת, *On the festival of Matzos, on the festival of Shavuos, and on the festival of Succos (Deut.* 16:16). In the *Mishnah* the festival of *Matzos* is called פֶּסַח, *Pesach* (Passover); the festival of *Shavuos* — עֲצֶרֶת, *Atzeres;* and the festival of *Succos* — חַג, *Chag* (lit. *festival).*

Most categories of work are forbidden on the first and last days of both Pesach and Succos and on the day of Shavuos. These days are referred to as יוֹם טוֹב, *Yom Tov* (lit., *good day).* The intermediate days of Pesach and Succos are called חוֹל הַמּוֹעֵד, *Chol HaMoed* (lit., *ordinary days of the festival*). See preface to tractate *Moed Katan.*]

R' Eliezer holds that the power of rain is mentioned beginning with the first שַׁחֲרִית, *morning prayer,* of Succos. The Gemara explains that the recitation of the praise is equated with the commandment to take the אַרְבָּעָה מִינִים, *four species (Lev.* 23:40) which are used in the observance of Succos. Since the four species [lulav, esrog, myrtle, and willow] are vegetation which cannot grow without rain, their use implies a plea to God that, on Succos when He decides upon the distribution of rain for the following year, He should decree abundant rainfall. Since the precept of taking the four species begins on the first morning of Succos, the recitation of the power of rain was also instituted for that time *(Tos. Yom Tov).*

רַבִּי יְהוֹשֻׁעַ אוֹמֵר: מִיּוֹם טוֹב הָאַחֲרוֹן שֶׁל חָג. — *R' Yehoshua says: From the last Yom Tov of the festival.*

[This day is called שְׁמִינִי עֲצֶרֶת, *Shemini Atzeres, the Eighth Day of Assembly.*]

R' Yehoshua begins to mention the powers of rain at the evening prayer of *Shemini Atzeres (Tif. Yis.; Tos. Yom Tov,* mishnah 2).]

אָמַר לוֹ רַבִּי יְהוֹשֻׁעַ: הוֹאִיל וְאֵין הַגְּשָׁמִים אֶלָּא סִימַן קְלָלָה בֶּחָג, לָמָּה מַזְכִּיר? — *R' Yehoshua said to him: Since rain is but a symptom of curse during the festival, why mention* [it]?

By bringing rain and thereby making it impossible to sit in the *succah,* God indicates that He rejects our performance of the *mitzvah.* This is a curse, a sign of Divine displeasure.

Rainfall on Succos is compared to the case of a servant who came to dilute his master's wine with water, as was customary in ancient times. His master humiliated the servant by taking the water and splashing it in the servant's face saying, 'I have

א
ב

אָמַר לוֹ רַבִּי אֱלִיעֶזֶר: אַף אֲנִי לֹא אָמַרְתִּי לִשְׁאוֹל, אֶלָּא לְהַזְכִּיר ,,מַשִּׁיב הָרוּחַ וּמוֹרִיד הַגֶּשֶׁם" בְּעוֹנָתוֹ.

אָמַר לוֹ: אִם כֵּן, לְעוֹלָם יְהֵא מַזְכִּיר!

[ב] **אֵין** שׁוֹאֲלִין אֶת־הַגְּשָׁמִים אֶלָּא סָמוּךְ לַגְּשָׁמִים.

רַבִּי יְהוּדָה אוֹמֵר: הָעוֹבֵר לִפְנֵי הַתֵּבָה בְּיוֹם טוֹב הָאַחֲרוֹן שֶׁל חַג — הָאַחֲרוֹן מַזְכִּיר,

יד אברהם

no desire for your service' (*Succah* 29a).[1]

אָמַר לוֹ רַבִּי אֱלִיעֶזֶר: אַף אֲנִי לֹא אָמַרְתִּי לִשְׁאוֹל, אֶלָּא לְהַזְכִּיר ,,מַשִּׁיב הָרוּחַ וּמוֹרִיד הַגֶּשֶׁם" בְּעוֹנָתוֹ. — *R' Eliezer replied to him: I, too, did not say to request [rain], but [merely] to mention 'He causes the wind to blow and the rain to fall,' in its proper season.*

R' Eliezer counters that he, too, agrees that Succos is not the time to pray that God should given rain immediately. The prayer for rain, וְתֵן טַל וּמָטָר, *Give dew and rain*, in the *blessing of the years*, is not begun until after Succos [see pref.; see also mishnah 3] *(Rashi)*.

However, on Succos we are to praise the Almighty for His kindness in bringing about rainfall in its proper season — after Succos, when rainfall is indeed beneficial. At that time, it will nourish the crops and fill the reservoirs, but will not prevent the performance of a commandment *(Tos. Yom Tov)*.

אָמַר לוֹ: אִם כֵּן, לְעוֹלָם יְהֵא מַזְכִּיר! — *He responded: If so, one should always mention [the powers of rain]!*

R' Yehoshua argues that if, as R' Eliezer contends, the mention of rainfall does not imply that God brings rainfall at any other than its proper time, then why should he prescribe recitation of powers of rain only from the first day of Succos? Why do we not mention it all through the year, even during the summer, when no rain is needed? *(Rav)*.

R' Eliezer holds that one *may* indeed mention the powers of rain all year long if he so desires. The Sages made it *obligatory*, however, only from the first day of Succos, which immediately precedes the rainy season. Thus, just prior to the rainy season, we praise God as the Giver of rain — then, when it is needed, we pray for it *(Tos.* 2a).

1. *Vilna Gaon* explains further that the master's action in effect says, 'I do not want you to dilute my wine.' So it is in the case of Israel. If a harsh decree had been promulgated by the Heavenly Court on the High Holy Days, the merit of performing the commandment of *succah* would dilute and weaken that decree. By causing rain on Succos, God prevents us from modifying His decrees against us *(Divrei Eliyahu*, p. 47).

R′ Eliezer replied to him: I, too, did not say to request [rain], but [merely] to mention 'He causes the wind to blow and the rain to fall,' in its proper season.

He responded: If so, one should always mention [the powers of rain]!

2. We do not request rain except close to the rainy season.

R′ Yehudah says: Of those [*chazanim*] who stand before the Ark on the last *Yom Tov* of the Festival — the last [*chazan*] mentions [the powers of rain, but]

YAD AVRAHAM

2.

אֵין שׁוֹאֲלִין אֶת־הַגְּשָׁמִים אֶלָּא סָמוּךְ לַגְּשָׁמִים. — *We do not request rain except close to the rainy season.*

Rav cites two interpretations of this passage offered by the Talmud:

— The request that rain be given, וְתֵן טַל וּמָטָר, *Give dew and rain,* should begin only with the arrival of the rainy season in *MarCheshvan.* This opinion is shared by both R′ Eliezer and R′ Yehoshua, the disputants of mishnah 1. Although they disagree about when to mention the powers of rain, which is an expression of praise rather than a request, they agree that the *prayer* for rain should begin in *MarCheshvan,* when the rain is needed.

— The word שׁוֹאֲלִין, *we request,* is synonymous with מַזְכִּירִין, *we mention,* of mishnah 1. Thus, our mishnah refers not to the request for rain, but to the praise of God as the Giver of rain. Accordingly, our mishnah follows only R′ Yehoshua who holds that the powers of rain are mentioned beginning from the *last* day of the festival, immediately before the season when rainfall is needed.

רַבִּי יְהוּדָה אוֹמֵר: הָעוֹבֵר לִפְנֵי הַתֵּבָה בְּיוֹם טוֹב הָאַחֲרוֹן שֶׁל חַג... — *R′ Yehudah says: Of those* [*chazanim*] *who stand before the Ark* [lit., *He who passes before the Ark*] *on the last Yom Tov of the Festival,*

הָאַחֲרוֹן מַזְכִּיר, — *the last* [*chazan*] *mentions* [*the powers of rain*],

Among the various *chazanim,* [*prayer leaders*], of the *Shemini Atzeres* services, the one who conducts מוּסָף [*Musaf*], *the additional prayer service,* inaugurates the recitation of the powers of rain (*Rav*).

[In Mishnaic times, it was not customary for the same *chazan* to conduct both שַׁחֲרִית [*Shacharis*], *the morning service,* and *Musaf.* Therefore, the two *chazanim* are referred to as the first one and the last one. The Tanna describes the *Musaf* leader as *last one,* despite the fact that מִנְחָה [*Minchah*], *the afternoon prayer,* is the last of the day. Nevertheless, *Musaf* is the last of the morning prayers while *Minchah* is generally recited late in the afternoon. Although *Musaf* may be

א
ב

הָרִאשׁוֹן אֵינוֹ מַזְכִּיר. בְּיוֹם טוֹב הָרִאשׁוֹן שֶׁל פֶּסַח — הָרִאשׁוֹן מַזְכִּיר, הָאַחֲרוֹן אֵינוֹ מַזְכִּיר.
עַד אֵימָתַי שׁוֹאֲלִין אֶת־הַגְּשָׁמִים? רַבִּי יְהוּדָה אוֹמֵר: עַד שֶׁיַּעֲבֹר הַפֶּסַח. רַבִּי מֵאִיר אוֹמֵר: עַד שֶׁיֵּצֵא נִיסָן, שֶׁנֶּאֱמַר: ,,וַיּוֹרֶד לָכֶם גֶּשֶׁם, מוֹרֶה וּמַלְקוֹשׁ בָּרִאשׁוֹן.״

יד אברהם

recited throughout the day, it is customarily recited immediately after the morning Torah reading.]

הָרִאשׁוֹן אֵינוֹ מַזְכִּיר. — [*but*] *the first* [*chazan*] *does not mention* [*it*].

The *chazan* who conducts *Shacharis* does not mention מוֹרִיד הַגֶּשֶׁם, *He causes the rain to fall...* but he does mention מוֹרִיד הַטָּל, *He makes the dew fall* *(Rav).*

Only according to the Sephardic rite is *dew* mentioned in the second blessing of *Shemoneh Esrei.* Ashkenazim, however, omit this mention entirely *(Tos. Yom Tov).*

Yerushalmi explains why the mention of powers of rain is not begun during מַעֲרִיב [*Maariv*], *the evening prayer,* which, since the halachic day begins with nightfall, is the first prayer service of the day. Since not everyone is in the synagogue in the evening, some people would be unaware that the recitation had already been announced. The following morning, some would recite the powers of rain, and others would not. Therefore, the Sages ordained that it begin during morning services, when the largest number of people would be present.

Why then, do we not start at *Shacharis?* Some might think that the recitation had commenced the previous evening and would erroneously begin too early the following year. This would lead to the undesirable situation of divergent groups, some beginning at *Maariv*, others at *Shacharis.*

Another reason is that one may not mention powers of rain until he hears it announced first. Such an announcement cannot be made during *Shacharis* because it is forbidden to interrupt for any reason between the blessing prior to the *Shemoneh Esrei* of *Shacharis,* and the *Shemoneh Esrei* itself *(Berachos* 9b). Therefore, it is postponed until *Musaf* *(Rosh,* 2), when the announcement may be made.

בְּיוֹם טוֹב הָרִאשׁוֹן שֶׁל פֶּסַח—הָרִאשׁוֹן מַזְכִּיר, — *On the first Yom Tov of Pesach, the first* [*chazan*] *mentions* [*the powers of rain*],

[Although the recitation of powers of rain will be discontinued on the first day of Pesach according to R' Yehudah, the *Shacharis* reader continues to mention it.]

הָאַחֲרוֹן אֵינוֹ מַזְכִּיר. — [*but*] *the last* [*chazan*] *does not mention* [*it*].

The *chazan* of *Musaf* makes no mention of גֶּשֶׁם, *rain. Yerushalmi* explains that the Sages wanted mention of טַל, *dew,* to be preeminent during all three festivals, because dew is symbolic of great blessing to the world. Thus, mention of rain is discontinued in favor of praise for the dew at the first *Musaf* of Pesach. Dew is mentioned throughout Pesach, Shavuos, and the seven days of Succos until the praise for rain is begun at *Musaf* of *Shemini Atzeres (Tos. Yom Tov; Pnei Moshe).*

[It is implicit in the above *Yerushalmi* that the prevalent practice

1 the first [*chazan*] does not mention [it.] On the first
2 *Yom Tov* of Pesach, the first [*chazan*] mentions [the powers of rain, but] the last [*chazan*] does not mention [it].

Until when do we request rain? R' Yehudah says: Until Pesach is over. R' Meir says: Until *Nissan* is over; as it is said: *He caused rain to fall for you — the early rain and the late rain — in the first month* [Joel 2:23].

was to mention dew in the second blessing of *Shemoneh Esrei,* as is the Sephardic custom (see *Tos. Yom Tov* to preceding phrase).]

[The mishnah discusses the *Shemoneh Esrei* at which the *chazan* ceases the recitation of powers of rain. Unmentioned, however, is the time when the silently praying congregation discontinues its recitation. In this matter, the Sephardic and Ashkenazic rituals differ. Since the Sephardim (and all communities in *Eretz Yisrael) recite* מוֹרִיד הַטָּל, *He causes the dew to fall,* the sexton announces before *Musaf* the congregation should begin recitation of the new phrase. Thus, praise for the powers of rain is replaced by praise for dew. Ashkenazim, however, never recite praise for the dew. As a result, there is no *positive* announcement to be made. Rather than make the *negative* announcement, 'Do *not* recite powers of rain,' the Rabbis preferred to continue praise for the rain until the *chazan's* repetition of *Shemoneh Esrei.* His omission of powers of rain then becomes the signal to the congregation that the season of rain is over.]

עַד אֵימָתַי שׁוֹאֲלִין אֶת־הַגְּשָׁמִים? — *Until when do we request rain?*

[The mishnah now speaks of the prayer וְתֵן טַל וּמָטָר, *and give dew and rain,* inserted into the ninth blessing of *Shemoneh Esrei.* Until when must this prayer be recited?]

רַבִּי יְהוּדָה אוֹמֵר: עַד שֶׁיַּעֲבֹר הַפֶּסַח. — *R' Yehudah says: Until Pesach is over.*

R' Yehudah holds that rains are still a source of blessing and benefit until Pesach ends. During Temple times, pilgrims from throughout *Eretz Yisrael* came to Jerusalem. As long as they remained in the city, rain was not a significant inconvenience. On the way home after Pesach, rain would cause the pilgrims considerable hardship. Therefore, the prayer for rain is discontinued after Pesach *(Tos. Yom Tov).*

[Apparently, the inconvenience to pilgrims on the way *to* Jerusalem was discounted because rain was still needed until Pesach.]

There is an obvious inconsistency in our mishnah. Earlier, R' Yehudah rules that the very mention of rain is discontinued at the first *Musaf* of Pesach. Here he rules that it is even *requested* until at the conclusion of Pesach. The *Gemara* (4b) concludes that there were conflicting versions of R' Yehudah's ruling; our mishnah lists both *(Rav).*

רַבִּי מֵאִיר אוֹמֵר: עַד שֶׁיֵּצֵא נִיסָן, — *R' Meir says: Until Nissan is over;*

[We pray for rain until the end of *Nissan,* since rainfall is beneficial

א
ג

[ג] בִּשְׁלֹשָׁה בְּמַרְחֶשְׁוָן שׁוֹאֲלִין אֶת־הַגְּשָׁמִים. רַבָּן גַּמְלִיאֵל אוֹמֵר: בְּשִׁבְעָה בוֹ, חֲמִשָּׁה עָשָׂר יוֹם אַחַר הֶחָג, כְּדֵי שֶׁיַּגִּיעַ אַחֲרוֹן שֶׁבְּיִשְׂרָאֵל לִנְהַר פְּרָת.

יד אברהם

throughout the entire month.]

שֶׁנֶּאֱמַר: ,,וַיּוֹרֶד לָכֶם גֶּשֶׁם, מוֹרֶה וּמַלְקוֹשׁ בָּרִאשׁוֹן.'' — *as it is said: He caused rain to fall for you — the early rain and the late rain — in the first month* [*Joel* 2:23].

Since Scripture praises God for giving rain בָּרִאשׁוֹן, *in the first* [*month*], i.e., *Nissan*, we infer that rain is beneficial throughout that entire month *(Meleches Shlomo)*.[1]

Those who disagree with R' Meir hold that no conclusions can be drawn from *Joel*, because the entire event was clearly miraculous (see footnote). Under normal circumstances, however, rain is of no benefit in *Nissan (Tos. Yom Tov)*.

Alternatively, the verse from *Joel* was not intended as proof for R' Meir's view. Rather, it was cited by the redactor of the *Mishnah* merely to demonstrate that rain can be of benefit during *Nissan*. R' Yehudah would agree — but he maintains that rain is of benefit only until the end of Pesach, while R' Meir holds that rain is a blessing all month *(Meleches Shlomo)*.

The accepted *halachah* is in accordance with the first version of R' Yehudah: The phrase, 'He causes the wind to blow and the rain to fall,' is added beginning with *Musaf* of *Shemini Atzeres* and ending with either *Shacharis* (Sephardim) or *Musaf* (Ashkenazim) on the first day of Pesach. The request for rain is recited last at *Minchah* of the day before Pesach.

3.

...בִּשְׁלֹשָׁה בְּמַרְחֶשְׁוָן — *On the third* [*day*] *of MarCheshvan...*

This is normally the first day of rain in *Eretz Yisrael (Tos. Yom Tov)*...

שׁוֹאֲלִין אֶת־הַגְּשָׁמִים. — *we request rain* [lit. *the rains*].

In the Ashkenazic rite the request for rain consists of the phrase וְתֵן טַל וּמָטָר לִבְרָכָה, *give dew and rain as a blessing*, which is inserted in the ninth blessing of *Shemoneh Esrei*, בִּרְכַּת הַשָּׁנִים, *Blessing of the Years*, which is a general prayer for prosperity.

The Sephardic rite, however, has two versions of the Blessing of the Years, one for the rainy season, a different one for the remainder of the year. (See *Tur Orach Chaim* 117; *Beis Yosef; Bach)*.

רַבָּן גַּמְלִיאֵל אוֹמֵר: בְּשִׁבְעָה בוֹ, חֲמִשָּׁה עָשָׂר יוֹם אַחַר הֶחָג, — *Rabban Gamliel says: On its seventh* [*day*], *fifteen*

1. This verse appears in the prophecy of *Joel*. In his time, there was a severe locust plague for four years followed by a three-year drought. At the end of the third year the month of *Adar* passed without rainfall. The early rain fell on the first of *Nissan*.

1 during *Shemitah,* and repair damaged ones during
2 [*Chol*] *HaMoed.*

We may repair damaged cisterns in the public domain and clear them out. We may repair roads, streets, and ritual baths; provide all public needs; mark graves; and even go out [to inspect the fields] for forbidden mixtures [of seeds, during *Chol HaMoed*].

YAD AVRAHAM

sanitation of the neighborhood is affected.]

This cleaning may be done even if it is not urgent for *Chol HaMoed,* since it is essentially a public necessity *(Gem.* 5a). Since people are unoccupied during *Chol HaMoed,* they can all join in making the necessary repairs. Were the repairs left for after the festival, however, everyone would return to his regular occupation and the repairs would never be made *(Tos. Yom Tov; Rosh; Nimukei Yosef).*

The general rule is that work needed to fulfill public necessities may be done during *Chol HaMoed* even if it entails exertion. However, for private needs — even those that are not forbidden on *Chol HaMoed* — unskilled labor not requiring undue exertion is permitted (*Mishnah Berurah* 544:1).

ומְתַקְּנִין אֶת־הַדְּרָכִים וְאֶת־הָרְחוֹבוֹת... — *We may repair roads, (and) streets.*

I.e., the thoroughfares used by the public. Though the custom was to undertake these repairs on the fifteenth of *Adar* [at the end of the rainy season, see *Shekalim* 1:1], it was common for the roads to deteriorate again by the time Pesach arrived since the repairs availed for only brief periods *(Tos. Yom Tov).*

וְאֶת־מִקְווֹת הַמַּיִם, — *and ritual baths;*

If a מִקְוָה, *mikvah,* [*ritual bath*], contains less than the required forty *seah* of rain water, we are permitted to fill it to the required level during *Chol HaMoed* as this, too, is deemed a public necessity *(Meiri; Gem.* 5a).

וְעוֹשִׂין כָּל־צָרְכֵי הָרַבִּים, — *(and we may) provide all public needs;*

This includes digging water holes that are needed by the public for the festival (*Gem.* 5a). Since water holes must be dug professionally, they may be dug only if they are needed for the festival. Otherwise, such skilled labor would be prohibited on *Chol HaMoed* [see pref. to tractate; see mishnah 8] *(Rosh; Rabad).*

Yerushalmi explains public needs to include the trying of civil cases, and cases involving capital or corporal punishment *(Makkos* 3); redemption of captives; estimating and paying of funds to redeem vows of *arachin* value (see *Lev.* 27:1-8), property consecrated for the Temple (see *Lev.* 27:9-25); preparing and administering the water given to a *sotah* [a woman accused by her husband of adultery] (See *Num.* 5:11-31); the burning of the Red Cow (see *Num.* 19:1-6); cutting the neck of the heifer (see *Deut.* 21:1-9); boring the ear of a Hebrew slave who wishes to remain

א
ג

[ג] **רַבִּי** אֱלִיעֶזֶר בֶּן־יַעֲקֹב אוֹמֵר: מוֹשְׁכִים אֶת־הַמַּיִם מֵאִילָן לְאִילָן, וּבִלְבַד שֶׁלֹּא יַשְׁקֶה אֶת־כָּל־הַשָּׂדֶה. זְרָעִים שֶׁלֹּא שָׁתוּ לִפְנֵי הַמּוֹעֵד, לֹא יַשְׁקֵם בַּמּוֹעֵד. וַחֲכָמִים מַתִּירִין בָּזֶה וּבָזֶה.

יד אברהם

in slavery after his six years (see *Ex.* 21:5-6); and purifying the *metzora* (see *Lev.* 14:1-32).

וּמְצַיְּנִין אֶת־הַקְּבָרוֹת, —*(and we may) mark graves;*

It was customary to clearly indicate the presence of graves by pouring lime over them. This would serve to caution passersby not to become טָמֵא, *contaminated,* by walking over the graves *(Rav).* [The Tanna is not referring to the construction of tombstones, as this is *obviously* prohibited during *Chol HaMoed.*]

Though the custom was to mark graves on the fifteenth of *Adar,* the Tanna is referring to a case where the lime had been washed away by unseasonal rains *(Tos. Yom Tov;* see *Shekalim* 1:1).

[Alternatively, the Tanna may be referring to freshly dug and hence unmarked graves of bodies buried after the fifteenth of *Adar.*]

וְיוֹצְאִין אַף עַל־הַכִּלְאַיִם. — *(and we may) even go out [to inspect the fields] for forbidden mixtures [of seeds, during Chol HaMoed].*

Court-appointed agents were dispatched during *Chol HaMoed* Pesach to inspect the fields and uproot the forbidden mixtures. Since such agents were paid with public funds, they were hired during *Chol HaMoed* when they were unoccupied and consequently would be willing to accept lower wages *(Rav).*

Although the inspection was usually carried out on the fifteenth of *Adar (Shekalim 1:1),* inspectors were sent out again during *Chol Hamoed* Pesach to check for forbidden mixtures in late-sprouting plants *(Gem.* 6a). [For further explanation of the prohibition of forbidden mixtures, see *Lev.* 19:9 and tractate *Kilayim.*]

3.

רַבִּי אֱלִיעֶזֶר בֶּן־יַעֲקֹב אוֹמֵר: מוֹשְׁכִים אֶת־הַמַּיִם מֵאִילָן לְאִילָן, — *R' Eliezer ben Yaakov says: We may divert water from one tree to another...*

If water is gathered around the base of one tree, we may divert it to another tree since doing so does not entail strenuous work *(Tif. Yis.).*

וּבִלְבַד שֶׁלֹּא יַשְׁקֶה אֶת־כָּל־הַשָּׂדֶה — *provided that [by so doing] one does not water the entire field.*

[Such large-scale watering would be considered excessive exertion.]

According to *Rav,* the mishnah refers to a field that can subsist on rainfall without added irrigation. As *Rav* commented to 1:1, irrigation of such fields is forbidden on *Chol HaMoed,* but mere *diversion* of water is permitted. *Tosefos Yom Tov,* however, questions this interpretation in view of the mishnah's next statement: *Seeds that*

1
3

3. On the third [day] of *MarCheshvan* we request rain. Rabban Gamliel says: On its seventh [day], fifteen days after the Festival, so that the last [pilgrim straggler] of Israel may reach the Euphrates River.

days after the Festival,

The seventh of *MarCheshvan* is fifteen days after Succos. *Shemini Atzeres* falls on the twenty-second of *Tishrei,* leaving eight more days in that month. This calculation is based on the calendar now in use. As formulated and introduced by R' Hillel in 4118 (358 C.E.; see *comm.* to *Megillah* 1:2), it provides that *Tishrei* always have thirty days. During earlier times, however, when the new month was declared only after witnesses testified that they had seen the first phase of the moon (מוֹלָד), it was possible for *Tishrei* to have twenty-nine days, depending on when the witnesses arrived (see *Rosh Hashanah,* ch. 2). In that case, the prayer for rain would commence on the eighth of *MarCheshvan,* exactly fifteen days after Succos. Rabban Gamliel specifies that there must always be an interval of fifteen days after the festival before rain is requested *(Tos. Yom Tov).*

כְּדֵי שֶׁיַּגִּיעַ אַחֲרוֹן שֶׁבְּיִשְׂרָאֵל לִנְהַר פְּרָת. — *so that the last* [*pilgrim straggler*] *of Israel may reach the Euphrates River.*

Even for those who delayed their homeward journey until the last minutes, fifteen rain-free days should be sufficient to reach the Euphrates River, which is the northern border of *Eretz Yisrael* and the one furthest from Jerusalem.

From Jerusalem to the river is one hundred fifty פַּרְסָאוֹת, *parasangs* [one parasang equals four מִיל, *mil;* each *mil* is 2000 cubits]. The average person travels ten parasangs a day. Hence, it takes fifteen days to travel one hundred fifty parasangs *(Tos. Yom Tov).*

If they were to begin requesting rain before all the pilgrims had reached home, the prayers might be answered immediately, with the result that the returning travelers would be hindered by rain and muddy roads *(Rav).*

In *Eretz Yisrael,* the accepted *halachah* follows Rabban Gamliel. In Babylonia, however, since the land was low and well irrigated, rainfall was not needed so early in the year. Therefore, the prayer for

Go out and sow,' ordered the prophet.

The people asked him, 'One who has [only] a *kav* of wheat or two *kabim* of barley — shall he eat it and live, or sow it and die [of starvation before the seeds produce a crop]?'

Joel answered them, 'Nevertheless, go out and sow.' A miracle occurred, and that grain which was concealed in the walls and in the ant hills was revealed to them. The people obeyed Joel. On the second, third, and fourth days of *Nissan* they planted. The second rain fell on the fifth of *Nissan.* Miraculously, grain that usually takes six months to grow was ready for harvest after only eleven days. From the produce of that newly planted crop, they brought the *omer* offering on its ordained day, the sixteenth of *Nissan (Gem.* 3a).

א
ד־ה

[ד] **הִגִּיעַ** שִׁבְעָה עָשָׂר בְּמַרְחֶשְׁוָן וְלֹא יָרְדוּ גְשָׁמִים, הִתְחִילוּ הַיְּחִידִים מִתְעַנִּין שָׁלֹשׁ תַּעֲנִיּוֹת. אוֹכְלִין וְשׁוֹתִין מִשֶּׁחֲשֵׁכָה, וּמֻתָּרִין בִּמְלָאכָה וּבִרְחִיצָה וּבְסִיכָה וּבִנְעִילַת הַסַּנְדָּל וּבְתַשְׁמִישׁ הַמִּטָּה.

[ה] **הִגִּיעַ** רֹאשׁ חֹדֶשׁ כִּסְלֵו וְלֹא יָרְדוּ גְשָׁמִים, בֵּית דִּין גּוֹזְרִין שָׁלֹשׁ

In a place where rain is needed before then, the Babylonian practice is nevertheless followed; however, each individual may insert his personal request for rain in the blessing of שׁוֹמֵעַ תְּפִלָּה, *He Who hears prayer (Tif. Yis.).*

rain was not begun until sixty days after the *Tishrei* cycle of the sun. This coincides with December 4 in most years and December 5 on others. The accepted practice throughout the Diaspora follows that of Babylonia *(Rav; Rashi).*

4.

After having given the dates for normal recitation of the various prayers for rain and dew, the Tanna moves on to the main topic of this chapter — the fasts and prayer services that are declared when rain fails to descend in its season.

הִגִּיעַ שִׁבְעָה עָשָׂר בְּמַרְחֶשְׁוָן וְלֹא יָרְדוּ גְשָׁמִים, — *If the seventeenth of MarCheshvan arrived but rain did not fall,*

According to R' Meir, this is the normal date of the third rain. The first rains usually fall on the third, seventh, and seventeenth of *MarCheshvan (Tos. Yom Tov; Gem.* 6a). R' Yehudah gives the dates as the seventh, seventeenth and twenty-third of the month; while R' Yose considers the seventeenth and twenty-third of *MarCheshvan* and the first of *Kislev* as the proper time for the first three rains (*Gem.* 6a).

The 'rain' mentioned here refers to a seven-day period during which rain falls each day (*Gem.* 6a).

These three times are halachically significant: The first is the time to begin the request for rain; the second is used in conjunction with vows which give the rainy season as a time limit; the third is the date on which fasts are declared [if rain has not fallen by that date] (*Gem.* 6a).

הִתְחִילוּ הַיְּחִידִים מִתְעַנִּין... — *the* [*distinguished*] *individuals would start fasting...*

One who is capable of answering questions in all tractates of the Talmud is considered a יָחִיד, *distinguished individual (Tos. Yom Tov; Rosh; Tos.).*

שָׁלֹשׁ תַּעֲנִיּוֹת. — [*a series of*] *three fasts.*

I.e., Monday, Thursday, and the following Monday *(Rav).*

Tosafos (Bava Kamma 82a) explains why the fasts were decreed for no days other than Mondays and Thursdays. The *Midrash* states that Moses ascended Mount Sinai on a Thursday to receive the second pair of Tablets. His descent on Yom

4. If the seventeenth [day] of *MarCheshvan* arrived but rain did not fall, the [distinguished] individuals would start fasting [a series of] three fasts. They may eat and drink after dark, and they are permitted to work, bathe, anoint [themselves with oil], wear shoes, and have marital relations.

5. If *Rosh Chodesh Kislev* arrived but rain did not fall, *Beth Din* decrees [a series of] three fasts

YAD AVRAHAM

Kippur with the Tablets took place on a Monday. Since those were days of Divine good will and forgiveness, the Rabbis chose them for Torah readings and fast days.

Just as the series of communal fasts was not begun on Thursday (2:9), so were the fast days of the distinguished individuals not commenced on a Thursday *(Tos. Yom Tov)*. [See 2:9 for the reason the fast day series were begun on Mondays.]

אוֹכְלִין וְשׁוֹתִין מִשֶּׁחֲשֵׁכָה, — *They may eat and drink after dark,*

During the night preceding the fasts, they may eat and drink until they retire. Once they go to sleep, however, they are prohibited from eating even if they wake up before dawn, because it may be assumed that one who has gone to sleep has no intention of getting up before dawn for a meal. Thus, his retiring to bed is tantamount to acceptance of the prohibitions of the fast. However, if he stipulates that he intends to awake before dawn to eat, then he may do so. Some authorities hold that for drinking, stipulation is not required, since people have no set time for drinking. Therefore, retiring is no indication that the person does not intend to drink anymore *(Tos. Yom Tov; Rav)*.

וּמֻתָּרִין בִּמְלָאכָה וּבִרְחִיצָה וּבְסִיכָה וּבִנְעִילַת הַסַּנְדָּל וּבְתַשְׁמִישׁ הַמִּטָּה. — *and they are permitted to work, bathe, anoint [themselves with oil], wear shoes, and have marital relations.*

[These activities are mentioned here because they are prohibited on Yom Kippur, *Tishah B'Av*, and on certain fasts decreed upon the community by the *Beth Din*. The forms of Rabbinically enacted fast days vary in severity. *Tishah B'Av*, for example, extends from sundown to nightfall of the next day, and includes many of the restrictions of Yom Kippur. The other communal fasts — *Tzom Gedaliah*, Tenth of *Teves*, *Taanis Esther*, and Seventeenth of *Tammuz* — begin in the morning and are less restrictive regarding other activities. Similar variations are found regarding the fasts imposed because of drought (see mishnah 6). The first and second series of fasts described in our mishnah are less stringent than those that are imposed later if the emergency continues.]

5.

הִגִּיעַ רֹאשׁ חֹדֶשׁ כִּסְלֵו וְלֹא יָרְדוּ גְשָׁמִים, — *If Rc-h Chodesh Kislev arrived but rain lid not fall,*

Kislev is the month after *MarCheshvan*, and *Rosh Chodesh Kislev* is nearly two weeks after the

א ו תַּעֲנִיּוֹת עַל־הַצִּבּוּר. אוֹכְלִין וְשׁוֹתִין מִשֶּׁחֲשֵׁכָה, וּמֻתָּרִין בִּמְלָאכָה וּבִרְחִיצָה וּבְסִיכָה וּבִנְעִילַת הַסַּנְדָּל וּבְתַשְׁמִישׁ הַמִּטָּה.

[ו] **עָבְרוּ** אֵלּוּ וְלֹא נַעֲנוּ, בֵּית דִּין גּוֹזְרִין שָׁלֹשׁ תַּעֲנִיּוֹת אֲחֵרוֹת עַל־הַצִּבּוּר. אוֹכְלִין וְשׁוֹתִין מִבְּעוֹד יוֹם, וַאֲסוּרִין בִּמְלָאכָה וּבִרְחִיצָה וּבְסִיכָה וּבִנְעִילַת הַסַּנְדָּל

יד אברהם

normal date of the third rain. For no rain to have fallen by then is indeed considered a calamity, since the third rain never falls later than the seventeenth of *MarCheshvan* in a normal year *(Tos. Yom Tov).*

בֵּית דִּין גּוֹזְרִין שָׁלֹשׁ תַּעֲנִיּוֹת... — *Beth Din decrees* [*a series of*] *three fasts...*

The series of fasts begins with a Monday and continues on Thursday and the following Monday *(Rav; Tif. Yis.).*

עַל־הַצִּבּוּר. — *upon the* [*entire*] *community.*

[Since the dimension of the drought had continued to worsen, the fasts were no longer voluntarily kept by individuals, but were decreed compulsory for the entire community.]

אוֹכְלִין וְשׁוֹתִין מִשֶּׁחֲשֵׁכָה, — *They may eat and drink after dark,*

They were permitted to eat and drink during the night preceding the fast *(Rav* 1:4).

וּמֻתָּרִין בִּמְלָאכָה וּבִרְחִיצָה וּבְסִיכָה וּבִנְעִילַת הַסַּנְדָּל וּבְתַשְׁמִישׁ הַמִּטָּה. — *and they are permitted to work, bathe, anoint* [*themselves with oil*], *wear shoes, and have marital relations.*

[These fasts were given the same degree of leniency as the fasts of the distinguished individuals mentioned in mishnah 4; but not the stringency of the ten fasts mentioned in mishnah 6.]

6.

עָבְרוּ אֵלּוּ וְלֹא נַעֲנוּ, — *If these* [*fasts*] *passed and they were not answered* [*with rain*],

[I.e., if the first three communal fasts went by without Heavenly response to the prayers for rain ...]

בֵּית דִּין גּוֹזְרִין שָׁלֹשׁ תַּעֲנִיּוֹת אֲחֵרוֹת עַל־הַצִּבּוּר. — *Beth Din decrees* [*a series of*] *three more* [lit. *other*] *fasts upon the entire community.*

[Perhaps these are designated as *other fasts* because their restrictions differ from those of the fasts mentioned previously.]

These fasts too are observed on Monday, Thursday, and Monday *(Tif. Yis.).*

אוֹכְלִין וְשׁוֹתִין מִבְּעוֹד יוֹם, — *They may eat and drink* [*only*] *while it is still daytime,*

Like Yom Kippur and *Tishah B'Av,* these fasts begin from the previous sunset *(Tos. Yom Tov).*

וַאֲסוּרִין בִּמְלָאכָה ... — *and they are forbidden to work,*

The *Gemara* bases the prohibi-

upon the [entire] community. They may eat and drink after dark, and they are permitted to work, bathe, anoint [themselves with oil], wear shoes, and have marital relations.

6. If these [fasts] passed and they were not answered [with rain], *Beth Din* decrees [a series of] three more fasts upon the [entire] community. They may eat and drink [only] while it is still daytime, and they are forbidden to work, bathe, anoint [themselves with oil], wear shoes, and have

tion of work on the verse: קַדְּשׁוּ־צוֹם קִרְאוּ עֲצָרָה, *Sanctify a fast, summon assembly (Joel* 2:15). The name given the fast day, עֲצָרָה is similar to עֲצֶרֶת, the name given to Shavuos (*Moed Katan* 3:6), and to *Shemini Atzeres (Numbers* 29:35). Since work is forbidden on those days, we derive that work is forbidden on fast days as well *(Tos. Yom Tov).*

Alshich (Joel 1:14) explains that one is more likely to repent when he abandons his mundane pursuits and takes time to meditate over his shortcomings than if he continues his daily routine. Therefore, work is forbidden on these fast days.

Similarly, *Rabbeinu Yonah* writes in *Shaarei Teshuvah* (2:14) concerning the Ten Days of Penitence: How foolish are those who go out to their activities and to their work until evening, during the Days of Awe, the Days of Judgment ... it is fitting for every God-fearing person to minimize his business and to humble his thoughts; to set times by day and by night to seclude himself in his chamber to search his ways; and to arise early, and to engage in the ways of repentance and in improving his deeds.

וּבִרְחִיצָה... — *bathe,*

Although the very activities that are forbidden on communal fasts are also forbidden on *Tishah B'Av,* the *Gemara* draws a distinction between them. On fast days such pursuits are forbidden because they afford pleasure; therefore the Rabbis prohibited only bathing the *entire* body with hot water. Washing the face, hands, and feet with hot water or bathing the entire body with cold water is permissible. The prohibitions of *Tishah B'Av,* however, are designed to demonstrate mourning for the destruction of the Temple. They are, therefore, similar to the prohibitions of שִׁבְעָה [*shivah*], *the seven*-day mourning period, when even partial bathing with warm and complete bathing with cold water are forbidden. There is, however, one particular in which *Tishah B'Av* is more stringent than *shivah.* A mourner may wash his face, hands, and feet with cold water, but on *Tishah B'Av,* even that is forbidden *(Rosh).* [See below on locking the bathhouses.]

וּבְסִיכָה... — *anoint* [*themselves with oil*],

Anointing is only forbidden when it is done for pleasure, but to remove filth it is permissible

א וּבְתַשְׁמִישׁ הַמִּטָּה, וְנוֹעֲלִין אֶת־הַמֶּרְחֲצָאוֹת.
ו עָבְרוּ אֵלּוּ וְלֹא נַעֲנוּ, בֵּית דִּין גּוֹזְרִין עֲלֵיהֶם
עוֹד שֶׁבַע שֶׁהֵן שְׁלֹשׁ עֶשְׂרֵה תַעֲנִיּוֹת עַל־
הַצִּבּוּר.

הֲרֵי אֵלּוּ יְתֵרוֹת עַל־הָרִאשׁוֹנוֹת, שֶׁבְּאֵלּוּ
מַתְרִיעִין וְנוֹעֲלִין אֶת־הַחֲנוּיוֹת. בַּשֵּׁנִי מַטִּין עִם
חֲשֵׁכָה, וּבַחֲמִישִׁי מֻתָּרִין מִפְּנֵי כְבוֹד הַשַּׁבָּת.

(*Orach Chaim* 575:3); and surely, if one has sores on his head, he may anoint them with oil (*Mishnah Berurah* 575:3).

וּבִנְעִילַת הַסַּנְדָּל... — *wear shoes,*

I.e., leather shoes or sandals (see *Orach Chaim* 554:16).

וּבְתַשְׁמִישׁ הַמִּטָּה, — *and have marital relations,*

This is forbidden even if the fast coincides with the night she immerses herself after her menstrual period *(Mishnah Berurah* 575:8; *Pri Megadim).*

וְנוֹעֲלִין אֶת־הַמֶּרְחֲצָאוֹת. — *Also, they must lock the* [*public*] *bathhouses.*

Lest people bathe with hot water, the bathhouses that provide such facilities must be locked. From the fact that the mishnah specifies bathhouses, the *Gemara* (13a) derives that only *hot* water bathing is forbidden on these fast days.

עָבְרוּ אֵלּוּ וְלֹא נַעֲנוּ, — *If these* [*fasts*] *passed and they were not answered* [*with rain*],

[If it still did not rain even after the second series of fasts...]

בֵּית דִּין גּוֹזְרִין עֲלֵיהֶם עוֹד שֶׁבַע... — *Beth Din decrees* [*a series of*] *seven more* [*fasts*] *upon them* —

Beginning, as always, on a Monday, the seven fasts would include four consecutive Mondays and three consecutive Thursdays *(Tif. Yis.).*

שֶׁהֵן שְׁלֹשׁ עֶשְׂרֵה תַעֲנִיּוֹת עַל־הַצִּבּוּר. — *totaling thirteen fasts upon the* [*entire*] *community.*

This total includes the two series of communal fasts enumerated in mishnayos 5 and 6. The three fasts of the distinguished individuals, (mishnah 4), however, are not included [since the phrase עַל־הַצִּבּוּר, *upon the community,* applies only to those fasts which were decreed upon the entire community] *(Rav).*

The Tanna supplies the apparently obvious total of the fasts for two reasons:

(1) The number 'thirteen' corresponds to God's Thirteen Attributes of Mercy (שְׁלֹשׁ עֶשְׂרֵה מִדּוֹת הָרַחֲמִים, *Exod.* 34:6, 7). By fasting thirteen times, we hope to evoke these merciful attributes.[1]

(2) Thirteen is the maximum

1. After Israel sinned by making the golden calf, Moses thought that the gravity of the sin was such that no forgiveness was possible. God appeared to him as a cantor wrapped in his *talis* [to indicate that he should pray] and taught him the liturgy of the Thirteen Attributes of Mercy. The Holy One, Blessed be He, assured Moses that whenever Israel sins, they should follow this order of prayer, and they would be forgiven (*Rosh HaShanah* 17b). [This is the basis for the *Selichos* prayers recited

1 marital relations. Also, they must lock the [public]
6 bathhouses.

If these [fasts] passed and they were not answered [with rain], *Beth Din* decrees [a series of] seven more [fasts] upon them — totaling thirteen fasts upon the [entire] community.

These [latter seven fasts] are more stringent than the earlier ones, for on these they sound the *shofar* and lock the stores. On Monday they may open [the store doors] partially toward evening; but on Thursday they are permitted [to keep the doors open] in honor of the Sabbath.

YAD AVRAHAM

number of fasts that *Beth Din* ever imposes on the community *(Tos. Yom Tov).*

Tosefos Yom Tov cites a *Beraisa* (14b) which notes a dispute between Rabi [R' Yehudah HaNassi] and Rabban Shimon ben Gamliel. Rabi holds that the number of public fasts decreed for any calamity is limited to thirteen because more would constitute a greater burden than the community could bear. If so, no more than thirteen would be imposed no matter what the emergency. Rabban Shimon ben Gamliel contends that by the time the thirteen fasts are over, the season when rains are most beneficial has ended, for it would be the end of *Teves* or the beginning of *Shevat.* Theoretically, therefore, more than thirteen fasts could be decreed if a calamity other than a drought came and lingered on.

הֲרֵי אֵלּוּ יְתֵרוֹת עַל־הָרִאשׁוֹנוֹת, — *These [latter seven fasts] are more stringent than the earlier ones,*

[The final seven fasts are more stringent than the three fasts immediately preceding them.]

...שֶׁבְּאֵלּוּ מַתְרִיעִין — *for on those they sound the shofar...*

[There are two types of shofar sounds: *tekiah* and *teruah.* (The *shevarim* blasts used on Rosh HaShanah are a form of *teruah*). The *tekiah* is a long, unbroken sound, while the *teruah* is a series of short, staccato sounds. Whenever the shofar is blown, both *tekiah* and *teruah* are sounded. That our mishnah uses only the term מַתְרִיעִין [lit. *they blow the teruah sound*] indicates that the *teruah* is one of special significance in connection with these fasts.]

Tiferes Yisrael explains that the *teruah* is mentioned here because it is reminiscent of sobbing, and is therefore appropriate to times of distress (*Num.* 10:9). The *tekiah,* although it must be sounded before and after the *teruah,* is of secondary importance during times of calamity.

וְנוֹעֲלִין אֶת־הַחֲנוּיוֹת. — *and lock the stores.*

All stores should be closed in order to facilitate the mood of repentance as explained above. As the mishnah goes on to explain, exceptions were made. However, the

during the weeks prior to Yom Kippur, and on fast days. The recitation of the Thirteen Attributes is repeated throughout the *Selichos.* (See also ArtScroll's *Tashlich and the Thirteen Attributes.)*]

א
ז

[ז] **עָבְרוּ** אֵלּוּ וְלֹא נַעֲנוּ, מְמַעֲטִין בְּמַשָּׂא וּמַתָּן, בְּבִנְיָן וּבִנְטִיעָה, בְּאֵרוּסִין וּבְנִשּׂוּאִין, וּבִשְׁאֵלַת שָׁלוֹם בֵּין אָדָם לַחֲבֵרוֹ, כִּבְנֵי אָדָם הַנְּזוּפִין לַמָּקוֹם.

הַיְּחִידִים חוֹזְרִים וּמִתְעַנִּים עַד שֶׁיֵּצֵא נִיסָן. יָצָא נִיסָן וְיָרְדוּ גְשָׁמִים, סִימַן קְלָלָה, שֶׁנֶּאֱמַר: ,,הֲלוֹא קְצִיר־חִטִּים הַיּוֹם, וגו׳.״

יד אברהם

...וּבַחֲמִישִׁי — *but on Thursday* [i.e., on fast days proclaimed on Thursdays]...

מַתִּרִין מִפְּנֵי כְבוֹד הַשַּׁבָּת. — *they are permitted [to keep the doors open] in honor of the Sabbath.*

They are permitted to keep food stores open [wide *(Tif. Yis.)*] all day *(Rav).*

Food stores are allowed to be open all day because the preparation and cooking of food requires considerable time. Since food had to be prepared for the Sabbath as well as for the evening, the Sages allowed more time for shopping *(Tos. Yom Tov).*

However, stores selling beverages *only* could not be opened until Friday because their wares are sold ready to drink and need no special preparation *(Orach Chaim* 575:4).

exceptions applied only to food stores; other commercial establishments were required to remain closed throughout the fast day (*Beis Yosef* 575).

בַּשֵּׁנִי מַטִּין עִם חֲשֵׁכָה, — *On Monday they may open [the store doors] partially toward evening;*

The doors were kept partly open to allow customers to enter and make their purchases, but merchandise was not taken into the street for display *(Rambam; Rav).* [The general principle is that while it might be necessary to enable people to purchase goods, the day should not be treated as a normal business day.]

This dispensation referred only to food stores so that the populace could purchase food and drink for the evening meal (*Rashi; Tos. Yom Tov; Orach Chaim* 575:4).

7.

...עָבְרוּ אֵלּוּ — *If these [fasts] passed...*

[I.e., if this last series of seven fasts went by.]

וְלֹא נַעֲנוּ, — *and they were not answered [with rain],*

[If no rain fell after the thirteen fast days ended, no more fasts are decreed, as explained in mishnah 6. Instead, a period of mourning is declared upon the community for the rest of the winter, including many of the restrictions associated with mourning. Its restrictions are similar to those observed during the first nine days of *Av.* See 4:6.]

מְמַעֲטִין בְּמַשָּׂא וּמַתָּן, — *they must decrease commerce,*

The restriction against business transactions is limited to the buying and selling of merchandise used for joyous occasions, such as weddings

7. If these [fasts] passed and they were not answered [with rain], they must decrease commerce, construction, planting, betrothals, marriages, and greeting one another — as [befits] people censured by the Omnipresent.

The [distinguished] individuals resume their fasting until *Nissan* is over. If after *Nissan* ended rain fell, it is a symptom of curse; as it says: *Is today not the wheat harvest...?* [*I Samuel* 12:17].

YAD AVRAHAM

and the like (*Magen Avraham, Orach Chaim* 575, note 6).

בְּבִנְיָן וּבִנְטִיעָה, — *construction, planting,*

The limitation applies only to building and planting for joyous purposes, e.g., building a house for a marriage feast or planting shade trees, but building dwellings and planting fruit trees are permitted (*Rav; Gem.* 14b).

The *Shulchan Aruch* rules that any building which is not needed for dwelling, and is built for profit, is considered a building of joy. Also, myrtle trees and other spice trees are considered plantings of joy (551:1).

בְּאֵרוּסִין וּבְנִשּׂוּאִין, — *betrothals, marriages,*

This prohibition applies only to one who had previously been married and has children; thus he has fulfilled the commandment of פְּרוּ וּרְבוּ, *Be fruitful and multiply (Gen.* 2:7). One who has no children, however, is permitted to betroth or marry (*Tif. Yis.; Orach Chaim* 575:8).

וּבִשְׁאֵלַת שָׁלוֹם בֵּין אָדָם לַחֲבֵרוֹ, כִּבְנֵי אָדָם הַנְּזוּפִין לַמָּקוֹם. — *and greeting one another — as [befits] people censured by the Omnipresent.*

[Just as people who are under a ban are not to be greeted (see *Moed Katan* 3:1), the individual members of a community that received no rain during the entire rainy season must consider one another as if they are under such a ban.]

It is as though the Almighty Himself had censured them, [since He had deprived them of essential rain for the entire rainy season (*Tif. Yis.*).

הַיְחִידִים חוֹזְרִים וּמִתְעַנִּים עַד שֶׁיֵּצֵא נִיסָן. — *The [distinguished] individuals resume their fasting until Nissan is over.*

The individual scholars resume their voluntary fasts on Mondays and Thursdays as described in mishnah 4 (*Orach Chaim* 575:8).

The *Nissan* in our mishnah refers not to the month in our lunar calendar, but to the solar equivalent of *Nissan* when the sun enters the sign of Taurus (*Tos. Yom Tov; Yerushalmi*). This occurs thirty days after the *Nissan* cycle of the sun, approximately April 2 (*Beer HaGolah* 575:7).

Since the individuals resume their fasting until the end of the solar *Nissan*, rainfall is beneficial until then. If so, why should fasting not be decreed upon the community at large? [See above, mishnah 6.]

The general community is absolved because rainfall so late in the season would be of no *natural* benefit, nevertheless, there is still

ב [א] סֵדֶר תַּעֲנִיּוֹת כֵּיצַד? מוֹצִיאִין אֶת־
א הַתֵּבָה לִרְחוֹבָהּ שֶׁל עִיר וְנוֹתְנִין
אֵפֶר מִקְלֶה עַל־גַּבֵּי הַתֵּבָה, וּבְרֹאשׁ הַנָּשִׂיא,
וּבְרֹאשׁ אַב בֵּית דִּין; וְכָל אֶחָד וְאֶחָד נוֹתֵן
בְּרֹאשׁוֹ.

יד אברהם

room for prayer that God will perform a miracle as He did in the time of Joel (see above 1:2). Fasts and prayers for such a miracle are offered by people of outstanding piety and Torah scholarship. These fasts and prayers are conducted privately by each individual in his own home. The public is not informed about these fasts, lest they despair if the prayers are not answered *(Ritva).*

יָצָא נִיסָן וְיָרְדוּ גְשָׁמִים, סִימַן קְלָלָה, — *If after Nissan ended rain fell, it is a symptom of curse;*

If no rain fell before the end of *Nissan* but it rained afterwards, that is a symptom of a curse. The presence of rain when it is of no benefit accentuates the displeasure indicated by God's refusal to give rain when it was needed *(Rav).*

Tosefos Yom Tov comments that our reading follows that found in the *Gemara, Rav,* and most accurate texts. Most traditional *Mishnah* texts read וְלֹא יָרְדוּ גְשָׁמִים, [*if Nissan passed*] *and no rain fell.* The meaning of the second reading is the same, however: post-*Nissan* rain is a curse if no rain fell before then.

שֶׁנֶּאֱמַר ,,הֲלוֹא קְצִיר־חִטִּים הַיּוֹם וְגוֹמֵר״. — *as it says, 'Is today not the wheat harvest...?'* [*I Samuel* 12:17].

[When the people made an improper request for a king and ignored Samuel's rebuke, he demonstrated God's displeasure by causing rainfall during the wheat harvest. The people responded that since the rain had fallen out of season, it was a curse, and they begged him to pray for them.]

Rav notes that the dates given in this chapter refer only to *Eretz Yisrael,* where rain is needed during the winter season, but not after the end of *Nissan.* In other countries, however, special prayers and fasts for rain are declared according to the particular needs and conditions of that country.

Chapter 2

1.

סֵדֶר תַּעֲנִיּוֹת כֵּיצַד? — *What is the order* [*of service*] *for fast days?*

The seven final and most stringent of the communal fasts have a unique order of prayers which the mishnah will now discuss [see 1:6] *(Rav; Gem.* 15b).

מוֹצִיאִין אֶת־הַתֵּבָה... — *They would bring out the Ark...*

The Ark was removed from the synagogue with the Torah scroll still in it *(Rashi* on *Rif; Tif. Yis.).*

This does not refer to the אֲרוֹן הַקֹּדֶשׁ, *Holy Ark,* which was built into the eastern wall of the synagogue, and toward which the congregation's prayers were directed. Rather, it refers to a long, narrow,

2
1

1. **W**hat is the order [of service] for fast days? They would bring out the Ark to the town square and place ashes upon the Ark, the head of the *Nassi* and the head of the chief of the court. Everyone [else] places [ashes] on his [own] head.

YAD AVRAHAM

portable box containing one Torah Scroll. It was placed either in front of the *chazan (Bach; Tur Orach Chaim* 150), or on the בִּימָה, *central platform,* before the reading of the Torah *(Bais Yosef 150).*

... לִרְחוֹבָהּ שֶׁל עִיר — *to the town square...*

The Ark's relatively secluded position in the synagogue symbolized the modest lack of ostentation that becomes Israel. Now, it was removed from its private place of honor and, so to speak, exposed to the gaze of all passersby in the public square. This was done as if to say: 'Behold! This secluded vessel was shamed through our sins' (*Rav; Gem.* 16a).

The people congregated in the public square as if to say: 'Our prayers in the synagogue were not answered; let us humiliate ourselves publicly — perhaps we will thus invoke Divine mercy' *(Rav; Tif. Yis.; Gem.* 16a).

Additionally, this service was held outdoors to symbolize the national condition of exile. Therefore, if services cannot be held in the town square for any reason, they should not be conducted in the synagogue but, rather, in the 'exile' of another building *(Tif. yis.; Magen Avraham 579:1).*

...וְנוֹתְנִין אֵפֶר מִקְלֶה — *and place ashes* [lit. *burnt ashes*]...

The mishnah adds the adjective מִקְלֶה, *burnt,* because אֵפֶר (which usually means *ashes*) is often used as a synonym for עָפָר, *earth (Rashi).*

Ashes are used as a reminder of Isaac's 'ashes.' We beseech God to have mercy on us in the merit of Abraham, who was ready to sacrifice his 'only' son and burn him to ashes in the service of God, and in the merit of Isaac who willingly agreed *(Gem.* 16a).

עַל־גַּבֵּי הַתֵּבָה, — *upon the Ark,*

Placing ashes upon the Ark, which had been brought to the public square, symbolizes that God joins us in our distress, so to speak, as it is written: עִמּוֹ אָנֹכִי בְצָרָה, *I* [God] *am with him* [Israel] *in distress (Psalms* 91:15); and בְּכָל־צָרָתָם לוֹ צָר, *in their every distress, He is in distress (Isaiah* 63:9). As R' Zeira said: 'When I saw the rabbis place ashes upon the Ark, my entire body trembled' (*Gem.* 16a).

Rambam adds that ashes are placed even on the Torah Scroll itself. [This follows the alternative version of *Rif* and *Rosh* who render נוֹתְנִין...עַל־גַּבֵּי סֵפֶר תּוֹרָה, *we place ... on the Torah Scroll*]. According to *Baal HaTzeroros,* this placing of ashes on the *Sefer Torah* was not required by the mishnah. It was, rather, a custom practised in Amoraic times. (See notes on *Pekudas HaLevi'im,* p. 15).

וּבְרֹאשׁ הַנָּשִׂיא, וּבְרֹאשׁ אַב בֵּית דִּין; — *(and upon) the head of the Nassi, and (upon) the head of the Chief of the Court;*

[Concerning these positions, see *Chagigah* 2:2.]

ב ב הַזָּקֵן שֶׁבָּהֶן אוֹמֵר לִפְנֵיהֶן דִּבְרֵי כִבּוּשִׁין: אַחֵינוּ, לֹא נֶאֱמַר בְּאַנְשֵׁי נִינְוֵה ,,וַיַּרְא הָאֱלֹהִים אֶת־שַׂקָּם וְאֶת־תַּעֲנִיתָם״, אֶלָּא ,,וַיַּרְא הָאֱלֹהִים אֶת־מַעֲשֵׂיהֶם, כִּי שָׁבוּ מִדַּרְכָּם הָרָעָה״. וּבַקַּבָּלָה הוּא אוֹמֵר: ,,וְקִרְעוּ לְבַבְכֶם וְאַל־בִּגְדֵיכֶם״.

[ב] **עָמְדוּ** בִתְפִלָּה. מוֹרִידִין לִפְנֵי הַתֵּבָה זָקֵן וְרָגִיל, וְיֵשׁ לוֹ בָנִים וּבֵיתוֹ

יד אברהם

The congregants would place ashes upon the heads of the *Nassi* and the Chief of the Court. Thus the humility of these great men was heightened because, as the nation's most prominent leaders, they were accustomed to the deference of all others *(Gem.* 15b-16a).

וְכָל אֶחָד וְאֶחָד נוֹתֵן בְּרֹאשׁוֹ. — *Everyone* [*else*] *places* [*ashes*] *upon his* [*own*] *head.*

In contrast to the two leaders who submitted to the humiliation of others, members of the community placed the ashes on their own heads. Common people are not more humiliated when others shame them than when they do so themselves. Therefore, it is sufficient for each to place the ashes himself *(Rashi* 16a).

הַזָּקֵן שֶׁבָּהֶן אוֹמֵר לִפְנֵיהֶן דִּבְרֵי כִבּוּשִׁין: — *The eldest among them would preach words of inspiration before them:*

[The word זָקֵן, *elder,* is meant to be understood as an acronym for זֶה קָנָה חָכְמָה, *this one acquired wisdom.* Thus the term implies not just old, but old and wise.]

The expression דִּבְרֵי כִבּוּשִׁין, from מַכְבֵּשׁ, *press,* connotes words that 'press' the heart and inspire it to repent *(Tos. Yom Tov; Rashi.* See also *Rambam, Hilchos Taaniyos* 4:2).

Another interpretation of דִּבְרֵי כִבּוּשִׁין is *words regarding hidden things.* A similar use of the words is found in the expression כַּבְשֵׁי דְרַחֲמָנָא, *hidden matters of the All Merciful* (as in *Berachos* 10a). The elders would preach that God knows man's thoughts even though man may strive to conceal them *(Eliyah Rabbah* 1:3).

[The elder would commence with the following words of inspiration:]

אַחֵינוּ, לֹא נֶאֱמַר בְּאַנְשֵׁי נִינְוֵה ,,וַיַּרְא הָאֱלֹהִים אֶת־שַׂקָּם וְאֶת־תַּעֲנִיתָם״, אֶלָּא, ,,וַיַּרְא הָאֱלֹהִים, אֶת־מַעֲשֵׂיהֶם כִּי שָׁבוּ מִדַּרְכָּם הָרָעָה.״ — *'Our brethren, it is not stated regarding the people of Nineveh: And God saw their sackcloth and their fast, but rather: And God saw their deeds, that they repented their evil ways (Jonah* 3:6).'

[Although all Ninevites wore sackcloth and fasted, God hearkened to their cries and relented only because they truly repented.]

Fasting and wearing sackcloth help foster humility and submissiveness. Their importance is that they *prepare* one for repentance, but they cannot substitute for it *(Maharsha).*

2
2 The eldest among them would preach words of inspiration before them: 'Our brethren, it is not stated regarding the people of Nineveh: *And God saw their sackloth and their fasting,* but [rather]: *And God saw their deeds, that they repented their evil ways* [*Jonah* 3:6]. And in the admonition he states: *Now rend your hearts and not your clothing* [*Joel* 2:13].'

2. They [then] began to pray.

They send before the Ark a well-versed elder who has children and whose house is empty, so that

YAD AVRAHAM

וּבַקַּבָּלָה הוּא אוֹמֵר: — *And in the admonition, he* [i.e., the prophet] *states:*

The Tanna refers to the following words of direct rebuke by the prophet Joel as קַבָּלָה [from the root קבל, *to cry (Shitah Mekubetzes, Bava Kamma* 2b)]. The quotation from *Jonah,* however, is not referred to as קַבָּלָה, *rebuke,* because it is a narrative *(Rashi).*

The word קַבָּלָה also means *tradition* and is used to refer to a quotation from the Prophets or Writings. This is not the intended meaning here [for then the verse from *Jonah* would also be so described] *(Pesach Einayim).*

,,וְקִרְעוּ לְבַבְכֶם... — *Now rend your hearts (Joel* 2:13),

— Tear all evil thoughts and wickedness from your hearts *(Targum Yonasan; Radak).*

— Remove from your hearts the block which prevents you from being receptive to thoughts of truth and repentance *(Ibn Ezra).*

— Subdue your hearts *(Metzudas David).*

וְאַל־בִּגְדֵיכֶם״. — *and not your clothing.'*

— Do not be content with rending only your clothing *(Metzudas David).*

— God does not take notice of the mere rending of your clothing [because it lacks sincerity] *(Rashi).*

— If you rend your hearts and sincerely repent, it will be unnecessary for you to rend your garments in mourning for your sons and daughters *(Rashi; Radak; Abarbanel; Pesikta d'Rav Kahana* 25; *Yerushalmi, Taanis* 2:1).

The elder continues to preach according to his ability until the congregation is humbled and inspired to repent (*Rambam, Taaniyos* 4:2).

2.

עָמְדוּ בִתְפִלָּה. — *They* [*then*] *began to pray* [lit. *stood in prayer*].

[In Talmudic usage, the word תְּפִלָּה, *prayer,* almost invariably refers to *Shemoneh Esrei.* On weekdays, the only days when public fasts are proclaimed, there are of course, three prayers. On the fasts for calamities the Rabbis instituted a נְעִילָה [*Ne'ilah*], *concluding prayer,* just as they did on Yom Kippur.]

Our mishnah begins with שַׁחֲרִית, [*Shacharis*], *the morning prayer.*

ב רֵיקָם, כְּדֵי שֶׁיְּהֵא לִבּוֹ שָׁלֵם בִּתְפִלָּה. וְאוֹמֵר
ג לִפְנֵיהֶם עֶשְׂרִים וְאַרְבַּע בְּרָכוֹת: שְׁמֹנֶה עֶשְׂרֵה
שֶׁבְּכָל־יוֹם, וּמוֹסִיף עֲלֵיהֶן עוֹד שֵׁשׁ.

[ג] **וְאֵלּוּ** הֵן: זִכְרוֹנוֹת; וְשׁוֹפָרוֹת; ,,אֶל־ה׳ בַּצָּרָתָה לִּי קָרָאתִי וַיַּעֲנֵנִי״; ,,אֶשָּׂא עֵינַי אֶל־הֶהָרִים וגו׳ ״; ,,מִמַּעֲמַקִּים קְרָאתִיךָ ה׳ ״; ,,תְּפִלָּה לְעָנִי כִי־יַעֲטֹף״.

יד אברהם

However, the order of the service as described here is repeated at מִנְחָה, [*Minchah*], *the afternoon prayer*, and *Ne'ilah (Tif. Yis.; Tur Orach Chaim 575, 579; Beis Yosef).*

[Although *Rambam* mentions only *Shacharis* and *Minchah* in *Taaniyos 3:7*, it is clear from *Taaniyos* 4:18 that *Ne'ilah*, too, is included.]

מוֹרִידִין לִפְנֵי הַתֵּבָה... — *They send* [lit. *lower*] *before the Ark* [as *chazan*]...

[I.e., before the small ark which had been was brought out to the town square. See above mishnah 1.]

זָקֵן וְרָגִיל, — *a well-versed elder,*

I.e., well-versed in prayer. They were apprehensive that one not well-versed might err and cause the people to fear an evil omen. *Berachos* 5:5 states that if one errs in his prayers, it is a bad sign for him. Similarly, if the delegate of the congregation errs, it is a bad sign for those who sent him *(Rashi).*

Rambam adds that the *chazan* should be well-versed in תּוֹרָה נְבִיאִים וּכְתוּבִים, *Pentateuch, Prophets, and Writings*, so that he would understand the additional passages of the fast day prayer.

וְיֵשׁ לוֹ בָנִים וּבֵיתוֹ רֵיקָם, — *who has children and whose house is empty,*

This can be understood literally: He has a family dependent on him for support, but his cupboard is bare.

Alternatively, וּבֵיתוֹ רֵיקָם, *whose house is empty*, means that his house should be free of sin; the *chazan* should be one whose reputation is impeccable *(Rav; Gem.* 16b).

Or, *his house is empty* of stolen goods *(Rashi).*

Alternatively, בֵּיתוֹ means *his household*, i.e., no member of his household is a sinner. The *chazan*, himself, surely must have an impeccable reputation, unblemished even by sins committed in his youth (*Tos. Yom Tov; Rambam).* [This last opinion is more stringent than the previous ones which require only that the *chazan* himself have an impeccable reputation.]

כְּדֵי שֶׁיְּהֵא לִבּוֹ שָׁלֵם בִּתְפִלָּה. — *so that his heart should be fully* [*devoted*] *in prayer.*

[Since he lacks the means to support his children, he is personally very distresssed, and will pray with great devotion and fervor. According to the other interpretations cited above, his personal, irreproachable piety will guarantee the sincerity of his prayer.]

וְאוֹמֵר לִפְנֵיהֶם עֶשְׂרִים וְאַרְבַּע בְּרָכוֹת: — *He recites before them twenty-four blessings:*

2 his heart should be fully [devoted] in prayer. He
3 recites before them twenty-four blessings: the eighteen which are [recited] every day, and six more which are added.

3. And they are as follows: *Zichronos, Shofaros;* To HASHEM in my distress I called and He answered me [Ps. 120]; I shall lift my eyes to the mountains etc. [Ps. 121]; From the depths have I called You, HASHEM [Ps. 130]; A prayer of the afflicted when he faints [Ps. 102].

YAD AVRAHAM

Individuals recite the normal weekday *Shemoneh Esrei,* but when the *chazan* repeats the *tefillah* aloud לִפְנֵיהֶם, *before them* [the congregation], his *Shemoneh Esrei* includes a total of twenty-four blessings (*Tur* 579).

שְׁמֹנֶה עֶשְׂרֵה שֶׁבְּכָל־יוֹם, — *the eighteen which are [recited] every day,*

[I.e., the regular weekday *Shemoneh Esrei.*]

וּמוֹסִיף עֲלֵיהֶן עוֹד שֵׁשׁ. — *and six more which are added* [lit. *and he adds six more to them*].

The six additional blessings, as delineated in the next mishnah, are inserted between the blessing that concludes: גּוֹאֵל יִשְׂרָאֵל, *Who redeems Israel,* and the blessing that concludes: רוֹפֵא חוֹלֵי עַמּוֹ יִשְׂרָאֵל, *Who heals the sick of His people Israel (Rav).* These additional blessings are recited only on fasts decreed because of calamities (*Tur* 579).

3.

וְאֵלּוּ הֵן: — *And they are as follows* [lit. *and these are they*]:

[These are the six blessings added to the fast day *Shemoneh Esrei.*]

זִכְרוֹנוֹת; וְשׁוֹפָרוֹת; — *Zichronos* [lit. *Remembrances*]; *Shofaros;*

The complete blessings of *Zichronos* and *Shofaros* that are recited in the *Musaf* of Rosh HaShanah are recited on communal fast days. These two blessings begin respectively with the words אַתָּה זוֹכֵר, *You remember,* and אַתָּה נִגְלֵיתָ, *You were revealed* [see *Rosh HaShanah* 4:5,6] *(Rav).*

[The mishnah now proceeds to list four psalms that are recited in their entirety. Each is concluded with a blessing as given in mishnah 4.]

,,אֶל־ה׳ בַּצָּרָתָה לִּי קָרָאתִי וַיַּעֲנֵנִי״; — *To HASHEM in my distress I called and He answered me [Psalms 120];*

,,אֶשָּׂא עֵינַי אֶל־הֶהָרִים וגו׳ ״; — *I shall lift my eyes to the mountains, etc. [Psalms 121].*

,,מִמַּעֲמַקִּים קְרָאתִיךָ ה׳ ״; — *From the depths have I called You,* HASHEM *[Psalms 130];*

,,תְּפִלָּה לְעָנִי כִּי־יַעֲטֹף״. — *A prayer of the afflicted when he faints [Psalms 102].*

These four psalms were recited after *Zichronos* and *Shofaros.* Altogether, they constitute the six

ב רַבִּי יְהוּדָה אוֹמֵר: לֹא הָיָה צָרִיךְ לוֹמַר
ד זִכְרוֹנוֹת וְשׁוֹפָרוֹת. אֶלָּא אוֹמֵר תַּחְתֵּיהֶן „רָעָב
כִּי־יִהְיֶה בָאָרֶץ, דֶּבֶר כִּי־יִהְיֶה וגו׳ ”; „דְּבַר־ה׳
אֲשֶׁר הָיָה אֶל־יִרְמְיָהוּ עַל־דִּבְרֵי הַבַּצָּרוֹת”.
וְאוֹמֵר חוֹתְמֵיהֶן.

[ד] **עַל־הָרִאשׁוֹנָה** הוּא אוֹמֵר: מִי שֶׁעָנָה אֶת־אַבְרָהָם בְּהַר הַמּוֹרִיָּה, הוּא יַעֲנֶה אֶתְכֶם וְיִשְׁמַע בְּקוֹל צַעֲקַתְכֶם הַיּוֹם הַזֶּה. בָּרוּךְ אַתָּה ה׳, גּוֹאֵל יִשְׂרָאֵל.

יד אברהם

additional blessings recited on fast days *(Tif. Yis.).*

רַבִּי יְהוּדָה אוֹמֵר: לֹא הָיָה צָרִיךְ לוֹמַר זִכְרוֹנוֹת וְשׁוֹפָרוֹת. — *R' Yehudah says: He was not obligated to say Zichronos and Shofaros.*

Tosefos Yom Tov explains that according to R' Yehudah, *Zichronos* and *Shofaros* are limited to Rosh HaShanah, the Jubilee Year, and time of war. The additional blessings of fast days, however, do not include *Zichronos* and *Shofaros (Tif. Yis.).*

אֶלָּא אוֹמֵר תַּחְתֵּיהֶן „רָעָב כִּי־יִהְיֶה בָאָרֶץ, דֶּבֶר כִּי־יִהְיֶה וגו׳ ”; — *But in their place he says: If there be a famine in the Land, if there be a pestilence...* [*I Kings* 8:37-40];

This prayer was recited by King Solomon upon the dedication of the Temple. In it he beseeched God to be responsive to prayers mercy in time of life-threatening natural disaster. According to R' Yehudah, these verses are recited in place of *Zichronos (Tif. Yis.).*

„דְּבַר־ה׳ אֲשֶׁר הָיָה אֶל־יִרְמְיָהוּ עַל־דִּבְרֵי הַבַּצָּרוֹת”. — *and The word of* HASHEM *which came to Jeremiah regarding the droughts* [*Jeremiah* 14:1-9].

These verses, describing the ravages of drought and concluding with pleas for Divine help even if we are unworthy, should be recited instead of the blessing of *Shofaros (Tif. Yis.).*

וְאוֹמֵר חוֹתְמֵיהֶן. — *He then says their* [*proper*] *endings.*

After digressing to give R' Yehudah's view, the mishnah now concludes the opinion of the first Tanna. After *Zichronos* and *Shofaros*, the reader concludes with the same blessings as those recited on Rosh HaShanah. Similarly, each of the other added blessings would be concluded with an appropriate concluding blessing as enumerated in mishnah 4 (Rav).

Tiferes Yisrael, however, maintains that this phrase is the conclusion of R' Yehudah's statement. Although R' Yehudah substitutes the passages from *Kings* and *Jeremiah* for recitation of *Zichronos* and *Shofaros,* he agrees, nevertheless, that the concluding blessings of those two passages are same as those of *Zichronos* and *Shofaros Tif. Yis.).*

R' Yehudah says: He was not obligated to say *Zichronos* and *Shofaros*. But in their place he says: *If there be a famine in the land, if there be a pestilence* ... [*I Kings* 8:35-40]; and *The word of* HASHEM *which came to Jeremiah regarding the droughts* [*Jer.* 14:1-9]. He then says their [proper] endings.

4. After the first he says: He Who answered Abraham on Mount Moriah, He shall answer you and hearken to the sound of your cry this day. Blessed are You, HASHEM Who redeems Israel.

YAD AVRAHAM

4.

[After having enumerated the substance of each of the fast day blessings, the mishnah goes on to delineate the conclusion of each one. According to *Tur Orach Chaim* 579, it was customary to precede the conclusion of each blessing with additional supplications. After the conclusion of each blessing, the shofar would be sounded and the Thirteen Divine Attributes of Mercy as well as other supplications would be recited before going on to the following blessing. As mentioned above, these special blessings were added only in the last series of seven fast days. See above 1:6.]

עַל הָרִאשׁוֹנָה הוּא אוֹמֵר: — *After* [lit., *on*] *the first he says:*

Our mishnah refers not to the first of the *additional* blessings, but to the blessing of רְאֵה נָא בְעָנְיֵנוּ, *Please see our affliction*, which is part of the daily *Shemoneh Esrei*. Unlike the other regular blessings, the text of this blessing is augmented on fast days. For this reason, our mishnah calls it the *first* blessing; it is the first blessing which includes additions for the fast *(Rav)*.

Below, the mishnah gives the insertion for fast days. However, before the text cited by the mishnah, two other paragraphs are added. The first begins עֲנֵנוּ ה' עֲנֵנוּ, *Answer us,* HASHEM, *answer us ...* , the paragraph that is recited on the regular, annual fast days. The blessing then incorporates a section before the conclusion of the Rosh HaShanah *Zichronos* prayer, beginning וְקַיֶּם־לָנוּ ה' אֱלֹהֵינוּ אֶת־הַבְּרִית וְאֶת־הַחֶסֶד..., *And fulfill for us,* HASHEM, *our God, the covenant and the loving-kindness...,* *(Tif. Yis.; Tur* 579).

[A total of seven blessings in the fast day *Shemoneh Esrei* deal with the special needs of the day — six additional blessings and this augmented blessing which the mishnah mentions first. Each of these leads up to its conclusion with a similar formula: ...מִי שֶׁעָנָה, *He Who answered* ... one of the great figures in Jewish history, ...הוּא יַעֲנֶה אֶתְכֶם, *He shall answer you...* on this fast day.]

מִי שֶׁעָנָה אֶת־אַבְרָהָם בְּהַר הַמּוֹרִיָּה, הוּא יַעֲנֶה אֶתְכֶם וְיִשְׁמַע בְּקוֹל צַעֲקַתְכֶם הַיּוֹם הַזֶּה. — *He who answered Abraham on Mount Moriah, He shall answer you and hearken to the sound of your cry this day.*

ב ד

עַל־הַשְּׁנִיָּה הוּא אוֹמֵר: מִי שֶׁעָנָה אֶת־אֲבוֹתֵינוּ עַל־יַם־סוּף, הוּא יַעֲנֶה אֶתְכֶם וְיִשְׁמַע קוֹל צַעֲקַתְכֶם הַיּוֹם הַזֶּה. בָּרוּךְ אַתָּה ה׳, זוֹכֵר הַנִּשְׁכָּחוֹת.

עַל־הַשְּׁלִישִׁית הוּא אוֹמֵר: מִי שֶׁעָנָה אֶת־יְהוֹשֻׁעַ בַּגִּלְגָּל, הוּא יַעֲנֶה אֶתְכֶם וְיִשְׁמַע קוֹל צַעֲקַתְכֶם הַיּוֹם הַזֶּה. בָּרוּךְ אַתָּה ה׳, שׁוֹמֵעַ תְּרוּעָה.

יד אברהם

Since Abraham was the first Jew to be saved through God's intervention, when he was thrown into the furnace by Nimrod, he is mentioned first *(Tos. Yom Tov; Tos.* 16b).[1]

בָּרוּךְ אַתָּה ה׳, גּוֹאֵל יִשְׂרָאֵל. — *Blessed are You, HASHEM, Who redeems Israel.*

Yerushalmi explains that when Isaac, the progenitor of Israel, was spared on Mount Moriah, it was as though all Israel had been redeemed; therefore, we conclude the blessing of Isaac's redemption by referring to God as Redeemer of [all] Israel *(Tos. Yom Tov; Ran).*

The congregants respond with *Amen,* and sound תְּקִיעָה תְּרוּעָה תְּקִיעָה, *tekiah, teruah, tekiah,* on the shofar.

The *chazan* continues with the Thirteen Divine Attributes of Mercy from *Exodus* 24:6-7.

He then adds: — *May Your loving-kindness with Your compassion come upon us today. Pour rain upon us today, whether [we are] like [Your] children or like [Your] servants. If like children, have compassion upon us as a father has compassion on his children. And if like servants, our eyes look to You until You are gracious to us* ... (For the continuation of the prayer, see *Tur Orach Chaim* 579.)

עַל־הַשְּׁנִיָּה הוּא אוֹמֵר: — *After the second he says:*

What the mishnah calls the *second* blessing, is the first of the additional fast day blessings. It is called the 'second' because, as explained above, an alteration had already been made in the regular

1. The Torah does not give the content of Abraham's prayer on Mount Moriah. He surely did not pray that Isaac be spared, since he was ready to carry out God's command; what, then, was his prayer?

Yerushalmi [*Taanis* 2:4] narrates that Abraham said before the Holy One, Blessed be He: Master of the Universe! It is known to You that when You commanded me to offer up my son Isaac, I could have answered, 'Yesterday You said to me, "כִּי בְיִצְחָק יִקָּרֵא לְךָ זָרַע, *since through Isaac will offspring be considered yours (Gen.* 21:12)," and now You say, "וְהַעֲלֵהוּ שָׁם לְעֹלָה, *and offer him up there as a burnt offering (Gen.* 22:2)." ' God forbid, I did not do so. Instead, I overpowered my temptation, and performed Your will. So may it be Your will, HASHEM, my God, that whenever my son Isaac's children will be in distress, and they will have no one to defend them, that *You* defend them. ה׳ יִרְאֶה, *HASHEM shall see (Gen.* 22:14) i.e., You shall remember for them the binding of Isaac and become filled with compassion for them.

2
4 After the second he says: He Who answered our forefathers at the Sea of Reeds, He shall answer you and hearken to the sound of your cry this day. Blessed are You, HASHEM, Who remembers the forgotten.

After the third he says: He Who answered Joshua in Gilgal, He shall answer you and hearken to the sound of your cry this day. Blessed are You, HASHEM, Who hearkens to the sounding of the shofar.

YAD AVRAHAM

blessing of רְאֵה נָא בְעָנְיֵנוּ, *Please see our affliction.* This second blessing consists of the Rosh HaShanah blessing which begins אַתָּה זוֹכֵר, *You remember...* This is the blessing of *Remembrances* mentioned in the previous mishnah *(Tif. Yis.; Tur).*

מִי שֶׁעָנָה אֶת־אֲבוֹתֵינוּ עַל־יַם־סוּף הוּא יַעֲנֶה אֶתְכֶם וְיִשְׁמַע קוֹל צַעֲקַתְכֶם הַיּוֹם הַזֶּה. — *He Who answered our forefathers at the Sea of Reeds, He shall answer you and hearken to the sound of your cry this day.*

This prayer is appropriate for the blessing of *Zichronos*, because God remembered our forefathers who were 'forgotten' in Egypt for so many years that they despaired of ever being redeemed. Hashem 'remembered' them and redeemed them, as is stated *(Exod. 6:5)*: וָאֶזְכֹּר אֶת־בְּרִיתִי, *and I remembered My covenant (Rashi).*

בָּרוּךְ אַתָּה ה׳, זוֹכֵר הַנִּשְׁכָּחוֹת. — *Blessed are You, HASHEM, Who remembers the forgotten.*

— God remembered our forefathers who were *forgotten* in Egypt *(Bach).*

This time the order of the *shofar* sounds is תְּרוּעָה תְקִיעָה תְּרוּעָה, *teruah, tekiah, teruah;* unlike the earlier series which began with the *tekiah* (see *Bach, Tur Orach Chaim* 579). The Thirteen Divine Attributes of Mercy are repeated. The reader then continues: *Today, let generous rain fall, O God. Today, fill the rivulet with water, O God. Today prepare of Your goodness for the poor, O God.* He concludes with, *Whether like children ...* [see comm. on first blessing] *(Tur 579).*

עַל־הַשְּׁלִישִׁית הוּא אוֹמֵר: — *After the third he says:*

For this blessing, which is the second of the additional blessings of the day, the *chazan* recites the blessing of *Shofaros* from the Rosh HaShanah *Shemoneh Esrei*, beginning with אַתָּה נִגְלֵיתָ, *You were revealed.* Then, *Joshua* 6:20 is recited, telling how the sound of the *shofar* caused the walls of Jericho to sink into the ground. The final Scriptural verse of this blessing is *Numbers* 10:9 which commands Israel to sound the *shofar* when it goes to war against an aggressive enemy.

The *chazan* concludes: וּזְכָר־לָנוּ ה׳ אֱלֹהֵינוּ זְכוּתוֹ שֶׁל יְהוֹשֻׁעַ עַבְדְּךָ הַיּוֹם וְרַחֵם עָלֵינוּ לְמַעַן שְׁמֶךָ, *Remember for us today HASHEM, our God, the merit of Joshua, Your servant, and have compassion on us for Your Name's sake (Tur, 579).*

מִי שֶׁעָנָה אֶת־יְהוֹשֻׁעַ בַּגִּלְגָּל, הוּא יַעֲנֶה אֶתְכֶם וְיִשְׁמַע קוֹל צַעֲקַתְכֶם הַיּוֹם הַזֶּה. — *He Who answered Joshua in Gilgal, He shall answer you and*

ב
ד

עַל־הָרְבִיעִית הוּא אוֹמֵר: מִי שֶׁעָנָה אֶת־שְׁמוּאֵל בַּמִּצְפָּה, הוּא יַעֲנֶה אֶתְכֶם וְיִשְׁמַע בְּקוֹל צַעֲקַתְכֶם הַיּוֹם הַזֶּה. בָּרוּךְ אַתָּה ה׳, שׁוֹמֵעַ צְעָקָה.

עַל־הַחֲמִישִׁית הוּא אוֹמֵר: מִי שֶׁעָנָה אֶת־אֵלִיָּהוּ בְּהַר הַכַּרְמֶל, הוּא יַעֲנֶה אֶתְכֶם וְיִשְׁמַע בְּקוֹל צַעֲקַתְכֶם הַיּוֹם הַזֶּה. בָּרוּךְ אַתָּה ה׳, שׁוֹמֵעַ תְּפִלָּה.

עַל־הַשִּׁשִּׁית הוּא אוֹמֵר: מִי שֶׁעָנָה אֶת־יוֹנָה

hearken to the sound of your cry this day.

The 'response to Joshua' refers to the miracle brought about by the *shofar* blast at Jericho. Joshua is described as being in Gilgal because Israel was encamped at Gilgal when the battle of Jericho took place (*Tos. Yom Tov; Rashi*).

בָּרוּךְ אַתָּה ה׳, שׁוֹמֵעַ תְּרוּעָה. — *Blessed are You, HASHEM, Who hearkens to the sounding of the shofar.*

The blessing follows the reference to Joshua's victory as a result of the *shofar* blast. Thus, it alludes to the prayers of the fast day which are accompanied by the blowing of the *shofar* (*Tos. Yom Tov; Rosh*).

After the blessing תְּקִיעָה תְּרוּעָה תְּקִיעָה, *tekiah, teruah, tekiah,* is sounded on the *shofar* and the Thirteen Divine Attributes of Mercy are repeated [see mishnah 4]. The *chazan* then says: *Today, do not remember for us the sins of the chastened ones. Today, do not make Your heavens brass-like. Today, remember for us the covenant of the three Patriarchs.* He concludes: *Whether like children ...* (*Tur* 579).

עַל־הָרְבִיעִית הוּא אוֹמֵר: — *After the fourth he says:*

[The *chazan* then recites the third of the six additional blessings, which begins with *Psalm* 120. He then continues: *We beseech You, HASHEM, our God, remember for us today the merit of Samuel, Your seer, and have compassion on us for Your Name's sake* (*Tur*, 579).

מִי שֶׁעָנָה אֶת־שְׁמוּאֵל בַּמִּצְפָּה, הוּא יַעֲנֶה אֶתְכֶם וְיִשְׁמַע בְּקוֹל צַעֲקַתְכֶם הַיּוֹם הַזֶּה. — *He Who answered Samuel in Mizpah, He shall answer you and hearken to the sound of your cry this day.*

The reference to Samuel alludes to the time he prayed that Israel be saved from the Philistines (*I Sam.* 7:9). This concluding portion of the blessing is similar to *Psalm* 120 which begins אֶל־ה׳ בַּצָּרָתָה לִּי קָרָאתִי וַיַּעֲנֵנִי, *To HASHEM in my distress I called and He answered me* (*Tos. Yom Tov; Rashi*).

בָּרוּךְ אַתָּה ה׳, שׁוֹמֵעַ צְעָקָה. — *Blessed are You, HASHEM, Who hearkens to a cry.*

As it is said, (*I Sam.* 7:9): *Samuel cried out and HASHEM answered him* (*Tos. Yom Tov; Rashi*).

They then sound, *teruah, tekiah, teruah,* and recite the Thirteen Divine Attributes. The leader concludes with the prayer: *Answer us today with rains of good will,*

2 After the fourth he says: He Who answered
4 Samuel at Mizpah, He shall answer you and hearken to the sound of your cry this day. Blessed are You, HASHEM, Who hearkens to a cry.

After the fifth he says: He Who answered Elijah on Mount Carmel, He shall answer you and hearken to the sound of your cry this day. Blessed are You, HASHEM, Who hearkens to prayer.

After the sixth he says: He Who answered Jonah

blessing, generosity and goodness. Answer us today, God revered in the great council of the holy [angels]. Answer us today and open for us Your storehouse of goodness. He concludes: *Whether like children ... (Tur* 579).

עַל־הַחֲמִישִׁית הוּא אוֹמֵר: — *After the fifth he says:*

As the Mishnah states below, the theme of this blessing is the mercy God showed Elijah when he challenged the false prophets to prove themselves in the presence of all Israel (*I Kings* 18). He and they stood atop Mount Carmel and offered sacrifices. After the idolatrous prophets were proven charlatans, Elijah prayed for the acceptance of his offering. To allude to Elijah's prayer on the mountaintop, this blessing is begun with the recitation of Psalm 121: אֶשָּׂא עֵינַי אֶל־הֶהָרִים, *I shall lift my eyes to the mountains (Tos. Yom Tov; Rashi).*

מִי שֶׁעָנָה אֶת־אֵלִיָּהוּ בְּהַר הַכַּרְמֶל הוּא יַעֲנֶה אֶתְכֶם וְיִשְׁמַע בְּקוֹל צַעֲקַתְכֶם הַיּוֹם הַזֶּה. בָּרוּךְ אַתָּה ה׳ שׁוֹמֵעַ תְּפִלָּה. — *He Who answered Elijah on Mount Carmel, He shall answer you and hearken to the sound of your cry this day. Blessed are You, HASHEM, Who hearkens to prayer.*

Following the blessing, they would sound *tekiah, teruah, tekiah*; and recite the Thirteen Attributes of Divine Mercy. Then the *chazan* continues: *Today let rain fall from Your heavens, rain on the surface of the ground. Today, let a mist rise from the ground and water the surface of the earth.* He continues with *Joel* 2:21-27 which begins: *Today, bring us good tidings with mercy. Fear not, O earth ...* And concludes: *Whether like children... (Tur* 579).

עַל־הַשִּׁשִּׁית הוּא אוֹמֵר: — *After the sixth he says:*

The theme of this blessing is the experience of the prophet Jonah as described in the book by that name. When Jonah, in frustration of his attempt to flee God's command to prophesy to the people of Nineveh, was swallowed by a huge fish, he prayed to God from the innards of the fish (see ArtScroll *Jonah*). To allude to Jonah's experience, all of *Psalm* 130 is recited. It begins: מִמַּעֲמַקִּים קְרָאתִיךָ ה׳, *From the depths have I called to You, HASHEM.* This suggests the plight of Jonah who cried out from deep within the fish *(Tos. Yom Tov; Rashi).*

The *chazan* then adds: *Please, HASHEM, our God, remember for us this day the merit of Your prophet Jonah, and be merciful to us for Your Name's sake (Tur* 579).

ב
ה

מִמְּעֵי הַדָּגָה, הוּא יַעֲנֶה אֶתְכֶם וְיִשְׁמַע בְּקוֹל צַעֲקַתְכֶם הַיּוֹם הַזֶּה. בָּרוּךְ אַתָּה ה׳, הָעוֹנֶה בְּעֵת צָרָה.

עַל־הַשְּׁבִיעִית הוּא אוֹמֵר: מִי שֶׁעָנָה אֶת־דָּוִד וְאֶת־שְׁלֹמֹה בְנוֹ בִירוּשָׁלַיִם, הוּא יַעֲנֶה אֶתְכֶם וְיִשְׁמַע בְּקוֹל צַעֲקַתְכֶם הַיּוֹם הַזֶּה. בָּרוּךְ אַתָּה ה׳, הַמְרַחֵם עַל־הָאָרֶץ.

[ה] **מַעֲשֶׂה** בִּימֵי רַבִּי חֲלַפְתָּא וְרַבִּי חֲנַנְיָה בֶן־תְּרַדְיוֹן שֶׁעָבַר אֶחָד לִפְנֵי הַתֵּבָה וְגָמַר אֶת־הַבְּרָכָה כֻּלָּהּ, וְלֹא עָנוּ אַחֲרָיו אָמֵן.

יד אברהם

מִי שֶׁעָנָה אֶת־יוֹנָה מִמְּעֵי הַדָּגָה, הוּא יַעֲנֶה אֶתְכֶם וְיִשְׁמַע בְּקוֹל צַעֲקַתְכֶם הַיּוֹם הַזֶּה. בָּרוּךְ אַתָּה ה׳, הָעוֹנֶה בְּעֵת צָרָה. — *He Who answered Jonah from the fish's belly, He shall answer you and hearken to the sound of your cry this day. Blessed are You, HASHEM, Who answers in time of distress.*

The text of the blessing is based on Jonah's prayer. He said, קָרָאתִי מִצָּרָה לִי אֶל ה׳ וַיַּעֲנֵנִי, *I called, in my distress, to HASHEM, and He answered me (Jonah 2:3).*

The *shofar* is sounded *teruah, tekiah, teruah,* the Thirteen Attributes are recited, and the prayer is continued: *Today, hearken to the prayer of the people who pour their hearts out like water. Today, give drink to the earth which has not been sated with water. Today, bring blessing with a spring of water. Whether like children ... (Tur 579).*

עַל־הַשְּׁבִיעִית הוּא אוֹמֵר: — *After the seventh he says:*

The theme of this final blessing is to beseech God to have mercy on the famished land as He did in response to the prayer of David, and as Solomon requested when he inaugurated the Temple (see below). Although David and Solomon preceded both Elijah and Jonah who were mentioned in earlier blessings, the Rabbis chose to conclude the entire series of additional blessings prayers with this specific historic reference to mercy upon a drought-stricken land. Thus, the blessings of the day are ended with a prayer directed toward the particular calamity, drought, which prompted the proclamation of the fasts *(Rav).*

Preceding the text about to be given by the mishnah, all of Psalm 102 was recited, beginning: תְּפִלָּה לְעָנִי כִי יַעֲטֹף, *A prayer of the afflicted when he faints.* [*Tiferes Yisrael* comments that this psalm is relevant since it alludes to someone fainting from hunger, the outcome of drought.] Then the *chazan* says: *Please, HASHEM, our God, recall for us the merit of David, Your anointed servant, and Solomon, his royal son, and have mercy on us for Your Name's sake (Tur 579).*

[Then he continues:]

2 from the fish's belly, He shall answer you and
5 hearken to the sound of your cry, this day. Blessed are You, HASHEM, Who answers in time of distress.

After the seventh he says: He Who answered David and his son Solomon in Jerusalem, He shall answer you and hearken to the sound of your cry this day. Blessed are You, HASHEM, Who has mercy on the Land.

5. It happened in the days of R' Chalafta and R' Chananyah ben Teradyon that one went before the Ark and completed the entire blessing, but they did not respond Amen after the blessing.

YAD AVRAHAM

מִי שֶׁעָנָה אֶת־דָּוִד וְאֶת־שְׁלֹמֹה בְנוֹ בִּירוּשָׁלַיִם, הוּא יַעֲנֶה אֶתְכֶם וְיִשְׁמַע בְּקוֹל צַעֲקַתְכֶם הַיּוֹם הַזֶּה. בָּרוּךְ אַתָּה ה׳ הַמְרַחֵם עַל־הָאָרֶץ. — *He Who answered David and his son Solomon in Jerusalem, He shall answer you and hearken to the voice of your cry this day. Blessed are You, HASHEM, Who has mercy on the land.*

Following the blessing, the *shofar* is sounded *tekiah, teruah, tekiah,* the Thirteen Attributes are recited, and the prayer is concluded with: *Today, favor our prayer that You allow a remnant to remain in the land. Today, may the rain not cease to water the land. Today, nullify Your anger with us and sate the land from Your goodness. Whether like children... (Tur 579).*

ה

◆§ Response to Blessings in the Temple

The custom in the בֵּית הַמִּקְדָּשׁ, *Holy Temple,* was that, instead of אָמֵן, *Amen,* the congregants would respond בָּרוּךְ שֵׁם כְּבוֹד מַלְכוּתוֹ לְעוֹלָם וָעֶד, *Blessed is the Name of His glorious kingdom for ever and ever,* at the conclusion of each blessing. Since the *kohen* who recited the blessing in the Temple used שֵׁם הַמְּפֹרָשׁ, *the Ineffable Name of HASHEM,* in the blessings, a response more appropriate to the holiness of the Name than *Amen* was required *(Rav).*

...מַעֲשֶׂה בִּימֵי רַבִּי חֲלַפְתָּא — *It happened* [lit. *a story*] *in the days of R' Chalafta...*

— The father of R' Yose *(Rashi, Sanhedrin* 32b).

...וְרַבִּי חֲנַנְיָה בֶּן־תְּרַדְיוֹן — *and R' Chananyah ben Teradyon...*

Although the term מַעֲשֶׂה generally refers to a *story* — an actual occurence — our mishnah uses it differently. It tells of a custom instituted by them in their communities, R' Chalafta in Sipphoris (Tzipori), and R' Chananyah ben Teradyon in Siknin *(Beraisa* 16b).

...שֶׁעָבַר אֶחָד לִפְנֵי הַתֵּבָה — *that one went before the Ark...*

[The *chazan* proceeded to lead the services during the concluding series of seven fast days.]

ב ה תִּקְעוּ הַכֹּהֲנִים, תְּקָעוּ! מִי שֶׁעָנָה אֶת־אַבְרָהָם אָבִינוּ בְּהַר הַמּוֹרִיָּה הוּא יַעֲנֶה אֶתְכֶם וְיִשְׁמַע בְּקוֹל צַעֲקַתְכֶם הַיּוֹם הַזֶּה. הָרִיעוּ בְּנֵי אַהֲרֹן, הָרִיעוּ! מִי שֶׁעָנָה אֶת־אֲבוֹתֵינוּ עַל־יַם־סוּף, הוּא יַעֲנֶה אֶתְכֶם וְיִשְׁמַע בְּקוֹל צַעֲקַתְכֶם הַיּוֹם הַזֶּה.

וּכְשֶׁבָּא דָבָר אֵצֶל חֲכָמִים, אָמְרוּ: לֹא הָיִינוּ נוֹהֲגִין כֵּן אֶלָּא בְשַׁעַר הַמִּזְרָח וּבְהַר הַבַּיִת.

יד אברהם

וְגָמַר אֶת־הַבְּרָכָה כֻּלָּהּ, — *and completed the entire blessing,*

As described in mishnah 4, the blessing of גּוֹאֵל יִשְׂרָאֵל, *Who redeems Israel,* was augmented, and six blessings were added to the fast day *Shemoneh Esrei.* The procedure described below by our mishnah, refers to all seven of these blessings.

וְלֹא עָנוּ אַחֲרָיו אָמֵן. — *but they* [i.e., the congregants] *did not respond Amen after the blessing.*

Instead of responding with the customary *Amen,* they responded with בָּרוּךְ שֵׁם כְּבוֹד מַלְכוּתוֹ לְעוֹלָם וָעֶד, *Blessed is the Name of His glorious Kingdom for ever and ever,* as was the custom in the Holy Temple *(Rav).*

תִּקְעוּ הַכֹּהֲנִים, תְּקָעוּ! — *Sound the tekiah, O kohanim, sound the tekiah.*

This announcement was made by a synagogue attendant, rather than by the *chazan.* The repetitive text of the *tekiah* command indicated that following *tekiah* and *teruah,* there should be another *tekiah (Tos. Yom Tov; Tif. Yis.).*

Although the sounding of the *shofar* on fast days was not restricted to *kohanim,* R' Chalafta and R' Chananyah instituted this custom to further liken the fast day service to that of the Temple where a *kohen* was required to sound the *shofar (Tif. Yis.).*

Tiferes Yisrael continues that the *kohen* did not sound the *shofar* immediately. Instead, he waited for the *chazan* to recite the following prayer:

מִי שֶׁעָנָה אֶת־אַבְרָהָם אָבִינוּ בְּהַר הַמּוֹרִיָּה הוּא יַעֲנֶה אֶתְכֶם וְיִשְׁמַע בְּקוֹל צַעֲקַתְכֶם הַיּוֹם הַזֶּה. — *He Who answered our father Abraham on Mount Moriah, He shall answer you and hearken to the sound of your cry this day.*

This prayer was recited *prior* to the blowing of the *shofar* in order to avoid the following misunderstanding: As R' Chalafta and R' Chananyah instituted, the people would respond to the blessing with בָּרוּךְ שֵׁם..., *Blessed is the Name...,* a rather long response that was almost a blessing in its own right. Were the *kohanim* to sound the shofar at this point, it would appear as though it were sounded in conjunction with the response of *Blessed is the Name...*rather than the special fast day prayers. In order to avoid this misapprehension, the leader would not recite the prayer: מִי שֶׁעָנָה, *He Who answered...* until after the conclusion of both the blessing and *Blessed is the Name...* Only then would he recite *He Who answered...* in conjunction with

2 Sound the *tekiah, O kohanim,* sound the *tekiah.*
5 He who answered our father Abraham on Mount Moriah, He shall answer you and hearken to the sound of your cry this day. Sound the *teruah, O* sons of Aaron, sound the *teruah.* He who answered our forefathers at the Red Sea, He shall answer you and hearken to the sound of your cry this day.

When the matter came before the Sages, they said: Such was not our custom except at the Eastern Gate and on the Temple Mount.

YAD AVRAHAM

which the *kohanim* would sound the *shofar.* Thus, *He...,* which should have been recited before the blessing, was moved to a different part of the prayer to avoid an erroneous impression. Alternatively, the possibility of error was avoided without removing *He Who answered...* from the body of the blessing. The prayer מִי שֶׁעָנָה, *He Who answered...,* was recited *within* the blessing, which is its proper place. However, it was repeated *after* the recitation of *Blessed is the Name...* Only then was the *shofar* sounded. Thus it was made apparent that the sounding of the *shofar* was related to the fast day prayer *(Tos. Yom Tov; Ran).*

Rambam, however, maintains that the prevalent custom on fast days was to sound the *shofar* after the completion of the services. R' Chalafta and R' Chananyah felt that since the service on fasts was so much more elaborate than on ordinary days, the Temple formula should be adopted. Therefore, they sounded the *shofar* after each blessing and responded to the blessings with *Blessed is the Name... (Tos. Yom Tov).*

[Similarly, at the conclusion of the next additional fast day blessing, the congregants would respond *Blessed is the Name...,* and the synagogue attendant would announce:]

הָרִיעוּ, בְּנֵי אַהֲרֹן, הָרִיעוּ! — *Sound the teruah, O sons of Aaron, sound the teruah.*

The repetition of הָרִיעוּ, *sound the teruah,* indicated *teruah, tekiah,* followed by another *teruah.* The earlier *shofar* sounding consisted of *tekiah* and then *teruah, tekiah.* The order of the sounds was alternated in each of the additional blessings between *tekiah, teruah, tekiah,* and *teruah, tekiah, teruah (Tos. Yom Tov; Tif. Yis.).*

[Again, the *kohen* did not sound the *shofar* immediately. Instead, he waited for the leader to recite:]

מִי שֶׁעָנָה אֶת־אֲבוֹתֵינוּ עַל־יַם־סוּף, הוּא יַעֲנֶה אֶתְכֶם וְיִשְׁמַע בְּקוֹל צַעֲקַתְכֶם הַיּוֹם הַזֶּה. — *He Who answered our forefathers at the Red Sea, He shall answer you and hearken to the sound of your cry this day.*

Similarly, after the conclusion of each of the additional blessings, the leader would recite the appropriate prayer (see previous mishnah) *before the sounding of the shofar (Tif. Yis.).*

וּכְשֶׁבָּא דָבָר אֵצֶל חֲכָמִים, אָמְרוּ: לֹא הָיִינוּ נוֹהֲגִין כֵּן אֶלָּא בְּשַׁעַר הַמִּזְרָח וּבְהַר הַבַּיִת. — *When the matter came before the Sages, they said: Such was not our custom except at the*

ב
ו

[ו] **שָׁלשׁ** תַּעֲנִיּוֹת הָרִאשׁוֹנוֹת, אַנְשֵׁי מִשְׁמָר מִתְעַנִּין וְלֹא מַשְׁלִימִין; וְאַנְשֵׁי בֵית־אָב לֹא הָיוּ מִתְעַנִּין כְּלָל. שָׁלשׁ שְׁנִיּוֹת, אַנְשֵׁי מִשְׁמָר מִתְעַנִּין וּמַשְׁלִימִין; וְאַנְשֵׁי בֵית־אָב מִתְעַנִּין וְלֹא מַשְׁלִימִין. שֶׁבַע אַחֲרוֹנוֹת,אֵלּוּ וָאֵלּוּ מִתְעַנִּין וּמַשְׁלִימִין; דִּבְרֵי רַבִּי יְהוֹשֻׁעַ.

יד אברהם

Eastern Gate and on the Temple Mount.

The institution of this custom in places other than the Temple Mount was not adopted by the Sages. They observed that custom only at the Eastern Gate of the Temple Mount.

Alternatively, at the Eastern Gate of the Women's Court *and* on the Temple Mount *(Tos. Yom Tov; Rashi, Rosh HaShanah* 27a).

Upon closer scrutiny of the commentary of *Ran*, it seems clear that his text of the mishnah regarding the enactment of R' Chalafta and R' Chananyah read: וְעָנוּ אַחֲרָיו אָמֵן, *and they responded Amen after the blessing.* Accordingly, the two rabbis instituted the recitation of the fast day prayer [*He Who answered...*] *after* the conclusion of the blessing even though the congregation responded *Amen* but not *Blessed is the Name...* When the matter came before the Sages, they disagreed with the practice of removing *He Who...* from the body of the blesing and reciting it afterward. They asserted that this practice was followed *only* at the Eastern Gate... Since on the Temple Mount the response was *Blessed be the Name...*, it was necessary to recite *He Who answered...* after this response to make it clear that the *shofar* was sounded in conjunction with the prayer rather than with the response. Outside of the Temple, however, since the congregants respond with Amen, the *shofar* should be sounded immediately after the conclusion of the blessing, and the prayer recited within the blessing only *(Chidushei Mahariach).*

6.

◆§ Kohanim of the Watch and Kohanim of the Family Group

The *kohanim* involved in the Temple service were divided into twenty-four extended families known as מִשְׁמָרוֹת [*mishmaros*, singular, *mishmar*], *watches*, each of which served for one week at a time on a rotating basis. Each watch was subdivided into six groups, each known as בֵּית־אָב [*beis av*], *family group* [lit., *father's house*]. Each family group served for one day of the week, and all the groups of the *mishmar* combined to serve on the Sabbath *(Rashi* and most commentators, *Menachos* 107b). *Rav*, however, comments that each *mishmar* was divided into *seven* groups. The privilege of performing the service on any day belonged to the family group assigned to that particular day, but all members of the *mishmar* were required to make themselves available in the event more *kohanim* were needed *(Rav; Tif. Yis.).*

This mishnah discusses the public fast days as they relate to the *kohanim* of the *mishmar* serving during the week in which the fast is proclaimed, and the *kohanim* of the *beis av* serving on the fast day itself.

6. On the first three fast days, the *kohanim* of the *mishmar* fast but do not complete [their fast]; the *kohanim* of the *beis av* do not fast at all. On the second three [fast days], the *kohanim* of the watch fast and complete [their fast]; the *kohanim* of the *beis av* fast but do not complete [their fast]. On the last seven [fast days], both groups fast and complete [their fast]; this is the opinion of R' Yehoshua.

שָׁלֹשׁ תַּעֲנִיּוֹת הָרִאשׁוֹנוֹת, אַנְשֵׁי מִשְׁמָר מִתְעַנִּין וְלֹא מַשְׁלִימִין; — *On the first three fasts, the kohanim* [lit. *men*] *of the mishmar fast, but do not complete* [*their fast*];

The laws of the first three communal fasts were not as stringent as those of the later ones (see 1:5). Therefore, the Sages are lenient in imposing the fasts upon the *kohanim* who are involved in the Temple service so that hunger would not interfere with their responsibilities. They fast part of the day to signify their wish to join in the suffering of the community. Because they do not fast until evening, however, it is not considered a fast with regard to reciting the prayer עֲנֵנוּ, *Answer us*, which each individual recites as an addition to the *Minchah Shemoneh Esrei* on fast days *(Meleches Shlomo)*.

וְאַנְשֵׁי בֵית־אָב לֹא הָיוּ מִתְעַנִּין כְּלָל. — *the kohanim of the beis av do not fast at all.*

This group is occupied all day with the Temple service, and fasting would impede their performance *(Tif. Yis.)*.

שָׁלֹשׁ שְׁנִיּוֹת, אַנְשֵׁי מִשְׁמָר מִתְעַנִּין וּמַשְׁלִימִין; — *On the second three* [*fast days*], *the kohanim of the mishmar fast and complete* [*their fast*];

Since the second series of three fasts is more stringent than the first (see 1:6), the *kohanim* of the *mishmar,* who are not members of that day's *beis av*, and who would, presumably, not be called upon to take part in the service, are required to fast the entire day *(Tif. Yis.)*.

וְאַנְשֵׁי בֵית־אָב מִתְעַנִּין וְלֹא מַשְׁלִימִין. — *the kohanim of the beis av fast but do not complete* [*their fast*].

[They are not required to complete the fast lest their ability to perform the service be impaired. However, due to the gravity of the situation, they are required to participate in the fast to a limited extent in order to share in the pain of the community. See above.]

שֶׁבַע אַחֲרוֹנוֹת, אֵלּוּ וָאֵלּוּ מִתְעַנִּין וּמַשְׁלִימִין דִּבְרֵי רַבִּי יְהוֹשֻׁעַ. — *On the last seven* [*fast days*], *both groups* [lit. *these and these*] *fast and complete* [*their fast*]; *this is the opinion of R' Yehoshua.*

[I.e., both the *kohanim* of the *mishmar* and the *kohanim* of the *beis av* are required to fast all day according to R' Yehoshua. He holds that the urgency of the third group of fasts (see 1:6) is sufficient cause to obligate even those engaging in performance of Temple service to fast.]

ב
ז

וַחֲכָמִים אוֹמְרִים: שָׁלֹשׁ תַּעֲנִיּוֹת הָרִאשׁוֹנוֹת, אֵלּוּ וָאֵלּוּ לֹא הָיוּ מִתְעַנִּין כְּלָל. שָׁלֹשׁ שְׁנִיּוֹת, אַנְשֵׁי מִשְׁמָר מִתְעַנִּין וְלֹא מַשְׁלִימִין; וְאַנְשֵׁי בֵית־אָב לֹא הָיוּ מִתְעַנִּין כְּלָל. שֶׁבַע אַחֲרוֹנוֹת, אַנְשֵׁי מִשְׁמָר מִתְעַנִּין וּמַשְׁלִימִין; וְאַנְשֵׁי בֵית־אָב מִתְעַנִּין וְלֹא מַשְׁלִימִין.

[ז] **אַנְשֵׁי** מִשְׁמָר מֻתָּרִים לִשְׁתּוֹת יַיִן בַּלֵּילוֹת, אֲבָל לֹא בַיָּמִים; וְאַנְשֵׁי בֵית אָב, לֹא בַיּוֹם וְלֹא בַלַּיְלָה.
אַנְשֵׁי מִשְׁמָר וְאַנְשֵׁי מַעֲמָד אֲסוּרִין מִלְּסַפֵּר

יד אברהם

וַחֲכָמִים אוֹמְרִים: שָׁלֹשׁ תַּעֲנִיּוֹת הָרִאשׁוֹנוֹת, אֵלּוּ וָאֵלּוּ לֹא הָיוּ מִתְעַנִּין כְּלָל. — *But the Sages say: On the first three fast days neither groups fasts at all.*

[The Sages rule more leniently than R' Yehoshua in all cases. Since the situation requiring the first group of fasts is the least urgent, the Sages exempt even the *kohanim* of the *mishmar*, from any participation in the fast.]

שָׁלֹשׁ שְׁנִיּוֹת, אַנְשֵׁי מִשְׁמָר מִתְעַנִּין וְלֹא מַשְׁלִימִין; וְאַנְשֵׁי בֵית־אָב לֹא הָיוּ מִתְעַנִּין כְּלָל. — *On the second three [fast days], the kohanim of the mishmar fast but do not complete [their fast]; the kohanim of the beis av do not fast at all.*

[Since the situation requiring this group of fasts is more grave than the first; the Sages require some participation in the fast on the part of the *mishmar*.]

שֶׁבַע אַחֲרוֹנוֹת, אַנְשֵׁי מִשְׁמָר מִתְעַנִּין וּמַשְׁלִימִין; וְאַנְשֵׁי בֵית־אָב מִתְעַנִּין וְלֹא מַשְׁלִימִין. — *On the last seven [fast days], the kohanim of the mishmar fast and complete [their fast]; the kohanim of the beis av fast but do not complete [their fast].*

[Due to the urgency of the third group of fasts, even the Sages agree that the *kohanim* of the *beis av* participate in the fast to show their sympathy for the community. However, they are not required to complete the fast.]

7.

Since the previous mishnah discussed the laws pertaining to אַנְשֵׁי מִשְׁמָר, *the kohanim of the watch,* and אַנְשֵׁי בֵית אָב, *the kohanim of the beis av* [family group], the mishnah now proceeds to discuss other laws concerning them *(Rav).*

◆§ Drinking Wine

Kohanim are prohibited from drinking wine prior to performing the Temple service (see *Lev.* 10:8-11). This prohibition applies mainly to the members of the day's *beis av,* for they are responsible for the service of the day. The other members of the

2 7 But the Sages say: On the first three fast days neither group fasts at all. On the second three [fast days], the *kohanim* of the *mishmar* fast but do not complete [their fast], and the *kohanim* of the *beis av* do not fast at all. On the last seven [fast days], the *kohanim* of the *mishmar* fast and complete [their fast], and the *kohanim* of the father's house fast but do not complete [their fast].

7. The *kohanim* of the *mishmar* are permitted to drink wine at night, but not during the day; the *kohanim* of the *beis av* [are] not [permitted to drink wine] during the day or during the night.

The *kohanim* of the *mishmar* and the men of the *maamad* are prohibited from hair cutting and

YAD AVRAHAM

mishmar are sometimes needed to assist the *beis av* in the service when sacrifices are offered in such great quantities that the *beis av* cannot handle them. Therefore, the other members of the *mishmar* must also refrain from drinking wine lest they be needed to assist in the service.

אַנְשֵׁי מִשְׁמָר מֻתָּרִים לִשְׁתּוֹת יַיִן בַּלֵּילוֹת, — *The kohanim of the mishmar are permitted to drink wine at night...*

There is no need for the *kohanim* of the watch to hold themselves ready for service at night, The only service done in the evening was הֶקְטֵר חֲלָבִים וְאֵבָרִים עַל־גַּבֵּי הַמִּזְבֵּחַ, *burning of the fats and limbs* [of the day's sacrifices] *upon the altar*. That task could be managed easily by the *kohanim* of the *beis av (Rav).*

אֲבָל לֹא בַיָּמִים; — *but not during the day;*

Since the daytime service is more laborious, there is a constant possibility that the other *kohanim* of the *mishmar*, will be called upon to assist in the service. Therefore, they must hold themselves in readiness and not drink wine during the day *(Tos. Yom Tov).*

וְאַנְשֵׁי בֵית־אָב, לֹא בַיּוֹם וְלֹא בַלָּיְלָה. — *and the kohanim of the beis av* [*are*] *not* [*permitted to drink wine*] *during the day or during the night.*

During the night they are engaged in the burning of fats and limbs of the day's sacrifices upon the altar. The *kohanim* of the *beis av* are responsible to insure the thorough burning of the fats and limbs of the previous day's offerings. They place the parts on the altar, turn over the unburned parts with a fork, and replace any unburned parts that fall off *(Rav; Tos. Yom Tov).*

אַנְשֵׁי מִשְׁמָר וְאַנְשֵׁי מַעֲמָד... — *The kohanim of the watch and the men of the maamad...*

[The Torah requires the בְּעָלִים, *owners* (of a sacrifice), to be present in the Temple during its service (see below 4:2). Theoretically, therefore,

ב
ח

וּמְלַכְּבִּים; וּבַחֲמִישִׁי, מֻתָּרִין מִפְּנֵי כְבוֹד הַשַּׁבָּת.

[ח] **כָּל־הַכָּתוּב** בִּמְגִלַּת תַּעֲנִית „דְּלָא לְמִסְפַּד", לְפָנָיו אָסוּר, לְאַחֲרָיו מֻתָּר. רַבִּי יוֹסֵי אוֹמֵר: לְפָנָיו וּלְאַחֲרָיו אָסוּר.

„דְּלָא לְהִתְעַנָּאָה בְּהוֹן", לְפָנָיו וּלְאַחֲרָיו מֻתָּר. רַבִּי יוֹסֵי אוֹמֵר: לְפָנָיו אָסוּר, לְאַחֲרָיו מֻתָּר.

יד אברהם

every Jew is required to be present during the offering of the תְּמִידִים, *daily sacrifices,* which are offered on behalf of the entire nation. In order to fulfill this requirement, the Sages ordained that representatives of the entire nation be appointed and divided into twenty-four groups corresponding to the *mishmaros* of the *kohanim.* On a rotating basis, part of each group comes to the Temple while the remaining members conduct special prayers in the towns and cities. Each group is known as a מַעֲמָד [*maamad*], *station.* As representatives of the nation, the group prays that the offerings be accepted favorably by God (*Rav.* See 4:2).]

אֲסוּרִין מִלְּסַפֵּר וּמִלְּכַבֵּס; — *are prohibited from haircutting and laundering.*

In order to assure that the *kohanim* of the *mishmar* and the people of the *maamad* groom themselves properly before beginning their duties, the Rabbis forbade such activity during the week of their service *(Rav).* [See *Moed Katan,* ch. 3 for similar restrictions on *Chol HaMoed.* There, the reason certain activities were prohibited during *Chol HaMoed* was in order to prod people to prepare for the festival in time.]

וּבַחֲמִישִׁי, — *However, on Thursday* [of the week of their watch]...

מֻתָּרִין מִפְּנֵי כְבוֹד הַשַּׁבָּת. — *these* [*activities*] *are permitted, in honor of the Sabbath.*

Since many people groom themselves on Thursday in honor of the Sabbath, *kohanim* of the watch and the people of the *maamad* of that week are similarly permitted to cut their hair and launder their clothing on Thursday in honor of the Sabbath. Although Friday would have been the more logical day, many people are so busy with Sabbath preparation then, that they advance their grooming to Thursday *(Rashi; Rav).*

8.

◆§ Megillas Taanis — Scroll of Fasts

מְגִלַּת תַּעֲנִית [*Megillas Taanis*], *Scroll of Fasts,* is an ancient document written by Chananyah ben Chizkiyah and his colleagues (*Shabbos* 13b) during the period of the Second Temple. In it are recorded all the days on which miracles occurred for the Jewish people during the Second Commonwealth — days which were celebrated

laundering. However, on Thursday these activities are permitted, in honor of the Sabbath.

8. Whenever it is written in the *Scroll of Fasts*, 'Not to eulogize [on a particular day],' [on the day] before it [fasting] is forbidden; [on the day] after it [fasting] is permitted.

R' Yose says: [Both] before and after it [fasting] is forbidden.

[Concering days about which it is written in the *Scroll of Fasts*,] 'Not to fast on them,' [both] before and after them [fasting] is permitted.

R' Yose says: Before them [fasting] is forbidden; after them [fasting] is permitted.

YAD AVRAHAM

every year as minor holidays. On some of these days, fasting was forbidden but eulogies were permitted; while on others, even eulogies were forbidden *(Rashi; Rav).*

After the destruction of the Temple, the prohibitions contained in the document were abrogated, except for those of Chanukah and Pruim. Hence, we may fast on all days enumerated in this scroll, except for Chanukah and Purim *(Rav; Rosh HaShanah* 19b).

כָּל־הַכָּתוּב בִּמְגִלַּת תַּעֲנִית ,,דְּלָא לְמִסְפַּד״, — *Whenever it is written in the Scroll of Fasts, 'Not to eulogize [on a particular day],'*

On days commemorating great miracles, the degree of celebration was such that even eulogies were forbidden *(Meiri).*

The mishnah stresses הַכָּתוּב, *is written,* with regard to *Megillas Taanis* because it was compiled and committed to writing during the period when the prohibition against transcribing the Oral Law was still in effect. Therefore, the mishnah notes the unusual fact that this particular compilation of laws was *written (Tos. Yom Tov).*

לְפָנָיו אָסוּר, — *[on the day] before it [fasting] is forbidden;*

— lest one do likewise on the festive day *(Rashi; Rav).*

Fasting is forbidden, but not eulogizing *(Meiri).*

לְאַחֲרָיו מֻתָּר. — *[the day] after it [fasting] is permitted.*

Since the festive day is over, there is no fear that one may erroneously deliver eulogies even on the festival *(Rav).*

רַבִּי יוֹסֵי אוֹמֵר: לְפָנָיו וּלְאַחֲרָיו אָסוּר. — *R' Yose says: [Both] before and after it [fasting] is forbidden.*

[— in order to assure the festivity of the day.]

,,דְּלָא לְהִתְעַנָּאָה בְּהוֹן״, — *[Concerning days about which it is written in the Scroll of Fasts,] 'Not to fast on them,'*

[These days of minor miracles required a lower degree of festivity, therefore, although fasting was forbidden, eulogies were permitted.]

לְפָנָיו וּלְאַחֲרָיו מֻתָּר. — *[both] before and after them [fasting] is permitted.*

ב
ט

[ט] **אֵין** גּוֹזְרִין תַּעֲנִית עַל־הַצִּבּוּר בַּתְּחִלָּה בַּחֲמִישִׁי, שֶׁלֹּא לְהַפְקִיעַ הַשְּׁעָרִים. אֶלָּא שָׁלֹשׁ תַּעֲנִיּוֹת הָרִאשׁוֹנוֹת שֵׁנִי וַחֲמִישִׁי וָשֵׁנִי; וְשָׁלֹשׁ שְׁנִיּוֹת, חֲמִישִׁי שֵׁנִי וַחֲמִישִׁי.

רַבִּי יוֹסֵי אוֹמֵר: כְּשֵׁם שֶׁאֵין הָרִאשׁוֹנוֹת בַּחֲמִישִׁי, כָּךְ לֹא שְׁנִיּוֹת וְלֹא אַחֲרוֹנוֹת.

יד אברהם

רַבִּי יוֹסֵי אוֹמֵר: לְפָנָיו אָסוּר, לְאַחֲרָיו מֻתָּר. — *R' Yose says: Before them [fasting] is forbidden, after them [fasting] is permitted.*

Meiri notes that only regarding festive days established by the Rabbis was the requirement of joy extended to the day before and the day following. He explains that the Sages feared that laxity might prevail on those days since they are merely Rabbinic enactments; hence they extended the degree of festivity to assure popular compliance. However, on festive days established by the Torah no fear of laxity existed.

9.

אֵין גּוֹזְרִין תַּעֲנִית עַל־הַצִּבּוּר בַּתְּחִלָּה בַּחֲמִישִׁי, — *We may not decree upon the community a* [*series of*] *fast*[s] *beginning on Thursday,*

— [The various series of fasts decreed upon the community in the absence of rain are never begun on Thursdays. See above 1:5.]

שֶׁלֹּא לְהַפְקִיעַ הַשְּׁעָרִים. — *so as not to cause a rise in the market prices.*

A Thursday fast will cause people to do an inordinate amount of shopping since they must prepare for the meal after the fast in addition to the regular Sabbath meals. Seeing this, the merchants will presume that the people are hoarding food for an impending famine, and they will raise the prices *(Rashi; Rav).*

Even if the storekeepers are Jewish, and thus aware of the fast, they might fail to associate the purchase of large quantities of food with the meal following the fast *(Tos. Yom Tov).*

Rambam explains that the mere fact that the Rabbis decreed a fast so close to the Sabbath will be taken as a sign that a famine is imminent.

Tiferes Yisrael, however, does not accept *Rambam's* reasoning. If the fast was decreed because of a drought, a Thursday fast might indeed cause the merchants to feel that famine was imminent. But if a fast were decreed for some other calamity, there would be no grounds for such a fear. If so, why should fasts not be decreed on Thursday in such cases?

אֶלָּא שָׁלֹשׁ תַּעֲנִיּוֹת הָרִאשׁוֹנוֹת, שֵׁנִי וַחֲמִישִׁי וְשֵׁנִי; — *Rather, the first three fasts are on Monday, Thursday, and Monday;*

Since the community already fasted on Monday, the storekeepers will realize that the purchase of large quantities of food on Thursday is simply for the meal following the fast *(Rashi; Rav).*

9. We may not decree upon the community a [series of] fast[s] commencing on Thursday, so as not to cause a rise in the market prices. Rather, the first three fasts are on Monday, Thursday, and Monday; the second three, on Thursday, Monday, and Thursday.

R' Yose says: Just as the first [three fasts] are not [to commence] on Thursday, so too, neither the second [three fasts] nor the final [seven fasts may commence on Thursday].

וְשָׁלֹשׁ שְׁנִיּוֹת, חֲמִישִׁי שֵׁנִי וַחֲמִישִׁי. — *the second three, are Thursday, Monday, and Thursday.*

Since the second series of fasts is a direct continuation of the first, the storekeepers will be prepared for large Thursday purchases and not raise the prices; hence, the second series of fasts may commence on Thursday *(Kehati).*

[The same reasoning is valid for the third and final series of fasts.]

רַבִּי יוֹסֵי אוֹמֵר: כְּשֵׁם שֶׁאֵין הָרִאשׁוֹנוֹת בַּחֲמִישִׁי, כָּךְ לֹא שְׁנִיּוֹת וְלֹא אַחֲרוֹנוֹת. — *R' Yose says: Just as the first [three fasts] are not [to commence] on Thursday, so too, neither the second [three fasts] nor the final [seven fasts commence on Thursday].*

Upon completion of a series of fasts, it is customary to wait a reasonable time for God's help before decreeing a new series. Moreover, it is customary to announce each series of fasts in the synagogues on the preceding Sabbath; thereby necessitating that further time elapse from series to series. Since there was such an interval, storekeepers might forget the buying habits of Thursday fast days that coincided with the need to purchase Sabbath provisions, and presume that people are buying large quantities of food on Thursday for fear of imminent famine; therefore they might raise prices *(Tos. Yom Tov).*

The *halachah* is in accordance with the opinion of R' Yose *(Tos. Yom Tov).*[1]

1. [A minimum of two weeks would have elapsed between the Thursday of the first series and the Thursday when the second series *might* have begun had it not been for R' Yose's prohibition. The first series consists of Monday, Thursday, and Monday. The following Thursday is not a fast day. On the Sabbath, the second series is announced. Were it to begin on the folloling Thursday, two weeks would have elapsed from the last time people purchased food in large quantities — sufficient time for the storekeepers to forget the shopping habits of Thursday fasts. However, if the second series also commences on Monday, the storekeepers will realize that the reason people purchase large quantities of food on Thursday is the fast rather than the fear of an imminent famine.]

ב
י

[י] **אֵין** גּוֹזְרִין תַּעֲנִית עַל־הַצִּבּוּר בְּרֹאשׁ חֹדֶשׁ, בַּחֲנֻכָּה, וּבְפוּרִים. וְאִם הִתְחִילוּ, אֵין מַפְסִיקִין; דִּבְרֵי רַבָּן גַּמְלִיאֵל. אָמַר רַבִּי מֵאִיר: אַף־עַל־פִּי שֶׁאָמַר רַבָּן גַּמְלִיאֵל אֵין מַפְסִיקִין, מוֹדֶה הָיָה שֶׁאֵין מַשְׁלִימִין.

וְכֵן תִּשְׁעָה בְּאָב שֶׁחָל לִהְיוֹת בְּעֶרֶב שַׁבָּת.

ג
א

[א] **סֵדֶר** תַּעֲנִיּוֹת אֵלּוּ הָאָמוּר — בִּרְבִיעָה רִאשׁוֹנָה. אֲבָל צְמָחִים שֶׁשָּׁנוּ,

יד אברהם

אֵין גּוֹזְרִין תַּעֲנִית עַל־הַצִּבּוּר בְּרֹאשׁ חֹדֶשׁ, בַּחֲנֻכָּה, וּבְפוּרִים; — *We may not decree a community fast on Rosh Chodesh, Chanukah, or Purim;*

Such fasts may not be scheduled for *Rosh Chodesh*, because the Torah refers to that day as מוֹעֵד, *festival* [lit. *appointed season*]. Consequently, fasts may not be decreed for חוֹל הַמּוֹעֵד, *Intermediate Days of festivals*, or the Sabbath, for the Torah refers to them, too, as מוֹעֵד, *festivals (Meiri)*. On Purim, fasts are forbidden because the *Megillah* ordains it as a day of feasting. As noted above *(comm.* to mishnah 8) the provisions of *Megillas Taanis* still apply to Purim and Chanukah. Accordingly, fasts and eulogies are forbidden on the fifteenth of Adar as well as on Purim, and on Chanukah *(Megillah* 5b).

וְאִם הִתְחִילוּ, אֵין מַפְסִיקִין; דִּבְרֵי רַבָּן גַּמְלִיאֵל. — *however, if they had* [*already*] *commenced* [*a series of fasts*], *they may not interrupt* [*it*]. *This is the opinion of Rabban Gamliel.*

If the court had already decreed a series of fasts and the first fast day had been observed, the subsequent fasts must be observed even if they occur on *Rosh Chodesh*, Chanukah, or Purim *(Rav; Tif. Yis.)*.

Such subsequent fasts must be observed even on *Rosh Chodesh* because, even though it is a מוֹעֵד, *festival,* it is not a day of feasting and gladness *(Rashi)*.

Similarly, although Purim *is* a day of feasting and gladness *(Esther* 9:22), it is not referred to as מוֹעֵד, *festival*. Only a day which has both gladness and the designation of *Moed* (the Sabbath, festivals, and *Chol HaMoed*) can supersede a fast after its series has already begun *(Tos. Yom Tov)*.

אָמַר רַבִּי מֵאִיר; אַף־עַל־פִּי שֶׁאָמַר רַבָּן גַּמְלִיאֵל אֵין מַפְסִיקִין, מוֹדֶה הָיָה שֶׁאֵין מַשְׁלִימִין. — *R' Meir says: Although Rabban Gamliel said, they may not interrupt* [*the series*], *he agrees that they should not complete* [*the fast*].

Although they fast, the people must eat shortly before sunset so as not to complete the fast *(Rav)*.

וְכֵן תִּשְׁעָה בְּאָב שֶׁחָל לִהְיוֹת בְּעֶרֶב שַׁבָּת. — *The same is true of Tishah B'Av which falls on the eve of the Sabbath.*

An incidence of *Tishah B'Av* on a

2
10

10. **W**e may not decree a community fast on *Rosh Chodesh,* Chanukah, or Purim, however, if they had [already] commenced [a series of fasts], they may not interrupt [it]. This is the opinion of Rabban Gamliel.

R' Meir says: Although Rabban Gamliel said, they may not interrupt [the series], he agrees that they should not complete [the fast].

The same is true of *Tishah B'Av* which falls on the eve of the Sabbath.

3
1

1. **T**he order of the fasts mentioned above [applies only] if the first rain [was withheld]. However,

YAD AVRAHAM

Friday could occur only when the *Sanhedrin* sanctified the New Moon based on the testimony of witnesses. Nowadays, however, the Hebrew calendar in use is the one formulated by R' Hillel in the year 4117 (358 C.E.). He planned his calendar to avoid the incidence of festivals or fasts on days that could cause halachic difficulties or serious hardship. As a result of his calculations, it became an impossibility for *Tishah B'Av* to fall on a Friday. R' Meir's device of not completing a Friday fast is not accepted in the *halachah;* accordingly, any fast that does take place on a Friday or the other days mentioned above must be completed (*Rav;* see *comm.* to *Megillah* 1:2).

Chapter 3

1.

סֵדֶר תַּעֲנִיּוֹת אֵלּוּ הָאָמוּר— — *The order of the fasts mentioned above...*

The mishnah refers to 1:5-7, which gives the order and severity of the fasts and other restrictions that are imposed in response to a lack of rain *(Tif. Yis.).*

According to *Kehati,* the *order* mentioned in our mishnah includes the voluntary fasts and self-imposed restrictions of the יְחִידִים, *distinguished individuals,* as delineated in 1:4.

בִּרְבִיעָה רִאשׁוֹנָה. — [*applies only*] *if the first rain* [*was withheld*].

The first rain usually falls on the third, seventh, and seventeenth of MarCheshvan [see above 1:3,4]. Only when rain has not come by then are the fasts and restrictions imposed in gradual order as outlined in 1:4-7. However, if other calamities, such as those outlined below, are the cause of the public fasting, the initial decree is for a more severe fast, commensurate with the severity of the emergency *(Rav; Tif. Yis.).*

These three rainfalls are sometimes described separately as the first, second, and third rainfalls. The Tanna of our mishnah, however, includes all three in

ג
ב

מַתְרִיעִין עֲלֵיהֶם מִיָּד. וְכֵן שֶׁפָּסְקוּ גְשָׁמִים בֵּין גֶּשֶׁם לְגֶשֶׁם אַרְבָּעִים יוֹם, מַתְרִיעִין עֲלֵיהֶם מִיָּד, מִפְּנֵי שֶׁהִיא מַכַּת בַּצֹּרֶת.

[ב] **יָרְדוּ** לַצְּמָחִין, אֲבָל לֹא יָרְדוּ לָאִילָן, לָאִילָן וְלֹא לַצְּמָחִים, לָזֶה וְלָזֶה

the general category of 'first' rain (*Gem.* 19a).

[By using the collective term to refer to all three early rains, the Tanna follows the pattern of *Deuteronomy* 11:14, which refers to them collectively as יוֹרֶה, the early rain. They are the fructifying rains that enable the crops to grow. The mishnah describes them as רְבִיעָה, from רבע, *breeding of animals* (see *Lev.* 19:11), because the early rains soften the soil, enabling seeds to take root and begin to grow or 'breed' *(Gem.* 6a).]

אֲבָל צְמָחִים שֶׁשָּׁנוּ, — *However, if plants changed* [*abnormally*],

If rain fell normally but the crops changed drastically, it is considered a major emergency. For example, if thistles grew instead of wheat, or extremely inferior barley grew instead of normal barley *(Rashi; Rav).*

Another interpretation is that the crops began to grow normally, but then wilted and dried out completely *(Rambam, Taanis* 2:16; *Tur, Orach Chaim* 575; *Aruch).*

מַתְרִיעִין עֲלֵיהֶם מִיָּד.—*we sound* [*the shofar*] *at once because of them;*

The term 'sounding of the *shofar*' is symbolic of the third and most severe series of communal fasts, as described in 1:6. Thus, in addition to the sounding of the *shofar*, the other provisions of 1:6 are instituted as well *(Rav).*

The abnormal changes in plants and the situations described below are all considered such emergencies that the gradual escalation mentioned in 1:4-7 is discarded. Instead, all provisions of 1:6 are instituted: sounding of the *shofar;* commencement of fasting from sundown; cessation of work; closing of stores; and prohibition of bathing, anointing the body with oil, wearing leather footwear, and having marital relations (*Ran,* see above 1:6).

Rambam (Hilchos Taaniyos 2:16) maintains that only public fasting must be decreed at once, but the other restrictions of 1:6 are not applicable. The commentators disagree on how *Rambam* renders our mishnah. *Beis Yosef (Tur, Orach Chaim* 575) explains that *Rambam* interprets מַתְרִיעִין as *they cry* rather than *they sound the shofar.* Thus the mishnah declares only that they fast and cry in prayer for deliverance from the calamity, but *not* that the *shofar* is sounded. Hence, the restrictions attendant upon *shofar* sounding are not implemented. According to *Lechem Mishneh,* however, *Rambam* renders מַתְרִיעִין as *sounding the shofar,* but maintains that the use of the *shofar* does not automatically involve the full complement of restrictions.

וְכֵן שֶׁפָּסְקוּ גְשָׁמִים בֵּין גֶּשֶׁם לְגֶשֶׁם אַרְבָּעִים יוֹם, — *similarly, if rains were interrupted between one rain and the next for forty days,*

Although the first rain fell on schedule, forty days of drought

3
2
if plants changed [abnormally], we sound the *shofar* at once because of them; similarly if rains were interrupted between one rain and the next for forty days, we sound [the *shofar*] at once because this represents a calamity of food shortage.

2. **I**f [suitable rain] fell for crops, but did not fall for trees; [or] for trees, but not for crops; for both,

passed before the second rain fell *(Rav).*

This is considered a major disaster, because the timely early rain caused the crops to begin growing, but the lack of further rain to nurture them as they develop will cause most of them to die *(Ran).*

מַתְרִיעִין עֲלֵיהֶם מִיָּד, מִפְּנֵי שֶׁהִיא מַכַּת בַּצֹּרֶת — *we sound the shofar at once because this represents a calamity of food shortage.*

Rav (Avos 5:8) explains בַּצֹּרֶת as a condition of inadequate rain with the result that food prices will be high.

An overly long interval between rainfalls is an indication of impending drought (*Rav; Gem.* 19a).

If no rain falls during Mar-Cheshvan, there is merely a possiblity of drought in the event rain does not come in time to salvage the growing season. If forty days elapse between rainfalls, however, it is a definite indication of impending drought because the growing crops are adversely affected *(Tif. Yis.).*

Tosefos Yom Tov comments that *Avos* 5:8 makes clear that בַּצּוֹרֶת, *food shortage*, is not as severe as רָעָב, *famine*. Our mishnah, therefore, means to say that although the presence of *some* rainfall may have been sufficient to prevent a *famine*, the lengthy interruption of rain augurs severe food shortages.

[Despite the fact that food shortage is not as severe as famine, it is still serious enough for the immediate sounding of the *shofar* and the attendant measures.]

2.

יָרְדוּ לִצְמָחִין, אֲבָל לֹא יָרְדוּ לָאִילָן, — *If [suitable rain] fell for crops, but did not fall for trees;*

A light rain benefits crops, but not trees *(Rav; Gem.* 9b). Light rains do not penetrate deeply into the soil, thus the moisture does not reach the roots of trees *(Meiri).*

לָאִילָן וְלֹא לִצְמָחִים, — [or] *for trees, but not for crops;*

Heavy rainfall penetrates deeply into the ground so that it reaches tree roots, but such rain is detrimental to crops *(Rav; Tif. Yis.; Gem.* 19b).

לָזֶה וְלָזֶה אֲבָל לֹא לְבוֹרוֹת לְשִׁיחִין וְלִמְעָרוֹת; — *for both, but not for [the filling of] waterholes, ditches, and caves;*

Even if both light and heavy rains fell — sufficient for crops and trees — but not in sufficient quantity to fill the waterholes used for drinking water and laundering *(Tif. Yis.).*

ג אֲבָל לֹא לַבּוֹרוֹת לַשִּׁיחִין וְלַמְּעָרוֹת —
ג מַתְרִיעִין עֲלֵיהֶן מִיָּד.

[ג] **וְכֵן** עִיר שֶׁלֹּא יָרְדוּ עָלֶיהָ גְשָׁמִים;— כַּכָּתוּב: ,,וְהִמְטַרְתִּי עַל־עִיר אֶחָת וְעַל־עִיר אַחַת לֹא אַמְטִיר, חֶלְקָה אַחַת תִּמָּטֵר וגו׳ ״— אוֹתָהּ הָעִיר מִתְעַנָּה וּמַתְרַעַת, וְכָל סְבִיבוֹתֶיהָ מִתְעַנּוֹת וְלֹא מַתְרִיעוֹת. רַבִּי עֲקִיבָא אוֹמֵר: מַתְרִיעוֹת וְלֹא מִתְעַנּוֹת.

יד אברהם

מַתְרִיעִין עֲלֵיהֶן מִיָּד. — *we sound [the shofar] at once.*

[Sounding of the *shofar* indicates the fast and other restrictions given in 1:6. See *comm.* to mishnah 1, above.]

Tosefos Yom Tov explains the nature of our mishnah's three emergencies situations. If Pesach arrives without sufficient rain to cause the trees to blossom, they will not produce normal fruit even if rain will fall later. If there *was* rainfall, but not the sort that would benefit crops, it can be presumed that further rain will not fall, because after Pesach it is totally dry in *Eretz Yisrael.* If rains fell without sufficient drinking water having been stored in the reservoirs, the emergency is immediate.

3.

וְכֵן עִיר שֶׁלֹּא יָרְדוּ עָלֶיהָ גְשָׁמִים, — *Similarly, if no rains fell on a [particular] city;*

If only one city is drought-stricken while the surrounding towns have enough rain, the indication is that the afflicted city is suffering Divine punishment; otherwise, the entire area would face similar circumstances *(Tos. Yom Tov).*

כַּכָּתוּב: ,,וְהִמְטַרְתִּי עַל־עִיר אֶחָת וְעַל־עִיר אַחַת לֹא אַמְטִיר, חֶלְקָה אַחַת תִּמָּטֵר וגו׳.״ — *as is stated, (Amos 4:7): 'I caused it to rain on one city, and on one city I caused no rains to fall; one field was rained upon...'*

[The verse concludes that the field without rain will dry out. The Tanna cites the verse to show that inconsistent rainfall can be presumed to indicate God's anger with a particular city or farm.]

אוֹתָהּ הָעִיר מִתְעַנָּה וּמַתְרַעַת, — *that city must fast and sound [the shofar],*

Though in the case of general drought, the gradual procedure outlined in chapter 1 is observed, if only one specific city is affected, the most stringent restrictions must be put into effect immediately. As explained above, the unique predicament of the afflicted city indicates that it had incurred the wrath of God. Since the lack of rain cannot be attributed to natural causes, a Divine decree has been directed against it alone. It is proper, therefore, to sound the *shofar* and observe the most stringent restrictions *(Tos. Yom Tov; Ran).*

3 but not for [the filling of] waterholes, ditches, and
3 caves; we sound [the *shofar*] at once.

3. Similarly, if no rains fell on a particular city—as is stated (*Amos* 4:7): *'I caused it to rain on one city and on one city I caused no rains to fall; one field was rained upon...'*—that city must fast and sound [the *shofar*], and all surrounding areas fast, but do not sound [the *shofar*], R' Akiva says, they sound [the *shofar*] but do not fast.

YAD AVRAHAM

וְכָל־סְבִיבוֹתֶיהָ מִתְעַנּוֹת וְלֹא מַתְרִיעוֹת. — *and all surrounding areas fast, but do not sound* [*the shofar*].

As residents of the same province, they must sympathize with the plight of the stricken city's residents; therefore, they are required to fast on the behalf of their brethren (*Tos. Yom Tov; Ran*).

Inasmuch as the residents of the stricken city will come to the neighboring towns to purchase food, stocks will dwindle throughout the area, causing even the surrounding towns to suffer food shortages (*Rashi; Rav*).

Rashi maintains that the entire country must participate in the fasts. Thus, if one city in *Eretz Yisrael* was stricken, fasting is decreed even in Ashkelon, which was not part of *Eretz Yisrael* during the Second Commonwealth (see mishnah 6). Inasmuch as Ashkelon was originally conquered by Joshua, it is considered part of the same province for purposes of joining in the fast (*Tos. Yom Tov; Ran*).

[However, because the surrounding cities are not directly affected by the drought, they do not adopt the full range of restrictions that is decreed upon the stricken city.]

רַבִּי עֲקִיבָא אוֹמֵר: מַתְרִיעוֹת וְלֹא מִתְעַנּוֹת. — *R' Akiva says: They sound* [*the shofar*] *but do not fast.*

R' Akiva is of the opinion that the day is comparable to Rosh HaShanah, when we sound the *shofar* without fasting. The *Tanna Kamma* [the anonymous first opinion cited in the Mishnah], on the other hand, compares it to Yom Kippur when we fast but do not sound the *shofar*. Inasmuch as the surrounding populations pray that they be spared a similar fate, the analogy to the two High Holidays is valid. Both agree that the afflicted people must fast and sound the *shofar* (*Ran; Yerushalmi*).

The *halachah* is in accordance with the *Tanna Kamma* (*Tif. Yis.*).

In contrast to the case of mishnayos 1 and 2, where all commentators (with the exception of *Rambam*) note that the 'sounding of the *shofar*' is taken to indicate that all restrictions are observed, R' Akiva holds that the two are not automatically connected. For this reason, the *Tanna Kamma* specifies both elements — *shofar* blowing *and* fasting. Although mention of the fast would seem superfluous in view of the *shofar* sounding, R' Akiva's contrary opinion necessitates that both be specified in order to clarify the severity of the fast (*Tos. Yom Tov; Tos.*).

ג
ד

[ד] **וְכֵן** עִיר שֶׁיֵּשׁ־בָּהּ דֶּבֶר אוֹ מַפֹּלֶת, אוֹתָהּ הָעִיר מִתְעַנָּה וּמַתְרַעַת, וְכָל סְבִיבוֹתֶיהָ מִתְעַנּוֹת וְלֹא מַתְרִיעוֹת. רַבִּי עֲקִיבָא אוֹמֵר: מַתְרִיעוֹת וְלֹא מִתְעַנּוֹת. אֵיזֶהוּ דֶבֶר? עִיר הַמּוֹצִיאָה חֲמֵשׁ מֵאוֹת רַגְלִי, וְיָצְאוּ מִמֶּנָּה שְׁלֹשָׁה מֵתִים בִּשְׁלֹשָׁה יָמִים זֶה אַחַר זֶה, הֲרֵי זֶה דֶבֶר; פָּחוֹת מִכָּאן אֵין זֶה דֶבֶר.

יד אברהם

4.

וְכֵן עִיר שֶׁיֵּשׁ־בָּהּ דֶּבֶר אוֹ מַפֹּלֶת, — *Similarly, a city in which there is pestilence or collapse* [*of buildings*],

Collapse of buildings is considered to be a calamity calling for immediate fasts with full stringency only if the collapsed walls were strong, and neither unusually high nor near a river, which would cause them to be weakened by excessive moisture. If the buildings collapsed due to natural causes leading to a predictable result, however, it cannot be considered a calamity (*Meiri*).

Rambam includes in this category an earthquake which causes buildings to collapse and people to die (*Taaniyos* 2:12).

אוֹתָהּ הָעִיר מִתְעַנָּה וּמַתְרַעַת, — *that city must fast and sound* [*the shofar*],

[Pestilence and unusual collapse of buildings are indications of Divine displeasure.]

The minimum number of walls that constitute *collapse* is not specified. *Ritva* conjectures that three walls constitute collapse just as three deaths constitute pestilence [see below].

וְכָל־סְבִיבוֹתֶיהָ מִתְעַנּוֹת וְלֹא מַתְרִיעוֹת. רַבִּי עֲקִיבָא אוֹמֵר: מַתְרִיעוֹת וְלֹא מִתְעַנּוֹת. — *and all surrounding areas fast but do not sound* [*the shofar*]. *R' Akiva says: They sound* [*the shofar*] *but do not fast.*

[The conflicting views are explained in the previous mishnah.]

Here, too, the *halachah* is in accordance with the *Tanna Kamma* (*Tif. Yis.*).

[The mishnah now goes on to give the size of the city and the number of victims of pestilence which constitute a calamity that requires fasting.]

אֵיזֶהוּ דֶבֶר? עִיר הַמּוֹצִיאָה חֲמֵשׁ מֵאוֹת רַגְלִי — *What is considered pestilence?* [*In*] *a city that can bring forth five hundred* [*men*] *on foot,*

The city in question has a population large enough to number at least five hundred adult males (*Rambam, Taanis* 2:5).

The commentators offer varying views of which part of the mishnah leads to the conclusion that it refers to five hundred adult males without the inclusion of women, children, and the elderly.

— *Maggid Mishneh* derives this

3
4

4. Similarly, a city in which there is pestilence or collapse [of buildings], that city must fast and sound [the *shofar*], and all surrounding areas fast but do not sound [the *shofar*]. R' Akiva says: They sound [the *shofar*] but do not fast. What is considered pestilence? [In] a city that can bring forth five hundred men on foot, [if] three men died on three successive days, it is considered pestilence. Fewer than this is not considered pestilence.

from the Tanna's use of the term רַגְלִי, *[men] on foot,* as in *Exodus* 12:37, where it refers to young adult males and excludes women, children, and aged men.

— *Ran* derives it from the term הַמּוֹצִיאָה *that brings forth,* which refers to those who *go out* to work, as opposed to those who do not work or whose primary field of activity is at home.

— Alternatively, הַמּוֹצִיאָה refers to people eligible for military duty who can be *brought forth* in the sense of being drafted and sent to war (*Pesach Einayim, Otzar HaGeonim*).

וְיָצְאוּ מִמֶּנָּה שְׁלֹשָׁה מֵתִים בִּשְׁלֹשָׁה יָמִים זֶה אַחַר זֶה, הֲרֵי זֶה דֶבֶר: פָּחוֹת מִכָּאן אֵין זֶה דֶבֶר. — *[if] three men died on three successive days, it is considered pestilence. Fewer than this is not considered pestilence.*

In order to prove that the deaths are caused by a Divinely inflicted pestilence rather than random, natural occurrences, the victims must be three healthy men. This is derived from the juxtaposition in the mishnah of *collapse* and *pestilence.* Just as *collapse* refers to strong walls that fell for no apparent natural reason, so too does *pestilence* refer to healthy men who died without apparent cause (*Yerushalmi*).

To constitute such proof, at least one man must die on each of three successive days (*Tif. Yis.*).

The death of women, though, does not constitute proof of pestilence, inasmuch as women's lives are often endangered by childbirth. Furthermore, the after-effects of childbirth often leave women more susceptible to early death (*Beis Yosef, Orach Chaim* 576; *Tif. Yis.*).

If *two* people died within three days, or three people died within *two* days, the deaths are not attributable to Divine displeasure with the *city*. Each death is deemed an individual case (*Tif. Yis.; Gem.* 21b).

5.

This mishnah speaks of a type of calamity different from those discussed heretofore. Those mentioned below are localized episodes, but they are of the sort that can spread to surrounding areas. Therefore, they must be considered general rather than local. Since these plagues spread, even people far from the immediate areas must fast and sound the *shofar* for they, too, may ultimately be affected (*Rashi; Rav*).

ג
ה־ו

[ה] **עַל** אֵלּוּ מַתְרִיעִין בְּכָל מָקוֹם: עַל־הַשִּׁדָּפוֹן וְעַל־הַיֵּרָקוֹן, עַל־הָאַרְבֶּה וְעַל־הֶחָסִיל וְעַל־חַיָּה רָעָה וְעַל־הַחֶרֶב. מַתְרִיעִין עָלֶיהָ, מִפְּנֵי שֶׁהִיא מַכָּה מְהַלֶּכֶת.

[ו] **מַעֲשֶׂה** שֶׁיָּרְדוּ זְקֵנִים מִירוּשָׁלַיִם לְעָרֵיהֶם, וְגָזְרוּ תַעֲנִית עַל־שֶׁנִּרְאָה כִמְלֹא פִי תַנּוּר שִׁדָּפוֹן בְּאַשְׁקְלוֹן.

יד אברהם

עַל־אֵלּוּ מַתְרִיעִין בְּכָל מָקוֹם: — *For these [plagues] we sound [the shofar] everywhere:*

The phrase *everywhere* is more inclusive than *all surrounding areas* (mishnah 3). The Tanna emphasizes that wherever news of such plagues arrives, people must fast for fear that the plague may spread and affect them *(Tos. Yom Tov).*

Rambam rejects *Rashi's* view that the mishnah refers even to very distant places which happen to hear the news. If people in distant places were required to fast simply because they may eventually be affected by a far-off calamity, all cities would have to fast constantly, for the world is never without some form of spreading plague or war.

Rambam maintains, therefore, that the mishnah, too, limits the participation only to close-by surrounding areas.

[*Tosefos Yom Tov* resolves *Rambam's* objection to *Rashi's* interpretation. He infers from *Rashi* that the fact that a particular far-off city heard about the calamity may be taken as an omen that it may eventually spread to affect it as well. Alternatively, *Rashi* holds that distant places must fast if they *fear* that they, too, may become victims of the same catastrophe. Unless they feel such a fear, they need not fast if they are very far away.]

Because our mishnah uses the expression מַתְרִיעִין, *sound the shofar* [as opposed to the Tanna Kamma of mishnah 3 who says וּמַתְרִיעִין מִתְעַנִּין, we fast and sound the *shofar*], we may infer that fasting is *not* required. The Tanna of our mishnah must be R' Akiva, who maintained in mishnah 3 that surrounding areas are required to sound the *shofar* only but not to fast *(Tos. Yom Tov; Beis Yosef).*

עַל־הַשִּׁדָּפוֹן... — *for wind blasts,*

I.e., gusts of wind so strong that they ruin the kernels of grain *(Rav; Tif. Yis.).*

וְעַל־הַיֵּרָקוֹן, — *and for yellowing [of grain];*

I.e., heat so intense that it causes grain to whither, pale, and yellow (*Rav.;* see also *Rashi, Deut.* 28:22).

Others interpret the term as jaundice — an illness which causes the *skin* to turn yellow *(Rav).*

This interpretation, however, is questionable since it is unlikely that the Tanna would have juxtaposed human illness with plagues affecting plants [wind blasts and locust] *(Tif. Yis.).*

Rashi, who translates the word as חולי, *malady* — a word usually used for human illness — may refer to a malady affecting vegetation, as in his commentary to the Torah *(Hoffman, Perush Talmid HaRamban;*

5. **F**or these [plagues], we sound [the *shofar*] everywhere: For wind blasts, and for yellowing [of grain]; for numerous-locusts and for finishing-locusts; for a wild beast, or for the sword. We sound [the *shofar*] on these occasions because each is considered a traveling plague.

6. **I**t once happened that the elders descended from Jerusalem to their cities and decreed a fast because wind blast the size of an oven's mouth was

Lichtenstein, Talmid HaRamban; Nimukei Yosef. See *Chiddushei Anshei Shem).*

עַל־הָאַרְבֶּה וְעַל־הֶחָסִיל... — *for numerous-locusts and for finishing-locusts;*

אַרְבֶּה, derived from the root רבה, *to multiply*, is the most numerous of the locust family. חָסִיל, derived from the root חסל, *to finish* or *destroy*, completely devours vegetation (see *Joel* 1:4).

וְעַל־חַיָּה רָעָה... — *for a wild beast,*

Only a beast brazen enough to threaten a city by day is deemed a calamity *(Rav; Tif. Yis. Gem.* 22a) [for it is not unusual for beasts to prowl the city at night in outlying agricultural areas].

וְעַל־הַחֶרֶב. — *or for the sword.*

Foreign armies passing through peacefully on their way to attack other countries are regarded as calamities because of the strong potential for bloodshed *(Rashi Gem. 22a).*

מַתְרִיעִין עָלֶיהָ מִפְּנֵי שֶׁהִיא מַכָּה מְהַלֶּכֶת. — *We sound [the shofar] on these occasions* [lit., *on it*] *because each is considered a traveling plague.*

All plagues mentioned in the mishnah are progressive plagues in that they spread quickly and increase in severity *(Tif. Yis.).*

6.

[Following the previous mishnah, which required that fasts be observed even in distant places in the case of calamities that may spread, our mishnah now cites cases where the elders saw fit to proclaim fasts in *Eretz Yisrael* because of calamities that occurred in territory that was no longer considered *Eretz Yisrael.* See above mishnah 3.]

מַעֲשֶׂה שֶׁיָּרְדוּ זְקֵנִים מִירוּשָׁלַיִם לְעָרֵיהֶם, — *It once happened that the elders descended from Jerusalem to their cities...*

The members of the *Sanhedrin* left Jerusalem to return to their native cities throughout *Eretz Yisrael (Rashi; Rav)* in order to proclaim a public fast *(Tif. Yis.).*

וְגָזְרוּ תַעֲנִית עַל־שֶׁנִּרְאָה כִמְלֹא פִּי תַנּוּר שִׁדָּפוֹן... — *and decreed a fast because wind blast the size of an oven's mouth was seen* [*on grain*]*...*

The quantity of grain stricken was only large enough to yield enough flour for a bread the size of an oven's opening *(Rav).*

[The sort of oven used in Mish-

ג
ז

וְעוֹד גָּזְרוּ תַעֲנִית עַל־שֶׁאָכְלוּ זְאֵבִים שְׁנֵי תִינוּקוֹת בְּעֵבֶר הַיַּרְדֵּן. רַבִּי יוֹסֵי אוֹמֵר: לֹא עַל שֶׁאָכְלוּ אֶלָּא עַל שֶׁנִּרְאוּ.

[ז] **עַל־** אֵלּוּ מַתְרִיעִין בַּשַּׁבָּת: עַל־עִיר שֶׁהִקִּיפוּהָ גוֹיִם אוֹ נָהָר, וְעַל־סְפִינָה

יד אברהם

previously mentioned calamities that require merely the sounding of the *shofar*, even fasting is required in distant areas if wind blast damage had reached the proportions of that of Ashkelon.]

Alternatively, *Rashi* suggests that the mishnah merely relates the fact of the Ashkelon calamity without implying that the *oven's mouth* is to be taken as a minimum size in determining the need to fast. Hence, the Ashkelon incident would have called for fasting even if the affected grain had been of a smaller amount. [Accordingly, the occurrence is related to support the previous mishnah, in that even in distant places people are required to fast and sound the *shofar*. If so, גָּזְרוּ תַעֲנִית, *they decreed a fast*, would include sounding the *shofar*. Hence, the Tanna of this mishnah can also be the *Tanna Kamma* of mishnah 3, who does not differentiate between fasting and *shofar* blowing.]

וְעוֹד גָּזְרוּ תַעֲנִית עַל־שֶׁאָכְלוּ זְאֵבִים שְׁנֵי תִינוּקוֹת בְּעֵבֶר הַיַּרְדֵּן. — *They further decreed a fast because wolves had devoured two children beyond the Jordan* [*River*].

[This is an example of *wild beasts* mentioned in mishnah 5 above.]

רַבִּי יוֹסֵי אוֹמֵר: לֹא עַל־שֶׁאָכְלוּ אֶלָּא עַל־שֶׁנִּרְאוּ. — *R' Yose says:* [*the fast was decreed*] *not because they*

naic times was made of clay and had a large opening. The baking method was to stick rows of dough onto the interior walls of the oven.] The Talmud gives three alternate interpretations of כִּמְלֹא פִּי תַנּוּר, *the size of a full oven's mouth:* (1) a loaf of bread the size of the opening of an oven, (2) the first row of loaves packed around the opening of an oven, and (3) the complete yield of one oven (*Rashi; Gem.* 2b).

בְּאַשְׁקְלוֹן. — *in Ashkelon.*
— a Philistine city *(Rashi; Rav)* [near the southwestern border of *Eretz Yisrael.*]

The mishnah related this incident to set a precedent concerning the minimum amount of destroyed grain to make the wind blast a calamity, requiring fasting and sounding of the *shofar (Rambam).*

Rashi maintains that this amount is the minimum that requires fasting even in distant places. However, the *shofar* must be sounded for wind blast damage of *any* quantity (22a). [According to this interpretation, the Tanna of our mishnah must be R' Akiva (mishnah 3), who holds that outside the immediate area of the calamity, the *shofar* is sounded, but fasting is not required; the *Tanna Kamma* of that mishnah, however, maintains that the *shofar* is never blown without a decree of fasting. In our mishnah, R' Akiva teaches that unlike the

seen [on grain] in Ashkelon. They further decreed a fast because wolves had devoured two children beyond the Jordan [River]. R′ Yose says, [the fast was decreed] not because they had devoured [the children], but [merely] because they were seen [in the city during the day].

7. In these cases we cry out even on the Sabbath: If a city is surrounded by [hostile] gentiles or by a [flooding] river, or if a ship is storm-tossed at sea. R′

YAD AVRAHAM

had devoured [*the children*], *but* [*merely*] *because they were seen* [*in the city during the day*].

[Thus, according to R′ Yose, *wild beasts* mentioned in mishnah 5 refers to the sighting of wild beasts in the city during the day. See *comm.* there.]

7.

[Because of the joyful nature of the Sabbath and holidays, we are normally forbidden to fast, sound the *shofar*, and trumpets, or offer prayers of supplication (see *Rambam, Hilchos Taaniyos* 1:6). In extraordinary circumstances, however, we are permitted to do so. The mishnah describes the circumstances which are deemed such emergencies.]

עַל־אֵלּוּ מַתְרִיעִין בַּשַּׁבָּת: — *In these cases we cry out* [*even*] *on the Sabbath:*

[In this mishnah, מַתְרִיעִין is interpreted as *cry out in prayer,* and not as *sound the shofar;* for there is a general prohibition against sounding the *shofar* on the Sabbath *(Tos. Yom Tov).* The prayer עֲנֵנוּ, *Answer us,* is recited *(Tos. Yom Tov; Rashi).* This is the prayer that is recited at the end of *Selichos:* עֲנֵנוּ אָבִינוּ עֲנֵנוּ, *Answer us, our Father, answer us! (Rashi* 14a).

However, neither the *shofar,* nor the silver trumpet *(Gem.* 19a) are sounded. Although we are commanded to violate the Sabbath in order to save lives, the *shofar* and trumpet are not sounded as part of the prayers, because there is no guarantee of their efficacy *(Maggid Mishnah; Tos. Yom Tov).*

Ran holds that even in the following extraordinary circumstances, fasting was not permitted on the Sabbath.

Rav, however, maintains that just as we may make supplication, we may also fast.

From this mishnah it may also be inferred that prayers may be recited for the critically ill on the Sabbath and festivals *(Tif. Yis.).*

עַל־עִיר שֶׁהִקִּיפוּהָ גוֹיִם... — *if a city is surrounded by* [*hostile*] *gentiles.*

I.e., if the city is under siege *(Rashi* 14a).

According to our version of the *Gemara,* and *Rashi* (14a) as quoted by *Meleches Shlomo,* the text of the mishnah should read גַּיִס, *a military unit.* The text in the *Rif* reads גַּיָסוֹת, *military units* (plural).

אוֹ נָהָר, — *or by a* [*flooding*] *river,*

ג ח הַמִּטָּרֶפֶת בַּיָּם. רַבִּי יוֹסֵי אוֹמֵר: לְעֶזְרָה וְלֹא לִצְעָקָה. שִׁמְעוֹן הַתִּמְנִי אוֹמֵר: אַף עַל־הַדֶּבֶר. וְלֹא הוֹדוּ לוֹ חֲכָמִים.

[ח] **עַל** כָּל צָרָה שֶׁלֹּא תָבֹא עַל הַצִּבּוּר, מַתְרִיעִין עָלֶיהָ, חוּץ מֵרֹב גְּשָׁמִים.

יד אברהם

I.e., an overflowing river that threatens to flood a city (*Rashi* 14a).

וְעַל־סְפִינָה הַמִּטָּרֶפֶת בַּיָּם. — *or if a ship is storm-tossed at sea.*

If it is in danger of sinking. In all the aforementioned circumstances, we may cry out even on the Sabbath (*Rav; Tif. Yis.*).

רַבִּי יוֹסֵי אוֹמֵר: לְעֶזְרָה וְלֹא לִצְעָקָה. — *R' Yose says:* [*We may call upon the people to assemble*] *for assistance, but not for supplication.*

The *shofar* may be used to assemble people to defend or save the endangered parties. It is also permitted to fast and pray in their behalf (*Rav*).

Meiri quotes authorities who hold that מַתְרִיעִין *does,* in fact, refer to the sounding of the *shofar* on the Sabbath. Hence, according to the *Tanna Kamma,* the *shofar* may be sounded both as a call to assemble for purposes of aid, and as part of the prayers. However, *Meiri* rejects this view, for he holds that the *shofar* may *not* be sounded on the Sabbath.

According to *Rambam* (*Hilchos Taaniyos* 1:6; see *Maggid Mishnah*), however, the *shofar may* be sounded to assemble people for assistance.

[Accordingly, *Rambam* interprets that there is no disagreement between the Tanna Kamma and R' Yose concerning the matter of blowing the *shofar* to alarm the population to assist the besieged city. His reason is simply that assembling people in order to defend others is a matter of פִּקּוּחַ נֶפֶשׁ, *saving lives.* The dispute in our mishnah concerns supplication: The *Tanna Kamma* asserts that the people may *cry out* in prayer (מַתְרִיעִין), even on the Sabbath, due to the gravity of the emergency. R' Yose disagrees because there is no assurance that supplications will avail them. He *does* permit a call to assembly for the purpose of *assistance,* i.e., to defend the people. If they cannot be assembled by word of mouth, however, they may be alarmed through use of a *shofar.*]

שִׁמְעוֹן הַתִּמְנִי אוֹמֵר: — *Shimon the Timnite says:*

Timna was a Philistine city [see *Judges* 15:16] (*Rashi; Beitzah* 21a). Another popular reading is תֵּימָנִי, *from Teiman,* the land named after Teiman, son of Eliphaz [*Gen.* 36:11] (*Lechem Shamayim*).

Shimon the Timnite died at a young age, before he could be ordained; hence, he is not referred to as רַבִּי, *Rabbi.* He studied with R' Yehoshua, R' Eliezer, and R' Akiva and was renowned for his ability to solve difficult problems (*Rashi, Sanhedrin* 17b).

אַף עַל־הַדֶּבֶר. — *Also concerning pestilence.*

I.e., we may also cry out on the Sabbath concerning pestilence (*Rav*).

3 Yose says, [we may call upon the people to assemble]
8 for assistance, but not for supplication. Shimon the Timnite says: Also concerning pestilence. But the Sages did not agree with him.

8. For every calamity that may befall the community we sound [the *shofar*] concerning them, except for excessive rain. It once happened that

וְלֹא הוֹדוּ לוֹ חֲכָמִים. — *But the Sages did not agree with him.*

They did not accept his opinion that we may cry out on the Sabbath concerning pestilence. They did, however, concur that we do so on weekdays *(Rav)*.

Rambam, however, maintains that the Sages did not concur with him even about weekdays. This is the conclusion of the *Gemara* (22b). Hence, only fasting is decreed but the *shofar* is not sounded.

Ran maintains that the Sages differentiate pestilence from the earlier cases in the mishnah in this manner: In the case of the other calamities, in addition to fasting, the *shofar* is sounded continuously, while in the case of pestilence, the *shofar* is sounded according to the procedure of the fasts described in earlier mishnayos. Neighboring cities fast but do not sound the *shofar*, according to the *Tanna Kamma* in mishnah 3 *(Tos. Yom Tov)*.

According to *Rashi*, the *shofar* is not sounded because it would be of no avail against a divine decree. [It seems that according to *Rashi*, pestilence is an irrevocable decree and there is no purpose in fasting in supplication.]

Accordingly, the mishnah follows the opinion of R' Akiva (mishnah 3) that in cases of pestilence, surrounding areas sound the *shofar* but need not fast and cry out *(Tos. Yom Tov)*.

Tiferes Yisrael explains that according to the Sages, we may not fast, supplicate, or sound the *shofar* in an instance of pestilence, because these actions may upset the people and make them more vulnerable to the pestilence. The Sages would, thus, disagree with both the *Tanna Kamma* and R' Akiva of mishnah 4, both of whom concur that those of the affected city are to accept the full severity of communal fasts.

Nowadays, we do not fast in times of plague, because fasting lowers people's resistance; thus, instead of helping the situation, it may cause more harm *(Magen Avraham, Orach Chaim* 576:2).

8.

עַל כָּל צָרָה שֶׁלֹּא תָבֹא עַל הַצִּבּוּר, — *For every calamity that may befall the community...*

The expression literally reads: *for every calamity that may 'not' befall the community*. It is meant euphemistically, like many others used throughout the Talmud. The Sages were reluctant to use expressions that signified suffering or calamities that would befall Israel. Instead, they would use expressions such as that of our mishnah, *that may not befall* or they would speak of mis-

ג
ח

מַעֲשֶׂה שֶׁאָמְרוּ לוֹ לְחוֹנִי הַמְעַגֵּל: ,,הִתְפַּלֵּל שֶׁיֵּרְדוּ גְשָׁמִים״. אָמַר לָהֶם: ,,צְאוּ וְהַכְנִיסוּ תַנּוּרֵי פְסָחִים, בִּשְׁבִיל שֶׁלֹּא יִמּוֹקוּ״. הִתְפַּלֵּל, וְלֹא יָרְדוּ גְשָׁמִים. מֶה עָשָׂה? עָג עוּגָה וְעָמַד בְּתוֹכָהּ, וְאָמַר לְפָנָיו: ,,רִבּוֹנוֹ שֶׁל עוֹלָם, בָּנֶיךָ שָׂמוּ פְנֵיהֶם עָלַי, שֶׁאֲנִי כְּבֶן בַּיִת לְפָנֶיךָ. נִשְׁבָּע אֲנִי בְשִׁמְךָ הַגָּדוֹל שֶׁאֵינִי זָז מִכָּאן, עַד שֶׁתְּרַחֵם עַל בָּנֶיךָ״. הִתְחִילוּ גְשָׁמִים מְנַטְּפִין. אָמַר: ,,לֹא כָךְ שָׁאַלְתִּי, אֶלָּא גִשְׁמֵי בוֹרוֹת שִׁיחִין

fortune that would befall שׂוֹנְאֵיהֶם שֶׁל יִשְׂרָאֵל, *the enemies of Israel;* thus, avoiding direct mention of a threat of calamity toward Israel. In our mishnah, the euphemism is meant to express the hope that the calamity may never come *(Tos. Yom Tov; Rashi)*. Many editions, avoiding the euphemism, read שֶׁתָּבֹא, *which may come (Nimukei Yosef; Shinuyei Nuschaos).*

מַתְרִיעִין עָלֶיהָ, — *we sound [the shofar] concerning them,*

— along with fast and supplication *(Tif. Yis.).*

חוּץ מֵרֹב גְּשָׁמִים. — *except for excessive rain.*

If the rain does not destroy crops, but is merely excessive and burdensome, we do not sound the *shofar* or pray for its cessation (*Rav* from *Rashi).*

When God bestows his bounty — such as rainfall, without which the crops would die — He does so lavishly. Thus, it is improper to pray for its removal *(Tos. Yom Tov* from *Ran).*

מַעֲשֶׂה שֶׁאָמְרוּ לוֹ לְחוֹנִי הַמְעַגֵּל, 'הִתְפַּלֵּל שֶׁיֵּרְדוּ גְשָׁמִים.' — *It once happened that the people said to Choni HaMe'agel* [lit. *Choni, the circle drawer*], *'Pray that rain should fall.'*

[This incident is cited to prove that we do not pray for the cessation of rain unless it causes damage.]

The righteous sage, Choni, was given the title *circle drawer,* because of the following episode (*Rashi, Menachos* 94b).

Others theorize that he was a roof plasterer; the roller [or trowel] used by roofers to smoothen their clay is called מַעֲגִילָה, *ma'agilah;* the one using it is a מְעַגֵּל, *me'agel* (see *Makkos* 2:1).

Choni was famed for his extreme piety and noted for his commitment to understanding the Torah and for the pain he suffered if something was beyond his comprehension. Therefore, the people turned to him to intercede with prayer when all else failed to end the drought *(Iyun Yaakov).*

אָמַר לָהֶם: צְאוּ וְהַכְנִיסוּ תַנּוּרֵי פְסָחִים, שֶׁלֹּא יִמּוֹקוּ. — *He said to them, 'Go and bring in the ovens* [*used*] *for* [*roasting*] *the Pesach sacrifices, lest they dissolve* [*because of the rain*].*'*

Ovens in Mishnaic times were made of clay, were portable, and stood in the yards exposed to the elements. Had they remained out-

3 [the people] said to Choni HaMe'agel, 'Pray that rain
8 should fall.' He said to them, 'Go and bring in the ovens [used] for [roasting] the Pesach sacrifices, lest they dissolve [because of the rain].' He prayed but no rain fell. What did he do? He drew a circle and stood within it and said before Him, 'Master of the Universe! Your children have turned to me because I am like a member of Your household. I swear by Your great Name that I shall not move from here until You have mercy on Your children.' Rain began to trickle. He said, 'Not for such [rains] have I prayed, but for rains [that will fill the] waterholes, ditches,

doors to be drenched by the immiment rain, they would have dissolved *(Rashi, Rav, Tif. Yis.)*.

The incident took place on the twentieth day of Adar. [The people had already prepared ovens for roasting the Paschal lamb which would be offered on the fourteenth of Nissan, a little over three weeks after Choni's prayers *(Yerushalmi)*.] The newly-made clay ovens were not yet dry; had they been left outdoors, they would have been ruined by the rain which Choni was confident would come in response to his entreaties *(Ran; Tif. Yis.)*.

הִתְפַּלֵּל וְלֹא יָרְדוּ גְשָׁמִים — *He prayed, but no rain fell.*

According to *Yerushalmi* (3:9), he was punished for his lack of humility in publicly predicting that his prayer would be successful.

מֶה עָשָׂה? עָג עוּגָה וְעָמַד בְּתוֹכָהּ — *What did he do? He drew a circle and stood within it* (following *Rashi* and *Rav*)...

Alternatively, he dug a *circular hole*, symbolic of a dungeon and stood within it. His intention was to graphically illustrate his pain by likening himself to a prisoner *(Rashi* on *Ein Yaakov, Tiferes Yisrael)*.

He learned this tactic from Habakuk who asked why God tolerates the success of the wicked. Habakuk dug a hole and stood within it, symbolizing that he was 'imprisoned' by the taunts and jibes of disbelievers who argued that Divine Providence was ח״ו unjust. Habakuk said that he would remain in his 'dungeon' until God revealed Himself to answer the question (see *Rashi* to *Habakuk* 2:1).

וְאָמַר לְפָנָיו: רִבּוֹנוֹ שֶׁל עוֹלָם, בָּנֶיךָ שָׂמוּ פְנֵיהֶם עָלַי שֶׁאֲנִי כְּבֶן־בַּיִת לְפָנֶיךָ. נִשְׁבָּע אֲנִי בְשִׁמְךָ הַגָּדוֹל שֶׁאֵינִי זָז מִכָּאן עַד שֶׁתְּרַחֵם עַל בָּנֶיךָ. הִתְחִילוּ גְשָׁמִים מְנַטְּפִין. — *and said before Him, 'Master of the Universe! Your children have turned to me because I am like a member of Your household. I swear by Your Great Name that I shall not move from here until You have mercy on Your children.' Rain began to trickle.*

[He was answered with a rainfall that was sufficient only for crops, but not for other needs.]

אָמַר: לֹא כַךְ שָׁאַלְתִּי אֶלָּא גִשְׁמֵי בוֹרוֹת, שִׁיחִין, וּמְעָרוֹת. — *He said, 'Not for such [rain] have I prayed, but for*

ג וּמְעָרוֹת״. הִתְחִילוּ לֵירֵד בְּזַעַף. אָמַר: ״לֹא כָךְ
ח שָׁאַלְתִּי, אֶלָּא גִשְׁמֵי רָצוֹן, בְּרָכָה וּנְדָבָה״. יָרְדוּ
כְּתִקְנָן, עַד שֶׁיָּצְאוּ יִשְׂרָאֵל מִירוּשָׁלַיִם לְהַר
הַבַּיִת מִפְּנֵי הַגְּשָׁמִים. בָּאוּ וְאָמְרוּ לוֹ: ״כְּשֵׁם
שֶׁהִתְפַּלַּלְתָּ עֲלֵיהֶם שֶׁיֵּרְדוּ, כָּךְ הִתְפַּלֵּל שֶׁיֵּלְכוּ
לָהֶן״. אָמַר לָהֶן: ״צְאוּ וּרְאוּ אִם נִמְחֵית אֶבֶן
הַטּוֹעִים״. שָׁלַח לוֹ שִׁמְעוֹן בֶּן־שָׁטַח: אִלְמָלֵא
חוֹנִי אַתָּה, גּוֹזְרַנִי עָלֶיךָ נִדּוּי. אֲבָל מָה אֶעֱשֶׂה

יד אברהם

rain [*that will fill the*] *water holes, ditches, and caves.'*

[Choni took it upon himself to insist that rain to water the crops was not sufficient because, as mishnah 2 stated, even if there was rainfall sufficient for the crops, as long as there was not enough to fill the reservoirs that were the source of drinking water, prayers and fasts were decreed.]

הִתְחִילוּ לֵירֵד בְּזַעַף. — *Rain began to fall with a vengeance* [lit. *anger*].

Every drop was as big as the mouth of a barrel. The Rabbis said that no drop was smaller than a *log* [approximately a pint] *(Gem. 23a)*.

אָמַר: ״לֹא כָךְ שָׁאַלְתִּי, אֶלָּא גִשְׁמֵי רָצוֹן, בְּרָכָה וּנְדָבָה. יָרְדוּ כְּתִקְנָן, עַד שֶׁיָּצְאוּ יִשְׂרָאֵל מִירוּשָׁלַיִם לְהַר הַבַּיִת מִפְּנֵי הַגְּשָׁמִים. — *He said, 'Not for this have I prayed, but for rains of good will, blessing, and grace.'* [*The rains*] *fell normally until the Jews left Jerusalem for the Temple Mount in the face of the rains.*

[Not for such heavy rain have I prayed, rather for rain that would benefit the people and reassure them of God's beneficence.]

They ascended the Temple Mount to seek shelter under its roof *(Tos. Yom Tov* from *Yerushalmi)*.

Alternatively, they left the inundated lowland for the higher terrain of the mountain *(Meiri)*.

בָּאוּ וְאָמְרוּ לוֹ: ״כְּשֵׁם שֶׁהִתְפַּלַּלְתָּ עֲלֵיהֶם שֶׁיֵּרְדוּ, כָּךְ הִתְפַּלֵּל שֶׁיֵּלְכוּ לָהֶן.״ אָמַר לָהֶן: ״צְאוּ וּרְאוּ אִם נִמְחֵית אֶבֶן הַטּוֹעִים.״ — *They came and said to him, 'Just as you prayed for them to fall, pray that they cease* [lit. *depart*]*.' He said to them, 'Go out and see whether the Stone of the Strayers has been washed away.'*

Choni implied: just as the large stone cannot be washed away, neither may one pray for the cessation of rain. For אֵין מִתְפַּלְּלִין עַל רוֹב הַטּוֹבָה, *we do not pray for* [*the cessation of*] *abundance of good (Ran; Yerushalmi; Tos. Yom Tov; Tif. Yis.)*.

Others render: 'Go out and see whether the Stone of the Strayers has been covered by water.' This could have happened only if there had been a deluge *(Rashi)*. [In that event, Choni would have prayed for the rain to cease].

The Stone of the Strayers served as a place for assembly of people who *strayed* from their property. One who found an article, would announce his find there. Those who had lost property would gather around and offer identifying signs

3
8

and caves.' [Rain] began to fall with a vengeance. He said, 'Not for this have I prayed, but for rains of good will, blessing,and grace.' [The rains] fell normally until the Jews left Jerusalem for the Temple Mount in the face of the rains. They came and said to him, 'Just as you prayed for them to fall, pray that they cease.' He said to them, 'Go out and see whether the Stone of the Strayers has been washed away.' Shimon ben Shatach sent him [a message] saying, 'Were you not Choni, I would pronounce a ban upon you. But what

as proof of ownership. Thus the name, Stone of the Strayers *(Rav* from *Yerushalmi).*

Elsewhere it is referred to as אֶבֶן הַטּוֹעֵן, *the Stone of the Claimant (Bava Metzia* 28b).

;שָׁלַח לוֹ שִׁמְעוֹן בֶּן שָׁטַח — *Shimon ben Shatach sent him* [*a message*]:

Shimon ben Shatach, along with Yehudah ben Tabbai, comprised one of the זוגות, *pairs,* who were the leaders of Jewry after the days of the אַנְשֵׁי כְּנֶסֶת הַגְּדוֹלָה, *members of the Great Assembly* (see *Chagigah* 2:2 and *Avos* 1:8). Each pair consisted of a נָשִׂיא, *President,* and an אַב בֵּית דִּין, *Chief of the Court.* R' Meir and the Sages disagree as to which member of this pair served as the former and which as the latter *(Chagigah* 16b).

,,אִלְמָלֵא חוֹנִי אַתָּה, גוֹזְרַנִי עָלֶיךָ נִדּוּי, — *'Were you not Choni, I would pronounce a ban upon you.*

You deserve to be banned, for you showed disrespect to God in having said, 'Not for such rain have I prayed' (*Rashi; Berachos* 19a).

The *beraisa (Taanis* 23a) elaborates on Shimon ben Shatach's reprimand. 'If these years were like the time of Elijah who controlled the rain, the Name of God would be profaned by your brazen action'. Then, Elijah swore that there would be no rain. Had such an oath been taken in Choni's time, only to have Choni take a contradictory oath that there *must* be rain, one of the two oaths would have been violated, resulting in a profanation of God's name. For Choni to have made such an oath without considering the possibility of a contrary oath having been made was a brazen act *(Tos. Yom Tov).*[1]

1. Chiel of Beth-El had rebuilt Jericho, in violation of the ancient ban of Joshua, and was subsequently punished by the death of his children. Elijah and Ahab, both having gone to console him, met at his home. Ahab asked Elijah how it was possible that the curse of the disciple (Joshua, who prohibited the rebuilding Jericho and placed a curse on anyone who did so) was fulfilled while the curse of the master (Moses who said that no rain would fall if the people practiced idolatry, as they were doing in the kingdom of Ahab) remained unfulfilled. Elijah thereupon swore that there would be neither rain nor dew except upon his decree. He prayed that God would ratify his oath, and God granted him the 'keys of rainfall' (*I Kings* 17; *Sanhedrin* 113a).

Elijah took his oath because of the potential profanation of God's Name inherent in Ahab's question.

ג ט

לְךָ, שֶׁאַתָּה מִתְחַטֵּא לִפְנֵי הַמָּקוֹם וְעוֹשֶׂה לְךָ רְצוֹנְךָ כְּבֵן שֶׁהוּא מִתְחַטֵּא עַל אָבִיו וְעוֹשֶׂה לוֹ רְצוֹנוֹ. וְעָלֶיךָ הַכָּתוּב אוֹמֵר ,,יִשְׂמַח אָבִיךָ וְאִמֶּךָ וְתָגֵל יוֹלַדְתֶּךָ״.

[ט] **הָיוּ** מִתְעַנִּין וְיָרְדוּ לָהֶם גְּשָׁמִים קֹדֶם הָנֵץ הַחַמָּה, לֹא יַשְׁלִימוּ: לְאַחַר הָנֵץ הַחַמָּה, יַשְׁלִימוּ. רַבִּי אֱלִיעֶזֶר אוֹמֵר: קֹדֶם חֲצוֹת לֹא יַשְׁלִימוּ, לְאַחַר חֲצוֹת יַשְׁלִימוּ. מַעֲשֶׂה שֶׁגָּזְרוּ תַעֲנִית בְּלֹד, וְיָרְדוּ לָהֶם גְּשָׁמִים

אֲבָל מָה אֶעֱשֶׂה לְךָ שֶׁאַתָּה מִתְחַטֵּא לִפְנֵי הַמָּקוֹם. — *But what can I do to you, since you are like a* [*favorite*] *child before the Omnipresent,*

מִתְחַטֵּא is from the Aramaic מַחְטַיי, *child,* implying: You make yourself like a child whose requests are granted even when they are requested in a disrespectful manner *(Tos. Yom Tov* from *Aruch; Tif. Yis.).*

Alternatively, *you sin before God* with your constant pleading; from חֵטְא, *sin (Rashi* on *Berachos* 19a);

You purify yourself, from חַטֵא, *to cleanse or purify as in (Numbers* 19:12) הוּא יִתְחַטָּא, *he is to purify himself (Rashi* on the mishnah)

— *You humble yourself (Rashi* on *Berachos* 57b); or *you walk before (Menachos* 67a). *Ran* renders: *you long for things.*

וְעוֹשֶׂה לְךָ רְצוֹנְךָ כְּבֵן שֶׁהוּא מִתְחַטֵּא עַל־אָבִיו וְעוֹשֶׂה לוֹ רְצוֹנוֹ וְעָלֶיךָ הַכָּתוּב אוֹמֵר; יִשְׂמַח אָבִיךָ וְאִמֶּךָ וְתָגֵל יוֹלַדְתֶּךָ.׳ — *And He fulfills your wishes as a son who makes himself like a young child before his father who fulfills his wish. Concerning* [*people like*] *you, Scripture states: May your father and mother be glad, and she who bore you rejoice' (Prov.* 23:25).

[Since I see that HASHEM grants your wishes, I cannot ban you.]

9.

הָיוּ מִתְעַנִּין וְיָרְדוּ לָהֶם גְּשָׁמִים קֹדֶם הָנֵץ הַחַמָּה, לֹא יַשְׁלִימוּ. — *If they had been fasting* [i.e., from daybreak], *and rain began to fall before sunrise, they need not complete* [*the fast*].

They need not fast at all. The binding status of the fast begins only at sunrise, but by that time, the reason for decreeing the fast no longer existed for rain had already fallen *(Tos. Yom Tov* from *Rashi).*

לְאַחַר הָנֵץ הַחַמָּה, יַשְׁלִימוּ. — [*If the rain began to fall*] *after sunrise, they must complete* [*the fast*].

[The people had begun fasting before it rained, and a fast that is commenced must be completed.]

רַבִּי אֱלִיעֶזֶר אוֹמֵר; קֹדֶם חֲצוֹת, לֹא יַשְׁלִימוּ, לְאַחַר חֲצוֹת יַשְׁלִימוּ — *R' Eliezer says, if* [*it began to rain*]

can I do to you, since you are like a [favorite] child before the Omnipresent, and He fulfills your wishes as a son who makes himself like a young child before his father and he fulfills his wish. Concerning [people like] you Scripture states (*Proverbs* 23:25): *May your father and mother rejoice and she who bore you be glad.*'

9. **I**f they had been fasting, and rain began to fall before sunrise, they need not complete [the fast]. [If the rain began to fall] after sunrise, they must complete [the fast]. R' Eliezer says, [if it began to rain] before midday, they need not complete [the fast but if the rain began] after midday, they must complete [the fast]. It once happened that a fast was decreed in Lod and rain fell before midday. R' Tarfon

before midday, they need not complete [*the fast, but if the rain began*] *after midday, they must complete* [*the fast*].

A fast is considered to have begun only once the midday meal was omitted. Before then, however, it is as if the fast had not yet commenced (*Tos. Yom Tov* from *Rashi*).

Alternatively, once half the day has passed in purity [fasting], the remainder of the day should be continued in the same manner (*Rif; Rosh, Yerushalmi*).

Another interpretation: Since it rained only after the people had begun the fast, it is an indication that God had indeedbeen displeased with them; therefore, they should continue their fast (*Tif. Yis.*).

The *halachah* is in accordance with R' Eliezer.

This is true only of public fasts, because the court ordains such fasts on the condition that the precipitating circumstance still exists at the time the fast takes effect. In the case of privately accepted fasts, unless a condition is explicitly stated at the time the individual imposes the fast upon himself, he must complete the fast (*Orach Chaim* 579:1). *Rashi* (10b) explains that unless the fast were completed, it would seem as though a person is, so to speak; making conditions with the Almighty: 'If the distress is alleviated, I will not fast; if it is not, I will fast.'

Others differentiate between a public fast, which would be harder for the entire community, and a private fast, which involves only the individual (*Ritva* from *Ramban, Maggid Mishnah*).

[The mishnah proceeds to support R' Eliezer by citing an actual occurrence:]

מַעֲשֶׂה שֶׁגָּזְרוּ תַעֲנִית בְּלֹד, וְיָרְדוּ לָהֶם גְּשָׁמִים קֹדֶם חֲצוֹת. אָמַר לָהֶם רַבִּי טַרְפוֹן, צְאוּ וְאִכְלוּ וּשְׁתוּ וַעֲשׂוּ יוֹם טוֹב. וְיָצְאוּ וְאָכְלוּ וְשָׁתוּ וְעָשׂוּ יוֹם טוֹב וּבָאוּ בֵּין הָעַרְבַּיִם וְקָרְאוּ הַלֵּל הַגָּדוֹל — *It once*

קֹדֶם חֲצוֹת. אָמַר לָהֶם רַבִּי טַרְפוֹן: ,,צְאוּ ג
וְאִכְלוּ וּשְׁתוּ וַעֲשׂוּ יוֹם טוֹב״. וְיָצְאוּ וְאָכְלוּ ט
וְשָׁתוּ וְעָשׂוּ יוֹם טוֹב, וּבָאוּ בֵּין הָעַרְבַּיִם וְקָרְאוּ
הַלֵּל הַגָּדוֹל.

happened that a fast was decreed in Lod and rain fell before midday. R' Tarfon said to them: Go out, eat, drink, and proclaim a holiday. They then went out, ate, drank, and proclaimed a holiday. In the afternoon, they returned [to the synagogue] and recited the Great Hallel.

R' Tarfon lived in Lod *(Kehati).*

As the day drew to a close, the people came to the synagogue and recited the *Great Hallel (Psalm* 136). This is in contrast to the more familiar *Hallel* known as הַלֵּל הַמִּצְרִי, *the Egyptian Hallel,* which comprises Psalms 113-118. [It is the *Egyptian Hallel* that we recite on festivals and on *Rosh Chodesh.* The *Great Hallel* is recited as part of the Pesach Seder.]. The *Great Hallel* was specified for the celebration of the rainfall because it contains the verse: נוֹתֵן לֶחֶם לְכָל־בָּשָׂר, *He gives food to all flesh,* an apt praise on a day when God was beseeched for salvation from famine. Since the verse is a statement of gratitude to God for having given sustenance, R' Tarfon inferred that it should be recited only when people are sated. Therefore, he advised the people to eat and drink, and then give thanks *(Tos. Yom Tov* from *Rashi ad. loc.).*

[Though Psalm 136 is recited as part of the morning prayers of the Sabbath *before* people have eaten, then it is not recited specifically in thanksgiving for food, but as general praise.]

When the *Great Hallel* is recited in thanksgiving for rain, it is preceded by Psalm 135 which states מַעֲלֶה נְשִׂאִים מִקְצֵה הָאָרֶץ, *He brings clouds from the ends of the earth,* a clear reference to rainfall. Afterward we say, מוֹדִים אֲנַחְנוּ לָךְ עַל כָּל טִפָּה וְטִפָּה, *we thank You for each and every drop (Tif. Yis.* from 575:11).

Chapter 4

1.

The Order of the Daytime Prayers

— שַׁחֲרִית, [*Shacharis*] *the Morning Prayer,* is recited every day during the first third of the day beginning with the הָנֵץ הַחַמָּה, *sunrise (Berachos* 4:11);

— מוּסָף, [*Musaf*] *the Additional Prayer* is recited on the Sabbath, *Rosh Chodesh,* and festivals in remembrance of the special additional sacrifices offered on these days during the time of the Temple. This prayer is recited after *Shacharis,* on those days.

— מִנְחָה, [*Minchah*] *the Afternoon Prayer,* is recited every day before sunset. In the time of the mishnah, it was generally recited in early afternoon;

— נְעִילָה, [*Ne'ilah*] *Prayer at the Closing of the Gates,* is a concluding prayer added to the prayers of Yom Kippur and any public fasts that were decreed in response to lack of rain or other calamities [see ch. 2]. This prayer is recited just

3 said to them, 'Go out, eat and drink, and proclaim a
9 holiday. They then went out, ate, drank and
proclaimed a holiday. In the afternoon, they returned
[to the synagogue] and recited the Great *Hallel*.

before sunset — a time when the 'Gates of Heaven,' through which prayers ascend to God, so to speak, are about to be closed.

The *Ne'ilah* prayer was added to the fast day service because the fasts were decreed primarily so that the community could unite in prayer to seek God's mercy. Therefore, on such fasts as Tishah B'Av and the Seventeenth of Tammuz which were established to mourn the Destructions rather than for prayer, there is no concluding prayer of *Ne'ilah*. On those days, however, *Minchah* is recited close to sunset rather than in the early afternoon; therefore, it bears a resemblance to *Ne'ilah*.

◆§ Bircas Kohanim

The *kohanim* are commanded to bless Israel (*Numbers* 6:22-27). Because they are required to raise their hands during its recitation, the blessing is known as נְשִׂיאַת כַּפַּיִם, *Raising of the Hands*. It is also known by the more obvious name בִּרְכַּת כֹּהֲנִים, [*Bircas Kohanim*] *Priestly Blessing*.

The halachah provides that the blessings be conferred by the *kohanim* every day at every public recitation of the *Shemoneh Esrei*. Thus, the maximum number of times the *kohen* can confer the blessing on any single day is four as will be seen below.

Although *Bircas Kohanim* should be recited at each public recitation of *Shemoneh Esrei*, the Rabbis decreed that it not be done during the *Minchah* services. Because *Minchah* follows the midday meal, there is a possibility that the *kohanim* drank alchoholic beverages during the meal, thereby disqualifying themselves from pronouncing the blessing (*Gem.* 26b). On fast days, however, since no such possibility exists, R' Meir, the Tanna of our mishnah, contends that *Bircas Kohanim* is indeed pronounced even at *Minchah*. R' Yose disagrees; he maintains that the Sages chose not to differentiate between the *Minchah* services of fast days and those of other days. However, on fast days when there is no *Ne'ilah* service, since *Minchah* is recited just prior to sunset, even R' Yose agrees that *Bircas Kohanim* is pronounced; for on those days *Minchah* is more similar to *Ne'ilah* than to the *Minchah* of other days. Despite the fact that our mishnah is to the contrary, the *halachah* follows R' Yose (*Gem.* 26b; *Shulchan Aruch, Orach Chaim* 129:1).

◆§ Bircas Kohanim Today

In Jerusalem as well as in Sephardic communities in the Diaspora, the above custom is still followed. However, in the Ashkenazic communities of the Diaspora, *Bircas Kohanim* is pronounced only during the *Musaf* services of festivals. *Rama* (*Orach Chaim* 128:44) maintains that *Bircas Kohanim* may be pronounced only in a joyous atmosphere; hence, on weekdays when people are preoccupied with earning a livelihood — and even on the Sabbath when such mundane thoughts are difficult to avoid — *Bircas Kohanim* may not be pronounced. However, on festivals when the *Musaf* service precedes the festive meal, a joyous mood does prevail; hence, *Bircas Kohanim* may be pronounced.

The fact that our mishnah discusses the Priestly Blessing on *fast days*, makes it clear that *Bircas Kohanim* was pronounced even on fast days when the atmosphere was surely not joyous. Therefore we must seek an explanation beyond that given by *Rama*.

ד
א

[א] **בִּשְׁלֹשָׁה** פְרָקִים בַּשָּׁנָה כֹּהֲנִים נוֹשְׂאִין אֶת־כַּפֵּיהֶן אַרְבַּע פְּעָמִים בַּיּוֹם — בַּשַּׁחֲרִית, בַּמּוּסָף וּבַמִּנְחָה וּבִנְעִילַת שְׁעָרִים: בַּתַּעֲנִיּוֹת וּבַמַּעֲמָדוֹת וּבְיוֹם הַכִּפּוּרִים.

יד אברהם

Sefer Moadim U'Zemanim notes that in the Temple, *Bircas Kohanim* was pronounced only at the time of עֲבוֹדָה, [*the sacrificial*] *service*, of a קָרְבַּן צִבּוּר, *communal offering (Tosafos, Sotah* 38a). The Sages frequently refer to *Shemoneh Esrei* as עֲבוֹדָה, *service*, for it is intenaed as a substitute for the *sacrificial service*, of the Temple. If a proper quorum listens attentively to חֲזָרַת הַשַּׁ״ץ, *the chazan's repetition of Shemoneh Esrei*, it can be considered equivalent to a *communal* offering. Given that explanation, we can understand the recitation of the Priestly blessing in the presence of ten men (*Megillah* 18a) as an extension of the communal Temple service.

In Talmudic times, when many people were unable to recite the prayers correctly, they fulfilled their obligation to pray by listening intently to the *chazan's* repetition and answering, "Amen." It was therefore taken as a matter of course that the *chazan's Shemoneh Esrei* was a communal service at which *Bircas Kohanim* should be recited. Nowadays, when people are well versed in prayers and have *siddurim* to pray from, they do not rely on the *chazan* to fulfill their obligation. Since the congregation is not very attentive to his recitation, it is not considered communal service, and *Bircas Kohanim* is not pronounced. On festivals, however, since people are not preoccupied with anything but the spirit of the festival, they will listen attentively to the leader even though they have already fulfilled their individual obligation.

Similarly in Jerusalem, since the early settlers dedicated their lives to the service of God and were not preoccupied with mundane thoughts, they adopted the Sephardic custom of pronouncing the blessing every day. Among the Sephardim, in turn, there were many worshipers who were unable to read the prayers, and, therefore, listened attentively to the *chazan* in order to fulfill their obligation.

Alternatively, *Responsa Beis Ephraim* theorizes that since very few *kohanim* have positive documentary proof of their כְּהֻנָּה, *priestly descent*, the recitation of *Bircas Kohanim*, which is a privilege permitted only to qualified priests, is kept to a minimum. However, the early inhabitants of Jerusalem who did not wander in exile as much as those living in the Diaspora, generally had such *documentation;* hence, the custom in Jerusalem to pronounce *Bircas Kohanim* every day. Once the custom was adopted, it remained in effect even after conditions changed.

בִּשְׁלֹשָׁה פְרָקִים בַּשָּׁנָה כֹּהֲנִים נוֹשְׂאִין אֶת־כַּפֵּיהֶן אַרְבַּע פְּעָמִים בַּיּוֹם; בַּשַּׁחֲרִית בַּמּוּסָף וּבַמִּנְחָה וּבִנְעִילַת שְׁעָרִים — *On three junctures of the year the kohanim raise their hands* [*to bless the people*] *four times during the day — at Shacharis, Musaf, Minchah, and Ne'ilah* [lit. the closing of the gates].

On the three occasions given below, *Bircas Kohanim* is pronounced at each *Shemoneh Esrei* of the day. The maximum possible number of times is four — *Shacharis, Musaf, Minchah,* and *Ne'ilah* — although not every one of the three occasions has a *Ne'ilah* prayer.

According to Rav, the Closing of the Gates' refers figuratively to the closing of the gates of Heaven [see below], while according to R'

4
1

1. On three junctures of the year, the *kohanim* raise their hands [to bless the people] four times during the day — at *Shacharis, Musaf, Minchah,* and *Ne'ilah* — on fast days, at *maamados,* and on Yom Kippur.

YAD AVRAHAM

Yochanan it refers literally to the closing of the Temple gates (*Yerushalmi, Berachos* 4:1).

The Gates of Heaven 'close' after nightfall when the daily prayers have ended *(Rashi).* Accordingly, Rav would begin to pray when the setting sun was visible just above the tree tops and, because he prayed very slowly and fervently, he would finish after nightfall. It is clear, therefore, that according to Rav, the time of *Ne'ilah* extends until after nightfall, provided it is begun before sunset.

R' Yochanan, however, rules that the *Ne'ilah* service must be completed no later than the closing of the Temple doors after the lighting of the *Menorah.* This was done before sunset. Hence, he maintains that *Ne'ilah* must be completed before sunset *(Rosh; Ran,* end of *Yoma). Yerushalmi* (end of *Yoma)* cites our mishnah as proof of R' Yochanan's view since it states that *Bircas Kohanim* is recited at *Ne'ilah;* since *Bircas Kohanim* is not pronounced at night, we must assume that *Ne'ilah* is completed before nightfall.

Despite much evidence in favor of R' Yochanan, the custom is to commence the *Ne'ilah* service before sunset, and to extend it even into the night *(Magen Avraham; Turei Zahav,* 623:1).

[What are the three occasions when *Bircas Kohanim* is said at every prayer?]

בְּתַעֲנִיּוֹת וּבַמַּעֲמָדוֹת וּבְיוֹם הַכִּפּוּרִים — *on fast days, on maamados, and on Yom Kippur.*

— On fast days that are decreed because of calamities, the *kohanim* pronounce *Bircas Kohanim* three times: at *Shacharis, Minchah,* and *Ne'ilah.* [There is, of course, no *Musaf* on fast days, but *Ne'ilah* is added on specially decreed fasts.] As noted in the preface, our mishnah follows R' Meir who holds that *Bircas Kohanim* is recited at the *Minchah* of fasts although it is omitted at the *Minchah* of other days. The halachah, however, follows R' Yose who omits *Bircas Kohanim* at *Minchah* on specially decreed fasts when *Ne'ilah* is recited *(Rav).*

— On Yom Kippur, when all four prayers were recited, *Bircas Kohanim* was pronounced four times.

— On *maamados* [see 2:7 for an explanation of *maamados,* and the next mishnah for its origin] it was pronounced three times each day from Monday through Thursday *(Rav).*[1]

1. During the week of their *maamad,* the people of the *ma..mad* would fast from Monday through Thursday. On Sunday, they were exempt because of the danger inherent in fasting after the heavy meals of the Sabbath. On Friday they were also exempt in order to be able to prepare for the Sabbath properly. *Rav* includes only the four days of fasting among the days when *Bircas Kohanim* is recited the maximum number of times. Apparently he rules that *Ne'ilah* was recited only on the

ד [ב] **אֵלּוּ** הֵן מַעֲמָדוֹת, לְפִי שֶׁנֶּאֱמַר ,,צַו
ב אֶת־בְּנֵי יִשְׂרָאֵל, וְאָמַרְתָּ אֲלֵהֶם
אֶת־קָרְבָּנִי לַחְמִי״; וְכִי הֵיאַךְ קָרְבָּנוֹ שֶׁל אָדָם
קָרֵב, וְהוּא אֵינוֹ עוֹמֵד עַל גַּבָּיו? הִתְקִינוּ
נְבִיאִים הָרִאשׁוֹנִים עֶשְׂרִים וְאַרְבָּעָה
מִשְׁמָרוֹת; עַל־כָּל־מִשְׁמָר וּמִשְׁמָר הָיָה מַעֲמָד
בִּירוּשָׁלַיִם שֶׁל כֹּהֲנִים, שֶׁל לְוִיִּם וְשֶׁל
יִשְׂרְאֵלִים. הִגִּיעַ זְמַן הַמִּשְׁמָר לַעֲלוֹת, כֹּהֲנִים
וּלְוִיִּם עוֹלִים לִירוּשָׁלַיִם. וְיִשְׂרָאֵל שֶׁבְּאוֹתוֹ

יד אברהם

According to *Rambam*, the people of the *maamados* recited an additional prayer known as *Musaf* each day; hence, the *kohanim* pronounced *Bircas Kohanim* four times a day on *maamados*.

2.

אֵלּוּ הֵן מַעֲמָדוֹת: — *These are the maamados:*

Having mentioned *maamados* in connection with *Bircas Kohanim*, the mishnah now goes on to define this institution and explain its purpose *(Rashi; Meiri).*

לְפִי שֶׁנֶּאֱמַר צַו אֶת־בְּנֵי יִשְׂרָאֵל וְאָמַרְתָּ אֲלֵהֶם אֶת־קָרְבָּנִי לַחְמִי, — *Since the Torah states: Command the Children of Israel and say to them: 'My sacrifice, My bread...' (Num.* 28:2),

[The verse begins the commandment of offering the קָרְבַּן תָּמִיד, *continual* (daily) *sacrifice.* As the introductory phrase clearly implies, the responsibility for the sacrifice is not that of the *kohanim,* but of all Israel. The offering is a קָרְבַּן צִבּוּר, *communal sacrifice* in which each individual Jew is a partner.]

וְכִי הֵיאַךְ קָרְבָּנוֹ שֶׁל אָדָם קָרֵב וְהוּא אֵינוֹ עוֹמֵד עַל גַּבָּיו? — *Now, how can a person's sacrifice be offered when he is not present?*

One who brings an offering to the Temple is required to be present while the sacrificial service is performed (*Sotah* 8a). Since the offering of the daily sacrifice is incumbent upon all Israel, theoretically it would require the presence of every Jew in the Temple Court during the service — a physical impossibility *(Tos. Yom Tov* from *Rav* 2:7).

The origin of the premise that one must be present when his sacrifice is offered is Balaam's statement to Balak *(Numbers* 23:3): הִתְיַצֵּב עַל־עֹלָתֶךָ, *Stand by your burnt offering.* This indicates that standing by one's sacrifice was common practice even among non-Jews *(Meleches Shlomo).*

Alternatively, it is only proper that the one for whom the animal is being sacrificed should stand nearby to demonstrate that the sacrifice

days when the people of the *maamad* actually fasted. *Ran* and *Meiri,* however, hold that *Ne'ilah* was recited even on Sunday and Friday even though the people of the maamad did not fast.

4
2

2. **T**hese are the *maamados*: Since the Torah states: *Command the Children of Israel and say to them, 'My sacrifice, my bread...' (Num.* 28:2). Now, how can a person's sacrifice be offered when he is not present? The early prophets instituted twenty-four *mishmaros.* Corresponding to every single *mishmar,* there was a *maamad* in Jerusalem of *kohanim,* Levites, and Israelites. When the time approached the *mishmar* to ascend, the *kohanim* and the Levites would ascend to Jerusalem, and the Israelites as-

YAD AVRAHAM

is being offered in his stead. As many commentators explain, an offering symbolizes that the sinner deserves to lose his life but that his property is offered in his place (*Beer Hagolah* 31:1).

הִתְקִינוּ נְבִיאִים הָרִאשׁוֹנִים עֶשְׂרִים וְאַרְבָּעָה מִשְׁמָרוֹת, — *The early prophets instituted twenty-four mishmaros,*

I.e., Samuel and David *(Tos. Yom Tov* from *Rashi).* This institution is referred to in *I Chron.* 9:22: הֵמָּה יִסַּד דָּוִיד וּשְׁמוּאֵל הָרוֹאֶה בֶּאֱמוּנָתָם, *they* [i.e., the heads of the watches of *kohanim*] *are those whom David and Samuel the Seer ordained in their set office (Tos. Yom Tov).*

David and Samuel divided the *kohanim* and the Levites into twenty-four groups which would go to Jerusalem and perform the sacrificial service a week at a time on a rotating basis (*Gemara* 27a; see above 2:7).

The early prophets established the practice of selecting from all Israel righteous, sin-fearing men to be emissaries of all Israel to stand over the sacrifices. They were lay divisions referred to as אַנְשֵׁי מַעֲמָד, [*Anshei Maamad*] *Men of the Station (Rambam, Klei HaMikdash* 6:1).

Just as the *kohanim* and Levites were divided into twenty-four groups, so were the Israelites divided into twenty-four groups whose purpose was to stand by the service and pray as described below *(Tos. Yom Tov).*

עַל כָּל־מִשְׁמָר וּמִשְׁמָר הָיָה מַעֲמָד בִּירוּשָׁלַיִם שֶׁל כֹּהֲנִים, שֶׁל לְוִיִּם, וְשֶׁל יִשְׂרְאֵלִים. — *Corresponding to every single mishmar, there was a maamad in Jerusalem of kohanim, Levites, and Israelites.*

[In this instance, *maamad* here is a collective noun including all three groups who participated in the Temple service.]

Thus, as explained above, a *maamad* of Israelites was designated to correspond to each *mishmar* of *kohanim (Rav).*

הִגִּיעַ זְמַן הַמִּשְׁמָר לַעֲלוֹת, כֹּהֲנִים וּלְוִיִּם עוֹלִים לִירוּשָׁלַיִם, — *When the time approached for the mishmar to ascend, the kohanim, and the Levites would ascend to Jerusalem,*

When their assigned weeks approached, all members of the *mishmar* would leave their home cities and assemble in Jerusalem. The *kohanim* would offer the sacrifices; the Levites would sing and play musical instruments during the service.

ד
ג

מִשְׁמָר מִתְכַּנְּסִין לְעָרֵיהֶן וְקוֹרְאִין בְּמַעֲשֵׂה בְרֵאשִׁית.

[ג] **וְאַנְשֵׁי** הַמַּעֲמָד הָיוּ מִתְעַנִּין אַרְבָּעָה יָמִים בַּשָּׁבוּעַ, מִיּוֹם שֵׁנִי וְעַד יוֹם חֲמִישִׁי; וְלֹא הָיוּ מִתְעַנִּין עֶרֶב שַׁבָּת, מִפְּנֵי כְבוֹד הַשַּׁבָּת. וְלֹא בְאֶחָד בְּשַׁבָּת, כְּדֵי שֶׁלֹּא יֵצְאוּ מִמְּנוּחָה וָעֹנֶג לִיגִיעָה וְתַעֲנִית וְיָמוּתוּ.

יד אברהם

Another version: כֹּהֲנָיו וּלְוִיָּו, *Its* [the *mishmar's*] *kohanim and Levites (Meleches Shlomo).*

וְיִשְׂרָאֵל שֶׁבְּאוֹתוֹ מִשְׁמָר מִתְכַּנְּסִין לְעָרֵיהֶן, — *and the Israelites assigned to that* [lit. *of that*] *mishmar would assemble in their cities.*[1]

[Above, the mishnah said that the Israelites of the *maamad* were stationed in Jerusalem where they represented the nation during the offering of the communal sacrifices. Here, the people of the *maamad* are described as going to their respective cities, thus indicating that there are different categories of *maamados.*]

The members of the *maamad* who lived *in or around* Jerusalem would enter the Temple along with the *mishmar* of the *kohanim* and Levites of that week; those who lived far from Jerusalem would gather in their local synagogue (*Rambam, Klei HaMikdash* 6:2; *Rav*).

Others maintain that only those who lived *in* Jerusalem would be present in the עֲזָרָה, *Temple Court,* during the sacrificial service. Those who lived *outside* Jerusalem, although they may have been nearby, were not required to travel to Jerusalem. They assembled in the synagogues of their own town to pray and fast on behalf of their brethren (*Rashi, Rabad* quoted by *Meiri,* and *Pesach Einayim).*

Still another version is that all people appointed to a *maamad* were required to make the pilgrimage to Jerusalem. When they aged and found it difficult to travel, they were not expected to resign from the *maamad;* instead, they would remain in their own cities, retaining their capacity of *Anshei Maamad,* and pray for their brethren *(Meiri).*

1. The *Gemara* (27b) explains that the *Anshei Maamad* would assemble in the *synagogue* to read the story of Creation. *Megillah* 21a, however, states that the people would gather in the *town square* to pray on fast days and *maamados,* implying that the *Anshei Maamad* prayed in the town square, rather than the synagogue.

Rashi (Megillah 21a) suggests that a synagogue was built in the town square for this purpose. The same synagogue was also used when people gathered with their *bikkurim* [first fruits] to embark to Jerusalem. Before their journey, they would remain overnight in the town square (*Bikkurim* 3:2).

Others claim that the word *maamados* in *Megillah* is an error. Accordingly, the synagogue in the town square was used only for the prayers of fast days, but not for *maamados (Rashi* quoting *R' Yitzchak HaLevi; Tosafos).*

4 signed to that *mishmar* would assemble in their cities,
3 and read from the Story of Creation.

3. The men of the *maamad* would fast four days of the week, from Monday through Thursday. They did not fast on Friday because of the honor due the Sabbath; nor on Sunday lest they go from rest and pleasure to toil and fast, and become faint.

YAD AVRAHAM

וְקוֹרִין בְּמַעֲשֵׂה בְרֵאשִׁית. — *and read from the story of Creation.*

All members of the *maamad*, those in the cities as well as those in Jerusalem *(Tos. Yom Tov; Tif. Yis.)*, would read the Torah's narrative of creation according to the order outlined in mishnah 3.

The reading symbolized that Creation exists in the merit of the sacrificial service (*Rav; Tif. Yis.* from *Gem.* 27b).[1]

3.

וְאַנְשֵׁי הַמַּעֲמָד הָיוּ מִתְעַנִּין... — [*And*] *the men of the maamad would fast...*

All members of the *maamad* would fast, both the groups that assembled in Jerusalem and those that assembled in their own cities (*Rambam, Klei HaMikdash* 6:3). [See above mishnah 2.]

אַרְבָּעָה יָמִים בַּשָּׁבוּעַ—מִיּוֹם שֵׁנִי וְעַד יוֹם חֲמִישִׁי... — *four days of the week, from Monday through Thursday.*

They did not fast *continuously* from Monday morning to Thursday night. Rather they fasted on each day from morning until night, when they would eat *(Tif. Yis.)*.

וְלֹא הָיוּ מִתְעַנִּין עֶרֶב שַׁבָּת מִפְּנֵי כְּבוֹד שַׁבָּת; — *They did not fast on Friday because of the honor due the Sabbath;*

It is improper to enter the Sabbath famished from the fast *(Tos. Yom Tov)*. It goes without saying that they refrained from fasting on the Sabbath itself (*Rav* from *Gem.* 27b).

וְלֹא בְאֶחָד בְּשַׁבָּת כְּדֵי שֶׁלֹּא יֵצְאוּ מִמְּנוּחָה וָעֹנֶג לִיגִיעָה וְתַעֲנִית וְיָמוּתוּ. — *nor on Sunday lest they go from rest and pleasure to toil and fast, and become faint* [lit. *and die*].

The contrast from feasting to fasting may unduly weaken the body; therefore, the Rabbis did not require it. Though the mishnah uses the term וְיָמוּתוּ, *they will die*, the expression is meant figuratively *(Tif. Yis.)*.

The above paragraph appears in the standard editions of the Mishnah, however its authenticity is doubtful. It is deleted in many editions of mishnayos and in *Yerushalmi*, and is in parentheses in *Bavli*.

A further indication that it is not part of the mishnah is the fact that the *Gemara* seeks reasons for not fasting on Sunday and ignores the reason given by the 'mishnah' *(Tos. Yom Tov)*.

1. Now that the *Beis HaMikdash* has been destroyed and sacrifices can no longer be offered, the recitation of Scriptural chapters concerning the sacrifices takes the place of the offerings (*Gem., ibid.*). These portions, too, were recited by the *Anshei Maamad*, before reading from the portion of Creation *(Otzar HaGeonim)*.

ד בַּיּוֹם הָרִאשׁוֹן — „בְּרֵאשִׁית" וְ„יְהִי רָקִיעַ";
ה בַּשֵּׁנִי — „יְהִי רָקִיעַ" וְ„יִקָּווּ הַמַּיִם". בַּשְּׁלִישִׁי
— „יִקָּווּ הַמַּיִם" וְ„יְהִי מְאֹרֹת". בָּרְבִיעִי —
„יְהִי מְאֹרֹת" וְ„יִשְׁרְצוּ הַמַּיִם". בַּחֲמִישִׁי —
„יִשְׁרְצוּ הַמַּיִם" וְ„תּוֹצֵא הָאָרֶץ"; בַּשִּׁשִּׁי —
„תּוֹצֵא הָאָרֶץ", וּ„וַיְכֻלּוּ הַשָּׁמַיִם". פָּרָשָׁה
גְדוֹלָה — קוֹרִין אוֹתָהּ בִּשְׁנַיִם, וְהַקְּטַנָּה —
בְּיָחִיד, בַּשַּׁחֲרִית וּבַמּוּסָף. וּבַמִּנְחָה נִכְנָסִין

Rav cites two of the *Gemara's* reasons:

—1) Since Adam was created on Friday, Sunday was the third day of his life. Just as we find that the people of Shechem were weak on the third day after their circumcision (*Gen.* 34:25), Adam was weak on the third day after his creation.

—2) On the Sabbath, one is granted a נְשָׁמָה יְתֵרָה, *additional soul,* so to speak. [See ArtScroll *Zemiroth* p. 113.] The departure of this soul at the close of the Sabbath leaves one weakened and in no condition to fast on Sunday.

⊱§ The Portions Read

The *Anshei Maamad* read the Torah from the beginning of *Genesis.* On each day, they read the verses describing the creation of that day. Each person called to the Torah must read at least three verses, and three people — a *kohen,* Levite, and Israelite — were called to the Torah each day. Since no single day's reading contains enough verses for all three readers, verses from the next day's reading would be read as well.

בַּיּוֹם הָרִאשׁוֹן „בְּרֵאשִׁית" וְ„יְהִי רָקִיעַ". — *On Sunday* [*they would read*], *'In the beginning' (Gen.* 1:1-5) *and 'Let there be a firmament'* (6-8).

The first day's portion consists of five verses. The *kohen* would read the first three verses, and the Levite would repeat the third verse and continue until the end of the portion. The Israelite would read the second day's portion. A similar procedure was followed every day.

בַּשֵּׁנִי—„יְהִי רָקִיעַ" וְ„יִקָּווּ הַמַּיִם". — *On Monday: 'Let there be a firmament' (ibid.), and 'Let the waters gather'* (9-13).

The *kohen* read the portion of the second day, which has only three verses. The portion of the third day, having five verses, was shared by the Levite and the Israelite. The third verse of the portion concluded the Levite's three verses, and the Israelite repeated it as the first of his three verses *(Rav; Tif. Yis.).*

Let there be a firmament to separate the waters corresponds with the prayer for the safety of sea-travelers *(Rashi,* 27b).

בַּשְּׁלִישִׁי—„יִקָּווּ הַמַּיִם" וְ„יְהִי מְאֹרֹת". — *On Tuesday: 'Let the waters gather'* (ibid.), and *'Let there be luminaries'* (14:19).

[— the portions of the third and fourth days.]

On the third day, God commanded: וְתֵרָאֶה הַיַּבָּשָׁה, *and let the dry land appear.* וְתֵרָאֶה can also be rendered *let* [the dry land] *become fit;* therefore it corresponds to the

4 On Sunday [they would read]: *In the beginning*
5 *(Gen.* 1:1-5), and *Let there be a firmament* (6-8). On Monday: *Let there be a firmament* (ibid.), and *Let the waters...gather (9-13).* On Tuesday: *Let the waters gather* (ibid.), and *Let there be luminaries (*14-19). On Wednesday: *Let there be luminaries* (ibid.), and *Let the waters swarm* (20-23). On Thursday: *Let the waters swarm* (ibid.), and *Let the earth bring forth* (24-31). On Friday: *Let the earth bring forth (ibid.), and the heaven was completed* (2:1-3).

A long section would be read by two [people] and a short one by one [person], at *Shacharis* and at *Musaf.*

prayer that the roads should become fit for travelers (*Rashi,* 27b).

בָּרְבִיעִי ,,יְהִי מְאֹרֹת" וְ,,יִשְׁרְצוּ הַמַּיִם". — *On Wednesday: 'Let there be luminaries'* (ibid.), *and 'Let the waters swarm'* (20-22).

[— the portions of the fourth and fifth days.]

מְאֹרֹת, *luminaries,* is spelled defectively, alluding to מְאֵרָה, *curse, plague.* [The Sages teach that this plague, namely croup can be attributed to the luminaries *(Abudraham)*]. Therefore, they prayed that children be saved from the croup *(Rashi, ibid.).*

בַּחֲמִישִׁי— ,,יִשְׁרְצוּ הַמַּיִם" וְ,,תוֹצֵא הָאָרֶץ." — *On Thursday: 'Let the waters swarm' (ibid.), and 'Let the earth bring forth'* (24-31).

[— the portions of the fifth and sixth days.]

On the fifth day, God bestowed the blessing of fertility. They would, therefore, pray for the safety of pregnant and lactating women *(Rashi, ibid.).*

בַּשִּׁשִּׁי ,,תוֹצֵא הָאָרֶץ" ,,וַיְכֻלּוּ הַשָּׁמַיִם." — *On Friday: 'Let the earth bring forth'* (ibid.) *and 'And the heavens was completed' (2:1-3).*

[— the portions of the sixth day and the Sabbath.]

פָּרָשָׁה גְדוֹלָה—קוֹרִין אוֹתָהּ בִּשְׁנַיִם וְהַקְּטַנָּה—בְּיָחִיד... — *A long portion would be read by two* [*people*] *and a short one by one* [*person*].

Since each reader was required to read a minimum of three verses, a long portion (consisting of a minimum of five verses) could be shared by two readers: the first person would read verses 1-3; the second would read verses 3-5. A short portion would be read in its entirety by one person *(Rav).*

בַּשַּׁחֲרִית וּבַמּוּסָף. — *at Shacharis and at Musaf.*

The *Anshei Maamad* who remained in their own cities would read the Torah after the *Shacharis* service and again after the *Musaf* service on days when *Musaf* was recited. Those in the Temple, however, were occupied with preparing wood and water for the *Musaf* offering (see 2:7). They did not read the Torah nor recite any special prayers *(Rav).*

According to *Rambam,* however, our mishnah refers to every *maamad,* whether in Jerusalem or elsewhere. In his interpretation, the

ד
ד

וְקוֹרִין עַל פִּיהֶן, כְּקוֹרִין אֶת־,,שְׁמַע״. עֶרֶב שַׁבָּת בַּמִּנְחָה לֹא הָיוּ נִכְנָסִין, מִפְּנֵי כְבוֹד הַשַּׁבָּת.

[ד] **כָּל** יוֹם שֶׁיֶּשׁ־בּוֹ הַלֵּל, אֵין בּוֹ מַעֲמָד בַּשַּׁחֲרִית. קָרְבַּן מוּסָף — אֵין בּוֹ בַּנְּעִילָה. קָרְבַּן עֵצִים — אֵין בּוֹ בַּמִּנְחָה; דִּבְרֵי

יד אברהם

Musaf of our mishnah is not the additional prayer of the Sabbath, *Rosh Chodesh*, and festivals, but a special prayer exclusive to the *Anshei Maamad*. They would recite it every day between *Shacharis* and *Minchah (Klei HaMikdash* 6:4). [See above mishnah 1.]

וּבַמִּנְחָה נִכְנָסִין וְקוֹרִין עַל פִּיהֶן, — *At Minchah, they would enter* [*the synagogue*] *and recite* [*the verses*] *by heart,*

Since the *Anshei Maamad* were fasting, the Sages eased their physical burden by excusing them from taking the *Sefer Torah* from the Ark at *Minchah (Rav).*

Even on Sundays, when there was no fast, the verses were recited by heart, in order not to make a distinction between one day and another *(Meleches Shlomo* from *Rabbeinu Yehonasan).*

כְּקוֹרִין אֶת־שְׁמַע. — *like those who read the Shema.*

[Just as the *Shema* is recited by heart, they would recite the verses of the Torah reading by heart.]

Although the Rabbis taught: דְּבָרִים שֶׁבִּכְתָב אִי אַתָּה רַשַּׁאי לְאָמְרָם בְּעַל פֶּה, *Words of Scripture may not be recited by heart*, it is permitted in such cases since each individual recites the verses on his *own* behalf, rather than to discharge the congregation of its obligation *(Tif. Yis.*; see *Tur Orach Chaim* 49).

עֶרֶב שַׁבָּת בְּמִנְחָה לֹא הָיוּ נִכְנָסִין מִפְּנֵי כְּבוֹד הַשַּׁבָּת. — *On Friday at Minchah they would not enter* [*the synagogue*] *because of the honor due the Sabbath.*

On Friday afternoon, the *Anshei Maamad* were not required to go to the synagogue or to read the appropriate verses privately. They were given an opportunity to prepare properly for the Sabbath *(Rav).*

4.

[In addition to fasting and praying, the *Anshei Maamad* of Jerusalem were occupied all day with other chores in the Temple. They would chop wood for the altar, and draw water to facilitate the flaying of the תָּמִיד, *daily sacrifice.*[1]

1. Although Joshua designated the Gibeonites as wood-cutters and water-drawers for the Temple *(Joshua* 9:27), they performed those services only for the *personal* use of the *kohanim* and Levites who served in the Temple. The *Anshei Maamad*, however, performed these services for actual sacrifices *(Tos. Yom Tov).*

At *Minchah*, they would enter [the synagogue] and recite [the verses] by heart, like those who read the *Shema*. On Friday at *Minchah*, they would not enter [the synagogue] because of the honor due the Sabbath.

4. On any day when *Hallel* is recited there is no *maamad* at *Shacharis*. [Whenever there was] a *Musaf* sacrifice, there is no [*maamad* even] at *Ne'ilah*. [Whenever there was] a wood offering, there was no [*maamad*] *at Minchah*. [This is] R' Akiva's

YAD AVRAHAM

On certain days they were required to perform chores in addition to the above. On such occasions, if the additional responsibilities were in conflict with the *maamad* prayers and Torah readings given in mishnah 3, the members of the *maamad* were excused from such prayers and readings. Such exemptions would not apply to the *Anshei Maamad* of other cities, who had no Temple duties.]

כָּל־יוֹם שֶׁיֵּשׁ־בּוֹ הַלֵּל, אֵין בּוֹ מַעֲמָד בַּשַּׁחֲרִית. — *On any day when Hallel is recited* [lit. *when there is Hallel*], *there is no maamad at Shacharis.*

The mishnah here refers to a day when *Hallel* is recited, but when no additional sacrifices are offered. Such a day is Chanukah. On Chanukah, the *Anshei Maamad* in Jerusalem would omit the portions from *Genesis* at *Shacharis* because they were occupied with the recitation of *Hallel (Rav).*

Some maintain that Hallel frees all *maamados* from their usual reading, even those outside Jerusalem *(Ritva).*

The *maamad* would omit its customary supplications as well *(Tif. Yis.).*

Some maintain that *Hallel* supersedes only the supplications, but not the Torah readings *(Ravad).*

קָרְבַּן מוּסָף, אֵין בּוֹ בַּנְּעִילָה. — [*Whenever there was*] *a Musaf sacrifice, there is no* [*maamad even*] *at Ne'ilah.*

The mishnah refers to *Rosh Chodesh* when additional sacrifices were offered in the Temple *(Rav).*

There was no *maamad* at *Musaf, Minchah,* or *Ne'ilah* because of the additional responsibilities of preparing wood and water for the *Musaf* sacrifices *(Rav).*

Tosefos Yom Tov explains that the *kohanim* were involved with the sacrificial service of the *Musaf* offering while the Israelites tended to its wood and water.

[At *Shacharis,* however, there was a *maamad,* although *Hallel* was recited, for the *Hallel* of *Rosh Chodesh* is not obligatory. See below next mishnah s.v. בְּאֶחָד בְּטֵבֵת לֹא הָיָה בּוֹ מַעֲמָד.]

Since a minimum of two animals was offered for the *Musaf* sacrifices, the *Anshei Maamad* were occupied with preparing wood and water throughout the day and did not have time for the *maamad* even at *Ne'ilah (Rashi).*

קָרְבַּן עֵצִים אֵין בּוֹ בַּמִּנְחָה, דִּבְרֵי רַבִּי עֲקִיבָא. — [*Whenever there was*] *a wood-offering, there was no* [*maamad*] *at Minchah.* [*This is*] *R' Akiva's view.*

ד ה

רַבִּי עֲקִיבָא. אָמַר לוֹ בֶן־עַזַּאי: „כָּךְ הָיָה רַבִּי יְהוֹשֻׁעַ שׁוֹנֶה: קָרְבַּן מוּסָף — אֵין בּוֹ בַמִּנְחָה. קָרְבַּן עֵצִים — אֵין בּוֹ בַנְּעִילָה". חָזַר רַבִּי עֲקִיבָא לִהְיוֹת שׁוֹנֶה כְּבֶן עַזַּאי.

[ה] **זְמַן** עֲצֵי כֹהֲנִים וְהָעָם תִּשְׁעָה: בְּאֶחָד בְּנִיסָן — בְּנֵי אָרַח בֶּן־יְהוּדָה;

יד אברהם

As described below (mishnah 5), specific families had the honor of contributing quantities of firewood for the needs of the altar at designated times of the year. In celebration of the occasion, they would bring sacrifices and celebrate the day as a family festival. Thus, the *Anshei Maamad* had extra responsibilities *(Tif. Yis.).*

However, the extra work of the day was not great enough to prevent the *Anshei Maamad* from performing the *maamad* at *Ne'ilah (Rav)* or at *Shacharis (Tif. Yis.).*

אָמַר לוֹ בֶן־עַזַּאי כָּךְ הָיָה רַבִּי יְהוֹשֻׁעַ שׁוֹנֶה; — *Ben Azzai said to him* [i.e., R' Akiva]: *R' Yehoshua would learn this way:*

[Ben Azzai wanted R' Akiva to retract his view. Since R' Akiva was a disciple of R' Yehoshua, Ben Azzai felt that he would be reluctant to dispute his teacher. See *Sanhedrin* 68a.]

קָרְבַּן מוּסָף, אֵין בּוֹ בַמִּנְחָה — [*Whenever there is a*] *Musaf sacrifice there is no* [*maamad*] *at Minchah;*

R' Yehoshua maintains that the labor necessitated by the *Musaf* sacrifice was not sufficient to require omission of the *Ne'ilah maamad.* The Rabbis, therefore, enacted that the *Musaf* preparations should supersede only the *maamad* of *Musaf* itself and *Minchah (Tif. Yis.).*

קָרְבַּן עֵצִים, אֵין בּוֹ בַנְּעִילָה. — [*whenever there is*] *a wood-offering, there is no* [*maamad*] *at Ne'ilah.*

As noted above, on days when individual families had the honor of bringing wood for the Temple service, they brought offerings and celebrated. Since the festive status of such a day of a wood-offering is Rabbinic in origin, there is a danger that people may tend to take it lightly and even ignore it. To avoid such laxity, special safeguards were often imposed in the case of Rabbinic enactments. Therefore, it was established that on days when the wood-offerings were brought they would supersede the *maamados* of both *Minchah* and *Ne'ilah.* Since wood-offerings were brought late in the day, they could come in conflict only with the last prayers, but not with *Musaf* or *Shacharis. Musaf,* however, because it is required by the Torah, would be observed conscientiously even without such safeguards. Hence, it was sufficient for the *Musaf* preparations to supersede the *maamad* of *Minchah,* but not of *Ne'ilah (Rav, Tif. Yis.).*

Others maintain that the wood-offering supersedes *only* the *maamad* of *Ne'ilah,* but not of *Minchah.* Since *Minchah* is of ancient origin dating back to the Patriarch Isaac, it is considered equivalent to a Torah obligation. Hence its *maamad* cannot be superseded except by that of

view. Said Ben Azzai to him, 'R' Yehoshua would learn this way: "[Whenever there is a] *Musaf* sacrifice, there is no [*maamad*] at *Minchah*; [whenever there is] a wood offering, there is no [*maamad*] at *Ne'ilah.*" ' R' Akiva retracted in order to comply with Ben Azzai.

5. The wood festival of the *kohanim* and the people [was celebrated] nine times [a year]. On the first of Nissan, the family of Arach of the tribe of

YAD AVRAHAM

Musaf, which is likewise a Torah obligation. The wood-offering, which is purely a Rabbinical enactment, cannot supersede the *maamad* of *Minchah,* but only that of *Ne'ilah,* which is likewise a Rabbinic enactment *(Rashi; Tos.).*

חָזַר רַבִּי עֲקִיבָא לִהְיוֹת שׁוֹנֶה כְּבֶן־עַזַּאי. — *R' Akiva retracted in order to comply* [lit. *to be learning like*] *Ben Azzai.*

[Upon hearing that his view was in conflict with that of his teacher, R' Yehoshua, R' Akiva withdrew.]

5.

When the Jews returned from Babylonian exile and prepared to offer sacrifices, there was no firewood in the Temple. In order to facilitate the sacrificial service, families came forward and volunteered to contribute wood. In recognition of their gesture, the prophets among them made a condition that, in future years, these families should continue to contribute even if the Temple wood chamber would be full. Scripture *(Nechemiah* 10:35) states: *And we the kohanim, the Levites, and the people cast lots for the wood offering, to bring into the House of our God according to our father's houses at appointed times, year by year, to burn upon the altar of HASHEM our God as it is written in the Torah (Gem.* 28a).

On the days when families brought the wood, they would offer a voluntary sacrifice [i.e., burnt offerings (*Tos. Yom Tov* from *Rav, Megillah* 1:3)] and would celebrate the day as a festival. Eulogies, fasting, and labor were proscribed on those days (*Rambam, Klei Hamikdash* 6:9). Others claim that a portion of the wood was placed on the altar and burned as a separate sacrifice and that no animal sacrifice was offered *(Ritva).*

An obvious question arises: How could the private festival of a single family exempt the *Anshei Maamad* from their public duties as expounded in mishnah 4?

One opinion is that, the exemptions applied only to *Anshei Maamad* who were members of the family donating the *wood offering;* other *maamad* members were required to fulfill their daily duties as usual *(Ritva* quoting *Rabad).*

Others maintain that *general* festivities would accompany the wood offerings. The *Anshei Maamad*, along with the entire population of Jerusalem, would go out to greet the family that was bringing the wood, Hence, all members of the *maamad* took part in the festivities. This honor accorded those who participated in the *mitzvah* superseded the recitation of the *maamad;* and was similar to honors accorded those who participated in the bringing of *bikkurim* [*first fruits*] (See *Bikkurim* 3:3. *Meiri; Meleches Shlomo; Rabbenu Yehonasan.)*

זְמַן עֲצֵי כֹהֲנִים וְהָעָם תִּשְׁעָה — *The wood festival of the kohanim and the people* [*was celebrated*] *nine times* [*a year*].

ד בְּעֶשְׂרִים בְּתַמּוּז — בְּנֵי דָוִד בֶּן־יְהוּדָה;
ה בַּחֲמִשָּׁה בְאָב — בְּנֵי פַרְעֹשׁ בֶּן־יְהוּדָה;
בְּשִׁבְעָה בוֹ — בְּנֵי יוֹנָדָב בֶּן־רֵכָב; בַּעֲשָׂרָה בוֹ
— בְּנֵי סְנָאָה בֶּן־בִּנְיָמִין; בַּחֲמִשָּׁה עָשָׂר בּוֹ —
בְּנֵי זַתּוּא בֶּן־יְהוּדָה, וְעִמָּהֶם כֹּהֲנִים וּלְוִיִּם וְכָל
מִי שֶׁטָּעָה בְשִׁבְטוֹ, וּבְנֵי גוֹנְבֵי עֱלִי, בְּנֵי קוֹצְעֵי

יד אברהם

On nine occasions during the year, the families named below would donate wood for the altar according to the precedent set by their forebears who returned from Babylonian exile *(Rav).*

בְּאֶחָד בְּנִיסָן בְּנֵי אָרַח בֶּן־יְהוּדָה — *On the first of Nissan, the family of Arach of the tribe of Judah* [lit. *the sons of Arach the son of Judah*] [*did so*].

This family is mentioned in *Ezra* 2:5 and *Nehemiah* 7:10. Since Judah and Benjamin were the only tribes that returned from Babylon [with the exceptions, of course, of *kohanim* and Levites], all the families mentioned here are of those tribes *(Tos. Yom Tov).*

When they returned from Babylon, the family of Arach made the first contribution of wood on *Rosh Chodesh* Nissan. The wood lasted until the twentieth of Tammuz, when the next family made its contribution *(Rashi).*

בְּעֶשְׂרִים בְּתַמּוּז בְּנֵי דָוִד בֶּן־יְהוּדָה. — *On the twentieth of Tammuz the family of David of the tribe of Judah* [*did so*].

I.e., the descendants of King David *(Tif. Yis.; Rashi).*

בַּחֲמִשָּׁה בְאָב בְּנֵי פַרְעֹשׁ בֶּן־יְהוּדָה — *On the fifth of Av, the family of Parosh of the tribe of Judah* [*did so*].

[This family is mentioned in *Ezra* 2:3 and *Nehemiah* 7:8 among the returnees to *Eretz Yisrael.*]

בְּשִׁבְעָה בוֹ בְּנֵי יוֹנָדָב בֶּן־רֵכָב. — *On the seventh of that month, the family of Jonadab the son of Rechab* [*did so*].

This was a family of proselytes that descended from Jethro, the father-in-law of Moses (*I Chron.* 2:55). To them was entrusted custody of the fertile land of Jericho until the building of the *Beis HaMikdash.* Then it would be given to the tribe in whose territory the *Beis HaMikdash* would be built. They refused this privilege, however, and went into the wilderness of Judea to study Torah under Othniel the son of Kenaz, also known as Yabetz (*Rashi, Judges* 1:16). Later, we find Jonadab the son of Rechab assisting Jehu in his destruction of the Baal worshippers (*II Kings* 10:15-26). We also find that Jonadab commanded his children to abstain from wine (*Jer.* 35:6). The prophet informed them in the name of God that since they kept their father's command, there would always be a member of the family serving God (*Jer.* 35:19).

בַּעֲשָׂרָה בוֹ בְּנֵי סְנָאָה בֶּן־בִּנְיָמִין. — *On the tenth of that* [*month*] *the family of Senaah of the tribe of Benjamin* [*did so*],

This family is mentioned in *Ezra* 2:35 and *Nehemiah* 7:38 among those who returned from Babylonian exile.

בַּחֲמִשָּׁה עָשָׂר בּוֹ בְּנֵי זַתּוּא בֶּן־יְהוּדָה, — *On the fifteenth of that* [*month*],

4 Judah [did so]. On the twentieth of Tammuz, the
5 family of David of the tribe of Judah [did so]. On the fifth of Av, the family of Parosh of the tribe of Judah [did so]. On the seventh of that month, the family of Jonadab, the son of Rechab [did so]. On the tenth of that month, the family of Senaah of the tribe of Benjamin [did so]. On the fifteenth of that month, the family of Zattu of the tribe of Judah [did so], and along with them were *kohanim* and Levites, and everyone who was uncertain of his tribe, and the family of the pestle smugglers, the family of the fig-

the family of Zattu of the tribe of Judah [did so],

This family is mentioned in *Ezra* 2:8 and *Nehemiah* 7:13.

וְעִמָּהֶם כֹּהֲנִים וּלְוִיִּם וְכָל־מִי שֶׁטָּעָה בְשִׁבְטוֹ, — *and along with them were kohanim and Levites, and anyone who was uncertain of his tribe,*

Anyone who was uncertain of his descent, and did not know with which family he was to bring his wood offering, would join the family of Zattu and bring his wood offering on the fifteenth of Av. Since it was celebrated as a festival in its own right [see last mishnah of this tractate], it was a fitting day for a general wood-bringing celebration.

Alternatively, the mishnah refers to those of uncertain lineage at the time of the return from exile. They joined the family of Zattu in bringing wood, and continued to do so in future years *(Tif. Yis.).*

וּבְנֵי גוֹנְבֵי עֱלִי בְּנֵי קוֹצְעֵי קְצִיעוֹת, — *and the family of the pestle-smugglers, the family of the fig-cutters.*

Once, the foreign overlords of *Eretz Yisrael* forbade the bringing of *bikkurim* (First Fruit) to Jerusalem and stationed sentries on the roads to prevent the Jews from doing so. Pious men of that generation arose and placed baskets of *bikkurim*, covered with dried figs into large wooden vessels shaped like a pestle, which was used for pressing dried figs into cakes, and carried them on their shoulders to Jerusalem. When the sentries inquired about the contents, the Jews would say that they were taking the dried figs to a mortar where they would press them with their pestle. Therefore, they were given the appelation of the family of the *pestle-smugglers* or *pestle-thieves* because they would *steal the hearts* i.e., deceive of the sentries with the pretext of the pestle. They were also known as the family of the *fig-cutters*, because they carried knives with which they would cut figs to facilitate the draining of the fig juice *(Rav; Gem.* 28a).

[In our versions of the *Gemara*, no mention is made of the date of this decree. The common version of the *Tosefta*, however, attributes it to the מַלְכֵי יָוָן, *the Syrian-Greek kings*. Accordingly, this occurred during the Second Commonwealth, while *Eretz Yisrael* was under Syrian rule. If so, this group joined the family of Zattu later than the other familes, who joined at the beginning of the Second Com-

ד
ו

קְצִיעוֹת. בְּעֶשְׂרִים בּוֹ — בְּנֵי פַּחַת מוֹאָב בֶּן־יְהוּדָה; בְּעֶשְׂרִים בֶּאֱלוּל — בְּנֵי עָדִין בֶּן־יְהוּדָה; בְּאֶחָד בְּטֵבֵת שָׁבוּ בְנֵי פַרְעֹשׁ שְׁנִיָּה. בְּאֶחָד בְּטֵבֵת לֹא הָיָה בוֹ מַעֲמָד, שֶׁהָיָה בוֹ הַלֵּל וְקָרְבַּן מוּסָף וְקָרְבַּן עֵצִים.

[ו] **חֲמִשָּׁה** דְבָרִים אֵרְעוּ אֶת־אֲבוֹתֵינוּ בְּשִׁבְעָה עָשָׂר בְּתַמּוּז וַחֲמִשָּׁה בְתִשְׁעָה בְאָב. בְּשִׁבְעָה עָשָׂר בְּתַמּוּז נִשְׁתַּבְּרוּ

יד אברהם

monwealth.

Yerushalmi attributes the decree to King Jeroboam. *Meiri* similarly states that this was in the time of the First Temple.

בְּעֶשְׂרִים בּוֹ בְּנֵי פַּחַת־מוֹאָב בֶּן־יְהוּדָה. — *On the twentieth of that* [*month*] *the family of Pachas-Moav of the tribe of Judah* [*did so*].

This family is mentioned in *Ezra* 2:6, and *Nehemiah* 7:20.

Some hold that this was the family of Joab the son of Zeruiah (*Gem.* 28a).

בְּעֶשְׂרִים בֶּאֱלוּל בְּנֵי עָדִין בֶּן־יְהוּדָה. — *On the twentieth of Elul, the family of Adin of the tribe of Judah* [*did so*].

Some maintain that *this* was the family of Joab (ibid.).

בְּאֶחָד בְּטֵבֵת שָׁבוּ בְנֵי פַרְעֹשׁ שְׁנִיָּה. — *On the first of Teves the family of Parosh returned a second time.*

Upon the return from Babylon, the wood that was brought on the twentieth of Elul lasted until the first of Teves. No other family had come forward, so lots were cast among those who already donated. The lot fell on the Parosh family which was required to bring enough wood to last until the first of Nissan when the cycle would repeat itself. It is noteworthy that Parosh whose first gift of wood had lasted for only two days, from the fifth to the seventh of Av, was now required to donate a three-month supply (*Tos. Yom Tov*).

בְּאֶחָד בְּטֵבֵת לֹא הָיָה בוֹ מַעֲמָד שֶׁהָיָה בוֹ הַלֵּל, וְקָרְבַּן מוּסָף, וְקָרְבַּן עֵצִים. — *On the first of Teves there was no maamad, since Hallel* [*was recited*] *and a musaf sacrifice and a wood offering* [*were brought*] *thereon.*

Since the first of Teves occurs during Chanukah, *Hallel*, which supersedes the *Maamad* of *Shacharis*, is recited. Since it is *Rosh Chodesh*, a *Musaf* sacrifice, which supersedes the *maamad* of *Musaf*, is offered and since there is a wood offering, it supersedes the *maamad* of *Neilah*. The mishnah did not mention *Rosh Chodesh* Nissan although then too, there was a combination of the same three festive occurrences, because the *Hallel* of an ordinary *Rosh Chodesh* does not supersede *Hallel*. That is because the *Hallel* of *Rosh Chodesh* was customary rather than obligatory in origin (as indicated by the fact that the *Hallel* of *Rosh Chodesh* is abridged); hence, it is not con-

4
6 cutters [did so]. On the twentieth of that month, the family of Pachas-Moav of the tribe of Judah [did so]. On the twentieth of Elul, the family of Adin of the tribe of Judah [did so]. On the first of Teves, the family of Paros of the tribe of Judah returned a second time. On the first of Teves, there was no *maamad*, since *Hallel* [was recited] and a *Musaf* sacrifice and a wood-offering were brought thereon.

6. Five incidents befell our ancestors on the Seventeenth of Tammuz, and five on the Ninth of Av. On the Seventeenth of Tammuz, the Tablets

sidered significant enough to supersede the *maamad* of *Shacharis*. On Chanukah, however *Hallel* is recited in accordance with the procedure established by the prophets that God is to be praised whenever he performs a miracle to rescue Israel from distress. Therefore, it is tantamount to a *mitzvah* of the Torah (*Rashi* 28b).

6.

After having delineated the laws of fasts decreed because of drought or other calamities in chapters 1-2, the mishnah now discusses the two main annual fasts that were proclaimed because of misfortunes which befell our ancestors (*Kehati*).

Although the principle reason for these fasts relates to the destruction of Jerusalem and the Temples, the mishnah recalls all the other misfortunes that occurred on those days because to recall them will make us repent the sins which caused them (*Meiri*).

As *Rambam* writes: [*Taaniyos* 5:1], There are days when all Israel fasts because of the misfortunes that occurred then, in order to awaken the hearts and to open the ways of repentance. Let this be a reminder of our evil deeds and our forefathers' deeds that were like our present deeds until they caused those misfortunes for them and for us. For through the recollection of these matters, we will repent to improve, as Scripture states (*Lev.* 26:40): *And they shall confess their transgression and the transgression of their fathers.*

חֲמִשָּׁה דְבָרִים אֵרְעוּ אֶת־אֲבוֹתֵינוּ בְּשִׁבְעָה עָשָׂר בְּתַמּוּז וַחֲמִשָּׁה בְּתִשְׁעָה בְּאָב. — *Five incidents befell our ancestors on the Seventeenth of Tammuz, and five on the Ninth of Av.*

בְּשִׁבְעָה עָשָׂר בְּתַמּוּז נִשְׁתַּבְּרוּ הַלּוּחוֹת, — *On the Seventeenth of Tammuz, the Tablets were broken,*

The Jews received the עֲשֶׂרֶת הַדִּבְּרוֹת, *Ten Commandments,* on the sixth of Sivan. On the morning of the seventh, Moses ascended Mount Sinai to receive the rest of the Torah. He remained there until the Seventeenth of Tammuz, when he was given the two stone tablets of the Law. Upon his descent from the mountain, he saw the reveling

ד
ו

הַלּוּחוֹת, וּבָטֵל הַתָּמִיד, וְהָבְקְעָה הָעִיר, וְשָׂרַף אַפּוֹסְטְמוֹס אֶת־הַתּוֹרָה, וְהֶעֱמִיד צֶלֶם בַּהֵיכָל. בְּתִשְׁעָה בְאָב נִגְזַר עַל אֲבוֹתֵינוּ שֶׁלֹּא יִכָּנְסוּ לָאָרֶץ, וְחָרַב הַבַּיִת בָּרִאשׁוֹנָה וּבַשְּׁנִיָּה,

יד אברהם

worshippers of the Golden Calf, whereupon he grasped the tablets and shattered them at the foot of the mountain *(Rav* from *Gemara* 28b).

וּבָטֵל הַתָּמִיד, — *the continual* [*daily*] *sacrifice was discontinued,*

We have a tradition from our forefathers that the daily sacrifices were discontinued on the Seventeenth of Tammuz *(Tos. Yom Tov, Gemara* 28a).

The sacrifice was discontinued at the time of Hyrcanus and Aristobolus, two feuding brothers who were scions of the Hasmonean dynasty, who vied for the throne of Judea. Hyrcanus was inside Jerusalem and Aristobolus attacked from outside and besieged the city. In order to purchase lambs for the daily sacrifice, the isolated inhabitants would lower bundles of gold coins over the wall to the flock owners below who would supply a lamb to be hoisted up. One day an old man outside the wall advised his cohorts to substitute a pig for the usual lamb. As it was being raised by the unsuspecting Jerusalemites, the pig thrust its claws into the wall, and all *Eretz Yisrael* quaked. On that day, the daily sacrifices were discontinued for the duration of the seige *(Tif. Yis.* from *Bava Kamma* 82b).

A second interpretation is that the mishnah refers to Nebuchadnezzar's three year siege of Jerusalem prior to the first Desturction. There was a famine and, by the Seventeenth of Tammuz, there were no more sheep available for the sacrifice *(Rav; Tif. Yis.).*

Rashi explains that the government forbade the offering of the daily sacrifices *(Rashi).*

[Support for *Rashi's* interpretation can be found in the *Gemara* 28b. It appears that Manasseh, king of Judah, who took the throne a century before the first Destruction, abolished the daily sacrifice and placed an idol in the Temple Court.]

וְהָבְקְעָה הָעִיר, — *the City* [*wall*] *was breached,*

Jerusalem's walls were breached on the *seventeenth* of Tammuz, three weeks before the final destruction of the Second Temple. The walls of Jerusalem in the period of the first Destruction, were breached on the ninth of Tammuz *(Gemara* 28b from *Jeremiah* 52:6,7). Although both the ninth and the seventeenth were tragic dates, the Rabbis chose not to burden the community with two separate fasts. They selected the seventeenth, rather than the ninth, as the fast day, because it recalls the Destruction preceding our current, still-enduring exile *(Tur Orach Chaim* 549).

According to *Yerushalmi,* both breaches occurred on the seventeenth, but because of their great distress, the people became confused and erred in their calculations. Jeremiah recorded the date according to the people's miscalculations.

4
6
were broken, the continual [daily] sacrifice was discontinued, the City [wall] was breached, Apostumos burned the Torah, and placed an image in the Sanctuary.

On the Ninth of Av, it was decreed upon our ancestors that they would not enter the Land, the Temple was destroyed for the first time, and the se-

וְשָׂרַף אַפָּסְטְמוֹס אֶת־הַתּוֹרָה, — *Apostumos burned the Torah,*

Apostumos, a Greek general, burned the Torah which was kept in the עֲזָרָה, *Temple Court.* Written by Ezra, it was the most authoritative copy of the Torah and was used to check the accuracy of other scrolls. Alternatively, he burned *all* the *Sifrei Torah* that he found. Obviously, his intention was to cause the Torah to be forgotten *(Rav; Meiri; Tif. Yis.).*

וְהֶעֱמִיד צֶלֶם בַּהֵיכָל. — *and placed an image in the Sanctuary.*

Apostumos, who burned the Torah, placed an image in the Temple during the Greek occupation of the Second Commonwealth. Another version is: וְהָעֳמַד צֶלֶם בַּהֵיכָל, *And an image 'was placed' in the Sanctuary;* this would refer to the image that Manasseh placed in the First Temple *(Rav; Tos. Yom Tov* from *Yerushalmi).*

בְּתִשְׁעָה בְאָב נִגְזַר עַל אֲבוֹתֵינוּ שֶׁלֹּא יִכָּנְסוּ לָאָרֶץ, — *On the Ninth of Av, it was decreed upon our ancestors that they would not enter the Land,*

The spies whom Moses sent to the land of Canaan, began their journey on the twenty-ninth of Sivan and returned after forty days [*Numbers* 13:25]. Since both Sivan and Tammuz consisted of thirty days that year, the forty-day period ended on the eighth of Av. Thus, they returned on the eve of the Ninth of Av and their malicious report and terrifying predictions caused the discontented and grief-stricken Jews to lose faith in God. In response to their loud weeping, God declared, 'You wept without cause; therefore, I shall set this day as a day for weeping throughout future generations'. It was then decreed that they would wander in the desert for forty years until all adult males of the generation were dead. Then, their children would inherit *Eretz Yisrael* [*Num.* 14:13] *(Gem.* 29a).

[For the *hashkofah*-philosophical significance of this decree, see *Overview* to ArtScroll *Eichah.*]

וְחָרַב הַבַּיִת בָּרִאשׁוֹנָה, — *the Temple was destroyed for the first time,*

It is written *(II Kings* 25:8,9): *Now in the fifth month, on the seventh day of the month, which was the nineteenth year of Nebuchadnezzar, king of Babylon, came Nebuzaradan, captain of the executioners, a servant of the king of Babylon, into Jerusalem, and he burned the House of* HASHEM. It is further written *(Jer.* 52:12,13): *Now in the fifth month, on the* tenth *of the month, which was the nineteenth year of King Nebuchadnezzar, king of Babylon, came Nebuzaradan, captain of the executioners. He stood before the king of Babylon in Jerusalem and burned the House of* HASHEM. How do we

ד וְנִלְכְּדָה בֵּתֵּר, וְנֶחְרְשָׁה הָעִיר. מִשֶּׁנִּכְנַס אָב
ז מְמַעֲטִין בְּשִׂמְחָה.

[ז] **שַׁבָּת** שֶׁחָל תִּשְׁעָה בְאָב לִהְיוֹת בְּתוֹכָהּ
אָסוּר מִלְּסַפֵּר וּמִלְּכַבֵּס, וּבַחֲמִישִׁי
מֻתָּרִין מִפְּנֵי כְבוֹד הַשַּׁבָּת. עֶרֶב תִּשְׁעָה בְאָב לֹא

יד אברהם

reconcile the passage which places the burning on the seventh of Av with the other passage which places it on the ninth? On the seventh, the heathens entered the Temple; they gorged themselves and reveled during the seventh and eighth days. On the ninth, towards evening, they set fire to it, and it burned throughout the tenth day (*Tos. Yom Tov* from *Gemara* 29a).

וּבַשְּׁנִיָּה, — *and the second time,*

Although the date of the first Destruction is recorded in Scripture, there is no such authoritative source for the date of the second destruction. However, the Rabbis reasoned that since the ninth was a day foreordained for tragedy from the early days in the Wilderness, the destruction of the Temple, which was definitely in Av, must have come to pass on the same day. *Good things come to pass on an auspicious day, and bad things on an inauspicious day (Gem.* 29a. See *Overview* to ArtScroll *Eichah).*

וְנִלְכְּדָה בֵּתֵּר, — *and Bethar was conquered,*

Tradition tells us that Bethar fell on *Tishah B'Av (Gem.* 29a).

The conquest of Bethar was a calamity as great as the destruction of the Temple *(Rambam, Tanniyos* 5:3).[1]

וְנֶחְרְשָׁה הָעִיר. — *and the City was plowed under.*

After the destruction of the First Temple, *Eretz Yisrael* was desolate for fifty-two years, and Jerusalem itself was razed and flattened like a plowed field *(Tif. Yis.).* This fulfilled Micah's prophecy (3:12) that Zion would be plowed under like a field *(Rashi).*

The *Gemara* (29a) relates that Turnus Rufus, a Roman officer, plowed the Temple under. According to *Tur (Orach Chaim* 549), this was the incident recorded in the Mishnah. *Rambam* adds that Turnus Rufus plowed the Sanctuary and its environs *(Taanis* 5:3).

Tradition tells us that this took place on *Tishah B'Av (Gem.* 29a).

מִשֶּׁנִּכְנַס אָב מְמַעֲטִין בְּשִׂמְחָה. — *Therefore, when Av begins* [lit.

1. Fifty-two years after the destruction of the Second Temple, a large Jewish army assembled in Bethar under the leadership of a great personality, Ben Kuziva, known as Bar Kochba. The great R' Akiva became his armor bearer and regarded him as the Messiah. Bar Kochba was very successful in battle and managed to hold off the Romans for three and a half years *(Tif. Yis.).*

So powerful were Bar Kochba and his army, that he arrogantly declared: 'Lord of the Universe, neither help nor hinder us. HASHEM, have You not deserted us [by permitting the destruction of the Temple]? Now, You shall not go out in our armies. That defiant belief that he could triumph without God's help led to his downfall.

cond time, Bethar was conquered, and the City was plowed under.

Therefore, when Av begins, we curtail joy.

7. During the week of *Tishah B'Av*, it is forbidden to cut hair or launder [clothes]. However, on Thursday it is permitted because of the honor due the Sabbath. On the afternoon before *Tishah B'Av*, a

YAD AVRAHAM

from the time that Av enters], we curtail joy.

This month was destined for calamity from the time of the spies *(Tif. Yis.)*. Accordingly, from *Rosh Chodesh* Av, we must limit business transactions and construction (see above 1:7).

We may betroth, but not marry; nor may we make feasts in celebration of betrothals *(Tur* 551 from *Yevamos* 43a).

7.

שַׁבָּת שֶׁחָל תִּשְׁעָה בְאָב לִהְיוֹת בְּתוֹכָהּ אָסוּר לְסַפֵּר וּלְכַבֵּס. — *During the week of Tishah B'Av it is forbidden to cut hair or launder* [*clothes*].

During the entire week from Sunday until after the fast, it is forbidden to cut hair or wash clothes even if they will not be worn until after *Tishah B'Av (Tif. Yis.; Gen.* 29b). The very act of laundering, even for later use, makes one appear to be distracted from mourning the destruction of the Temple *(Rashi)*.

וּבַחֲמִישִׁי מֻתָּרִין מִפְּנֵי כְבוֹד הַשַּׁבָּת. — *However, on Thursday it is permitted because of the honor due the Sabbath.*

The mishnah refers to a case of *Tishah B'Av* falling on Friday. Since no laundering could be done on *Tishah B'Av* itself, there would be no opportunity to prepare for the Sabbath unless certain chores were permitted before *Tishah B'Av*. Therefore, the Rabbis permitted laundering on Thursday even though it was the day before the fast. [In the Hebrew calendar which has been in use for the last sixteen centuries, *Tishah B'Av* cannot fall on a Friday. In earlier times, however, when the Beth Din would sanctify *Rosh Chodesh* according to the testimony of witnesses, as set forth by the Torah, *Tishah B'Av* could fall on a Friday. The law of our Mishnah was applicable in such

For three and a half years the Roman general, Hadrian, surrounded Bethar, but could not pierce its defenses because the righteous Sage, R' Eleazar of Modin sat in sackcloth and ashes and prayed: 'Lord of the Worlds, do not sit in judgment today! Do not sit in judgment today!'

Hadrian decided to abandon the siege and leave Bethar, when a Cuthite approached and told him that the prayers of R' Eleazer were protecting Bethar. The Cuthite said that he had a plan to bring about the conquest of the fortress. He entered through the gate *(Eichah Rabbah* 2:4; *Mattenos Kehunah)* or the sewer *(Yerushalmi; Yefei Anaf* on *Midrash)* of the city, sought out and found R' Eleazar and pretended to whisper in his ear. The sage, engrossed in prayer, was not even

ד יֹאכַל אָדָם שְׁנֵי תַבְשִׁילִין, לֹא יֹאכַל בָּשָׂר וְלֹא
ז יִשְׁתֶּה יַיִן. רַבָּן שִׁמְעוֹן בֶּן גַּמְלִיאֵל אוֹמֵר:
יְשַׁנֶּה. רַבִּי יְהוּדָה מְחַיֵּב בִּכְפִיַּת הַמִּטָּה; וְלֹא
הוֹדוּ לוֹ חֲכָמִים.

cases] (*Rashi*).

However, haircutting was forbidden even in this case. Since people do not generally take haircuts every week, it is not considered disrespectful to the Sabbath not to cut hair in its honor (*Magen Avraham* 551:14).

This above distinction between laundering and haircutting is derived from the fact that *Rashi*, followed by *Rav*, specifies only *laundering* as being permitted on the Thursday before *Tishah B'Av*, implying that the other subject of our Mishnah, haircutting, is not permitted on such Thursdays. *Tosafos*, however, maintains that both are permitted on a Thursday before *Tishah B'Av* (*Tos. R' Akiva Eiger*).

If *Tisha B'Av* falls on Thursday, one must wait until Friday to cut his hair and launder his clothes (*Magen Avraham* 551:18).

In later generations, it became customary to refrain from laundering clothes during the 'Nine Days' from *Rosh Chodesh* Av until after *Tishah B'Av*, and to refrain from haircuts and weddings during the 'Three Weeks' beginning with the Seventeenth of Tammuz. Other mourning customs originally limited to the week of *Tishah B'Av* were extended to be in effect during the 'Nine Days,' beginning with *Rosh Chodesh Av* (*Orach Chaim* 551).

עֶרֶב תִּשְׁעָה בְּאָב — *On the afternoon before Tishah B'Av,*

The mishnah refers to the last meal before the fast begins. The laws about to be given apply only to the last meal that is eaten that afternoon (*Rav* from *Gem.* 30a).

[It is known as סְעוּדָה הַמַּפְסֶקֶת, *the concluding meal*, i.e., final meal before the fast begins. The meal introduces the mournful atmosphere of *Tishah B'Av;* therefore one eats it while sitting on the floor or a low stool. Therefore, too, the choice of food is restricted as given below.]

לֹא יֹאכַל אָדָם שְׁנֵי תַבְשִׁילִין, — *a person may not eat two cooked foods,*

[The menu of that last meal may include a single cooked dish, but not more than one.]

Any cooked or roasted food is considered a cooked dish, even if it can be eaten raw (*Tif. Yis.* from *Shulchan Aruch* 552:3).

In the above respect, the definition of *cooked food* with relation to the *concluding meal* is unique. For example, with regard to the restric-

conscious of the Cuthite's presence, but guards reported to Ben Kuziva, 'Your uncle, R' Eleazer, is plotting to surrender the city.'

He sent for the Cuthite and asked him to divulge what he had whispered to R' Eleazar. According to *Yerushalmi*, he replied, 'If I tell you, the king will kill me. If I do not tell you, you will kill me. Rather let the king kill me and not you. He [R' Eleazar] *said that he was ready to surrender the city.*'

Bar Kuziva confronted with the Cuthite's allegation. When the sage denied any knowledge of the alleged conversation, Ben Kuziva became angry and kicked him, killing him instantly.

After R' Eleazer's demise, the city was captured and Ben Kuziva was

4 person may not eat two cooked foods; nor may one
7 eat meat nor drink wine. Rabban Shimon ben Gamliel says: He need [merely] make some variance. R' Yehudah requires overturning the beds, but the Sages did not agree with him.

tion against food cooked by non-Jews [בִּשּׁוּל עַכּוּ״ם], the prohibition applies only to food that is *not* edible when raw. Fish and meat, for example, are forbidden, but apples and peanuts are not. For the *concluding meal,* however, *all* cooked foods, even those edible when raw, are regarded as 'cooked,' because the purpose of the decree was that the last meal before the fast should bear no semblance of luxury or pleasure *(Rosh).*

It is customary to eat cold, hard-boiled eggs at the the last meal, since that is a dish traditionally served to mourners upon their return from a burial (*Orach Chaim* 552:5; *Magen Abraham).* Since a boiled egg is considered a cooked dish may be eaten (*Mishnah Berurah* ibid. 14).

In order to facilitate fasting, a larger meal is served before *Minchah* in the late afternoon of the eighth of Av. The *division meal,* customarily consisting of bread dipped in ashes, a hard-boiled egg, and a glass of water, is eaten after *Minchah (Rama* ibid.).

וְלֹא יֹאכַל בָּשָׂר וְלֹא יִשְׁתֶּה יַיִן. — *nor may one eat meat nor drink wine.*

One may not eat meat even if it is the only cooked dish served at the meal *(Rav).*

It is customary to abstain from meat and wine from *Rosh Chodesh* Av until the afternoon of the tenth of Av *(Shulchan Aruch* 551:9, 558:1 *Rama).*

רַבָּן שִׁמְעוֹן בֶּן־גַּמְלִיאֵל אוֹמֵר יְשַׁנֶּה — *Rabban Shimon ben Gamaliel says: He need* [*merely*] *make some variance.*

The *concluding meal* is not necessarily limited to only one cooked dish. The point is that it be noticeably more frugal that one's ordinary meal. Hence, one who is accustomed to eating three cooked dishes, may eat only one. One who is accustomed to drinking three cups of wine, may drink only two (*Gem.* 30a).

According to this opinion, even meat may be eaten *(Tiferes Yisrael).*

The *halachah* is in accordance with the Tanna Kamma *(Rav).*

רַבִּי יְהוּדָה מְחַיֵּב בִּכְפִיַּת הַמִּטָּה. — *R' Yehudah requires overturning the beds.*

— Similar to a mourner who is required to overturn all his beds and sleep on the reverse side. This aspect of the mourning laws does not apply nowadays (*Tur Yoreh Deah* 387).

Rav comments that the beds must

killed. His head was brought to Hadrian. Later, they found his body with a snake curled up on his neck. Hadrian, himself, acknowledged that had not God delivered Ben Kuziva into his hands, he would never have been able to defeat him.

According to *Tiferes Yisrael,* the Romans killed 580,000 Jews in Bethar. Judging from statements in the *Midrash, Yerushalmi,* and *Bavli Gittin* 58a, however, this appears to be an understatement.

Horses were actually submerged in blood up to the nose. The blood flowed into the Mediterranean Sea, a distance of approximately forty miles, carrying huge rocks along with it *(Yerushalmi, Eichah Rabbah* 2:4).

ד
ח

[ח] **אָמַר** רַבָּן שִׁמְעוֹן בֶּן גַּמְלִיאֵל: לֹא הָיוּ יָמִים טוֹבִים לְיִשְׂרָאֵל כַּחֲמִשָּׁה עָשָׂר בְּאָב וּכְיוֹם הַכִּפּוּרִים, שֶׁבָּהֶן בְּנוֹת

be overturned and not used on *Tishah B'Av.* People must sleep on the ground.

According to *Yerushalmi,* R' Yehudah's view is that the beds must be overturned during the *dividing meal,* for he requires that mourning commence at that time.

The Rabbis, however, compare this meal to אֲנִינוּת, *the period following death and preceding burial,* when the mourners are not yet required to observe the formal requirements of mourning, just as they are excused from the performance of other positive commandments. During that period, however, the mourner may not sleep or eat on either a bed or couch. Hence, our custom to sit on a low stool or on the floor while eating the meal (*Beur HaGra* 552:15).

Others explain that this manner of eating indicates that we are partaking of a humble, poor repast (*Magen Avraham, Taz* ibid.).

According to *Bavli,* R' Yehudah requires the overturning of beds during the entire fast of *Tishah B'Av (Keren Orah).*

.וְלֹא הוֹדוּ לוֹ חֲכָמִים — *but the Sages did not agree with him.*

They permit sleeping on beds in the normal fashion on *Tishah B'Av.* However, one should reduce the level of sleeping comfort to which he is accustomed. For example, someone accustomed to two pillows should use only one (555:2).

8.

אָמַר רַבָּן שִׁמְעוֹן בֶּן גַּמְלִיאֵל: לֹא הָיוּ יָמִים טוֹבִים לְיִשְׂרָאֵל כַּחֲמִשָּׁה עָשָׂר בְּאָב — *Rabban Shimon ben Gamliel said: Israel had no days as festive as the Fifteenth of Av...*

The *Gemara* gives many reasons for the festivities on *Chamishah Asar B'Av.*

(1) On this day, the tribes were permitted to intermarry. In the generation that entered the Holy Land with Joshua, any woman who had inherited land was prohibited from marrying out of her שֵׁבֶט, *tribe,* lest their inherited property be transferred permanently to her husband's tribe upon her death (*Numbers* ch. 36). This prohibition was limited to the generation that entered *Eretz Yisrael,* and it was left for the Sages to determine when it was no longer in force. They reached the decision on a fifteenth of Av.

This occasion was a cause of greater joy for women than for men, because the prior restriction against them had been more severe: an heiress could marry only within her tribe, while men could marry women from any tribe provided they were not heiresses. Therefore, as the mishnah depicts below, the *maidens* rather than the men, would go forth and dance in the vineyards on that day (*Maharsha* to *Bava Basra* 121a).

(2) On the fifteenth of Av, the tribes decided that the tribe of Benjamin be permitted to *reenter* the congregation of Israel. After the incident of the concubine in Gibeah (*Judges ch.* 19,20), all the tribes swore that they would not give their

8. Rabban Shimon ben Gamliel said: Israel had no days as festive as the Fifteenth of Av and Yom Kippur, for on those days, the maidens of Jerusalem

YAD AVRAHAM

daughters in marriage to the Benjaminites (ibid. ch. 21). Subsequently, on the fifteenth of Av, they ruled that the oath had restricted only the first generation, but the next generation was permitted to give its daughters to the tribe of Benjamin.

(3) On that day, the decree of death was lifted from the surviving members of the generation that spent forty years in the Wilderness. After the spies returned from their journey to the land of Canaan and discouraged the people from attempting to enter the land, HASHEM swore that all men between the ages of twenty and sixty would die by the time they reached sixty. Every year, each man in that age group dug a grave on the eve of *Tishah B'Av* and lay down to sleep in it. The next morning an announcement would be made: 'Let the living separate themselves from the dead!' And all those who remained alive would rise and leave their graves. They did this year after year. In the fortieth year, when the announcement was made, everyone arose. Seeing that no one had died, they suspected that they had erred in their calculation of the dates, so they returned to their graves and slept there every night until the fifteenth of the month. Upon seeing the full moon, they realized that it was indeed the middle of the month, and the decree had expired. Therefore, they established it as a festival. They had calculated the forty years from the time of the decree, the second year after the Exodus. Actually, however, the forty years had commenced from the first *Tishah B'Av* after the Exodus (*Rashi* and *Tos.* from *Pesichta d'Midrash Eichah; Yerushalmi*).

The *Gemara* adds that as long as those destined to die in the desert had not all died, there was no Divine communication to Moses, as it is stated, *And it came to pass, when all the men of war had stopped dying that HASHEM spoke to me* (*Deut.* 2:16,17). Since the Fifteenth of Av was the day when God resumed speaking to Moses for the benefit of Israel, it became a time of celebration (*Rashi*).[1]

(4) On that day Hosea the son of Elah removed the sentries that Jeroboam the son of Nebat had stationed on the roads to prevent

1. Moses had lost his exalted level of prophecy when the nation, having become the object of God's wrath, was considered as if excommunicated. This reduced status was to continue until the last member of the generation died. Thereupon, the decree of excommunication would have ended and the nation would have returned to its earlier status. As events were to prove, the ban had already ended the year before that last Fifteenth of Av; that is why no one died on the last *Tishah B'Av*. If so, however, why wasn't Moses' prophecy restored?

A prerequisite of prophecy is that the prophet must feel joyous. Since Moses did not know the decree had run its course, he was still aggrieved; therefore, the *Shechinah* did not rest on him. On the following fifteenth of Av, when it was discovered that the decree had expired, Moses was jubilant; hence, the *Shechinah* returned to him and he was restored to his previous level of prophecy (*Rabbeinu Bachya, Devarim*).

ד יְרוּשָׁלַיִם יוֹצְאוֹת בִּכְלֵי לָבָן שְׁאוּלִין, שֶׁלֹּא
ח לְבַיֵּשׁ אֶת־מִי שֶׁאֵין לוֹ; כָּל־הַכֵּלִים טְעוּנִין
טְבִילָה. וּבְנוֹת יְרוּשָׁלַיִם יוֹצְאוֹת וְחוֹלוֹת
בַּכְּרָמִים. וּמֶה הָיוּ אוֹמְרוֹת? ,,בָּחוּר, שָׂא־נָא

יד אברהם

Jews from going to the Temple.

(5) The Romans permitted the burial of the Jews slain in the conquest of Bethar. Their bodies had lain exposed throughout the reign of Hadrian, who forbade their burial. Miraculously, their bodies did not decay.

(6) On that day, they stopped felling trees for the altar. By the middle of Av, the most intense heat of summer is over and the sunlight is weaker. Wood cut thereafter is not sufficiently dry to prevent it from becoming wormy and unfit for the altar (*Tos.* 31a). Since the Fifteenth of Av marked the completion of a *mitzvah*, it was proclaimed a festive occasion (*Rashbam, Bava Basra* 121a).

וּבְיוֹם הַכִּפּוּרִים — *and Yom Kippur.*

Yom Kippur commemorates the giving of the second set of tablets of the Ten Commandments. As mentioned above, Moses broke the first tablets on the Seventeenth of Tammuz. He ground up the golden calf on the eighteenth and returned to Mount Sinai where he prayed for forty days, until God accepted his entreaties and agreed to spare Israel. Moses remained there another forty days, when he received the second tablets. If we add the last twelve days of Tammuz (which had twenty-nine days), thirty days of Av, and twenty-nine days of Elul, we arrive at the total of seventy-one days. By the ninth of Tishrei, eighty days had elapsed since his ascension. However, since Moses had ascended the mountain on the eighteenth of Tammuz by day, a *full* eighty days had not yet elapsed. The following night completed the total of eighty days and eighty nights. [According to *Rashi* on *Deuteronomy* 9:18, Moses descended from the mountain on the twenty-ninth of Av and ascended again on *Rosh Chodesh* Elul.] Hence, Moses descended with the tablets on the morning of the tenth of Tishrei, Yom Kippur (*Tos. Yom Tov* from *Rashi*).

On that day, God forgave the Jews the sin of the Golden Calf. It was therefore proclaimed as a day of forgiveness for all generations (*Tif. Yis.*).

שֶׁבָּהֶן בְּנוֹת יְרוּשָׁלַיִם יוֹצְאוֹת בִּכְלֵי לָבָן שְׁאוּלִין—שֶׁלֹּא לְבַיֵּשׁ אֶת מִי שֶׁאֵין לוֹ. — *For on those days the maidens of Jerusalem would go out* [*dressed*] *in white, borrowed garments—in order not to embarrass one who had none.*

On Yom Kippur and the Fifteenth of Av, the girls of Jerusalem would wear white, *borrowed* clothing. Even the wealthy maidens were forbidden to wear their *own* clothing lest they embarrass girls from poor families, who had no suitable garments of their own (*Rav* and *Tif. Yis.* from *Gem.* 31a).

Therefore, even the king's daughter would not wear her own clothing. She would borrow from the *kohen gadol's* daughter; the *kohen gadol's* daughter from the deputy-*kohen gadol's* daughter; the deputy-*kohen gadol's* daughter from the daughter of the *kohen*

4 would go out [dressed] in white, borrowed garments
8 — in order not to embarrass one who had none. All
the garments [worn on these occasions] required immersion.

The maidens of Jerusalem would go out and dance in the vineyards. And what did they say? 'Young

YAD AVRAHAM

anointed for battle; who, in turn, would borrow from the daughter of a כֹּהֵן הֶדְיוֹט, *ordinary kohen.* All the others would borrow from one another (*Gem.* 31a).

Thus, even the daughters of Israel's most distinguished families would borrow from others of slightly lower status. If they were to borrow from one another — the daughters of the king and *kohen gadol* exchanging dresses, for example — it would seem as though the elite of the society had merely traded with one another, but the poorest girls who had no garment worthy of exchange, would still feel humiliated (*Maharsha*).

Rashash, however, cites *Yerushalmi* which states that the daughters of the king and *kohen gadol* did indeed exchange with one another.

[The material required for these garments is not specified. Although *Tiferes Yisrael* claims they were silk, I have found no basis for this statement.]

That the garments were white, the symbol of purity, indicated that those participating in this activity were innocent of any evil temptation or erotic thoughts. Therefore, there was no objection to this procedure being carried out even on the pure and holy day of Yom Kippur (*Ritva, Bava Basra* 121a).

כָּל־הַכֵּלִים טְעוּנִין טְבִילָה. — *All the garments* [*worn on these occasions*] *required immersion.*

I.e., ritual immersion in a valid *Mikvah.*

[It must be kept in mind that during the existence of the Temple, and even afterwards, the people scrupulously observed טֻמְאָה וְטָהֳרָה, *the laws of ritual purity.* See *Chagigah* 4.]

Since one could not be sure that the lender was strict in her observance of the laws of purity, the borrower was required to immerse the garment before wearing it since it might have become טָמֵא, *contaminated* (*Rav*).

In order not to embarrass anyone, even a garment that had been locked away in a trunk and was unquestionably pure, required immersion (*Gem.* 31a).

Yerushalmi interprets this to imply that the Rabbis decreed that *all* white garments stored away in trunks and drawers had to be removed and immersed whether or not they would be worn. This would help insure that their owners would be willing to lend them. Otherwise, people whose clothing was stored away would hesitate to unpack their trunks in order to lend out the white garments. But since they had to remove and immerse their garments anyway, they might as well lend them to others.

וּבְנוֹת יְרוּשָׁלַיִם יוֹצְאוֹת וְחוֹלוֹת בַּכְּרָמִים. — *The maidens of Jerusalem would go out and dance in the vineyards.*

Unmarried men, too, would go there (*Gem.* 31a).

ד עֵינֶיךָ וּרְאֵה, מָה אַתָּה בוֹרֵר לָךְ. אַל תִּתֵּן
ח עֵינֶיךָ בַּנּוֹי, תֵּן עֵינֶיךָ בַּמִּשְׁפָּחָה: „שֶׁקֶר הַחֵן
וְהֶבֶל הַיֹּפִי, אִשָּׁה יִרְאַת ה׳ הִיא תִתְהַלָּל״;
וְאוֹמֵר „תְּנוּ־לָהּ מִפְּרִי יָדֶיהָ, וִיהַלְלוּהָ
בַשְּׁעָרִים מַעֲשֶׂיהָ״. וְכֵן הוּא אוֹמֵר „צְאֶינָה
וּרְאֶינָה בְּנוֹת צִיּוֹן בַּמֶּלֶךְ שְׁלֹמֹה, בָּעֲטָרָה
שֶׁעִטְּרָה־לּוֹ אִמּוֹ בְּיוֹם חֲתֻנָּתוֹ וּבְיוֹם שִׂמְחַת
לִבּוֹ״; „בְּיוֹם חֲתֻנָּתוֹ״ — זֶה מַתַּן תּוֹרָה;
„וּבְיוֹם שִׂמְחַת לִבּוֹ״, — זֶה בִּנְיַן בֵּית הַמִּקְדָּשׁ
שֶׁיִּבָּנֶה בִּמְהֵרָה בְיָמֵינוּ. אָמֵן.

יד אברהם

וּמֶה הָיוּ אוֹמְרוֹת? בָּחוּר שָׂא נָא עֵינֶיךָ, — *And what would they say? Young man, lift up your eyes...*

[The mishnah will now allude to three types of maidens mentioned in the *Gemara:* beautiful ones, well-born ones, and homely ones. The beautiful ones would say:]

וּרְאֵה מָה אַתָּה בוֹרֵר לָךְ. — *and see what you choose for yourself.*

See that we are beautiful, for a wife is primarily for beauty (*Eliyah Rabbah* 580:10).

— Since one may not marry a woman unless he first sees her, he is urged to look first (*Etz Yosef* on Ein Yaakov, Kiddushin 41a).

Daughters of distinguished families would say:

אַל תִּתֵּן עֵינֶיךָ בַּנּוֹי, תֵּן עֵינֶיךָ בַּמִּשְׁפָּחָה — *Do not consider* [lit. *fix your eyes on*] *beauty; consider family.*

Pay no heed to the beautiful maidens. Fix your eyes on family, for a wife is primarily for child-bearing, and one who has a good upbringing will tend to raise her own children well (*Eliyah Rabbah,* ibid.).

'Noble' families are those that are descended from Torah scholars and righteous people *(Tos. Yom Tov)* [For this is considered nobility among Jews.]

The homely ones would say:

שֶׁקֶר הַחֵן וְהֶבֶל הַיֹּפִי אִשָּׁה יִרְאַת ה׳ הִיא תִתְהַלָּל. — *Grace is false and beauty is vain. A woman who fears HASHEM, she shall be praised (Proverbs* 31:30).

Pay no heed to the grace of the nobility nor to the beauty of the fair ones, for both are deceitful. Rather, take note of the woman who fears God. Marry a woman for the sake of Heaven, and adorn her with golden jewelry; the lack of natural beauty and charm can be compensated for by fine jewelry and beautiful clothing (*Eliyah Rabbah, Orach Chaim* 580:10).

וְאוֹמֵר תְּנוּ לָהּ מִפְּרִי יָדֶיהָ וִיהַלְלוּהָ בַשְּׁעָרִים מַעֲשֶׂיהָ. — *And it is stated: Give her but the fruits of her own hands, and let her be praised in the gates by her very own deeds (ibid.* 31).

A woman can be praised only for

4 man, lift up your eyes and see what you choose for
8 yourself. Do not consider beauty. Consider family. *Grace is false and beauty is vain; a woman who fears HASHEM, she shall be praised (Proverbs* 31:30). And it is further stated: *Give her but the fruits of her own hands, and let her be praised in the gates by her very own deeds (ibid* 31). Similarly, it says: *Go forth and gaze, O daughters of Zion, upon the King Shlomo, adorned with the crown His nation made Him on the day of His wedding and on the day of the joy of His heart (Shir HaShirim* 3:11). On the day of His wedding — this is the giving of the Torah; *and on the day of the joy of His heart* — this is the building of the Holy Temple may it be rebuilt speedily in our days! Amen.

her good deeds, not for external features (*Eliyah Rabbah* ibid.).

וְכֵן הוּא אוֹמֵר: — *Similarly it* [*Scripture*] *says (Shir HaShirim* 3:11):

The following verse was not quoted by the maidens; rather Rabban Shimon expounds on it *(Tos. Yom Tov).*

צְאֶינָה וּרְאֶינָה בְּנוֹת צִיּוֹן... — *go forth and gaze, O daughters of Zion...*

This alludes to the maidens going forth to dance in the vineyards [on Yom Kippur] *(Ran).*

בַּמֶּלֶךְ שְׁלֹמֹה... — *upon the King Shlomo...*

I.e., HASHEM, מֶלֶךְ שֶׁהַשָּׁלוֹם שֶׁלּוֹ, *the King, to Whom peace belongs (Rav).*

בָּעֲטָרָה שֶׁעִטְּרָה־לוֹ אִמּוֹ בְּיוֹם חֲתֻנָּתוֹ וּבְיוֹם שִׂמְחַת לִבּוֹ. — *adorned with the crown His nation made Him on the day of his wedding and on the day of the joy of his heart.*

אִמּוֹ is rendered as אֻמָּתוֹ, *His nation (Rashi, Prov.* 1:8).

Others explain that the Jewish people is allegorically called the mother of HASHEM, as it were, since the *tzaddikim* among them can nullify His decrees, as a mother refuses the wishes of her child *(Tif. Yis.).*

,,בְּיוֹם חֲתֻנָּתוֹ''—זֶה מַתַּן תּוֹרָה. — *'On the day of His wedding,' this is the giving of the Torah,*

I.e., Yom Kippur the day God gave the second tablets and was united through them to Israel as bride and groom are united one to the other *(Rav).*

Moreover, since HASHEM forgave the sin of the golden calf, it was as though they had reestablished their union with Him *(Tif. Yis.).*

וּבְיוֹם שִׂמְחַת לִבּוֹ''—זֶה בִּנְיַן בֵּית הַמִּקְדָּשׁ — *'and on the day of His heart's gladness' — this is the building of the Holy Temple.*

King Solomon dedicated the First Temple from the seventh to the fourteenth of Tishrei. Thus, Yom Kippur is described as a day of

God's gladness because it was part of the feast of dedication (*Tos. Yom Tov* from *Moed Katan* 9a).[1]

שֶׁיִּבָּנֶה בִּמְהֵרָה בְיָמֵינוּ אָמֵן — *May it be built speedily in our days! Amen.*

Since the Tanna mentioned the Temple, he prayed that it be rebuilt speedily in our days, Amen *(Tif. Yis.).*

סליק מסכת תענית

1. [For an allegorical translation of *Song of Songs* as perceived by the Sages, see ArtScroll *Shir HaShirim.*]

מסכת מגילה

Tractate Megillah

Translation and anthologized commentary by
Rabbi Avrohom Yoseif Rosenberg

Mesorah Publications, ltd

◆§ Tractate Megillah

וְהַיָּמִים הָאֵלֶּה נִזְכָּרִים וְנַעֲשִׂים בְּכָל־דּוֹר וָדוֹר, *Consequently, these days should be remembered and celebrated by every single generation (Esther 9:28).*

נִזְכָּרִים, *remembered* — by reading the *Megillah;* וְנַעֲשִׂים, *and celebrated* — with feast, gladness, festivities, and giving portions [to friends] and gifts [to the poor] *(Rashi).*

T*ractate Megillah*, as its name implies, deals with the laws of reading מְגִלַּת אֶסְתֵּר, *the Megillah* or *Scroll of Esther*, on Purim. It begins with a detailed listing of the days on which the *Megillah* is to be read. The Tanna deemed it unnecessary to inform us that there is a *mitzvah* to read the *Megillah;* that is well-known by all Jews. His purpose is to acquaint us with the details of this *mitzvah*. Similarly, although The Five Books of Moses could also be called as *megillos,* [literally *scrolls*,] the Tanna does not specify that our tractate refers to the *Scroll of Esther*, because it was obvious which *megillah* he meant.

The word *megillah* comes from the root גלל, *to roll*, because ancient books were written on parchment scrolls and rolled up. Though all books were once written in this manner, as are our Torah scrolls, only five 'short' books were called *megillos: Esther, Ruth, Shir HaShirim* [*Song of Songs*], *Koheles* [*Ecclesiastes*], and *Eichah* [*Lamentations*]. Of the five, the only *megillah* whose reading is obligatory is *Megillas Esther*. The reading of the other four is based on custom — *Shir HaShirim* on Pesach, *Ruth* on Shavuos, *Koheles* on Succos, and *Eichah* on *Tishah B'Av (Responsa Rama* 35). Even according to the *Vilna Gaon* who holds that the reading of all *megillos* is obligatory, this obligation applies only in the presence of a *minyan* [*a quorum of ten*]. The reading of *Megillas Esther*, however, is incumbent upon every man and woman even when no *minyan* is available. Even young children must listen if they are capable of following the reading *(Peulas Sachir, Maaseh Rav* 175).

As cited above, the *Megillah* itself alludes to this reading. This makes it מִצְוַת עֲשֵׂה מִדִּבְרֵי קַבָּלָה, *a positive commandment from tradition* [i.e., the Prophets or the Writings.]

According to some authorities, such a commandment is more stringent than an ordinary Rabbinical enactment *(Turei Even, Megillah* 5a, 7a). There is a further reason for assigning greater weight to the *Megillah* reading, for the commandment to read it annually was ratified by the Heavenly Tribunal, as the Talmud expounds on the passage קִיְּמוּ וְקִבְּלוּ, *they confirmed and they undertook (Esther 9:27),* they [the Heavenly Tribunal] confirmed above what they [the Jews] undertook below *(Gemara* 7a).

Chapter One

◆§Purim — Either of Two Days

The *Sanhedrin* established Purim as a holiday לְפַרְסוּמֵי נִיסָא, *to publicize the miracle,* of the deliverance. Since the spontaneous celebration throughout the Persian Empire originally took place on the fourteenth of *Adar* — the day the Jews gained relief from their enemies after having battled and defeated them on the thirteenth — Mordechai proclaimed that day as an annual festival (*Esther* 9:19). The Jews of Shushan, however, had a miracle all their own, because they fought their enemies on the fourteenth day as well. Hence its original celebration was on the *fifteenth* of *Adar (Esther* 9:18). In commemoration of that miracle, the fifteenth was proclaimed as the Purim of Shushan.

The law of celebrating Purim and reading the *Megillah* on the fifteenth in walled cities is not stated specifically in the *Megillah,* but it is implied.

The *Megillah* states clearly that both the fourteenth and fifteenth days are celebrated *(Esther* 9:21). Verse 19 limits the celebration to one day in each place: עַל־כֵּן הַיְּהוּדִים הַפְּרָזִים הַיֹּשְׁבִים בְּעָרֵי הַפְּרָזוֹת עֹשִׂים אֵת יוֹם אַרְבָּעָה עָשָׂר, *Therefore, the Jewish townsmen who live in unwalled towns celebrate the fourteenth.* The implication is that only the townsmen living in *unwalled towns* celebrate the fourteenth, but citizens of walled cities celebrate the fifteenth *(Gemara* 2b).

Rather than limit that celebration to Shushan the Sages ordained that, on the fifteenth of *Adar,* Shushan Purim be celebrated in all cities which, like Shushan, had walls around them. However, this created a problem: *Eretz Yisrael* lay in ruins at that time, and even Jerusalem's wall had been destroyed by Nebuchadnezzar's conquering army. Therefore, Jerusalem and all other cities of *Eretz Yisrael* would have to celebrate Purim on the fourteenth like ordinary unwalled cities; the Holy City, indeed, the entire Holy Land, would have a status inferior to that of Shushan and other walled cities.

◆§Walled From Joshua's Times

To accord honor to Jerusalem and to *Eretz Yisrael,* and to attach the remembrance of *Eretz Yisrael* to the miracle in some way, the Rabbis decreed that all cities that were walled מִימוֹת יְהוֹשֻׁעַ בִּן־נוּן, *from the days of Joshua son of Nun* (who led the conquest of *Eretz Yisrael*), would celebrate Purim on the fifteenth of *Adar,* thus including Jerusalem in the category of the world's celebrated cities. Shushan itself was unwalled in the time of Joshua, but it was accorded a privileged status because the miracle [being celebrated] was performed there (see *Gemara* 2b; *Rambam, Hilchos Megillah* 1:5; *Yerushalmi* 1:1).

Since it was Joshua who led the nation in its first battle against Amalek *(Exodus* 17:8-16), it is fitting to connect the holiday which commemorates the defeat of Haman, who was an Amalekite, with Joshua. Furthermore, those killed by the Jews on the thirteenth and fourteenth of Adar *(Esther* 9:1-2,15) were all of Amalekite descent *(Rav; Yerushalmi).* [See pref. to mishnah 1.]

There were, of course, many walled cities in the days of Joshua, when such fortifications were common. All of them were destroyed during the course of history, however, and, although many have been rebuilt, there is no way of knowing whether they stand today on their original sites. Even Shushan was eventually destroyed. As a result, the only city in the world that *definitely* celebrates its Purim on the fifteenth is Jerusalem, which, despite frequent conquest and pillage, remains on its ancient site. The other walled cities of antiquity read the *Megillah* with a blessing on the fourteenth, and again, this time without a blessing, on the fifteenth. Thus the *mitzvah* is fulfilled even if they stand today on the same sites they occupied in Joshua's day. These cities are Ashdod, Ashkelon, Beer Sheva, Beit Sh'an, Gush Khalav, Hebron, Haifa, Tiberias, Jaffa, Lod, Gaza, Acco, Safed, Ramleh, and Shechem *(Ziv HaMinhagim).*

1.

◆§ Allowances for Villagers

Mishnayos 1 and 2 provide that villagers may, in certain years, read the *Megillah* on the eleventh, twelfth, and thirteenth days of *Adar*, a clear exception to the rule discussed above. Generally, the villagers were unlearned and unable to read the *Megillah*. Furthermore, the outlying farms and villages usually lacked a *minyan*, which, although not required, is preferable for the *Megillah* reading. Hence, the villagers would have been forced to travel to the cities to hear the *Megillah*, a distinct hardship. Because the villages supplied the cities with food and water, the Sages saw fit to make special allowances for them with regard to the *Megillah* reading (see comm. end of mishnah 1). Since the villagers customarily came to the cities on Mondays and Thursdays [referred to as יוֹם הַכְּנִיסָה, *day of entry*] to present their grievances before the *Beth Din* which convened on those days, and to hear the regular reading of the Torah, the Rabbis permitted them to hear the *Megillah* read on the Monday or Thursday immediately preceding Purim, so as not to burden them with an additional journey to town on Purim *(Rashi).*

◆§ Who Reads for Villagers?

According to *Rashi*, a townsman would read for the villagers for they were generally unlearned and incapable of reading for themselves. *Ran* contends that the townsmen were disqualified from reading at any time other than the day of their own obligation; therefore, one of the villagers would read the *Megillah*. It could be assumed that among the many people from all the surrounding villages, surely at least one who was qualified to read the *Megillah* could be found.

Others explain that the villagers would *assemble* in their *own* synagogues every Monday and Thursday to hear the reading of the Torah. Since taking time from their work to go to the synagogue again on Purim would entail great hardship for them, they were permitted to read the *Megillah* on the Monday or Thursday preceding Purim *(Tos., Yevamos* 14a; *Rambam, Megillah* 1:6). The authority to grant the villagers the privilege of reading the *Megillah* on the day of entry is alluded to in the *Megillah* itself: לְקַיֵּם אֶת־יְמֵי הַפֻּרִים הָאֵלֶּה בִּזְמַנֵּיהֶם, *to establish these days of Purim in their times (Esther* 9:31). The plural phrase *in their times* [rather than בִּזְמַנָּם, *in their time*] indicates that the *Megillah* may be read on *many days* in addition to the specifically assigned fourteenth and fifteenth *(Gemara* 2a).

א
א

[א] **מְגִלָּה** נִקְרֵאת בְּאַחַד עָשָׂר, בִּשְׁנֵים עָשָׂר, בִּשְׁלֹשָׁה עָשָׂר, בְּאַרְבָּעָה עָשָׂר, בַּחֲמִשָּׁה עָשָׂר, לֹא פָּחוֹת וְלֹא יוֹתֵר. כְּרַכִּין הַמֻּקָּפִין חוֹמָה מִימוֹת יְהוֹשֻׁעַ בִּן־נוּן, קוֹרִין בַּחֲמִשָּׁה עָשָׂר. כְּפָרִים וַעֲיָרוֹת גְּדוֹלוֹת קוֹרִין בְּאַרְבָּעָה עָשָׂר, אֶלָּא שֶׁהַכְּפָרִים מַקְדִּימִין לְיוֹם הַכְּנִיסָה.

יד אברהם

מְגִלָּה נִקְרֵאת... — *The Megillah* [lit. *scroll*] *may be read...*

The *Megillah*, the *Scroll of Esther*, may be read on any of the following days under the appropriate conditions which will be outlined by the mishnah *(Rav)*.

[See pref. to the tractate for the obligation to read the *Megillah* on Purim. See 2:3 for how much of the *Megillah* must be read.]

בְּאַחַד עָשָׂר, בִּשְׁנֵים עָשָׂר, בִּשְׁלֹשָׁה עָשָׂר, בְּאַרְבָּעָה עָשָׂר, בַּחֲמִשָּׁה עָשָׂר, — *on the eleventh, twelfth, thirteenth, fourteenth, and fifteenth* [*day of Adar*],

לֹא פָּחוֹת וְלֹא יוֹתֵר. — *but never earlier nor later.*

The *Megillah* is never read *earlier* than the *eleventh* nor is it read *later* than the *fifteenth (Tif. Yis.)*.

[The specific sets of circumstances are discussed here and in the following mishnah.]

כְּרַכִּין... — *Cities...*

Only fortified cities surrounded by walls fall under this category. [The Hebrew word מִבְצָרִים, *fortresses (Num.* 13:19), is rendered in Aramaic as כְּרַכִּין.]

הַמֻּקָּפִין חוֹמָה מִימוֹת יְהוֹשֻׁעַ בִּן־נוּן, — *that were surrounded by walls at the time of Joshua son of Nun...*

This status belongs only to cities that were walled when Joshua conquered the Land of Israel from the Canaanites, even though their walls have long since been destroyed *(Ran)*. [See pref.]

The *Gemara* (2b) bases this ruling on the similarity of the word פְּרָזִים, *townsmen (Esther* 9:19), to the word פְּרָזִי, *open cities*, used in reference to the cities of Sichon *(Deut.* 3:5). Just as the latter refers to cities existent in the time of Joshua's conquest, so does the former refer to dwellers of such towns *(Rav)*.

קוֹרִין בַּחֲמִשָּׁה עָשָׂר. — *read on the fifteenth.*

כְּפָרִים וַעֲיָרוֹת גְּדוֹלוֹת קוֹרִין בְּאַרְבָּעָה עָשָׂר, — *Villages and large towns read on the fourteenth,*

[This reading is in accordance with the verse: עַל־כֵּן הַיְּהוּדִים הַפְּרָזִים הַיֹּשְׁבִים בְּעָרֵי הַפְּרָזוֹת עֹשִׂים אֵת יוֹם אַרְבָּעָה עָשָׂר, *Therefore, the Jewish townsmen who live in unwalled towns celebrate the fourteenth ... (Esther* 9:19).]

[Since walled cities read on the *fifteenth* and all others read on the *fourteenth*, where is the *Megillah*

1 **1.** The *MEGILLAH* may be read on the eleventh,
1 twelfth, thirteenth, fourteenth, and fifteenth [day of *Adar*] but never earlier nor later. Cities that were surrounded by walls at the time of Joshua son of Nun read on the fifteenth. Villages and large towns read on the fourteenth; however, villages [sometimes] advance [their reading] to the day of entry [into the towns].

YAD AVRAHAM

read on the thirteenth, twelfth, or eleventh as mentioned above?]

אֶלָּא שֶׁהַכְּפָרִים מַקְדִּימִין לְיוֹם הַכְּנִיסָה. — *however, villages* [*sometimes*] *advance* [*their reading*] *to the day of entry* [*into the towns*].

I.e., the Monday or Thursday preceding Purim. Ezra ordained that the Torah be read on Mondays and Thursdays to assure that no one would let three full days go by without studying Torah. He likewise ordained that on those days when people assemble to hear the Torah being read, a *Beth Din* [*rabbinical court*] be in session so that they could gain redress for the grievances (*Bava Kama* 82a).

For these two purposes, villagers established Mondays and Thursdays as the market days when they would come to town. Since the villagers were not fluent in reading the *Megillah*, they were permitted to take advantage of their day of entry into the town when they could conveniently find someone to read for them *(Rav)*.

According to the *Gemara's* conclusion, it was in recognition of the service the villagers performed in providing the townspeople with food and water that the Rabbis afforded them the convenience of advancing their reading of the *Megillah* to their 'day of entry' *(Tos. Yom Tov)*.

R' Achai Gaon renders יוֹם הַכְּנִיסָה as *the day of assembly (Sh'iltos D'Rav Achai Gaon* on *Parshas Vayakhel* 67). According to him, the *day of assembly* refers to the thirteenth of Adar. On that date each year, we assemble to observe the Fast of Esther by reading the Torah, and reciting *Selichos*, prayers for forgiveness. This commemorates the day when the Jews battled their enemies *(Esther* 9:16). We assume that the Jews of Persia fasted on that day to beg divine assistance, just as Moses presumably fasted on the day of the battle against Amalek *(Ran; Rosh; Rabbeinu Tam)*.

Thus, according to *Rav Achai Gaon*, since the villagers had already assembled for the fast, they were permitted to hear the *Megillah* reading on that day to avoid the hardship of requiring them to assemble again the next day.

Hence, if the thirteenth fell on a Sabbath or Friday and was therefore observed earlier (because fasts are avoided on those days) the *Megillah* could be read on the eleventh or on the twelfth; i.e., if the thirteenth is on the Sabbath, the fast is observed on Thursday, the eleventh, and if Friday is the

א
ב

[ב] כֵּיצַד? חָל לִהְיוֹת יוֹם אַרְבָּעָה עָשָׂר בַּשֵּׁנִי — כְּפָרִים וַעֲיָרוֹת גְּדוֹלוֹת קוֹרִין בּוֹ בַּיּוֹם, וּמֻקָּפוֹת חוֹמָה לְמָחָר. חָל לִהְיוֹת בַּשְּׁלִישִׁי אוֹ בָרְבִיעִי — כְּפָרִים מַקְדִּימִין לְיוֹם הַכְּנִיסָה, וַעֲיָרוֹת גְּדוֹלוֹת קוֹרִין בּוֹ בַּיּוֹם, וּמֻקָּפוֹת חוֹמָה לְמָחָר. חָל לִהְיוֹת בַּחֲמִישִׁי — כְּפָרִים וַעֲיָרוֹת גְּדוֹלוֹת קוֹרִין בּוֹ בַּיּוֹם, וּמֻקָּפוֹת חוֹמָה לְמָחָר. חָל לִהְיוֹת עֶרֶב שַׁבָּת — כְּפָרִים מַקְדִּימִין לְיוֹם הַכְּנִיסָה,

יד אברהם

thirteenth, the fast is observed on Thursday, the twelfth.

Although most commentators trace the institution of the Fast of Esther to the Gaonic period, R' Achai obviously considered that fast to have been enacted in Talmudic times.

Whether the mishnah refers only to unwalled villages or even to walled villages is discussed by the commentators. *Tosafos* maintains that only unwalled villages are permitted to advance their reading, however, no such dispensation is granted walled villages. *Ran* allows the residents of a walled village to choose whether to advance their reading to the day of entry [since they are a village] or read on the fifteenth [since they are surrounded by walls]. *Ramban* likewise allows the residents to choose which day to read, but limits the choice to the fourteenth or fifteenth *(Tos. R' Akiva Eiger).*

2.

כֵּיצַד? — *How is this possible?*

[I.e., how is it possible for the *Megillah* reading, which is essentially required on the fourteenth or fifteenth — to be done on the eleventh, twelfth, or thirteenth of *Adar?* The mishnah proceeds to outline the circumstances making possible such unusual readings.]

חָל לִהְיוֹת יוֹם אַרְבָּעָה עָשָׂר בַּשֵּׁנִי— כְּפָרִים וַעֲיָרוֹת גְּדוֹלוֹת קוֹרִין בּוֹ בַּיּוֹם, — *If the fourteenth* [*of Adar*] *fell on a Monday, villages and large towns read on that very day;*

[I.e., on Monday, the fourteenth of *Adar* (fig. 1). Since the villagers assembled in the towns on Mondays in any case, there was no reason for them to advance their reading.

S	M	T	W	T	F	S
13	14 PURIM	15 SHUSHAN PURIM	16	17	18	19

Figure 1

Even according to R' Achai Gaon (see *comm.* to preceding mishnah), villagers read on Monday, the fourteenth, rather than on Sunday, the thirteenth, because they would assemble on Mondays and Thursdays as well as on the Fast of Esther. Therefore, if Purim fell on Monday, the villagers would be assembled for the reading of the Torah, and they

1 2. How is this possible? If the fourteenth [of *Adar*]
2 fell on a Monday, villages and large towns read on that very day; walled cities [read] on the next day. If it fell on a Tuesday or Wednesday, villages advance [their reading] to the day of entry; large towns read on that very day; and walled cities read the next day. If it fell on a Thursday, villages and large towns read on that very day; walled cities on the next day. If it fell on the eve of the Sabbath, villages advance their reading to the day of entry; large

could listen to the *Megillah* along with the city dwellers (*Nimukei Yosef*).

וּמֻקָּפוֹת חוֹמָה לְמָחָר. — *walled cities* [*read*] *on the next day* [i.e., on Tuesday, the fifteenth of Adar].

חָל לִהְיוֹת... — *If it* [i.e., the fourteenth of *Adar*] *fell...*

The mishnah always starts with the fourteenth since that is the date when most communities read (*Tos. Yom Tov*).

בַּשְּׁלִישִׁי אוֹ בָרְבִיעִי—כְּפָרִים מַקְדִּימִין לְיוֹם הַכְּנִיסָה, — *on a Tuesday or Wednesday, villages advance* [*their reading*] *to the day of entry;*

[I.e., if the fourteenth falls on a Tuesday (fig. 2), the villagers read

S	M	T	W	T	F	S
12	13 DAY OF ENTRY	14 PURIM	15 SHUSHAN PURIM	16	17	18

Figure 2

the *Megillah* on Monday, the thirteenth. If it falls on a Wednesday (fig. 3), they read the *Megillah* on Monday, the twelfth.]

S	M	T	W	T	F	S
11	12 DAY OF ENTRY	13	14 PURIM	15 SHUSHAN PURIM	16	17

Figure 3

וַעֲיָרוֹת גְּדוֹלוֹת קוֹרִין בּוֹ בַיּוֹם, — *large towns read on that very day* [i.e., on either Tuesday or Wednesday, the fourteenth];

וּמֻקָּפוֹת חוֹמָה לְמָחָר. — *and walled cities read the next day* [i.e., on Wednesday or Thursday, the fifteenth].

חָל לִהְיוֹת בַּחֲמִישִׁי—כְּפָרִים וַעֲיָרוֹת גְּדוֹלוֹת קוֹרִין בּוֹ בַיּוֹם, — *If it* [i.e., the fourteenth of *Adar*] *fell on a Thursday, villages and large towns read on that very day* (fig. 4);

S	M	T	W	T	F	S
10	11	12	13	14 PURIM	15 SHUSHAN PURIM	16

Figure 4

[I.e., on Thursday, the fourteenth of Adar. Since the villagers assembled in the towns on Thursdays, there was no reason for them to read earlier.]

וּמֻקָּפוֹת חוֹמָה לְמָחָר. — *walled cities on the next day* [i.e., Friday the fifteenth].

חָל לִהְיוֹת עֶרֶב שַׁבָּת—כְּפָרִים מַקְדִּימִין לְיוֹם הַכְּנִיסָה, — *If it* [i.e., the fourteenth of *Adar*] *fell on the eve of the Sabbath* [i.e., Friday], *villages advance their reading to the day of entry* [i.e., Thursday, the thirteenth] (fig. 5);

S	M	T	W	T	F	S
9	10	11	12	13 DAY OF ENTRY	14 PURIM	15 SHUSHAN PURIM

Figure 5

א וַעֲיָרוֹת גְּדוֹלוֹת וּמֻקָּפוֹת חוֹמָה קוֹרִין בּוֹ בַּיּוֹם.
ב חָל לִהְיוֹת בַּשַּׁבָּת — כְּפָרִים וַעֲיָרוֹת גְּדוֹלוֹת מַקְדִּימִין וְקוֹרִין לְיוֹם הַכְּנִיסָה, וּמֻקָּפוֹת חוֹמָה

יד אברהם

וַעֲיָרוֹת גְּדוֹלוֹת וּמֻקָּפוֹת חוֹמָה קוֹרִין בּוֹ בַּיּוֹם. — *large towns and walled cities read on that very day.*

I.e., on Friday, the fourteenth. Even the walled cities must advance their reading to the fourteenth since, fearing possible desecration of the Sabbath, the Sages ruled that the *Megillah* should never be read on the Sabbath. As Rabbah explains, the Sages feared that since every individual is required to read the *Megillah,* whether or not a *minyan* is present, an unqualified person may attempt to read it for himself. Upon encountering difficulty, he may carry the *Megillah* through the street to seek instruction from an expert, thereby inadvertently desecrating the Sabbath. For this same reason, the precepts of *shofar* and *lulav* [which are incumbent upon each individual] are not performed on the Sabbath *(Rav).*[1] [That the Sanhedrin and Talmudic Sages of comparable stature were empowered to set aside a positive precept of the Torah under certain circumstances is discussed in *Yevamos* 90a, b.]

Alternatively, R' Yosef explains that the *Megillah* is not read on the Sabbath because the poor expect to receive gifts on the day of the reading. Were gifts to be distributed on the Sabbath, the result might be its desecration *(Gemara* 4b).

The reading is not postponed until Sunday because it is never done later than the fourteenth in unwalled cities. This is derived from the verse (*Esther* 9:27): וְלֹא יַעֲבוֹר, *and it* [the *Megillah* reading] *shall not pass;* i.e., the reading may not be postponed to a date later than that prescribed in the *Megillah* itself (*Gemara* 5a).

Hence, if the fifteenth of *Adar* falls on a Sabbath, the *Megillah* reading is advanced to the fourteenth in walled cities. The fifteenth, however, is considered Purim and the *Al Hanisim* prayer is said in the *Shemoneh Esrei* and in *Bircas HaMazon*; the Torah reading of a weekday Purim (see below 3:6) is read as the *maftir*, and the *haftarah* of *Parshas Zachor* is repeated (see below 3:4).

Concerning the day on which the citizens of a walled city eat the Purim feast when the fifteenth falls on a Sabbath, the commentators disagree. Some maintain that it is eaten on the Sabbath. Many are of the opinion, however, that a festive repast which is eaten on the Sabbath cannot be considered as the Purim feast, for the verse states: לַעֲשׂוֹת אוֹתָם יְמֵי מִשְׁתֶּה וְשִׂמְחָה, *to make them days of feasting and joy (Esther* 9:22), i.e., days whose joy is dependent on Purim and not days whose joy was or-

1. A fear that one might carry on the Sabbath to find a competent reader was felt by the Sages only with regard to *Megillah,* but not with regard to the reading of the Torah. Since the *Megillah* reading is incumbent upon each individual even in the absence of a *minyan,* the danger existed that an unlearned person would carry his *Megillah* and go in search of a competent reader. The Torah reading, however, is incumbent upon the congregation rather than the individual. We, therefore, assume that within the group there will be someone capable of reading; or, one will remind the others that carrying is not permitted on the Sabbath *(Lechem Shamayim).*

1 towns and walled cities read on that very day. If it fell
2 on the Sabbath, villages and large towns advance
[their reading] to the day of entry; walled cities read

dained for another reason [i.e., the Sabbath]. *Rif,* based on *Yerushalmi* 1:4, rules that the feast is observed on Sunday, the sixteenth.

Others are of the opinion that precepts connected with Purim can be performed only on days when the *Megillah* may be read; thus, the sixteenth is excluded. They rule, therefore, that the festive meal is served on Friday, the fourteenth *(R' Aharon HaLevi; Ran; Rav).*[1]

חָל לִהְיוֹת בְּשַׁבָּת — *If it* [i.e., the fourteenth of Adar] *fell on the Sabbath* (fig. 6),

S	M	T	W	T	F	S
8	9	10	11	12 DAY OF ENTRY	13	14 PURIM
15 SHUSHAN PURIM	16	17	18	19	20	21

Figure 6

It was possible for Purim to fall on the Sabbath when the months were proclaimed by the Sanhedrin on the testimony of witnesses who observed the appearance of the מוֹלָד, *the moon's first phase* [see *Rosh HaShanah,* Chap. I] *(Tif. Yis.).*

[Nowadays, however, we use a לוּחַ, *calendar,* formulated in 4118 (358 C.E.) by R' Hillel HaSheini, the son of R' Yehudah Nesia *(Seder Hadoros).* According to this calendar, the fourteenth of *Adar* cannot fall on the Sabbath, Monday, or Wednesday. The *Shulchan Aruch* 428:1 provides us with a mnemonic by which to remember it. It is: לא זְבַ״ד פּוּרִים, *Purim cannot fall on* ז׳, *the seventh,* ב׳, *the second, or* ד׳, *the fourth* day of the week.]

כְּפָרִים וַעֲיָרוֹת גְּדוֹלוֹת מַקְדִּימִין וְקוֹרִין לְיוֹם הַכְּנִיסָה, — *villages and large towns advance* [*their reading*] *to the day of entry;*

The villages advance their reading to Thursday, the twelfth of *Adar.* Moreover, even the large towns advance their reading to that day; since they must advance their date of reading from the Sabbath, they advance it to the villagers' day of entry (*Tos. Yom Tov; Gem.* 4b).

וּמֻקָּפוֹת חוֹמָה לְמָחָר — *walled cities read the next day* [i.e., on Sunday, the fifteenth of *Adar*].

1. The *Shulchan Aruch* (688:6) decides in favor of *Rif,* and for a period this was the practice in Jerusalem, the only city definitely known to be walled since the time of Joshua's conquest. However, when R' Levi ben Chaviv came to Jerusalem, he refuted this ruling, and argued convincingly that the festive meal and *mishloach manos* [gifts of food to friends] were to be observed on the Sabbath *(Responsa Maharal Bach* 232). Although his arguments were subsequently refuted by other authorities *(Magen Avraham; Taz; Beur HaGra),* a *three-day Purim* [פּוּרִים מְשֻׁלָּשׁ] came to be observed in Jerusalem.

Thus, on Friday, the fourteenth, the *Megillah* is read and gifts are distributed to the poor. In addition, סְעוּדַת פּוּרִים, *the Purim feast,* and מִשְׁלוֹחַ מָנוֹת, *sending of food,* are observed by some following the view of *Ra'ah* cited by *Rav.* On the Sabbath, the *Al Hanisim* prayer is added, the *maftir* is the reading of Purim, and the *haftarah* is that of *Parshas Zachor.* A second festive meal is served, in accordance with the view of R' Levi ben Chaviv. On Sunday, the sixteenth, a third festive meal is served and gifts are again sent, in accordance with the view of *Rif.*

א
ג

לְמָחָר. חָל לִהְיוֹת אַחַר הַשַּׁבָּת — כְּפָרִים מַקְדִּימִין לְיוֹם הַכְּנִיסָה, וַעֲיָרוֹת גְּדוֹלוֹת קוֹרִין בּוֹ בַּיּוֹם, וּמֻקָּפוֹת חוֹמָה לְמָחָר.

[ג] **אֵיזוֹ** הִיא עִיר גְּדוֹלָה? כָּל־שֶׁיֵּשׁ־בָּהּ עֲשָׂרָה בַטְלָנִים. פָּחוֹת מִכָּאן הֲרֵי זֶה כְּפָר.

בְּאֵלּוּ אָמְרוּ: מַקְדִּימִין וְלֹא מְאַחֲרִין. אֲבָל זְמַן עֲצֵי כֹהֲנִים, וְתִשְׁעָה בְאָב, וַחֲגִיגָה, וְהַקְהֵל

חָל לִהְיוֹת אַחַר הַשַּׁבָּת—כְּפָרִים מַקְדִּימִין לְיוֹם הַכְּנִיסָה, — *If it* [the fourteenth of *Adar*] *fell after the Sabbath* [on Sunday], *villages advance* [*their reading*] *to the day of entry* (fig. 7);

S	M	T	W	T	F	S
7	8	9	10	11 DAY OF ENTRY	12	13
14 PURIM	15 SHUSHAN PURIM	16	17	18	19	20

Figure 7

[Villagers cannot postpone their reading to the next day of entry, Monday, the fifteenth, so they advance their reading to Thursday, the eleventh. This is the earliest date on which the *Megillah* can be read.]

וַעֲיָרוֹת גְּדוֹלוֹת קוֹרִין בּוֹ בַּיּוֹם, — *large towns read on that very day* [Sunday, the fourteenth of *Adar*];

וּמֻקָּפוֹת חוֹמָה לְמָחָר. — *walled cities read the next day* [Monday, the fifteenth of *Adar*].

[The question כֵּיצַד, *how is this possible?* raised at the beginning of this mishnah has been answered. Illustrations have been provided for each of the possible alternative reading days enumerated in mishnah 1. They are as follows:

In villages, the Megillah may be read on Monday, the eleventh, if the fourteenth falls on Sunday (fig. 7); it may be read on Monday or Thursday, the twelfth, if the fourteenth falls on Wednesday (fig. 3); or the Sabbath (fig. 6); it may be read on Monday or Thursday, the thirteenth, if the fourteenth falls on Tuesday (fig. 2) or Friday (fig. 5); or it may be read on Monday or Thursday, the fourteenth, when Purim falls on either of those days (figs. 1, 4).

In unwalled cities, the *Megillah* may be read on Thursday, the twelfth, if the fourteenth falls on the Sabbath (fig. 6), or on the fourteenth when it falls on any weekday.

In walled cities, the *Megillah* may be read on Friday, the fourteenth, if the fifteenth falls on the Sabbath (fig. 5), or on the fifteenth when it falls on any weekday.]

3.

אֵיזוֹ הִיא עִיר גְּדוֹלָה? — *What is considered a large town?*

[What is the criterion for designating a city as 'large' (1:1), thus disqualifying its citizens from advancing their day of reading?]

כָּל שֶׁיֵּשׁ־בָּהּ עֲשָׂרָה בַטְלָנִים. — *Any in which there are ten unoccupied men.*

1 the next day. If it fell after the Sabbath, villages ad-
3 vance [their reading] to the day of entry; large towns
read on that very day; walled cities read the next day.

3. What is considered a large town? Any in which there are ten unoccupied men. [If there are] fewer than that it is [considered] a village.

As regards these times, they said to advance rather than postpone; but the time of the wood offering of the *kohanim*, [the fast of] *Tisha B'Av*, the festival sacrifice, and the Assembly are postponed and not

YAD AVRAHAM

I.e., ten men supported by the community, who remain in the synagogue to insure the constant presence of a *minyan (Rav).*

Alternatively, these men are supported by the community to devote themselves exclusively to Torah study and communal affairs *(Rambam).* Other authorities do not require them to be community-supported. It is sufficient if they are always in the synagogue at the time of prayers *(Ran).*

The practice of having ten unoccupied men is based on the anthropomorphic Rabbinical saying that God is angered when ten men are not present in the synagogue [at prayer time] *(Berachos* 6b). Therefore, ten men were appointed to be available in the synagogue at times of prayer *(Rashi).*

פָּחוֹת מִכָּאן... — *[If there are] fewer than that...*

[If a place does not have ten unoccupied men in the synagogue ...]

הֲרֵי זֶה כְּפָר. — *it is [considered] a village* [and may read the *Megillah* earlier than the fourteenth].

בְּאֵלּוּ אָמְרוּ: מַקְדִּימִין... — *As regards these times* [when the *Megillah* may be read] *they* [i.e., the Sages] *said to advance* [the reading]...

It is *only* regarding the case of Purim which fell on Sabbath that the performance of the *mitzvah* is advanced to a prior day *(Rav).*

וְלֹא מְאַחֲרִין. — *rather than postpone;*

[I.e., rather than postpone the *mitzvah* until after the Sabbath.]

אֲבָל... — *but...*

[In the case of other *mitzvos*, however, if they cannot be performed on the Sabbath, they are postponed to Sunday. For example:]

זְמַן עֲצֵי כֹהֲנִים, — *the time of the wood offering of the kohanim,*

[According to *Taanis* 4:5, the text should read: *The time of the wood offering of* הַכֹּהֲנִים וְהָעָם, *the kohanim and the people.*]

Certain families obligated themselves to provide wood for the altar annually on certain days, and accompanied their donations with voluntary burnt offerings. If the day of their offering fell on the Sabbath, it was postponed until Sunday. The offering could not be advanced to Friday because, under the terms of the vow, the obligation

א ג — מְאַחֲרִין וְלֹא מַקְדִּימִין. אַף עַל פִּי שֶׁאָמְרוּ מַקְדִּימִין וְלֹא מְאַחֲרִין, מֻתָּרִין בְּהֶסְפֵּד וּבְתַעֲנִיּוֹת וּמַתָּנוֹת לָאֶבְיוֹנִים.

יד אברהם

would not begin until the Sabbath *(Rav).*

Moreover, if they had brought their offering earlier, they would have encroached on the rights of the previous donor who had the right to provide wood until a specific date; i.e., the wood that the previous donor brought was to be used until the next time of the wood offering *(Rashi* on *Rif).*

וְתִשְׁעָה בְּאָב, — *[the fast of] Tisha B'Av,*

If *Tishah B'Av* [the Ninth of *Av*], falls on the Sabbath, a day when it is forbidden to fast, the observance takes place on Sunday, the tenth of *Av.* Other fasts, [such as the Seventeenth of *Tammuz* and *Tzom Gedaliah*] which fall on the Sabbath are also observed on the next day *(Rav).* Because those fasts are mourning periods commemorative of calamities, the recollection of such vexing memories should be postponed rather than hastened (*Gemara* 5a; see *Taanis* 4:6).

[If, however, the Fast of Esther falls on the Sabbath, the fast is advanced to the preceding Thursday. This fast is not in mourning for past troublesome times, rather it commemorates the supplications to God to aid the nation in defeating its adversaries. The day was not one of פּוּרְעָנוּת, *troubles,* but of נִצָּחוֹן, *victory.* Thus, there is no objection to advancing its observance when the thirteenth of *Adar* falls on the Sabbath.

That the fast is not observed on Friday in this instance is to avoid entering the Sabbath in a weakened state. A *rescheduled* fast is, therefore, never observed on Friday. (If a fast falls on Friday — as is sometimes the case with the Tenth of *Teves* — it is observed on that day.)

In the event that Yom Kippur falls on the Sabbath, the fast *is* observed on that day because the Torah specifies that Yom Kippur must take place on the Tenth of *Tishrei,* regardless of which day of the week it falls.]

וַחֲגִיגָה, — *the festival sacrifice,*

This refers to the שְׁלָמִים, *peace offering,* that everyone was required to bring on the first day of each of the שָׁלֹשׁ רְגָלִים, *three pilgrimage festivals.* If one neglected to do so, he had seven days in which to fulfill his obligation (*Chagigah* 1:6).

[The peace offering may be brought on festivals when slaughter and preparation of meat are permitted. On the Sabbath, however, only Scripturally required communal offerings may be brought.]

Thus, if the first day of the holiday fell on the Sabbath, the sacrifice was postponed. It could not be brought earlier, as the time of the obligation would not have arrived *(Rav).*

— וְהַקְהֵל — *and the Assembly ...*

The Torah states [*Deut.* 31:10-12]: מִקֵּץ שֶׁבַע שָׁנִים בְּמֹעֵד שְׁנַת הַשְּׁמִטָּה בְּחַג הַסֻּכֹּת...תִּקְרָא אֶת־הַתּוֹרָה הַזֹּאת נֶגֶד כָּל־יִשְׂרָאֵל בְּאָזְנֵיהֶם הַקְהֵל אֶת־הָעָם הָאֲנָשִׁים וְהַנָּשִׁים וְהַטַּף..., *At the end of seven years, at the appointed time of Shemitah during the festival of Succos ... you shall read this Torah before all Israel in their hearing. Assemble the people, the men, the women, and the young children ... .*

During the Assembly, the king would read the book of *Deutero-*

1 advanced. Even though [the Sages] said to advance
3 [the reading] rather than postpone, eulogies, fasts
and gifts to the poor are permitted [on the earlier
dates].

nomy. The event took place on the evening following the first day of Succos, in the year *following* the שְׁמִטָּה, *Sabbatical Year (Sotah* 7:8).

If the night following the first day of Succos fell on the Sabbath, the Assembly was postponed until the next night.

The following reasons are given for postponing the Assembly:

— The Torah states: הַקְהֵל אֶת־הָעָם הָאֲנָשִׁים וְהַנָּשִׁים וְהַטַּף, *Assemble the people, the men, the women, and the young children (Deut.* 31:12). This includes babies too small to walk. Since it is forbidden to carry them in the public domain on the Sabbath, the Assembly was delayed until the following evening *(Rav).*

— That night a wooden platform on which the king stood was constructed (see *Sotah* 7:8). It could not be constructed before the Sabbath because it would obstruct the Temple court *(Rashi)*... [nor on the Sabbath because building is one of the forbidden labors of the Sabbath.]

— Silver trumpets were sounded and supplications were recited at the Assembly. This was forbidden on the Sabbath *(Rambam).*

מְאַחֲרִין וְלֹא מַקְדִּימִין. — *are postponed and not advanced.*

[I.e., all four of the previously mentioned *mitzvos* are postponed until Sunday, unlike the *Megillah* reading which is advanced to Friday.]

☙[We have learned that the *Megillah* reading may be advanced to Monday or Thursday for the benefit of villagers, or to Friday if Purim falls on the Sabbath. Do those days have the status of the Purim festival with regard to the prohibitions (e.g., fasting and eulogizing) and other precepts (e.g., gifts to the poor, festive meal) of Purim? The mishnah proceeds to discuss this:]

אַף עַל פִּי שֶׁאָמְרוּ ... — *Even though [the Sages] said...*

In reference to the reading of the *Megillah (Tif. Yis.).*

מַקְדִּימִין וְלֹא מְאַחֲרִין, — *to advance [the reading] rather than postpone,*

[I.e., if Purim falls on the Sabbath, and for the benefit of villagers.]

מֻתָּרִין בְּהֶסְפֵּד וּבְתַעֲנִיּוֹת ... — *eulogies, fasts ... are permitted* [*on the earlier dates*].

The earlier dates on which the *Megillah* may be read are not considered holidays. Therefore, eulogies and fasts are permitted on those days. However, if the fourteenth fell on a Friday and the villagers read on the thirteenth, eulogies were prohibited for the special reason that that day was known as the Day of Nikanor, in commemoration of the defeat of Nikanor, one of the Greek generals in Hasmonean times (see *Taanis* 18b). [Obviously, since the thirteenth of Adar was celebrated as the Day of Nikanor, the Fast of Esther was not observed while the Temple stood. See comm. end of mishnah 1.]

וּמַתָּנוֹת לָאֶבְיוֹנִים. — *and gifts to the poor are permitted* [*on the earlier dates*].

One can discharge his obligation of מַתָּנוֹת לָאֶבְיוֹנִים, *gifts to the poor*, on the earlier dates. However, if one

א אָמַר רַבִּי יְהוּדָה: אֵימָתַי? מָקוֹם שֶׁנִּכְנָסִין
ד בַּשֵּׁנִי וּבַחֲמִישִׁי; אֲבָל מָקוֹם שֶׁאֵין נִכְנָסִין לֹא
בַּשֵּׁנִי וְלֹא בַחֲמִישִׁי, אֵין קוֹרִין אוֹתָהּ אֶלָּא
בִּזְמַנָּהּ.

[ד] **קָרְאוּ** אֶת־הַמְּגִלָּה בַּאֲדָר הָרִאשׁוֹן וְנִתְעַבְּרָה הַשָּׁנָה, קוֹרִין אוֹתָהּ בַּאֲדָר הַשֵּׁנִי.

יד אברהם

sent מִשְׁלוֹחַ מָנוֹת, *gifts to friends*, on the earlier dates, he must do so again on the fourteenth as this precept is connected with the festive meal which is eaten on the fourteenth, even though the *Megillah* may have been read earlier *(Tos. Yom Tov)*.

אָמַר רַבִּי יְהוּדָה: אֵימָתַי? — *R' Yehudah says: When* [*may the reading be advanced*]*?*

I.e., when do we apply the ruling of 1:2, that the villagers may advance the reading to the preceding Monday or Thursday *(Tif. Yis.)?*

מָקוֹם שֶׁנִּכְנָסִין בַּשֵּׁנִי וּבַחֲמִישִׁי; — *In a place where they enter* [*the towns*] *on Monday and Thursday.*

Villagers may advance their reading only in cases where they enter the cities on Mondays and Thursdays to go to the *Beth Din* or to hear the Torah reading. According to this interpretation, villagers would travel to the cities to hear the *Megillah*. According to other commentators, the advanced reading takes place not in the cities but in the villages. If the village has its own *minyan* that meets on Mondays and Thursdays to hear the reading of the Torah, the villagers advance the *Megillah* reading in their own villages so as to read it with a *minyan (Meiri)*.

אֲבָל מָקוֹם שֶׁאֵין נִכְנָסִין לֹא בַשֵּׁנִי וְלֹא בַחֲמִישִׁי, — *However, in a place where they do not enter* [*the towns*] *on Monday and Thursday,*

I.e., if there is neither *Beth Din* nor synagogue in the neighboring towns. Alternatively, if there is no *minyan* for reading the Torah in the village on Monday and Thursday *(Meiri)*.

אֵין קוֹרִין אוֹתָהּ אֶלָּא בִזְמַנָּהּ. — *they may read it only on the proper date.*

They may read the *Megillah* only on the fourteenth of *Adar* and the rule in 1:2 does not apply. Thus, nowadays that villagers do not enter the towns on Mondays and Thursdays, the practice of reading the *Megillah* earlier has been abandoned.

Even when the villagers did enter the towns on Mondays and Thursdays, the practice of advancing the *Megillah* reading did not always apply. This lenient ruling was applicable only when the Jews were in their land and when the months were established by the *Sanhedrin*. In those times, everyone would take note when *Rosh Chodesh Nissan* was proclaimed and observed Pesach accordingly. However, since the adoption of R' Hillel's calendar [see comm. Mishnah 3], *Adar* always has twenty-nine days. Thus, Pesach is always thirty days after Purim. הוֹאִיל וּמִסְתַּכְּלִין בָּהּ אֵין קוֹרִין אוֹתָהּ אֶלָּא בִּזְמַנָּהּ,

1
4 R' Yehudah says: When [may the reading be advanced]? — In a place where they enter [the towns] on Monday and Thursday. However, in a place where they do not enter [the towns] on Monday and Thursday, they may read it only on the proper date.

4. If they read the *Megillah* during the first *Adar* and an extra month [of *Adar*] was added to the year, they must read it [again] in the second *Adar*.

YAD AVRAHAM

since they [the common people] *look to that day* [of Purim, in order to know when to begin Pesach], *therefore, we only read it at its proper time* [i.e., the fourteenth]; for were we to continue the practice of reading the *Megillah* earlier than the fourteenth, people might erroneously begin Pesach thirty days from the twelfth or the thirteenth. If so, they would mistakenly end the Pesach holiday a day or two early and eat *chametz* on its last day (*Gem.* 2a; *Rashi*).

Based on an alternative reading, *Sefer HaMichtam* interprets this Talmudic dictum in a different light: The practice was abandoned הוֹאִיל וּמִסְתַּכְּנִים בָּהּ, *since they became endangered on that day*, i.e., religious persecution made observance of the precepts hazardous. The gentile authorities were particularly opposed to Purim, which commemorates a victory over a gentile oppressor. An extended celebration would arouse even more hostility. [*Since they* (the gentiles) *look to that day* (to vent their hatred), *therefore, we only read it at its proper time* (and do not extend the reading period).]

Only during prosperous times could the *Megillah* be read earlier. In years of dire poverty, however, the poor, who receive their gifts on the day the *Megillah* is read, might consume their meager grants before the fourteenth and be left with nothing with which to celebrate the holiday *(Rif)*.

Even though this practice has been abandoned, if one is embarking on a voyage making it impossible for him to secure a *Megillah* on the fourteenth, he should read on the eleventh, twelfth, or thirteenth, without reciting a blessing. Some authorities even permit him to read from the first of *Adar*, if he is leaving before the eleventh. If he reads earlier than the fourteenth, he may do so only in the presence of ten men. Moreover, if he does secure a *Megillah* on the fourteenth, he must repeat the reading and recite the blessings *(Orach Chaim* 688:7).

4.

קָרְאוּ אֶת־הַמְּגִלָּה בַּאֲדָר הָרִאשׁוֹן וְנִתְעַבְּרָה הַשָּׁנָה, — *If they read the Megillah during the first Adar and an extra month* [*of Adar*] *was added to the year,*

I.e., if after Purim, the *Sanhedrin* proclaimed the addition of an extra month *(Kehati)*.

[During the period when the Sanhedrin sat and consecrated the months, they decided on a year-to-year basis whether or not it was necessary to add an extra month. This thirteenth month was called אֲדָר שֵׁנִי, *the second Adar*. In some years, the determination could not be made until after Purim. Nowadays when we rely on the perma-

א
ה

אֵין בֵּין אֲדָר הָרִאשׁוֹן לַאֲדָר הַשֵּׁנִי אֶלָּא קְרִיאַת הַמְּגִלָּה וּמַתָּנוֹת לָאֶבְיוֹנִים.

[ה] **אֵין** בֵּין יוֹם טוֹב לְשַׁבָּת אֶלָּא אֹכֶל נֶפֶשׁ בִּלְבָד.

יד אברהם

קוֹרִין אוֹתָהּ בַּאֲדָר הַשֵּׁנִי. — *they must read it [again] in the second Adar.*

I.e., they must reread the *Megillah* since they did not discharge their duty by reading it in the first *Adar (Kehati).*

nent calendar computed by R' Hillel, the situation posed by our mishnah is mostly academic. This law can nowadays be relevant only if a community erred by reading the *Megillah* in the first *Adar,* forgetting that there would be a second *Adar.*]

☙There is no difference ... except ...

[The mishnah now compares and contrasts the twin months of *Adar* with regard to a specific topic (namely, the laws of Purim). Although not every aspect of the month is included here (e.g., the four special portions are discussed later, in 3:4), the Tanna, nevertheless, uses the all inclusive phrase, אֵין בֵּין ... אֶלָּא, *there is no difference ... except.* Thus, the phrase should be understood as: With reference to the particular aspect of *Adar* under discussion, *there is no difference between the first Adar and the second ... except.*]

Mishnayos 5-11 are related neither to *Megillah* reading and the other laws of Purim, nor to each other. They have been included [probably as a mnemonic device since mishnayos were originally not written but were studied from memory] because of the similarity of phraseology. Just as the mishnah here begins אֵין בֵּין, *there is no difference,* so do all the rest of the mishnayos in this chapter. Just as our mishnah compares and contrasts two things with reference to a specific aspect, so do the following mishnayos (*Meiri;* see also *Tos. Bava Kama* 62b, ד״ה מי קתני אין בין).

אֵין בֵּין אֲדָר הָרִאשׁוֹן לַאֲדָר הַשֵּׁנִי... — *There is no difference between the first Adar and the second Adar ...*

I.e., the fourteenth and fifteenth of the first *Adar,* and the fourteenth and fifteenth of the second *Adar* are identical in that it is forbidden to fast and deliver eulogies on all four of these days *(Rav).* This inference is derived from the statement, *There is no difference between the first Adar and the second (Tur* 697; *Rambam; S'mag).*

אֶלָּא קְרִיאַת הַמְּגִלָּה וּמַתָּנוֹת לָאֶבְיוֹנִים. — *except [as regards] the reading of the Megillah and the giving of gifts to the poor* [which apply to the second *Adar* only *(Kehati)*].

The *Megillah* reading was prescribed for the *Adar* which precedes *Nissan,* i.e., the second *Adar,* in order to celebrate one period of redemption close to another (*Gem.* 6b). [Thus, the *Megillah,* which commemorates the redemption from Haman's decree, should be read close to *Nissan,* the month of the redemption from Egyptian bondage.]

The gifts to the poor, as we have seen, are dependent on the reading of the *Megillah.* Accordingly, if one performed these two precepts in the first *Adar,* he must do so again in the second

There is no difference between the first *Adar* and the second *Adar* except [as regards] the reading of the *Megillah* and the giving of gifts to the poor.

5. There is no difference between [the laws applying to] a holiday and [those applying to] Sabbath except [in laws pertaining to] food.

to discharge his duty. The same ruling applies to *mishloach manos [gifts of food to friends] (Tos. Yom Tov).*

Other authorities are of the opinion that this is true only if the *Megillah* was read on the first *Adar*, and the second *Adar* was added on that very day. In that case, the days would retain the festive nature that had originally been intended for them. If, however, it was known beforehand that there would be a second *Adar*, fasts and eulogies would be permitted on the fourteenth and fifteenth of the first *Adar (Rosh).*

Still other authorities maintain that not only are we forbidden to fast on the fourteenth of the first *Adar*, but we are even required to partake of a festive meal on that day *(Tur; Rif).* Though this last opinion has not been accepted in practice, nevertheless, the fourteenth and fifteenth of the first *Adar* are referred to as פּוּרִים קָטָן, *Minor Purim.* No *Tachanun* is recited and Psalm 20 is omitted, as it is on all minor holidays, because it begins with the words, יַעַנְךָ ה׳ בְּיוֹם צָרָה, *May HASHEM answer you on the day of distress.* It is not fitting to say this on festive occasions. In addition, it is praiseworthy, though not mandatory, to partake of a festive meal *(Shulchan Aruch* 697).

The *Gemara* (6a) notes, however, that the months are dissimilar also with regard to the reading of אַרְבַּע פָּרָשִׁיּוֹת, *four special portions*, discussed in 3:4. They are read only in conjunction with the second *Adar*.

5.

אֵין בֵּין יוֹם טוֹב לְשַׁבָּת... — *There is no difference between [the laws applying to] a holiday and [those applying to] Sabbath ...*

Whatever types of work are forbidden on the Sabbath, are forbidden on festivals as well (with the exception of the labors listed below).

Although the days have this in common, there is a vast difference between the *stringency* of Sabbath and that of festivals. The transgression of the Sabbath is a capital offense, whereas the penalty for profaning a festival is never more serious than מַלְקוּת, *lashes (Rashi; Tos.; Meiri).*

אֶלָּא אֹכֶל נֶפֶשׁ בִּלְבָד. — *except [in laws pertaining to] food.*

On the Sabbath, all types of work are forbidden, even if they are needed for the preparation or the acquisition of food; whereas on festivals, such work is permitted. This exception is specified by Scripture, for after forbidding labor on festivals, it is stated *(Exod.* 12:16): אַךְ אֲשֶׁר יֵאָכֵל לְכָל־נֶפֶשׁ הוּא לְבַדּוֹ יֵעָשֶׂה לָכֶם, *Only that which is eaten by any person, that alone may be done for you.*

Our mishnah implies clearly that even the forms of labor permitted in food-preparation, such as carrying

א
ו

אֵין בֵּין שַׁבָּת לְיוֹם הַכִּפּוּרִים אֶלָּא שֶׁזֶּה זְדוֹנוֹ בִּידֵי אָדָם וְזֶה זְדוֹנוֹ בְּכָרֵת.

[ו] **אֵין** בֵּין הַמֻּדָּר הֲנָאָה מֵחֲבֵרוֹ לַמֻּדָּר מִמֶּנּוּ מַאֲכָל אֶלָּא דְרִיסַת הָרֶגֶל וְכֵלִים שֶׁאֵין עוֹשִׂין בָּהֶן אֹכֶל נֶפֶשׁ.

יד אברהם

in the public domain and cooking, are forbidden for other purposes. The question appears in *Beitzah* 5:2, where it is discussed in detail by the *Gemara* and the commentaries. There, the *Gemara* explains that this is the view only of Beis Shammai. Beis Hillel, however, maintains that whatever types of works are permitted to prepare food, are also permitted for other necessities. For example, according to Beis Hillel, one may carry a child, a *lulav*, or a *Sefer Torah* into a public domain on a holiday, while Beis Shammai forbid such work *(Beitzah* 1:5). As usual, the *halachah* is in accordance with Beis Hillel *(Rav).*

אֵין בֵּין שַׁבָּת לְיוֹם הַכִּפּוּרִים... — *There is no difference between* [*the laws applying to*] *Sabbath and* [*those applying to*] *Yom Kippur* ...

The mishnah refers only to the *severity* of the penalties inflicted upon willful desecrators of the Sabbath and Yom Kippur. Regarding *restrictions*, however, there *are* differences between the two days. On Yom Kippur one must fast and abstain from washing, wearing leather shoes, and so on. On the Sabbath, however, there are no such restrictions *(Meiri).*

Alternatively, the 'similarity' referred to by the mishnah refers only to restrictions of labor common to both. Concerning *those* restrictions, there is no difference except ... *(Tif. Yis.).*

אֶלָּא שֶׁזֶּה זְדוֹנוֹ בִּידֵי אָדָם... — *except that the deliberate desecration of one* [i.e., Sabbath] *is punishable by man,*

[If one desecrates the Sabbath intentionally, after having been warned of the prohibition and the penalty, and witnesses testify to that effect, he is sentenced to סְקִילָה, *skilah* (lit., *stoning)*, by the Court. This punishment was first meted out by the tribunal of Moses which, at God's command, sentenced the wood gatherer to *skilah (Num.* 15:32-36).]

וְזֶה זְדוֹנוֹ בְּכָרֵת. — *but the deliberate desecration of the other* [i.e., Yom Kippur] *is punishable by kares.*

[The deliberate desecration of Yom Kippur is punishable by כָּרֵת, *(kares) spiritual excision and premature death*, decreed by בֵּית דִּין שֶׁל־מַעְלָה, *the Heavenly Tribunal.* This punishment for desecration of Yom Kippur is given in *Lev.* 23:29, 30.]

Although the main punishment for desecration of Yom Kippur is *kares*, one who transgresses willfully is punished by lashes if he does so in the presence of witnesses after having been warned. If lashes are inflicted, the sinner is absolved of *kares (Tos. Yom Tov; Gemara).*

1 6 There is no difference between [the laws applying to] Sabbath and [those applying to] Yom Kippur except that the deliberate desecration of one is punishable by man, but the deliberate desecration of the other is punishable by *kares*.

6. There is no difference between one forbidden by vow to have any benefit from someone else and one forbidden by vow to receive food from him, except for setting foot [on his property] and utensils with which people do not prepare food.

YAD AVRAHAM

6.

◆§ Vows

[This mishnah, which also appears in *Nedarim* 4:1, is based on the verse, אִישׁ כִּי־יִדֹּר נֶדֶר לַה׳ אוֹ־הִשָּׁבַע שְׁבֻעָה לֶאְסֹר אִסָּר עַל־נַפְשׁוֹ לֹא יַחֵל דְּבָרוֹ כְּכָל־הַיֹּצֵא מִפִּיו יַעֲשֶׂה, *If a man makes a vow to HASHEM, or makes an oath to take a prohibition upon himself, he shall not profane his word; according to whatever proceeds from his mouth, he shall do* (*Num.* 30:3).

The mishnah interprets this verse to mean that by means of a vow, a person can prohibit himself from deriving benefit from someone else's property. He may similarly prohibit someone else from deriving benefit from *his* property. Such an interdiction may embrace all conceivable forms of benefit or it may be limited only to benefits which may result in the accumulation or production of food. Although the effects of the vows may be essentially the same, because virtually every form of benefit or profit can enable one to buy, make, or achieve a saving that will indirectly result in having food, there are differences between the vows. The mishnah enumerates the differences.

...אֵין בֵּין הַמֻּדָּר הֲנָאָה מֵחֲבֵרוֹ — *There is no difference between one forbidden by vow to have any benefit from someone else ...*

[One may voluntarily effect such a prohibition by pronouncing a נֶדֶר, *vow*, prohibiting himself from deriving benefit from another's property; or, a person may place a prohibition on his *own* property, thereby forbidding another individual to derive benefit from it.]

...לַמֻּדָּר מִמֶּנּוּ מַאֲכָל — *and one forbidden by now to receive food from him,*

By means of such a vow, one prohibits only benefits connected with *food*. Obviously, it would place a prohibition upon eating the food to which the vow applies. In addition, such vows prohibit any action or contact which will result in a monetary gain or an avoidance of expense, because such money could be used to purchase food (*Nedarim* 33a).

...אֶלָּא דְרִיסַת הָרֶגֶל — *except for setting foot* [*on his property*] ...

Although this is considered a benefit, it is not a benefit for which people receive remuneration. Therefore, since it has no monetary value, it is not considered a benefit from which food is derived. Thus, one whose vow forbids him *any* benefit from another may not even

אֵין בֵּין נְדָרִים לִנְדָבוֹת אֶלָּא שֶׁהַנְּדָרִים חַיָּב א
בְּאַחֲרָיוּתָן, וּנְדָבוֹת אֵינוֹ חַיָּב בְּאַחֲרָיוּתָן. ז

[ז] **אֵין** בֵּין זָב הָרוֹאֶה שְׁתֵּי רְאִיּוֹת לְרוֹאֶה שָׁלֹשׁ אֶלָּא קָרְבָּן.

set foot on his property, whereas he may walk on the property if the vow was limited to benefits solely connected with food *(Rav).*

וְכֵלִים שֶׁאֵין עוֹשִׂין בָּהֶן אֹכֶל נֶפֶשׁ. — *and utensils with which people do not prepare food.*

Only utensils that are not used to prepare food, and that are not customarily rented are referred to here. Since they do not assist in food preparation, nor does their free use constitute a monetary gain, no food can result from their use. If, however, the vow prohibited even non-food use, such utensils are forbidden *(Rav).*

אֵין בֵּין נְדָרִים... — *There is no difference between vows...*

In making a vow one says: הֲרֵי עָלַי, *I take upon myself* to bring a sacrifice. By this declaration, one undertakes a *personal obligation* to designate the animal and bring it as an offering *(Rav).*

לִנְדָבוֹת... — *and gifts ...*

If one says הֲרֵי זוּ, *'This* animal *shall be* a sacrifice' [in which case the obligation is not a *personal* one, as explained below] *(Rav).* The Mishnah's declaration that there is no difference between vows and gifts concerns the precept of לֹא תְאַחֵר, *you shall not delay (Deut.* 23:22), which forbids one to delay the bringing of his offering, whether it be a vow or a gift. This is based on the verse מוֹצָא שְׂפָתֶיךָ תִּשְׁמֹר וְעָשִׂיתָ כַּאֲשֶׁר נָדַרְתָּ לַה' אֱלֹהֶיךָ נְדָבָה, *The expression of your lips you shall observe and do, as* [נָדַרְתָּ] *you have vowed to HASHEM, your God,* [נְדָבָה] *a free will offering ... (Deut.* 23:24). Thus, the Torah compares the gift offering to the vow offering: in both instances delay is prohibited *(Rav).*

[The Talmud derives the positive *mitzvah* that one must bring his offering before the next festival passes. If he tarries past that time he is guilty of noncompliance. If, however, he delays fulfilling his pledge beyond three festival periods, then he has violated an additional negative *mitzvah* (see *Rosh HaShanah* 1:1).]

אֶלָּא שֶׁהַנְּדָרִים חַיָּב בְּאַחֲרָיוּתָן, — *except that concerning vows one is responsible for their security,*

For if one has obligated himself through a vow, he remains responsible for its fulfillment. Therefore, if he set aside a specific animal as his offering, and the animal dies or is stolen through no fault of his own, he must still replace it with another animal *(Rav).*

וּנְדָבוֹת אֵינוֹ חַיָּב בְּאַחֲרָיוּתָן. — *but concerning gifts one is not responsible for their security.*

If he set aside a specific animal for a gift offering, and the animal is no longer available — for example, if the animal died or was stolen — he is not required to replace it with another *(Rav).*

[In the case of the נֶדֶר, *vow offering,* since he assumed a personal obligation to offer a sacrifice, his

There is no difference between vow offerings and gift offerings except that concerning vows one is responsible for their security, but concerning gifts one is not responsible for their security.

7. There is no difference between a *zav* who experiences two issues and one who experiences three, other than [bringing] an offering.

YAD AVRAHAM

obligation is not cancelled by the fact that the animal he chose is no longer available. However, in the case of נְדָבוֹת, *gift offerings,* he obligated himself only to offer a specific animal, but assumed no personal responsibility. Therefore, if that animal becomes unavailable, he is not obligated to offer another animal in its place.]

7.

◆§ Zav

The law of *zav* is found in *Leviticus* 15:1-15: אִישׁ אִישׁ כִּי יִהְיֶה זָב מִבְּשָׂרוֹ זוֹבוֹ טָמֵא הוּא... וְאִישׁ אֲשֶׁר יִגַּע בְּמִשְׁכָּבוֹ יְכַבֵּס בְּגָדָיו וְרָחַץ בַּמַּיִם... וְכִי יִטְהַר הַזָּב מִזּוֹבוֹ וְסָפַר לוֹ שִׁבְעַת יָמִים לְטָהֳרָתוֹ... וּבַיּוֹם הַשְּׁמִינִי יִקַּח לוֹ שְׁתֵּי תֹרִים אוֹ שְׁנֵי בְּנֵי יוֹנָה..., *Any man who will have an issue from his flesh, his issue is contaminated... And any man who will touch his bed shall wash his clothes and bathe himself in water... And when one is cleansed of his issue, he shall count for himself seven days of his cleansing... On the eighth day, he shall take for himself two turtledoves or two young pigeons...*

Scripture teaches that a male who has experienced a gonorrheal issue becomes טָמֵא, *ritually contaminated.* If such issue was repeated, he becomes contaminated to the extent that even a bed or chair upon which he lies or sits becomes contaminated. He transmits this contamination even though his flesh does not come in direct contact with his seat. For example, if a number of cushions are on a chair, and the *zav* sits on them, even the bottom cushion becomes contaminated. When the issue stops, he must count seven 'clean' days during which he experiences no issue. Then he must immerse himself in spring water. If such issue occurred a third time, then in addition to the above counting he must also bring two birds as sacrifices.

The mishnah clarifies which of these laws apply even to a male who experiences two gonorrheal issues, and which apply only to one who experiences three or more.

אֵין בֵּין זָב... — *There is no difference between a zav* [i.e., a male who experienced a gonorrheal issue *(Lev.* 15:1-15)].

הָרוֹאֶה שְׁתֵּי רְאִיּוֹת... — *who experiences two issues* [lit. *sees two sightings*] ...

[Such issues may occur on the same day or two consecutive days.]

לְרוֹאֶה שָׁלֹשׁ... — *And one who experiences three* ...

The three issues may occur in any of the following combinations of days: on one day, on three consecutive days, or two on one day and one on the next *(Rav).*

Such issues render him טָמֵא, *contaminated.* The Torah requires him to count seven consecutive days during which he experiences no issue, and then to immerse himself in a מַעְיָן, *spring.* Thereupon, he becomes cleansed. During this period of *contamination,* any bed upon which he lies and any chair or saddle upon which he sits becomes

א
ו

אֵין בֵּין מְצֹרָע מֻסְגָּר לִמְצֹרָע מֻחְלָט אֶלָּא פְּרִיעָה וּפְרִימָה.

One who experienced three issues is obligated to bring an offering of two turtledoves or two young doves as prescribed by the Torah (*Lev.* 15:14,15). One who experienced only two issues, however, is not required to do so *(Rav)*. [These laws are discussed in the first two chapters of *Zavim.*]

an אַב הַטֻּמְאָה, [*av hatumah*] *contamination of the first grade.* Regarding these laws, one who experienced two issues is no less a *zav* than one who experienced three *(Rav).*

.אֶלָּא קָרְבָּן — *other than* [*bringing*] *an offering.*

◆§ Metzora

צָרַעַת, *tzaraas,* is an affliction mentioned in the Torah. The person stricken with this affliction is known as a מְצֹרָע, *metzora,* or צָרוּעַ, *tzarua.* The symptoms of this ailment are white spots which appear on the skin (*Lev.* 13:1-46). Although *tzaraas* is usually translated as leprosy, the symptoms described by Scripture are not those of leprosy. Moreover, the spontaneous cure mentioned in connection with *tzaraas* is unknown as a cure for leprosy.

From the case of the prophetess Miriam, who was stricken with *tzaraas* for speaking disrespectfully about her brother Moses, the Sages derive that this ailment is a punishment for לְשׁוֹן הָרַע, *slander* (see *Num.* 12:1-16 and commentaries). The Torah exhorts us to remember what God did to Miriam and to beware of the plague of *tzaraas (Deut.* 24:8,9).

Since the *metzora* is guilty of causing strife between friends and discord between husband and wife, he is paid in kind, and is isolated from his friends and family, and even from other contaminated persons.

In the wilderness, the desert habitation of Israel was divided into three camps, and the *metzora* was excluded from all three. In the center of the nation was the מִשְׁכָּן, *Tabernacle,* which was known as מַחֲנֵה שְׁכִינָה, *the camp of the Shechinah* [*Divine Presence*]. All contaminated persons were prohibited from entering this area. Surrounding the Tabernacle area was מַחֲנֵה לְוִיָּה, *the camp of the Levites.* People who had become contaminated through contact with human corpses or other defiling objects were permitted to remain in this camp. *Zavim* (see above) however, were excluded from it. Surrounding the camp of the Levites was מַחֲנֵה יִשְׂרָאֵל, *the camp of the Israelites,* the area of the twelve tribes. In this section, all contaminated persons with the exception of a *metzora* were allowed to remain. *Metzoraim* were expelled from all three camps (see *Rashi* to *Lev.* 13:46).

In *Eretz Yisrael,* the Temple and עֶזְרַת יִשְׂרָאֵל, *the Court of Israelites,* were equivalent to the camp of the *Shechinah;* עֶזְרַת נָשִׁים, *the Women's Court,* and the entire Temple Mount area were equivalent to the camp of the Levites; and the walled Old City of Jerusalem was equivalent to the camp of the Israelites. (See *Rashi, Num.* 5:2.)

Scripture states: וְהַצָּרוּעַ אֲשֶׁר־בּוֹ הַנֶּגַע בְּגָדָיו יִהְיוּ פְרֻמִים וְרֹאשׁוֹ יִהְיֶה פָרוּעַ וְעַל־שָׂפָם יַעְטֶה, *and as for the tzarua in whom is the plague, his garments shall be torn and* [*the hair of*] *his head shall grow wild, and he shall cover his upper lip ... (Lev.* 13:45). The *metzora* must rend his garments like a mourner. His hair must be left to grow wild and remain uncut as long as he is afflicted. He must also cover his head, and his face must be covered as far down as his upper lip. These practices are also similar to those of a mourner. [According to *Minchas Chinuch,* 171, he differs from

There is no difference between a confined *metzora* and a confirmed *metzora* except letting the hair grow wild and rending the garments.

YAD AVRAHAM

the mourner in that he may wear a previously rent garment, whereas a mourner must rend his garment *after* the death of his close relative.]

The primary symptom of *tzaraas* is a white spot on the body. If the spot contains two hairs that have turned white, the person is adjudged a מְצֹרָע מֻחְלָט, *confirmed metzora,* in which case he is subject to all the laws of *tzaraas.* If the hairs are not present, he is isolated for a seven-day period, after which the development of the spot is observed and evaluated. During this stage, he is a מְצֹרָע מֻסְגָּר, *confined metzora,* who is subject to most, but not all laws of *tzaraas.* The determination of whether a particular affliction is or is not *tzaraas* must be made by a *kohen.* The similarities and differences between the *confirmed* and the *confined metzora* are discussed here.

...אֵין בֵּין מְצֹרָע מֻסְגָּר — *There is no difference between a confined metzora...*

If a white spot indicating possible *tzaraas* appears on someone's skin, the potential *metzora* is confined for seven days. At the end of that period, the *kohen* studies the spot once again. If the spot has spread, the *metzora's* status is confirmed (*Lev.* 13:4-8).

There are varying opinions concerning the form of the confinement. According to some commentaries, the *metzora* is confined in a house during these seven days (*Rashi; Ibn Ezra, Lev.* 13:5).

It is not necessary, however, for the *metzora* to be locked in the house like a prisoner. It means merely that his house is not to be open for passersby to visit (*HaKesav VeHakabbalah, Lev.* 13:5).

Radak in *Sefer Hashorashim,* however, states that he must be quarantined so that no one should see him and so that he should not go out among people.

Other commentaries maintain that there is no mention in the Talmud that the confined *metzora* must be isolated in a house. They explain that the 'confinement' is done to the *spot on the skin,* rather than to the afflicted person. A line is drawn outlining the spot so that it can be determined at the end of the week whether it has spread (*Meiri; Tur; Rosh; Sefer HaShorashim* of *R' Yonah Ibn Janach*).

...לִמְצֹרָע מֻחְלָט — *and a confirmed metzora ...*

There are two symptoms which confirm a white spot as *tzaraas* rather than a skin disease: If two or more hairs within the spot changed to white, or if the spot became enlarged during the week of confinement. The white hairs confirm it as *tzaraas* whether they appeared originally or were observed after the week of confinement (*Lev.* 13:3, 7,8).

Regarding the degree of contamination, and the requirement of expulsion from Jerusalem, there is no difference between the two types of *metzoraim* (*Rav; Gem.* 8b).

.אֶלָּא פְּרִיעָה וּפְרִימָה — *except letting the hair grow wild and rending the garments.*

[The מְצֹרָע מֻחְלָט, *confirmed metzora,* must let his hair grow wild and rend his garments. The מְצֹרָע מֻסְגָּר, *confined metzora,* however, is exempt from these requirements.]

Tosefos Yom Tov notes that the

א
ח

אֵין בֵּין טָהוֹר מִתּוֹךְ הֶסְגֵּר לְטָהוֹר מִתּוֹךְ הֶחְלֵט אֶלָּא תִגְלַחַת וְצִפֳּרִים.

[ח] **אֵין** בֵּין סְפָרִים לִתְפִלִּין וּמְזוּזוֹת, אֶלָּא שֶׁהַסְּפָרִים נִכְתָּבִין בְּכָל־לָשׁוֹן, וּתְפִלִּין וּמְזוּזוֹת אֵינָן נִכְתָּבוֹת אֶלָּא אַשּׁוּרִית. רַבָּן שִׁמְעוֹן בֶּן־גַּמְלִיאֵל אוֹמֵר: אַף בַּסְּפָרִים לֹא הִתִּירוּ שֶׁיִּכָּתְבוּ אֶלָּא יְוָנִית.

יד אברהם

confined *metzora* is likewise exempt from the requirement of covering his head as far down as his upper lip [see pref.] but the Mishnah only mentions the first two requirements listed in the verse.

אֵין בֵּין טָהוֹר מִתּוֹךְ הֶסְגֵּר... — *There is no difference between [the laws pertaining to] one who was [pronounced] cleansed after having been confined ...*

[I.e., if the confined *metzora* was pronounced cleansed by the *kohen* because the requisite symptoms for confirmation did not appear.]

לְטָהוֹר מִתּוֹךְ הֶחְלֵט... — *and [those pertaining to] one who was [pronounced] cleansed after having been confirmed ...*

If the white spot disappeared, darkened, or became smaller than the required measurement, the *metzora* is pronounced cleansed. He must, however, immerse himself and his garments. This is also required of a *metzora* who has been pronounced cleansed after having been confined. See *Lev.* 13:6, 14:8 (*Rav; Gem.* 8b).

אֶלָּא תִגְלַחַת וְצִפֳּרִים. — *except for shaving and [bringing] birds.*

The procedure of the cleansing of the *metzora* is given in *Leviticus* 14:1-32. On the first day, he must shave his entire body and carry out a ritual involving two birds, one of which was slaughtered, and the other set free. This procedure was required of a confirmed *metzora,* but not of a confined *metzora.* The sacrifices brought by the confirmed *metzora* on the eighth day were not brought by the confined *metzora.* Our mishnah, however, does not mention this difference because it deals only with those ceremonies performed on the day of cleansing (*Rav; Rashi* 8b).

8.

אֵין בֵּין סְפָרִים... — *There is no difference between [the laws pertaining to] Books [of Scripture] ...*

I.e., Torah, Prophets, and Holy Writings *(Rashi; Tif. Yis.).*

לִתְפִלִּין וּמְזוּזוֹת, — *And [those pertaining to] tefillin and mezuzos...*

Parchment scrolls containing the four paragraphs *Exodus* 13:1-10 and 11-16; *Deuteronomy* 6:4-9 and 11-24, are inserted into *tefillin.* The *mezuzah* is a parchment scroll containing *Deuteronomy* 6:4-9 and 11-24.

There is no difference between them as regards the obligation of sewing them together with sinews;

There is no difference between [the laws pertaining to] one who was [pronounced] cleansed after having been confined and [those pertaining to] one who was [pronounced] cleansed after having been confirmed except for shaving and [bringing] birds.

8. There is no difference between [the laws pertaining to] Books [of Scripture] and [those pertaining to] *tefillin* and *mezuzos* except that Books [of Scripture] may be written in any language, but *tefillin* and *mezuzos* may be written only in Assyrian [script]. Rabban Shimon ben Gamliel says that even Books [of Scripture] were not authorized to be written except [in] Greek.

YAD AVRAHAM

this is required both for Books of Scripture and for *tefillin* and *mezuzos.*

Moreover, all such scrolls are alike in that the hands of one who touches them become contaminated *(Rav; Gem.* 8b). The Rabbis enacted this contamination as a deterrent from touching Torah scrolls without their wrappings (*Shabbos* 14a).

אֶלָּא שֶׁהַסְּפָרִים נִכְתָּבִין בְּכָל־לָשׁוֹן, — *except that Books [of Scripture] may be written in any language,*

Scripture may be written in any language and in any script [i.e., it may be translated into other languages and the Hebrew text may be transliterated in non-Hebrew script *(Rav).*

וּתְפִלִּין וּמְזוּזוֹת אֵינָן נִכְתָּבוֹת אֶלָּא אַשּׁוּרִית. — *but tefillin and mezuzos may be written only in Assyrian [script].*

I.e., Hebrew written in Assyrian characters. The Torah was originally written in ancient Hebrew script like that found on ancient monuments and coins. In the time of King Belshazzar of Babylon, a hand wrote on the wall in a script which no one present could read (*Daniel* 5:7, 8). By conveying His prophecy in this manner, God indicated that there was to be a new holy script to be used for writing Scripture. Ezra wrote the Torah in this new script and called it כְּתָב הַנִּשְׁתְּוָן, *the script that was changed (Ezra* 4:7). This script is used to this very day for Torah Scrolls, Prophets, Megillos, *tefillin,* and *mezuzos (Rashi, Sanhedrin* 22a).

This script is also called כְּתַב אַשּׁוּרִי, *Assyrian* [*Asshuri*] *script,* because it is the most מְאוּשָּׁר, *praiseworthy* of all scripts, and because it was brought to *Eretz Yisrael* via אַשּׁוּר, *Assyria (Yerushalmi).* According to *Piskei HaTosafos* (23) this honor of calling the Torah script אַשּׁוּרִי, *Asshuri,* was accorded Asshur when he went forth from the land of Shinar leaving his children who were rebelling against God by following Nimrod. (See *Rashi, Gen.* 10:11).

רַבָּן שִׁמְעוֹן בֶּן־גַּמְלִיאֵל אוֹמֵר: אַף בַּסְּפָרִים לֹא הִתִּירוּ שֶׁיִּכָּתְבוּ אֶלָּא יְוָנִית. — *Rabban Shimon ben Gamliel says that even Books [of Scripture] were*

א
ט

[ט] אֵין בֵּין כֹּהֵן מָשׁוּחַ בְּשֶׁמֶן הַמִּשְׁחָה לִמְרֻבֵּה בְגָדִים אֶלָּא פַּר הַבָּא עַל-כָּל-הַמִּצְוֹת.
אֵין בֵּין כֹּהֵן מְשַׁמֵּשׁ לְכֹהֵן שֶׁעָבַר אֶלָּא פַּר יוֹם הַכִּפּוּרִים וַעֲשִׂירִית הָאֵיפָה.

not authorized to be written except [*in*] *Greek.*

The only permitted script and language, other than Hebrew, was Greek. This is based on the verse, יַפְתְּ אֱלֹהִים לְיֶפֶת וְיִשְׁכֹּן בְּאָהֳלֵי־שֵׁם, *the most beautiful language with which God endowed Japheth will dwell in the house of Shem (Gen.* 9:27). This is interpreted as referring to Greek, the most beautiful of languages of Japheth. As noted in ArtScroll *Bereishis*, the verse implies that the Greek language and script will be found in the study halls of the descendants of Shem, intimating that Scripture may be written in Greek. Although R' Shimon ben Gamliel's opinion was accepted as halachah, Greek is no longer used for holy texts because, with the passage of time, ancient Greek has been corrupted by other dialects. Thus, books of Scripture must be written in the Hebrew language using Assyrian script (*Rav; Tif. Yis.; Rashi; Gem.* 9b; *Rambam, Tefillin* 1:19).

R' Yehuda maintains that Rabban Shimon ben Gamliel permitted only Torah Scrolls but not other Scriptural books to be written in Greek *(Gem.* 9a; *Rashi).*

9.

אֵין בֵּין כֹּהֵן מָשׁוּחַ בְּשֶׁמֶן הַמִּשְׁחָה... — *There is no difference between the kohen* [*gadol*] *anointed with the oil of anointment...*

Every *kohen gadol* [high priest] from the time of Aaron was anointed with the oil prepared in the wilderness by Moses. This practice was discontinued from the time of King Josiah, when the sanctified oil was hidden *(Rashi; Rav).*

לִמְרֻבֵּה בְגָדִים... — *and the one who donned the additional vestments...*

Kohanim gedolim from King Josiah's time, through the time of the Second Temple were initiated into the high priesthood by donning the שְׁמֹנָה בְגָדִים, *eight special vestments* of the *kohen gadol* as opposed to the כֹּהֵן הֶדְיוֹט, *ordinary kohen,* who wore only four garments (see *Yoma* 7:5). Despite the absence of the oil of anointment, they were, nevertheless, deemed *kohanim gedolim (Rav).*

Thus, the mishnah teaches that there was no difference between the status of *kohanim gedolim* as regards the offering of the *kohen gadol* on Yom Kippur and the meal offering which the *kohen gadol* offered every day — half in the morning and half in the evening *(Tos. Yom Tov ; Gem.* 9b).

אֶלָּא פַּר הַבָּא עַל־כָּל־הַמִּצְוֹת. — *except the bull offered for violation of any of the precepts.*

If the anointed *kohen gadol* renders an incorrect halachic decision permitting a prohibition which

1
9

9. There is no difference between the *kohen* [*gadol*] anointed with the oil of anointment and the one who donned the additional vestments except the bull offered for violation of any of the precepts.

There is no difference between a *kohen* [*gadol*] who is serving and a *kohen* [*gadol*] who is no longer serving except the bull offered on Yom Kippur and the tenth of the *ephah*.

would have been punishable by *kares*, had it been committed willfully, and then acted upon his own decision, he is required to bring a bull as a חַטָּאת, *sin-offering*.

If, however, such an offense is committed by the *kohen gadol* who was invested only through wearing the additional garments, his offering is a ewe or a female goat, like that of an ordinary person. This is deduced from Scripture (*Lev.* 4:3): אִם הַכֹּהֵן הַמָּשִׁיחַ יֶחֱטָא לְאַשְׁמַת הָעָם וְהִקְרִיב עַל חַטָּאתוֹ אֲשֶׁר חָטָא פַּר בֶּן־בָּקָר תָּמִים לַה׳ לְחַטָּאת, *If the anointed kohen sins, causing the guilt of the people, he shall bring for his sin which he committed an unblemished bull to HASHEM for a sin offering*. Here the Torah specifies *the anointed kohen* (*Rav; Rashi*).

אֵין כֹּהֵן מְשַׁמֵּשׁ... — *There is no difference between a kohen* [*gadol*] *who is serving...*

I.e., a *kohen gadol* who was returned to office after having been temporarily disqualified (*Rav*).

לְכֹהֵן שֶׁעָבַר... — *and a kohen* [*gadol*] *who is no longer serving...*

[If the *kohen gadol* becomes contaminated, thereby becoming disqualified from performing the Temple service, another *kohen* is appointed to substitute for him temporarily. When the *kohen gadol* is reinstated, the deposed substitute is known as a כֹּהֵן שֶׁעָבַר, *kohen who is no longer serving*, in contrast to כֹּהֵן מְשַׁמֵּשׁ, *the kohen who is serving*. The mishnah clarifies the status of the substitute *kohen* whose service has ended and differentiates between him and a *kohen gadol* who has been returned to office.]

There is no difference between the two, for though he no longer serves as the *kohen gadol*, the substitute retains that title and its attendant obligations. He continues to wear the eight garments of the *kohen gadol* when he serves in the Temple; he may marry only a virgin; and he may not marry a widow even if she is a virgin. Furthermore, he may continue to serve even while he is an אוֹנֵן, *one whose relative died on that day, or whose dead relative has not yet been buried*. Our mishnah follows the view of R' Meir. However, the *halachah* follows R' Yose who holds that the substitute *kohen gadol* may no longer serve; he has neither the duties of a *kohen gadol*, nor of an ordinary *kohen*. He may not return to wearing the four vestments of an ordinary *kohen* since he once wore the eight vestments of a *kohen gadol*, and we follow the principle that one's degree of holiness may be elevated, but not

א
י

[י] **אֵין** בֵּין בָּמָה גְדוֹלָה לְבָמָה קְטַנָּה אֶלָּא פְסָחִים. זֶה הַכְּלָל: כָּל שֶׁהוּא נִדָּר

יד אברהם

lowered (see *Tos., Yoma* 12b). He may not continue to serve as a *kohen gadol* lest he arouse the jealousy of the original *kohen gadol* *(R' Akiva Eiger; Yoma* 12b).

אֶלָּא פַּר יוֹם הַכִּפּוּרִים... — *except the bull offered on Yom Kippur...*

This sacrifice was brought by the *kohen gadol* as a sin-offering to atone for sins of his fellow *kohanim* (see *Lev.* 16:3, 6, 11).

According to this mishnah, the *kohen* who passed from office has the status of a *kohen gadol* in all respects. Nevertheless, because the Torah provides for only *one* such offering on Yom Kippur, and this is brought by the *kohen gadol*, his erstwhile substitute may not offer a second one *(Rashi; Rav).*

וַעֲשִׂירִית הָאֵיפָה. — *and the tenth of the ephah.*

This is the מִנְחָה, *meal-offering,* known as חֲבִתֵּי כֹּהֵן גָּדוֹל, *pan offering of the kohen gadol.* It was offered every day, half in the morning and half in the evening *(Lev.* 6:12-15).

This too, can be brought only once. Therefore, only the serving *kohen gadol* may bring it *(Rashi; Rav).*

10.

◆§ Bamos

Originally, one who desired to sacrifice to God did so anywhere he chose. Thus, we find that Adam, Cain, Abel, Noah, Abraham, Isaac, and Jacob offered sacrifices in various locations on altars erected by them. No specific place was designated by God for such altars; rather each individual chose a location suited to his needs or connected to an experience that influenced him to offer the sacrifice. Such a private altar was called a בָּמָה [*bamah*], *high place.*

When our forefathers were redeemed from Egypt, they were commanded to erect a מִשְׁכָּן [*Mishkan*], *Tabernacle, (Exod.* 25-27) which would be the dwelling of the *Shechinah,* and which would be the only altar used for offering sacrifices. The Torah strictly prohibited the use of *bamos* during the forty years of wandering in the desert (see *Lev.* 17:1-9). After Israel crossed the Jordan, the nation erected the Tabernacle in Gilgal, where it remained during the fourteen year period of conquest and apportionment of the land. During this era, the use of *bamos* was sanctioned. The *Mishkan* of Gilgal, however, did not have the same status as the *Mishkan* of the wilderness but of a בָּמָה גְדוֹלָה [*bamah gedolah*], *major high place.* Private altars, known as בָּמוֹת קְטַנּוֹת, *minor high places,* or simply, *bamos,* were permitted during this period.

After the land had been apportioned to the tribes, and the people settled in their respective territories, they erected a *Mishkan* in Shiloh *(Joshua* 18:1). The Torah alludes to this *Mishkan* by the term מְנוּחָה, *resting place (Deut.* 12:9), where the Jews rested after their wanderings. During the 369-year era of Shiloh, the use of *bamos* was once again forbidden.

In the time of Eli, Shiloh was destroyed by the Philistines *(I Samuel* 3). The *Mishkan* was then transferred to Nob, the priestly city. After Saul had the *kohanim*

1 10 **10.** There is no difference between [the laws pertaining to] a major *bamah* and [those pertaining to] a lesser *bamah* except [as regards] the *Pesach* sacrifices.

This is the general rule: Any sacrifice which is a vow offering or a gift offering, may be brought on a

YAD AVRAHAM

of Nob executed for collaborating with David (*I Samuel* 22:19), the Tabernacle was transferred to Gibeon. The era of Nob and Gibeon lasted for fifty-seven years, during which *bamos* were again permitted. Nob and Gibeon themselves were deemed *bamos gedolos*, but they lacked the status of the *Mishkan* of Shiloh.

After the construction of the First Temple, *bamos* were again prohibited. Because Jerusalem was referred to as נַחֲלָה, *inheritance* (*Deut.* 12:9), the permanent dwelling of the *Shechinah*, *bamos* remained forbidden even after the destruction of the Temple.

Mishnah 10 describes the similarities and differences between a major *bamah* (such as Gilgal, Nob, or Gibeon) and a minor *bamah* (such as any private altar).

Mishnah 11 describes the similarities and differences between Shiloh and Jerusalem. (For details, see *Zevachim* 14:4-8.)

אֵין בֵּין בָּמָה גְדוֹלָה... — *There is no difference between [the laws pertaining to] a major bamah...*

I.e., an altar used by the entire people of Israel, such as Gilgal, Nob, and Gibeon (*Rav*).

Even though the copper altar in Gibeon was originally fashioned for Moses' *Mishkan*, it was nevertheless deemed a *bamah*, as Scripture states, וַיֵּלֶךְ הַמֶּלֶךְ גִּבְעֹנָה לִזְבֹּחַ שָׁם כִּי־הִיא הַבָּמָה הַגְּדוֹלָה, *And the king went to Gibeon to sacrifice there, for the major high place was there* [*I Kings* 3:4] (*Tos. Yom Tov*).

לְבָמָה קְטַנָּה... — *and [those pertaining to] a lesser bamah...*

I.e., a private altar which anyone could erect for his own personal use during the periods when such *bamos* were permitted (*Rav*).

אֶלָּא פְּסָחִים. — *except [as regards] the Pesach sacrifices.*

Which could be offered on a major *bamah* but not on a private *bamah*. Although the mishnah specifies the Pesach sacrifices, the same law applies to any obligatory sacrifices for whose offering the Torah fixes a time. All such sacrifices are similar to the Pesach lamb which had to be offered on the fourteenth of *Nissan*. This category includes תְּמִידִים, *daily burnt offerings*, and מוּסָפִים, *additional sacrifices*, offered on the Sabbath, *Rosh Chodesh*, and festivals. Obligatory sacrifices which have no fixed time, such as sin offerings, were not offered there (Rav).

זֶה הַכְּלָל: כָּל־שֶׁהוּא נֶדֶר... — *This is the general rule: Any sacrifice which is a vow offering...*

[I.e., any voluntary sacrifice which one may obligate himself to bring by vowing to do so, and subsequently designating an animal for that sacrifice. This includes the עוֹלָה [*olah*], *burnt offering*, and שְׁלָמִים [*shelamim*], *peace offering*.]

וְנִדָּב... — *or a gift offering...*

[I.e., by merely designating an animal for an *olah* or a *shelamim* without accepting personal responsibility by means of a vow.]

א
יא

וְנָדָב קָרֵב בַּבָּמָה. וְכָל שֶׁאֵינוֹ לֹא נָדָר וְלֹא נָדָב אֵינוֹ קָרֵב בַּבָּמָה.

[יא] **אֵין** בֵּין שִׁילֹה לִירוּשָׁלַיִם אֶלָּא שֶׁבְּשִׁילֹה אוֹכְלִים קָדָשִׁים קַלִּים וּמַעֲשֵׂר שֵׁנִי בְּכָל־הָרוֹאֶה, וּבִירוּשָׁלַיִם לִפְנִים מִן הַחוֹמָה. וְכָאן וְכָאן קָדְשֵׁי קָדָשִׁים נֶאֱכָלִים לִפְנִים מִן הַקְּלָעִים.

קְדֻשַּׁת שִׁילֹה יֵשׁ אַחֲרֶיהָ הֶתֵּר וּקְדֻשַּׁת יְרוּשָׁלַיִם אֵין אַחֲרֶיהָ הֶתֵּר.

יד אברהם

קָרֵב בַּבָּמָה. — *may be brought on a bamah,*

I.e., on a lesser *bamah (Rashi; Tif. Yis.).*

וְכָל שֶׁאֵינוֹ לֹא נָדָר וְלֹא נָדָב אֵינוֹ קָרֵב בַּבָּמָה. — *but any sacrifice that is not a vow offering or a gift offering may not be brought on a bamah.*

[I.e., on a lesser *bamah*. On a major *bamah*, however, any mandatory sacrifice which has a fixed time may be offered (see above). The principle stated by the mishnah is that a lesser *bamah* may be used for any offering which one may choose whether to bring or not.]

11.

אֵין בֵּין שִׁילֹה... — *There is no difference between [the laws pertaining to the Tabernacle at] Shiloh...*

I.e., when the national *Mishkan* was standing at Shiloh *(Tif. Yis.;* see pref. to mishnah 10).

לִירוּשָׁלַיִם... — *and [those pertaining to the Temple in] Jerusalem...*

I.e., after the building of the Temple *(Tif. Yis.).*

אֶלָּא שֶׁבְּשִׁילֹה אוֹכְלִים קָדָשִׁים קַלִּים... — *except that in Shiloh one was permitted to eat kodoshim kallim...*

These are sacrifices of lesser sanctity, such as בְּכוֹר, *firstborn animals;* מַעֲשֵׂר בְּהֵמָה, *animal tithes;* שְׁלָמִים, *peace offerings;* and פֶּסַח, *Pesach.* (For details, see *Zevachim,* ch. 5).

וּמַעֲשֵׂר שֵׁנִי... — *and second tithes...*

After the *first tithe* has been given to the Levite, the owner of the grain or fruit separates a second tithe which he himself eats in Jerusalem *(Deut.* 14:12-27).

During the era of Gilgal, while the land was being conquered and apportioned, there was no obligation to tithe produce. During the period of Shiloh, however, when the land had already been apportioned, there was an obligation to tithe produce *(Tif. Yis.; Rav; Zevachim* 14:6).

1
11

bamah, but any sacrifice that is not a vow offering or a gift offering cannot be brought on a *bamah.*

11. There is no difference between [the laws pertaining to the Tabernacle at] Shiloh and [those pertaining to the Temple in] Jerusalem except that in Shiloh one was permitted to eat *kodoshim kallim* and second tithes anywhere within sight [of Shiloh], but in Jerusalem [one was only permitted to do so] within the walls. Both here and there *kodshei kodoshim* were permitted to be eaten only within the curtains.

After the sanctity of Shiloh, *bamos* were permitted, but after the sanctification of Jerusalem, *bamos* were not permitted.

בְּכָל־הָרוֹאֶה, — *anywhere within sight [of Shiloh],*

I.e., any location from which the *town* of Shiloh is visible. Others explain that קָדָשִׁים קַלִּים, *sacrifices of lesser sanctity*, and the second tithe might be eaten only in places from which the *Mishkan* of Shiloh was visible *(Rambam, Zevachim* 14:6).

וּבִירוּשָׁלַיִם לִפְנִים מִן הַחוֹמָה. — *but in Jerusalem, [one was only permitted to do so] within the walls.*

[I.e., such foods may be eaten only within Jerusalem's walls, rather than merely within sight of the city.]

וְכָאן וְכָאן... — *Both here and there* [i.e., both in Shiloh and in Jerusalem]...

קָדְשֵׁי קָדָשִׁים... — *Kodshei kodoshim ...*

These are sacrifices of the highest sanctity, such as חַטָּאת, *sin-offering*, and אָשָׁם, *guilt-offering (Zevachim*, ch. 5).]

נֶאֱכָלִים לִפְנִים מִן הַקְּלָעִים. — *were permitted to be eaten only within the curtains.*

I.e., *kodshei kodoshim* were eaten only within the confines of the Temple court, or within the courtyard of *Mishkan* Shiloh. Since the yard of the *Mishkan* in the desert was enclosed by curtains, the Temple court, which was enclosed by a wall is described as 'within the curtains' *(Rav, Zevachim* 5:3; *Rashi).*

Others explain that the expression is used in deference to Shiloh, which was also enclosed by curtains *(Ritva).*

קְדֻשַּׁת שִׁילֹה יֵשׁ אַחֲרֶיהָ הֶתֵּר... — *After the sanctity of Shiloh, bamos were permitted* [lit., *there was permission*],

I.e., after Shiloh was destroyed, *bamos* were permitted during the era of Nob and Gibeon. (See pref. to Mishnah 10).

ב
א

[א] הַקּוֹרֵא אֶת־הַמְּגִלָּה לְמַפְרֵעַ, לֹא יָצָא. קְרָאָהּ עַל פֶּה, קְרָאָהּ תַּרְגּוּם, בְּכָל לָשׁוֹן — לֹא יָצָא. אֲבָל קוֹרִין אוֹתָהּ לַלּוֹעֲזוֹת בְּלַעַז. וְהַלּוֹעֵז שֶׁשָּׁמַע אַשּׁוּרִית, יָצָא.

יד אברהם

וּקְדֻשַּׁת יְרוּשָׁלַיִם אֵין אַחֲרֶיהָ הֶתֵּר. — *but after the sanctification of Jerusalem, bamos were not permitted* [lit. *there was no permission*].

Jerusalem is called נַחֲלָה, *heritage*, i.e., the *permanent* home of the *Shechinah*. [Therefore, even after the destruction of the Temple, *bamos* remain forbidden] *(Tos. Yom Tov, Zevachim* 14:8).

Chapter 2

1.

הַקּוֹרֵא אֶת־הַמְּגִלָּה לְמַפְרֵעַ, — *If someone read the Megillah out of sequence,*

I.e., if one read a later section before an earlier one *(Tif. Yis.)*.

לֹא יָצָא. — *he has not fulfilled his obligation.*

Thus, if one reads the first verse, omits the next, continues with the third and then goes back to the second, after which he reads the fourth verse, he has not fulfilled his obligation because he has not read the verses in their proper sequence. Therefore, if one omitted a verse, he cannot merely read that verse itself, but must read the entire *Megillah* from the omitted verse to the end *(Shulchan Aruch, Orach Chaim* 690:6).

The verse states, וְהַיָּמִים הָאֵלֶּה נִזְכָּרִים וְנַעֲשִׂים, *and these days should be remembered and celebrated (Esther* 9:28). Just as the order of days cannot be reversed (i.e., the fifteenth day cannot come before the fourteenth), so too the remembrance (i.e., the reading of the *Megillah* itself) cannot be in reverse order *(Rav)*.

If one were to read the *Megillah* out of sequence, the narrative would be completely distorted. Since the purpose of the reading is פִּרְסוּמֵי נִיסָא, *publicizing the miracle,* he would be presenting an improper picture of the occurrence. Therefore, he would not have fulfilled his obligation *(Meiri)*.

קְרָאָהּ עַל פֶּה, — *If he read it by heart,*

If one read the *Megillah* from memory instead of from a written text, he did not fulfill his obligation. We derive this with an analogy to the Torah's statement, כְּתֹב זֹאת זִכָּרוֹן בַּסֵּפֶר, *write this us a remembrance in the Book (Exod.* 17:14): Just as the remembrance mentioned in connection with Amalek must be written in the Book, so too, the *remembrance* of the miracle of Purim — which is an instance of a battle against Amalek — must be from a written text *(Rav)*.

If the precept is simply to remember the miracle of Purim, why is it necessary to read the words *aloud?* Could one not fulfill the obligation by *glancing* at the text? In reply, the *Talmud* draws another analogy to the verse concerning Amalek. The Torah says, זָכוֹר ... לֹא תִּשְׁכָּח, *remember ... do not forget (Deut.* 25:17-19). Had the precept been

2 1. If someone read the *Megillah* out of sequence, he
1 has not fulfilled his obligation. If he read it by heart, or if he read it in *Targum* or in any other language, he has not fulfilled his obligation. However, we may read it for those who speak a foreign language in a foreign language. One who speaks a foreign language and heard it [read in Hebrew that was written] in Assyrian [script] has fulfilled his obligation.

simply to remember the evil of Amalek, the Torah could have merely said *do not forget.* The added admonition *remember* teaches us that we must read the words aloud *(Tos. Yom Tov).*

קְרָאָהּ תַּרְגּוּם, — [*or*] *if he read it in Targum ...*

I.e., if one read the *Megillah* in its Aramaic translation, but did not understand what he read *(Tif. Yis.).*

בְּכָל־לָשׁוֹן — לֹא יָצָא. — *Or in any other language, he has not fulfilled his obligation.*

I.e., if one reads the *Megillah* in any language which he does not understand [with the exception of Hebrew], he has not fulfilled his obligation *(Tif. Yis.).*

This statement is a continuation of the previous one; just as one who reads the *Megillah* in Aramaic has not fulfilled his obligation [unless he understands Aramaic], so too, one who reads it in any other foreign language has obviously not fulfilled his obligation unless he understands what he has read *(Tos. Yom Tov; Rashi).*

[Lest one think that he may read the *Megillah* in Aramaic even without understanding it, because Aramaic is a holy tongue, the Tanna informs us that one can fulfill the obligation only in Hebrew or in a language which he understands.]

אֲבָל קוֹרִין אוֹתָהּ לְלוֹעֲזוֹת בְּלַעַז. — *However, we may read it for those who speak a foreign language in a foreign language.*

Foreigners may hear the *Megillah* in their own language provided it is written in that language. But, for example, if one translates aloud in English as he reads from a Hebrew text, it is considered to have been read by heart *(Rav).*

Most authorities maintain that one who understands Hebrew may not fulfill his obligation to read the *Megillah* by reading in any other language. Thus, one who understands Hebrew may not read the *Megillah* in another language to discharge the obligation of those who do not understand Hebrew. Since he cannot fulfill his *own* obligation in that language, he cannot discharge the obligation of others *(Ramban; Rashba; Ran).*

Other authorities, however, maintain that even one who understands Hebrew may read the *Megillah,* and thereby fulfill his obligation, in a foreign language which he understands *(Rashi; Rambam).*

[In practice, it is virtually impossible to consider reading the *Megillah* in a foreign language. The scroll would have to be written on proper parchment and with kosher ink, with the care required in holy

ב ב [ב] **קְרָאָהּ** סֵרוּגִין וּמִתְנַמְנֵם, יָצָא. הָיָה כּוֹתְבָהּ, דּוֹרְשָׁהּ וּמַגִּיהָהּ: אִם כִּוֵּן לִבּוֹ, יָצָא; וְאִם לָאו, לֹא יָצָא.

יד אברהם

scrolls. Furthermore, the translation would have to be literal and accurate, a condition that even the early sages found difficult to fulfill. Other difficulties are enumerated in *Shulchan Aruch* 690:8-11 (see *Mishnah Berurah).*]

לַעַז denotes any language other than Hebrew. The word is found in its adjectival form in *Psalms* 114:1, מֵעַם לֹעֵז, *from a people who speak a foreign tongue (Tos. Yom Tov).* Hence, the expression בְּלַעַז often found in *Rashi's* commentary is a Hebrew word meaning *in a foreign tongue.* The word is not an abbreviation of לְשׁוֹן עַם זָר, *tongue of a strange people,* as is often supposed *(Berliner).*

וְהַלּוֹעֵז שֶׁשָּׁמַע אַשּׁוּרִית, — *One who speaks a foreign language and heard it* [read in Hebrew that was written] *in Assyrian* [script] ...

[He heard the *Megillah* read in Hebrew from a scroll that was written, not in ancient Hebrew script, but in the script the Jews brought back from Assyria. Assyrian script came to be used for all sacred scrolls: Torahs, *tefillin, mezuzos,* and *megillos.* See above 1:8.]

The same is true if the *Megillah* was read in ancient Greek, as seen previously [1:8] *(Rav).*

Ancient Greek was considered different from other foreign languages in that it was widely understood and spoken. Under Ptolemy, the Torah had been translated into Greek. This translation, known as the Septuagint, was very popular. Thus, one who heard it read in ancient Greek would understand most of what was being read. In this sense, it was the same as Hebrew *(Rambam).*

According to *Rambam's* interpretation, the Tanna specifically mentioned Aramaic because that language was widely spoken and understood. Today, however, ancient Greek and Aramaic are no longer spoken languages; therefore, we read the *Megillah* in Hebrew only (see *Rav* 1:8).

יָצָא. — *has fulfilled his obligation.*

I.e., even if he does not understand Hebrew. Just as most of us fulfill our obligation although we do not understand the meaning of the Persian phrases in the *Megillah* [e.g., הָאֲחַשְׁתְּרָנִים בְּנֵי הָרַמָּכִים *(Esther* 8:10)], so too, one who understands no Hebrew fulfills his obligation inasmuch as the reading and the publicizing of the miracle have been accomplished (*Tos. Yom Tov* from *Gem.* 18a).

One who hears the *Megillah* being read will ask others to explain the parts he does not understand; thus the story of the miracle will be publicized *(Rashi* 1:8).[1]

1. [Although one could say about any language that listeners will inquire about the parts which they do not understand, Hebrew is uniquely preeminent as the language in which the *Megillah* should be read because it is the language in which it was written originally. Also, because it is inherently sacred. Therefore, if one reads the *Megillah* in Hebrew, he discharges his obligation even though he fails to understand the language.

The other element involved in the reading of the *Megillah,* that of פִּרְסוּמֵי נִיסָא, *publicizing the miracle,* is supplementary to the *mitzvah* of the reading. This is ac-

2. If one read it discontinuously, or while half asleep, he has fulfilled his obligation. If one was writing it, expounding upon it, or correcting it, provided he had intent, he fulfilled his obligation; if not, he did not fulfill his obligation.

YAD AVRAHAM

2.

קָרְאָהּ סֵרוּגִין... — *If one read it discontinuously,*

I.e., if one reads part of the *Megillah*, pauses, and then resumes reading. Even if the entire reading could have been completed during the pause, he has, as the Mishnah proceeds to teach, fulfilled his obligation *(Rav).*

If one conversed during this pause, although he is deserving of reprimand, he has fulfilled his obligation *(Rama* 690:5).

If, however, one conversed during the reading itself, even if he missed hearing only one word, he has not fulfilled his obligation (*Mishnah Berurah; Pri Megadim* 690:19).

וּמִתְנַמְנֵם, יָצָא. — *or, while half asleep, he has fulfilled his obligation.*[1]

Half asleep is described as 'asleep, yet not asleep; awake, yet not awake.' If one calls him, he will answer, but he cannot give an answer that requires thought. If he is reminded of what was said, however, he remembers *(Gem.* 18b, according to *Rashi).*

Pri Megadim explains that though one is half asleep, he can still be considered sufficiently awake to have the degree of intent necessary to fulfill his obligation. *Mishnah Berurah*, however, questions this ruling and maintains that the Mishnah is referring to one who *began* the reading with proper intent while mentally alert. He *subsequently* became drowsy during the reading *(Shaar HaTziun* 690:39).

[Although according to the above-cited reasoning, one who woke up and is still drowsy could not have the necessary degree of intent, *Beur Halachah* quotes the vast number of *poskim* who maintain that there is no difference whether one is half asleep on the way to falling into deeper sleep, or if he is half asleep while awakening. In either case he fulfills his obligation.]

הָיָה כּוֹתְבָהּ, — *If one was writing it,*

When a scribe is in the process of writing a new *Megillah*, he copies from a complete *Megillah*, and reads each sentence aloud before transcribing it. Accordingly, this Mishnah teaches that since he reads from a complete *Megillah*, a scribe can fulfill his obligation of reading the *Megillah* in this manner *(Rav).*

Even though he pauses after each sentence in order to write, he fulfills his obligation [provided that when

complished by arousing the curiosity of the listeners and answering their questions.

If one reads the *Megillah* in a language other than Hebrew, the *mitzvah* is accomplished primarily through פִּרְסוּמֵי נִיסָא, *publicizing the miracle*, since his reading lacks the sanctity of Hebrew. If, however, one does not understand the language, the reading has accomplished nothing.]

1. There is a well known controversy in the Talmud as to whether מִצְוֹת צְרִיכוֹת כַּוָּנָה, *precepts need intent*, or not — i.e., when one fulfills a precept, is he required to

ב ב הָיְתָה כְתוּבָה בְּסַם וּבְסִקְרָא וּבְקוֹמוֹס וּבְקַנְקַנְתּוֹם, עַל־הַנְּיָר וְעַל־הַדִּפְתְּרָא — לֹא יָצָא, עַד שֶׁתְּהֵא כְתוּבָה אַשּׁוּרִית עַל־הַסֵּפֶר וּבִדְיוֹ.

יד אברהם

he reads the sentences, he does so with intent to fulfill the precept] *(Tif. Yis.)*.

...דּוֹרְשָׁהּ — *expounding upon it,*

If, as one read each sentence, he paused to explain it, he has fulfilled his obligation despite the verbal interruption *(Tif. Yis.)*.

:וּמַגִּיהָהּ — *or correcting it,*

I.e., he was reading the *Megillah* to check for misspellings, occasionally pausing to make corrections *(Tif. Yis.)*.

;אִם כִּוֵּן לִבּוֹ, יָצָא — *provided he had intent* [lit. *he directed his heart*], *he fulfilled his obligation.*

In the three cases cited above, one fulfills his obligation *provided he had conscious intent to do so (Rav)* [for one can have dual intent: to check the *Megillah* and, at the same time, to fulfill the obligation of reading it.]

.וְאִם לָאו, לֹא יָצָא — *if not* [i.e., if he did not consciously intend that his reading serve to fulfill his obligation *(Rav)*], *he did not fulfill his obligation.*

☙The second part of this Mishnah deals with the materials necessary for writing a *Megillah.* All such requirements relate only to the reader's scroll, the one used for the reading which discharges the listeners of their obligation. For purposes of study or *following* the *Megillah* reading, any printed or written copy is adequate.

...הָיְתָה כְתוּבָה בְּסַם — *If it was written with orpiment...*

The translation follows *Rashi* who renders yellow arsenic. *Rambam* and *Rav* render an ink derived from a grass root.

be mindful that his act is intended to fulfill a specific precept, or is it sufficient to perform the act without any conscious intent? The question is discussed in reference to reciting the *Shema*, eating *matzah*, blowing *shofar*, reading the *Megillah*, and numerous other *mitzvos*. Those who maintain that precepts require intent, base their view on the Mishnah (*Berachos* 2:1) which rules that one fulfills the precept of reading the *Shema* only if such were his intentions at the time of his recital. This is the accepted ruling, and we shall explain this Mishnah accordingly (see *Shulchan Aruch* 60:3; 690:12).

Some maintain that only Torah precepts require intent whereas Rabbinical enactments do not *(Magen Avraham; Radbaz* 60:3).

The *Megillah* reading, though of Rabbinic origin, has many of the stringencies of Torah precepts (see pref. to the tractate). Thus, its reading also requires intent. However, this is only true of the daytime reading which is ordained by the *Megillah* (*Esther* 9:27); the nighttime reading, however, is solely a Rabbinical enactment *(Shaar HaTziun* 690:41).

Other authorities maintain that there is no difference between Torah precepts and Rabbinical ordinances as regards the requirement of intent. Thus, both readings must be done with intent to fulfill the obligation *(Mishnah Berurah* 60:10; *Shaar HaTziun* 690:41).

2
2 If it was written with orpiment, vermilion, gum, or ferrous sulfate, or on paper, or on unfinished parchment, he did not fulfill his obligation, unless it is written in Assyrian [script] on parchment and with ink.

YAD AVRAHAM

וּבְסִקְרָא... — *(or with) vermilion,*

Rashi translates this as a red dye. *Rav* and *Tiferes Yisrael* maintain that it is a red chalk.

וּבְקוֹמוֹס... — *(or with) gum,*

Rashi, Rav, and *Tiferes Yisrael* render this as gum arabic which is used in the manufacture of ink. According to *Rambam,* it is a type of yellow earth.

וּבְקַנְקַנְתּוֹם, — *(or with) ferrous sulfate,*

This is also known as copperas or vitriol *(Tosafos; Rambam; Rav).*

עַל־הַנְּיָר... — [*or if it were written*] *on paper,*

This paper was manufactured from grass *(Rashi; Rav)* [and although the Mishnah probably refers to papyrus, today's modern papers would apparently fall into this category].

וְעַל־הַדִּפְתְּרָא — — *or on unfinished parchment,*

I.e., on animal skin treated with salt and flour, but not with gall-nuts *(Rav).*

לֹא יָצָא, — *he did not fulfill his obligation.*

[I.e., if he read from a *Megillah* written with one of the aforementioned inks or on unfinished parchment.]

עַד שֶׁתְּהֵא כְתוּבָה אַשּׁוּרִית... — *unless it is written in Assyrian* [*script*] ...

[I.e., if written in Hebrew, it must be written in Assyrian script (see 1:8).]

עַל־הַסֵּפֶר... — *on parchment* [lit. *on the book*] ...

[A *Megillah* must be written on the same type of material on which other סִפְרֵי קֹדֶשׁ, *holy Books,* must be written.]

וּבִדְיוֹ. — *and with ink.*

I.e., with black ink that maintains its color on parchment *(Tif. Yis.).*

Nowadays, it is customary to make ink for sacred use from a combination of ferrous sulfate, gall-nuts and gum arabic, which form a stable thick black compound *(Mishnah Berurah* 32:8).

3.

Residency requirements

Our interpretation of Mishnah 3 follows *Mishnah Berurah's* introduction and explanation of the *halachah* discussed here. It is based on the *Kessef Mishneh, Maggid Mishnah,* and *Beur HaGra.*

Three principles should be kept in mind:

1. One who lives in a place for even one day reads the *Megillah* as do the

ב
ג

[ג] **בֶּן־עִיר** שֶׁהָלַךְ לִכְרַךְ וּבֶן כְּרַךְ שֶׁהָלַךְ לְעִיר: אִם עָתִיד לַחֲזוֹר לִמְקוֹמוֹ, קוֹרֵא כִּמְקוֹמוֹ; וְאִם לָאו, קוֹרֵא עִמָּהֶן.

מֵהֵיכָן קוֹרֵא אָדָם אֶת־הַמְּגִלָּה וְיוֹצֵא בָהּ יְדֵי חוֹבָתוֹ? רַבִּי מֵאִיר אוֹמֵר: כֻּלָּהּ. רַבִּי יְהוּדָה אוֹמֵר: מֵ ,,אִישׁ יְהוּדִי". רַבִּי יוֹסֵי אוֹמֵר: מֵ ,,אַחַר הַדְּבָרִים הָאֵלֶּה".

יד אברהם

citizens of that place — on the fourteenth in an unwalled city, or on the fifteenth in a walled city. This is true only if he is in that place on the day the *Megillah* is read *there*, irrespective of the reading date in his permanent residence.

2. The main reading of the *Megillah* is the daytime reading, as has been noted in the pref. to the tractate. Hence, acquiring the status of a city or town dweller, is contingent upon one's intended presence in that locale in the daylight hours of Purim.

3. In order to acquire the status of a resident in any place other than his home city, one must have left his home with the intention of spending Purim in the new location. For example, if one went to Jerusalem (where Purim is celebrated on the fifteenth) with the intention of being there on the fifteenth, he reads the *Megillah only* on the fifteenth as do Jerusalemites, but *not* on the fourteenth, the day of reading in his hometown. If, however, he planned to be home before Purim, then he would read on the fourteenth even if he was detained and forced to remain in Jerusalem throughout the fourteenth *and* fifteenth.

בֶּן־עִיר שֶׁהָלַךְ לִכְרַךְ... — *A townsman who went to a walled city,*

If one who lives in an unwalled town or city where the *Megillah* is read on the fourteenth of *Adar* went to a walled city where the *Megillah* is read on the fifteenth of *Adar* *(Rashi; Rav).*

וּבֶן־כְּרַךְ שֶׁהָלַךְ לְעִיר: — *or a city dweller who went to a town,*

[I.e., if one who lives in a walled city where the *Megillah* is read on the fifteenth of *Adar* went to a city where the *Megillah* is read on the fourteenth.]

אִם עָתִיד לַחֲזוֹר לִמְקוֹמוֹ, — *if he intends to return to his home* [lit. *place*],

At the time he left, he intended to return home before the day on which the *Megillah* was to be read in the place he is visiting. He was delayed, however, and could not return home in time *(Tif. Yis.).*

קוֹרֵא כִּמְקוֹמוֹ: — *he reads* [at the same time] *as in his home;*

Although he was detained in the place he is visiting, he reads the *Megillah* on the day it is read in his *home* city, even though that is dif-

2
3

3. A townsman who went to a walled city, or a city dweller who went to a town, if he intends to return to his home, he reads [at the same time] as in his home; but if not, he reads with them.

From what part of the *Megillah* must one read in order to fulfill his obligation? R' Meir says: All of it. R' Yehudah says: From *'There was a Jewish man.'* R' Yose says: From *'After these things.'*

ferent from the day it is to be read where he is spending Purim (*Mishnah Berurah* 688:12).

וְאִם לָאו, — *but if not,*

I.e., if he does not intend to return home before dawn of the day on which the *Megillah* is read in the place he is visiting *(Rav).*

קוֹרֵא עִמָּהֶן. — *he reads with them.*

I.e., he assumes the status of a resident of the place he is visiting and reads *Megillah* on the same day as the other residents of that locale *(Rav).*

Thus, someone who goes to a walled city with the intention of remaining there until after dawn of the fifteenth, reads the *Megillah* on the fifteenth. Similarly, if a walled city resident goes to a town and intends to remain there until after dawn of the fourteenth, he reads the *Megillah* on the fourteenth. However, if he returns home before dawn of the fifteenth, he must read the *Megillah* again (*Mishnah Berurah* 688:12).

מֵהֵיכָן קוֹרֵא אָדָם אֶת־הַמְּגִלָּה וְיוֹצֵא בָהּ יְדֵי חוֹבָתוֹ? — *From what part of the Megillah must one read in order to fulfill his obligation?*

From which verse must one commence his reading in order to fulfill the obligation derived from the verse וַתִּכְתֹּב אֶסְתֵּר ... וּמָרְדֳּכַי ... אֶת־כָּל־תֹּקֶף, *And Esther ... and Mordechai ... wrote all the acts of power (Esther* 9:29); i.e., what part of the *Megillah* is meant by *acts of power? (Tos. Yom Tov: Gem.* 19a).

ר' מֵאִיר אוֹמֵר: כֻּלָּהּ. — *R' Meir says: All of it.*

R' Meir explains that תֹּקֶף refers to the *power* of Ahasuerus; therefore, one must read the *entire Megillah* [which begins with a description of the vastness of Ahasuerus' realm] (*Gem.* 19a).

ר' יְהוּדָה אוֹמֵר: מֵ"אִישׁ יְהוּדִי". — *R' Yehudah says: From 'There was a Jewish man'* [*Esther* 2:5].

R' Yehudah explains that the reference is to the *power* of Mordechai; therefore, one begins the reading from the section describing Mordechai's accomplishments (*Gem.* 19a).

ר' יוֹסֵי אוֹמֵר: מֵ"אַחַר הַדְּבָרִים הָאֵלֶּה". — *R' Yose says: From 'After these things'* [*Esther* 3:1].

R' Yose explains that the *power* of Haman is referred to here; therefore, one need begin the reading only from the narration of Haman's rise to power (*Gem.* 19a).

The *halachah* is in accordance with R' Meir *(Rav).* [Therefore, to fulfill the obligation, one must read the entire *Megillah.*]

ב [ד] **הַכֹּל** כְּשֵׁרִין לִקְרוֹת אֶת־הַמְּגִלָּה, חוּץ
ד מֵחֵרֵשׁ, שׁוֹטֶה וְקָטָן. רַבִּי יְהוּדָה
מַכְשִׁיר בְּקָטָן.

יד אברהם

4.

הַכֹּל כְּשֵׁרִין לִקְרוֹת אֶת־הַמְּגִלָּה, — *All are qualified to read the Megillah...*

This includes women. Though the reading of the *Megillah* is a מִצְוַת עֲשֵׂה שֶׁהַזְּמַן גְּרָמָא, *a positive precept dependent upon a set time,* and women are normally not required to observe such precepts (see *Kiddushin* 1:7), nevertheless because they were included in the decree to be killed, and were thus beneficiaries of the miracle of salvation — they are required to observe the precept. Some authorities maintain that their obligation is equal to that of men; therefore, they may even read the *Megillah* for men *(Rashi, Arachin* 3a).

There is a dispute as to whether the argument that *women were included in the miracle* is strong enough to obligate them equally with men, or whether it was the reasoning for a separate Rabbinic enactment requiring women to *hear* the *Megillah* reading but not obligating them to read it. [According to this latter opinion, there are two distinct *mitzvos* regarding reading the *Megillah:* the *original precept* of reading the *Megillah* on a specific day, inherently excluding women since the precept is dependent upon a set time; and, a second enactment *extending the obligation* to women.] Thus, women may read for other women but not for men. [The accepted practice is for women to listen to the *Megillah* being read by a man *(Tif. Yis.).*] Although such *reading* may be accomplished by an agent, that agent must be obligated to at least the same degree as the one for whome he is reading (*Halachos Gedolos; Tos.* 4a).

Other reasons that women do not read the *Megillah* to enable men to fulfill their obligation are:

— *Megillah* reading is comparable to Torah reading, concerning which the Talmud states that a woman should not read, out of respect for the congregation *(Magen Avraham* 689:5);

— קוֹל בְּאִשָּׁה עֶרְוָה, [for a man to listen to] *a woman's [singing] voice is an act of immodesty (Orchos Chaim).*

חוּץ מֵחֵרֵשׁ, — *except one who is deaf,*

Although חֵרֵשׁ generally refers to a *deaf-mute* totally devoid of hearing and speech (*Terumos* 1:2), the Mishnah here obviously refers to one who is capable of speech and is fully intelligent; deafness is his only handicap *(Tosafos).*

Our Mishnah is in accordance with R' Yose *(Berachos* 2:3) who maintains that if one reads the *Shema* without hearing the words, he has not fulfilled his obligation. The same rule applies to *Megillah* reading. Thus, one who is deaf cannot fulfill the obligation. The *halachah* however, is in accordance with R' Yehudah who maintains that one fulfills his obligation of reading the *Shema* [and the *Megillah*] even if he does not hear the words that he is reading *(Rav; Tos. Yom Tov).*

Others differentiate between the readings of *Shema* and of the *Megillah.* Since the purpose of reading the *Megillah* is to publicize

2 **4.** All are qualified to read the *Megillah* except one
4 who is deaf, an imbecile, or a minor. R' Yehudah declares a minor qualified.

YAD AVRAHAM

the miracle of Purim, one can only fulfill his obligation by reading it aloud or hearing it read. The precept of the *Shema*, on the other hand, is simply to recite it; hence, one can fulfill his obligation even if he cannot hear himself *(Beis Yosef* 689).[1]

[Thus our Mishnah can be in accordance with the halachically accepted view of R' Yehudah that a deaf person is obligated in the reading of the *Shema*. Since the *Megillah* reading has the additional purpose of publicizing the miracle, R' Yehudah would agree that deaf people are excluded.]

...שׁוֹטֶה — *Or an imbecile,*

[The word 'imbecile' is not used here in its technical sense of one whose mental development does not exceed that of a seven or eight year old. It refers to one who is wont to commit senseless acts. One example of 'imbecile' is given in *Chagigah* (4a) as: הַמְאַבֵּד כָּל־מַה שֶׁנּוֹתְנִין לוֹ, *one who destroys whatever is given to him.*

Because of his limited mental capacity, he is not required to read the *Megillah* himself, therefore, he cannot discharge the obligation of others by reading for them.]

.וְקָטָן — *or a child.*

I.e., a minor who is old enough to be trained to read the *Megillah*. There is a superficial similarity between the obligations of adults and minors in that both are required by Rabbinic enactment to hear the *Megillah* — adults, because the basic *Megillah* reading is Rabbinic in origin, and minors, because the Sages ordained that they be trained to perform commandments. Nevertheless, the obligation of minors is inferior because their *Megillah* reading involves two Rabbinic obligations: (1) their obligation to perform *mitzvos* in general, and (2) the obligation to read the *Megillah;* whereas adults are required by the Torah to perform *mitzvos*. Hence, the obligation to read the *Megillah* involves only one Rabbinic obligation. Therefore, a minor cannot discharge and adult of his obligation (*Tos.* 19b).

Others maintain that a minor has no obligation whatsoever. Although his father is required to train him in the performance of precepts, the minor has no personal obligation of his own *(Ramban).*

1. Still others differentiate between one who *can* hear, but does not read loudly enough to hear himself, and one who cannot hear at all. This follows the dictum כָּל־הָרָאוּי לְבִילָה אֵין בִּילָה מְעַכֶּבֶת בּוֹ, [*any meal-offering containing flour and oil*] *that can be mixed is acceptable even though it is not mixed.* However, if the proportion of flour to oil is so great that the two *cannot* be properly mixed, the failure to mix the flour with oil renders the offering unacceptable *(Menachos* 12:4). This ruling is extended to other instances where the potential for fulfillment is considered equivalent to actual fulfillment. In the case of *Megillah* reading, one who is physically capable of hearing fulfills his obligation, even though he does not hear his own reading. A deaf person, however, who is completely incapable of hearing, cannot discharge his own obligation. Hence, he cannot discharge the obligation of his listeners *(Taz* 689:1).

ב
ד

אֵין קוֹרִין אֶת־הַמְּגִלָּה, וְלֹא מָלִין, וְלֹא טוֹבְלִין, וְלֹא מַזִּין: וְכֵן שׁוֹמֶרֶת יוֹם כְּנֶגֶד יוֹם לֹא תִטְבֹּל, עַד שֶׁתָּנֵץ הַחַמָּה. וְכֻלָּן שֶׁעָשׂוּ מִשֶּׁעָלָה עַמּוּד הַשַּׁחַר, כָּשֵׁר.

יד אברהם

ר׳ יְהוּדָה מַכְשִׁיר בְּקָטָן. — *R' Yehudah declares a minor qualified.*

R' Yehudah [disputing the logic of distinguishing between particular Rabbinical enactments] maintains that since a minor is obligated by virtue of a Rabbinical enactment to hear the *Megillah*, he can discharge the obligation of adults who are also obligated by virtue of a Rabbinical enactment *(Tif. Yis.)*.

The *halachah* is not in accordance with the view of R' Yehudah *(Rav)*.

☙ Daytime Precepts

According to the Torah, day begins with עֲלוֹת הַשַּׁחַר, *the moment when the first rays of the rising sun are visible in the night sky.* All the precepts of the day may be performed from that time. However, since it is difficult to determine that instant with precision, the Rabbis have decreed that we wait until sunrise before performing precepts which must be done during daylight hours. This latter time is referred to as הָנֵץ הַחַמָּה, *sprouting of the sun;* i.e., the time when the sun is first visible on the horizon (see *Mishnah Berurah* 58:7). The Mishnah proceeds to list those precepts which are performed during the daytime.

אֵין קוֹרִין אֶת־הַמְּגִלָּה, — *we may not read the Megillah,*

The daytime reading of the *Megillah* may not be performed until sunrise. The basis for reading the *Megillah* by day is the verse וְהַיָּמִים הָאֵלֶּה נִזְכָּרִים וְנַעֲשִׂים, *And these days, should be remembered and celebrated (Esther* 9:28).

[See commentary to 4:1 (s.v., "Blessings Recited Upon Reading the Megillah") regarding the relationship between the day reading and the reading of the *Megillah* at night.]

וְלֹא מָלִין, — *nor circumcise,*

The Torah states, וּבַיּוֹם הַשְּׁמִינִי יִמּוֹל בְּשַׂר עָרְלָתוֹ, *And on the eighth day, the flesh of his surplusage shall be circumcised (Lev.* 12:3); thus, circumcision must be performed by day *(Rav)*.

וְלֹא טוֹבְלִין, וְלֹא מַזִּין: — *nor perform ritual immersion, nor sprinkle [purification water]—*

If one became טָמֵא, *contaminated*, through contact with a corpse, he can be cleansed only through 'sprinkling and immersion.' To make the formula for sprinkling — מֵי חַטָּאת, *water of purification* — the ashes of the Red Cow are mixed with water and sprinkled upon the contaminated person on the third and seventh day from his contamination. On the seventh day he must immerse himself in a מִקְוֶה [*mikvah*], *ritual pool.* The Torah states, ... *And a pure person shall sprinkle on the*

2
4
We may not read the *Megillah*, nor circumcise, nor perform ritual immersion, nor sprinkle [purification water] — similarly, a woman who counts a day corresponding to a day may not immerse herself until the sun has risen. However, if any of them did so after the [first] ray of dawn appeared, the act is valid.

contaminated person on the third day, and on the seventh day (Num. 19:19) indicating that the sprinkling must be done by day. The same verse continues, וְרָחַץ בַּמַּיִם, *and he shall bathe in water,* which is contextually interpreted to mean that the immersion on the seventh day must also be done by day. If the immersion takes place after the seventh day, however, it may be performed at night *(Rav).*

[The same rule applies to others who must immerse themselves on the seventh day of their contamination; e.g., a *metzora* or a *zav (Tif. Yis.).*]

וְכֵן שׁוֹמֶרֶת יוֹם כְּנֶגֶד יוֹם... — *similarly, a woman who counts* [lit. *watches*] *a day corresponding to a day.*

The Mishnah refers to טֻמְאַת זָבָה, *contamination of a zavah,* i.e., a woman who experiences bleeding during specific portions of her cycle (see *Lev.* 15:25-30) [and should not be confused with נִדָּה, *niddah (Lev.* 15:19-24)]. The *zavah* is required to wait one day free from bleeding corresponding to the day of flow. On the day after the flow she immerses herself and is cleansed. This immersion may be done by day *(Rav).* If the flow continues for three or more days, the cleansing process is the same as that of a *zav* (see pref. to 1:7).

[For a more detailed discussion of the differences between a *zavah* and a נִדָּה, *niddah,* see *Chochmas Adam* 107:1-9.]

לֹא תִטְבֹּל, — *may not immerse herself* [i.e., on the day following the flow *(Rav)*]...

עַד שֶׁתָּנֵץ הַחַמָּה. — *until the sun has risen.*

The above-mentioned acts may not be performed until the edge of the sun becomes visible on the horizon *(Rav).*

וְכֻלָּן שֶׁעָשׂוּ מִשֶּׁעָלָה עַמּוּד הַשַּׁחַר, — *However, if any of them did so after the* [*first*] *ray of dawn appeared.*

I.e., if any of the above acts was done after the first rays of light appeared in the sky *(Tos. Yom Tov, Berachos* 1:1)

כָּשֵׁר — *the act is valid.*

Since, in fact, day begins with the appearance of the first ray of dawn, any act performed thereafter is deemed to have been performed during the day. The Sages ordained sunrise as the preferred time only because it is difficult to establish the exact time of the first ray of dawn.

The appearance of the first ray of dawn is calculated as one and one-fifth hours before sunrise *(Rambam;* see *Berachos* 1:1 for a discussion of the method used to compute the time).

ב
ה

[ה] **כָּל** הַיּוֹם כָּשֵׁר לִקְרִיאַת הַמְּגִלָּה, וְלִקְרִיאַת הַהַלֵּל, וְלִתְקִיעַת שׁוֹפָר, וְלִנְטִילַת לוּלָב, וְלִתְפִלַּת הַמּוּסָפִין, וְלַמּוּסָפִין, וּלְוִדּוּי הַפָּרִים, וּלְוִדּוּי הַמַּעֲשֵׂר, וּלְוִדּוּי יוֹם הַכִּפּוּרִים, לִסְמִיכָה, לִשְׁחִיטָה, לִתְנוּפָה,

יד אברהם

5.

כָּל הַיּוֹם כָּשֵׁר... — *The entire day is valid...*

The zealous perform precepts as soon as possible, as exemplified by Abraham, who arose early in the morning to bring Isaac to the mountain where he was to be sacrificed (*Gen.* 22:3). Nevertheless, the *entire day* is valid for the performance of the following precepts (*Rashi 20b*).

לִקְרִיאַת הַמְּגִלָּה, — *for reading the Megillah,*

Scripture states: וְהַיָּמִים הָאֵלֶּה נִזְכָּרִים, *And these days should be remembered (Esther* 9:28). From this, the *Gemara* (20b) infers that the *Megillah* reading, which constitutes the 'remembrance,' may be performed throughout the day (*Tos. Yom Tov*).

וְלִקְרִיאַת הַהַלֵּל, — *(and for) the reciting the Hallel.*

The verse states, זֶה הַיּוֹם עָשָׂה ה׳, *This is the day which HASHEM has wrought (Psalms* 118:24). This implies that *Hallel* may be recited throughout the day (*Tos. Yom Tov; Gem.* 20b).

[Hence, if one failed to recite the *Hallel* during the morning prayer (*Shacharis*), he may do so until evening.]

וְלִתְקִיעַת שׁוֹפָר, — *(and for) blowing the shofar,*

The Torah describes Rosh HaShanah as יוֹם תְּרוּעָה, *a day of* [*shofar*] *blowing (Numbers* 29:1), implying that the *shofar* may be sounded throughout the day (*Tos. Yom Tov; Gem.* 20b).

[Thus, if the *shofar* was not sounded during *Musaf*, it must be sounded before evening.]

וְלִנְטִילַת לוּלָב, — *(and for) taking the lulav,*

The Torah states: וּלְקַחְתֶּם לָכֶם בַּיּוֹם הָרִאשׁוֹן, *And you shall take for yourselves on the first day* [*of Succos*] *(Lev.* 23:40); implying that one may perform the precept all day (*Tos. Yom Tov; Gem.* 20b).

וְלִתְפִלַּת הַמּוּסָפִין, — *(and for)* [reciting] *the Musaf prayer,*

The additional prayer [*Musaf*] is recited on the Sabbath, festivals, and *Rosh Chodesh* — when *Musaf* sacrifices were offered in the Temple. The mishnah equates the *Musaf* prayer with the *Musaf* sacrifices which it commemorates; just as the sacrifices could be brought all day long, so may the prayer be recited all day long (*Tos. Yom Tov, Gem.* 20b).

וְלַמּוּסָפִין, — *(and for)* [offering] *the Musaf sacrifices,*

The Torah says of these sacrifices, דְּבַר־יוֹם בְּיוֹמוֹ, *the offering of each day on its day (Lev.* 23:37); implying that they may be offered throughout the day (*Tos. Yom Tov; Gem.* 20b).

Although the *Musaf* sacrifice should neither precede the daily morning sacrifice nor follow the daily afternoon sacrifice, the *Musaf*

5. The entire day is valid for reading the *Megillah*; reciting the *Hallel*; blowing the *shofar*; taking the *lulav*; [reciting] the *Musaf* prayer; [offering] the *Musaf* sacrifices; the confession [recited with the offering] of the bulls; the confession [recited with] the tithe; the confession of Yom Kippur; leaning the hands [on the head of a sacrificial animal]; slaughtering [of sacrifices]; waving [of sacrifices]; bringing

YAD AVRAHAM

is valid even if offered before the former or after the latter. Therefore, the Tanna describes its period of validity as *all day long (Ran).*

וּלְוִדּוּי הַפָּרִים, — *(and for) the confession* [*recited with the offering*] *of the bulls.*

The *bulls* referred to are the unique sacrifices offered of the *kohen gadol* and the *Sanhedrin* in matters involving a negative commandment for which the potential punishment is *kares*. If the *kohen gadol* makes an erroneous halachic decision which results in the violation of such a precept, or if the *Sanhedrin* makes a similar error and *a majority of the nation*, relying on the *Sanhedrin's* ruling, violates the precept, the *kohen gadol* [or the court] must bring a bull as a sin offering (*Lev.* 4:1-21). As part of the sacrificial service, they must confess their sins. These confessions are similar to the confession of Yom Kippur which is recited during the day *(Rav).*

וּלְוִדּוּי הַמַּעֲשֵׂר, — *(and for) the confession* [recited with] *the tithe.*

This confession (*Deut.* 26:12-15) is recited on the last day of Pesach of the fourth and seventh years of the Sabbatical cycle. It is a declaration that by the first day of Pesach, all previously undistributed tithes had been delivered to their proper recipients. Included in the declaration is the phrase הַיּוֹם הַזֶּה, *on this day,* implying that the confession was recited by day (*Tos. Yom Tov; Gem.* 20b).

וּלְוִדּוּי יוֹם הַכִּפּוּרִים, — *(and for) the confession of Yom Kippur,*

The confession is recited by the *kohen gadol* on the bull he offered as a sin-offering of the *kohanim*. The Torah refers to this sacrifice as a כַּפָּרָה, *atonement (Lev.* 16:6). Thus, the sacrifice is likened to יוֹם כִּפּוּר, *Yom Kippur*, which, as its name literally means, is a day of atonement. Of Yom Kippur the Torah states (*Lev.* 16:30): כִּי־בַיּוֹם הַזֶּה יְכַפֵּר עֲלֵיכֶם, *for on this day he shall atone for you;* implying that the atonement of Yom Kippur is accomplished during the day (*Gem.* 20b).

לִסְמִיכָה, — *(for) leaning the hands* [*on the head of a sacrificial animal*],

[See preface to *Chagigah* 2:2.]

The Torah states: וְסָמַךְ יָדוֹ עַל רֹאשׁ הָעוֹלָה, *And he shall place his hand on the head of the burnt offering (Lev.* 1:4). The very next verse begins וְשָׁחַט, *And he shall slaughter*. Thus, the *placing of the hands* is likened to the *slaughter* of the sacrifice; just as the latter is performed by day (see below), so too is the former *(Gem.* 20b).

לִשְׁחִיטָה, — *(for) slaughtering* [of sacrifices];

The Torah states: בְּיוֹם זִבְחֲכֶם, *On*

ב לְהַגָּשָׁה, לִקְמִיצָה וּלְהַקְטָרָה, לִמְלִיקָה,
ו וּלְקַבָּלָה, וּלְהַזָּיָה, וּלְהַשְׁקָיַת סוֹטָה, וְלַעֲרִיפַת
הָעֶגְלָה, וּלְטָהֳרַת הַמְּצֹרָע.

[ו] **כָּל־הַלַּיְלָה** כָּשֵׁר לִקְצִירַת הָעֹמֶר וּלְהֶקְטֵר חֲלָבִים וְאֵבָרִים.

יד אברהם

the day of your slaughter, (Lev. 19:6), which implies that the slaughtering is performed by day *(Gem.* 20b).

לִתְנוּפָה, — *(for) the waving* [of sacrifices];

The *Omer* offering and the breast and shank of peace offerings are raised, and lowered, and waved in all directions by the *kohen* performing the service. The Torah states: בְּיוֹם הֲנִיפְכֶם אֶת הָעֹמֶר, *On the day of your waving of the Omer (Lev.* 23:12), which implies that waving is done by day *(Tif. Yis.; Gem.* 20b).

לְהַגָּשָׁה, — *(for) bringing* [the vessel with the meal-offering near the altar];

I.e., to its southwest corner *(Rav).*

The Torah compares the bringing of the vessel to its waving; just as the latter is performed by day, so too, is the former (*Gem.* 20b).

לִקְמִיצָה וּלְהַקְטָרָה, — *(for) taking a handful* [*of the meal offering*] *and (for) burning it;*

At the southwest corner of the altar, the *kohen* removes a handful of the meal offering and places it upon the fire of the altar. That these two aspects of the service must be done by day is not specifically expressed by Scripture. The same is true of the next three parts of the service: מְלִיקָה, קַבָּלָה, הַזָּיָה, *nipping, receiving,* and *sprinkling.* The *Gemara* (20b) derives the requirement from the verse: בְּיוֹם צַוֹּתוֹ אֶת־בְּנֵי יִשְׂרָאֵל לְהַקְרִיב אֶת־קָרְבְּנֵיהֶם לַה׳, *On the day He commanded the Children of Israel to bring near their offerings to HASHEM (Lev.* 7:38). The implication is that everything which is an integral part of הַקְרָבָה, *bringing* [the offerings] *near,* must be done by day. All these five acts fall under that category. (See *Rashi* to *Gem.* 20b).

לִמְלִיקָה, — *(for) nipping* [the neck of bird offerings];

[Bird offerings were slaughtered in a manner unique to the sacrificial service. The *kohen* nipped the back of the bird's neck with the sharp pressure of his thumbnail (see *Lev.* 1:15; 5:8).]

וּלְקַבָּלָה, — *(and for) receiving* [the blood of sacrifices];

Following its slaughter, the blood of an offering is caught in a basin from which it will be placed on the altar *(Rav).*

וּלְהַזָּיָה, — *(and for) sprinkling* [the blood of sacrifices].

The term הַזָּיָה, *sprinkling,* is used by Scripture only in relation to sin offerings, from which the blood is brought inside the Temple building and sprinkled either toward the Holy of Holies or upon the inner, golden altar. Our mishnah, however, uses it in its broader sense as referring to the placement of blood from offerings in whatever manner and place Scripture prescribed for the respective offerings *(Rav).*

וּלְהַשְׁקָיַת סוֹטָה, — *(and for) causing the sotah to drink;*

2 near [the vessel with the meal-offering to the altar];
6 taking a handful [of the meal-offering] and burning it; nipping [the neck of the bird-offerings]; receiving [the blood of sacrifices]; sprinkling [the blood of sacrifices]; causing the *sotah* to drink; cutting [the neck of] the heifer; and the cleansing of the *metzora*.

6. The entire night is valid for the reaping of the *omer*, and for the burning of [sacrificial] fats and limbs.

YAD AVRAHAM

A *sotah* is a woman whose husband accuses her of adultery. Although there is no proof of guilt, there are grounds for suspicion. The Torah prescribes that her guilt or innocence is tested by means of having her drink specially prepared water on the Temple grounds. The full procedure is given in *Numbers* 5:11-31.

After describing the conditions under which a wife becomes a *sotah*, and the bitter waters which she must drink, Scripture sums up the chapter of *sotah* with the words: אֶת כָּל־הַתּוֹרָה הַזֹּאת, *This entire* [Torah] *teaching (Numbers* 5:30). In discussing the courts of law, Scripture again uses the term הַתּוֹרָה, *the Torah (Deut.* 17:11). The similarity of terms teaches that certain rules relating to the law courts also relate to *sotah*. Namely just as courts hand down decisions only by day *(Rosh HaShanah* 25b), so too, the *sotah* process is carried out only by day *(Gem.* 20b).

וְלַעֲרִיפַת הָעֶגְלָה, — *(and for) cutting the neck of the heifer;*

[If a person is found murdered in a field and the identity of the perpetrator is unknown, the elders of the court determine the city closest to the scene of the crime. The elders of that city are required to take a heifer to a valley that was never tilled nor planted, decapitate the animal there, and declare that they bear no responsibility for the tragedy.] The *kohanim* then pray, כַּפֵּר לְעַמְּךָ יִשְׂרָאֵל, *Atone for Your people Israel (Deut.* 21:8-9). The term כַּפֵּר, *atone*, is commonly used in connection with sacrifices (see above וּלְוִדּוּי יוֹם הַכִּפּוּרִים); just as sacrifices are offered by day, so too is the decapitation of the heifer performed by day *(Gem.* 21a).

וּלְטָהֳרַת הַמְּצֹרָע. — *and (for) the cleansing of the metzora.*

[For *metzora*, see 1:7.]

The cleansing procedure involves two birds, a cedar branch, scarlet wool, and hyssop (see *Lev.* 14:1-8). The Torah introduces this chapter with the words, בְּיוֹם טָהֳרָתוֹ, *on the day of his cleansing*, implying that the procedure must be performed by day *(Gem.* 21a).

6.

כָּל הַלַּיְלָה כָּשֵׁר... — *The entire night is valid ...*

[The mishnah now teaches that just as daytime precepts may be performed throughout the day, so too, nighttime precepts may be per-

ג
א

זֶה הַכְּלָל: דָּבָר שֶׁמִּצְוָתוֹ בַּיּוֹם, כָּשֵׁר כָּל הַיּוֹם; דָּבָר שֶׁמִּצְוָתוֹ בַּלַּיְלָה, כָּשֵׁר כָּל הַלָּיְלָה.

[א] **בְּנֵי** הָעִיר שֶׁמָּכְרוּ רְחוֹבָהּ שֶׁל עִיר, לוֹקְחִין בְּדָמָיו בֵּית הַכְּנֶסֶת; בֵּית

יד אברהם

formed throughout the night.]

לִקְצִירַת הָעֹמֶר... — *for the reaping of the omer,*

The *omer* was a measure of barley brought as a meal offering on the sixteenth of *Nissan (Lev.* 23:9-14). The reaping was done on the previous night (see *Menachos* 10:3).

וּלְהֶקְטֵר חֲלָבִים וְאֵבָרִים. — *and for the burning of [sacrificial] fats and limbs.*

Fats and limbs of the תָּמִיד שֶׁל בֵּין הָעַרְבַּיִם, *the daily afternoon burnt offering*, may be burned on the altar throughout the night as Scripture *(Lev.* 6:2) specifies עַל־הַמִּזְבֵּחַ כָּל־הַלַּיְלָה, *on the altar throughout the night (Rav).*

Tosafos Yom Tov (Berachos 1:1) adds that the same rule applies to all parts of offerings that are burned on the altar.

זֶה הַכְּלָל: דָּבָר שֶׁמִּצְוָתוֹ בַּיּוֹם, כָּשֵׁר כָּל הַיּוֹם, — *This is the general rule: Any rite which is to be done by day may be performed throughout the day;*

It is a principle of *mishnah* interpretation that the phrase זֶה הַכְּלָל, *this is the general rule*, implies that other situations have the same rule though the mishnah omits them. These other cases need have no similarity to the previous situations, other than this general rule. In our case, the *Gemara* extends the rule stated here to include לְבֹנָה, *frankincense*, which was placed upon the לֶחֶם הַפָּנִים, *loaves of showbread* [see *Lev.* 24:5-9] *(Rav);* and the showbread itself *(Tif. Yis.).* [The verse there *(Lev.* 24:8) states בְּיוֹם הַשַּׁבָּת בְּיוֹם הַשַּׁבָּת, *on each Sabbath day*, indicating that the showbread and accompanying frankincense be placed on the שֻׁלְחָן, *Table*, by day.]

דָּבָר שֶׁמִּצְוָתוֹ בַּלַּיְלָה, כָּשֵׁר כָּל־הַלָּיְלָה. — *any rite which is to be done at night may be performed throughout the night.*[1]

Since the phrase זֶה הַכְּלָל, *this is the rule*, which introduces the first half of this statement also applies to the second half, the Talmud again extends this rule to include similar cases which have not been included in the mishnah. *This is the rule* includes the eating of the Pesach sacrifice on the first night of Pesach, which may be done throughout the night *(Rav).*[2]

1. Surprisingly, there is no mention of the *Megillah* reading as one of the precepts applicable at night. Some say that since the primary precept is the daytime reading, the Tanna did not mention the evening reading at all *(Ran).*

Others maintain that at the time the Mishnah was written, the Sages had not yet instituted the evening reading *(Beur HaGra* 692:4, *Binyan Shlomo* 58).

2. The Sages, however, ordained that it should not be eaten after midnight so as to prevent people from delaying their eating so long that they forget or fall asleep (see *Berachos* 1:1; *Rav).*

Others however, hold that the prohibition against eating of the Paschal sacrifice

3 This is the general rule: Any rite which is to be
1 done by day, may be performed throughout the day; any rite which is to be done at night, may be performed throughout the night.

1. If the representatives of a town sell the town square, they must use the proceeds [of that sale]

YAD AVRAHAM

Chapter 3

1.

◆§ Sanctity of the Synagogue

After completing the laws of the reading of the *Megillah*, the Tanna goes on to the laws of the reading of the Torah. Since the Torah reading is an enactment of the prophets, it is similar to the *Megillah* reading, which was ordained by the Men of the Great Assembly [among whose members were counted many prophets (see *Gem.* 17b)]. Because the Torah is read in the synagogue, the *Tanna* devotes the first three mishnayos to general laws relating to the sanctity of the synagogue *(Tos. Yom Tov).*

Mishnah 1 enumerates the various parts of the synagogue in ascending order of their holiness. This order is applied to the disposition of the proceeds realized from the sale of sanctified property. Such proceeds acquire the same degree of sanctity possessed by the items which had been sold. In keeping with the rule that מַעֲלִין בְּקֹדֶשׁ וְאֵין מוֹרִידִין, *levels of sanctity may be raised, but not lowered,* the use of such proceeds is limited as specified below.

בְּנֵי הָעִיר... — *[If] the representatives* [lit. *people*] *of a town...*

I.e., those with the authority to sell community property. They are the שִׁבְעָה טוֹבֵי הָעִיר, *the seven trustees of the city,* the town fathers or city council elected to conduct the city's affairs. Their general authority to conduct community business did not include specific authorization to sell community-owned sacred articles *(Ran).*

שֶׁמָּכְרוּ... — *sell* [lit. *that sold*] ...

The limitations specified below apply only if the council sold the articles without explicit authorization from the residents of the town *(Rav).*

If the residents of the town sold any of the articles without the authorization of the council, the same restrictions apply to their use of the proceeds as apply to the council's: As the mishnah continues, they may only buy articles of higher sanctity. Thus, neither the council nor the general citizenry may act in unrestricted independence of one another *(Ran).*

However, if the trustees were authorized by the community's citizens to sell the town square or other property, they had the right to

after midnight is Scriptural in origin (see *Pesachim* 10:9 and *Zevachim* 5:8). Since the precept of eating the *afikoman* at the *seder* is linked to the eating of the Paschal sacrifice, one should be careful to eat the *afikoman* before midnight *(Shulchan Aruch* 477:1).

ג
א

הַכְּנֶסֶת — לוֹקְחִין תֵּבָה; תֵּבָה — לוֹקְחִין מִטְפָּחוֹת; מִטְפָּחוֹת — לוֹקְחִין סְפָרִים; סְפָרִים — לוֹקְחִין תּוֹרָה.

יד אברהם

designate any legitimate purpose for the use of the proceeds *(Rav).*

Although the proceeds of the sale acquire a degree of sanctity, the sacred property had *its own* holiness, while the money became merely *a substitute* for the property it replaced. Therefore, the Sages ruled that if the sale was made with the mutual agreement of the council and the residents, the proceeds do not acquire any sanctity, but may be used for any purpose *(Ran).*

רְחוֹבָהּ שֶׁל עִיר — *the town square,*

Each town had an open area where the people gathered on fast days for prayer (see *Taanis* 2:1). The mishnah follows the opinion of R' Menachem ben R' Yose, who holds that because the area was occasionally used for prayer, it acquired a degree of sanctity, albeit lower than that of a synagogue, which is used constantly. Thus, if the square is sold, the proceeds may be used only to purchase articles of higher sanctity — in accordance with the principle מַעֲלִין בְּקֹדֶשׁ וְאֵין מוֹרִידִין, *levels of sanctity may be raised, but not lowered.* Because of its infrequent use for prayer, however, the Sages disagree with R' Menachem's view and do not ascribe sanctity to the town square. Consequently, according to the Sages, the proceeds of the sale may be used for any purpose *(Rav).*

לוֹקְחִין בִּדְמָיו בֵּית הַכְּנֶסֶת: — *they must use the proceeds* [*of that sale*] *to purchase a synagogue.*

[The mishnah does not restrict the proceeds of the sale only to use in the purchase of a synagogue. The money may also be used to purchase items of a higher degree of holiness, such as those listed further in the mishnah.]

The money received for the sale of the article becomes invested with the sanctity of the article itself. Thus, [according to R' Menachem ben R' Yose, whom our mishnah follows], if the town square was sold without the mutual agreement of the council and the residents, the proceeds may be used only to purchase articles of higher sanctity, such as a synagogue *(Ran).*

בֵּית הַכְּנֶסֶת— — [*If they sell*] *a synagogue,*

The mishnah refers only to a *village* synagogue, because it was built for the use of the villagers. A *town* synagogue, however, may not be sold since it was constructed to be used even by travelers; consequently, everyone in the nation must agree to the sale *(Rav; Gem.* 26a).

Nowadays, however, even a town synagogue may be sold if the sale is made with the consent of the residents and council, provided the residents of the town built it at their own expense. Moreover, if the council announces the proposed sale and no objections are raised, the sale is presumed to have the approval of all the residents. Finally, if an old synagogue was razed to construct a new one, the materials of the old synagogue may be sold for any purpose, provided the residents and council agree *(Tif. Yis.; Magen Avraham* 133:7, 37).

לוֹקְחִין תֵּבָה; — *they must purchase an Ark;*

[The Ark is an enclosure in which the Torah scrolls are placed, and

3
1 to purchase a synagogue. [If they sell] a synagogue, they must purchase an ark; [if they sell] an ark, they must purchase wrappings [for the Torah scrolls]; [if they sell] wrappings, they must purchase Books [of Scripture]; [if they sell] Books [of Scripture], they must purchase a Torah scroll.

YAD AVRAHAM

which has a higher degree of sanctity than the synagogue building. The commentaries differ concerning the form of this Ark]:

According to *Ran*, the Ark was built into the wall of the synagogue.

Other commentaries maintain that the Ark referred to in the mishnah is a box containing a single Torah, which was placed on the floor in front of the cantor *(Bach; Tur Orach Chaim* 150). According to some, the תֵּבָה, *Ark*, was placed on the בִּימָה, *central platform*, when the Torah scroll was to be read *(Rambam, Hilchos Tefillah* 11:3; *Kessef Mishneh; Beis Yosef; Tur*, ch. 150). According to these commentaries, the mishnah does not refer to a *built-in* Ark, because, since it is part of the building, such an Ark has no greater sanctity than the synagogue itself *(Tif. Yis.)*.

תֵּבָה—לוֹקְחִין מִטְפָּחוֹת; — [*If they sell*] *an Ark, they must purchase wrappings* [*for the Torah scrolls*];

[The Torah covers are considered to be of higher sanctity than the Ark since they come in direct contact with the Torah scrolls.]

מִטְפָּחוֹת—לוֹקְחִין סְפָרִים; — [*if they sell*] *wrappings, they must purchase Books* [*of Scripture*];

They must use the proceeds to purchase parchment scrolls of נְבִיאִים וּכְתוּבִים, *Prophets and Holy Writings (Rav)*.

Alternatively, סְפָרִים, *Books*, are individual volumes of the *Chumashim* written on parchment [see above 2:2] *(Rambam)*.

The *halachah* is that any of these scrolls may be purchased with the proceeds, though individual volumes of *Chumash* have a higher degree of sanctity than do Prophets or Writings. The latter two, however, are of equal sanctity *(Magen Avraham* 153:2).

Many authorities maintain that printed Books of the Torah or Scripture are of equal sanctity to parchment scrolls. Thus, for the purpose of purchase — although not, of course, for discharging the obligation of reading the Torah — such Books may be purchased with the proceeds of sales of articles of lesser sanctity *(Tif. Yis.)*.

סְפָרִים—לוֹקְחִין תּוֹרָה. — [if they sell] *Books* [of Scripture], *they must purchase a Torah scroll.*

A Torah scroll has the highest degree of sanctity. However, if an error was found in the Torah, it is considered to be of the same degree of sanctity as individual volumes of *Chumash* since it cannot be used for public reading *(Shulchan Aruch Orach Chaim* 153:3).

◆§ Proceeds of Sale of Scroll

Until this point, the mishnah has stressed that the proceeds of a sale of holy articles must be used to purchase an item of greater sanctity than the sold article. This implies that an item of equal sanctity may not be bought. The next part of the mish-

ג
א

אֲבָל אִם מָכְרוּ תוֹרָה, לֹא יִקְחוּ סְפָרִים; סְפָרִים — לֹא יִקְחוּ מִטְפָּחוֹת; מִטְפָּחוֹת — לֹא יִקְחוּ תֵבָה; תֵּבָה — לֹא יִקְחוּ בֵית הַכְּנֶסֶת; בֵּית הַכְּנֶסֶת — לֹא יִקְחוּ אֶת־הָרְחוֹב. וְכֵן בְּמוֹתְרֵיהֶן.

אֵין מוֹכְרִין אֶת־שֶׁל רַבִּים לְיָחִיד, מִפְּנֵי שֶׁמּוֹרִידִין אוֹתוֹ מִקְּדֻשָּׁתוֹ; דִּבְרֵי רַבִּי יְהוּדָה.

יד אברהם

nah insists that the proceeds of such a sale not be used to purchase any article of lesser sanctity, indicating that items of equivalent holiness may be purchased. This apparent contradiction is discussed by the Talmud and commentaries.

Kessef Mishneh takes the רֵישָׁא, *first part*, of the mishnah as decisive. Only articles of *greater* sanctity may be purchased. However, once the list reaches the level of Torah scrolls, no item of greater holiness exists. In this one instance, therefore, the Tanna must specify: *However, if they sold a Torah scroll, they may not use the proceeds to purchase Books of Scripture;* for on this level only an equivalent article [i.e., another Torah scroll] may be bought. Once the Tanna makes this statement in reference to Torah scrolls, he continues through the entire list.

Tosefos Yom Tov, on the other hand, understands the סֵיפָא, *latter section*, of the mishnah to be decisive. Holy items of equivalent sanctity may be purchased with the proceeds of any of the sales mentioned here. The mishnah initially speaks of the *preferential* use of the monies — for increased sanctity. Then, the mishnah continues with the minimum requirement that the original sanctity not be lowered [see also *Shulchan Aruch* and *Beis Yosef* cited below].

אֲבָל אִם מָכְרוּ תוֹרָה, לֹא יִקְחוּ סְפָרִים; — *However, if they sold a Torah scroll, they may not [use the proceeds to] purchase Books [of Scripture];*

Since Torah scrolls have the highest degree of sanctity, the proceeds may not be used to purchase articles of lesser sanctity *(Rav).*

[The proceeds of the sale of a Torah scroll can be used, however, for pressing public needs, such as redeeming captives (see *Tos., Bava Basra* 8b).]

The *Gemara* (27a) discusses the question of whether an old Torah scroll may be sold to purchase a new one. Since the question was not resolved, we adopt the more stringent opinion and do not permit the sale *(Shulchan Aruch, Yoreh Deah* 270:1). [According to this view the mishnah speaks of a case where the Torah scroll has already been sold. However, had the townsmen asked the *Beth Din* whether it is permissible to sell it, they would have been told not to.]

סְפָרִים—לֹא יִקְחוּ מִטְפָּחוֹת; — *[if they sold] Books [of Scripture], they may not purchase wrappings [for the Torah scrolls];*

The authorities differ as to whether they may use the proceeds of this sale to purchase *other* books of a sanctity equivalent to the one that was sold. According to *Ran*, the proceeds may be used only to purchase articles of *higher* sanctity. If a Torah is sold, however, since there is nothing of greater sanctity, only another Torah may be purchased. Others maintain that while the proceeds of such sales may not be used to purchase articles

3 However, if they sold a Torah scroll, they may not
1 [use the proceeds to] purchase Books [of Scripture]; [if they sold] Books [of Scripture], they may not purchase wrappings [for the Torah scrolls]; [if they sold] wrappings, they may not purchase an Ark; [if they sold] an Ark, they may not purchase a synagogue; [if they sold] a synagogue, they may not purchase a square. [Moreover], the same is true of any left over [proceeds].

Communal property may not be sold to an individual for this would lessen the sanctity of the article — this is the opinion of R' Yehudah. They said

YAD AVRAHAM

of *lesser* sanctity, they *may* be used to purchase articles of *equal* sanctity, such as equivalent Books of Scripture. While it is *praiseworthy* to use the proceeds to purchase articles of higher sanctity, it is not a requirement *(Beis Yosef; Tur Orach Chaim* 153; *Kessef Mishneh; Tos. Yom Tov;* see pref.).

מִטְפָּחוֹת—לֹא יִקְחוּ תֵּבָה: תֵּבָה—לֹא יִקְחוּ בֵּית הַכְּנֶסֶת: בֵּית הַכְּנֶסֶת—לֹא יִקְחוּ אֶת הָרְחוֹב. — [*if they sold*] *wrappings, they may not purchase an Ark;* [*if they sold*] *an Ark, they may not purchase a synagogue;* [*if they sold*] *a synagogue, they may not purchase a square.*

[In all these instances, the article or property purchased is of lesser sanctity than the one that was sold.]

וְכֵן בְּמוֹתְרֵיהֶן. — [*Moreover,*] *the same is true of any leftover* [*proceeds*].

If funds were still left after the purchase of a more sacred article, such funds retain the same restriction as the original money: They may not be used to buy anything of lesser sanctity *(Rav).*

Similarly, if money was collected to purchase an article and some is left over, that money may not be used to purchase articles of lesser sanctity than the article for which the money was initially collected *(Tif. Yis.).*

אֵין מוֹכְרִין אֶת־שֶׁל רַבִּים לְיָחִיד, — *Communal property may not be sold to an individual...*

According to *Yerushalmi,* this stricture against selling to an individual refers only to a Torah. A synagogue, however, may be sold to an individual, provided there is an option to repurchase [according to R' Meir], or as long as it is not used for the four demeaning purposes outlined in mishnah 2 [according to the Sages].

Ran maintains, however, that the prohibition of our mishnah refers only to a synagogue which was sold unconditionally; according to R' Meir, the sale is not valid and it must remain a synagogue. In this case, a public synagogue may not be sold to an individual since a private synagogue has less sanctity than a public one.

A 'private synagogue' in the context of our mishnah is one in which an individual will pray alone; it will not be used by a *minyan (Tos. Yom Tov).*

ג
ב

אָמְרוּ לוֹ: אִם כֵּן, אַף לֹא מֵעִיר גְּדוֹלָה לְעִיר קְטַנָּה.

[ב] **אֵין** מוֹכְרִין בֵּית הַכְּנֶסֶת, אֶלָּא עַל תְּנַאי שֶׁאִם יִרְצוּ יַחֲזִירוּהוּ; דִּבְרֵי רַבִּי מֵאִיר. וַחֲכָמִים אוֹמְרִים: מוֹכְרִים אוֹתוֹ מִמְכַּר עוֹלָם, חוּץ מֵאַרְבָּעָה דְבָרִים — לְמֶרְחָץ וּלְבֻרְסְקִי וְלִטְבִילָה וּלְבֵית הַמָּיִם. רַבִּי יְהוּדָה אוֹמֵר: מוֹכְרִין אוֹתוֹ לְשֵׁם חָצֵר, וְהַלּוֹקֵחַ מַה־שֶּׁיִּרְצֶה יַעֲשֶׂה.

יד אברהם

מִפְּנֵי שֶׁמּוֹרִידִין אוֹתוֹ מִקְּדֻשָּׁתוֹ; — *for this would lessen the sanctity of the article—*

Since prayers of קְדֻשָּׁה, *holiness*, (such as *Kaddish, Kedushah*, and *Borchu*) can be recited only in the presence of a *minyan*, the communal synagogue is of higher sanctity than an individual one *(Rashi)*.

דִּבְרֵי ר׳ יְהוּדָה. — *this is the opinion of R' Yehudah.*

Some editions record this as the view of R' Meir.

אָמְרוּ לוֹ: אִם־כֵּן, — *They* [i.e., the Sages] *said to him: If so,*

[I.e., according to your opinion that a communal synagogue may not be sold to an individual] ...

אַף לֹא מֵעִיר גְּדוֹלָה לְעִיר קְטַנָּה. — [*they may*] *not even sell* [*the synagogue*] *of a large town to* [*the residents*] *of a small town.*

Since the synagogue of a large town has a greater attendance than that of a small town, such a sale would diminish the synagogue's sanctity. The verse בְּרָב־עָם הַדְרַת־מֶלֶךְ, *the King's glory is in the multitudes* [that serve Him] *(Proverbs* 14:28) indicates that there is greater merit — and, hence, greater sanctity — in a place where God is served by *larger* numbers *(Tos. Yom Tov; Gem.* 27b).

According to R' Yehudah, this sale would not represent a lessening of sanctity since the synagogue will still be used by a *minyan*, whereas if sold to an individual, holy prayers requiring a *minyan* would no longer be recited therein *(Tif. Yis.; Gem.* 27b).

2.

אֵין מוֹכְרִין בֵּית הַכְּנֶסֶת, — *They may not sell a synagogue...*

One community may not sell a synagogue to another community even though the buyers will maintain it in the same degree of sanctity as did the previous owners *(Rashi; Rav).*

אֶלָּא עַל תְּנַאי שֶׁאִם יִרְצוּ יַחֲזִירוּהוּ; — *except under the condition that, if they wish, they may repurchase it —*

3 unto him: If so, [they may] not even sell [the syn-
2 agogue] of a large town to [the residents of] a small town.

2. They may not sell a synagogue except under the condition that, if they wish, they may repurchase it — this is the opinion of R' Meir. The Sages say, however, they may sell it permanently [and for any purpose] except for [the following] four uses: as a bathhouse, a tannery, a ritualarium, or a water closet. R' Yehudah says: They may sell it as a courtyard and the purchaser may do as he pleases.

YAD AVRAHAM

Were they to sell the synagogue unconditionally, it would appear that they were doing so because it was worthless to them *(Rav)*.

By virtue of the option to repurchase, the buyer will be deterred from using the synagogue for any unseemly purpose *(Meiri)*.

.דִּבְרֵי ר׳ מֵאִיר — *this is the opinion of R' Meir.*

[According to the editions that cite R' Meir as the Tanna who prohibits the sale of a public synagogue to an individual, or to a smaller town (see previous mishnah), this case must refer to a sale made with the agreement of the council and the town's residents.]

וַחֲכָמִים אוֹמְרִים: מוֹכְרִין אוֹתוֹ מִמְכַּר עוֹלָם, — *The Sages say, however, they may sell it permanently* [and for any purpose]...

If the sale was made with the agreement of the council and the residents (see above), it may be sold to an individual who may use it for any purpose *(Rav)*.

—חוּץ מֵאַרְבָּעָה דְבָרִים — *except for [the following] four uses:*

At the time of the sale, a stipulation must be made that the buyer will not use the synagogue for any of the four purposes listed below *(Meiri)*:

.לְמֶרְחָץ וּלְבֻרְסְקִי וְלִטְבִילָה וּלְבֵית הַמָּיִם — *as a bathhouse, a tannery, a mikvah or water closet.*

[Either because people use these facilities when they are unclothed, or because of the foul odors emanating from them, they are considered as a degrading use for a former house of worship.]

בֵּית הַמָּיִם [lit., *water house*] may also refer to a laundry *(Rav)*.

The *Shulchan Aruch* (153:9) rules that if the synagogue was sold with the mutual agreement of the council and the residents of the town, the buyer may use it for any purpose. Thus, the mishnah must be referring only to a case where the council sold it without first publicizing the sale. *Mishnah Berurah*, however, questions this ruling (see *Beur Halachah*, 153).

ר׳ יְהוּדָה אוֹמֵר: מוֹכְרִין אוֹתוֹ לְשֵׁם חָצֵר, — *R' Yehudah says: They may sell it as a courtyard...*

According to R' Yehudah the buyer may use it without restriction for any purpose, but only if he bought it as a courtyard (see below). However, if it was sold outright

[ג] **וְעוֹד** אָמַר רַבִּי יְהוּדָה: בֵּית הַכְּנֶסֶת ג
שֶׁחָרַב, אֵין מַסְפִּידִין בְּתוֹכוֹ, וְאֵין ג
מַפְשִׁילִין בְּתוֹכוֹ חֲבָלִים, וְאֵין פּוֹרְשִׂין לְתוֹכוֹ
מְצוּדוֹת, וְאֵין שׁוֹטְחִין עַל גַּגּוֹ פֵּרוֹת, וְאֵין
עוֹשִׂין אוֹתוֹ קַפַּנְדַּרְיָא, שֶׁנֶּאֱמַר ,,וַהֲשִׁמּוֹתִי
אֶת־מִקְדְּשֵׁיכֶם" — קְדֻשָּׁתָן אַף כְּשֶׁהֵן שׁוֹמֵמִין.
עָלוּ בוֹ עֲשָׂבִים, לֹא יִתְלשׁ, מִפְּנֵי עָגְמַת נֶפֶשׁ.

without specification, it retains its holiness; hence it may not be used for any of the above four purposes *(Tos. Yom Tov; Tos.* 28a).

Most authorities maintain that the *halachah* is not in accordance with R' Yehudah *(Rav).*

.וְהַלּוֹקֵחַ מַה־שֶּׁיִּרְצֶה יַעֲשֶׂה — *and the purchaser may do as he pleases.*

[If the sale is made with the agreement of the council and residents, as noted previously, both the Sages and R' Meir agree that a condition must be made at the time of the sale to demonstrate that the sellers were not selling the synagogue because they deemed it worthless. Once such a stipulation was made, the sale was permitted. R' Yehudah maintains that the sellers must show that they appreciate the sanctity of the synagogue, but need neither attach a repurchase option (R' Meir's opinion), nor limit the buyer's potential use (the Sages' opinion). By specifying that the synagogue is being sold as a courtyard rather than for some demeaning purpose, they show that they are aware of its sanctity. Once purchased, the buyer may proceed to use it as he pleases, for the limitations outlined in the mishnah apply only to the *sellers;* i.e., they may not *sell* it for purposes that are deemed degrading.]

3.

:וְעוֹד אָמַר ר׳ יְהוּדָה — *R' Yehudah said further:*

In addition to his stringent ruling that a former synagogue may be used for degrading purposes only if the sale specifies that it is being sold as a courtyard (see above), R' Yehudah also made other rulings regarding the sanctity of synagogues in general (*Tos. Yom Tov; Tos.* 28a). The mishnah proceeds to enumerate them:

,בֵּית הַכְּנֶסֶת שֶׁחָרַב, אֵין מַסְפִּידִין בְּתוֹכוֹ — *In a synagogue that has been destroyed one may not offer eulogies,*

Although a synagogue may fall to ruins, it still maintains its sanctity, and eulogies may not be offered therein. However, eulogies for the scholars of the town or their relatives are permitted even in a functioning synagogue *(Tif. Yis.).*

Since *all* residents of a town customarily attend eulogies for outstanding scholars, such occasions are regarded as public, rather than private, functions and, as such, do

3
3

3. R' Yehudah said further: In a synagogue that has been destroyed one may not offer eulogies, twist ropes, spread nets, spread produce on its roof, nor use as a shortcut — for the Torah states, *And I shall make desolate your sanctuaries* [*Lev.* 26:31]; [this implies that] they are holy even when they are desolate.

If grass grew [in the ruins], one may not detach it, because of grief.

not demean the sanctity of the synagogue (*Shulchan Aruch,* 151:1).

וְאֵין מַפְשִׁילִין בְּתוֹכוֹ חֲבָלִים, — *(nor may one) twist ropes (therein),*

One may not use the ruins as a work space. The *Tanna* used the example of twisting ropes since that requires a large open space for which the ruins of a synagogue are ideal *(Rav; Rashi).*

וְאֵין פּוֹרְשִׁין לְתוֹכוֹ מְצוּדוֹת, — *(nor may one) spread nets (therein)* [to trap the birds and animals that are wont to roam there *(Tif. Yis.)*],

וְאֵין שׁוֹטְחִין עַל גַּגּוֹ פֵּרוֹת, — *(nor may one) spread produce on its roof* [to dry in the sun *(Kehati)*],

וְאֵין עוֹשִׂין אוֹתוֹ קַפֶּנְדַּרְיָא, — *nor use it as a shortcut —*

A synagogue may not be used to shorten the way by walking through its ruins instead of going around them. The *Gemara* (29a) explains קַפֶּנְדַּרְיָא, *shortcut,* as a contraction of אַדְּמַקִּיפְנָא אַדָּרֵי אֵיעוּל בְּהָא, *instead of going around the rows of houses, I will go through here (Rav; Gem.* 29a).

Others maintain that the word is of Greek origin (*Tif. Yis., Pesachim* 10:8).

שֶׁנֶּאֱמַר ,,וַהֲשִׁמּוֹתִי אֶת־מִקְדְּשֵׁיכֶם״— קְדֻשָּׁתָן אַף כְּשֶׁהֵן שׁוֹמֵמִין. — *For the Torah states, 'And I shall make desolate your sanctuaries'* [*Lev.* 26:31]; [*this implies that*] *they are holy even when they are desolate.*

Since the synagogue is described as מִקְדָּשׁ מְעַט, *a small sanctuary* (*Ezek.* 11:16),the Torah's statement is also interpreted as referring to synagogues and not only to the Temple in Jerusalem; hence the mishnah's ruling (*Gem.* 29a).

The Tanna infers that desolate synagogues retain their sanctity from the order of the Torah's words: first the verse says *I shall make desolate*; then it refers to them as *sanctuaries.* This suggests that even after their desolation, they retain their sanctity *(Tos. Yom Tov).*

Alternatively, the verb וַהֲשִׁמּוֹתִי, *I shall make desolate,* is from the root שמם, which is applicable only to ruins that have been desolate for many years. [This is in contrast to חרב, *destroy,* which indicates recent destruction.] Thus, we infer that they are still considered *sanctuaries,* even many years after their destruction *(R' Akiva Eiger).*

עָלוּ בוֹ עֲשָׂבִים, — *If grass grew* [*in the ruins*],

[I.e., if weeds grew on the site.]

לֹא יִתְלֹשׁ, — *one may not detach it* [either to use as fodder for his animals or even merely to destroy the grass],

ג
ד

[ד] **ראש** חֹדֶשׁ אֲדָר שֶׁחָל לִהְיוֹת בַּשַּׁבָּת, קוֹרִין בְּפָרָשַׁת שְׁקָלִים. חָל לִהְיוֹת בְּתוֹךְ הַשַּׁבָּת, מַקְדִּימִין לְשֶׁעָבַר

יד אברהם

מִפְּנֵי עַגְמַת נֶפֶשׁ. — *because of grief.*

By leaving the site overgrown with weeds, the people will grieve, [and be inspired to repent their evil ways *(Rambam)*]. They will make every effort to rebuild the synagogue or at least pray that the site be restored *(Rav).* One may, however, cut the weeds and leave them where they fall *(Rav; Rambam; Gem.* 29a).

Alternatively, the mishnah's statement may be read as *one should not detach it because of grief,* i.e., in such a way that will alleviate grief; for if the weeds were cut and removed from the ruins, grief over the desolation would be partially alleviated. At the same time, the weeds should not be permitted to grow wild for it would appear that the former synagogue site is being left for animals. The people should cut the weeds and leave them at the site to show their grief and to indicate the sanctity of the site. If a new synagogue is built elsewhere, however, the desolate site need only be fenced in out of respect for its sanctity *(Tif. Yis.).*

4.

◆§ Public Torah Reading

The practice of publicly reading portions from the Torah dates back to antiquity. While the Torah mentions only the reading of *Deuteronomy* at the הַקְהֵל, *Assembly,* service (see 1:3 above and *Deut.* 31:12), tradition tells us that Moses instituted the practice of reading the Torah on Shabbos, festivals, *Rosh Chodesh,* and during חוֹל הַמּוֹעֵד [*Chol HaMoed*], *the Intermediate Days of festivals.* Ezra and the members of the Great Assembly instituted the reading of the Torah on Mondays, Thursdays, and at *Minchah* on the Sabbath *(Yerushalmi).*

According to this tradition, it would appear that before Ezra's time, the Torah was not read on Mondays and Thursdays. The *Talmud (Bava Kama* 82a), however, relates that the practice of reading on Mondays and Thursdays dates back to the time when the Jews were in the desert. This is alluded to in the verse, וַיֵּלְכוּ שְׁלֹשֶׁת־יָמִים בַּמִּדְבָּר וְלֹא־מָצְאוּ מָיִם, *and they traveled three days in the desert but did not find water (Exod.* 15:22). When this occurred the nation complained bitterly to Moses (*v.* 24). *Water* is allegorically interpreted as a reference to Torah (see *Isaiah* 55:1). Hence, we infer that the Jews complained because they had not heard words of Torah for three days. To prevent such situations in the future, the prophets [Moses and the members of his court *(Rambam)*] among them ordained that no three-day period should pass without the Torah being read. Thus, the practice of reading the Torah on Mondays and Thursdays would seem to predate Ezra. The Talmud resolves this dilemma by telling us that in the desert the practice was that three verses were read, either by one man or by three, corresponding to the three classes of Jews: *kohanim,* Levites, and Israelites; whereas Ezra ordained that three men be called to read a total of ten verses. The ten verses corresponding to the ten unoccupied men described above in 1:3.

The Talmud (29b) relates that in *Eretz Yisrael* the practice was to read the entire Torah over a period of three years. In Babylon, however, the practice was to finish

3 4. **O**n the first day of Adar which falls on a
4 Sabbath, we read the portion of *Shekalim* [*Exod.* 30:11-16]. If it falls on a weekday, we advance [the reading of *Shekalim*] to [the Sabbath] before and

the entire reading in one year. These two practices prevailed during the Gaonic period (see *Otzar HaGaonim, Berachos* 36).

Rambam (Hilchos Tefillah 13:1) relates that in his time, the overwhelming majority of communities followed the tradition of Babylon and read the entire Torah every year.

◆§ The Four Portions

Since this tractate deals primarily with the reading of the *Megillah* in the month of *Adar*, the Tanna now proceeds (mishnah 4) to discuss אַרְבַּע פָּרָשִׁיוֹת, *the Four* [*special*] *Portions* — the special Torah readings during and just prior to the month of *Adar*. The portions are: *Shekalim* [*Exod.* 30:11-16], which deals with the half-shekel per capita tax which paid for the purchase of communal offerings; *Zachor* [*'Remember'*; *Deut.* 25:17-19] which sets forth the commandment to exterminate Amalek; *Parah* [*'Cow'*; *Numb.* 19:1-22], which contains the laws of פָּרָה אֲדֻמָּה, the *Red Cow*, and *HaChodesh* [*'This month'*; *Exod.* 19:1-22], which describes the commandments of *Rosh Chodesh* and the month of *Nissan*. Once the subject of special Torah readings is mentioned, the Tanna concludes the chapter (mishnayos 5-6) with a listing of the special chapters that are read at other times *(Meiri; Tos. Yom Tov)*.

רֹאשׁ חֹדֶשׁ אֲדָר שֶׁחָל לִהְיוֹת בְּשַׁבָּת — [*On*] *the first day of Adar, which falls on a Sabbath,*

[The mishnah refers only to the month of *Adar* that immediately precedes *Nissan*. In years when there are two *Adars* these rules apply to the second *Adar* (see 1:4).]

קוֹרִין בְּפָרָשַׁת שְׁקָלִים — *We read the portion of Shekalim* [*Exod.* 30:11-16].

This portion is read as the *maftir* to announce the collection of the annual half-*shekel* tax which was to commence on the first of *Adar* (see *Shekalim* 1:1). The proceeds of the tax were used to purchase animals for communal sacrifices, e.g., תְּמִידִים, *daily burnt offerings*, and מוּסָפִים, *additional offerings*, for Sabbath, *Rosh Chodesh* and festivals. The tax was collected during *Adar*, and the people were obligated to pay it before *Rosh Chodesh Nissan*, because sacrifices offered from then on were to be purchased with funds from the newly contributed taxes. This annual collection was announced in the synagogue on the Sabbath prior to *Adar (Rav)*.

In ancient times, the portion of *Shekalim* was read to serve as a reminder to pay the tax *(Meiri)*. Nowadays, the reading serves as a remembrance of the tax (*Mishnah Berurah* 685:1).

[In Messianic times, when the Holy Temple will be rebuilt, the half-*shekel* will once again serve its original purpose. Thus, we read *Shekalim* nowadays so as not to forget our obligation then.]

חָל לִהְיוֹת בְּתוֹךְ הַשַּׁבָּת, — *If it falls on a weekday* [lit. *during the week*],

I.e., if the first day of *Adar* [on

ג וּמַפְסִיקִין לְשַׁבָּת אַחֶרֶת. בַּשְּׁנִיָּה — ,,זָכוֹר״,
ד בַּשְּׁלִישִׁית — ,,פָּרָה אֲדֻמָּה״, בָּרְבִיעִית —
,, הַחֹדֶשׁ הַזֶּה לָכֶם״, בַּחֲמִישִׁית חוֹזְרִין
לְכִסְדְרָן.

which day the collection of the half-*shekel* tax was to begin] falls on a weekday *(Rav)*...

מַקְדִּימִין לְשֶׁעָבַר, — *we advance [the reading of Shekalim] to [the Sabbath] before...*

Even if the first of *Adar* falls on a Friday, we read the portion of *Shekalim*, which serves notice of the impending collection, on the previous Sabbath so that the full month of *Adar* could be devoted to collection of the half-*shekels*] *(Rav; Gem.* 30a).

וּמַפְסִיקִין לְשַׁבָּת אַחֶרֶת. — *and interrupt [the reading of the four parshios] on the next Sabbath.*

On the Sabbath following the reading of *Shekalim*, no special portion is read. The Sabbath after the interruption, i.e., the second Sabbath of *Adar*, would be the Sabbath before Purim. At that time, *Zachor* is read [see below]. Thus, the reading of *Zachor*, which deals with the precept of eradicating the memory of Amalek, is linked with the *Megillah's* narrative of the downfall of Haman, the scion of Amalek *(Rav)*.

בַּשְּׁנִיָּה— — *On the second [Sabbath]...*

I.e., on the second Sabbath of the month. If the first of *Adar* falls on the Sabbath, we read *Shekalim* then and *Zachor* on the next Sabbath [see below]. If *Adar* begins during the week, we read *Zachor* on the Sabbath following the interruption *(Tif. Yis.; Gem.)*.

Others explain that the mishnah is referring not to the second Sabbath of the month, but to the second Sabbath on which a special portion is read. The 'first' Sabbath is that of *Shekalim*; the 'second' is that of *Zachor (Meiri)*.

,,זָכוֹר״, — [we read the portion of] *Zachor ['Remember,' Deut.* 25:17-19].

For *maftir*, we read the section containing the precepts to remember Amalek's attack on our ancestors, and to avenge it until no trace of Amalek remains.

As noted above, the reading of this portion always takes place on the Sabbath immediately preceding Purim. Many authorities maintain that the reading of this portion is a Torah precept (מִדְּאוֹרַיְיתָא). Therefore, villagers who have no *minyan* are required to come to a town where there is a *minyan*, in order to hear the reading (*Shulchan Aruch* 685:7).

בַּשְּׁלִישִׁית— — *On the third [Sabbath]...*

If *Adar* began on a weekday other than Friday, *Parah* will be read on the third Sabbath of the month. For example, if *Adar* began on a Wednesday (fig. 8), the third Sabbath will be the eighteenth of the month. Since it will be the Sabbath before the reading of the chapter of *HaChodesh*, *Parah* will be read on that day [see below]. If, however, *Adar* began on a Sabbath (fig. 9), the third Sabbath of *Adar*

3 4 interrupt [the reading of the four *parshios*] on the next Sabbath. On the second [Sabbath we read the portion of] *Zachor*, ['Remember what Amalek did,' *Deut.* 25:17-19]. On the third [Sabbath we read the portion of] *Parah Adumah*, ['The Red Cow,' *Num.* 19:1-22]. On the fourth [Sabbath we read the portion of] *HaChodesh hazeh lachem*, ['This month shall be to you,' *Exod.* 19:1-20]. On the fifth [Sabbath] we resume [reading] the regular order.

YAD AVRAHAM

S	M	T	W	T	F	S
						PARSHAS SHEKALIM
			1 ROSH CHODESH ADAR	2	3	4
5	6	7	8	9	10	11 PARSHAS ZACHOR
12	13	14 PURIM	15	16	17	18 PARSHAS PARAH
19	20	21	22	23	24	25 PARSHAS HACHODESH
26	27	28	29	ROSH CHODESH NISSAN		

Figure 8

S	M	T	W	T	F	S
						1 ROSH CHODESH ADAR PARSHAS SHEKALIM
2	3	4	5	6	7	8 PARSHAS ZACHOR
9	10	11	12	13	14 PURIM	15
16	17	18	19	20	21	22 PARSHAS PARAH
23	24	25	26	27	28	29 PARSHAS HACHODESH
ROSH CHODESH NISSAN						

Figure 9

will be the fifteenth. The Sabbath before *HaChodesh* will be the twenty-second, and that will be the day of the *Parah* reading. If *Adar* began on Friday (fig. 10), the third Sabbath will be the sixteenth of *Adar*. The Sabbath before *HaChodesh* will be the twenty-third, and *Parah* will be read on that day *(Tos. Yom Tov)*.

S	M	T	W	T	F	S
						PARSHAS SHEKALIM
					1 ROSH CHODESH ADAR	2
3	4	5	6	7	8	9 PARSHAS ZACHOR
10	11	12	13	14 PURIM	15	16
17	18	19	20	21	22	23 PARSHAS PARAH
24	25	26	27	28	29	ROSH CHODESH NISSAN PARSHAS HACHODESH

Figure 10

Alternatively, as noted, the reference is not to the third Sabbath of the month, but to the third Sabbath on which a special portion is read *(Meiri; Rivav)*.

,,פָּרָה אֲדֻמָּה'' — *[We read the portion of] Parah Adumah ['The Red Cow,' Num.* 19:1-22].

This portion deals with the slaughtering and burning of a completely red cow whose ashes were used for the preparation of the mixture needed to cleanse those who were contaminated by a corpse. This portion was read before Pesach to caution the people to cleanse themselves so as to be able to take part in the Pesach sacrifice *(Rashi; Rav).*

[The familiar translation of פָּרָה אֲדֻמָּה is *Red Heifer.* We have rejected this as erroneous because the word פָּרָה refers to *a cow* in its third year or older *(Parah* 1:1). A *heifer* is defined as 'a cow that has not produced a calf and is under three years of age' *(The Random House Dictionary of the English Language).*]

According to some authorities, this reading, too, is a Torah obligation. Therefore, villagers should go to the cities to hear the reading with a *minyan (Shulchan Aruch* 685:7).

בָּרְבִיעִית— – *On the fourth* [*Sabbath*]...

[I.e., the Sabbath preceding *Rosh Chodesh Nissan;* or on *Rosh Chodesh,* if it is falls on the Sabbath.]

If *Adar* began on a weekday other than Friday (fig. 11), this would be the fourth Sabbath counting from the interruption between the reading of *Shekalim* and *Zachor.* [If the first of *Adar* was on a Sabbath (fig. 9), this is the fourth Sabbath after the reading of *Shekalim.* If *Rosh Chodesh Adar* fell on Friday (fig. 10), however, *Rosh Chodesh Nissan* will be on the fifth Sabbath thereafter, and that day *HaChodesh* would be read.] As previously noted, no special portion was read on the Sabbath after Purim if the first of *Nissan* fell on a Sabbath (fig. 10) or Sunday (fig. 9) *(Ran).*

S	M	T	W	T	F	S
						PARSHAS SHEKALIM
	1 ROSH CHODESH ADAR	2	3	4	5	6
7	8	9	10	11	12	13 PARSHAS ZACHOR
14 PURIM	15	16	17	18	19	20 PARSHAS PARAH
21	22	23	24	25	26	27 PARSHAS HACHODESH
28	29	ROSH CHODESH NISSAN				

Figure 11

Alternatively, this refers to the fourth Sabbath on which a special portion is read *(Meiri; Rivav).*

הַחֹדֶשׁ הַזֶּה לָכֶם, – [*we read the portion of*] *HaChodesh hazeh lachem* [*'This month shall be to you,' Ex* 19:1-20].

...the portion dealing with the proclamation of *Rosh Chodesh* and the designation of *Nissan* as the first month of the year. This portion was read before Pesach since it contains the laws of Pesach *(Rav).*

The sequence of the four special portions warrants further explanation: Historically the מִשְׁכָּן, *Tabernacle,* was constructed on the first of *Nissan* whereas the Red Cow was slaughtered only on the second. Why then, does the portion of *Parah* precede that of *HaChodesh?*

Rashi cites *Yerushalmi,* which explains that the reading of *Parah* was advanced because of the paramount importance of purity. Thus, people who heard the reading would be reminded to cleanse themselves before Passover.

◆§ Maftir and Haftarah

The practice of concluding the Sabbath Torah reading with the הַפְטָרָה, *haftarah;* i.e., a selection from the Prophets, orginated later. According to *Sefer HaTishbi,* the practice dates from the time when Antiochus Epiphanes, the Syrian-Greek ruler of *Eretz Yisrael,* proscribed the public reading of the Torah. In order to prevent the Torah from being completely forgotten, the Sages ordained the reading of a selection from the Prophets related to the weekly portion. On festivals, too, a related selection from the Prophets was substituted for the pertinent Torah reading. When the Greeks were driven out of *Eretz Yisrael,* the original practice of reading from the Torah was reinstituted. Nevertheless, the custom of reading a related selection from the Prophets was maintained.

As we have noted, the selection from the Prophets is called the *haftarah.* The reader of this selection is referred to as the *maftir.* There are three theories as to the root of these terms:

— The term is derived from the root פטר, *to free.* During the period of Greek domination, the one who read the Prophetic selection would free, or release, the other members of the congregation of their obligation to hear the Torah reading *(Machzor Vitry).*

— The root פטר in this case means *to open.* After the reading of the *haftarah* one may open his mouth to speak. During the reading of the Torah, however, this is forbidden *(Abudraham; Rabbeinu Tam).*

— The root פטר in this case means *to conclude* (as in אֵין מַפְטִירִין אַחַר הַפֶּסַח אֲפִיקוֹמָן, *we may not conclude with dessert after eating the Pesach lamb).* Thus, the *haftarah* concludes the Torah reading *(Abudraham).*

On an ordinary Sabbath, the *maftir* reading is a repetition of the final three or more verses of the portion. On festivals and special Sabbaths such as *Rosh Chodesh* and the Four Portions, the *maftir* reading is a special portion of the Torah relating specifically to the uniqueness of that day. The *haftarah* reading on such days also relates to the day. Thus, on festivals the *maftir* reading is from the relevant verses in *Numbers* 28-29. Additionally, reading these verses, which speak of the festival sacrifices, fulfills the *Gemara's* statement (31a) that reading the order of the sacrifices is tantamount to having brought them.

בַּחֲמִישִׁית... — *On the fifth* [*Sabbath*]...

[If *Adar* began on any day other than Friday, this refers to the fifth Sabbath after *Rosh Chodesh Adar.* If *Adar* began on Friday (fig. 10), however, *Rosh Chodesh Nissan* would fall on the Sabbath and the regular order (see below) would resume on the sixth Sabbath. According to *Meiri's* alternative interpretation (see above), the four preceding ones are not necessarily in *Adar;* they are those on which the four portions were read.]

חוֹזְרִין לְכִסְדְרָן. — *we resume* [*reading*] *the regular order* [*of haftaros*].

We resume the reading of *haftarah* selections that are linked to the regular portions of the Torah. On Sabbaths when one of the four special sections is read as *maftir,* the *haftarah* selection from the Prophets is related to the special portions. Thus, for example, when *Shekalim* is read, the *haftarah* is taken from *II Kings* 11:17-12:17 (according to the Sephardim), or 12:1-17 (according to the Ashkenazim). This selection deals with the money collected in the days of King Yoash for the repair of the Temple.

The *haftarah* of *Zachor* is from *I Samuel* 15:1-35 (according to the Sephardim) or 15:2-35 (according to the Ashkenazim). It tells of Saul's battle with Amalek and his failure to kill Agag — Haman's progenitor.

The *haftarah* of *Parah* is from *Ezekiel* 36:16-36 (according to the Sephardim), or 36:16-38 (according to the Ashkenazim). It deals with God's promise to cleanse the Jewish people of their impurities.

The *haftarah* of *HaChodesh* is read from *Ezekiel* 45:18-46:15 (according to

ג לַכֹּל מַפְסִיקִין: בְּרָאשֵׁי חֳדָשִׁים, בַּחֲנֻכָּה,
ד וּבְפוּרִים, בְּתַעֲנִיּוֹת, וּבְמַעֲמָדוֹת, וּבְיוֹם
הַכִּפּוּרִים.

the Sephardim), or 45:16-46:18 (according to the Ashkenazim). It deals with the Sabbath, *Rosh Chodesh*, and festival sacrifices that will be offered in the Third Temple *(Rav)*.

לַכֹּל מַפְסִיקִין: — *For all [the following occasions] we interrupt [the regular order]:*

There are three approaches to this next section of the mishnah:

1) For all holidays — Pesach, Shavuos, Succos, Rosh HaShanah, Yom Kippur — we interrupt the regular order of the Torah readings whether they fall on the Sabbath, Monday or Thursday. There is a second category of days for which only the regular *weekday* Torah reading is interrupted — *Rosh Chodesh*, Purim, Chanukah, fasts, *maamados*. If these days fall on the Sabbath, however, the regular order of Torah reading is followed, but *maftir* and *haftarah* portions are chosen to commemorate the special nature of the day *(Ran; Rashi)*.

2) Whenever only three people are called to the Torah — Monday, Thursday, Sabbath *Minchah* — the regular reading may be superseded. Thus when *Rosh Chodesh*, Chanukah, Purim, fasts or *maamados*, fall on Monday or Thursday, the regular reading is set aside in favor of the special portion relating to the event of the day. Similarly, should Yom Kippur fall on a Sabbath, the regular *Minchah* reading is replaced by the Yom Kippur *Minchah* reading (*Tos.* 29a).

3) If any of the following falls on Sabbath, the *haftarah* is selected from a portion relevant to *it* rather than to the Sabbath portion. Thus we interrupt the regular order of *haftarah* readings *(Rav)*.

בְּרָאשֵׁי חֳדָשִׁים, — *on Rosh Chodesh,*

If *Rosh Chodesh* falls on the Sabbath, the *haftarah* is taken from *Isaiah* 66 [which contains the verse (23): וְהָיָה מִדֵּי־חֹדֶשׁ בְּחָדְשׁוֹ וּמִדֵּי שַׁבָּת בְּשַׁבַּתּוֹ, *And it shall be month after month and Sabbath after Sabbath*]. *If Rosh Chodesh* falls on a Sunday, the *haftarah* is from *I Samuel* 20:18-42 [which begins, *Jonathan said to him (David), 'Tomorrow is Rosh Chodesh!'*] (*Gem.* 31a).

בַּחֲנֻכָּה, — *on Chanukah,*

On the Sabbath that falls during Chanukah, the *haftarah* is read from *Zechariah* 3:14-4:7. It describes the prophet's vision of a *menorah* with seven candles. If there is a second Sabbath in Chanukah, [i.e., the first and eighth days of Chanukah fall on the Sabbath], the *haftarah* is read from *I Kings* 7:40-51, which describes the construction of the vessels used in the First Temple.

The reading from *Zechariah* takes precedence over that from *Kings* because the former is the form of a *prophecy* [whereas the latter is written as a historic narrative] *(Ran)*.

Alternatively, the reading from *Zechariah* takes precedence since it speaks of the Second Temple — the scene of the Chanukah miracle [whereas *Kings* refers to the First Temple] *(Meiri)*.

Though the miracle of Chanukah occurred after that of Purim, the Tanna mentions it first since it is

3
4 For all [the following occasions] we interrupt [the regular order] on *Rosh Chodesh*, on Chanukah, on Purim on [public] fasts, on *maamados* and on Yom Kippur.

celebrated before Purim in the calendar year. Alternatively, Chanukah is mentioned first because it is an eight-day festival [and therefore always contains at least one Sabbath *haftarah* reading] whereas Purim is but one day [and unless it falls on the Sabbath, no *haftarah* reading is interrupted] *(Tos. Yom Tov).*

וּבְפוּרִים, — *on Purim,*

If the fifteenth of Adar falls on a Sabbath, residents of walled cities read the *haftarah* of *Zachor* instead of the regular Sabbath selection *(Rav).*

בְּתַעֲנִיּוֹת, — *on* [*public*] *fasts,*

In the context of the mishnah, this would seem to discuss a fast day which falls on the Sabbath. It is impossible, however, since public fasts are not observed on the Sabbath. Therefore, the subject of the mishnah must be the interruption of the regular order of *weekday* Torah reading in favor of the fast day portion (see 3:6; *Gem.* 30b). [The same logic applies to *maamados*, below.]

וּבְמַעֲמָדוֹת, — *on maamados*

Maamados were twenty-four groups of Israelites who represented the entire nation during the daily sacrifices. The members of the *maamad* on duty would pray together and read from the account of Creation (*Gen.* 1:1-2:3; see *Taanis* 4:2-3). Those who lived near Jerusalem would go to the Temple to be present when the sacrifices were offered. Those who lived far away from the Holy City would gather in the synagogue and pray for their brethren. The twenty-four groups would serve on a rotating basis, a week at a time (see *Taanis* 4:1-4). This reading superseded the regular weekday Torah reading on Monday and Thursday *(Tif. Yis.).*

וּבְיוֹם הַכִּפּוּרִים. — *and on Yom Kippur.*

The *haftarah* of Yom Kippur is read even when the day falls on the *Sabbath*. The *haftarah*, from *Isaiah* 57:14-58:14, describes the type of repentance expected on a fast day *(Rav).*

Although Yom Kippur had been included with holidays in the phrase *all occasions*, [see above] it is repeated here in conjunction with the fast days mentioned above *(Ran; Rashi).*

Another reason for enumerating Yom Kippur separately is because it is unique in that it has its own *Minchah* reading, a feature which other festivals do not have. It supersedes the Sabbath *Minchah* reading. Thus, it is the only case dealing with a *Minchah* reading.

Alternatively, since Scripture refers to Yom Kippur as a 'Sabbath' (*Lev.* 23:32) and it is as stringent in its prohibition of work as the Sabbath, it would be possible to think that the regular Sabbath reading should be recited as usual.

Furthermore, since the Torah is read twice on Yom Kippur, we might think that the Sabbath portion should be read in the morning and the Yom Kippur portion in the afternoon *(Tos. Yom Tov).*

ג [ה] **בְּפֶסַח** קוֹרִין בְּפָרָשַׁת מוֹעֲדוֹת שֶׁל
ה תּוֹרַת כֹּהֲנִים. בַּעֲצֶרֶת —
,,שִׁבְעָה שָׁבֻעֹת״. בְּרֹאשׁ הַשָּׁנָה — ,,בַּחֹדֶשׁ
הַשְּׁבִיעִי בְּאֶחָד לַחֹדֶשׁ״. בְּיוֹם הַכִּפּוּרִים —
,,אַחֲרֵי מוֹת״. בְּיוֹם טוֹב הָרִאשׁוֹן שֶׁל חָג

יד אברהם

5.

...בְּפֶסַח — *On Pesach,*

I.e., on the first day of *Pesach* (*Rav* from 31a).

קוֹרִין בְּפָרָשַׁת הַמּוֹעֲדוֹת שֶׁל תּוֹרַת כֹּהֲנִים. — *We read the portion of the festivals in Leviticus (23).*

This portion contains the precepts connected with the observance of the Festivals. It is customary to commence the reading from 22:26 (*Rav; Rashi* from 31a).

[The concluding verses of *Leviticus* 22 discuss the minimum age at which an animal may be brought as a sacrifice, a law which is relevant to all the festival offerings. The chapter ends [22:32-33]: *I am HASHEM Who sanctifies you, Who has brought you forth from the Land of Egypt...* Thus these verses also relate to Pesach in particular.][1]

בַּעֲצֶרֶת—,,שִׁבְעָה שָׁבֻעֹת״. — *On*

1. [As can be seen from the end of this chapter, some portions relating to each festival must be read on that festival.] The practice today is not based upon these mishnayos but upon various other ancient sources [among others, the *Gemara, Pesikta* and *Maseches Soferim* (see *Tos.* 31b; *Mabit,* vol. 2, 129)].

On the first day of Pesach the portion (*Exod.* 12:21-51) dealing with the Exodus from Egypt and the eating of the Pesach sacrifice was read since these both occurred on that day (*Tif. Yis.*).

On the second day of Pesach, the day of the reaping and counting of the *omer,* the portion of the festivals (*Lev.* 22:26-23:44) is read since it contains the precepts of the day (*Tos. Yom Tov; Tiferes Yisrael; Ran*).

[In *Eretz Yisrael,* the second day of Pesach is the first day of *Chol HaMoed;* the reading, however, is the same as that in the Diaspora.]

The portions prescribed for *Chol HaMoed* and the last days of Pesach are not mentioned in the mishnah. *Tosefta* 3:3 rules that one must select Scriptural portions that deal with Pesach. Thus, on the third day of the festival, the reading is קַדֵּשׁ, *Sanctify* (*Exod.* 13:1-17), dealing with the sanctification of the firstborn, and the laws of Pesach.

On the fourth day, the reading is כֶּסֶף, [*When you lend*] *money* (*Exod.* 22:24 — 23:19), dealing with the three pilgrimage festivals. On the fifth day, the reading is פְּסָל, *Hew,* (*Exod.* 34:1-25) dealing with the Pesach sacrifice and the three pilgrimage festivals. On the sixth day, the reading is בְּמִדְבַּר, *In the desert,* (*Numbers* 15:1-4) dealing with the Pesach sacrifice that was offered in the desert. It also states that people who were contaminated, and therefore unable to bring the Pesach offering, would be given an opportunity to bring it on the fourteenth of *Iyar,* [פֶּסַח שֵׁנִי, *Second Pesach*].

On the seventh day of Pesach, we read the portion (*Exod.* 13:17-15:26) that deals with the splitting of the Red Sea, which took place on that date.

On the eighth day (not applicable in *Eretz Yisrael*) we read כָּל־הַבְּכוֹר, *Every first-*

3
5

5. On Pesach, we read the portion of the festivals in *Leviticus* (23). On Shavuos [we read the portion of] *'Seven Weeks'* [*Deut.* 16:9-12]. On Rosh HaShanah [we read the portion of] *'In the seventh month, on the first day'* [*Lev.* 23:23-25]. On Yom Kippur [we read the portion of] *'After the death'* [*Lev.* 16]. On the first day of the Festival we read the

Shavuos [*we read the portion of*] *'Seven weeks'* [*Deut.* 16:9-12].

[We read the entire portion that includes these verses. Since we must call up five persons to the reading, we must read at least fifteen verses, allowing the minimum number of three verses for each one. However, the chapters chosen for the reading must comprise a logical unit, rather than fifteen haphazard verses. We therefore commence the reading from כָּל־הַבְּכוֹר, *every firstborn* (15:19), and conclude with 16:17.]

Since this section was not read on Pesach in *Eretz Yisrael*, it was selected to be read on Shavuos *(Tos. Yom Tov; Ran).* Current practice in Eretz Yisrael is to read *Exod.* 19-20 on the first day (*Orach Chaim* 494:1).

Outside of *Eretz Yisrael*, this section is read on the second day of the festival. On the first day, the narrative of the day is read, i.e., the giving of the Ten Commandments *(Exodus* 19-20), since the event occurred on Shavuos *(Rashi* 31a; *Tif. Yis.).*

[Although *Tiferes Yisrael* states that the portion of שִׁבְעָה שָׁבֻעֹת, *Seven Weeks*, is read as the *maftir*, this is not the common practice. Like every festival *maftir*, this one is taken from the relevant verses in *Numbers* 29 which describes the מוּסָפִים, *additional offerings*, of the festivals.]

בְּרֹאשׁ הַשָּׁנָה—,,בַּחֹדֶשׁ הַשְּׁבִיעִי בְּאֶחָד לַחֹדֶשׁ". — *On Rosh HaShanah,* [*we read the portion of*] *'In the seventh month, on the first day'* [*Lev.* 23:23-25].

We read the entire portion of the festivals which includes that of Rosh HaShanah. [See comm. beginning of this mishnah] *(Tif. Yis.).*

Our custom on the first day is to read *Genesis* 21, which begins וַה' פָּקַד אֶת־שָׂרָה, *And HASHEM remembered Sarah.* According to tradition, Sarah conceived Isaac on that day *(Rav; Tif. Yis.).*

[For *maftir*, we read *Numbers* 29:1-6. Although *Tiferes Yisrael* states that we read *Lev.* 23:23-25 for *maftir*, this is not the common practice. (See also *Tiferes Yaakov).*]

בְּיוֹם הַכִּפּוּרִים—,,אַחֲרֵי מוֹת". — *On Yom Kippur* [*we read the portion of*] *'After the death'* [*Lev.* 16].

This chapter is read at *Shacharis.* It describes the sacrificial service performed on Yom Kippur and is read to express the wish that our prayers may be as acceptable to God as would be the sacrifices *(Tiferes Yisrael).*

At *Minchah*, we read the portion (*Lev.* 18) dealing with forbidden sexual unions. One reason given for the selection of this portion is to inspire repentance on the part of people guilty of

born (Deut. 15:19-16:17) which deals with all three pilgrimage festivals and their attendant precepts. It is read on the last day of festivals as a remembrance of Temple times, when the last day of the festival was the final opportunity one had to fulfill these precepts *(Tos. Yom Tov; Gem.* 31a).

ג קוֹרִין בְּפָרָשַׁת מוֹעֲדוֹת שֶׁבְּתוֹרַת כֹּהֲנִים.
ו וּבִשְׁאָר כָּל יְמוֹת הֶחָג בְּקָרְבְּנוֹת הֶחָג.

[ו] **בַּחֲנֻכָּה** — בַּנְּשִׂיאִים. בְּפוּרִים — „וַיָּבֹא עֲמָלֵק". בְּרָאשֵׁי

יד אברהם

such sins (*Rashi; Rambam, Tefillah* 13:11).

Tosafos explains that the portion was chosen to caution men not to be tempted by the women dressed in their holiday finery.

Others interpret the choice allegorically. Scripture refers to forbidden unions as גִּלוּי עֲרָיוֹת, *the uncovering of nakedness*, and it exhorts us not to uncover what should be left concealed. Similarly, we ask God not to uncover our nakedness; i.e., our shame for failing to have lived up to the Torah's standards (*Tos.; Abudraham*).

בְּיוֹם טוֹב הָרִאשׁוֹן שֶׁל חָג... — *On the first day of the Festival.*

[In Talmudic terminology, Succos is called simply חָג, *Festival.*]

קוֹרִין בְּפָרָשַׁת מוֹעֲדוֹת שֶׁבְּתוֹרַת כֹּהֲנִים. — *we read the portion of the festivals in Leviticus* [22:26-23:44];

Since we read כָּל-הַבְּכוֹר, *'Every firstborn' (Deut.* 15:19) on Shavuos, we alternate and read the section in *Leviticus* on Succos (*Tos. Yom Tov; Ran*).

In the Diaspora this section is repeated on the second day as well (*Rav; Gemara* 31a).

וּבִשְׁאָר כָּל יְמוֹת הֶחָג... — *and on all the remaining days of the Festival...*

[I.e., on *Chol HaMoed* Succos.]

בְּקָרְבְּנוֹת הֶחָג. — [*we read the portion of*] *the sacrifices of the festival* [*Num.* 29:12-30:1].

[On each day of *Chol HaMoed* Succos we read the portion that details the sacrifices offered on that day.]

In *Eretz Yisrael*, only the verses dealing with the day's sacrifices are read. Since four people are called to the Torah on intermediate days of festivals, the portion is repeated four times (*Shulchan Aruch* 663).

Outside of Israel, the order of the reading is complicated by סְפֵיקָא דְיוֹמָא, *doubt concerning the day*. We retain the status of ancient times when Jews living far from the *Sanhedrin* could not know which day had been proclaimed as *Rosh Chodesh*. As a result, each festival day was in doubt, and two days were observed.

Concerning the *Chol HaMoed* reading, there are two customs: Ashkenazim accept the ruling of *Rama* (*Shulchan Aruch* 663): On the first day, since doubt exists as to whether it is really the second or third day of Succos, the first person reads the verses dealing with the sacrifice of the second day. The second person reads the verses of the third day. The third person continues with the verses of the fourth day. (The fourth day's verses are added to provide the minimum reading of ten verses.) The fourth person rereads the first two sections. This procedure is followed throughout the festival except that on the seventh day. On this last intermediate day, we begin the reading with the verses of the fifth day and the fourth person rereads the portions dealing with the sixth and seventh day.

Sefardim follow the opinion of *Beis Yosef (663)*, who objected to reading the verses dealing with the sacrifices offered on the fourth day, because the doubt was only whether the day in question was the second or third; it was definitely not the fourth. Instead, the third person repeats the section read by the second person and the last person

3
6

portion of the festivals in *Leviticus* [22:26-23:44] and on all the remaining days of the Festival [we read the portion of] the sacrifices of the Festival [*Num.* 29:12-30:1].

6. On [the eighth day of] Chanukah [we read the portion of] the princes [*Num.* 7:12-89]. On Purim [we read the portion of] *'And Amalek came'*

YAD AVRAHAM

repeats both sections. This practice was also preferred by the *Vilna Gaon* and some Chassidic dynasties.

Although not mentioned in the mishnah, the custom is to read the verses dealing with the sacrifice offered on the first day as the *maftir* on the festival itself. This is based on the *Gemara's* statement (31b) that following the destruction of the Temple, Scriptural portions relating to the Temple service are read as a substitute for the sacrifices themselves (*Gem.* 31b). Following this principle, the Rabbis instituted as the festival *maftir* reading those verses of the portion of the *musaf* sacrifices (*Numb.* 28-29) relevant to the particular day (*Tos.* 30b).

On the eighth day of the Festival — *Shemini Atzeres* — we read כָּל־הַבְּכוֹר (*Deut.* 15:19-16:17) as is the custom on all festivals outside of *Eretz Yisrael.*

According to some authorities, the reading is begun from עַשֵּׂר תְּעַשֵּׂר (*Deut.* 14:22), which deals with tithes and gifts to the poor, both of which are to be given at the conclusion of Succos (Rashi). The *maftir* is read from the verses dealing with the sacrifices offered on that day.

In *Eretz Yisrael,* Simchas Torah is celebrated together with *Shemini Atzeres* and we read וְזֹאת הַבְּרָכָה, the last portion of the Torah *(Deut.* 33-34).

6.

בַּחֲנֻכָּה—בַּנְּשִׂיאִים. — *On [the eight days of] Chanukah [we read the portion of] the princes [Numb. 7:12-89].*

The reading prescribed by the mishnah includes the sections describing the sacrifices offered by the princes of the tribes when the *Mishkan* was dedicated. Since the Hasmoneans too, dedicated a new altar to replace the one that had been defiled by the Greeks, this reading is appropriate for Chanukah *(Rashi;Ran).*

It is customary, however, to start the reading of the first day from וַיְהִי בְּיוֹם כַּלּוֹת מֹשֶׁה לְהָקִים אֶת הַמִּשְׁכָּן, *And it was on the day that Moses finished erecting the Mishkan* (7:1). Although those eleven verses are not mentioned by the mishnah and do not deal with the offerings of the princes, the verses are read in accordance with the *Pesikta,* which states that the construction of the *Mishkan* was completed on the twenty-fifth day of *Kislev,* the same date when the Chanukah miracle took place. We, therefore, begin the Chanukah reading with that section. The *Mishkan* was not set up, however, until the first day of *Nissan* in order to honor the month in which the patriarch Isaac was born. We, therefore, begin the Chanukah reading with that section *(Bach; Tur* 684).

Some commence the reading from *Numbers* 6:22, in order to include the priestly blessing in the reading. Thus they commemorate the miracle of

ג חֳדָשִׁים — „וּבְרָאשֵׁי חָדְשֵׁיכֶם". בְּמַעֲמָדוֹת
ו — בְּמַעֲשֵׂה בְרֵאשִׁית. בְּתַעֲנִיּוֹת — בְּרָכוֹת
וּקְלָלוֹת.

אֵין מַפְסִיקִין בַּקְּלָלוֹת, אֶלָּא אֶחָד קוֹרֵא אֶת־כֻּלָּן.

בַּשֵּׁנִי וּבַחֲמִישִׁי וּבַשַּׁבָּת בַּמִּנְחָה קוֹרִין

יד אברהם

Chanukah which came about through the priestly family of Mattathias *(Tur).*

On the eighth day of Chanukah, it is customary to conclude the reading with *Numbers* 8:1-4 which deals with lighting the *Menorah*, an act which is most appropriate for Chanukah *(Tur).*

For the order of the daily Chanukah reading, see *Orach Chaim* 684.

בַּפּוּרִים — „וַיָּבֹא עֲמָלֵק". — *On Purim [we read the portion of] 'And Amalek came'* [*Exodus 17:8-16*].

[The portion describes our first encounter with Amalek. These verses were chosen since Purim deals with our later deliverance from this same enemy.]

Although this portion contains only nine verses and the normal requirement is ten, the rule here is waived since this is a complete topic [which is totally unrelated to either the preceding or the following verses] *(Rif).*

בְּרָאשֵׁי חֳדָשִׁים — „וּבְרָאשֵׁי חָדְשֵׁיכֶם". — *On Rosh Chodesh [we read the portion of] 'On your New Moons'* [*Numb.* 28:11-15].

[The portion describes the sacrifices offered on *Rosh Chodesh.* Since the portion contains only four verses, we include the sections dealing with the daily burnt offerings and the *Musaf* offering of the Sabbath *(Shulchan Aruch* 423:2).

If *Rosh Chodesh* falls on the Sabbath, this portion is read as the *maftir* but the verses dealing with the daily burnt offerings are omitted *(ibid.* 425:1).

בְּמַעֲמָדוֹת — *On maamados* [lit. *groups of people assigned to stand*].

The *maamados* were groups of individuals who were assigned to gather in Jerusalem and in local cities to pray for the acceptance of the communal offerings of the Temple (see mishnah 4 and *Taanis* 4:1-4).

בְּמַעֲשֵׂה בְרֵאשִׁית. — [*we read the portion of*] *the creation* [*Gen.* 1-2:4].

This reading was prescribed to indicate that the very existence of the heavens and earth is dependent upon the observance of the sacrificial service *(Rav; Gem.* 31b; see *Taanis* 4:3).

בְּתַעֲנִיּוֹת — *On [public] fasts...*

These fast days are not those which are permanent fixtures of the calendar [i.e., 3 *Tishrei*, 10 *Teves*, 17 *Tammuz*, and 9 *Av*] but are those enacted as the need arises when such calamities as drought befall the nation *(Rambam, Tefillah* 13:18; see *Taanis* 1:3-3:9).

בְּרָכוֹת וּקְלָלוֹת. — [*we read the portion of the*] *blessings and* [*the*] *curses* [*Lev.* 26:3-47].

This section is read to teach the people that their distress was caused by sinfulness; conversely, if they repent, they will be saved *(Rashi; Rav; Rambam, Tefillah* 13:18).

Rambam rules that the reading

[*Exod.* 17:8-16]. On *Rosh Chodesh* [we read the portion of] *'On your New Moons'* [*Num.* 28:11-15]. On *maamados* [we read the portion of] the Creation [*Gen.* 1-2:4]. On [public] fasts [we read the portion of] the blessings and curses [*Lev.* 26:3-47].

We may not interrupt [the reading of] the curses; therefore, one [person] reads them in their entirety.

On Mondays, Thursdays, and at *Minchah* on the Sabbath we read the regular order [of portions] but

YAD AVRAHAM

prescribed by our mishnah is binding on specially proclaimed fast days. On the regular annual fast days, however, we read וַיְחַל מֹשֶׁה, *and Moses supplicated (Exod.* 32:11-14; 34:1-10).

Rosh (4:10) interprets our mishnah as referring to all fast days and rules that the halachah does not follow our mishnah. Instead, based on *Soferim* 17:7, the reading from *Exodus* is used for regular annual fasts.

אֵין מַפְסִיקִין בַּקְּלָלוֹת, — *We may not interrupt* [*the reading of*] *the curses;*

The reading of the curses is not interrupted to allow a second person to be called to the Torah. Rather, the curses are read as a single, uninterrupted unit. Were one to stop during the reading of the curses, he would appear to despise God's admonitions. Another reason for avoiding such an interruption is that when a person concludes his Torah reading, he recites a blessing. The following reader recites a blessing prior to his reading. The result would be that two people will recite blessings over the curses. God says, as it were, 'It is not proper that My children should be cursed while I am being blessed' *(Gem.* 31b).

This applies also to the annual Sabbath reading of the curses in בְּחֻקֹּתַי [*Bechukosai*] *(Lev.* 26), but not to the curses in כִּי תָבֹא [*Ki Savo*] *(Deut.* 28), which, although Divinely inspired, were composed by Moses. Furthermore, they were spoken in the singular, making them less stringent to the community, whereas those in *Bechukosai* were said in the plural, implying much more general anger against Israel *(Gem.* 31b).

The widely accepted custom is, however, not to interrupt the reading of the curses in *Ki Savo (Rambam, Tefillah* 13:7; *Shulchan Aruch* 428:6).

אֶלָּא אֶחָד קוֹרֵא אֶת־כֻּלָּן. — *therefore, one* [*person*] *reads them in their entirety.*

The *kohen* and the Levite read the verses of blessings which introduce the curses, and the Israelite reads the curses *(Rashi; Tos. Yom Tov).*

The Israelite must commence at least three verses before the section dealing with the curses, since we never begin a Torah reading with curses *(Tos.* 31b).

בַּשֵּׁנִי וּבַחֲמִישִׁי וּבַשַּׁבָּת בַּמִּנְחָה קוֹרִין כְּסִדְרָן, — *On Mondays, Thursdays and at Minchah on the Sabbath we read the regular order* [*of portions*].

On these occasions, we read the

כְּסִדְרָן, וְאֵין עוֹלִין לָהֶם מִן־הַחֶשְׁבּוֹן. ד
שֶׁנֶּאֱמַר ,,וַיְדַבֵּר מֹשֶׁה אֶת־מֹעֲדֵי ה׳ אֶל־ א
בְּנֵי יִשְׂרָאֵל״ — מִצְוָתָן שֶׁיְּהוּ קוֹרִין כָּל־אֶחָד
וְאֶחָד בִּזְמַנּוֹ.

[א] **הַקּוֹרֵא** אֶת־הַמְּגִלָּה עוֹמֵד וְיוֹשֵׁב. קְרָאָהּ אֶחָד, קְרָאוּהָ שְׁנַיִם — יָצְאוּ.

יד אברהם

beginning of the following weekly portion *(Rashi; Rav).*

[The Monday and Thursday readings were instituted by Moses. See *pref.* to mishnah 4.]

The Sabbath afternoon reading was instituted by Ezra the Scribe. His motive was to afford an additional reading for people who are unfortunately so involved with their work or business that they neither study Torah nor hear the readings on Monday and Thursday *(Bava Kama* 82a).

Although the sanctity of the Sabbath would dictate that its reading be listed first, our mishnah mentions it after that of Monday and Thursday because the Sabbath *Minchah* reading was enacted as a supplement to the readings of Monday and Thursday.

וְאֵין עוֹלִין לָהֶם מִן־הַחֶשְׁבּוֹן. — *but this* [*reading*] *is not taken into account.*

Although the first section of the weekly portion already has been read three times [i.e., Monday, Thursday and the previous Sabbath afternoon], when the Sabbath arrives, this reading is repeated as part of the full portion *(Rav).*

שֶׁנֶּאֱמַר ,,וַיְדַבֵּר מֹשֶׁה אֶת־מֹעֲדֵי ה׳ אֶל־בְּנֵי יִשְׂרָאֵל״ — *As it is said, 'And Moses declared the appointed seasons of HASHEM to the children of Israel' (Lev.* 23:44).

The simple meaning of the verse is that Moses transmitted to Israel all the festival laws that had been given in that chapter *(Lev.* 23). However, some additional implication must lie in the verse, for it should not be necessary to tell us that Moses taught the people the commandments with which he had been charged *(Rashi* 31a). The Tanna derives support from this verse for the Rabbinic enactment to read relevant Torah portions on all the festivals *(Rashi; Rav).*

מִצְוָתָן שֶׁיְּהוּ קוֹרִין כָּל־אֶחָד וְאֶחָד... — *The precept is that each* [portion] *should be read...*

[I.e., the *mitzvah* of Torah readings on the festivals is that each section dealing with a festival be read ...]

בִּזְמַנּוֹ. — *at the appropriate time* [lit., *in its season*].

I.e., in the season when it is to be observed. Thus, the Torah tells us that in addition to observing the rituals of the festivals, Moses commanded Israel to read the relevant sections of the Torah on those days.

Although the mishnah quotes a Biblical verse on which it bases this practice, it is not considered a *mitz-*

this reading is not taken into account.

As it is said, *'And Moses declared the appointed seasons of HASHEM to the children of Israel'* [*Lev.* 23:44]; the precept is that each portion should be read at the appropriate time.

1. **O**ne who reads the *Megillah* may stand or sit. Whether one person read it or two read it, they have fulfilled their obligation.

YAD AVRAHAM

vah of the Torah. Since the practice of reading the Torah in public was an enactment of Moses and his court, followed by Ezra, the festival readings were obviously not made mandatory by the Torah. Hence this is a case of אַסְמַכְתָּא, *support* from a Biblical implication for a Rabbinical enactment (*Kesef Mishneh, Tefillah* 13:8).

Based on this verse Moses also enacted that Israel inquire into and expound upon the laws of each festival in its season *(Gem.* 32a).

Chapter 4

1.

◈ Reading the Megillah and the Torah

After enumerating the readings for all occasions (ch. 3), the Tanna proceeds to discuss such procedures as the number of people called to read and the order of the blessings. Since the reading of the *Megillah* is the main theme of this tractate, he turns first to *its* laws.

Originally, each person called to the Torah would read his own portion aloud, a practice that still obtains among Sephardim. Although there is evidence that the sexton would *assist* readers **(*Rashi, Shabbos* 12b)**, he would not *read* for them. Among Ashkenazim, however, one person [called the קוֹרֵא, *reader*, or, בַּעַל קְרִיאָה, *master of the reading*] is appointed to read aloud on behalf of all those called up.

According to one opinion, this practice of appointing one reader was initiated to avoid embarrassment to people who were not well versed in reading the Torah *(Tos.* 21b). Others maintain that the practice was instituted to prevent unlearned people from reading, since they were likely to make such errors that the listening congregation could not discharge its obligation to hear a proper reading *(Rosh* 3:2).

Although there is a reader, the one called to the Torah should read along with him quietly *(Shulchan Aruch* 139:2-3; *Rama; Magen Avraham).*

הַקּוֹרֵא אֶת־הַמְּגִלָּה... — *One who reads the Megillah*

[I.e., the Scroll of *Esther* on Purim.]

עוֹמֵד וְיוֹשֵׁב. — *may stand or sit.*

He fulfills his obligation in either manner *(Rav).*

Although one may read the

ד
א

מָקוֹם שֶׁנָּהֲגוּ לְבָרֵךְ, יְבָרֵךְ; וְשֶׁלֹּא לְבָרֵךְ, לֹא יְבָרֵךְ.

יד אברהם

Megillah even while seated if he so chooses, only one who reads privately has this option. In the presence of a congregation of ten or more, however, the reader should stand out of respect for the listeners (*Rambam, Megillah* 2:7; *Shulchan Aruch* 690:1).

According to *Meiri*, the requirement to honor a congregation by standing is a post-Talmudic custom.

According to *Rambam's* interpretation of the mishnah, preference that one stand is of Mishnaic origin. Nevertheless, *Rambam* agrees that בְּדִיעֲבַד, if one has *already* read while sitting, he had discharged his obligation although he should not have done so.

Magen Avraham (Orach Chaim 690:1) points out that the blessings must be recited while standing according to all opinions.]

The lenient ruling of the mishnah applies to the *Megillah* only. One who reads the Torah, however, is required to stand. This is derived from God's command to Moses: וְאַתָּה פֹּה עֲמֹד עִמָּדִי, *And you stand here with Me (Deut.* 5:28), which implies that God stood, as it were, when He conveyed the words of the Torah to Moses *(Gem.* 21a). Surely then, *we* must stand while reading the Torah, to afford it its proper awe and reverence *(Mishnah Berurah* 141:1).[1]

קְרָאָהּ אֶחָד, קְרָאוּהָ שְׁנַיִם—יָצְאוּ. — *Whether one person read it, or two read it, they [the listeners] have fulfilled their obligation.*

The obligation is fulfilled even if two read aloud simultaneously *(Rav).*

Although, as a rule, one cannot differentiate between two simultaneous voices, such differentiation *is* possible when one concentrates on sounds that are important to him. Because the *Megillah* reading is beloved, one listens especially closely *(Rav; Gem.* 21b).

People pay closer attention to the *Megillah* reading since it is a rare occurrence. Since the Torah, however, is read so frequently that it is taken for granted, it may be read by one person only *(Tos. Yom Tov).*

1. With regard to standing, the distinction between the Torah reading and the *Megillah* reading is not clear. The Torah reading discussed here is a congregational one, as *Rashi* states explicitly. Likewise, when one reads the *Megillah* before a congregation, he must stand. If so, there is no distinction between the two, yet the *Gemara* states emphatically that the Torah reading is more stringent in this respect.

[However, according to *Meiri*, who holds that the obligation to stand while reading the *Megillah* before a congregation is post-Talmudic (see above) the distinction is clear. The Mishnaic obligation to stand applies to the Torah reading only, not to that of the *Megillah.*]

According to *Bach*, there is indeed a difference between the two. He rules that if one read the *Megillah* for a congregation while sitting, he need not reread it, but if one read the Torah while sitting, he must repeat his reading *(Bach; Tur,* 141:1). However, this stringent view of the Torah reading is rejected by the majority of *poskim (Baer Hetev* 141:1).

Alternatively, one who reads the Torah is always required to stand, even if he reads for himself, without a congregation and without a blessing. Were he to read the *Megillah* for himself or for fewer than ten people, he could remain seated *(R' Avraham of Montpelier).*

4 Where they are accustomed to recite a blessing
1 [afterward], one should recite the blessing. [Where the custom is] not to recite a blessing, one need not recite the blessing.

◆§ Blessings Recited upon Reading the Megillah

Three blessings are pronounced before the reading of the *Megillah:*

בָּרוּךְ אַתָּה יהוה אֱלֹהֵינוּ מֶלֶךְ הָעוֹלָם אֲשֶׁר קִדְּשָׁנוּ בְּמִצְוֹתָיו וְצִוָּנוּ עַל מִקְרָא מְגִלָּה.

Blessed are You, HASHEM our God, King of the universe, Who has sanctified us with His commandments and has commanded us concerning the reading of the Megillah.

בָּרוּךְ אַתָּה יהוה אֱלֹהֵינוּ מֶלֶךְ הָעוֹלָם שֶׁעָשָׂה נִסִּים לַאֲבוֹתֵינוּ בַּיָּמִים הָהֵם בַּזְּמַן הַזֶּה.

Blessed are You, HASHEM our God, King of the universe, Who performed miracles for our forefathers in those days, at this time.

בָּרוּךְ אַתָּה יהוה אֱלֹהֵינוּ מֶלֶךְ הָעוֹלָם שֶׁהֶחֱיָנוּ וְקִיְּמָנוּ וְהִגִּיעָנוּ לַזְּמַן הַזֶּה.

Blessed are You, HASHEM our God, King of the universe, Who has kept us alive and sustained us and brought us to this time.

These three blessings were instituted by the Sages and are mandatory as an integral part of the *mitzvah* of *Megillah* reading. [Customs vary regarding the recitation of שֶׁהֶחֱיָנוּ, *Who has kept us alive,* at the morning reading. Since this is usually recited only the first time a seasonal *mitzvah* is performed each year (e.g., the first time one takes a *lulav), Rav* maintains that it is recited only at the night reading. This is the custom in Sephardic and German communities. Jews of Eastern European origin, on the other hand, repeat the blessing at the morning reading, owing to the fact that the main reading of the Megillah with its accompanying *pirsumei nissa* is the daytime reading. At that time the blessing also applies to the other precepts of Purim (gifts to friends and the poor; the Purim feast) which do not have their own special blessings and which apply only by day (see *Shulchan Aruch,* 692:1).]

Following the *Megillah* reading a longer blessing is pronounced:

בָּרוּךְ אַתָּה יהוה אֱלֹהֵינוּ מֶלֶךְ הָעוֹלָם, הָרָב אֶת רִיבֵנוּ וְהַדָּן אֶת דִּינֵנוּ וְהַנּוֹקֵם אֶת נִקְמָתֵנוּ וְהַנִּפְרָע לָנוּ מִצָּרֵינוּ וְהַמְשַׁלֵּם גְּמוּל לְכָל אֹיְבֵי נַפְשֵׁנוּ. בָּרוּךְ אַתָּה יהוה הַנִּפְרָע לְעַמּוֹ יִשְׂרָאֵל מִכָּל צָרֵיהֶם הָאֵל הַמּוֹשִׁיעַ:

Blessed are You, HASHEM our God, King of the Universe, Who argues our cause, judges our case, avenges our vengeance, exacts punishment of our oppressors for us, and pays just deserts to all our mortal enemies. Blessed are You, HASHEM, Who exacts punishment for His people, Israel, from all their oppressors — the God Who redeems.

This blessing does not relate specifically to Purim. Rather, it alludes to various wars waged against Amalek: Those of Moses and Joshua *(Exod.* 18:8-13); Saul *(I Samuel* 15:2-8); David *(I Samuel* 30); Jehoshafat *(II Chronicles* 20:1); and, finally, the battle related in the *Megillah (Sefer HaMichtam).*

According to *Ran,* this final blessing is unrelated to the *Megillah* reading — it is merely a general expression of thanksgiving. For this reason, *Sefer HaIttur* rules that one who converses before the recitation of this blessing is not to be rebuked, for such conversation does not constitute an interruption of the *mitzvah* of *Megillah* reading. *Tur,* however, disagrees, maintaining that any interruption between the reading and the recitation of this final blessing is forbidden (*Tur Orach Chaim* 692; see also *Shaar HaTziun* 692:12).

ד בַּשֵּׁנִי וּבַחֲמִישִׁי וּבַשַּׁבָּת בַּמִּנְחָה קוֹרִין
א שְׁלֹשָׁה. אֵין פּוֹחֲתִין וְאֵין מוֹסִיפִין עֲלֵיהֶן, וְאֵין
מַפְטִירִין בַּנָּבִיא.
הַפּוֹתֵחַ וְהַחוֹתֵם בַּתּוֹרָה מְבָרֵךְ לְפָנֶיהָ
וּלְאַחֲרֶיהָ.

יד אברהם

מָקוֹם שֶׁנָּהֲגוּ לְבָרֵךְ, יְבָרֵךְ; — *Where they are accustomed to recite a blessing* [*afterward*], *one should recite the blessing.*

The reference to a 'customary' blessing, as opposed to a mandatory one, applies only to the blessing *after* the *Megillah*. The blessings *before* the *Megillah*, however, are not merely customary; they were instituted and required by the Sages *(Rav).*

[Generally, it is forbidden to pronounce בְּרָכָה לְבַטָּלָה, *a blessing which serves no purpose,* or בְּרָכָה שֶׁאֵינָהּ צְרִיכָה, *an unnecessary blessing.* Blessings require reverence and have sanctity, hence they may be recited only when required. For example, one blesses God before eating a grape, but it is stringently forbidden to pronounce the blessing if one is not eating. It is also forbidden to recite it ten times when one is eating ten grapes; since one blessing is sufficient, additional blessings are unnecessary. In the case of our mishnah, however, this concluding blessing does not fall within that forbidden category even though it was introduced by custom, rather than by law, since the Sages composed it with the stipulation that communities should have the option to adopt it or not (See *Rosh Yosef).*]

וְשֶׁלֹּא לְבָרֵךְ, — [*Where the custom is*] *not to recite a blessing,*

[I.e., in communities that never accepted the tradition of reciting a blessing following the reading of the *Megillah.*]

לֹא יְבָרֵךְ. — *one need not recite the blessing.*

[The translation follows *Rashi* who uses the expression אֵין צָרִיךְ, *he is not required* (to bless), apparently implying that one *may* bless if he wishes to.]

בַּשֵּׁנִי וּבַחֲמִישִׁי וּבַשַּׁבָּת בַּמִּנְחָה קוֹרִין שְׁלֹשָׁה. — *On Monday and Thursday and on Sabbath afternoon three* [*people*] *read* [*the Torah*];

The Tanna now discusses the various numbers of people called to the Torah reading. He begins this discussion with the smallest number ever called; this is in fulfillment of the Talmud's dictum מַעֲלִין בְּקֹדֶשׁ וְלֹא מוֹרִידִין, *in* [matters of] *sanctity, we increase rather than decrease,* i.e., we deal with or perform the least sanctified matter first and progress upwards *(Tos. Yom Tov).*

The number of readers corresponds to the three categories of Scripture, תּוֹרָה, נְבִיאִים, וּכְתוּבִים, *Torah, Prophets, and Holy Writings.* Alternatively, the three people correspond to the treble nature of the Jewish people — *kohanim,* Levites, and Israelites (*Gem.* 21b).

אֵין פּוֹחֲתִין וְאֵין מוֹסִיפִין עֲלֵיהֶן, — [*we*] *may not decrease them nor add to them.*

We may not call more or fewer than three people on the above days. Were we to call more than three, it might prove burdensome to the congregation. Mondays and Thursdays are workdays, and *Minchah* of the Sabbath was usually recited shortly before nightfall as

4 On Monday and Thursday and on Sabbath after-
1 noon, three [people] read [the Torah]; we may not decrease them nor add to them. We do not conclude [the reading with a section] from the Prophets.

The one who commences and the one who concludes [the reading of] the Torah [respectively] recite the blessings said before it and after it.

the congregation would spend most of the day listening to rabbis teaching the law *(Rashi; Rav).*

וְאֵין מַפְטִירִין בַּנָּבִיא. — *We do not conclude* [*the reading*] *with a section from the Prophets.*

Again, to do so would elongate the service and might prove burdensome to the congregation *(Rashi; Rav).* [For the origin of the word מַפְטִיר, see pref. 3:4.]

[At the *Minchah* service of fast days and Yom Kippur, however, a *haftarah* is read because people do not work at those times in any case.]

הַפּוֹתֵחַ וְהַחוֹתֵם בַּתּוֹרָה... — *The one who commences and the one who concludes* [*the reading of*] *the Torah...*

I.e., the first and the last persons to be called *(Rav).*

מְבָרֵךְ לְפָנֶיהָ וּלְאַחֲרֶיהָ. — [*respectively*] *recite the blessings before it and after it.*

The entire Torah reading, no matter how many individuals participate, is considered a single *mitzvah.* Therefore it is sufficient for blessings to be pronounced only by the first and last readers. If, however, each portion were to be considered a separate *mitzvah,* then each reader would be required to pronounce blessings before and after *(Rav; Tif. Yis.).*

All readers must be *present,* however, when the preliminary and concluding blessings are recited; otherwise, they will be reading the Torah without having heard the proper blessings *(Meiri).*

Because of the growing prevalence during Amoraic times for transients to arrive at the synagogue after the Torah reading had begun or leave before it was completed the practice of each reader reciting two blessings was instituted. In either instance these transients might mistakenly assume that the Torah could be read without one or the other of the blessings. In Amoraic times, therefore, the tradition arose for *each* person called to the Torah to recite a blessing both before and after *(Rav; Gem.* 21b).

According to many authorities, the recitation of the blessings by the middle reader, or readers, was optional even during the period of the Mishnah. Our mishnah, however, discusses only the *mandatory* blessings, those which begin and conclude the reading *(Meiri; Taz* 428:8; *Responsa Chasam Sofer, Orach Chaim* 66).

Though, as we have noted, the middle blessings were optional, the *Yerushalmi* implies that it was always customary to recite them before and after certain sections of the Torah, such as עֲשֶׂרֶת הַדִּבְּרוֹת, *Ten Commandments,* or שִׁירַת הַיָּם, *the Song of the Sea.* Perhaps that is the source of the tradition of calling the most esteemed member of the congregation to read those sections *(Meleches Shlomo).*

ד
ב

[ב] **בְּרָאשֵׁי** חֳדָשִׁים וּבְחוּלוֹ שֶׁל מוֹעֵד קוֹרִין אַרְבָּעָה. אֵין פּוֹחֲתִין מֵהֶן וְאֵין מוֹסִיפִין עֲלֵיהֶן, וְאֵין מַפְטִירִין בַּנָּבִיא. הַפּוֹתֵחַ וְהַחוֹתֵם בַּתּוֹרָה, מְבָרֵךְ לְפָנֶיהָ וּלְאַחֲרֶיהָ.

זֶה הַכְּלָל: כָּל שֶׁיֵּשׁ־בּוֹ מוּסָף וְאֵינוֹ יוֹם טוֹב, קוֹרִין אַרְבָּעָה; בְּיוֹם טוֹב — חֲמִשָּׁה; בְּיוֹם הַכִּפּוּרִים — שִׁשָּׁה; בַּשַּׁבָּת — שִׁבְעָה. אֵין

יד אברהם

2.

בְּרָאשֵׁי חֳדָשִׁים וּבְחוּלוֹ שֶׁל מוֹעֵד קוֹרִין אַרְבָּעָה. – *On Rosh Chodesh and on Chol HaMoed four read* [the Torah].

[Both *Rosh Chodesh* and the Intermediate Days of Succos and Pesach have more sanctity than weekdays, as indicated by the fact that *Musaf* is recited. Both have partial prohibitions against work: on *Chol HaMoed* work is proscribed unless the specific task is such that failure to do it would result in דָבָר הָאָבֵד, *an irrevocable loss* (see pref. to Tractate *Moed Katan*); on *Rosh Chodesh,* it is customary for women to refrain from work. Thus, to indicate the increased sanctity of these days, four people, instead of three, are called to the Torah.][1]

אֵין פּוֹחֲתִין מֵהֶן... – *we may not decrease them...*

[i.e., the required four people. If fewer people are called, the reading is not valid].

וְאֵין מוֹסִיפִין עֲלֵיהֶן, – *nor add to them.*

Since certain types of work are permitted (see above) it could be burdensome to the congregation to call more than four people to the Torah and thereby lengthen the services with the result that necessary work would be unduly delayed *(Rav).*

וְאֵין מַפְטִירִין בַּנָּבִיא. – *We do not conclude* [*the reading with a section*] *from the Prophets.*

[This omission is in order not to

1. *Pirkei d'Rabbi Eliezer* maintains that *Rosh Chodesh* was given as a holiday to women in reward for their reticence to contribute their jewelry to the construction of the Golden Calf. Whereas the men gladly gave gold to make the calf but hesitated when asked to contribute towards the construction of the *Mishkan,* the women reacted in the opposite manner. In recognition, they were given a unique share in *Rosh Chodesh.* Moreover, the original custom had been for everyone to refrain from working on *Rosh Chodesh* in recognition of what it commemorates *(Rashi* 22b). Each festival was given in honor of one of the Patriarchs: Pesach for Abraham (see *Bereishis Rabbah* 48:12); Shavuos for Isaac; and Succos for Jacob *(Bereishis Rabbah* 33:16). The twelve *Roshei Chodashim* honored the twelve tribes and had been considered holidays regarding the prohibition of work. Due to the zeal of the men in taking part in the making of the Golden Calf, the special observance of the holiday was taken from them and left to the women (see *Responsa Tashbetz* 3:244).

4
2 **2.** On *Rosh Chodesh* and on *Chol HaMoed,* four [people] read [the Torah]; we may not decrease them nor add to them. We do not conclude [the reading with a section] from the Prophets. The one who commences and the one who concludes [the reading of] the Torah [respectively] recite the blessings said before it and after it.

This is the general rule: On any day on which there is a *Musaf* but which is not a festival, four [people] read [the Torah]. On festivals, five [people read]; on Yom Kippur, six [people read]; and on the Sabbath, seven [people read]. We may not decrease

YAD AVRAHAM

lengthen the services.[1]

הַפּוֹתֵחַ וְהַחוֹתֵם בַּתּוֹרָה — *The one who commences and the one who concludes [the reading of] the Torah...*

[I.e., the ones called first and last.]

מְבָרֵךְ לְפָנֶיהָ וּלְאַחֲרֶיהָ — *[respectively] recite the blessings said before it and after it.*

Even though an additional person is called, no additional blessings are recited *(Tif. Yis).*

זֶה הַכְּלָל: — *This is the general rule:*

[Usually the expression זֶה הַכְּלָל, *this is the general rule,* implies that specific situations omitted by the mishnah would be covered by this rule (e.g., 2:6). Here, however, the listing is complete.] The expression זֶה הַכְּלָל, *this is the rule,* is used by our mishnah to introduce a mnemonic device for remembering the number of people called (*Gem.* 22b).

כָּל־שֶׁיֵּשׁ בּוֹ מוּסָף וְאֵינוֹ יוֹם טוֹב, קוֹרִין אַרְבָּעָה; — *[On] any day on which there is a Musaf but which is not a festival, four [people] read [the Torah].*

[For example, *Rosh Chodesh* and *Chol HaMoed,* when *Musaf* sacrifices were offered in the Temple, and the *Musaf* prayer is recited today.]

בְּיוֹם טוֹב—חֲמִשָּׁה; — *On festivals, five [people read];*

Since the laws of festivals are more stringent than those of *Rosh Chodesh* or *Chol HaMoed* (see 1:5), one additional person is called, to indicate the increased sanctity of the day *(Rav; Gem.* 22b).

בְּיוֹם הַכִּפּוּרִים—שִׁשָּׁה; — *on Yom Kippur, six [people read];*

Since the desecration of Yom Kippur is an act punishable by *kares [excision of the soul; see 1:5] an additional person is called to indicate the increased sanctity of the day (Rav; Gem.* 22b).

1. [As noted above, the reading from the Prophets was introduced in reaction to the Greek prohibition against reading from the Torah. The Rabbis maintained the tradition in the case of holidays and the Sabbath even after the prohibition was annulled, but they discontinued the reading from Prophets in cases where it might prove burdensome to the congregation. This is a clear indication of how sensitive they were to טִרְחָה דְצִבּוּרָא, *unnecessary burden on the congregation.*]

ד
ג

פּוֹחֲתִין מֵהֶן, אֲבָל מוֹסִיפִין עֲלֵיהֶן, וּמַפְטִירִין בַּנָּבִיא. הַפּוֹתֵחַ וְהַחוֹתֵם בַּתּוֹרָה, מְבָרֵךְ לְפָנֶיהָ וּלְאַחֲרֶיהָ.

[ג] **אֵין** פּוֹרְסִין אֶת־שְׁמַע, וְאֵין עוֹבְרִין לִפְנֵי הַתֵּבָה, וְאֵין נוֹשְׂאִין אֶת כַּפֵּיהֶם,

יד אברהם

בַּשַּׁבָּת—שִׁבְעָה. — *and on the Sabbath, seven* [*people read*].

The sanctity of the Sabbath is the greatest of all since its desecration is punishable by סְקִילָה, *skilah* [lit. *stoning*]. Therefore, an additional person reads *(Rav).*

Alternatively, seven people are called on the Sabbath so congregants would hear and respond to *Borchu* seven times. Thereby, if someone had not prayed with a congregation during the week, he could compensate for the seven times that he missed the recitation of *Borchu* during the week *(Shibolei HaLeket).*

[Apparently it was customary, during the Mishnaic period, for each reader to pronounce *Borchu* even though the middle readers did not recite blessings (see 4:1).]

אֵין פּוֹחֲתִין מֵהֶן, אֲבָל מוֹסִיפִין עֲלֵיהֶן, — *We may not decrease them but we may increase them;*

[I.e., we do not decrease the number of people called to the Torah; but we may call more than the number specified in the Mishnah.]

Although on the days enumerated above it is forbidden to call *less* than the numbers specified for each day, *additional* readers may be called. Since the congregants are enjoined from working on these days, the lengthened service caused by the additional readers is not deemed an unreasonable burden *(Tos. Yom Tov).*

Other authorities maintain that the permission to call additional people refers only to the Sabbath. To do so on festivals or on Yom Kippur, however, might lead people to mistakenly assume that those days are equal in sanctity to the Sabbath *(Ran).*

This latter view is the prevailing custom with the exception of *Simchas Torah* when *all* present are called to the Torah *(Rama, Orach Chaim* 282:1).

וּמַפְטִירִין בַּנָּבִיא. — *And we conclude* [the reading with a section] *from the Prophets.*

[See above 3:4.].

Even after the removal of oppressive prohibitions against Torah reading [see pref. in 3:4], the Sages continued the custom of reading from the Prophets. In order to avoid any misconception that the Prophets were of equal status with the Torah, the Sages ordained that the person called to read from the Prophets should first read from the Torah, thus demonstrating that the Prophets alone were not adequate to validate a reading (see *Gem.* 23a; *Rashi; Tos.).*

The *halachah* is that the reader of the *maftir* could be counted among the seven, six, or five required readers, as the case may be. There is a view in the *Gemara* (23a), however, that the *maftir* should *not* be counted. Therefore, on festivals and the Sabbath when, according to most views, it is permitted to call more than the minimum number,

4 them but we may increase them; and we conclude
3 [the reading with a section] from the Prophets. The one who commences and the one who concludes [the reading of] the Torah [respectively] recite the blessings said before it and after it.

3. We may not divide the *Shema*; nor go before the Ark; nor [may the *kohanim*] lift their hands [to recite the priestly blessings]; nor do we

YAD AVRAHAM

the *maftir* is called in *addition* to the required minimum. On fast days, when additions to the three readers are forbidden, the third reader is the *maftir* (*Orach Chaim* 282:4).

הַפּוֹתֵחַ וְהַחוֹתֵם בַּתּוֹרָה, מְבָרֵךְ לְפָנֶיהָ וּלְאַחֲרֶיהָ. — *The one who commences and the one who concludes [the reading of] the Torah [respectively] recite the blessings said before it and after it.*

Even though additional people are called, no additional blessings are recited (*Tif. Yis.*).

3.

◆§ Minyan

Continuing his discussion of the laws relating to readings from the Torah and Prophets, the Tanna goes on to the requirement that the reading take place in the presence of a *minyan* [ten adult males]. In this connection, he mentions other rituals which also can be performed only in the presence of a *minyan*. The general rule is that a *minyan* is required for all sections of the prayers which the Sages describe as דְּבָרִים שֶׁבִּקְדֻשָּׁה, *matters of holiness*, such as *Kaddish, Kedushah* and so on.

This requirement is derived from the verse, וְנִקְדַּשְׁתִּי בְּתוֹךְ בְּנֵי יִשְׂרָאֵל, *And I shall be sanctified in the midst of the children of Israel* (*Lev.* 22:32). The Sages expound that the term בְּתוֹךְ, *midst*, alludes to the presence of ten adult males. This is derived from the use of the same term with reference to the rebellion of Korach. God commanded Moses and Aaron הִבָּדְלוּ מִתּוֹךְ הָעֵדָה הַזֹּאת, *Separate yourselves from the midst of this congregation* (*Numbers* 16:21). That verse also uses the term עֵדָה, *congregation*. That this word is defined as a group of at least ten people is indicated in *Numbers* 14:27, where the ten traitorous מְרַגְּלִים, *spies*, are described as עֵדָה, *a congregation*. The combination of these three verses leads us to the conclusion that 'sanctification' should take place among a 'congregation of ten' adult males (*Gem.* 23b).

אֵין פּוֹרְסִין אֶת־שְׁמַע, — *We may not divide the* Shema;

It was customary in Mishnaic times that if ten people came into the synagogue after the congregation had already recited the *Shema*, one of them would recite aloud *Kaddish*, *Borchu*, and בִּרְכַּת הַמְּאוֹרוֹת, *the Blessing of the Luminaries*, — the first of the two blessings said before the *Shema* (see *Berachos* 1:4). Since only one of the two blessings is recited, the Tanna describes it as dividing the *Shema*.

ד וְאֵין קוֹרִין בַּתּוֹרָה, וְאֵין מַפְטִירִין בַּנָּבִיא, וְאֵ

ג עוֹשִׂין מַעֲמָד וּמוֹשָׁב, וְאֵין אוֹמְרִים בִּרְכַּ

The term פּוֹרֵס is from the root פרס, *to break* or *divide*, and is used here to describe the recitation of only 'part' of the blessings. This 'dividing', as we learn in our mishnah, may not be done unless a *minyan* is present *(Rav)*.

The mishnah refers to a case where they had already prayed individually, but came to the synagogue to participate in those portions of the service that require a *minyan: Kaddish, Borchu,* and *Kedushah (Rashi).* [Had they not prayed previously, these ten people would conduct their own complete prayer service].

[According to this interpretation, why must they recite the first blessing of the *Shema* when they had already recited it as part of their own prayers?]

Tosefos Yom Tov cites an opinion that when this blessing is said by an individual the verses of the *Kedushah* said by the angels are omitted because it is considered a דָּבָר שֶׁבִּקְדֻשָּׁה, *matter of holiness,* which requires a *minyan.* Others maintain that even though it may be recited by an individual, it is nevertheless repeated by the *minyan* as the logical conclusion of *Borchu.* The leader's proclamation of *Borchu* [*come bless*] is a call to the congregants to bless God. They respond with the first of the blessings preceding the *Shema.*

Our practice is to recite *both* blessings of the *Shema* when praying individually *(Shulchan Aruch, Orach Chaim* 59:3; *Rama).* Moreover, individuals who have already prayed, but gather to recite *Borchu,* do *not* go on to recite the first blessing *(Shulchan Aruch* 133:1; *Rama; Ateres Zekeinim).*

Rambam interprets our mishnah in an entirely different manner. The mishnah refers not to those who had already prayed, but to the communal service in the synagogue. In Mishnaic times when prayers were recited by heart, many people were unversed in the texts. For their benefit, the reader would recite the blessings aloud in their entirety, thereby discharging his listeners of their obligation. With reference to this congregational procedure, our mishnah rules that it was done only in the presence of a *minyan.* פּוֹרְסִין אֶת־שְׁמַע is rendered *spread out the Shema;* i.e., recite it and its accompanying blessings in their entirety.

Others render the phrase פּוֹרְסִין אֶת־שְׁמַע: *blesses the Shema (Meiri);* or *commences the Shema (Ran).* Despite these variations of translation, these authorities all interpret the mishnah as referring to the practice that the reader would discharge the congregation of its obligation to recite the blessings of the *Shema.*

וְאֵין עוֹבְרִין לִפְנֵי הַתֵּבָה, — *nor* [*may we*] *go before the Ark,*

I.e., the *Shemoneh Esrei* is not repeated by the שְׁלִיחַ צִבּוּר, *prayer leader* [lit. *representative of the congregation*], unless a *minyan* is present *(Rashi; Rav).*

The Tanna did not find it necessary to specify that he was referring only to the *Shemoneh Esrei,* since it was customary for the prayer leader to go before the Ark only when reciting that section of the prayers *(Ran; Meiri).*

By making separate references to *Shema* and *Shemoneh Esrei,* the Tanna indicates that they are to be treated as separate categories. Thus, if a *minyan* were present when the reader started to recite the blessings of *Shema,* and subsequently several persons left, he may conclude those blessings. He may not *commence* the repetition of the *Shemoneh Esrei,* however, since it is not a con-

4
3
read [publicly] from the Torah; nor do we conclude [with a section] from the Prophets; nor do we make standing and sitting [tributes at a funeral]; nor do we

tinuation of the *Shema*, but a separate part of the service that requires a *minyan* in its own right. The same applies to all parts of the service which are enumerated separately *(Tos. Yom Tov; Yerushalmi).*

וְאֵין נוֹשְׂאִין אֶת־כַּפֵּיהֶם — *nor [may the kohanim] lift their hands [to recite the priestly blessing (Rav)];*

[The Talmud refers to the priestly blessing as נְשִׂיאַת כַּפַּיִם, *lifting of the hands,* because the *kohanim* are required to lift their hands when bestowing the blessing upon the people (see *Taanis* 4:1).]

That the priestly blessing may be said only in the presence of a *minyan* is based upon the similarity of terms in the two verses כֹּה תְבָרְכוּ אֶת־בְּנֵי יִשְׂרָאֵל, *so shall you* [the *kohanim*] *bless the children of Israel (Num.* 6:23), and וְנִקְדַּשְׁתִּי בְּתוֹךְ בְּנֵי יִשְׂרָאֵל, *And I shall be sanctified in the midst of the children of Israel (Lev.* 22:32). Just as matters of sanctity require a *minyan* [see above], so too does the priestly blessing. This derivation, however, is אַסְמַכְתָּא, *a Rabbinical ruling supported by a Scriptural allusion.* The pronouncement of the priestly blessing during prayers is surely Rabbinic since the formal order of our prayers is itself Rabbinic in origin *(Ran).*

Alternatively, inasmuch as the priestly blessing is a דָּבָר שֶׁבִּקְדֻשָּׁה, *matter of sanctity,* it may be said only in the presence of a *minyan (Meiri).*

וְאֵין קוֹרִין בַּתּוֹרָה — *nor do we read [publicly (Rav)] from the Torah;*

When the Sages instituted the public reading of the Torah, they ordained that it be performed only in the presence of a *minyan (Ran).*

[Although the practice originates from an enactment of Moses, it has the status of a Rabbinic ordinance, because the command came from Moses, not from God.]

וְאֵין מַפְטִירִין בַּנָּבִיא, — *nor do we conclude [with a section] from the Prophets.*

The *haftarah* reading was Rabbinically enacted to be performed only in the presence of a *minyan (Tos. Yom Tov).*

Alternatively, all the cases mentioned to this point are considered דְּבָרִים שֶׁבִּקְדֻשָּׁה, *matters of sanctity,* and as such require the presence of a *minyan (Tif. Yis.).*

וְאֵין עוֹשִׂין מַעֲמָד וּמוֹשָׁב, — *nor do we make standing and sitting [tributes at a funeral];*

On the way to a burial, it was the custom to halt the procession to bemoan the loss of the deceased, and deliver eulogies. Our mishnah limits the procedure to processions that included at least a *minyan.* The procedure was as follows: The leader would tell the people, 'Sit, dear ones, sit!' They would sit and weep while listening to eulogies. He would then tell them, 'Stand, dear ones, stand!' After proceeding a short distance, the procession would again be halted as before. This procedure was repeated seven times *(Rashbam, Bava Basra* 100b).

Rambam comments that the procedure was ignored if no *minyan* was present so that the leader would

ד ד אֲבֵלִים וְתַנְחוּמֵי אֲבֵלִים וּבִרְכַּת חֲתָנִים, וְאֵין מְזַמְּנִין בַּשֵּׁם פָּחוֹת מֵעֲשָׂרָה. וּבַקַּרְקָעוֹת תִּשְׁעָה וְכֹהֵן, וְאָדָם כַּיּוֹצֵא בָהֶן.

[ד] **הַקּוֹרֵא** בַּתּוֹרָה לֹא יִפְחֹת מִשְּׁלֹשָׁה פְסוּקִים. לֹא יִקְרָא לַמְתֻרְגְּמָן

יד אברהם

not be forced to deliver eulogies before such a small group.

Rashi comments: Were we to bestow the title of 'dear ones' on a gathering of fewer than ten, what title would we bestow on a larger gathering?

וְאֵין אוֹמְרִים בִּרְכַּת אֲבֵלִים... — *nor do we say the mourners' blessing,*

On the way back home from a burial, it was customary to sit in the street and recite a series of blessings: One in honor of God, one on behalf of the mourners, one on behalf of those who console the mourners, and one on behalf of all Israel *(Tif. Yis.).*

Others explain that these blessings were recited during the *mourners' meal,* which is served by his friends, and which, in Mishnaic times, was eaten in the street *(Rashi, Kesubos* 8b).

These blessings were enacted by the Rabbis to be recited only with a *minyan (Tos. Yom Tov).*

וְתַנְחוּמֵי אֲבֵלִים... — *nor the consolations to the mourners;*

After burial, those present form שורות, *rows,* through which the mourners pass as consolations are offered. This is done only in the presence of a *minyan (Rav).*

This *minyan* must consist of ten men offering consolation to the mourners. Since the mourners are obviously not consoling themselves, they cannot be counted as part of the *minyan (Tos. Yom Tov; Meleches Shlomo).*

וּבִרְכַּת חֲתָנִים, — *nor [are] the wedding blessings [recited];*

Also requiring a *minyan* are the seven blessings recited under the marriage canopy, and following the Grace after Meals during the seven festive days after the wedding *(Rav).*

The requirement of a *minyan* is based on the precedent set by Boaz, who summoned ten men when he married Ruth (see *Ruth* 4:2).

Unlike the previous case of the mourners, the groom himself may be counted as part of the *minyan (Tos. Yom Tov; Gem.* 23b).

וְאֵין מְזַמְּנִין בַּשֵּׁם פָּחוֹת מֵעֲשָׂרָה. — *nor is [God's] Name mentioned in the invitation [to the Grace after Meals] in the presence of fewer than ten [men].*

Since the מְזַמֵּן, *one who invites,* says נְבָרֵךְ אֱלֹהֵינוּ, *Let us bless our God,* it is not deemed proper to do so unless at least ten adult males (including himself) are present *(Gem.* 23b). [If fewer than ten men, but at least three, are reciting the Grace, then the invitation is extended, with the omission of God's Name.]

וּבַקַּרְקָעוֹת תִּשְׁעָה וְכֹהֵן, — *In [the appraisal of] lands, nine [men] and a kohen [are required];*

If someone wishes to redeem con-

4 say the mourners' blessing, nor the consolations to
4 the mourners; nor [are] the wedding blessings [recited]; nor is [God's] Name mentioned in the invitation [to the Grace after Meals] in the presence of fewer than ten [men]. In [the appraisal of] lands, nine [men] and a *kohen* [are required] and [the appraisal of] a human is the same.

4. One who reads the Torah may not read fewer than three verses. He may not read more than one verse [at a time] for the translator. In the section

YAD AVRAHAM

secrated land, it must be appraised by ten people to arrive at a fair value. One of those appraising the land must be a *kohen*. The Talmud (*Sanhedrin* 15a) derives this requirement from the verses in *Leviticus* 27 (*Rav; Tos. Yom Tov*).

וְאָדָם כְּיוֹצֵא בָהֶן. — *and [the appraisal of] a human is the same.*

If one vowed to consecrate an amount of money equivalent to his own value, the appraisal is to be made by ten people, one of whom must be a *kohen*. A person's value is equivalent to the price he would receive were he sold as a slave. Since non-Jewish slaves are likened to land in terms of their property status, the laws of land appraisal are applied to the appraisal of people, as well (*Rav; Gem.* 23b).

4.

Meturgeman

Already in the time of Nechemiah in the fifth century B.C.E. (see *Nedarim* 37b), it was customary to employ a מְתַרְגְּמָן, [*meturgeman*] *translator* or *interpreter* to explain the Torah reading to the congregation. This was necessitated by the fact that Hebrew had ceased to be the spoken language of the people, who had adopted Aramaic during the Babylonian exile. Therefore, a scholar, the *meturgeman*, would be appointed by the synagogue, to give a verse-by-verse Aramaic translation of the Torah reading. The reader read one verse of the Torah and paused; the *Meturgeman* then gave an Aramaic paraphrase of the verse, sometimes including brief halachic or midrashic commentaries. The reader would read the second verse, the *Meturgeman* would translate, and so on [*Akdamus*, ArtScroll p. xv].

Later, however, when Aramaic ceased to be the common language of all Jews, the Aramaic translation fell into disuse. The liturgical poem אַקְדָּמוּת, *Akdamus*, is a vestige of this custom. In Medieval times, it was used as an introduction for the translator, who still functioned on Pesach and Shavuos (*Havanas HaMikra, Exod.* p. 28). The languages of other countries of Jewish exile were never adopted as substitutes for Aramaic for two reasons: Aramaic is unique in that it lends itself to the brevity necessary for such a translation; and the *Targum* was introduced through רוּחַ הַקֹּדֶשׁ, *Divine Inspiration* (*Tif. Yis.*).

ד יוֹתֵר מִפָּסוּק אֶחָד; וּבַנָּבִיא—שְׁלֹשָׁה. הָיוּ
ה שְׁלָשְׁתָּן שָׁלֹשׁ פָּרָשִׁיּוֹת, קוֹרִין אֶחָד אֶחָד.
מְדַלְּגִין בַּנָּבִיא וְאֵין מְדַלְּגִין בַּתּוֹרָה. וְעַד
כַּמָּה הוּא מְדַלֵּג? עַד כְּדֵי שֶׁלֹּא יִפְסֹק
הַמְתֻרְגְּמָן.

[ה] **הַמַּפְטִיר** בַּנָּבִיא הוּא פּוֹרֵס עַל שְׁמַע,
וְהוּא עוֹבֵר לִפְנֵי הַתֵּבָה,

יד אברהם

הַקּוֹרֵא בַּתּוֹרָה... — *One who reads the Torah...*

[I.e., one who is called to read from the Torah.]

לֹא יִפְחֹת מִשְּׁלֹשָׁה פְסוּקִים. — *may not read fewer than three verses.*

The minimum of three verses per person corresponds to the three categories of Scripture: Torah, Prophets, and Holy Writings *(Gem.* 24a).

לֹא יִקְרָא לַמְתֻרְגְּמָן יוֹתֵר מִפָּסוּק אֶחָד: — *He may not read more than one verse [at a time] for the translator.*

The reader must pause after each verse, to allow the translator to render it into Aramaic. Since the translator did not use a written text, he might err or become confused were more than one verse to be read at a time *(Rav).*

וּבַנָּבִיא—שְׁלֹשָׁה. — *In the section from the Prophets [he may not read more than] three [verses at a time].*

He need pause only after reading *three* verses, to allow the translator to translate. Although a long pause may cause the translator to err, potential errors in the translation are not as serious as similar ones in the Torah, since no laws are derived from the Prophets *(Rashi; Rav).*

הָיוּ שְׁלָשְׁתָּן שָׁלֹשׁ פָּרָשִׁיּוֹת, קוֹרִין אֶחָד אֶחָד.— *If the three [verses] are three paragraphs, we read them one by one.*

If the three verses from the Prophets represent three paragraphs *(Rav)* or three topics *(Ran),* the reader should pause after each one. Since the verses are diverse, errors would be likely if they were translated in groups of three *(Meiri).*

מְדַלְּגִין בַּנָּבִיא... — *One is permitted to skip in [the reading of] the Prophets,*

The *haftarah* may be composed of two sections, although they are not consecutive and do not deal with the same topic *(Rav; Gem.* 24a).

It may not, however, be taken from two different books of the Prophets, except in the case of תְּרֵי עָשָׂר, *The Twelve Prophets,* which is considered one book *(R' Akiva Eiger; Gem.* 24a).

וְאֵין מְדַלְּגִין בַּתּוֹרָה. — *but one may not skip [in the reading of] the Torah.*

Were one to skip from one portion to another, the listeners might become confused *(Rashi* 4a).

However, one may skip from one portion to another if the two topics are related. Thus, the reading of the *kohen gadol* on Yom Kippur was included the entire chapter 16 of

4
5 from the Prophets [he may not read more than] three [verses at a time]. If the three [verses] are three paragraphs, we read them one by one.

One is permitted to skip in [the reading of] the Prophets, but one may not skip in [the reading of] the Torah. How much is one permitted to skip? No more than what would cause the translator to pause.

5. The one who concludes with the section from the Prophets is the one who divides the *Shema*, and goes before the Ark, and lifts his hands [to bless

YAD AVRAHAM

Leviticus, followed by 23:26-32, for these portions all discuss the laws pertaining to Yom Kippur *(Rav)*.

וְעַד כַּמָּה הוּא מְדַלֵּג? — *How much is one permitted to skip?*

How much may be skipped in the *haftarah*, or in the Torah, provided that the texts deal with the same subject? *(Rav)*.

עַד כְּדֵי שֶׁלֹּא יִפְסֹק הַמְתֻרְגְּמָן. — *No more than what would cause the translator to pause.*

The reader may roll the scrolls of the Torah or Prophets to a different section only while the translator is translating, so that the congregation will not be forced to wait for him to find the place. Thus, the reader may skip not more than the number of columns which can be rolled while the translator is rendering the previously read material *(Rav; Tif. Yis.; Yoma* 70a).

For this same reason, the Torah scroll should be prepared before the reading so that the congregation will not be forced to wait (see *Yoma* 7:1).

5.

הַמַּפְטִיר בַּנָּבִיא הוּא פוֹרֵס עַל שְׁמַע, — *The one who concludes with the section from the Prophets is the one who divides the Shema,*

[For *dividing the Shema* see mishnah 3.]

Maftir is the least significant of the Scriptural readings. Therefore, the person called to read the *haftarah* is compensated with other honors *(Rav)*.

וְהוּא עוֹבֵר לִפְנֵי הַתֵּבָה, — *and (he) goes before the Ark,*

I.e., to serve as the שְׁלִיחַ צִבּוּר, *prayer leader*, who repeats the *Shemoneh Esrei* aloud *(Rav)*.

Since the repetition of the *Shemoneh Esrei* precedes the reading of the Torah, how do we know then who will serve as *maftir? Tosefos Yom Tov* comments that if a congregant consistently volunteers to serve as *maftir*, we assume that he will do so today, and we honor him by selecting him to act as prayer leader. [This is probably the origin of our custom of honoring the *maftir* to serve as prayer leader for *Musaf*.]

ד וְהוּא נוֹשֵׂא אֶת־כַּפָּיו. וְאִם הָיָה קָטָן, אָבִיו אוֹ
ד רַבּוֹ עוֹבְרִין עַל־יָדוֹ.

[ו] **קָטָן** קוֹרֵא בַתּוֹרָה וּמְתַרְגֵּם, אֲבָל אֵינוֹ פּוֹרֵס עַל־שְׁמַע, וְאֵינוֹ עוֹבֵר לִפְנֵי הַתֵּבָה, וְאֵינוֹ נוֹשֵׂא אֶת־כַּפָּיו.
פּוֹחֵחַ פּוֹרֵס עַל־שְׁמַע וּמְתַרְגֵּם, אֲבָל אֵינוֹ

יד אברהם

Alternatively, he serves as prayer leader at *Minchah (Nimukei Yosef);* or on the following weekdays when no *haftarah* is read because he served as *maftir* on the previous Sabbath *(Meiri).*

Others explain that the mishnah was recorded during an ancient era when the Torah may have been read before *Shacharis.* Thus, one who volunteered to serve as *maftir* could be chosen to repeat the *Shemoneh Esrei* of *Shachris (R' Avraham of Montpelier).*

וְהוּא נוֹשֵׂא אֶת־כַּפָּיו. — *and (he) lifts his hands* [*to bless the people*];.

[I.e., if he is a *kohen.* For *lifting the hands* see mishnah 3.]

[This ruling is somewhat difficult to understand, since *all kohanim* are required to bless the people. A number of solutions are offered by later commentators.]

Tosefos Yom Tov explains that the *maftir* leads the other *kohanim* in the blessing.

Turei Even maintains that the Tanna is referring to a congregation composed solely of *kohanim;* if there is more than a *minyan* present, ten refrain from reciting the blessing and respond *Amen* to the blessings of the other *kohanim.* The *maftir* is honored by being chosen as one of those blessing.

וְאִם הָיָה קָטָן, — *If he is a minor,*

If the one who serves as *maftir* is a minor and, therefore, cannot serve as prayer leader [see mishnah 6] *(Rav).*

אָבִיו אוֹ רַבּוֹ עוֹבְרִין עַל־יָדוֹ. — *his father or teacher go* [*before the Ark*] *on his behalf.*

I.e., the honor due the *maftir* is given either to the minor's father or teacher *(Rav).* Thereby, it is as if the *maftir* himself were honored *(Tos. Yom Tov; Rambam).*

6.

קָטָן קוֹרֵא בַתּוֹרָה... — *A minor may read the Torah...*

Although the minor himself is not obligated to read the Torah, he may, nevertheless, discharge adults of their obligation by reading on their behalf. We cannot do so in the case of *Megillah* (see 2:3), because there is an essential difference between the two obligations: Everyone has an individual obligation to read the *Megillah.* A listener discharges his obligation through the principle of שׁוֹמֵעַ כְּעוֹנֶה, *one who listens is considered as if he had uttered.* Since the listener attains the status of the reader, the reader's obligation must be equal to

4 the people]. If he is a minor, his father or teacher go
6 [before the Ark] on his behalf.

6. A minor may read the Torah or serve as translator. However, he may not divide the *Shema*, nor may he go before the Ark, nor may he lift his hands [to bless the people].

One whose clothes are tattered may divide the *Shema* and serve as translator. However, he may not

YAD AVRAHAM

the listener's. The reading of the Torah, however, is a general *communal* obligation. The community is required to hear the public Torah reading, but there is no obligation on each individual to have *read* it. This general obligation can be fulfilled even through the reading of a minor.

A minor, however, may not read the entire weekly section, nor should a majority of those called to the Torah be minors *(Ran).*

Others permit a minor to be called only from the third reader onwards *(Rambam, Rav).*

Our custom is to limit the calling of minors to *maftir (Magen Avraham* 282:6).

וּמְתַרְגֵּם, — *or serve as translator.*

Since he is permitted to read the Torah on behalf of the community, he is surely permitted to serve as the translator *(Meiri).*

אֲבָל אֵינוֹ פּוֹרֵס עַל־שְׁמַע, וְאֵינוֹ עוֹבֵר לִפְנֵי הַתֵּבָה, — *However, he may not divide the Shema, nor may he go before the Ark...*

[See commentary to mishnah 3 where the concepts of dividing *Shema*, going before the Ark, and lifting the hands are explained.]

Since the reader fulfills the obligation of the congregation in these two cases, only one who is himself obligated can discharge others of their obligation *(Rav).*

וְאֵינוֹ נוֹשֵׂא אֶת־כַּפָּיו. — *nor may he lift his hands* [*to bless the people*].

A minor may not ascend to offer the priestly blessing [except in the company of adult *kohanim*] as it is deemed degrading for the congregation to be dependent on a child's blessing *(Rav).*

פּוֹחֵחַ... — *One* [i.e., an adult] *whose clothes are tattered...*

The commentators differ as to what degree the clothing is torn:

— the clothes are in shreds and the limbs are exposed *(Rav);*

— the knees are bared *(Rashi);*

— he is stripped to the waist *(Rambam);* or

— his shirt sleeves are ripped off *(R' Chananel; Aruch).*

פּוֹרֵס עַל־שְׁמַע... — *may divide the Shema...*

Since he is personally obligated to recite the blessings of the *Shema*, he may serve as the prayer leader and thus fulfill the obligations of the congregation despite his demeaning lack of proper attire *(Rav).*

Moreover, since the one who recited the blessings did not stand before the Ark, the fact that his clothes are tattered is not considered demeaning to the congregation *(Tos. Yom Tov; Ran).*

ד קוֹרֵא בַתּוֹרָה וְאֵינוֹ עוֹבֵר לִפְנֵי הַתֵּבָה, וְאֵינוֹ
ז נוֹשֵׂא אֶת־כַּפָּיו.

סוּמָא פּוֹרֵס אֶת־שְׁמַע, וּמְתַרְגֵּם. רַבִּי יְהוּדָה אוֹמֵר: כָּל־שֶׁלֹּא רָאָה מְאוֹרוֹת מִיָּמָיו, אֵינוֹ פּוֹרֵס עַל־שְׁמַע.

[ז] **כֹּהֵן** שֶׁיֵּשׁ בְּיָדָיו מוּמִין, לֹא יִשָּׂא אֶת־כַּפָּיו. רַבִּי יְהוּדָה אוֹמֵר: אַף מִי שֶׁהָיוּ יָדָיו צְבוּעוֹת אִסְטִיס וּפוּאָה, לֹא יִשָּׂא אֶת־כַּפָּיו, מִפְּנֵי שֶׁהָעָם מִסְתַּכְּלִין בּוֹ.

יד אברהם

וּמְתַרְגֵּם, — *and serve as translator.*

Inasmuch as this is a function of minor importance, the tattered condition of his clothing is not considered demeaning *(Ran).*

אֲבָל אֵינוֹ קוֹרֵא בַתּוֹרָה, וְאֵינוֹ עוֹבֵר לִפְנֵי הַתֵּבָה, — *However, he may not read the Torah, nor may he go before the Ark* [*to repeat the Shemoneh Esrei*],

It demeans the Torah's honor for one whose clothes are tattered to serve as reader. Similarly, one so exposed may not demean the congregation by being its agent to repeat the *Shemoneh Esrei (Rashi; Rav).*

[The *Shemoneh Esrei* repetition, is recited before the Ark and is more stringent than the division of the *Shema.*]

וְאֵינוֹ נוֹשֵׂא אֶת־כַּפָּיו. — *nor may he lift his hands.*

I.e., if he is a *kohen,* for this is demeaning for the congregation *(Rav,* see above).

סוּמָא פּוֹרֵס אֶת־שְׁמַע — *A blind man may divide the Shema...*

The division of the *Shema* includes בִּרְכַּת הַמְּאוֹרוֹת, *The Blessing of the Luminaries,* which would seem to be of no benefit, and thus inapplicable to an unsighted person. Nevertheless, even a blind man can properly pronounce this blessing because he benefits indirectly from the sun and moon, since, thanks to their light, sighted people prevent him from stumbling *(Rav; Gem.* 24b).[1]

וּמְתַרְגֵּם. — *and serve as translator.*

[Since the translation was recited by heart, there is no reason why a blind man cannot so serve.]

ר׳ יְהוּדָה אוֹמֵר: כָּל שֶׁלֹּא רָאָה מְאוֹרוֹת מִיָּמָיו, אֵינוֹ פּוֹרֵס עַל־שְׁמַע. — *R' Yehudah says: Anyone who has never seen the luminaries* [i.e., one who was born blind *(Gem.* 24b)] *may not divide the Shema.*

Since he never directly benefited from the light, he does not recite the blessing יוֹצֵר אוֹר, *He Who formed light.* The *halachah* is not in accordance with R' Yehudah's opinion *(Rav).*

1. R' Yose says: I was once walking at night and saw a blind man walking with a torch. I asked him, 'What use is the torch to you?'

He answered, 'As long as the torch is in my hand, people see me and prevent me from falling into pits' *(Gem.* 24b).

4
7 read the Torah nor may he go before the Ark, nor may he lift his hands.

A blind man may divide the *Shema* and serve as translator. R' Yehudah says: Anyone who has never seen the luminaries may not divide the *Shema.*

7. A *kohen* whose hands are blemished may not lift his hands. R' Yehudah says: Even one whose hands are stained with woad or madder may not lift his hands because the people will stare at him.

YAD AVRAHAM

7.

כֹּהֵן שֶׁיֵּשׁ בְּיָדָיו מוּמִין, — *A kohen whose hands are blemished...*

I.e., one whose hands are badly freckled, bent inwards, or bent sideways *(Gem.* 24b). The last case refers to one who cannot separate his fingers *(Ran).* [His deformity prevents him from pronouncing the blessings properly, since his fingers must be spread in the prescribed manner.]

A *kohen* whose face or feet are disfigured is also ineligible (*Rav; Gem.* 24b).

לֹא יִשָּׂא אֶת־כַּפָּיו. — *may not lift his hands.*

He may not ascend to bless the people. The deformities will cause people to stare at his hands while he pronounces the blessing, a practice which is forbidden. *Rashi,* citing *Chagigah* 16a, explains that the *Shechinah* rests upon the *kohen's* hands while he blesses the people; to stare at them can cause blindness.

Tosafos (Chagigah 16a) objects to this reasoning because the Shechinah is present on the *kohen's* hands only in the Temple and only then can blindness result from staring at them. Consequently, *Tosafos* explains that the Tanna objects to staring at the hands of the *kohanim* simply because the congregation will be distracted from listening to the blessing.

רַבִּי יְהוּדָה אוֹמֵר: אַף מִי שֶׁהָיוּ יָדָיו צְבוּעוֹת אִסְטִיס וּפוּאָה. — *R' Yehudah says: Even one whose hands are stained with woad or madder...*

אִסְטִיס [Latin, *Isatis tinctoria*], *woad,* is a bluish dye similar to תְּכֵלֶת, *techeiles.* פּוּאָה [*Rubia tinctorum*], *madder,* is a red dye made from roots *(Rav).*

לֹא יִשָּׂא אֶת־כַּפָּיו מִפְּנֵי שֶׁהָעָם מִסְתַּכְּלִין בּוֹ. — *may not lift his hands because the people will stare at him.*

Although he has no physical deformity, his stained hands will cause people to stare *(Tos. Yom Tov).*

Nevertheless, if the *kohen* was a long time resident of the town or if the majority of the city are also dyers, he may lift his hands to bless, as the discoloration is too common to make people stare *(Rav; Gem.* 24b).

Nowadays, *kohanim* customarily cover their hands and faces with their *talisos* when offering the priestly blessing. They may therefore, lift their hands to bless the people if their hands have such deformities or discoloration *(Shulchan Aruch, Orach Chaim* 128:32).

ד
ח

[ח] **הָאוֹמֵר:** „אֵינִי עוֹבֵר לִפְנֵי הַתֵּבָה בִּצְבוּעִין", אַף בִּלְבָנִים לֹא יַעֲבֹר; „בְּסַנְדָּל אֵינִי עוֹבֵר", אַף יָחֵף לֹא יַעֲבֹר.

הָעוֹשֶׂה תְפִלָּתוֹ עֲגֻלָּה, סַכָּנָה וְאֵין בָּהּ מִצְוָה. נְתָנָהּ עַל־מִצְחוֹ אוֹ עַל־פַּס יָדוֹ, הֲרֵי זוֹ דֶרֶךְ הַמִּינוּת. צִפָּן זָהָב, וּנְתָנָהּ עַל בֵּית אֻנְקְלִי שֶׁלּוֹ, הֲרֵי זוֹ דֶרֶךְ הַחִיצוֹנִים.

יד אברהם

8.

Statements of Heresy

The previous mishnayos have discussed people who are ineligible to perform various synagogue rites for *physical* reasons. The next two continue with a listing of those ineligible because of a grounded suspicion of heresy.

One who makes a statement which may be construed as indicative of heretical practices is considered ineligible to lead the prayers (mishnah 8).

When one utters a statement of heresy, his companions are obliged to silence him. However, in certain cases, where the statement is ambiguous enough to be considered righteous, although it may contain heretical overtones, the speaker is not silenced. Nevertheless, one must certainly refrain from such statements (mishnah 9).

הָאוֹמֵר: „אֵינִי עוֹבֵר לִפְנֵי הַתֵּבָה בִּצְבוּעִין" — *If one says, 'I will not go before the Ark in colored clothing,'*

If one refuses to serve as prayer leader because he is wearing colored clothing, we have reason to suppose that his refusal is based on the heretical practice of praying only in white clothing *(Meiri).*

Rashi, as quoted by *Nimukei Yosef,* maintains that this was the practice of the early Christians. Our version of *Rashi* states that it is the practice of 'idol worshipers.' This version was probably inserted by Christian censors *(Be'er Mosheh* on *Nimukei Yosef).*

Alternatively, his refusal may not be based on the practice of a specific group, but may represent a personal heresy *(Ran; Rivash* 224).

אַף בִּלְבָנִים לֹא יַעֲבֹר; — *he may not go even in white clothing.*

[I.e., even if he happens to be wearing white clothing, we disqualify him.]

The authorities disagree as to the duration of his disqualification. *Rambam* rules that he is prevented from serving as prayer leader only for that specific prayer whereas the *Ra'avad* maintains that he is permanently disqualified (see *Rambam, Hilchos Tefillah* 10:5; *Kessef Mishneh; Lechem Mishneh).*

"בְּסַנְדָּל אֵינִי עוֹבֵר", אַף יָחֵף לֹא יַעֲבֹר. — *[If he says] 'I will not go [before the Ark] in sandals,' he may not go even barefoot.*

Although it is permitted to pray barefoot, it is not a Jewish practice to insist on it. His *insistence* on praying barefoot is a heretical practice and, as such, it disqualifies him under all circumstances (*Tos. Yom Tov;* see above).

8. If one says, 'I will not go before the Ark in colored clothing,' he may not even go in white clothing. [If he says], 'I will not go [before the Ark] in sandals,' he may not even go barefoot.

One who makes his *tefillin* round endangers himself and does not fulfill the precept. If he places [the *tefillin*] on his forehead, or in his palm, it is the manner of heresy. If he covered them with gold, or if he placed it on his sleeve, this is considered the way of the outsiders.

YAD AVRAHAM

הָעוֹשֶׂה תְפִלָּתוֹ עֲגֻלָּה, סַכָּנָה... — *One who makes his tefillin round endangers himself...*

[The mishnah does not indicate why someone should wish to change the shape of his *tefillin*, especially since, as the mishnah says below, the *mitzvah* is not fulfilled unless the *tefillin* are square. As *Tiferes Yisrael* notes, the mishnah does not describe the practice as heretical. Perhaps it was a misguided attempt to beautify through innovation. The mishnah warns that it is not only inappropriate but also dangerous.]

One whose head-*tefillin* are oval-shaped endangers himself because, if he bumps it while entering a low doorway, the capsule might penetrate his head *(Tos. Yom Tov; Tiferes Yisrael* from *Rashi, Menachos* 35a).

Alternatively, he may bump the *tefillin* when he lowers his head to recite תַּחֲנוּן, *supplications (R' Chananel; Aruch).*

Others explain that if there is a decree prohibiting the wearing of *tefillin*, one who wears round *tefillin* — which are halachically unfit — is in more danger than one who wears square *tefillin* as prescribed by the *halachah* because ...

וְאֵין בָּהּ מִצְוָה. — *and does not fulfill the precept* [lit., *and there is no mitzvah in it*].

Accordingly, since he is not fulfilling a *mitzvah*, he cannot hope for a miracle to protect him in time of danger *(Tos.)*.

נְתָנָהּ עַל־מִצְחוֹ... — *If he places* [*the tefillin*] *on his forehead,* [instead of above the hairline as the *halachah* requires *(Ran)*].

אוֹ עַל־פַּס יָדוֹ, — *or on his palm* [instead of on the biceps *(Ran)*],

הֲרֵי זוֹ דֶּרֶךְ הַמִּינוּת. — *it is the manner of heresy.*

Such was the way of the צְדוּקִים, *Sadducees,* who interpreted the Torah literally in defiance of the authority of the Oral Law. In this instance, they placed their *tefillin* on the forehead and palm in literal obedience to the Torah's commandment that the *tefillin* be placed: עַל יָדְךָ, *on your hand,* and בֵּין עֵינֶיךָ, *between your eyes* [*Exod.* 13:9, 16; *Deut.* 6:8; 11:18] *(Rav).*

צִפָּן זָהָב, — *If he covered them with gold,*

I.e., if someone improperly covered the parchment of the *tefillin* with gold. The *tefillin* parchments must be in a receptacle made

ד
ט

[ט] **הָאוֹמֵר:** ,,יְבָרְכוּךָ טוֹבִים״, הֲרֵי זוֹ דֶּרֶךְ הַמִּינוּת; ,,עַל־קַן־צִפּוֹר

from the hide of a kosher animal. This is derived from the verse which, in discussing *tefillin,* states: לְמַעַן תִּהְיֶה תּוֹרַת ה׳ בְּפִיךָ, *in order that the teaching of* HASHEM *shall be in your mouth (Exod.* 13:9), which is Rabbinically interpreted to mean that the Torah [in this case, *tefillin*] must be written on something which may be put *in your mouth,* i.e., a kosher source *(Rashi; Ran; Rav).* The letter ש, *shin,* embossed on the receptacle is also considered Torah writing, therefore, the receptacle must also come from a kosher source (*Shabbos* 28b).

Tosefos R' Akiva Eiger raises the difficulty that gold, though not a food, is nonetheless not non-kosher. He cites *Rashi* to *Menachos* 42b that Moses was instructed at Sinai that the required material for both the boxes and straps is leather, thus gold is excluded. From the interpretation cited by *Rashi* to our mishnah, the Talmud (Menachos 45b) excludes non-kosher leather.

Another reading of the mishnah is צִפָּה זָהָב, *he covered* [*it*] *with gold* — i.e., the *Tanna* is referring to one who covered properly made *tefillin* boxes with gold and wore them that way. He would not fulfill the requirement since the box must be exposed to the air *(Bach; Tur* 32; *Mishnah Berurah* 32:221).

וּנְתָנָהּ עַל בֵּית אֻנְקְלִי שֶׁלּוֹ. — *or if he placed it on his sleeve,*

If he placed the *tefillin* on his sleeve rather than on his bicep, he would not fulfill the precept, as the Torah states, לְאוֹת עַל־יָדְךָ, *as a sign on your hand (Deut. 6:8)*; a sign for the *wearer* rather than for others, indicating that they are not to be worn in a manner visible to all — i.e., over the clothing — but directly on the arm and covered by the sleeve *(Rav).*

הֲרֵי זוֹ דֶּרֶךְ הַחִיצוֹנִים. — *This is considered the way of the outsiders.*

Outsiders are people who follow their own judgments even when their opinions are *outside* [i.e., not in accord with] the judgments of the Sages *(Rav).*

Though this practice is not *heretical* nor indicative of Sadducean leanings, it displays a disregard for the Rabbinical interpretation of the Torah *(Rav).*

Tiferes Yisrael maintains that the mishnah's cases are an indication of mistaken piety, as the person covered the *tefillin* with gold to beautify them or placed them on his sleeve to show how proud he is to wear them. If his intention were different, then it would be an indication of heresy rather than the way of the outsiders.

9.

[While one is permitted to add personal requests within relevant blessings of the *Shemoneh Esrei,* one must be careful that his additions not be misconstrued as heretical. Our mishnah discusses additions of varying degrees of unacceptability.]

הָאוֹמֵר: ,,יְבָרְכוּךָ טוֹבִים״, הֲרֵי זוֹ דֶּרֶךְ הַמִּינוּת; — *If one says* [as part of his prayer *(Rashi)*], *'Good men shall bless you,' this is heresy.*

This statement reflects heretical ideas and should therefore, not be said as part of the prayer *(Meiri).*

4
9
9. If one says, 'Good men shall bless You,' this is heresy. [If one says], 'Your mercy extends [even] to a bird's nest,' or 'For Your goodness is Your Name

YAD AVRAHAM

This statement implies that prayer is only for the righteous, whereas, in truth, the wicked must also be included in the prayers. This is derived from the fact that חֶלְבְּנָה, *galbanum*, was included in the preparation of the Temple's; קְטֹרֶת, *incense*, despite its foul odor (*Rashi; Rav; Kerisus* 6b).

Alternatively, the statement is considered heretical since it implies that the world was created so that only the *righteous* shall bless God, whereas *all* were created for that purpose (*R' Yonah; Berachos* 5:3).

Possibly, the statement is heretical because it suggests that only those who enjoy good fortune are required to bless God. This was based on a misinterpretation of the verse: וְאָכַלְתָּ וְשָׂבָעְתָּ וּבֵרַכְתָּ אֶת ה׳, *And you shall eat, be sated, and bless HASHEM (Deut.* 8:10); i.e., one is only required to bless God if he has eaten and been sated or more generally, if he enjoys good fortune. The statement disregards the Rabbinic enactment which requires *Bircas HaMazon* to be pronounced even after a small meal consisting of an olive-size or egg-size piece of bread *(Talmid HaRamban)*.

Others maintain that this statement is an indication of the acceptance of the Zoroastrian belief in two gods — one the god of good, the other the god of evil. Thus, he prays: May the good, i.e., those who are in Your jurisdiction with whom You have dealt favorably, bless You *(Ran)*.

However, one who uses the statement is not silenced as he may have innocent motives; his intent may be that only the righteous can honestly bless Hashem *(Tif. Yis.)*.

Tosefos HaRosh comments that the prayer itself is not heretical; on the contrary, it is a statement of blessing. In fact, *Rabbeinu Tam* made it a practice to conclude his personal correspondence with the blessing יְבָרְכוּךְ טוֹבִים, *may good men bless you.* Clearly, therefore, the objection is only to its use as part of the prayers where it can be misconstrued.

Indeed, *Rabbeinu Tam* interpreted this mishnah as referring to the blessing of מוֹדִים, [*Modim*], *we thank You,* in *Shemoneh Esrei,* which includes וְכָל־הַחַיִּים יוֹדוּךָ, *and all the living will thank You.* Substituting the word הַטּוֹבִים, *the good,* for *the living,* is heretical *(Meleches Shlomo)*.

[The mishnah now describes three forbidden additions to the prayer concerning which the law is: מְשַׁתְּקִין אוֹתוֹ, *we silence him.* Clearly, the statements are not considered heretical, but, as explained below, they betray serious errors.]

„עַל־קַן־צִפּוֹר יַגִּיעוּ רַחֲמֶיךָ״, — *[If one says], 'Your mercy extends [even] to a bird's nest,'*

We silence one who prays: Have mercy on us just as Your mercies extend to a bird's nest, as seen from Your commandment: לֹא־תִקַּח הָאֵם עַל־הַבָּנִים, *You shall not take the mother while she is on the children (Deut.* 22:6).

Two reasons are given for this ruling: (1) One who makes such a claim provokes jealousy, for by specifying God's mercy only in connection with a bird's nest, he

ד ט

יַגִּיעוּ רַחֲמֶיךָ״, וְ,,עַל־טוֹב יִזָּכֵר שְׁמֶךָ״, ,,מוֹדִים מוֹדִים״ — מְשַׁתְּקִין אוֹתוֹ.
הַמְכַנֶּה בָעֲרָיוֹת, מְשַׁתְּקִין אוֹתוֹ.

יד אברהם

implies that God has no mercy on His other creatures. Thus, it is as if he makes other creatures feel jealous of the birds. (2) Instead of recognizing that God's commandments are like royal decrees which must be obeyed whether or not they appeal to us, he suggests that God's authority is dependent on some perceived moral value *(Gem.* 25a, *Rashi).*

Others explain that the imputation of God's mercy as the cause of the commandment is totally unjustified. Were God to have been motivated by compassion for a mother, there would be no reason to distinguish between the bird's nest and the dwellings of other creatures. It is a decreee for which human intelligence cannot fathom a definite reason *(Nimukei Yosef).*[1]

Alternatively, although it is surely true that *His mercy is on all of His works (Psalms* 145:9), mercy is not the reason for the *mitzvah;* God's motives are too profound for human intellect to grasp *(Tif. Yis.).*

Tosefos Yom Tov (Berachos 5:3) comments that although one may homiletically attribute a *mitzvah* to Divine mercy, he may not do so in prayer, because then he is declaring his own perception of the reason to be absolute truth.

וְ,,עַל־טוֹב יִזָּכֵר שְׁמֶךָ״ — *or, 'For goodness is Your Name remembered,'*

If one says in his prayers that one is required to thank Hashem only for the good things He bestows, he is silenced. Man is required to thank Hashem for the bad just as he blesses Him for the good (see *Berachos* 9:5, *Rav).*

Man must recognize that there is reason for his misfortune; it may be an atonement for his sins or a trial to prove his merit. Misfortune can be compared to a painful operation necessary to effect a cure *(Aruch; Nimukei Yosef).*

,,מוֹדִים, מוֹדִים״, —מְשַׁתְּקִין אוֹתוֹ. — *or, 'We give thanks; we give thanks,' he is silenced.*

If one repeats the word מוֹדִים, [*Modim*], *we give thanks,* in the *Shemoneh Esrei,* it appears as if he is offering thanks to two gods, ח״ו *(Rav).* According to *Yerushalmi* this is objectionable only if said aloud in the repetition of the *Shemoneh Esrei.* If said silently, however, the repetition is seen as an implied sup-

1. Apparently, these commentators hold that the *mitzvos* must be accepted as having no reason other than the Divine will. This opinion is shared by *Rambam* in *Moreh Nevuchim* (3:48). He quotes many *Midrashim,* however, that *do* attribute reasons to the *mitzvos.* He therefore draws the conclusion that there is a difference of opinion among the Rabbis concerning whether or not reasons can be attributed to the *mitzvos.*

Ramban, however, maintains that there is no discrepancy between the various sources. The *mitzvos* indeed *have* reasons. They were given not for God's benefit, but for ours. We must send away the mother bird, not because He has pity on the

remembered,' or 'We give thanks; we give thanks,' he is silenced.

If one gives symbolic interpretations to [the prohibitions against] forbidden unions, we silence him.

plication since it reinforces our acknowledgment of our dependence on God.

Nimukei Yosef comments that all of the above are silenced in fulfillment of the verse, יִסָּכֵר פִּי דוֹבְרֵי־שָׁקֶר, *may the mouth of those who speak lies be stopped (Psalms* 63:12).

הַמְכַנֶּה בָּעֲרָיוֹת, — *If one gives symbolic interpretations to [the prohibitions against] forbidden unions.*

Instead of taking the injunctions against immorality in their literal sense, he interprets them as euphemisms. For example, Scripture forbids parental incest saying, עֶרְוַת אָבִיךָ וְעֶרְוַת אִמְּךָ לֹא תְגַלֵּה, *your father's nakedness and your mother's nakedness you shall not uncover (Lev.* 18:7). This person interprets *nakedness* to mean that you may not disclose anything uncomplimentary about them *(Rashi),* in public *(Rav).*

Alternatively, instead of reading the prohibitions in second person as they are given in Scripture — *you shall not* — he reads them in third person — *one shall not (Rambam; R' Chananel; Aruch; Yerushalmi;* see *Meleches Shlomo).* The reason the reader may choose to do so is to avoid making it seem as though he is directly admonishing a particular guilty individual, telling him *you* are prohibited from the forbidden unions *(Otzar HaGeonim* from *R' Hai).*

Sefer HaEshkol understands the mishnah as referring not to the reader but the *meturgeman* [see pref. mishnah 4] who translates the verses in the third person.

מְשַׁתְּקִין אוֹתוֹ. — *we silence him.*

According to the first explanation, we silence him because he is misinterpreting the passage by saying that one who disgraces his father or mother is punished as if he had committed adultery with them *(Ran).*

According to the second explanation, he is silenced because he tampers with the Masoretic text of the Torah.

Sefer HaEshkol explains that although he is not misinterpreting the passage, since the sense of the verse is the same whether one interprets it in second or third person, nevertheless, he is not translating it correctly.

birds; on the contrary, for our own use, we may slaughter animals and fowl despite the pain we are causing them. Why then must we send away the mother bird? The reason is that because God wishes to inculcate the trait of mercy in us; therefore, He gave us certain commandments that imbue that property. It is wrong, therefore, to say that He Himself was moved by pity for a helpless mother bird, for we have no right to attribute human emotions to Him *(Ramban, Deut.* 22:6).

ד
י

הָאוֹמֵר: ,,וּמִזַּרְעֲךָ לֹא־תִתֵּן לְהַעֲבִיר לַמֹּלֶךְ, וּמִזַּרְעָךְ לָא־תִתֵּן לְאַעְבָּרָא בְּאַרְמָיוּתָא״, מְשַׁתְּקִין אוֹתוֹ בִנְזִיפָה.

[י] **מַעֲשֵׂה** רְאוּבֵן נִקְרָא וְלֹא מִתַּרְגֵּם. מַעֲשֵׂה תָמָר נִקְרָא וּמִתַּרְגֵּם.

יד אברהם

הָאוֹמֵר: ,,וּמִזַּרְעֲךָ לֹא־תִתֵּן לְהַעֲבִיר לַמֹּלֶךְ, — וּמִזַּרְעָךְ לָא־תִתֵּן לְאַעְבָּרָא בְּאַרְמָיוּתָא״, *If one says, '[The verse:] And of your children you shall not give over to Molech* [*Lev.* 18:21] [*means,*] *that you shall not give of your seed to impregnate a gentile* [lit. *Aramean*] *woman,'*

I.e., if instead of translating correctly that the worship of the idol Molech is forbidden, the *meturgeman* translates the Torah's statement as a prohibition against having intercourse with a gentile woman, since the children will *eventually* worship idols *(Rav).*

Such an erroneous translation would render the word לְהַעֲבִיר as deriving from the term עִבּוּר, *conception (Tif. Yis.).*

[Thus the phrase is erroneously interpreted to imply: *And with your seed you shall not impregnate one from whom there shall descend those who will serve the idol Molech.*]

מְשַׁתְּקִין אוֹתוֹ בִנְזִיפָה. — *he is silenced with a condemnation.*

By translating the verse in this manner he distorts its meaning and places a penalty of כָּרֵת, *excision,* on an act which has no such punishment *(Rav).*

Targum Yonasan ben Uziel does interpret the verse in this manner. However, it is not intended there to reflect the literal translation of the words. That *Targum* often cites homiletic interpretations which do not adhere to פְּשָׁט, *the simple sense,* of the verse as opposed to the *meturgeman* whose function was to teach the simple meaning to the populace *(Reiach Dudaim).*

Alternatively, the objection is to the use of the term אַרְמָיוּתָא, literally *an Aramean woman,* which implies that cohabitation with other gentile women who do not worship Molech is not proscribed. Since this error may lead to a grave infraction of the law, we silence him with a condemnation. In the previous case of one who gives symbolic interpretations to the prohibitions of forbidden unions, since the error will not lead to any infraction of the law, we merely silence him, but without the added condemnation *(Tos. Yom Tov; Aruch).*

[According to *Rashi* and *Rav,* who explain that we silence the translator merely because he distorts the meaning of the verse, there is apparently no difference between this case and the previous one. Indeed, *Meiri* groups them both under the heading, מְשַׁתְּקִין אוֹתוֹ בִנְזִיפָה, *we silence him with condemnation.* Possibly, *Rashi* and *Rav* had the same version as *Meiri.*

If one says, '[The verse:] *And of your children you shall not give over to Molech* [*Lev.* 18:21] [means] that you shall not give of your seed to impregnate a gentile woman,' he is silenced with a condemnation.

10. The episode of Reuben is read but not translated. The episode of Tamar [however] is read and translated. The first narration of the

YAD AVRAHAM

10.

⌘ Portions Not to be Read or Translated

This mishnah enumerates certain sections of the Torah and the Prophets that are not translated, and certain sections of the Prophets that are not selected as *haftaros.* The sections of the Torah that contain narratives uncomplimentary to our ancestors, or that can be misconstrued by the populace, are read but not translated. Similar sections of the Prophets are not even read as *haftaros.*

It is apparent that at the time of the mishnah, the *haftaros* read on Sabbaths, and even on some festivals, were not uniform, but were chosen by each congregation. Therefore, some of the guidelines for selecting the *haftaros* are set down in this mishnah.

...מַעֲשֵׂה רְאוּבֵן — *The episode of Reuben...*

The episode is mentioned in *Genesis* 35:22: וַיֵּלֶךְ רְאוּבֵן וַיִּשְׁכַּב אֶת־בִּלְהָה פִּילֶגֶשׁ אָבִיו, *And Reuben went, and lay with Bilhah, his father's concubine.* The Rabbis tell us that this is not to be understood literally. The intention is that Reuben, upon seeing that his father had set up his bed in the tent belonging to Bilhah, Rachel's maidservant, rather than in the one belonging to Leah, Reuben's mother, felt that his mother had been slighted. Impetuously, he upset his father's bed. Reuben's lofty degree of righteousness was such that even so minor a misdeed could be equated to an act of adultery committed by a lesser person (*Shabbos* 55b). [See *Overview* to ArtScroll *Ruth.*]

...נִקְרָא — *is read...*

It is read in the synagogue as part of the regular order of Sabbath Torah reading, without fear of dishonoring Reuben *(Rashi).*

.וְלֹא מִתַּרְגֵּם — *but not translated.*

Since the *Targum* does not clarify the true meaning of this passage, a literal reading of the familiar Aramaic translation would degrade Reuben *(Rashi).*

Alternatively, the episode would degrade Jacob *(Ran).*

...מַעֲשֵׂה תָמָר — *The episode of Tamar...*

Rashi interprets this as the incident of Tamar and Judah related in *Genesis* 38.

Rav, however, maintains that the Tanna is referring to the narrative of Amnon and Tamar in *II Samuel* 13:1-22. Accordingly, the question is whether the episode may be chosen as a *haftarah.*

.נִקְרָא וּמִתַּרְגֵּם — [*however*] *is read and translated.*

Since Judah confessed his sin, the sum total of the story is complimentary *(Rashi).*

ד י מַעֲשֵׂה עֵגֶל הָרִאשׁוֹן נִקְרָא וּמִתַּרְגֵּם, וְהַשֵּׁנִי נִקְרָא וְלֹא מִתַּרְגֵּם.

בִּרְכַּת כֹּהֲנִים, מַעֲשֵׂה דָוִד וְאַמְנוֹן, לֹא נִקְרָאִין וְלֹא מִתַּרְגְּמִין.

אֵין מַפְטִירִין בַּמֶּרְכָּבָה. וְרַבִּי יְהוּדָה מַתִּיר. רַבִּי אֱלִיעֶזֶר אוֹמֵר: אֵין מַפְטִירִין בְּ„הוֹדַע אֶת־יְרוּשָׁלַיִם״.

יד אברהם

According to *Rav,* only those verses that do not describe Amnon as the son of David may be read and translated.

מַעֲשֵׂה עֵגֶל הָרִאשׁוֹן... — *The first narration of the* [*Golden*] *Calf...*

[Scripture's first account of the making of the Golden Calf is found in *Exodus* 32:1-20.]

נִקְרָא וּמִתַּרְגֵּם — *is read and translated;*

We are not concerned with degrading the Jews who worshiped it, since embarrassment is a vehicle that helps bring atonement *(Rav).*

Alternatively, reading and translating the episode will serve to inspire the people since it shows that even a serious transgression can be atoned for *(Tif. Yis.).*

וְהַשֵּׁנִי — *the second* [account of the episode *(Exod.* 32:21-24) as related by Aaron to Moses *(Rashi)*]...

נִקְרָא וְלֹא מִתַּרְגֵּם. — *is read but not translated.*

The conclusion of *Exodus* 32:24: וַיֵּצֵא הָעֵגֶל הַזֶּה, *And out* [of the fire] *came this calf,* may mislead the ignorant into believing that the calf possessed power since it seemed to come into existence miraculously. Therefore, it is read but not translated *(Rashi).*

Alternatively, since the narrative speaks of Aaron's role in the making of the golden calf, it is not translated out of respect for him. *Exod.* 32:25 is also left untranslated since it, too, speaks of Aaron's role *(Tos.; Yerushalmi).* For the same reason *Exod.* 32:35 is not translated *(Rif; Rambam; Rav).*

בִּרְכַּת כֹּהֲנִים, — *The priestly blessing* [*Numbers* 6:22-27]...

מַעֲשֵׂה דָוִד וְאַמְנוֹן, — *and the episode of David and Amnon...*

This refers to those verses in *II Samuel* 13 (*v.* 1 and 4) which refer to Amnon, violator of Tamar, as David's son *(Rav; Gem.* 25b).

לֹא נִקְרָאִין וְלֹא מִתַּרְגְּמִין. — *are neither read nor translated.*

In the case of Amnon, those verses are not read publicly out of respect for David. In the case of the priestly blessings, since the verse states, יִשָּׂא ה׳ פָּנָיו אֵלֶיךָ, *may* HASHEM *show you His countenance,* the ignorant may misconstrue it to mean that Hashem shows undeserved favoritism to Israel. Such critics fail to realize that

4
10 [Golden] Calf is read and translated; the second is read but not translated.

The priestly blessing and the episode of David and Amnon are neither read nor translated.

We do not read the [vision of the] chariot as a *haftarah*. R' Yehudah, however, permits it. R' Eliezer says: We do not read *'Make known to Jerusalem'* (*Ezekiel* 16) as a *haftarah*.

YAD AVRAHAM

Israel merits God's favor *(Rav)*.

According to *Rav*, the blessings are read, but not translated, whereas the offensive references to David are neither read nor translated. Our text, however, states that neither is read nor translated. To explain why the priestly blessing should not be read, *Tiferes Yisrael* cites *Yerushalmi* that the passage was meant for a blessing but not for reading. *Tiferes Yisrael* suggests that even according to this version, the blessings *would* be read as part of the Scriptural section, but they should not be read in isolation.

אֵין מַפְטִירִין בַּמֶּרְכָּבָה. — *We do not read the* [*vision of the*] *chariot as a haftarah.*

I.e., the vision described in *Ezekiel* (ch. 1). Were it read, people might attempt to delve into its profound mysteries. Since such knowledge is beyond the comprehension of all but the very greatest, lesser people might err in basic principles of faith *(Rav)*.

וְרַבִּי יְהוּדָה מַתִּיר. — *R' Yehudah, however, permits it.*

This is the accepted ruling *(Rav)*, and the section is read as the *haftarah* on the first day of Shavuos (see 3:4).

R' Yehudah maintains that the vision expressed in *Ezekiel* is not more potentially dangerous than the story of creation which *is* read *(Tos. Yom Tov)*.

ר׳ אֱלִיעֶזֶר אוֹמֵר: אֵין מַפְטִירִין בְּ,,הוֹדַע אֶת־יְרוּשָׁלַיִם״. — *R' Eliezer says: We do not read 'Make known to Jerusalem'* [*Ezekiel* 16] *as a haftarah.*

Since this chapter speaks of the degradation of Jerusalem, it is not read as a *haftarah*. The halachah, however, is not in accordance with this view *(Rav)*.

Alternatively, the chapter is not read because it contains the figurative description (*v.* 3): אָבִיךְ הָאֱמֹרִי וְאִמֵּךְ חִתִּית, *Your father was an Emorite and your mother a Hittite.* Thus it could be taken as casting aspersions on the genealogy of the Jews (*Tos. Yom Tov; Levush* 493).

סליק מסכת מגילה

מסכת מועד קטן

Tractate Moed Katan

Translation and anthologized commentary by

Rabbi Avrohom Yoseif Rosenberg

Mesorah Publications, ltd

◆§ Tractate Moed Katan

The festivals of Pesach and Succos both begin and end with holy days during which work is forbidden. The intermediate days of each festival are known as חוֹל הַמּוֹעֵד, *Chol HaMoed*, or חוּלוֹ שֶׁל מוֹעֵד, *Cholo shel Moed* [lit. *the ordinary part of the festival*]. (In *Eretz Yisrael*, only the first and last days of the festivals are full holy days — *Chol HaMoed* thus consists of the second through the sixth day of Pesach and the second through the seventh day of Succos. Outside of Israel, however, since we celebrate the first *two* and last *two* days of each festival with a full degree of holiness, *Chol HaMoed* is the third through the sixth day of Pesach, and the third through the seventh day of Succos.) The name *Chol HaMoed* alludes to the fact that, unlike the beginning and concluding days which have a degree of holiness so great that nearly all forms of labor are forbidden, the intermediate days are relatively חוֹל, *ordinary*, in that many forms of work are permitted on these days. Against some forms of work, however, there *is* a prohibition, the definition of which is a major theme of our tractate. Because these intermediate days are of lesser sanctity than the first and last days of the festival, the tractate which discusses them is called מוֹעֵד קָטָן, *Moed Katan* [lit. *minor festival*].

The Talmud (*Chagigah* 18a) derives this prohibition from the verse (*Deut.* 16:8) concerning Pesach: שֵׁשֶׁת יָמִים תֹּאכַל מַצּוֹת וּבַיּוֹם הַשְּׁבִיעִי עֲצֶרֶת ... לֹא תַעֲשֶׂה מְלָאכָה, *six days shall you eat matzos, but on the seventh day, restrain* [from work] ... *do not perform work.* The Talmud expounds on this verse: Although work of some sort is prohibited throughout Pesach, only on the seventh day is there a blanket prohibition on work. [Whatever prohibition applies to the seventh day would also apply to the first day, since both are specified as festivals.] The implication is that on *Chol HaMoed* some forms of work are prohibited and some are permitted.

Concerning the halachic status of the prohibitions on *Chol HaMoed*, there are two schools of thought. One (*Rashi, Rashbam, Rif, Shiltos d'R' Achai Gaon, Shibolei HaLeket, Eshkol,* and *R' Eliezer of Metz*) holds that it is a Scriptural prohibition. Unlike other prohibitions which are specified and unconditional, however, the Torah authorized the Rabbis to determine which forms of work to permit and which to prohibit on *Chol HaMoed*. The other view (*Tosafos, Rambam, Rosh, Tur, Mordechai,* and *Rashbatz*) holds that the prohibition is a Rabbinic enactment; the verse cited above upon which the prohibition is based is an אַסְמַכְתָּא, Scriptural text in *support* of a Rabbinic law; i.e., the Sages found their ordinance suggested, though not commanded, by the verse. According to this opinion, the Rabbis enacted the law in order to preserve the festive atmosphere of the holiday for the entire week, thereby enabling us to rejoice and to engage in the study of Torah, unburdened by mundane affairs (*Mishnah Berurah* 530).

◆§ ◆§ ◆§ ◆§

Basically, the forms of work permitted on *Chol HaMoed* are divided into five categories:

1) דָּבָר הָאָבֵד, [work that must be done to avoid] *an irretrievable loss,* [see 1:1];

2) צוֹרֶךְ הַמּוֹעֵד, [work] *needed for the festival* [see 2:4];

3) פּוֹעֵל שֶׁאֵין לוֹ מַה יֹּאכַל, *a laborer who has nothing to eat,* and must engage in gainful employment to support himself [see 2:4];

4) צָרְכֵי רַבִּים, *community* [as opposed to private] *needs* [see 1:2], and;

5) מַעֲשֵׂה הֶדְיוֹט, *work performed in a nonprofessional manner* [see 1:8] (*Tur* 530).

The main purpose of this tractate is to delineate which labors are forbidden and which are permitted on *Chol HaMoed,* as well as other Rabbinic enactments pertaining to the period. Since many of the prohibitions of *Chol HaMoed* also apply to the שְׁמִטָּה, *Shemitah* [*Sabbatical year*] (see *Lev.* 25:1-7), this period is also mentioned in much of the tractate.

א
א

[א] **מַשְׁקִין** בֵּית הַשְּׁלָחִין בַּמּוֹעֵד וּבַשְּׁבִיעִית, בֵּין מִמַּעְיָן שֶׁיָּצָא בַתְּחִלָּה בֵּין מִמַּעְיָן שֶׁלֹּא יָצָא בַתְּחִלָּה. אֲבָל אֵין מַשְׁקִין לֹא

יד אברהם

Chapter 1

1.

◆§ Irretrievable Loss

One of the categories of work permitted on *Chol HaMoed* (see above) is דָּבָר הָאָבֵד, work done to avoid *an irretrievable loss.* Such work may be done in the usual manner (see pref. mishnah 4). However, טִרְחָא יְתֵירָה, *excessive exertion,* must be avoided. Thus, if two methods will accomplish the same end, the less taxing one is to be used.

Often confused with *irretrievable loss* is the situation of מְנִיעַת הָרֶוַח, *prevention of profit,* i.e., denial of potential gain. דָּבָר הָאָבֵד refers only to an *irretrievable loss,* which is tangible, but not to the failure to capitalize on a potential gain.

Mishnah 1 discusses the relationship between *irretrievable loss* and *excessive exertion.* By implication, *prevention of profit* is not a ground to permit work.

◆§ Shemitah — The Sabbatical Year

Just as the first six days of each week are designated for physical labor while the seventh day is the Sabbath, a day of rest *(Exodus* 20:8-11), so, too, are the first six years of each שָׁבוּעַ, *seven-year period,* designated for working the land while the seventh year is Sabbath, a year of abstention from working the land *(Leviticus* 25:1-7). During that year, called שְׁבִיעִית [*Sheviis*], *seventh,* or שְׁמִטָּה [*Shemitah*], *release,* we are enjoined from cultivating and harvesting the fields, vineyards, and orchards of *Eretz Yisrael.*

Presumably, the category of the Sabbatical year is included in our mishnah because it bears a similarity to *Chol HaMoed* in that certain types of labor are permitted in specific situations.

מַשְׁקִין בֵּית הַשְּׁלָחִין... — *We may water an irrigated field...*

I.e., a field that cannot subsist on rainfall alone; unless it is watered it would be ruined *(Tiferes Yisrael).*

בֵּית הַשְּׁלָחִין is literally a *tired* or *thirsty field.* The *Targum* of עָיֵף, *tired,* is מְשַׁלְהֵי [שלח=שלה] *(Rashi* on 2a).

בַּמּוֹעֵד... — *during* [*Chol Ha*]*-Moed...*

The term מוֹעֵד, *festival,* in our mishnah refers to the intermediate days of Pesach and Succos. Our custom is to refer to these days as חוֹל הַמּוֹעֵד, *Chol HaMoed,* lit. *the ordinary part of the festival (Tos. Yom Tov).* [See pref. to this tractate for the implications of this expression. Throughout *Moed Katan* the word מוֹעֵד usually refers to *Chol HaMoed,* but in some instances (see 1:3, 10), the entire festival period is meant. Generally, the more sanctified portion of the festival is referred to as רֶגֶל, *pilgrimage* (see 3:5,6).]

Though work is generally forbidden during *Chol HaMoed,* such work *may* be performed if failure to do so will result in irretrievable loss [see pref.]. Since an irrigated field is affected adversely as soon as the watering is halted, an irretrievable loss would result. However,

1
1 **1.** **W**e may water an irrigated field during [*Chol*] *HaMoed* or during *Shemitah,* either from a spring that has just begun to flow or from a spring that has not just begun to flow. However, we may

YAD AVRAHAM

orchards may not be watered during *Chol HaMoed* since they will not suffer permanent damage *(Rav).*[1]

Others do not distinguish between fields and orchards *(Meiri).*

Similarly, a field that can subsist without irrigation may not be watered even though the field would be improved by watering it. Since failure to irrigate would result in no irretrievable tangible loss, but rather, in מְנִיעַת הָרֶוַח, *loss of further profit,* irrigation is forbidden *(Ran).*

Finally, although one is permitted to water an irrigated field without a שִׁנּוּי, *deviation* [from the usual manner], he is permitted to do so only in a manner which does not entail undue exertion; e.g., by redirecting water with his foot so that it flows into the field. However, drawing water with a pail is considered work entailing exertion and is prohibited [see below] *(Beis Yosef* on *Tur* 537).

וּבַשְּׁבִיעִית, — *and during Shemitah,*

The Tanna permits farmers to water their fields during the Sabbatical year even though they are forbidden to work their fields (see *Lev.* 25:1-7). The prohibition against watering is a Rabbinical ordinance, thus, if failure to do so will cause the plants to suffer one may irrigate, as the Rabbis did not apply their edict where it would cause a loss *(Tif. Yis.).*

There is a dispute among the commentaries as to whether during *Shemitah,* the Tanna permitted irrigating even a field that can subsist on rainfall alone *(Rashi; Rav);* or permitted watering only fields that would suffer without artificial irrigation *(Rambam, Shemitah V'Yovel* 1:8. See also *Tos.* 6b).

בֵּין מִמַּעְיָן שֶׁיָּצָא בַּתְּחִלָּה... — *either from a spring that has just begun to flow...*

We need not fear that its walls will collapse and that one might therefore engage in work requiring exertion in order to repair it *(Rav).*

[Though the next mishnah rules that one may repair damaged irrigation canals, this is only true if doing so does not entail undue exertion. In the context of our mishnah, however, were the spring's walls to collapse, the necessary repair would be considered strenuous, and therefore forbidden, work.]

בֵּין מִמַּעְיָן שֶׁלֹּא יָצָא בַּתְּחִלָּה. — *or from a spring that has not just begun to flow.*

I.e., a spring which has been tested by use, we surely have no reason to fear that its walls might collapse *(Rav).*

אֲבָל אֵין מַשְׁקִין... — *However, we may not water* [*irrigated fields*]...

I.e., on *Chol HaMoed.* This activity, and the next one as well, are forbidden on *Chol HaMoed* because

1. *Magen Avraham* 537 rules that even if it is not definite that failure to do such work will result in an irretrievable loss, the work is, nevertheless, permissible.

Machatzis HaShekel and *Pri Megadim* maintain that this is true only according to the authorities who consider the prohibition of work on *Chol HaMoed* a Rabbinical prohibition (see preface to tractate). Thus, a doubtful case falls into the category of סְפֵיקָא דְרַבָּנַן לְקוּלָא, *a case of doubt concerning a Rabbinic prohibition calls for a*

א
ב

מִמֵּי הַגְּשָׁמִים וְלֹא מִמֵּי הַקִּילוֹן. וְאֵין עוֹשִׂין עוּגִיּוֹת לַגְּפָנִים.

[ב] **רַבִּי** אֶלְעָזָר בֶּן־עֲזַרְיָה אוֹמֵר: אֵין עוֹשִׂין אֶת־הָאַמָּה בַּתְּחִלָּה בַּמּוֹעֵד וּבַשְּׁבִיעִית.
וַחֲכָמִים אוֹמְרִים: עוֹשִׂין אֶת־הָאַמָּה בַּתְּחִלָּה

יד אברהם

they involve, or can lead to, exertion [see below]. Therefore, the restrictions do not apply to *Shemitah*, where no distinction is drawn between work that does or does not require exertion. The criterion for *Shemitah* prohibitions is that the work be related to planting, growing, or harvesting; excessive exertion and strenuous labor are permitted if they are not connected with production of crops *(Tos. Yom Tov).*

לֹא מִמֵּי הַגְּשָׁמִים וְלֹא מִמֵּי הַקִּילוֹן. — *neither with rain water, nor with water from a cistern.*

Rain water may accumulate in a pond, from which it can be diverted into the field by one's foot, or rain may accumulate in a cistern from which it must be drawn with a pail.

Although diverting water from a pond is not strenuous, permission to use such water may be confused with the use of water drawn from a cistern, for both are rain water. If pond water were permitted, people might err and use cistern water as well; therefore, both are prohibited *(Rav).*

Furthermore, since the rain water in the pond may reach a level so low that it can be moved only with a pail, the Rabbis prohibited drawing rain water from a pond even when its water level is still high *(Beis Yosef* 537).

However, one may use rain water for irrigation provided there is a continuous supply of water to replace whatever is drawn; in such a case there is no chance that the water will reach a level low enough to necessitate the use of a pail. For example, one may divert water by foot from a stream that is continuously fed from pools of rain water, as this will not lead to a situation requiring exertion *(Shulchan Aruch, Orach Chaim* 537:3; *Mishnah Berurah* 9).

וְאֵין עוֹשִׂין עוּגִיּוֹת לַגְּפָנִים. — *nor may we dig* [lit. *make*] *ditches around grapevines.*

I.e., around the roots of the vines to collect rain water *(Rav),* because this is deemed work requiring exertion *(Rashi* 4b).

This prohibition applies only to

lenient decision. According to those who consider it a Torah prohibition, however, doubtful cases are forbidden, since they fall under the category of סְפֵיקָא דְאוֹרַיְיתָא לְחוּמְרָא, *a case of doubt concerning a Torah prohibition calls for a stringent decision.*

Nishmas Adam disagrees with the lenient ruling of *Magen Avraham.* He holds that even those who consider the prohibition to be Rabbinic proscribe the performance of work on *Chol HaMoed* unless a definite loss will result.

Beur Halachah refers us to 3:3, where the Tanna lists documents that may be

1 not water [irrigated fields], neither with rain water
2 nor with water from a cistern; nor may we dig ditches around grapevines.

2. R' Elazar ben Azaryah says: We may not dig a new irrigation canal during [*Chol*] *HaMoed* or during *Shemitah*.

The Sages say: We may dig a new irrigation canal

YAD AVRAHAM

Chol HaMoed. During *Shemitah* however, Rabbinically forbidden labor is permitted in the face of loss, regardless of the degree of exertion [for, as mentioned above, exertion is not a criterion for prohibiting work during *Shemitah*] (*Gem.* 3a; *Rambam, Shemitah V'Yovel* 1:9, 10).

2.

רַבִּי אֶלְעָזָר בֶּן־עֲזַרְיָה אוֹמֵר: אֵין עוֹשִׂין אֶת־הָאַמָּה בַּתְּחִלָּה... — *R' Elazar ben Azaryah says: We may not dig a new irrigation canal...*

The prohibition applies to the digging of a new canal where none existed. [Below, the mishnah will discuss the law of an old canal that became partially or totally clogged.] The canal (called an אַמָּה, *cubit*, because it was usually a cubit wide and a cubit deep) was used to direct water through the field or from one field to another (*Rav*).

[Halachic authorities differ as to the exact measurement of a cubit; opinions range from 18 to over 24 inches.]

בַּמּוֹעֵד... — *during* [*Chol*] *HaMoed...*

Digging irrigation canals in virgin soil is deemed strenuous work and is therefore prohibited (*Rav*).

וּבַשְּׁבִיעִית. — *or during Shemitah.*

Though there is no prohibition during *Shemitah* on labor unrelated to planting, R' Elazar prohibited the digging of irrigation canals because such labor is similar to hoeing, a task that is proscribed during *Shemitah* (*Tos. Yom Tov; Tif. Yis; Gem.* 4b).

וַחֲכָמִים אוֹמְרִים: עוֹשִׂין אֶת־הָאַמָּה בַּתְּחִלָּה בַּשְּׁבִיעִית, — *The Sages say: We may dig a new irrigation canal during Shemitah,*

The Sages maintain that since the earth dug out is flung far away, such digging cannot be confused with hoeing, which is meant to turn the soil in place; consequently, it is permitted during *Shemitah* (*Meiri; Tos. Yom Tov; Nimukei Yosef*).

Alternatively, R' Elazar prohibits digging irrigation canals during *Shemitah* since doing so renders

written on *Chol HaMoed* lest the witnesses of a transaction die or embark on a journey, and not be available for future testimony. This proves conclusively that work is permissible to prevent even a *possible* loss. He concludes that this is true only if a loss is *likely* to occur. Otherwise, it is proscribed.

Even in the case of an irretrievable loss, only work that does not involve exertion is permitted. Work that involves exertion is proscribed even in this case, as our mishnah clearly indicates.

בַּשְּׁבִיעִית, וּמְתַקְּנִין אֶת־הַמְקֻלְקָלוֹת בַּמּוֹעֵד. א
וּמְתַקְּנִין אֶת־קִלְקוּלֵי הַמַּיִם שֶׁבִּרְשׁוּת ב
הָרַבִּים, וְחוֹטְטִין אוֹתָן. וּמְתַקְּנִין אֶת־הַדְּרָכִים
וְאֶת־הָרְחוֹבוֹת וְאֶת־מִקְווֹת הַמַּיִם, וְעוֹשִׂין כָּל־
צָרְכֵי הָרַבִּים, וּמְצַיְּנִין אֶת־הַקְּבָרוֹת, וְיוֹצְאִין
אַף עַל־הַכִּלְאַיִם.

their banks suitable for sowing. This is an improvement in the land related to tilling the soil. The Sages, however, permit such digging, for since the prohibition is Rabbinic in origin, it is waived in instances of irretrievable loss. In our case failure to water the soil would allow the buildup of salt deposits which would render the soil infertile (*Rambam, Shemitah V'Yovel* 1:9,10; *Gem.* 4b).

וּמְתַקְּנִין אֶת־הַמְקֻלְקָלוֹת בַּמּוֹעֵד. — *and repair damaged ones during* [*Chol*] *HaMoed.*

If earth fell into the canal preventing the water from flowing freely, we may remove the earth and return the canal to its original dimensions. However, the Sages agree that new canals may not be dug on *Chol HaMoed (Rav).*

Dredging of a partially clogged canal is not deemed excessive exertion since the canal already exists. However, were it to become clogged to the extent that the flow is reduced substantially — so that less than one handbreadth (one-sixth of a cubit) is clear for water to flow through — one would not be permitted to remove the earth on *Chol HaMoed.* The clogged waterway would no longer be considered a preexisting canal and dredging it is tantamount to digging a new canal, which is forbidden (*Gem.* 4b).

The *halachah* in accordance with the Sages' view *(Rav).*

☙ Community Needs

וּמְתַקְּנִין אֶת־קִלְקוּלֵי הַמַּיִם שֶׁבִּרְשׁוּת הָרַבִּים, — *We may repair damaged cisterns in the public domain...*

Such cisterns were used to collect drinking water for the public *(Rav).*

Nimukei Yosef explains that public cisterns may be repaired on *Chol HaMoed* if they are cracked, and dirty water seeps in from nearby sewage pipes.

וְחוֹטְטִין אוֹתָן. — *and clear them out.*

I.e., we may clear them of any pebbles or splinters that may have fallen into them *(Rav; Nimukei Yosef).*

Others explain this section of the mishnah as referring to the sewage pipes, rather than irrigation canals and cisterns. It was customary to run one main sewage pipe through the streets of the city, to which pipes were connected from each house. Our mishnah teaches that even if an individual pipe became clogged, מְתַקְּנִין, *we may repair it,* on *Chol HaMoed.* If the waste adheres to the pipes so that a simple cleaning will not suffice, then חוֹטְטִין, *we may even scrape them out,* on *Chol HaMoed,* though this would require exertion *(Meiri).* [Such chores are considered *public* needs since the

3. R' Eliezer ben Yaakov says: We may divert water from one tree to another provided that [by so doing] we do not water the entire field. Seeds that were not watered before the festival may not be watered during [*Chol*] *HaMoed.*

The Sages, however, permit [watering] in both these cases.

YAD AVRAHAM

were not watered before the festival may not be watered during Chol HaMoed. Since that sentence obviously refers to an irrigated field, why should we interpret the first sentence as referring to a different type of field?

Tosefos Yom Tov therefore explains that the mishnah refers to orchards which are usually irrigated to improve their yield. Though they may not be watered during *Chol HaMoed* because they can subsist without watering, we *may* divert water that is gathered at the base of one tree to another.

Thus, there are three categories, according to *Tosefos Yom Tov:* (1) Fields that are usually irrigated may be watered during *Chol HaMoed,* since not doing so will cause the crops to fail, an irretrievable loss. (2) Orchards, which are irrigated to improve their yield, but can survive by rainfall, may not be watered, but water may be diverted from one tree to another. (3) Fields that subsist on rainfall may not be watered at all, even by diverting water from place to place by pushing it with one's foot.

זְרָעִים שֶׁלֹּא שָׁתוּ לִפְנֵי הַמּוֹעֵד, — *Seeds that were not watered before the festival...*

I.e., that were not *consistently* watered *(Rashi).*

לֹא יַשְׁקֵם בַּמּוֹעֵד. — *may not be watered during* [*Chol*] *HaMoed.*

Since they are growing even though they were not consistently watered before the festival, obviously they can survive for a few days without being watered. Thus, they may not be watered during the festival *(Rashi).*

Alternatively, if they are dying because they were not watered before the festival, watering them now will be of no avail *(Nimukei Yosef).*

Alternatively, since they had not been watered consistently before the festival, they would need a great amount of water during the festival. To provide it would require strenuous work and is therefore proscribed *(Rambam).*

If the field was moist before the festival and is now completely dry, it may be watered during *Chol HaMoed* because the situation is similar to that of seeds that were watered consistently before the festival and cannot survive without irrigation *(Rav).*

וַחֲכָמִים מַתִּירִין בָּזֶה וּבָזֶה. — *The Sages, however, permit* [*watering*] *in both these cases* [lit. *in this and in this*].

One may water seeds during *Chol HaMoed* regardless of whether they were watered before the festival or not. Moreover, the Rabbis permit even the irrigation of

א
ד

[ד] **צָדִין** אֶת־הָאִישׁוּת וְאֶת־הָעַכְבָּרִים מִשְּׂדֵה הָאִילָן וּמִשְּׂדֵה הַלָּבָן כְּדַרְכּוֹ, בַּמּוֹעֵד וּבַשְּׁבִיעִית. וַחֲכָמִים אוֹמְרִים: מִשְּׂדֵה הָאִילָן כְּדַרְכּוֹ, וּמִשְּׂדֵה הַלָּבָן שֶׁלֹּא כְדַרְכּוֹ. וּמְקָרִין אֶת־הַפִּרְצָה בַּמּוֹעֵד, וּבַשְּׁבִיעִית בּוֹנֶה כְדַרְכּוֹ.

יד אברהם

a field that can subsist on rainfall alone, because they do not proscribe work that is done to increase the field's yield. The *halachah*, however, follows the opinion of R' Eliezer ben Yaakov *(Rav)*.

4.

◆§ Usual vs. Unusual Manner

Although דָּבָר הָאָבֵד, work done to prevent *an irretrievable loss*, is permitted in many instances on *Chol HaMoed*, there are, nevertheless, certain classes of work which may not be done כְּדַרְכּוֹ, *in the usual manner*, but may be done only שֶׁלֹּא כְדַרְכּוֹ, *in an unusual manner*. Presumably, the requirement that the work be done with a שִׁנּוּי, *change*, from the normal manner, will serve as a constant reminder that the day is not a regular workday. This will make one cognizant of the prohibition against labor that is not required to prevent irretrievable loss.

צָדִין אֶת הָאִישׁוּת וְאֶת־הָעַכְבָּרִים... — *We may trap moles and mice...*

[Since these rodents destroy crops, they may be trapped then to prevent irretrievable loss.]

מִשְּׂדֵה הָאִילָן וּמִשְּׂדֵה הַלָּבָן... — *in* [lit. *from*] *an orchard or in a grain field...*

A treeless field used exclusively for raising crops is referred to as a שְׂדֵה הַלָּבָן, literally *a white field*, since it has no natural shade *(Aruch)*.

Alternatively, a grain field is referred to as שְׂדֵה הַלָּבָן since the grain turns white when it ripens *(Rash, Peah* 3:1).

כְּדַרְכּוֹ, בַּמּוֹעֵד וּבַשְּׁבִיעִית. — *in the usual manner during* [*Chol*] *HaMoed and during Shemitah.*

[There are two versions of the text of this mishnah. Our reading follows the mishnah as printed in most editions of the Talmud, *Rav* and *Tosefos Yom Tov*. In many editions of *Mishnah*, however, the word כְּדַרְכּוֹ, *in the usual manner*, is replaced with שֶׁלֹּא כְּדַרְכּוֹ, *in an unusual manner*. The question of which reading is the correct one is academic, since *halachah* follows the Sages cited later in the mishnah and not this Tanna.]

Since moles and mice ruin fields and cause substantial damage to the crops, trapping them is considered prevention of irretrievable loss and is permitted. This Tanna permits trapping in the usual manner which was by digging holes and placing nets inside them *(Rav)*.

By digging holes to set traps, one also prepares the land for planting, an activity forbidden during both *Chol HaMoed* and *Shemitah*. However, since the intent is to catch the

1
4

4. We may trap moles and mice in an orchard or in a grain field in the usual manner during [*Chol*] *HaMoed* and during *Shemitah*.

The Sages, however, say: In an orchard [we may trap] in the usual manner, but in a grain field [we may do so only] in an unusual manner.

We may block up a breach during [*Chol*] *HaMoed*, but during *Shemitah* we may build it up in the usual manner.

YAD AVRAHAM

rodents rather than to improve or prepare the land, one may dig the needed holes (*Rashi*).

Alternatively, since the form of digging is essentially different from that used in working the field, we do not fear that the digger will appear to be plowing (*Nimukei Yosef*).

וַחֲכָמִים אוֹמְרִים: מִשְּׂדֵה הָאִילָן כְּדַרְכּוֹ, — *The Sages, however, say: In an orchard* [*we may trap*] *in the usual manner,*

Since the rodents wreak extensive damage in an orchard, the Sages permitted farmers to dig a hole and hang a net in it (*Rav*).

וּמִשְּׂדֵה הַלָּבָן שֶׁלֹּא כְדַרְכּוֹ. — *but in a grain field* [*we may do so only*] *in an unusual manner.*

Since damage the rodents might cause to a grain field is not great, we may not set traps in the usual manner. It is permitted, however, to hammer a stake with an attached net into the ground. By moving the stake around the rodents are forced to emerge from their lairs and are trapped in the net (*Rashi* ms.; *Rashi* on *Rif; Meiri*).

Rashi (7a) comments that one uses the stake to flatten the rodent holes, thus forcing the occupants to come into the open where they can be caught and destroyed.

The stringent ruling applies to a grain field. However, if the grain field is situated near an orchard, trapping in the usual manner is permitted since the presence of the rodents constitutes a danger to the near-by orchard where they could cause extensive damage (*Rav; Gem.* 7a).

The *halachah* is in accordance with the opinion of the Sages (*Rav*). [See *Orach Chayim* 537:13.]

וּמְקָרִין אֶת־הַפִּרְצָה בַּמּוֹעֵד, — *We may block up a breach during* [*Chol*] *HaMoed,*

If a wall surrounding a garden fell down, the breach may be repaired by being blocked up with stones. They may not, however, be cemented into position as that would constitute work done in a professional manner which is prohibited [see mishnah 8]. However, if the wall of a dwelling place caves in, it may be repaired professionally to prevent thieves from entering (*Rav; Gem.* 7a).

Similarly, if the wall of a home is shaky, one may repair it professionally as failure to do so constitutes a danger to life (*Tif. Yis.*).

וּבַשְּׁבִיעִית בּוֹנֶה כְדַרְכּוֹ. — *but during Shemitah, we may build it up in the usual manner.*

Even though it may appear that

א
ה

[ה] רַבִּי מֵאִיר אוֹמֵר: רוֹאִין אֶת־הַנְּגָעִים בַּתְּחִלָּה לְהָקֵל, אֲבָל לֹא לְהַחֲמִיר. וַחֲכָמִים אוֹמְרִים: לֹא לְהָקֵל וְלֹא לְהַחֲמִיר.
וְעוֹד אָמַר רַבִּי מֵאִיר: מְלַקֵּט אָדָם עַצְמוֹת אָבִיו וְאִמּוֹ, מִפְּנֵי שֶׁשִּׂמְחָה הִיא לוֹ.

יד אברהם

he is doing so in order to guard his fruit from outsiders, an act forbidden during *Shemitah* [see pref. mishnah 1], he may, nevertheless, build the walls. [However, if his intention is in fact to prevent others from taking the fruit, it is prohibited] (*Gem.* 7a).

5.

Sadness and Mourning on Chol HaMoed

Certain acts are forbidden on *Chol HaMoed* because they lead to sadness, and are contrary to the spirit of joy which should dominate the festive season. Two examples are inspection of *tzaraas* and acts which induce mourning for the dead.

Tzaraas

Tzaraas is a disease characterized by skin lesions called נְגָעִים, *negaim* [singular, נֶגַע, *nega*]. One contracting this disease is called a מְצֹרָע, *metzora* (see tractate *Megillah* 1:7).Only *kohanim* are authorized to confirm or deny the lesion as true *tzaraas*. Upon being confirmed the *metzora* is isolated from the community. Since this confirmation and subsequent isolation is a source of grief to the *metzora*, examination of *negaim* will often prove contrary to the joyous spirit of the festive season.

In some instances the *nega* is immediately recognizable to the *kohen* as *tzaraas*, in others only some symptoms of the disease are manifest. In such cases the afflicted person is isolated for a seven-day period during which the affliction increases or decreases in intensity, or remains stable. Based upon an examination of these changes, the *kohen* declares the person to be either contaminated by *tzaraas* or free of it.

רַבִּי מֵאִיר אוֹמֵר: רוֹאִין אֶת־הַנְּגָעִים בַּתְּחִלָּה לְהָקֵל, — *R' Meir says: We may examine negaim for the first time in order to render a lenient verdict,*

A *kohen* may inspect a נֶגַע, *skin lesion*, to determine that the stricken individual is not contaminated with *tzaraas*. If the examination results in a decision that the lesion is not *tzaraas*, then the victim will have been given cause for great joy *(Rav).*

[The word בַּתְּחִלָּה, *for the first time*, indicates that the mishnah refers to the very first examination following the appearance of the earliest symptoms of *tzaraas*.]

אֲבָל לֹא לְהַחֲמִיר. — *but not to render a stringent one.*

If the *kohen* discerns that the *nega* warrants confinement, either for a second evaluation or because he confirms that the *nega* is *tzaraas*, he should remain silent so as not to necessitate banishment of the stricken person from the community during the festival *(Rav).*

R' Meir is of the opinion that the *kohen* has the right to refrain from

1
5

5. R' Meir says: We may examine *negaim* for the first time to render a lenient verdict, but not to render a stringent one.

The Sages say: [We may] not [examine a *nega* whether] for a lenient or for a stringent verdict.

R' Meir also said: A person may gather his father's and mother's bones [for burial], as it is a [source of] joy for him.

rendering an immediate determination even though he has examined the *nega* and knows it to be contaminated. Since only the *kohen* has the power to render a judgment, the effect of his silence is that the victim will remain clean throughout the festival (*Tos. Yom Tov; Gem.* 7b).

וַחֲכָמִים אוֹמְרִים: לֹא לְהָקֵל וְלֹא לְהַחֲמִיר. — *The Sages say: We may not* [*examine a nega whether*] *for a lenient or for a stringent verdict.*

The Sages hold that a *kohen* must render a decision upon viewing a *nega*. Therefore, since the *kohen* must examine the *nega* to render a lenient decision, he would also have to render a stringent one if the lesion is indeed *tzaraas*, as he has no right to keep silent. Thus, it is preferable completely to refrain from any examination, for as long as the *kohen* does not examine the stricken person, that person is not considered contaminated and is not isolated (*Tos. Yom Tov; Gem.* 7b).

Our text follows the reading of the mishnah as it appears in *Yerushalmi* and as cited by *Tosefos Yom Tov* and *Tiferes Yisrael*. *Talmud Bavli, Rashi* and *Rav* omit the word בַּתְּחִילָּה, *for the first time*. According to their reading the examination referred to in the mishnah is that which takes place after a week of confinement. In this view, the Sages agree with R' Meir that the *kohen* is under *no* obligation to render a decision before any confinement has taken place. Thus, in the event early symptoms have appeared, all would agree that the *kohen* need not examine the *nega* during a festival nor need he render a decision even if he had seen it. The dispute recorded in our mishnah relates only to the second examination after an initial week of confinement.

R' Meir holds the *kohen* may remain silent, therefore, the examination should be made. If he finds the individual to be free of *tzaraas*, he will tell him so, thereby causing him great joy. If, however, the *kohen* finds him contaminated, he should remain silent until after the festival.

The Sages, however, hold that the *kohen* does not have the option to remain silent. Therefore, the examination should not be made, for the chance of joy that would be caused by pronouncing him clean is outweighed by the grief which would result should the victim be pronounced a *metzora*.]

The *halachah* does not follow R' Meir's view (*Rav*).

◆§ Acts Inducing Mourning

וְעוֹד אָמַר רַבִּי מֵאִיר: — *R' Meir also said:*

I.e., R' Meir permitted the following as well (*Tos. Yom Tov; Tif. Yis.*).

רַבִּי יוֹסֵי אוֹמֵר: אֵבֶל הוּא לוֹ. ג:
לֹא יְעוֹרֵר אָדָם עַל־מֵתוֹ וְלֹא יַסְפִּידֶנּוּ קֹדֶם ו
לָרֶגֶל שְׁלֹשִׁים יוֹם.

[ו] **אֵין** חוֹפְרִין כּוּכִין וּקְבָרוֹת בַּמּוֹעֵד, אֲבָל מְחַנְּכִים אֶת־הַכּוּכִין בַּמּוֹעֵד. וְעוֹשִׂין

יד אברהם

לֹא יְעוֹרֵר אָדָם עַל־מֵתוֹ... — *A person may not inspire [lamentations] for his dead [relative],*

In order to prevent relatives from forgetting their kinsman who had died some time ago, it was customary to engage professional lamenters to summon the relatives of a deceased. The lamenters would announce 'Weep with me, all embittered souls'. The relatives would thus be aroused to eulogize the deceased *(Rav)*.

וְלֹא יַסְפִּידֶנּוּ... — *nor eulogize him...*

I.e., nor hire someone to eulogize his newly deceased relative *(Rav)*.

קֹדֶם לָרֶגֶל שְׁלֹשִׁים יוֹם. — *during the thirty days preceding a festival.*

One should neither inspire lamentations for, nor eulogize his dead relatives during the thirty days prior to a festival. The *Talmud* (8b) cites two reasons:

Thirty days prior to a festival, the rabbis begin teaching the relevant laws. Prompted by that event people begin saving money to cover the festival expenses. Were people permitted to hire eulogists during this month, we fear that they might expend their festival funds to hire a eulogist.

Secondly, the saddening effects of the eulogy last for thirty days. Therefore, so as not to lessen the joy of the festival, eulogies should not be given during this period *(Rav)*.

The halachic difference between the two reasons is that according to

מְלַקֵּט אָדָם עַצְמוֹת אָבִיו וְאִמּוֹ, — *A person may gather his father's and mother's bones [for burial],*

In Mishnaic times, the custom was to bury the dead in a deep moist grave so that the flesh would decay rapidly. Afterwards, the bones were gathered and reburied in a cedar coffin in a proper burial place *(Yerushalmi)*. R' Meir permitted this reinterment during *Chol HaMoed* *(Tif. Yis.)*.

מִפְּנֵי שֶׁשִּׂמְחָה הִיא לוֹ. — *as it is a [source of] joy for him.*

He is happy to see the bones of his loved ones reburied properly *(Rav)*.

Alternatively, though one is required to mourn on the day of the reburial, the sadness is tempered by the joy of the festival *(Rashi)*.

Others maintain that the requirement of rejoicing on the festival takes precedence over the requirement of mourning upon reburying one's parents *(Nimukei Yosef)*.

רַבִּי יוֹסֵי אוֹמֵר: אֵבֶל הוּא לוֹ. — *R' Yose says: It is [a source of] mourning for him.*

Though the joy of the festival supersedes the requirement to mourn, nevertheless, he will be saddened at the reburial. Therefore, the reburial should be delayed until after the festival *(Nimukei Yosef; see Sfas Emes)*.

The *halachah* does not follow R' Meir's view in this case either *(Rav)*.

R' Yose says: It is [a source of] mourning for him.

A person may not inspire [lamentations] for his dead [relative], nor eulogize him during the thirty days preceding a festival.

6. We may not hew burial niches nor [build] tombs during [*Chol*] *HaMoed;* but we may adapt burial niches during [*Chol*] *HaMoed;* dig wash

YAD AVRAHAM

the latter reason, a eulogist may not be engaged on *Chol HaMoed* even if he performs without remuneration (*Gem.* 8b).

The prohibition against eulogizing is even for a person who had just died *(Rav).*

According to others, the mishnah refers only to eulogies for those who died more than thirty days before the festival. However, if a person died within thirty days of the festival, he may be eulogized. Since the relatives are already grieving during the thirty-day mourning period, the eulogy will not add to their grief *(Orach Chaim* 547:3; *Magen Avraham* 547:1).

6.

[Having mentioned the prohibition against acts of mourning during the festival season, the Tanna now discusses work relating to burials and graves.]

אֵין חוֹפְרִין כּוּכִין... — *We may not hew burial niches...*

I.e., we may not hew niches in underground burial caves *(Rav).*

וּקְבָרוֹת בַּמּוֹעֵד, — *nor* [*build*] *tombs during* [*Chol*] *HaMoed,*

The mishnah refers to hewing or building caves for future use *(Rav).* For immediate need, how r, we are surely permitted to do .o as it falls within the criteria of צָרְכֵי רַבִּים, *public need (Tos. Yom Tov),* and צֹרֶךְ הַמּוֹעֵד, *requirement of the festival (Tif. Yis.)* [see pref. to this tractate]. Moreover, since we are permitted to dig graves for the newly deceased on יוֹם טוֹב שֵׁנִי שֶׁל גָּלֻיּוֹת, *the additional day of festival celebrated in the Diaspora (Beitzah* 6a); we are surely permitted to do so during *Chol HaMoed.*

Meiri, on the other hand, maintains that the mishnah refers to new niches and tombs even for immediate use. The *Gemara* permits digging graves of the type commonly used today, on the additional day of the festival. Hewing niches and building tombs, however, is forbidden even on *Chol HaMoed* as it requires excessive exertion. Thus, according to *Meiri,* during *Chol HaMoed* we may expand existing niches, whereas according to *Rav,* we may prepare new ones for immediate use.

[Obviously, even according to the Meiri, if there is no possibility of expanding existing graves, we may prepare a new one for immediate use, as burial may not be delayed.]

אֲבָל מְחַנְּכִין אֶת־הַכּוּכִין בַּמּוֹעֵד. — *but we may adapt burial niches during* [*Chol*] *HaMoed;*

I.e., we may lengthen them or shorten them to make them suitable for use *(Rav).*

א
ו

נִבְרֶכֶת בַּמּוֹעֵד, וְאָרוֹן עִם־הַמֵּת בֶּחָצֵר. רַבִּי יְהוּדָה אוֹסֵר, אֶלָּא אִם־כֵּן יֵשׁ עִמּוֹ נְסָרִים.

יד אברהם

Even though they are not needed for immediate use [according to *Rav*, see above], one is permitted to adapt them as it falls into the category of public need. Just as we are permitted to repair damaged cisterns (see mishnah 2) though they may not necessarily be needed during *Chol HaMoed*, so too are we permitted to adapt burial niches though they are not needed for immediate use *(Tos. Yom Tov)*.

[According to *Meiri*, however, the two cases are not comparable, since the reason for permitting cisterns to be repaired is because all members of the community are free on *Chol HaMoed* to join in the repairs. Were they not to make the repairs on *Chol HaMoed*, the repairs would never be made and the cistern would eventually collapse. However, in the case of burial niches, this is not so; for just as they can be adapted now for future use, they can be adapted at a future time when they are needed.]

Alternatively, adapting existing ones is not deemed strenuous work and is thus not proscribed *(Tif. Yis.)*.

וְעוֹשִׂין נִבְרֶכֶת בַּמּוֹעֵד, — *(and we may) dig* [lit. *make*] *wash ponds during* [*Chol*] *HaMoed;*

I.e., a pond in which to wash laundry *(Rashi; Rambam; Rav)*.

Though laundering is normally prohibited during *Chol HaMoed*, in certain instances it is permitted (see 3:2). The Tanna here permits digging ponds for those exceptional cases (*Tos.* 8b). This fits into the category of work permitted for the needs of the festival *(Tos. Yom Tov)*.

Alternatively, the ponds referred to are those used for washing the dead and their shrouds *(Tos.* 8b; *Meiri)*, or for the participants in the funeral to wash their hands *(Meiri)*.

Alternatively, the term נִבְרֶכֶת refers to *a temporary grave*, [see *comm.* mishnah 5 s.v. מְלַקֵּט]. If there were no previously dug crypts in the walls of a cave, the deceased would be interred in a temporary grave until after the festival *(Rabad* cited by *Rosh)*.

Still others explain נִבְרֶכֶת as an *adaptation of a tomb.* Just as a sepulchral chamber was permitted to be adapted during *Chol HaMoed* to fit the body of someone who died then, so was a tomb permitted to be adapted. If it is not deep enough, the bottom may be dug out, and stones may be placed around the recess.

Ramban notes that the context of the mishnah favors the last four interpretations which, like the rest of the mishnah, deal with matters pertaining to burial.

וְאָרוֹן עִם־הַמֵּת בֶּחָצֵר. — *and (we may)* [*construct*] *a coffin in the courtyard with the deceased.*

If the work is done in the same courtyard in which the deceased is lying, then it is permitted. Elsewhere, the noise of the sawing and banging would lead people to believe that a non-essential construction project was being worked on *Chol HaMoed*. However, if the deceased was well known or in a small community where the demise of any person is known to all, this

1
6

ponds during [*Chol*] *HaMoed;* and [construct] a coffin in the courtyard with the deceased.

R' Yehudah prohibits [the latter], unless the boards are at hand.

YAD AVRAHAM

provision does not apply, as people will be aware of the reason for the work *(Rav; Rashi; Tif. Yis.).*

.רַבִּי יְהוּדָה אוֹסֵר — *R' Yehudah prohibits* [*the latter*],

I.e., preparing wood for a coffin *(Rav).*

.אֶלָּא אִם־כֵּן יֵשׁ עִמּוֹ נְסָרִים — *unless the boards are at hand* [lit., *unless there are boards with him.*]

Since the work is strenuous and ready made boards are usually available, R' Yehudah ruled that sawing new boards is prohibited *(Tif. Yis.).* The *halachah* is not in accordance with R' Yehudah's view *(Rav).*

7.

◆§ Intermingling Joy with Joy

Mishnah 5 enumerated activities that are forbidden during *Chol HaMoed* because they cause grief. This mishnah discusses marriages which are forbidden during *Chol HaMoed* because they cause joy. The *Gemara* offers four explanations for the prohibition.

(1) R' Elazar bases it on the principle of אֵין מְעָרְבִין שִׂמְחָה בְשִׂמְחָה, *we may not intermingle one joyous occasion with another.* When one celebrates a joyous event, his heart should be completely permeated by the joy of the occasion, not diluted by any other joy. This is derived from the precedent set by King Solomon in his dedication of the First Temple, which commenced seven days before Succos, so as not to coincide with, and thereby conflict with, Succos *(Gem.* 8b-9a).

Yerushalmi derives this principle from the incident of the Patriarch Jacob, who was charged by Laban, מַלֵּא שְׁבֻעַ זֹאת, *complete the week of this one (Gen.* 29:27), i.e., complete the seven days of feasting following your marriage to Leah, and then you may marry Rachel. Thus, Jacob could not marry Rachel while he was still involved in the celebration of his marriage to Leah. To have entered into another marriage would have interfered with the separate joy of each event (*Tos.* 8b).

(2) Rabbah bar R' Huna bases the prohibition against marriage on *Chol HaMoed* on the verse וְשָׂמַחְתָּ בְּחַגֶּךָ, *and you shall rejoice with your festival (Deut.* 16:14), which can be interpreted: You shall rejoice with your festival, not with your wife. When one has a newly acquired wife, he is apt to become engrossed in that joy, and will neglect the joy of the festival (*Gem.* 8b).

(3) Ullah bases the prohibition on the excessive exertion expended in preparing the marriage feast. Because of the joy generated by the marriage the participants will overexert themselves, ignoring the sanctity of the day *(Gem.* 8b; *Tos.).*

(4) R' Yitzchak Nafcha understands that if marriages were permitted during *Chol HaMoed*, the precept פְּרוּ וּרְבוּ, *be fruitful and multiply (Gen.* 9:1) would be postponed for insufficient reason. Because it is a joyous occasion, one might postpone his wedding until *Chol HaMoed* when his joy would be enhanced by both the festive atmosphere and the free time. This would lead to a delay in fulfillment of the precept of bearing children.

א
ז

[ז] אֵין נוֹשְׂאִין נָשִׁים בַּמּוֹעֵד, לֹא בְתוּלוֹת וְלֹא אַלְמָנוֹת. וְלֹא מְיַבְּמִין, מִפְּנֵי שֶׁשִּׂמְחָה הִיא לוֹ, אֲבָל מַחֲזִיר הוּא אֶת־גְּרוּשָׁתוֹ.

וְעוֹשָׂה אִשָּׁה תַּכְשִׁיטֶיהָ בַּמּוֹעֵד. רַבִּי יְהוּדָה אוֹמֵר: לֹא תָסוּד, מִפְּנֵי שֶׁנִּוּוּל הוּא לָהּ.

יד אברהם

אֵין נוֹשְׂאִין נָשִׁים בַּמּוֹעֵד, לֹא בְתוּלוֹת וְלֹא אַלְמָנוֹת. — *We may not take wives during the* [*Chol*] *HaMoed, neither virgins nor widows,*

One is not permitted to marry during *Chol HaMoed*, regardless of the woman's previous marital status. Even the marriage of a widow, for which the celebration of שִׁבְעַת יְמֵי הַמִּשְׁתֶּה, *seven days of feasting*, is not required, is considered a joyous occasion, and is forbidden on *Chol HaMoed (Tif. Yis.)*. [See pref.]

וְלֹא מְיַבְּמִין, — *nor may levirate marriage may be entered into,*

If a man dies without offspring, his brother is required to marry the widow (see *Deut.* 25:5-10). This is known as יִבּוּם, *levirate marriage.*

Although it results from his brother's death — a tragic occurrence — the levirate marriage is nevertheless deemed a joyous occasion, and is forbidden on *Chol HaMoed (Tif. Yis.).*

מִפְּנֵי שֶׁשִּׂמְחָה הִיא לוֹ, — *because it is a* [*source of*] *joy for the one who does* [lit. *for him*].

[See pref.]

אֲבָל מַחֲזִיר הוּא אֶת־גְּרוּשָׁתוֹ. — *However, one may remarry his divorcee.*

Since she is familiar to him, the joy is not as intense as that of taking a new bride. Therefore, we need not fear that the joy of the marriage will intermingle with and detract from that of the festival *(Rav).*

Nor do we fear excessive exertion on preparing the marriage feast in this case. Likewise, the precept of *be fruitful and multiply* usually does not apply to a remarriage for in most cases there will have been offspring from the previous period of marriage *(Tos.* 8b),

וְעוֹשָׂה אִשָּׁה תַּכְשִׁיטֶיהָ בַּמּוֹעֵד. — *A woman may make her adornments during* [*Chol*] *HaMoed.*

This refers to matters of personal hygiene and grooming such as the application of cosmetics and the shaving of body hair *(Rav).*

Such acts may be done in the usual manner on *Chol HaMoed* because, as part of the physical needs of the body, they are comparable to food preparation. Haircutting and laundering should fall into this category, too, but are forbidden lest one schedule them for *Chol HaMoed*, thereby detracting from the honor of the festival [see 3:1]. This fear is absent regarding application of cosmetics and removal by women of body hair for they are done daily *(Ritva).*

רַבִּי יְהוּדָה אוֹמֵר: לֹא תָסוּד, — *R' Yehudah says: She may not apply lime,*

She may not apply to her skin a paste made of dissolved lime, as a depilatory *(Tif. Yis.).*

1
7

7. We may not take wives during [Chol] HaMoed, neither virgins nor widows, nor may levirate marriage be entered into, because it is a [source of] joy for the one who does. However, one may remarry his divorcee.

A woman may make her adornments during [Chol] HaMoed.

R' Yehuda says: She may not apply lime, because it is a disfigurement to her.

YAD AVRAHAM

מִפְּנֵי שֶׁנִּוּוּל הוּא לָהּ. — *because it is a disfigurement to her.*

Since she must leave the paste on her skin until after the festival for it to be effective, it would disfigure her until the end of the festival and cause her unhappiness *(Rashi; Tos. Yom Tov).*

The *Gemara* (9b) explains that lime may be applied provided she can remove it before the conclusion of *Chol HaMoed.* Since she will be pleased on the festival by her improved appearance, she may apply the paste although she suffers distress at the beginning of the treatment (see *Rashi).*

Rav follows *Rambam's Commentary to Mishnah* in deciding the *halachah* against R' Yehudah's view. *Tosefos Yom Tov,* however, notes that in *Mishneh Torah, Rambam* retracted that decision.

Shulchan Aruch (546:5) also decides the *halachah* in accordance with R' Yehudah.

Although the *halachah* usually follows the majority, it is possible that the first Tanna concurs with R' Yehudah in this matter. The *Baraisa* cited in the *Gemara* (9b) omits the application of lime from the list of cosmetic applications permitted on *Chol HaMoed;* thus we may infer that the application of lime is forbidden *(Maggid Mishnah, Yom Tov* 7:20).

8.

◈ Work Done in a Nonprofessional Manner

As mentioned in the preface to this tractate, one of the forms of work permitted on *Chol HaMoed* [provided it is needed for the festival (*Tos.* 10a)] is מַעֲשֵׂה הֶדְיוֹט, *work done in a nonprofessional manner.* The mishnah will now cite some examples, and delineate some restrictions concerning this form of work.

The first subject of the mishnah is sewing. The general rule is that sewing not needed for the festival is forbidden. If garments are needed for the festival, they may be sewn on *Chol HaMoed* provided the work is done with a noticeable שִׁנּוּי, *modification* of the conventional manner. This restriction applies to a tailor whose work is professional in quality. The work of an amateur is not considered creative work and is not forbidden *(Meiri).*

א
ח־ט

[ח] **הַהֶדְיוֹט** תּוֹפֵר כְּדַרְכּוֹ, וְהָאֻמָּן מַכְלִיב. וּמְסָרְגִין אֶת־הַמִּטּוֹת. רַבִּי יוֹסֵי אוֹמֵר: אַף מְמַתְּחִין.

[ט] **מַעֲמִידִין** תַּנּוּר וְכִירַיִם וְרֵחַיִם בַּמּוֹעֵד.

הַהֶדְיוֹט... — *An unskilled* [lit. *common*] *person...*

The *Gemara* (10a) gives two illustrations of an unskilled person:

— one who cannot draw a needleful of stitches in one sweep;

— one who cannot make an even seam on the hem of his tunic.

According to some, the second opinion cited above refers to linen, the material from which tunics were commonly made. The former opinion refers to wool, which is soft and is usually sewn by drawing a needleful of stitches in one sweep. An unskilled person, who cannot sew straight in this manner, would pull the needle through after every stitch *(Talmido shel R' Yechiel of Paris).*

תּוֹפֵר... — *may sew...*

An unskilled person may sew during *Chol HaMoed* only such garments as are needed during the festival (*Tif. Yis.; Rambam, Yom Tov* 7:5, *Shulchan Aruch* 541:5).

כְּדַרְכּוֹ, — *in his usual manner,*

[He may sew in the manner he sews throughout the year. He need not make an effort to sew with rough, uneven stitches, since his usual manner is nonprofessional.]

וְהָאֻמָּן... — *but an artisan...*

A skilled tailor is one who can sew an even seam on the hem of his tunic, or can draw a needleful of stitches in one sweep (*Rosh* 16; *Tur* 541; *Magen Avraham* 541:8).

מַכְלִיב. — *may sew only with irregular stitches* [lit. *make doglike*].

I.e., he must make one stitch longer and the next one shorter, so that they resemble dog's teeth (*Rav; Gem.* 10a).

Alternatively, he may only use basting stitches (*Gem.* 10a).

The required deviation must be one that is noticeable in the finished product. [To hold the needle or garment in an unconventional manner could constitute a halachically recognized deviation in terms of Sabbath labor, where the manner of *performance* is crucial, but has no bearing regarding sewing a garment on *Chol HaMoed*] *(Rama* 541:5; *Terumos HaDeshen).*

וּמְסָרְגִין אֶת־הַמִּטּוֹת. — *We may interlace* [*supports for*] *beds.*

Beds in Mishnaic times were supported by interlaced cords instead of springs. The art of interlacing is similar to weaving except that there is space between the cords, whereas in weaving, the cords are woven tightly (*Rama* 541:2).

It is permitted only to reinsert old cords which have become disarranged or removed, but not to replace them with new cords *(Tur* 541:2).

According to others, however, if cords became worn or disarranged, even new interlacing may be inserted though it appears as though a new bed is being made *(Rashi* 10a; *Rambam* [see *Maggid Mishnah*], *Yom Tov* 8:13; *Rabbeinu Yerucham* 4:5).

8. An unskilled person may sew in his usual manner, but an artisan may sew only with irregular stitches.

We may interlace [supports for] beds.

R' Yose says: We may even tighten them.

9. We may set up an oven, a stove, or millstones during [Chol] HaMoed.

YAD AVRAHAM

Since it is nonprofessional work, it may be done if needed for the festival week *(Rabbeinu Yerucham* 4:5; *Tur* 541).

Alternatively, it is permissible even if not needed immediately, because unless the bed is promptly repaired it will deteriorate further, resulting in דָּבָר הָאָבֵד, *irretrievable loss.* Since the cords are torn, were one to lie on the bed the excessive pressure on the remaining cords would cause them to break, and the entire bed would have to be interlaced again *(Rosh).*

רַבִּי יוֹסֵי אוֹמֵר: אַף מְמַתְּחִין. — *R' Yose says: We may even tighten them.*

If its cords become loose, they may be tightened. This is permitted even though the bed could be used simply by placing utensils under it to support the sagging places. R' Yose's use of the word אַף, *even,* indicates that he permits more than the first Tanna. He surely agrees, then, that if the cords became disarranged or completely removed, they may be interlaced *(Tif. Yis.).*

This interpretation holds true only according to the reading found in most editions of the *Mishnah, Rif,* and *Yerushalmi* which have the word אַף, *even,* in R' Yose's statement.

The *Gemara* (10a), however, omits this word from R' Yose's statement Accordingly, R' Yose permits only tightening but not interlacing, since interlacing demands more work. However, the first Tanna who permits interlacing, surely permits tightening which is less work (see *Tos. Yom Tov).*

[Thus, the two versions differ concerning the point of conflict between R' Yose and the first Tanna. According to the first version in which R' Yose uses the word אַף, *even,* he is more permissive than the first Tanna. The reason for the first Tanna's prohibition to tighten is that since propping up the bed is adequate temporarily, there is no reason to permit more strenuous labor. According to the second version which omits אַף, *even,* R' Yose is more restrictive in that he forbids interlacing on the ground that it is strenuous.]

The *halachah* is in accordance with the first Tanna, thus both interlacing and tightening are permissible during *Chol HaMoed (Rav).*

9.

מַעֲמִידִין תַּנּוּר וְכִירַיִם וְרֵחַיִם בַּמּוֹעֵד. — *We may set up an oven, a stove, or millstones during [Chol] HaMoed.*

We may build and set in place any of the above provided they are needed for the festival. Since the

א
י

רַבִּי יְהוּדָה אוֹמֵר: אֵין מְכַבְּשִׁין אֶת־הָרֵחַיִם בַּתְּחִלָּה.

[י] **עוֹשִׂין** מַעֲקֶה לְגַג וּלְמַרְפֶּסֶת מַעֲשֵׂה הֶדְיוֹט, אֲבָל לֹא מַעֲשֵׂה אֻמָּן. שָׁפִין אֶת־הַסְּדָקִין וּמַעֲגִילִין אוֹתָן בְּמַעֲגִילָה

יד אברהם

ovens and stoves used in Mishnaic times were movable, the mishnah uses the term מַעֲמִידִין, *set up, erect* *(Rav).*

Both ovens and stoves were made of clay, which was molded to shape and dried. Only after it dried and hardened could it be used. A תַּנּוּר, *oven,* was wide at the base and narrow on top and had room for one pot on top. A כִּירַיִם, *stove,* had a base and top of equal dimension and could hold more than one pot (*Rav, Shabbos* 3:1,2).

Others maintain that one may set up an existing stove or oven but may not build a new one *(Tos.* 10a).

Alternatively, the mishnah teaches that one is permitted to reinsulate an existing stove by applying *wet* plaster to its walls, whether or not the plaster will dry before the end of the festival; for even if the plaster does not dry, the stove is usable *(Mishnah Berurah* 540:20). A new stove, however, may be built only if the clay will dry during the festival, for then the building of it would serve a useful festival purpose *(Rambam, Yom Tov* 8:13).

According to all opinions, the stove and oven must be both usable and necessary during the festival. Though their construction requires both professional and strenuous labor, ovens and stoves may be built in the normal manner, since they are needed for the preparation of food for the festival *(Maggid Mishnah; Yom Tov* 8:7; *Ramban).*

The רֵחַיִם, *millstones,* may also be constructed and set up, for they, too, will be used in the preparation of food for the festival *(Tif. Yis.; Tos.* 10a).

ר׳ יְהוּדָה אוֹמֵר: אֵין מְכַבְּשִׁין אֶת הָרֵחַיִם בַּתְּחִלָּה. — *R' Yehudah says: We may not roughen the millstones initially.*

Smooth new millstones must be roughened so that the grain will be ground more finely. Roughening the grooves of a new millstone requires skilled labor. However, reroughening the surface of an old millstone is not considered skilled work *(Meiri).*

The *halachah,* however, is not in accordance with R' Yehudah *(Rav),* [for even professional labor is permitted if it is required for preparation of food for the festival].

10.

עוֹשִׂין מַעֲקֶה לְגַג וּלְמַרְפֶּסֶת... — *We may build a railing for a roof or for a balcony...*

The Torah requires that one build a safety railing around a roof, balcony, or any other high place from which people might fall (see *Deut.* 22:8). Thus, one is permitted to construct the railing during *Chol HaMoed* because of the danger in-

1 R' Yehudah says: We may not roughen the mill-
10 stone initially.

10. We may build a railing for a roof or for a balcony in an unskilled manner, but not in a professional manner. We may replaster the cracks and smooth them [as if] with a roller, with the hand

YAD AVRAHAM

volved in leaving it unprotected *(Tif. Yis.)*.

A מַרְפֶּסֶת, *balcony,* as used in the mishnah, is a walk or platform upon which the tenants of the upper story walk and descend to the yard below by means of a ladder *(Rav)*.

מַעֲשֵׂה הֶדְיוֹט, — *in an unskilled manner* [lit. *the work of an amateur*],

One may construct the parapet in a temporary fashion. Two such temporary means of construction are described by the *Gemara.* The first is by the use of הוּצָא וְדַפְנָא, variously rendered as *reeds and rushes (Rambam, Yom Tov* 8:6); *palm and chestnut branches (Rashi, Bava Basra* 4a); or *blossoms of vines and branches of trees (Rav, Bava Basra* 1:1).

It may also be constructed by piling stones one upon the other, without cementing them with mortar *(Gem.* 10a).

Whether there is a dispute as to which method may be used, or whether both are acceptable is not made clear by the *Gemara.* However, *Rif* and *Rosh* cite both methods without a decision; *Rambam* cites the first method, adding the words *and all similar means;* and *Tur* and *Shulchan Aruch* quote both. It is obvious therefore, that all these authorities understood the *Gemara* to mean that there is no dispute, and that either method is acceptable.

Others distinguish between wooden structures and stone structures. For wooden structures, we may build a parapet of branches, and for stone structures we may build a parapet of stones without mortar *(Talmido shel R' Yechiel of Paris)*.

אֲבָל לֹא מַעֲשֵׂה אֻמָּן. — *but not in a professional manner* [lit. *but not the work of a craftsman*].

[I.e., not in the usual fashion. Since the prevention of accidents until after the festival does not necessitate skilled work, one may not build the railing in the usual fashion.]

Some authorities maintain that the mishnah is referring to a roof or balcony used only for storage or one with no public access; hence, a railing is not halachically required. It is built as an extra precaution, or for privacy. Had the mishnah been referring to a regular roof, there would be no reason to build the railing in an unprofessional manner, since protecting people from danger is no less important than preparing food for which the previous mishnah permits the exercise of professional skills *(Rabad; Tos. HaRosh; Meiri; Ritva)*.

שָׁפִין אֶת־הַסְּדָקִין... — *We may replaster the cracks...*

We may plaster cracks in a roof on *Chol HaMoed,* lest the rain seep in and cause damage *(Tife. Yis.)*.

In Mishnaic times, the roofs were flat and were daubed with clay to keep out the rain *(Rav)*.

א בְּיָד וּבְרֶגֶל, אֲבָל לֹא בְמַחְלְצַיִם.

י הַצִּיר וְהַצִּנּוֹר וְהַקּוֹרָה וְהַמַּנְעוּל וְהַמַּפְתֵּחַ שֶׁנִּשְׁבְּרוּ, מְתַקְּנָן בַּמּוֹעֵד, וּבִלְבַד שֶׁלֹּא יְכַוֵּן מְלַאכְתּוֹ בַּמּוֹעֵד.

וְכָל־כְּבָשִׁין שֶׁהוּא יָכוֹל לֶאֱכֹל מֵהֶן בַּמּוֹעֵד, כּוֹבְשָׁן.

יד אברהם

וּמַעֲגִילִין אוֹתָן בְּמַעֲגִילָה בְּיָד וּבְרֶגֶל, — *and roll them [as if] with a roller, with the hand and the foot,*

Rav translates literally, *and roll them with a roller. A roller* is the tool used by roofers to smoothen the clay with which the roof is repaired. The repair may be completed in the normal professional manner.

The *Gemara* notes this apparent incongruity of this statement: if even a roller is permitted, surely hand labor is allowed! Therefore the *Gemara* interpolates the words *as if:* Thus, one may smooth the clay or plaster by hand or foot although the results are as good as with a roller, which is the proper tool for this work *(Tos. Yom Tov).*

אֲבָל לֹא בְמַחְלְצַיִם. — *but not with a trowel.*

When plastering roofs, a roller was used for flattening out the plaster or clay. A trowel was used after the roller to finish whatever was left undone by the roller *(Nimukei Yosef).*

[Hence, according to the *Gemara,* the mishnah teaches us that we may use the hand and foot even if they do as satisfactory a job as a roller. However, neither a trowel nor a roller may be used.]

Alternatively, the מַעֲגִילָה is a *trowel.* This was the usual tool used. However, there was another tool called מַחְלְצַיִם, which was a sort of *hammer,* and could be used to pound or press down the plaster. Even this was not permitted *(Meiri).*

This restriction against using tools when repairing a roof applies only in the case of *possible* rain. If it is raining, however, a leaky roof is considered an irretrievable loss, since there will inevitably be damage to the house or to household articles; hence, the work may be done in a professional manner with a roller and trowel *(Meiri).*

Others hold that since the rain will cause the inhabitants discomfort on the festival, the repair is considered צוֹרֶךְ הַמּוֹעֵד, *work needed for the festival,* and may be done in a professional manner *(Ritva).*

הַצִּיר... — *A hinge* [of a door *(Rav)*],

וְהַצִּנּוֹר... — *or a socket* [into which the hinge is inserted],

In Talmudic times, this was a hole in the threshold *(Rashi; Rav).*

וְהַקּוֹרָה... — *or a beam* [that supports the house *(Rav)*],

Kehati interprets this as a beam above the door. [This would seem to fit the context better since it, like the other cases in this clause, involves a damage that prevents proper locking of the house.]

וְהַמַּנְעוּל וְהַמַּפְתֵּחַ שֶׁנִּשְׁבְּרוּ, — *or a lock, or a key that broke,*

1 and the foot, but not with a trowel.
10 A hinge, or a socket, or a beam, or a lock, or a key that broke may be repaired during [*Chol*] *HaMoed*, provided that one does not plan his work for [*Chol*] *HaMoed*.

All pickled food that can be eaten during the festival may be pickled [during *Chol HaMoed*].

YAD AVRAHAM

Even if any of these broke before the festival, and it was possible to repair them before the festival (*Nimukei Yosef*)...

מִתַקְּנָן בַּמּוֹעֵד, — *may be repaired during* [*Chol*] *HaMoed.*

This falls into the category of preventing irretrievable loss; since thieves will be able to enter at will (*Tos. Yom Tov; Rambam; Yom Tov* 8:7).

וּבִלְבַד שֶׁלֹּא יְכַוֵּן מְלַאכְתּוֹ בַּמּוֹעֵד. — *provided that one does not plan his work for* [*Chol*] *HaMoed.*

One may not say to himself before the festival, 'I will leave this work for *Chol HaMoed* when I have more time' (*Rav*).

וְכָל־כְּבָשִׁין... — *All pickled foods...*

I.e., foods that are usually pickled in vinegar and salt, such as fish and vegetables (*Rashi* on *Rif; Rav*).

שֶׁהוּא יָכוֹל לֶאֱכֹל מֵהֶן בַּמּוֹעֵד, — *that can be eaten during the festival...*

I.e., foods that can be pickled quickly and will be ready to eat during the festival (*Rav*).

כּוֹבְשָׁן. — *may be pickled* [*during Chol HaMoed*].

[This is considered a necessary preparation for the festival.]

Chapter 2

1.

Irretrievable Loss: Planned vs. Accidental

We have learned in the first chapter that one category of labor permitted on *Chol HaMoed* is work done to prevent דָּבָר הָאָבֵד, *an irretrievable loss.* Mishnah 1:10, however, ruled that if one intentionally delayed a job until *Chol HaMoed* at which time the work became essential to avoid an irretrievable loss, the labor is forbidden lest people purposely schedule for *Chol HaMoed* activities that could have been done sooner.

It follows that any form of production requiring a lengthy process should not be initiated prior to the festival if its continuation will require labor during *Chol HaMoed.* The foreknowledge that such work will be required constitutes an intention to allow an irretrievable loss to develop during *Chol HaMoed;* under such circumstances the Sages did not relax their prohibition against work not needed for the festival.

The mishnah now will teach that in case the process was initiated with sufficient time to allow for its completion before the festival, but unpredictable events caused a delay that extended the process into *Chol HaMoed,* work is permitted.

ב
א

[א] **מִי** שֶׁהָפַךְ אֶת־זֵיתָיו וְאֵרְעוֹ אֵבֶל אוֹ אֹנֶס, אוֹ שֶׁהִטְעוּהוּ פוֹעֲלִים, טוֹעֵן קוֹרָה רִאשׁוֹנָה וּמַנִּיחָהּ לְאַחַר הַמּוֹעֵד; דִּבְרֵי רַבִּי יְהוּדָה.

יד אברהם

◆§ Mourning

One of the situations mentioned by the mishnah is אֵבֶל, *mourning*, whose obligations fall upon the burial of one of seven close relatives: spouse, father, mother, son, daughter, brother, sister (see *Lev.* 21:2-3). During the seven-day mourning period, the mourner is forbidden to work. The extent of the prohibition is the subject of a dispute in the *Gemara* (11b) between R' Shisha and R' Ashi.

R' Shisha interprets our mishnah as a listing of situations which made it impossible for work to be completed before *Chol HaMoed*, even though the failure to do so may result in irretrievable loss. Therefore, one who was required to observe a mourning period before *Chol HaMoed* was forbidden to do *any* work; thus, he would be permitted to engage in necessary labor during *Chol HaMoed* since his failure to do so earlier was not a result of negligence or intentional postponement. Since the Tanna lists mourning as a reason for *not* working, but gives no instances where an economic hardship supersedes mourning, R' Shisha infers that there are *no* exceptions to the prohibition against labor.

R' Ashi differs. In his interpretation the mishnah likens mourning to *Chol HaMoed*; whatever exigencies permit work on *Chol HaMoed* would also permit it during mourning. He reasons as follows: if labor to avoid irretrievable loss is permitted even on *Chol HaMoed* on which the Torah prohibits work (see preface to tractate), then surely such work would be permitted during mourning when the prohibition against work is Rabbinic in origin. [The *general* laws of mourning have a Scriptural basis; only the prohibition against *work* is Rabbinic *(Tos.* 14b s.v. עשה).]

The *halachah* follows R' Shisha's view that *all* work is forbidden during mourning *(Rambam, Hilchos Eivel* 5:10; *Yoreh Deah* 380:10).

מִי שֶׁהָפַךְ אֶת־זֵיתָיו... — *One who turned over his olives [to soften them]....*

The process of producing oil from olives is lengthy. First, the olives are placed in a vat to soften. After a certain length of time, they are turned over in the vat to complete the softening process. Once the olives are turned over, only a short time may elapse before the olives are pressed; otherwise they will rot *(Tif. Yis.)*.

וְאֵרְעוֹ אֵבֶל... — *and then mourning...befell him...*

Rashi interprets the case of *mourning* as unrelated to *Chol HaMoed*, i.e., the mishnah discusses the case of one who became a mourner at *any* time of the year, but faces the predicament of olives in his vat that will rot unless the pressing *process* is begun. According to this interpretation, which follows R' Ashi in the *Gemara* (see preface), the pressing process may be begun by a mourner, just as it may on *Chol HaMoed* (see below), to avoid an irretrievable loss.

Rav, following the *halachah*, interprets the mishnah according to R' Shisha: The death occurring just before the festival; because *all* labor

2
1 **1.** One who turned over his olives [to soften them] and then mourning befell him, or an accident [befell him,], or [his] workers misled him, may place the first beam and leave it until after the festival. This is the opinion of R' Yehudah.

is forbidden during mourning, the pressing had to be delayed with the result that an irretrievable loss will result unless it is done during *Chol HaMoed*. *Rashi* on *Rif* also follows this interpretation.

או אֹנֶס, — *or an accident* [*befell him*],

Uncontrollable circumstances prevented him from completing the processing of the olives before the festival. Such accidents include the cases of one who forgot about the forthcoming festival or assumed that the olives would not spoil if left until after the festival (*Tif. Yis.*).

[Although hardly comparable to the case of one who became a mourner, such occurrences are sufficient grounds for permitting work during *Chol HaMoed*. Despite the fact that he is partially at fault, he is permitted to tend to his olives because he did not consciously delay the work for *Chol HaMoed*.]

או שֶׁהִטְעוּהוּ פּוֹעֲלִים, — *or* [*his*] *workers misled him,*

They promised to complete the job before the festival but did not report for work (*Rav*).

Even in a case where other workers were available for hire, it would be considered an extenuating circumstance if their hiring entailed additional expense. Hence he would be permitted to delay the work until *Chol HaMoed* (*Ritva*).

טוֹעֵן קוֹרָה רִאשׁוֹנָה... — *may place the first beam...*

I.e., he may place a heavy beam on top of the olives during *Chol HaMoed*, thereby causing their oil to begin to flow. This is the first step in the actual pressing process. After a time, the beam is lifted and once again dropped atop the olives to remove the remaining oil. This second placement of the beam to *increase* the flow is forbidden since the partially pressed olives will no longer spoil (*Rav*).

וּמַנִּיחָהּ לְאַחַר הַמּוֹעֵד; דִּבְרֵי רַבִּי יְהוּדָה. — *and leave it until after the festival. This is the opinion of R' Yehudah.*

He may process the olives only to the point of preventing spoilage. He may not *complete* the procedure, however, for the second pressing is not for preventing an irretrievable loss (*Rav*).

According to this interpretation, placement of the first beam is sufficient to prevent further spoilage.

Other commentators maintain that *some* spoilage would occur if the beam were not placed over the olives a second time. Since the losses are minimal, R' Yehudah would prohibit this. His reasoning is that even work permitted on grounds of irretrievable loss may be done only with a שִׁנּוּי, *modification*, of the usual manner of performing the work. For the beam to be emplaced a second time, a modification would be required, but the simple task of putting a beam atop olives does not lend itself to modification.

ב
ב

רַבִּי יוֹסֵי אוֹמֵר: זוֹלֵף וְגוֹמֵר וְגָף כְּדַרְכּוֹ.

[ב] **וְכֵן** מִי שֶׁהָיָה יֵינוֹ בְּתוֹךְ הַבּוֹר וְאֵרְעוֹ אֵבֶל אוֹ אֹנֶס, אוֹ שֶׁהִטְעוּהוּ פוֹעֲלִים, זוֹלֵף וְגוֹמֵר וְגָף כְּדַרְכּוֹ; דִּבְרֵי רַבִּי יוֹסֵי. רַבִּי יְהוּדָה אוֹמֵר: עוֹשֶׂה לוֹ לְמוּדִים, בִּשְׁבִיל שֶׁלֹּא יַחֲמִיץ.

יד אברהם

Therefore, he may place the beam but one time and must forgo the second (*Ritva; Meiri*).

רַבִּי יוֹסֵי אוֹמֵר: זוֹלֵף... — *R' Yose says: He may pour [the olives into the press],*

The translation of זוֹלֵף follows *Rashi, Rav* and *Tiferes Yisrael.* Others render *press out the oil* (*Rashi* on *Rif; Meiri*), or, *remove from the vat* (*Rambam*).

וְגוֹמֵר... — *complete [the process],*

He may perform all the usual steps necessary to draw out *all* the oil from the olives (*Tif. Yis.*).

וְגָף... — *and seal [the barrels]...*

The barrels may be sealed to prevent spillage should they be moved, to keep out insects and reptiles, or to prevent the oil from losing its taste (*Tos.; Rashi;* see *Bach* on *Tur* 538).

כְּדַרְכּוֹ. — *in his usual manner.*

He may complete the *entire* process as is customary throughout the year.

R' Yose rules that in the case of a irretrievable loss, work may be done without any deviation (see 1:10). Therefore, the pressing process may be carried through to completion although a loss could be averted even if some steps were omitted (*Rabbeinu Yerucham* 4:5, quoted in *Darchei Moshe* 537:1; see *Ritva,* ed. *Mosad HaRav Kook*).

[However, since sealing the barrels is not an integral part of olive pressing, it would be permitted only if the sealing itself prevented loss. (See above, s.v. וְגָף. Also see *Hagahos HaBach* for *Rashi's* primary interpretation, where he omits וְגָף, *and seal,* for the reason that sealing is extraneous to the pressing process and failure to do so will not result in a loss).]

The *halachah* is in accordance with R' Yose (*Rav*).

The nature of the disagreement between R' Yose and R' Yehudah may have a further explanation. The two Tannaim disagree concerning the very nature of the permission to work in a case of irretrievable loss. R' Yose holds that work was never forbidden in such a case; no exception to the rule is involved for no prohibition ever existed in such circumstances. That being the case, there is no reason to do the work in an unusual manner any more than cooking requires a modification. R' Yehudah, however, maintains that since labors such as pressing do fall under the ban, a case like ours is an exception for which the Sages provided a dispensation. Therefore, they required that it must be accomplished in a manner that would necessitate the least amount of work or that the work be done in an unusual fashion (*R' David Landesman*).

2 R′ Yose says: He may pour [the olives into the
2 press], complete [the process], and seal [the barrels] in his usual manner.

2. Similarly, one whose wine was in the vat and then mourning befell him, or an accident [befell him], or [his] workers misled him, may pour [the wine into barrels], complete [its processing], and seal [the barrels] in his usual manner. This is the opinion of R′ Yose.

R′ Yehudah says: He may cover [the barrels] with boards so that [the wine] does not sour.

YAD AVRAHAM

2.

וְכֵן מִי שֶׁהָיָה יֵינוֹ בְּתוֹךְ הַבּוֹר... — *Similarly, one whose wine was in the vat...*

This refers to the cement vat below the wine-press *(Rav).*

וְאֵרְעוֹ אֵבֶל אוֹ אֹנֶס, אוֹ שֶׁהִטְעוּהוּ פּוֹעֲלִים, — *and then mourning befell him, or an accident [befell him], or [his] workers misled him,*

See mishnah 1.

זוֹלֵף וְגוֹמֵר וְגָף כְּדַרְכּוֹ. — *may pour [the wine into barrels], complete [its processing], and seal [the barrels] in his usual manner.*

The interpolations follow *Rashi, Nimukei Yosef,* and *Tosefos Yom Tov.*

Alternatively, the mishnah speaks of a case where part of the wine is in the vat: He may draw the remaining wine until it is completely in the vat, then seal the vat in his usual manner *(Rashi* on *Rif).*

[To prevent the wine from souring he may seal the barrels (or the vat) in the usual manner and need not utilize the modification demanded by R′ Yehudah (see below).]

דִּבְרֵי רַבִּי יוֹסֵי. — *This is the opinion of R′ Yose.*

In the previous mishnah, and throughout the Talmud, R′ Yehudah precedes R′ Yose. In our mishnah, the order of the Tannaim is reversed in order to state R′ Yose's rulings together *(Tos.* 12a).

רַבִּי יְהוּדָה אוֹמֵר: עוֹשֶׂה לוֹ לְמוּדִים, בִּשְׁבִיל שֶׁלֹּא יַחֲמִיץ. — *R′ Yehudah says, he may cover [the barrels] with boards so that [the wine] does not sour.*

Only the minimum amount of work necessary to prevent souring may be done (see previous mishnah).

Though this mishnah seems identical to the previous one, the Tanna found it necessary to teach us both. Had he only stated the disagreement between R′ Yose and R′ Yehudah in the case of *oil,* one might think that only in that instance does R′ Yose permit completion of the process, since a considerable loss would be suffered if the olives were permitted to rot. In the case of wine however, where the potential loss is less, perhaps R′ Yose agrees that one is permitted to do only the minimum neces-

ב [ג] **מַכְנִיס** אָדָם פֵּרוֹתָיו מִפְּנֵי הַגַּנָּבִים,
ג וְשׁוֹלֶה פִּשְׁתָּנוֹ מִן הַמִּשְׁרָה
בִּשְׁבִיל שֶׁלֹּא תֹאבַד, וּבִלְבַד שֶׁלֹּא יְכַוֵּן אֶת־
מְלַאכְתּוֹ בַּמּוֹעֵד. וְכֻלָּן אִם כִּוְּנוּ מְלַאכְתָּן
בַּמּוֹעֵד יֵאָבֵדוּ.

יד אברהם

sary to prevent souring. Conversely, had the Tanna mentioned only the second case, one might think that only in that instance does R' Yehudah maintain that one is only permitted to do the minimum amount of work, since the potential loss is small. In the case of oil, however, since the loss may be great, perhaps R' Yehudah agrees with R' Yose's opinion that one may complete the process *(Tos. Yom Tov; Gem.* 12a).

In the case of wine, too, the *halachah* is in accordance with R' Yose *(Rav).*

3.

מַכְנִיס אָדָם פֵּרוֹתָיו מִפְּנֵי הַגַּנָּבִים, — *A person may bring in his fruit because of thieves,*

[If one fears that thieves may steal his crops, he may take them in from his garden or orchard. Despite the fact that bringing in the fruit entails strenuous work it is permitted, for possible theft of the crops is considered irretrievable loss.]

Work to prevent potential loss is permitted only if the loss is *probable,* not just possible (*Beur Halachah* 537).

The fruit should be brought in inconspicuously *(Gem.* 12b); for if it were done publicly, people unaware that prevention of loss was involved would conclude that work is generally permitted on *Chol HaMoed,* with the result that observance of *Chol HaMoed* would deteriorate *(Rashi* ms.; *Rashi* on *Rif; Nimukei Yosef).*

Only in cases where the loss is *potential* rather than definite is one required to be inconspicuous in his performance of the chore. Where the work is to prevent *definite* loss, however, one need not be discreet *(Maggid Mishnah;* quoting *Ramban, Hilchos Yom Tov* 7:3).

Ritva quoting *Ramban* maintains that if the potential loss results from external causes, such as fear that the fruit may be stolen, one must be discreet. If, however, the loss may result from inherent conditions such as those mentioned in the first two mishnayos of the chapter, there is no such requirement.

Others reject such differentiations maintaining that in *all* cases permitted work should be done discreetly (*Darchei Moshe; Mordechai* 538:3). However, if this is impossible, the work may proceed openly *(Rama* 538).

וְשׁוֹלֶה פִּשְׁתָּנוֹ מִן הַמִּשְׁרָה... — *and remove his flax from the soaking pond...*

Before flax is dried and combed, it is soaked in order to soften it *(Tif. Yis.).*

בִּשְׁבִיל שֶׁלֹּא תֹאבַד, — *so that it does not become ruined,*

If left too long, the flax begins to decay *(Tif. Yis.).*

Alternatively, תֹּאבַד means *become lost;* he may remove the

3. A person may bring in his fruit because of thieves, and remove his flax from the soaking pond so that it does not become ruined, provided he does not plan his work for the [*Chol*] *HaMoed*. In all these cases, if they planned their work for [*Chol*] *HaMoed* it shall be forfeited.

YAD AVRAHAM

flax from the soaking pond lest it be stolen *(Meiri)*.

וּבִלְבַד שֶׁלֹּא יְכַוֵּן אֶת־מְלַאכְתּוֹ בַּמּוֹעֵד. — *provided he does not plan his work for* [*Chol*] *HaMoed.*

One may not consciously postpone the work until *Chol HaMoed*, when he will have more free time. Should he do so, he is forbidden to do the work on [*Chol*] *HaMoed* (*Nimukei Yosef*, see above 1:10).

Moreover, one may not place the flax in the soaking pond if he knows that he will not be able to remove it before the festival, as that would be tantamount to planning the work for [*Chol*] *HaMoed* *(Rivav)*.

However, if it happened that there was no time to remove the flax before *Chol HaMoed*, this would not be considered as planning of the work for [*Chol*] *HaMoed (Rashi)*.

וְכֻלָּן... — *In all these cases*, [where work is permitted to prevent an irretrievable loss],

אִם כִּוְּנוּ מְלַאכְתָּן בַּמּוֹעֵד יֹאבְדוּ. — *if they planned their work for* [*Chol*] *HaMoed, it* [lit. *they*] *shall be forfeited* [lit. *lost*].

The commentators differ on the intent of the mishnah. We list the three interpretations in order of their severity.

Tosefos Yom Tov interprets this as an order to the owner of the property. Having intentionally left his work for *Chol HaMoed*, he is told that he is forbidden to do it despite the irretrievable loss: *it shall be lost.*

Rambam and *Rav* interpret the phrase as referring to the case where one transgressed, and performed the work on *Chol HaMoed*, contrary to the mishnah's prohibition. The mishnah issues a command to the courts: יֹאבְדוּ, *it shall be forfeited.* The court is to seize the goods and rule them הֶפְקֵר, *ownerless property*, thus allowing everyone access to them. Hence, יֹאבְדוּ, *it shall be forfeited* — by the owners. The *halachah* follows this interpretation.

Rashi goes one step further and maintains that the courts are to *condemn* the goods, thereby prohibiting *everyone* from benefiting from them. Hence, יֹאבְדוּ, *it shall be lost* — to everyone.

4.

⁂ Commerce

Just as labor during *Chol HaMoed* detracts from the festive atmosphere of the day, so does commerce. Hence, the Sages forbade buying and selling during this period.

In the preface to this tractate, five exceptions to the prohibition

ב
ד

[ד] **אֵין** לוֹקְחִין בָּתִּים, עֲבָדִים וּבְהֵמָה, אֶלָּא לְצֹרֶךְ הַמּוֹעֵד, אוֹ לְצֹרֶךְ הַמּוֹכֵר, שֶׁאֵין לוֹ מַה־יֹּאכַל.

אֵין מְפַנִּין מִבַּיִת לְבַיִת, אֲבָל מְפַנֶּה הוּא לַחֲצֵרוֹ.

אֵין מְבִיאִין כֵּלִים מִבֵּית הָאֻמָּן; אִם חוֹשֵׁשׁ לָהֶם, מְפַנָּן לְחָצֵר אַחֶרֶת.

יד אברהם

however, are permitted in all instances.

אֵין לוֹקְחִין בָּתִּים, עֲבָדִים וּבְהֵמָה... — *We may not purchase homes, nor slaves, nor domestic animals,*

Some editions of the *Mishnah* add אֲבָנִים, *stones* [i.e., building materials] *(Rif; Rosh; Yerushalmi).*

אֶלָּא לְצֹרֶךְ הַמּוֹעֵד, — *except for use during the festival,*

The purchase is permitted only if the homes, slaves, or animals will be used during the festival. One may buy, for example, a home to live in during the festival, a slave to serve him during the festival, and animals to be slaughtered for the festival *(Rav).*

According to the reading of *Rif* and *Rosh*, stones may be purchased if needed for work that is permitted during *Chol HaMoed*, such as the repair of a breached wall (see 1:4; *Tos. Yom Tov).*

אוֹ לְצֹרֶךְ הַמּוֹכֵר, שֶׁאֵין לוֹ מַה־יֹּאכַל. — *or [to provide] for the needs of the seller who [otherwise] has nothing to eat.*

One may purchase goods that will not be used during the festival if the seller needs the money to spend for the festival *(Rav).*

Similarly, one may do work during *Chol HaMoed* if he needs the wages to purchase festival supplies. Prohibitions against work are enumerated. When applicable in cases of commerce, these same exemptions hold. Thus, an animal may be sold if it will be slaughtered for the festival meal (צֹרֶךְ הַמּוֹעֵד), or if the seller will otherwise not have the means with which to feed his family (שֶׁאֵין לוֹ מַה יֹּאכַל).

Opinions differ as to whether the prohibition against commerce applies to all buying and selling or only to those cases specified in the mishnah. *Tosafos* (13a) maintains that any items may be sold, but only if they fit into the exempted categories. The specific items mentioned in the mishnah are usually sold in the public marketplace and their purchase could easily be mistaken as a flagrant desecration of the sanctity of *Chol HaMoed*. The Tanna therefore states that despite this possibility, their sale is permitted. However, items not fitting the exempted categories may not be bought and sold in any circumstances, not even privately.

Tosefos Yom Tov, on the other hand, cites *Maggid Mishnah's* opinion that only items usually sold publicly, like those listed in the mishnah, which may not be sold during *Chol HaMoed* unless they are needed for the festival, or are similarly exempt. Private sales,

2 4

4. **W**e may not purchase homes, nor slaves, nor domestic animals, except for use during the festival, or [to provide] for the needs of the seller who [otherwise] has nothing to eat.

We may not move [objects] from one house to another, but one may move [objects from one house to another] within his courtyard.

We may not bring vessels from the artisan's shop; but if one fears for them, he may move them into a different courtyard.

YAD AVRAHAM

Moreover, he is even permitted to do work that serves no festival need if the wages are necessary for sustenance on the festival. Thus, a construction worker who depends on his earnings may work on a building that will not be ready until later (*Tos. Yom Tov*).

Accordingly, a buyer or employer may do business with, or hire a needy person in order to enable him to earn money for his festival needs. It is not necessary that the buyer or employer have a personal festival need for the item or labor (*Mishnah Berurah* 538:42).

אֵין מְפַנִּין מִבַּיִת לְבַיִת, — *We may not move* [*objects*] *from one house to another,*

One may not move goods or grain a great distance from where the goods are stored, as this is considered strenuous work (*Rav*). This applies only if the goods or grain need not be moved for use during the festival (*Tos. Yom Tov; Tur* 535).

אֲבָל מְפַנֶּה הוּא לַחֲצֵרוֹ. — *but one may move* [*objects from one house to another*] *within his courtyard.*

One may move goods into another house within the same courtyard because this can be accomplished discreetly. If the moving necessitates transporting the goods through a public thoroughfare, however, it is not permitted (*Rav*).

Some authorities permit one to move from rented quarters into his own home, although it will necessitate transporting through a public thoroughfare. Since moving into one's own home causes happiness, it will add to the joy of the festival; hence it is considered as a festival need (*Tur* 535). Moreover, one may move from a non-Jewish neighborhood into a rented apartment in a Jewish neighborhood for similar reasons (*Magen Avraham*).

אֵין מְבִיאִין כֵּלִים מִבֵּית הָאֻמָּן; — *We may not bring vessels from the artisan's shop;*

On *Chol HaMoed* one may not remove goods previously sent to the craftsman for repair unless they are to be used during the festival (*Rav*).

If the removal of the goods from the craftsman entails strenuous work, it is prohibited for that reason (*Rashi, Pesachim* 55b). In any case, however, it is prohibited since people might assume that the craftsman did the work during *Chol HaMoed* (*Meiri*).

אִם חוֹשֵׁשׁ לָהֶם, — *but if one fears for them,*

The goods may be taken from the

ב
ה

[ה] מְחַפִּין אֶת־הַקְּצִיעוֹת בְּקַשׁ. רַבִּי יְהוּדָה אוֹמֵר: אַף מְעַבִּין.

מוֹכְרֵי פֵרוֹת, כְּסוּת וְכֵלִים, מוֹכְרִים בְּצִנְעָה לְצֹרֶךְ הַמּוֹעֵד.

הַצַּיָּדִין וְהַדָּשׁוֹשׁוֹת וְהַגָּרוֹסוֹת, עוֹשִׂין בְּצִנְעָה לְצֹרֶךְ הַמּוֹעֵד. רַבִּי יוֹסֵי אוֹמֵר: הֵם הֶחֱמִירוּ עַל־עַצְמָן.

יד אברהם

craftsman on *Chol HaMoed* if their owner fears that they will be stolen *(Rav);* that the craftsman will use them as his own *(Meiri);* or that the craftsman will charge him for storage *(Meleches Shlomo).*

מְפַנָּן לְחָצֵר אַחֶרֶת. — *he may move them into a different courtyard.*

If he has such fears, he may move them into another courtyard in close proximity to the craftsman. This will allay the owner's fears, and at the same time avoid the impression that forbidden work was done. However, if he fears for their security even in a different courtyard, and has no choice but to bring the repaired goods home, he may remove them in a discreet manner *(Rambam; Meiri).*

Though one is permitted to bring his fruit from his field into his home (see mishnah 3), that case is different from this one since the potential for theft of the fruit is more likely *(Meiri).*

5.

מְחַפִּין אֶת־הַקְּצִיעוֹת בְּקַשׁ. — *We may cover drying figs with straw.*

Even though this entails strenuous work, one may cover the figs to protect them from the rain *(Rav).*

רַבִּי יְהוּדָה אוֹמֵר: אַף מְעַבִּין. — *R' Yehudah says: We may even stack them* [lit. *thicken them*].

In this way the top figs protect those underneath [even though this entails more strenuous work than covering them with straw] *(Rav).*

Alternatively, the figs may be gathered together in order to facilitate covering them with straw *(Rashi).*

The *halachah* is in accordance with the first Tanna *(Shulchan Aruch* 538:4).

The above interpretation is based on the reading אַף, *even,* which indicates that R' Yehudah is more lenient than the first Tanna. R' Yehudah not only permits what his colleague does, he *even* permits the piling up of figs.

Yerushalmi, however, deletes the word אַף, *even.*

According to *Yerushalmi,* the first Tanna permits even cutting the straw, while R' Yehudah permits covering only with available straw. According to this, the reading is רַבִּי יְהוּדָה אוֹמֵר: מְעַבִּין, *R' Yehudah says: We may stack them* — deleting the word אַף, *even,* for R' Yehudah's ruling is stricter than that of the first Tanna *(P'nei Moshe* 2:5).

2
5

5. We may cover drying figs with straw.

R' Yehudah says: We may even stack them.

Vendors of fruit, clothing and utensils may sell [their wares] in private, for use during the festival. Trappers, cereal makers, and bean pounders may ply their trade in private for festival needs.

R' Yose says: They imposed a stringency upon themselves.

YAD AVRAHAM

Alternatively, the first Tanna permits covering the figs with straw even if they were not covered at all before the festival. R' Yehudah permits only *adding* straw to *thicken* an existing covering. If the figs were not covered at all, R' Yehudah does not permit covering them *(Meiri)*. [Obviously, *Meiri* did not have the word אַף, *even*, in his edition of the *Mishnah*.]

Tiferes Yisrael, however, explains that R' Yehudah's ruling is more lenient than that of the first Tanna. Whereas the first Tanna permits only covering the figs with straw, R' Yehudah permits piling the straw on *thickly*, even though he appears to be storing the figs rather than merely protecting them.

מוֹכְרֵי פֵרוֹת, כְּסוּת וְכֵלִים, מוֹכְרִים בְּצִנְעָה לְצֹרֶךְ הַמּוֹעֵד. — *Vendors of fruit, clothing and utensils may sell [their wares] in private, for use during the festival.*

Even though they are selling goods for use during the festival, they must do so only in private, so that people should not suspect them of selling goods for use after the festival *(Rashi)*.

What is meant by *in private?* — If the store front faces a public thoroughfare, the vendor should open only one door. However, if it faces an alley, he may open the doors in the usual manner *(Tos. Yom Tov)*.

[Many commentators find rationales for the common practice of opening stores in the usual manner during *Chol HaMoed* (see *Machatzis HaShekel*, *Eliyah Rabbah* and *Aruch HaShulchan*, 539:11).]

הַצַּיָּדִין, — *Trappers* [of beasts, fowl, and fish *(Tos. Yom Tov; Nimukei Yosef)*],

וְהַדָּשׁוֹשׁוֹת וְהַגָּרוֹסוֹת... — *cereal makers, and bean pounders* [lit. *groat and bean pounders (Rav)*]...

עוֹשִׂין בְּצִנְעָה לְצֹרֶךְ הַמּוֹעֵד. — *may ply their trade in private for festival needs.*

Professional trappers may engage in their work discreetly on *Chol HaMoed*. Since they trap large numbers of animals, people might assume that they are preparing goods for use *after* the festival. Individuals, however, need not be discreet, since it is obvious that they are trapping for immediate use *(Tos. Yom Tov)*.

Even fishermen, who ply their trade to provide food for the festival, must do so discreetly *(Tif. Yis.)*.

רַבִּי יוֹסֵי אוֹמֵר: הֵם הֶחֱמִירוּ עַל־עַצְמָן. — *R' Yose says: They* [i.e., the professionals just mentioned] *imposed a stringency upon themselves.*

Even though they were permitted

ג
א

[א] **וְאֵלּוּ** מְגַלְּחִין בַּמּוֹעֵד: הַבָּא מִמְּדִינַת הַיָּם, וּמִבֵּית הַשִּׁבְיָה, וְהַיּוֹצֵא מִבֵּית הָאֲסוּרִין, וְהַמְנֻדֶּה שֶׁהִתִּירוּ לוֹ חֲכָמִים.

יד אברהם

to work discreetly, they extended the prohibition upon themselves even in private [and are thus forbidden to ply their trade during *Chol HaMoed*] *(Rav; Gem.* 13b).

In fact, it is not proper for these food suppliers to abstain from plying their trades, lest the people have insufficient food for the festival *(Meiri* from *Yerushalmi).*

The *halachah* is not in accordance with R' Yose *(Rav).*

Chapter 3

1.

◆§ Rabbinical Prohibitions Against Permitted Work

In the latter part of the second chapter, the mishnah discussed work that is permitted on *Chol HaMoed* for the sake of the festival. Here, the mishnah discusses work that is necessary for the festival, but is, nevertheless, prohibited during *Chol HaMoed.* However, exceptions to these prohibitions do exist when even these tasks are permissible on *Chol HaMoed (Tos.* 13b).

◆§ Haircutting and Laundering on Chol HaMoed

Haircutting and laundering should, indeed, have been permitted on *Chol HaMoed,* since they are essentially for the sake of the (remaining days of the) festival (*Tif. Yis.; Tos.* 14a).

Since haircutting and laundering are essential to proper preparation for the festival, the Rabbis wanted to insure that people would cut their hair and launder their clothing *before* the beginning of the festival. They did so by enacting a prohibition against haircutting and laundering during *Chol HaMoed,* thereby assuring that people would do their grooming and cleaning beforehand (*Gem.* 14a).

Mishnah 1 lists those who are permitted to cut their hair during *Chol HaMoed* due to extenuating circumstances. Mishnah 2 discusses exemptions to the prohibition against laundering.

וְאֵלּוּ מְגַלְּחִין בַּמּוֹעֵד: — *(And) these* [*people*] *may cut their hair during* [*Chol*] *HaMoed*:

[Despite the Rabbinic prohibition against haircutting during *Chol HaMoed,* exceptions were made in the following cases:]

הַבָּא מִמְּדִינַת הַיָּם, — *One who arrived from abroad* [lit. *from a maritime state*];

The Tanna refers both to one who arrived from abroad during *Chol HaMoed (Rav)* and to one who arrived late on the eve of the festival. In either case, he did not have the opportunity to cut his hair before the festival *(Tos. Yom Tov).*

The mishnah uses the term הַבָּא מִמְּדִינַת הַיָּם, *one who has arrived from abroad,* since his arrival would be common knowledge with the result that the public would be aware that the traveler had no op-

3
1

1. These [people] may cut their hair during [Chol] *HaMoed*: One who arrived from abroad; [was released] from captivity; left prison; or the excommunicate whose ban was lifted by sages. Similarly,

portunity to cut his hair before the festival. The same reasoning would apply if one arrived from any distant city, not necessarily from abroad *(Machatzis HaShekel* 531:6). [However, if one arrived from a nearby city, since such journeys are common, it is usually not well-known that he was away, and cutting his hair is prohibited on *Chol HaMoed*, for people would suspect that he brazenly disobeyed the prohibition without cause.]

The Rabbis made this exception to the general prohibition of haircutting only for travelers who went abroad for business or some other necessary purpose. If the trip was merely a pleasure cruise, however, the Rabbis made no exceptions. Hence, a traveler returning from a pleasure cruise on *Chol HaMoed* may not cut his hair, although it is public knowledge that he could not do so earlier *(Rav)*.

Rosh maintains that the restriction in the case of a pleasure cruise pertains only to one who had taken a trip away from *Eretz Yisrael* because it is forbidden to leave *Eretz Yisrael* except for a valid purpose (see *Avodah Zarah* 13a and *Yerushalmi)*. In the case of one who lives elsewhere, there is no difference between a business trip and a pleasure cruise.

וּמִבֵּית הַשִּׁבְיָה, וְהַיּוֹצֵא מִבֵּית הָאֲסוּרִין, — *[was released] from (the house of) captivity; left prison;*

Release from captivity or imprisonment is in itself sufficient grounds for permitting haircutting. No distinction is made between one imprisoned in his hometown and one incarcerated abroad *(Ritva)*.

In the case of יוֹצֵא מִבֵּית הָאֲסוּרִין, *one who left prison*, the dispensation applies equally to one who was imprisoned by Jewish courts even though the Jewish jailkeepers would have permitted him to cut his hair in honor of the festival. Nevertheless, since a prisoner is usually not in the proper state of mind to be concerned with grooming himself, it is considered as if he had no opportunity to do so; hence, he is permitted to cut his hair during *Chol HaMoed (Rav)*.

Similarly, one who recovered from illness during *Chol HaMoed* is permitted to cut his hair if it is clear that he had not previously been in the proper frame of mind to be concerned with his appearance *(Meiri)*.

◆§ Nidui — Ban

The term נִדּוּי, *nidui*, is rendered as *ban*. It is basically a curse pronounced on a violator of religious law. *Rambam (Talmud Torah* 6:14) enumerates twenty-four transgressions for which one is liable to a *nidui*. According to *Ran (Nedarim* 7b), one deserves *nidui* for any infraction of religious law. (See *Yoreh Deah* 334:1). The violations fall into three general categories: (1) showing disrespect to Torah scholars; (2) infraction of religious law, whether Scriptural or Rabbinic in origin; and (3) refusal to obey a court order regarding monetary matters.

The person under the ban is prohibited from doing certain things, much like a mourner. He may not cut his hair nor launder his garments (*Gem.* 15a), and, ac-

ג
א

וְכֵן מִי שֶׁנִּשְׁאַל לְחָכָם וְהֻתַּר; וְהַנָּזִיר, וְהַמְּצֹרָע הָעוֹלֶה מִטֻּמְאָתוֹ לְטָהֳרָתוֹ.

יד אברהם

cording to many authorities, he may not wear leather shoes (*Yoreh Deah* 334:12).

In many respects he is isolated from other Jews. No one may sit within four cubits of him. He may not even be counted as one of a *minyan (Rambam, Talmud Torah* 7:4; *Yoreh Deah* 334:2).

The duration of a *nidui* is generally thirty days (*Gem.* 16a). Under certain circumstances, however, it may be rescinded prior to the termination of this period. (See *Ran, Nedarim* 7b; *Rif, Rosh, Moed Katan* 16a; *Yoreh Deah* 334:13).

The mishnah here speaks of one whose period of *nidui* ended, or was rescinded, either during *Chol HaMoed (Rav)* or just prior to the festival *(Meiri).*

...וְכֵן מִי שֶׁנִּשְׁאַל לְחָכָם — *Similarly, one who applied to a sage* [to be released from his vow]...

One who had taken a vow not to cut his hair [or to become a *nazir (Meiri)*] could have had his vow annulled by a sage or court under certain conditions. Failing to find a sage before the festival, he made his appeal for annulment during *Chol HaMoed.*

Alternatively, our mishnah refers to a case where grounds for annulment were not discovered until the festival had begun. [In order to annul a vow, the sage must discover a fact or an outcome of the vow that, had it been known previously to the vower, would have been sufficient to deter him from taking the vow. (The guidelines of such grounds are given in tractate *Nedarim.*) Only if such grounds exist, may a qualified sage or court annul the vow as having been made in error] *(Rav; Yerushalmi).*

According to *Bavli (Nedarim* 22b), however, since a sage may annul a vow merely on the grounds of the person's regret at having taken it, our mishnah can refer only to one who could not find a sage before the festival *(Rosh).*

Others maintain that the mishnah refers to one who decided to ap-

וְהַמְּנֻדֶּה שֶׁהִתִּירוּ לוֹ חֲכָמִים. — *or the excommunicate whose ban was lifted by sages.*

According to *Yerushalmi,* the dispensation applies only to a banned individual who was unable to have his *nidui* rescinded before the festival. However, if he could have had the ban lifted before the festival — for example, by appealing to the court at the end of his thirty-day *nidui* — but negligently failed to do so earlier, he may not cut his hair on *Chol HaMoed.*

Rambam, however, holds that in certain circumstances, although the person under ban could have done something to cause the lifting of the ban before the festival, his failure to do so does not constitute negligence. For example, an individual placed under ban for refusal to obey the courts regarding monetary matters (see pref.) could have had the ban lifted by appeasing his litigant. If he chose not to appease him, the court was compelled to maintain the ban; this is not considered negligence on the part of the banned individual. Hence, if he had a change of heart and settled his case during *Chol HaMoed,* the court could then lift the ban and he would be permitted to cut his hair on *Chol HaMoed.*

3 one who applied to a sage who released [him from his
1 vow]; the *nazir* or the *metzora* who returns from [a
state of] contamination to [a state of] purity.

ply for annulment during *Chol HaMoed*. [This agrees with the principle of *Rambam* (see above) that failure to undertake a course of action that will result indirectly in the lifting of a ban does not constitute negligence.]

;וְהִתִּיר — *who released [him from his vow];*

I.e., the sage annulled the vow during *Chol HaMoed (Tif. Yis.).*

,וְהַנָּזִיר — *(and) the nazir...*

One who imposes upon himself the status of *nazir* is prohibited from cutting his hair, drinking wine, eating grapes, and coming into contact with a corpse for a minimum period of thirty days [see *Numb.* 6:1-7]. Thus, the mishnah refers to an instance where the period terminated during *Chol HaMoed (Rav).*

Alternatively, the Tanna may refer even to one whose period of *nezirus* terminated before the festival but who neglected to cut his hair. Nevertheless, the Sages did not enforce the prohibition against a former *nazir*. Since he is required to offer specified sacrifices upon the conclusion of his period of *nezirus*, and he is required to cut his hair prior to doing so, the Sages did not want him to delay his sacrifices even further because he could not cut his hair on *Chol HaMoed (Tos. Yom Tov; Gem.* 14b). [For a fuller treatment of this subject, see tractate *Nazir*.]

.וְהַמְּצֹרָע הָעוֹלֶה מִטֻּמְאָתוֹ לְטָהֳרָתוֹ — *or the metzora who returns from [a state of] contamination to [a state of] purity.*

Once the symptoms of *tzaraas* disappear (see *Megillah* 1:7) the afflicted one is required to cut his hair on the seventh day of his period of purification (see *Lev.* 14:8,9). If the seventh day fell during *Chol HaMoed*, he is permitted to cut his hair as that act is a prerequisite to the bringing of the sacrifice that completes the purification process *(Rav).*

Other editions of the *Mishnah* read הַמְּצֹרָע וְהָעוֹלֶה מִטֻּמְאָתוֹ לְטָהֳרָתוֹ, *the metzora 'and' one who returns from contamination to purity*. If so, the mishnah refers to two separate people — a *metzora* and one who had been rendered impure by contact with a corpse. He, too, must undergo a seven-day purification process, and he, too, is permitted to cut his hair during *Chol HaMoed*. This however, is somewhat difficult to comprehend, since a person contaminated by contact with a corpse is not proscribed from cutting his hair during his purification process. *Maggid Mishnah (Yom Tov* 7:19) suggests that any contaminated person should not groom himself, therefore it would have been improper for him to have cut his hair before the festival. Others reject this as having no legal basis and suggest simply that the contaminated person may not have been able to have his hair cut before the festival since others may avoid physical contact with him in order not to contaminate themselves *(Dikdukei Sofrim).*

ג
ב

[ב] **וְאֵלּוּ** מְכַבְּסִין בַּמּוֹעֵד: הַבָּא מִמְּדִינַת הַיָּם, וּמִבֵּית הַשִּׁבְיָה, וְהַיּוֹצֵא מִבֵּית הָאֲסוּרִים, וְהַמְנֻדֶּה שֶׁהִתִּירוּ לוֹ חֲכָמִים; וְכֵן מִי שֶׁנִּשְׁאַל לְחָכָם וְהֻתַּר; מִטְפְּחוֹת הַיָּדַיִם וּמִטְפְּחוֹת הַסַּפָּרִים וּמִטְפְּחוֹת הַסְּפָג; הַזָּבִין וְהַזָּבוֹת וְהַנִּדּוֹת וְהַיּוֹלְדוֹת, וְכָל־הָעוֹלִין מִטֻּמְאָה לְטָהֳרָה, הֲרֵי אֵלּוּ מֻתָּרִין; וּשְׁאָר כָּל־אָדָם אֲסוּרִין.

יד אברהם

2.

וְאֵלּוּ מְכַבְּסִין בַּמּוֹעֵד: — *And these* [*people*] *may launder* [*their clothing*] *during* [*Chol*] *HaMoed:*

[I.e., the following are granted dispensations from the Rabbinic prohibition. See preface to mishnah 1.]

הַבָּא מִמְּדִינַת הַיָּם, וּמִבֵּית הַשִּׁבְיָה, וְהַיּוֹצֵא מִבֵּית הָאֲסוּרִים, וְהַמְנֻדֶּה שֶׁהִתִּירוּ לוֹ חֲכָמִים. — *One who arrived from abroad;* [*was released*] *from captivity; left prison; or the excommunicate whose ban was lifted by sages.*

[See above mishnah 1 — just as they were unable to cut their hair before the festival, so too, they were unable to launder their clothing.]

וְכֵן מִי שֶׁנִּשְׁאַל לְחָכָם וְהֻתַּר; — *Similarly, one who applied to a sage who released him* [*from his vow*].

I.e., one who vowed not to launder his clothing and had the vow annulled by a sage during *Chol HaMoed* (*Rav;* see above, mishnah 1).

מִטְפְּחוֹת הַיָּדַיִם... — *Hand towels...* [*may also be laundered*],

This refers to napkins used to wipe the hands during the meal (*Rav; Meiri*). Because they are in steady use, such napkins require constant laundering and even if they were laundered before the festival, they must be relaundered during *Chol HaMoed*. For this same reason, diapers may be laundered during *Chol HaMoed* (*Tif. Yis.*).

וּמִטְפְּחוֹת הַסַּפָּרִים... — *barbers' cloths...* [*may also be laundered*],

Barbers place cloths atop the clothing of their customers. The cloths may be laundered for the benefit of those who are permitted to have their hair cut during *Chol HaMoed* (*Rav*).

An alternative reading is: מִטְפְּחוֹת סוֹפְרִים, *scholars'* [lit. *scribes*] *cloths*. Cloths were spread over the desks on which the students placed the pages from which they studied. These cloths required constant laundering because they often became soiled from the drippings of the candles used during night study (*Meiri*).

Another variant reading is: מִטְפְּחוֹת סְפָרִים, *book cloths*, i.e., the coverings in which scrolls were wrapped, which also required frequent cleaning since they were constantly handled (*Nimukei Yosef*).

וּמִטְפְּחוֹת הַסְּפָג; — *and bath towels* [*may also be laundered*].

Bath towels require frequent

3 **2.** And these [people] may launder [their clothing]
2 during [*Chol*] *HaMoed:* One who arrived from abroad; [was released] from captivity; left prison; or the excommunicate whose ban was lifted by sages. Similarly, one who applied to a sage who released [him from his vow].

Hand towels, barbers' cloths, and bath towels [may also be laundered].

Zavim, zavos, menstruants, women who have given birth, and all who return from [a state of] contamination to [a state of] purity, these are permitted [to launder their clothing], but all others are forbidden.

laundering for they become thoroughly soiled with each use. Hence, they would require laundering on *Chol HaMoed,* even if they had been washed immediately prior to the festival *(Meiri).*

However, the mishnah permits such laundering only where no other towels are available. If sufficient towels are available for use, the soiled ones may not be washed on *Chol HaMoed (Aruch HaShulchan* 543:3-4).

Similarly, clothing that became soiled on the festival may be cleaned if one has no clean clothes left for the festival (*Aruch HaShulchan* 543:3-4).

הַזָּבִין וְהַזָּבוֹת וְהַנִּדּוֹת וְהַיּוֹלְדוֹת, — *Zavim, zavos, menstruants, women who have given birth,*

[For a lengthy exposition on these terms and variations, see pref. to *Megillah* 1:7.]

Because of their physiological condition, they soil their clothing frequently, therefore they are permitted to launder their clothing during *Chol HaMoed.*

Moreover, they are required to wear clean white clothing during the seven 'clean' days following the conclusion of the flow *(Meiri).*

וְכָל־הָעוֹלִין מִטֻּמְאָה לְטָהֳרָה, — *and all who return from [a state of] contamination to [a state of] purity.*

All whose garments require immersion — such as a *metzora* or one defiled by a corpse — may cleanse them during *Chol HaMoed* provided that it could not have been done before the festival *(Tos. Yom Tov).*

הֲרֵי אֵלּוּ מֻתָּרִין; — *These are permitted [to launder their clothing],*

Linen garments may be laundered during *Chol HaMoed* because they are easily soiled *(Rav).* Nowadays, however, we do not launder even linen garments (*Orach Chayim* 534:2) except if one has nothing else to wear (*Mishnah Berurah* 534:9).

If one has only one suit, he may launder it if it became soiled during the festival, provided he makes it obvious that he is laundering it only because he has nothing else to wear; for example, by washing it while

ג
ג

[ג] **וְאֵלּוּ** כּוֹתְבִין בַּמּוֹעֵד: קִדּוּשֵׁי נָשִׁים, גִּטִּין, וְשׁוֹבָרִין, דְּיַתִּיקִי, מַתָּנָה,

he stands wrapped in a towel *(Rav; Gem.* 18a).

וּשְׁאָר כָּל־אָדָם אֲסוּרִין. — *but all others are forbidden.*

[People not falling under the above guidelines may not do laundry on *Chol HaMoed.*]

3.

◆§ Writing

We have learned previously (end of chapter 1) that work requiring skill of a professional caliber is prohibited on *Chol HaMoed*. Therefore, calligraphy, which is a skilled craft is prohibited. Some authorities prohibit even writing in a non-calligraphic manner, for they consider the simple act of writing to be a professional form of labor [see *Mishnah Berurah* 545:5].

Mishnah 3 lists exceptions when writing is permitted on *Chol HaMoed*.

וְאֵלּוּ כּוֹתְבִין בַּמּוֹעֵד: — *(And) these [documents] may be written* [lit. *these may write*] *during [Chol] HaMoed:*

The following may be written on *Chol HaMoed*, for if they were not written immediately irretrievable loss might occur *(Tif. Yis.).*

קִדּוּשֵׁי נָשִׁים, — *Instruments of betrothal* [lit. *betrothal of women*],

One of the means of betrothal is a שְׁטָר, *contract.* The groom writes the words הֲרֵי אַתְּ מְקֻדֶּשֶׁת לִי, *You are consecrated to me,* on paper (or any other suitable material) and hands it to the bride before two witnesses (see *Kiddushin* 1:1). This instrument may be written on *Chol HaMoed*, for if it is postponed until after the festival, the prospective bride might renege on her previous consent and marry another, causing irretrievable loss to the prospective groom (*Rav; Gem.* 18b).

Similarly, it is permissible to write תְּנָאִים, *engagement contracts,* delineating various financial obligations pertaining to the marriage. These, too, may be written and signed on *Chol HaMoed*; for if they were to wait until after the festival, one of the parties might reconsider the terms earlier agreed upon *(Tif. Yis.).*

גִּטִּין, — *divorces,*

If the husband is about to set out on a hazardous trip from which he might not return (such as a soldier going to war, or a traveler to a very distant land), he may write his wife a conditional divorce on *Chol HaMoed,* so that if he does not return she will not remain an עֲגוּנָה, *a woman prevented from remarrying* [for lack of evidence of her husband's death]. The divorce would state that it would take effect only if he were not to return *(Rav; Rashi* on *Rif; Rashi* ms.; *Nimukei Yosef; Tif. Yis.).*

[Ordinarily, however, divorce proceedings should be delayed until after the festival unless the delay might cause irretrievable loss, for example, if there is reasonable fear that the husband might change his

3
3 **3.** And these [documents] may be written during [*Chol*] *HaMoed*: Instruments of betrothal, divorces, receipts, testaments, gifts, *prozbulin*,

mind and leave his wife without granting her a divorce, or that he might demand money in return for the divorce.]

וְשׁוֹבָרִין, — *receipts,*

A debtor always has the right to request a receipt upon payment of a debt.[1] Therefore, if the debtor is leaving town during *Chol HaMoed*, his creditor may write a receipt, for otherwise the debtor will leave without paying him *(Rav; Rashi* on *Rif).*

Even if the debtor is not leaving, the creditor may write a receipt on *Chol HaMoed* for it is possible that the debtor may no longer have money available after the festival *(Tif. Yis.).*

דְּיַתִּיקִי, — *testaments,*

[I.e., a document attesting to the bequest of a terminally ill person. Although the Sages prescribed that מַתְּנַת שְׁכִיב מְרַע, *the verbal bequest of a terminally ill person*, takes effect without the usual means of transfer of property, the דְּיַתִּיקִי, *testament*, would serve as proof that the gift had been made. Since such documentation might be needed as proof against possible claims from heirs, it may be written on *Chol HaMoed*.]

מַתָּנָה, — *gifts,*

[I.e., gifts of land given by a healthy person].

Real estate may be transferred by means of a שְׁטָר, *contract*. In making a gift of such property, the owner writes: 'I transfer this property to...', and hands the document to the recipient. This document is both a legal means of transfer, and proof that the property did indeed change hands. If the benefactor wishes to make such a gift on *Chol HaMoed*, a document may be written in order to make the transfer final. Otherwise, the giver may renege on his gift, resulting in an irretrievable loss to the recipient *(Rashi* on *Rif, Rashi* ms.; *Meiri, Rav; Tif. Yis.).*

Other commentators maintain that even if title to the property were transferred by other than a written contract, a document may be written even on *Chol HaMoed* to serve as proof of the transfer *(Nimukei Yosef; Tos. Yom Tov).*

Ran maintains that even if there were witnesses to the transfer, the document may be written on *Chol HaMoed*, if it will be the only proof of the transfer in the event the witnesses decide to leave town.

◆§ Prozbul

Among the laws pertaining to שְׁמִטָּה [*Shemitah*], *Sabbatical year*, is the nullification of all debts incurred before the end of the *Shemitah* (see *Deut.* 15:1-3). Concurrent with this law, there is a negative commandment against refraining from

1. This rule applies only in the case where the creditor lost his note for indebtedness. If, however, he does possess the note, he must return the note to the debtor upon payment of the debt, thereby removing the need for a receipt *(Ran; Nimukei Yosef; Tos. Yom Tov).*

ג
ג

וּפְרוֹזְבּוּלִין, אִגְּרוֹת שׁוּם, וְאִגְּרוֹת מָזוֹן, שְׁטָרֵי חֲלִיצָה, וּמֵאוּנִים, וּשְׁטָרֵי בֵרוּרִין, וּגְזֵרוֹת בֵּית דִּין, וְאִגְּרוֹת שֶׁל רָשׁוּת.

יד אברהם

lending before *Shemitah* for fear of losing the debt *(Deut.* 15:9). However, for fear of losing their money, people transgressed this commandment and did not lend money prior to *Shemitah*. To combat this flagrant violation of the Torah, Hillel enacted the *prozbul.*

The *prozbul* is a legal document based on the rule (*Shvi'is* 10:2) that one's debts are not nullified if they have been transferred to the court. Hillel, therefore enacted the *prozbul* which constitutes such a transfer. Since the debts technically become owned by the court, they are not nullified and the debtor is permitted to collect them (see *Shvi'is* 10:3-4).

וּפְרוֹזְבּוּלִין, — *prozbulin,*

Since the *prozbul* may be written at any time before the end of *Shemitah*, why do we permit it to be written on *Chol HaMoed* of Succos or Pesach — at least half a year before the end of *Shemitah?*

The mishnah refers to a community which usually does not have a *Beth Din* but there happens to be a court in session during *Chol HaMoed (Meiri)*; or someone embarking on a journey to a place without a *Beth Din*. Hence if he cannot write a *prozbul* on *Chol HaMoed*, he might not get a chance to write one before the end of *Shemitah (Nimukei Yosef).*

אִגְּרוֹת שׁוּם, — *evaluation documents,*

I.e., certificates written by the courts evaluating the debtor's property for purposes of liens. This certificate is handed over to the creditor by the courts and serves the creditor as proof of ownership *(Rav).*

Once the courts have evaluated the property, the promissory note would be destroyed prior to the writing of the certificate of evaluation, in order to prevent the creditor from collecting his debt twice (*Bava Basra* 169a). Thus, if the note had been destroyed but the courts were not permitted to write this certificate on *Chol HaMoed*, the creditor might be left without any proof *(Ran).*

The certificate also enables the creditor to transfer the assigned property to someone else as it serves as proof of title *(Talmido Shel Rabbeinu Yechiel MiParis).*

Alternatively, the document was written by the court as evidence of the value of a field which was awarded to one heir while other fields of equal value were awarded to the others *(Rashi).*

וְאִגְּרוֹת מָזוֹן, — *support documents,*

Upon marriage, the bride receives from the groom a כְּתֻבָּה, *marriage contract*, which provides, among other things, that she and their daughters will receive support from the estate in case of the husband's death. When there was no money at hand, the courts would sell a part of the estate to raise funds for their support. In order to prevent the heirs from contesting the sale, the courts would then write a support document.

Alternatively, if one obligates himself to support his stepdaughter for a given period, a certificate is written to that effect. This certificate may be written during *Chol HaMoed* since witnesses may not be

3
3

evaluation documents, support documents, *chalitzah* certificates, refusals, selection contracts, court edicts and government documents.

available afterwards to attest to the obligation *(Rav).*

שְׁטָרֵי חֲלִיצָה, — *chalitzah certificates,*

If a man dies childless, and is survived by a widow and the brother, the widow may not marry anyone other than a brother of her late husband. The brother has the option to perform יִבּוּם, *levirate marriage* [a practice that has been prohibited by the Sages], or חֲלִיצָה, *chalitzah* [lit. *removal*], a rite which releases the widow from her obligation to her brother-in-law and permits her to marry whomever she pleases (*Deut.* 25:5-10). (See tractates *Kiddushin* and *Yevamos).*

The *Beth Din* gives the widow a written verification of her *chalitzah* as evidence of her release from her brother-in-law, and as a sanction for remarriage. If she wishes to embark on a voyage on *Chol HaMoed,* the court may write her this certificate to enable her to remarry abroad *(Talmido shel Rabbeinu Yechiel MiParis).*

Alternatively, she may meet a prospective husband who may not be present after the festival. Since he will not marry her without the certificate of *chalitzah,* it may be written on *Chol HaMoed* since failure to do so may cause an irretrievable loss *(Meiri).* [Although she is not permitted to marry during *Chol HaMoed* (see 1:7) she is permitted to be betrothed (see beginning of this mishnah).]

וּמֵאוּנִים, — *refusals,*

Though the Torah gives only a father the right to give an under-age girl in marriage, in the event he was not living the Rabbis assigned this right to her mother or brothers. They added the proviso that she has the authority to invalidate the marriage before attaining her majority. This מֵאוּן, *refusal* [to continue the marriage], was certified by the court to enable her to marry someone else *(Rav).*

Ran explains that this constitutes a case of irretrievable loss in a case where she will come of age during or immediately after the festival. Thus, if we do not give her the certificate during *Chol HaMoed* she will lose her authority to invalidate the marriage.

Meiri maintains that even if there is no chance of her reaching puberty soon after the festival, it is still a case of irretrievable loss, for she might meet a prospective husband during the festival who may be leaving immediately after the festival. Hence, if she does not possess the certificate during the festival, she will lose her chance to marry him.

וּשְׁטָרֵי בֵרוּרִין, — *selection contracts,*

Each of the two litigants in a civil suit has the right to select one of the three judges who hear the case. This selection is documented lest the litigants recant.

The documentation may be done on *Chol HaMoed* since other acceptable, competent judges might not be found after the festival *(Meiri).*

Or the judge might leave if he is not certified, thereby jeopardizing the prospects for a peaceful settlement *(Nimukei Yosef; Tos. Yom Tov).*

ג
ד

[ד] **אֵין** כּוֹתְבִין שְׁטָרֵי חוֹב בַּמּוֹעֵד, וְאִם אֵינוֹ מַאֲמִינוֹ, אוֹ שֶׁאֵין לוֹ מַה־יֹּאכַל, הֲרֵי זֶה יִכְתֹּב.

יד אברהם

Alternatively, these are documents evidencing the distribution of the property of an estate. The *Beth Din* selects one piece of property for one heir and another one for the other heir. Without this document, the division may be contested, thereby resulting in a loss for one of the heirs *(Rashi; Ran).*

וּגְזֵרוֹת בֵּית דִּין, — *court edicts,*

I.e., rulings handed down by a court during *Chol HaMoed.* If the verdict is not recorded immediately, it may be forgotten and the court may not reach the same decision again. Thus, it fits the criterion of irretrievable loss *(Tos. Yom Tov).*

Alternatively, edicts prescribing flogging or *nidui* [see mishnah 1] of an individual who violated certain laws. If the harsh decision is not recorded, the punishment might not be meted out; hence, people might forget the severity of the violation *(Meiri).*

וְאִגְּרוֹת שֶׁל רָשׁוּת. — *and government documents.*

This refers to either official decrees *(Rashi; Tos.),* or letters written to the government concerning the needs of the community *(Rashi* as quoted by *Ran* and *Ritva).*

These explanations follow the vowelization רָשׁוּת [*rashus*], *government.* Other authorities, however, read רְשׁוּת [*reshus*], *permission,* and understand the mishnah to refer to certificates of permission granted by the *Nassi,* certifying individuals as judges. Since unauthorized judges are liable for damages stemming from certain forms of erroneous decisions, unlike judges authorized by the *Nassi,* lack of such a document is an irretrievable loss and, therefore, it may be written on *Chol HaMoed (Ritva; Ran; Nimukei Yosef).*

Others interpret אִגְּרוֹת שֶׁל רְשׁוּת as *permissible letters,* i.e., social correspondence *(Yerushalmi).*

There are two schools of thought concerning the permissibility of social correspondence during *Chol HaMoed.* One holds that social correspondence contributes to the festive joy of both the recipient who hears from his loved ones, and the sender who contacts his loved ones. However, since the sanction is based on festive needs, it is permissible only if written in an unprofessional manner *(Rambam, Yom Tov 7:14; Ramban; Maggid Mishnah; Ritva).*

The second school holds that the mishnah permits social correspondence only in the case of irretrievable loss, e.g., he might not find a messenger after the festival to convey important information. Accordingly, there is no restriction against writing these letters even professionally *(Ravad; Tos. HaRosh; Ran; Meiri).*

It is customary to write all social correspondence with a שִׁנּוּי, *modification,* such as writing the first line crooked or left-handed. This is permissible only with our cursive writing, which is usually written casually. However, if one tries to write in a beautiful, meticulous manner like a scribe writing official documents, it is forbidden *(Mish-*

3
4

4. We may not write loan contracts during [*Chol*] *HaMoed*. However, if he does not trust him, or if he has nothing to eat, then he may write.

nah Berurah 545:34,35, see *Beur Halachah*). [See *comm.* of *Rama* quoting *Terumos HaDeshen* 87 that the required deviation must be one that is evident in the finished product. Writing left-handed will usually produce a sloppy handwriting and is thus permitted.]

4.

The following may not be written on *Chol Hamoed*, because failure to do so is not considered an irretrievable loss.

אֵין כּוֹתְבִין שְׁטָרֵי חוֹב בַּמּוֹעֵד. — *We may not write loan contracts during* [*Chol*] *HaMoed.*

No loss will occur if the writing of the contract is delayed until after the festival, since the creditor and the debtor trust one another. Therefore, the contract may not be written during *Chol HaMoed (Rav).*

However, if either the debtor or creditor will not be present after the festival, the contract may be written on *Chol HaMoed (Tos. Yom Tov).*

וְאִם אֵינוֹ מַאֲמִינוֹ, — *However, if he does not trust him,*

If the creditor suspects that the debtor will deny having received the loan, or that he will dispute the amount, he will refuse to lend the money unless he receives a note in return. If so, the note may be written since the debtor needs the loan during *Chol HaMoed (Rav).*

There are three differing opinions regarding the sort of loan for which the mishnah permits the writing of a note during *Chol HaMoed.*

Rashi maintains that it may be done even if the borrower needs the money only for investment purposes, rather than to purchase festival needs.

Tur (545) requires that the loan be needed to provide for the festival.

Rambam, however, rules that it is sufficient that the funds will be used during the festival, although not specifically for the festival.

All agree, however, that if it will be impossible for the borrower to obtain the loan after the festival, the note may be written on *Chol HaMoed*, even though the funds will not be needed until afterward *(Magen Avraham* 545:23).

אוֹ שֶׁאֵין לוֹ מַה־יֹּאכַל, הֲרֵי זֶה יִכְתֹּב. — *or if he* [the scribe *(Rashi; Rav)*] *has nothing to eat, then he may write.*

The scribe may practice his craft on *Chol HaMoed* to earn money only if he has *literally* nothing to eat — not even bread and water *(Magen Avraham* 542:1).

Others permit the scribe to write as long as he lacks sufficient food to celebrate the festival properly (*Eliyah Rabbah* 542:3).

Any highly skilled work is permissible in the case of a laborer who has nothing to eat, although the work itself is not needed for the festival (*Shulchan Aruch* 542:2) [see above 2:4].

ג אֵין כּוֹתְבִין סְפָרִים, תְּפִלִּין וּמְזוּזוֹת בַּמּוֹעֵד;
ד וְאֵין מַגִּיהִין אוֹת אַחַת, אֲפִילוּ בְּסֵפֶר הָעֲזָרָה.
רַבִּי יְהוּדָה אוֹמֵר: כּוֹתֵב אָדָם תְּפִלִּין
וּמְזוּזוֹת לְעַצְמוֹ, וְטוֹוֶה עַל יְרֵכוֹ תְּכֵלֶת
לְצִיצִיתוֹ.

יד אברהם

אֵין כּוֹתְבִין סְפָרִים, תְּפִלִּין, וּמְזוּזוֹת בַּמּוֹעֵד; — *We may not write Books [of Scripture], nor tefillin, nor mezuzos during [Chol] HaMoed.*

Even though they are all connected with the performance of precepts, they may not be written — whether for profit or for personal use — unless they are needed for use during the festival itself *(Nimukei Yosef).*

Others maintain that such items may be written on *Chol HaMoed* if they are needed for personal use after the festival *(Ran)* [see *Tos. s.v.* רַבִּי יוֹסֵי]. However, if the writing was purposely delayed for *Chol HaMoed*, it would be prohibited in any case [see above 1:10, 2:3] *(Tif. Yis.).*

וְאֵין מַגִּיהִין אוֹת אַחַת, — *(And) we may not correct a single letter...*

[If an error was detected in a *Sefer Torah*, it may not be corrected during *Chol HaMoed.*]

אֲפִילוּ בְּסֵפֶר הָעֲזָרָה. — *even in the [Torah] Scroll of the Temple court.*

Even the סֵפֶר תּוֹרָה [*Sefer Torah*], *Torah scroll,* from which the *kohen gadol* reads on Yom Kippur may not be repaired, although it is used for a public function at that time *(Rav).*

The scroll is needed by the community only on Yom Kippur. If, however, it were needed for the festival reading, the scribe would be permitted to make the necessary corrections *(Tos. Yom Tov).*

If a congregation has no other *Sefer Torah,* except for one that requires correcting, it may be corrected on *Chol HaMoed (Beis Yosef* 545; *Shulchan Aruch* 545:2).

Other editions of the *Mishnah* read אֲפִילוּ בְּסֵפֶר עֶזְרָא, *even in the Sefer Torah of Ezra.* Ezra the Scribe wrote a *Sefer Torah* which was kept in the Temple area and which was used as the authoritative text whenever questions arose regarding the accuracy of variant renditions *(Rashi).*

רַבִּי יְהוּדָה אוֹמֵר: כּוֹתֵב אָדָם תְּפִלִּין וּמְזוּזוֹת לְעַצְמוֹ, — *R' Yehudah says: A person may write tefillin or mezuzos for his personal use;*

One may write them provided they are not intended for sale or rental *(Rav).* We may infer that one *may* write for others provided he does not do so for profit *(Tos. Yom Tov; Semag; Yerushalmi).*

Magen Avraham (545:3) adds that for personal use, one may write *tefillin* or *mezuzos* even if he will have no need for them until after the festival.

Ran, however, contends that לְעַצְמוֹ, *for his personal use,* is specific. Hence, one would not be allowed to write for others even if he were to give them away gratis.

Maggid Mishnah infers from R' Yehudah's omission of סְפָרִים, *books,* that only *tefillin* and *mezuzos* may be written for personal use after the festival since they can be completed during *Chol HaMoed.* But Torah scrolls cannot usually be

3 We may not write Books [of Scripture], nor *tefil-*
4 *lin,* nor *mezuzos,* during [*Chol*] *HaMoed.* We may not correct a single letter even in the [Torah] scroll of the Temple court. R' Yehudah says: A person may write *tefillin* or *mezuzos* for his personal use; and he may spin the blue thread for his *tzitzis,* on his thigh.

YAD AVRAHAM

completed during the few days of *Chol HaMoed* and their writing would have to be continued after the festival in any case. Therefore, the Sages did not permit the writing of such scrolls.

Some commentators deduce from this mishnah that we are obliged to wear *tefillin* on *Chol HaMoed.* Otherwise, we would not be allowed to write them on *Chol HaMoed* for they would not be needed during the festival.[1]

Others hold that *Chol Hamoed* is not a time for wearing *tefillin,* since the festival itself with all its *mitzvos* is equivalent to the Sabbath when *tefillin* are not worn *(Tos. Menachos* 36b; *Rosh, Halachos Ketanos).* Why, then, are we permitted to write them on *Chol HaMoed*?

The mishnah is referring to a case where the *tefillin* are needed immediately after the festival. Since there would not be sufficient time to prepare them after the festival, they may be written on *Chol HaMoed (Meiri).*

וְטֹוֶה עַל יְרֵכוֹ תְּכֵלֶת לְצִיצִיתוֹ. — *and he may spin the blue thread for his tzitzis, on his thigh.*

[As part of the commandment of צִיצִית, *fringes,* which must be affixed to four corners of garments having the proper size and configurations, one thread of the fringes must be תְּכֵלֶת, *wool dyed a special sky-blue shade (Numbers* 15:38). The dye was made from חִלָּזוֹן, *chalazon,* a rare amphibian whose identity is no longer known. Therefore, the particular commandment of adding *techeiles* to the *tzitzis* cannot be observed, although the general commandment of wearing *tzitzis* can still be fulfilled. The mishnah permits the twisting of the *techeiles* wool into thread for use with *tzitzis,* but only provided it is done with a שִׁנּוּי, *modification,* of the normal manner. Thus, it is made apparent to all observers that although material is being prepared for the essential performance of a *mitzvah,* the sanctity of *Chol HaMoed* is maintained by not engaging in the typical, workday manner of spinning thread.]

The thread may be spun only by rolling the wool against the thigh, but it may not be done in a more professional manner, whether by the use of a spinning wheel or even twisting by hand. The *halachah,* however, is that *techeiles* may be spun without a deviation. Only the use of a spinning wheel is forbidden because it is so conspicuous *(Rav;* see also 545:3).

1. The question of the obligation to wear *tefillin* during *Chol HaMoed* was not resolved. The custom of Ashkenazic communities (with the exception of those in *Eretz Yisrael*) is to put on *tefillin* though some do so without reciting a blessing *(Taz* 31:2; *Mishnah Berurah).* According to the ruling of *Beis Yosef* and *Vilna Gaon, tefillin* are not worn during *Chol HaMoed.* This is the custom of Sephardic and Chassidic communities, and the Ashkenazic community in *Eretz Yisrael.*

ג
ה

[ה] **הַקּוֹבֵר** אֶת־מֵתוֹ שְׁלֹשָׁה יָמִים קֹדֶם לָרֶגֶל, בָּטְלָה הֵימֶנּוּ גְּזֵרַת שִׁבְעָה; שְׁמֹנָה, בָּטְלָה הֵימֶנּוּ גְּזֵרַת שְׁלֹשִׁים — מִפְּנֵי שֶׁאָמְרוּ: שַׁבָּת עוֹלָה וְאֵינָהּ מַפְסֶקֶת, רְגָלִים מַפְסִיקִין וְאֵינָן עוֹלִין.

יד אברהם

5.

◆§ Mourning Periods

The remainder of our chapter deals with the laws of mourning as they are affected by the incidence of a festival. Simultaneous observance of both is impossible since the festival laws require joy, while mourning requires the absence of joy.

Mourning must be observed by the relatives enumerated in *Leviticus* 21:2-3. They are: parent, child, spouse, and sibling. For a parent, one must observe laws of mourning for twelve months; for the other relatives, restrictions apply for thirty days following burial. The laws apply to three distinct periods of time with diminishing severity: The first and strictest is שִׁבְעָה [*shivah*], *seven*, i.e., the initial seven-day period; next comes the period from *shivah's* conclusion to the end of שְׁלֹשִׁים [*sheloshim*], *thirty*, days; then, for children mourning their parents, the remainder of the twelve month period.

...הַקּוֹבֵר אֶת־מֵתוֹ — *He who buries his dead* [*relative*]...

A close relative died and was buried. [Although the mishnah speaks of one who buries his dead, the laws of mourning apply to close relatives whether or not they participated physically in the burial.] The mishnah stresses burial because אֲבֵלוּת, *mourning*, does not commence until after the burial *(Tos. Yom Tov; Tos.)*.

,שְׁלֹשָׁה יָמִים קֹדֶם לָרֶגֶל — *three days before a festival,*

I.e., if one observed the regulations of mourning for three days prior to the advent of a festival *(Rav; Rashi* on *Rif; Rashi* ms.).

;בָּטְלָה הֵימֶנּוּ גְּזֵרַת שִׁבְעָה — *has the edict of seven* [*days of mourning*] *annulled;*

Once he has observed three days of mourning before the onset of the festival, it is considered as if he has completed the entire *shivah*. If, however, the mourner had mourned for only two days, the festival interrupts, but does not annul the *shivah*. Thus, the remaining days would be observed after the festival.

The reason for this distinction is that the first three days are the main part of *shivah*. The mourning is more intense on these days, as the *Gemara* (27b) states: ,שְׁלֹשָׁה לְבֶכִי [the first] *three* [*days*] *are for weeping (Tos.* 19a; *Nimukei Yosef)*.

Halachically, there are differences between the regulations of the first three days and those of the remainder of the *shivah*. For example, we find that during the former period the mourner may not acknowledge a greeting — rather he must inform the people who greet him of his status — whereas during the latter period he may acknowledge the greeting (*Gem.* 21b).

Moreover, if a mourner is poor, he may work secretly in the confines of his house from the fourth

3 5. He who buries his dead [relative] three days
5 before a festival has the edict of the seven [days of mourning] annulled. [He who buries his dead relative] eight [days before a festival] has the edict of thirty [days of mourning] annulled. [This is so] because they said: Sabbath is included [in the period of mourning] but does not interrupt [it]. Festivals [however], interrupt but are not included.

day on. During the first three days, however, he may not perform any work *(Gem.* 21b).

Rabbeinu Yerucham (28:2) quotes *Rabad* who bases this stringency on the maxim [*Gem.* 27b cited above]: שְׁלֹשָׁה לְבֶכִי, *Three days are for weeping.* If one is occupied with his work, he is distracted from weeping for the dead.

In the case of one who has mourned for three days, the festival annuls only the regulations pertaining to *shivah;* those obligations related to *sheloshim,* however, are still applicable after the festival.

The *halachah* is that the advent of a festival annuls the regulations of *shivah* even if only an hour of mourning had been observed *(Rav).*

,שְׁמֹנָה — [*He who buries his dead relative*] *eight* [*days before a festival*]...

Thus, he had completed the entire *shivah* period plus one day of the *sheloshim* before the advent of a festival *(Rav).*

—בָּטְלָה הֵימֶנּוּ גְּזֵרַת שְׁלֹשִׁים — *has the edict of thirty* [*days of mourning*] *annulled.*

Since he observed one day of the *sheloshim* period before the festival, the rest of the period is annulled and he need not observe it after the festival *(Rav).*

The *halachah* is that even if one had completed only the seven day period of *shivah,* the *sheloshim* is annulled, for the last day of *shivah* is also considered the first day of *sheloshim.* This is based on the principle that מִקְצַת הַיּוֹם כְּכֻלּוֹ, *part of a day is considered like an entire day.* For this reason, *shivah* is always considered as having ended a short while after the morning of the seventh day begins. Therefore, the remainder of the seventh day is regarded as the first day of *sheloshim* and, since the *sheloshim* is annulled, the mourner may cut his hair and launder his clothing on the eve of the festival in honor of the festival *(Yoreh Deah* 399:2).

:מִפְּנֵי שֶׁאָמְרוּ — [*This is so*] *because they* [i.e., the Sages] *said:*

Since the regulations of the mourning period are Rabbinically ordained, the Sages are empowered to prescribe the procedures pertaining to mourning periods interrupted by the advent of a festival *(Ritva).*

,שַׁבָּת עוֹלָה וְאֵינָהּ מַפְסֶקֶת — *Sabbath is included* [*in the period of mourning*] *but does not interrupt* [*it*].

Because some regulations of mourning [those observed in private, such as abstention from marital relations] are observed on the Sabbath, it is counted as a day of *shivah* rather than as an interruption. Hence, if one began *shivah*

[ו] **רַבִּי** אֱלִיעֶזֶר אוֹמֵר: מִשֶּׁחָרַב בֵּית הַמִּקְדָּשׁ, עֲצֶרֶת כַּשַּׁבָּת. רַבָּן גַּמְלִיאֵל אוֹמֵר: רֹאשׁ הַשָּׁנָה וְיוֹם הַכִּפּוּרִים כָּרְגָלִים. וַחֲכָמִים אוֹמְרִים: לֹא כְדִבְרֵי זֶה וְלֹא כְדִבְרֵי זֶה; אֶלָּא עֲצֶרֶת כָּרְגָלִים, רֹאשׁ הַשָּׁנָה וְיוֹם הַכִּפּוּרִים כַּשַּׁבָּת.

יד אברהם

three days prior to the Sabbath, the Sabbath is considered the fourth day *(Rav).*

The obligations of mourning are incompatible with a festival since festivals must be celebrated with שִׂמְחָה, *joy.* Even private expressions of mourning interfere with joy which is an attitude and feeling rather than a form of behavior. On the Sabbath, however, the observance of the day calls not for joy but for עֹנֶג, *pleasure,* hence the laws of mourning are relaxed, but not interrupted. The only restrictions that are relaxed are those that are incompatible with עֹנֶג, *pleasure,* such as wearing leather shoes *(Tos. Yom Tov; Nimukei Yosef).* [The *halachah* is, however, that if one did not learn of his relative's death until the festival, or if the demise took place during the festival, then private expressions of mourning are observed even during the festival. See *Yoreh Deah* 399:1,2.]

Additionally, *Tur (Yoreh Deah* 400) and *Ramban* point out that the Sages must have intended that the Sabbath be counted as one of the days of *shivah* since every seven-day *shivah* period must include a Sabbath *(Tos. Yom Tov).*

...רְגָלִים מַפְסִיקִין — *Festivals* [*however,*] *interrupt...*

The laws of *shivah* are annulled by the onset of a festival if it falls after part of the *shivah* had been observed *(Meiri).*

.וְאֵינָן עוֹלִין — *but are not included.*

If burial takes place less than two days before the festival (according to the mishnah) or during the festival (according to the *halachah*), the *shivah* period must be completed after the festival *(Rav).*

Since the festival week is one of joy, it cannot be included in the days of mourning *(Nimukei Yosef).*

6.

רַבִּי אֱלִיעֶזֶר אוֹמֵר: מִשֶּׁחָרַב בֵּית הַמִּקְדָּשׁ, .עֲצֶרֶת כַּשַּׁבָּת — *R' Eliezer says: From the time the Temple was destroyed Shavuos is like the Sabbath.*

I.e., it is included in the mourning period of *shivah,* and does not interrupt it (see previous mishnah).

R' Eliezer maintains that festivals should have had the same status as the Sabbath in that they should become part of *shivah* with only a relaxation of the mourning. However, since Pesach and Succos are at least a week long, in the event burial took place immediately before the festival or on a festival day (see *Beitzah* 6a) there would be no proper manifestation of mourning;

3
6

6. R′ Eliezer says: From the time the Temple was destroyed Shavuos is like the Sabbath.

Rabban Gamliel says: Rosh HaShanah and Yom Kippur are like the festivals.

The Sages, however, do not agree with either of the two. Rather, Shavuos is like the festivals; Rosh HaShanah and Yom Kippur are like the Sabbath.

hence the Sages ordained that those festivals would not be counted as part of the *shivah*. Therefore, if no part of *shivah* had been observed prior to the festival, a full seven-day observance begins upon the festival's conclusion. Since the seven day festival period is not part of the mourning observance, it is considered an interruption.

However, in Temple times, Shavuos, too, was regarded as tantamount to a week long, because the חֲגִיגָה, *festival offering*, could be brought for a full seven-day period [during which there was general rejoicing]. Following the destruction of the Temple, Shavuos reverts to its status as a brief festival, and is, for the purpose of *shivah*, treated like the Sabbath *(Tos. Yom Tov; Nimukei Yosef)*.

According to R′ Eliezer, Rosh HaShanah and Yom Kippur are certainly considered to be like the Sabbath since they are always brief festivals *(Tos. Yom Tov; Tos.)*.

רַבָּן גַּמְלִיאֵל אוֹמֵר: רֹאשׁ הַשָּׁנָה וְיוֹם הַכִּפּוּרִים כָּרְגָלִים. — *Rabban Gamliel says: Rosh HaShanah and Yom Kippur are like the festivals.*

Not only is Shavuos considered to be like the other festivals [even after the festival offering was discontinued], but so are Rosh HaShanah and Yom Kippur. All festivals are likened to one another for they are equally termed מוֹעֲדֵי ה׳, *appointed seasons of HASHEM (Lev.* 23:4). Therefore, they all interrupt the *shivah* period *(Tos. Yom Tov)*.

וַחֲכָמִים אוֹמְרִים: לֹא כְּדִבְרֵי זֶה וְלֹא כְּדִבְרֵי זֶה; — *The Sages, however, do not agree with either of the two;*

[I.e., in contrast to the rulings of R′ Eliezer and of Rabban Gamliel, they hold that there is a basic difference between Shavuos and Rosh HaShanah and Yom Kippur.]

אֶלָּא עֲצֶרֶת כָּרְגָלִים, רֹאשׁ הַשָּׁנָה וְיוֹם הַכִּפּוּרִים כַּשַּׁבָּת. — *Rather, Shavuos is like the festivals; Rosh HaShanah and Yom Kippur are like the Sabbath.*

[Shavuos is considered like the other festivals, for it, too, requires joy, thus it is excluded from mourning; whereas Rosh HaShanah and Yom Kippur are like the Sabbath for neither of them has the requirement of joy.]

The *halachah* is in accordance with Rabban Gamliel's opinion that all three are considered as festivals since the Torah describes them equally as *appointed seasons of HASHEM*. As such, they interrupt either *shivah* or *sheloshim*, as the case may be *(Rav)*.

ג
ז

[ז] **אֵין** קוֹרְעִין, וְלֹא חוֹלְצִין, וְאֵין מַבְרִין, אֶלָּא קְרוֹבָיו שֶׁל מֵת. וְאֵין מַבְרִין אֶלָּא עַל מִטָּה זְקוּפָה.

יד אברהם

7.

◆§ Rending Garments in Mourning

[Although the restrictions of *shivah* and *sheloshim* are suspended on festivals, some mourning practices are observed during *Chol HaMoed*. The next two mishnayos specify them and their applicability on *Chol HaMoed*. Concerning the first two laws of mishnah 7 where the word מוֹעֵד, [*Chol*] *HaMoed*, is not used, there is a difference of opinion among the commentators as to whether these laws are general and apply all year round rather than only to *Chol HaMoed*. The varying interpretations will be discussed in the commentary.]

The laws of קְרִיעָה [*keriah*], *rending*, of garments are derived from [or supported by] Scriptural sources. It is first indicated in *Leviticus* 10:6 where Aaron instructed his surviving sons, Elazar and Isamar, that because of their responsibilities to continue performing the Tabernacle service, they were not to tear their clothing in mourning over the death of their brothers Nadav and Avihu. From this is derived that all seven relatives — father, mother, brother, sister, son, daughter, and spouse — who are required to observe the laws of mourning *(Lev.* 21:2-3) are required to rend their garments. See *Yoreh Deah* 340 for the complete laws of rending as they have been formulated in the *halachah*.

אֵין קוֹרְעִין, — *Garments may not be rent,*

Rav interprets this law as limited to *Chol HaMoed*. Thus, garments may be torn in mourning on *Chol HaMoed* only for one of the seven relatives. [At other times, one is *permitted* but not required to rend garments in mourning even for others.] However, if the deceased is a great sage, this limitation does not apply. Similarly, this limitation does not apply to those present at the time of the demise of any Jew *(Rav* from *Gem.* 24a).[1]

The prevalent custom is to rend the clothing only when present at the demise of one noted for his piety (*Rama, Yoreh Deah* 340:6).

Alternatively, this portion of mishnah is *not* limited to *Chol HaMoed*. Rather, it refers to tearing one's garment in mourning *at any time*. Accordingly, one may not rend his garments unless the deceased is a relative for whom he is required to observe the laws of mourning. Otherwise, for one to tear his garments falls within the prohibition לֹא תַשְׁחִית, *do not cause unnecessary destruction* or *waste* [*Deut.* 20:19]. (See *Meiri, Otzar HaGeonim*, p. 45).

According to this interpretation, since the mishnah allows *keriah* only for relatives even during ordinary days, such rending would be prohibited on *Chol HaMoed* even

1. The practice of tearing one's garment as a sign of mourning for the death of a sage or a man noted for his piety dates from Talmudic times, but was later discarded. However, one is required to tear upon the death of a teacher from whom he acquired most of his Torah wisdom, for a teacher is considered to be like a father in terms of the honor due him (see *Aruch HaShulchan* 340).

3
7

7. Garments may not be rent, shoulders may not be bared, and the mourner's meal may not be served, except by relatives of the deceased. The mourner's meal is only served on a set up bed.

for relatives *(Beis Yosef; Bach; Yoreh Deah* 340; *Raviah).*

Because of this dispute, it is the practice of the German Jewish community to perform *keriah* on *Chol HaMoed* only for a father or mother, and to wait until after the festival to tear garments in mourning for other relatives. The custom of Polish Jews, however, is to perform *keriah* for all relatives on *Chol HaMoed (Rama; Yoreh Deah* 340:31; *Shach).*

וְלֹא חוֹלְצִין, — *shoulders may not be bared,*

It was customary to tear one's clothes at the shoulder and walk before the bier with the shoulder and arm exposed as a sign of mourning (*Rav; Rashi, Bava Kamma* 17a); or they would tear the garment and thrust the arm through the tear *(Rif);* or the collar opening would be extended to expose the arm *(Nimukei Yosef).* However, this custom is no longer practiced *(Tif. Yis.).*

וְאֵין מַבְרִין, — *and the mourner's meal may not be served,*

The first meal partaken of by mourners after burial is not their own; it is paid for, prepared, and served by others. In Mishnaic times, the meal was served publicly, in the street. During *Chol HaMoed,* however, it was served by relatives in the privacy of the home *(Rav).*

The origin of this practice is found in *Ezekiel* 24:17 וְלֶחֶם אֲנָשִׁים לֹא תֹאכֵל, *and the food of* [*other*] *people you shall not eat.* Since the mourning prophet was instructed not to eat other people's food, the implication is that ordinarily, mourners should eat food paid for and prepared by others.

According to the interpretation that the mishnah is dealing only with *Chol HaMoed* (see above), the mishnah prohibits this meal from being served for nonmourners on *Chol HaMoed.* However, during weekdays when the meal is served, even nonmourners may partake of it.

According to the interpretation that the mishnah refers not to *Chol HaMoed,* but to all cases of mourning, the mishnah prohibits nonmourners from partaking of the meal. On *Chol HaMoed,* however, no mourner's meal is served *(Ritva).*

אֶלָּא קְרוֹבָיו שֶׁל מֵת; — *except by relatives of the deceased.*

According to the first interpretation cited above, only those required to observe mourning may perform these acts during *Chol HaMoed.* According to the second interpretation, these acts of mourning apply only to relatives required to observe the laws of mourning, whatever the time of year *(Ritva).*

וְאֵין מַבְרִין אֶלָּא עַל מִטָּה זְקוּפָה. —*The mourner's meal is only served on a set up bed.*

One of the mourning practices observed during *shivah* in Mishnaic times was that the beds and sofas of the mourners were overturned. The above dispute over whether the mishnah refers only to *Chol*

ג ח

אֵין מוֹלִיכִין לְבֵית הָאֵבֶל לֹא בְטַבְלָא וְלֹא בְאִסְקוּטְלָא וְלֹא בְקָנוֹן, אֶלָּא בְסַלִּים. וְאֵין אוֹמְרִים בִּרְכַּת אֲבֵלִים בַּמּוֹעֵד, אֲבָל עוֹמְדִין בַּשּׁוּרָה וּמְנַחֲמִין; וּפוֹטְרִין אֶת־הָרַבִּים.

[ח] **אֵין** מַנִּיחִין אֶת־הַמִּטָּה בָּרְחוֹב, שֶׁלֹּא לְהַרְגִּיל אֶת־הַהֶסְפֵּד; וְלֹא שֶׁל נָשִׁים לְעוֹלָם, מִפְּנֵי הַכָּבוֹד.

HaMoed applies to this part of the mishnah as well.

According to *Rav's* interpretation, the mishnah refers only to mourning during *Chol HaMoed*. Although the year round practice is to serve the meal while the mourners sit on overturned couches, on *Chol HaMoed* this practice is not observed; the couches remain erect.

Alternatively, the mishnah states that all year round couches are not overturned by mourners until the consolers leave upon completion of the mourner's meal. As long as the visitors are present, the couches are left erect. On *Chol HaMoed*, however, the mourner's meal is not served at all according to this view (*Otzar HaGeonim*, p. 46).

אֵין מוֹלִיכִין לְבֵית הָאֵבֶל... — *We may not bring* [*food*] *to the house of mourning...*

For the mourner's meal *(Rav, Tif. Yis.; Ran).*

לֹא בְטַבְלָא... — *neither on a tray,*

I.e., on an elaborate tray *(Tif. Yis.)* even though it demonstrates esteem for the mourner *(Ran).*

Alternatively, a טַבְלָא is a *table* of silver, gold, or glass. The word is derived from the Latin *tabula (Aruch).*

וְלֹא בְאִסְקוּטְלָא... — *nor on a salver,*

I.e., a silver bowl. The term is derived from the Latin *skutella (Aruch; Nimukei Yosef; Rav; Tif. Yis.).*

Alternatively, it means a small table *(Rashi* on *Rif; Ran; Nimukei Yosef; Rav).*

וְלֹא בְקָנוֹן, — *nor in a decorative basket,*

The translation follows *Tiferes Yisrael.* Others render a large woven reed basket *(Aruch; Ran)* or a large basket used for measuring wheat *(Rashi* on *Rif).*

אֶלָּא בְסַלִּים. — *but only in* [*plain*] *baskets.*

The meal must be brought in ordinary baskets of peeled willow twigs (*Ran; Rav; Gem.* 27a).

This regulation was instituted for the benefit of the poor, who could ill afford expensive vessels in which to bring the food. Lest they be embarrassed, the Rabbis instituted that all visitors bring their food to the house of mourning in ordinary willow baskets (*Rav; Gem.* 27a).

Even on *Chol HaMoed*, the food is brought in simple willow baskets; we do not honor the festival by adorning the meal to give it the appearance of an elaborate gift rather than a mourner's repast *(Nimukei Yosef; Rivav; Ramban).*

3 We may not bring [food] to the house of mourning
8 neither on a tray, nor on a salver, nor on a decorative basket; but only in [plain] baskets.

We do not say the mourner's blessing during [*Chol*] *HaMoed*, but we stand in rows and offer consolation. They then dismiss the public.

8. We do not set down the bier in the street, so as not to encourage eulogies. [The biers] of women are never [set down], out of respect.

YAD AVRAHAM

וְאֵין אוֹמְרִים בִּרְכַּת אֲבֵלִים בַּמּוֹעֵד, — *We do not say the mourner's blessing during* [*Chol*] *HaMoed,*

I.e., the blessing recited when the mourners partake of the mourner's meal in the town square after returning from the burial (see *Megillah* 4:3).

אֲבָל עוֹמְדִים בַּשּׁוּרָה... — *but we stand in rows...*

Those who accompany the bier form two rows through which the mourners pass after the burial to receive the consolation of bystanders (see *Megillah* 4:3).

וּמְנַחֲמִין... — *and offer consolation.*

To the mourners as they pass between the rows (see *Berachos* 3:2).

וּפוֹטְרִין אֶת־הָרַבִּים. — *They then dismiss the public.*

The mourners dismiss the public immediately, omitting the usual rite of reciting the mourner's blessing in the public square (*Rashi* on *Rif; Nimukei Yosef; Ran* quoting *Rabbeinu Yehonasan; Rav).*

Alternatively, *they free the public* from repeating this rite even after the festival (*Rabad* quoted by *Nimukei Yosef; Meiri).*

Alternatively, they dismiss the public with the *usual* blessing of לְכוּ לְשָׁלוֹם לְאָהֳלֵיכֶם, *Go to your homes in peace.* Even though mourners are generally forbidden to greet, it is permissible for them to greet during the festival *(Ran).*

Alternatively, the mourners dismiss those standing in the rows and permit them to leave immediately, contrary to the usual procedure whereby the consolers accompany the mourners *(Tif. Yis.).*

8.

אֵין מַנִּיחִין אֶת־הַמִּטָּה בָּרְחוֹב, — *We do not set down the bier in the street,*

Though the bier is usually set down to permit eulogies, the practice is dispensed with during *Chol HaMoed.* Although the mishnah does not specify *Chol HaMoed*, it is clear from the context which period is meant *(Meiri; Nimukei Yosef; Rav).*

According to *Rashi* on the *Rif*, the word בַּמּוֹעֵד, *on* [*Chol*] *HaMoed*, does appear in the mishnah's text...

שֶׁלֹּא לְהַרְגִּיל אֶת־הַהֶסְפֵּד; — *so as not to encourage eulogies.*

ג נָשִׁים בַּמּוֹעֵד מְעַנּוֹת, אֲבָל לֹא מְטַפְּחוֹת.
ט רַבִּי יִשְׁמָעֵאל אוֹמֵר: הַסְּמוּכוֹת לַמִּטָּה מְטַפְּחוֹת.

[ט] **בְּרָאשֵׁי** חֳדָשִׁים, בַּחֲנֻכָּה וּבְפוּרִים, מְעַנּוֹת וּמְטַפְּחוֹת בָּזֶה וּבָזֶה; אֲבָל לֹא מְקוֹנְנוֹת. נִקְבַּר הַמֵּת, לֹא מְעַנּוֹת וְלֹא מְטַפְּחוֹת. אֵיזֶהוּ עִנּוּי? שֶׁכֻּלָּן עוֹנוֹת כְּאַחַת; קִינָה? שֶׁאַחַת מְדַבֶּרֶת וְכֻלָּן עוֹנוֹת אַחֲרֶיהָ, שֶׁנֶּאֱמַר: „וְלַמֵּדְנָה בְנֹתֵיכֶם נֶהִי, וְאִשָּׁה רְעוּתָהּ קִינָה". אֲבָל לֶעָתִיד לָבֹא הוּא אוֹמֵר „בִּלַּע הַמָּוֶת לָנֶצַח, וּמָחָה ה' אֱלֹהִים דִּמְעָה מֵעַל כָּל־פָּנִים, וגו' (וְחֶרְפַּת עַמּוֹ יָסִיר מֵעַל כָּל־הָאָרֶץ, כִּי ה' דִּבֵּר)."

יד אברהם

Were the bier to be put down for any reason, people would be encouraged to eulogize, a practice which is forbidden on *Chol HaMoed (Tif. Yis.).*

Alternatively, the bier is not set down on the way to burial, as it encourages weeping which is contrary to the spirit of the holiday *(Ran).*

וְלֹא שֶׁל נָשִׁים לְעוֹלָם, — [*The biers*] *of women are never set down,*

Even if burial takes place on a weekday, the practice of setting the bier down in the street is dispensed with *(Tif. Yis.).*

מִפְּנֵי הַכָּבוֹד. — *out of respect.*

I.e., out of respect for the deceased woman, as the corpse may still secrete fluids *(Rashi).*

Alternatively, it is degrading to living women to have a deceased woman clothed only in burial shrouds set down in front of men *(Nimukei Yosef).*

R' Eliezer (*Gem.* 28a) finds support for this law in the implication of the Torah's statement: וַתָּמָת שָׁם מִרְיָם וַתִּקָּבֵר שָׁם, *and Miriam died there and was buried there (Num.* 20:1); she was buried immediately after death *(Rav; Gem.* 28a).

נָשִׁים בַּמּוֹעֵד מְעַנּוֹת, — *Women may sing dirges during* [*Chol*] *HaMoed,*

Although eulogies are proscribed, the women may sing dirges as described in the next mishnah *(Tif. Yis.).*

אֲבָל לֹא מְטַפְּחוֹת. — *but may not clap.*

They may not pound their hands together as a sign of sorrow. However, if the deceased was a sage, they may do so, as the death of a great person takes precedence over the restrictions of *Chol HaMoed.* Nowadays, however, no one is deemed a sage of a high enough degree to override the honor of *Chol HaMoed (Tif. Yis.).*

Women may sing dirges during [*Chol*] *HaMoed*, but may not clap. R' Yishmael says: Those near the bier may clap.

9. On *Rosh Chodesh*, Chanukah, and Purim, [they] may sing dirges and clap on any of these days, but they may not engage in [responsive] wailing.

Once the deceased is buried, they may neither sing dirges, nor clap.

What is meant by dirges? That all lament in unison. [And what is meant by] wailing? That one speaks and all others respond after her; as the verse states: *And teach your daughters a lament and each woman* [shall teach] *her neighbor a wailing* [*Jer.* 9:19].

However, as regards the future, the verse states: *He will destroy death forever, and my Lord, HASHEM/ELOHIM, will wipe tears from upon every face, (He will remove the shame of His people from the entire earth — for HASHEM has spoken)* [*Isa.* 25:8].

YAD AVRAHAM

Alternatively, they may not beat their chests as an expression of pain (*Rashi* on *Rif; Nimukei Yosef*).

רַבִּי יִשְׁמָעֵאל אוֹמֵר, הַסְּמוּכוֹת לְמִטָּה מְטַפְּחוֹת. — *R' Yishmael says: Those near the bier may clap.*

Rav amends the text to read R' Shimon. *Maggid Mishnah* amends it to read: *Rabban Shimon Ben Gamliel.*

Rav notes that the *halachah* does not recognize a difference between those close to the bier and those at a distance. None may clap.

9.

בְּרָאשֵׁי חֳדָשִׁים, בַּחֲנֻכָּה וּבְפוּרִים, מְעַנּוֹת וּמְטַפְּחוֹת בָּזֶה וּבָזֶה: — *On Rosh Chodesh, Chanukah and Purim, [they] may sing dirges and clap on any of these days* [lit. *on this and on this*],

[The women mentioned in the preceding mishnah, who were wont to sing dirges and clap their hands at funerals, may do so if the funeral falls on *Rosh Chodesh*, Chanukah, or Purim. In this respect, these days are less stringent than *Chol HaMoed* when such expressions of grief are forbidden.]

אֲבָל לֹא מְקוֹנְנוֹת; — *but they may not engage in [responsive] wailing.*

Below, the mishnah describes what is meant by 'responsive wailing.' It is regarded as a greater expression of grief than either clapping or wailing, and is therefore forbidden *(Tif. Yis.)*.

We have presented the reading of most editions of *Mishnah* and *Yerushalmi*. However, the reading of the *Gemara, Rif, Rosh,* and *Maggid Mishnah* is בָּזֶה וּבָזֶה לֹא מְקוֹנְנוֹת, *on* [*both*] *these and on those* [i.e., *Chol HaMoed* and the other occasions mentioned above] *it is forbidden to engage in responsive wailing.*

נִקְבַּר הַמֵּת, לֹא מְעַנּוֹת וְלֹא מְטַפְּחוֹת. — *Once the deceased is buried, they may neither sing dirges, nor clap.*

Although they are permitted to sing dirges and clap they may do so only *before* the burial on *Rosh Chodesh,* Chanukah, and Purim, but they must cease once the burial is completed *(Nimukei Yosef; Tos. Yom Tov).*

אֵיזֶהוּ עִנּוּי? שֶׁכֻּלָּן עוֹנוֹת כְּאַחַת. — *What is meant by dirges* [*mentioned above*]*? That all lament in unison.*

[The permissible dirges are recited by all the women in unison.]

קִינָה? שֶׁאַחַת מְדַבֶּרֶת וְכֻלָּן עוֹנוֹת אַחֲרֶיהָ; — [*And what is meant by*] *wailing? When one speaks and all others respond after her;*

[One woman leads the lament and the others repeat after her. This form of lamentation, with a leader and chorus, is more moving and causes more grief on the part of the participant.]

שֶׁנֶּאֱמַר: ,,וְלַמֵּדְנָה בְנֹתֵיכֶם נֶהִי וְאִשָּׁה רְעוּתָהּ קִינָה.'' — *as the verse states: And teach your daughters a lament and each woman* [*shall teach*] *her neighbor a wailing (Jeremiah 9:19).*

The implication of the verse is that קִינָה, *wailing,* is said by one and repeated by the assembled listeners *(Rav).*

אֲבָל לֶעָתִיד לָבֹא הוּא אוֹמֵר: — *However, as regards the future, the verse states:*

Regarding the time of תְּחִיַּת הַמֵּתִים, *resurrection of the dead,* the applicable verse is ... *(Tif. Yis.).*

,,בִּלַּע הַמָּוֶת לָנֶצַח, וּמָחָה ה' אֱלֹהִים דִּמְעָה מֵעַל כָּל־פָּנִים.'' — *He will destroy death forever, and my Lord* HASHEM/ELOHIM, *will wipe away tears from upon every face.*

There will be no reason for lamenting or wailing since death will be done away with. Instead it will be a time to sing new songs of praise to God *(Tif. Yis.).*

Although it is irrelevant to the subject of *Chol HaMoed,* the Tanna cites this verse because it is customary to end a tractate on a cheerful note *(Rav).*

סליק מסכת מועד קטן

◆§ מסכת חגיגה

◆§ Tractate Chagigah

Translation and anthologized commentary by
Rabbi Avrohom Yoseif Rosenberg

Mesorah Publications, ltd

◆§ Tractate Chagigah

They shall not appear before Me empty-handed... three times during the year all your males shall appear before the Master, HASHEM *(Exodus 23:15,17).*

Three pilgrimages shall you celebrate to Me each year (Exodus 23:14).

You shall be joyful before HASHEM *your God... you shall be joyful on your festivals (Deuteronomy 16:11,14).*

You shall slaughter peace offerings, and you shall eat there; and you shall be joyful before HASHEM *your God (Deuteronomy 27:7).*

◆§ Olas Re'eyah

Pesach, Shavuos, and Succos are the שָׁלֹשׁ רְגָלִים, *three pilgrimage festivals.* Every Jewish male is commanded to appear at the בֵּית הַמִּקְדָּשׁ [*Beis HaMikdash*], *Holy Temple,* during these festivals. However, he must not appear with empty hands, but should bring an עוֹלָה [*olah*], *burnt offering,* as a קָרְבָּן [*korban*], *sacrifice.* This pilgrimage to the *Beis HaMikdash* is called רְאִיָּה [*re'eyah*], *appearance,* and the accompanying *korban* is known as עוֹלַת רְאִיָּה [*olas re'eyah*], *burnt offering of appearance,* or just רְאִיָּה, *re'eyah.*

◆§ Shalmei Chagigah

Concomitant with the command of appearance is the command תָּחֹג, *you shall celebrate (Exod.* 23:14). The *Gemara* (10b) cites various verses which indicate that celebration requires the bringing of שְׁלָמִים [*shelamim*], *peace offerings.* Hence, along with the *olas re'eyah,* each male must bring שַׁלְמֵי חֲגִיגָה [*shalmei chagigah*], *peace offerings of celebration,* or *festival.* The name of this sacrifice is often shortened to just *chagigah.* It is from the name of this *korban* that tractate *Chagigah* gets its name.

◆§ Shalmei Simchah

There is yet another sacrifice to be offered alongside these two. The Jew is enjoined to be joyful before his God when he appears before Him during the festivals. But how is this joyfulness to be manifested? By slaughtering *shelamim* and partaking of their meat. If the *shalmei chagigah* do not supply enough meat, then additional *shelomim* must be brought. These additional *korbanos* are called שַׁלְמֵי שִׂמְחָה [*shalmei simchah*], *peace offerings of joy.*

Although named *Chagigah,* this tractate's central theme is a discussion of all three of these sacrifices (based on *Meiri).*

◆§Yom Tov and Chol HaMoed

To distinguish between that part of the Succos and Pesach festivals which are of greater sanctity [i.e., the first and last day(s)] and the days of lesser sanctity [i.e., the intermediate days] we use the expressions יוֹם טוֹב [*Yom Tov*], *holiday* [lit., *good day*], for the former, and חוֹל הַמּוֹעֵד [*Chol HaMoed*], *intermediate days* [lit., *ordinary day of the festival*], for the latter. (See preface to tractate *Moed Katan.*)

א
א

[א] **הַכֹּל** חַיָּבִין בִּרְאִיָּה, חוּץ מֵחֵרֵשׁ, שׁוֹטֶה, וְקָטָן, וְטֻמְטוּם, וְאַנְדְּרוֹגִינוֹס, וְנָשִׁים, וַעֲבָדִים שֶׁאֵינָם

יד אברהם

Chapter 1

1.

הַכֹּל חַיָּבִין בִּרְאִיָּה, — *All are obligated in re'eyah...*

All Jews, with the exception of those enumerated further, are obligated to ascend to Jerusalem for the three pilgrimage festivals, Pesach, Shavuos, and Succos, in fulfillment of the precept [*Exod.* 23:17]: שָׁלֹשׁ פְּעָמִים בַּשָּׁנָה יֵרָאֶה כָּל־זְכוּרְךָ אֶל־פְּנֵי הָאָדֹן ה׳, *three times during the year all your males shall appear before the Master,* HASHEM *(Rashi; Gem.* 2a).

In mishnah 2 the word רְאִיָּה, *re'eyah,* obviously refers to *olas re'eyah* [see preface to tractate]. In our mishnah the word connotes both the precept of appearing and the *olas re'eyah* brought in conjunction with that appearance *(Tos.* 2a).

חוּץ... — *except for...*

The following categories of people are exempt from both the obligation to appear at the Temple Mount during the pilgrimage festivals and from the obligation to bring burnt offerings even if they appear voluntarily *(Tos.).*

מֵחֵרֵשׁ, — *a deaf person,*

Although the term חֵרֵשׁ in Talmudic usage usually refers to a deaf-mute, the *Gemara* (3a) rules that even one who is deaf but not mute is freed from the obligation of appearing. This exemption is derived from the precept of הַקְהֵל, *Assembly,* in which the people were obligated to assemble during the Succos following *Shemitah* to hear the king read the Book of *Deuteronomy.* Concerning that precept, the Torah states: לְמַעַן יִשְׁמְעוּ, *so that they may hear (Deut.* 31:12). This teaches that only hearing people are obligated to assemble. In both its exposition of רְאִיָּה, *appearance,* and הַקְהֵל, *Assembly,* Scripture uses a form of the root ראה, *seeing* or *appearing.* This similarity of expression [גְּזֵרָה שָׁוָה] implies that both precepts share the same rules. Thus, just as a deaf person, although not mute, is exempt from *Assembly,* so is he exempt from *re'eyah.*

Similarly, a mute who can hear is also exempt from the precept of *appearing.* This too is deduced from the precept of *Assembly.* Concerning *Assembly,* the Torah states: וּלְמַעַן יִלְמְדוּ, *and so that they may learn* [from the king's reading]. The word יִלְמְדוּ, *they may learn,* can also be vowelized יְלַמְּדוּ, *they may teach.* Teaching involves speaking; since a mute is incapable of teaching, he is exempt from the precept of *Assembly.* The similarity of expression in the precept of *re'eyah* teaches that he is exempt from that precept, too *(Ran).*

שׁוֹטֶה, — *an imbecile,*

[As explained in *comm.* to *Megillah* 2:4, the 'imbecile' in

1
1

1. All are obligated in *re'eyah* except for a deaf person, an imbecile, a minor, a person of undetermined sex, a hermaphrodite, women, slaves who

Talmudic usage who is excused from the performance of commandments is not equivalent to the dictionary definition of the term. Rather it refers to the sort of extremely foolish behavior described by the Talmud.]

וְקָטָן, — *a minor,*

Like an imbecile, a minor below the age of *bar mitzvah* is not obligated in the performance of commandments because he lacks the requisite degree of understanding and judgment. However, as the mishnah sets forth below, at a certain stage of a child's development, it becomes his father's responsibility to train him in the performance of commandments. That obligation, however, is Rabbinic in origin, not Scriptural *(Rashi; Rav).*

⚘§Non-Male Status

In the precept of appearing at the Temple Mount during pilgrimage festivals the Torah specifies: יֵרָאֶה כָּל זְכוּרְךָ, *all your males shall appear... (Exodus* 23:17). Women, therefore, are clearly excluded from the requirement. The *Gemara* (4a) derives from this phrase that all categories of people who are not positively of the *male* sex, and those who have the halachic status of females, are likewise exempt. These categories are now enumerated by the mishnah. These people are exempt from both the commandment to appear and the attendant *olas re'eyah.*

וְטֻמְטוּם, — *a person of undetermined sex* [lit. *stopped up*],

A טֻמְטוּם [*tumtum*] is *a person whose sex is undetermined* because a membrane covers the genitalia preventing a determination of the person's sex *(Tif. Yis.).*

Because the Torah specifies that only *definite* males are required to appear, a *tumtum* is exempt *(Rav; Gem.* 4a).

Tosafos (4a) adds that a *tumtum* would be forbidden to bring an *olas re'eyah* on the chance that he may be a male because it would constitute a possibility of חוּלִין בָּעֲזָרָה, *non-sacred offerings in the Temple courtyard,* since a female is not required to bring such offerings.

וְאַנְדְּרוֹגִינוֹס, — *a hermaphrodite,*

I.e., one who has both male and female genitalia and, as a result, can be identified neither as male nor as female *(Tif. Yis.).*

The word אַנְדְּרוֹגִינוֹס is from the Greek *androgynos.,* lit., man/woman *(Tishbi).*

וְנָשִׁים, וַעֲבָדִים שֶׁאֵינָם מְשֻׁחְרָרִים, — *women, (and) slaves who have not been freed,*

Women are clearly exempt (see above). The *Talmud* derives that non-Jewish slaves have a responsibility to fulfill commandments equal to that of women (*Kiddushin* 23a). Therefore, since women are exempt from appearing during pilgrimages, slaves, too, are exempt *(Rav; Gem.* 4a). *Rav* adds that the precept of *Assembly* specifies בְּבוֹא כָל־יִשְׂרָאֵל, *when all of Israel comes (Deut.* 31:11); although a non-Jewish slave is obligated to keep most commandments, as is a woman, unlike a woman he lacks the status of *Israel,* and is therefore exempt from *appearing.* And, as

א
א

מְשֻׁחְרָרִים, הַחִגֵּר, וְהַסּוּמָא, וְהַחוֹלֶה, וְהַזָּקֵן, וּמִי שֶׁאֵינוֹ יָכוֹל לַעֲלוֹת בְּרַגְלָיו.

אֵיזֶהוּ קָטָן? כָּל־שֶׁאֵינוֹ יָכוֹל לִרְכֹּב עַל־כְּתֵפָיו שֶׁל־אָבִיו וְלַעֲלוֹת מִירוּשָׁלַיִם לְהַר הַבַּיִת; דִּבְרֵי בֵית שַׁמַּאי. וּבֵית הִלֵּל אוֹמְרִים: כָּל־שֶׁאֵינוֹ יָכוֹל לֶאֱחֹז בְּיָדוֹ שֶׁל־אָבִיו וְלַעֲלוֹת מִירוּשָׁלַיִם לְהַר הַבַּיִת, שֶׁנֶּאֱמַר: „שָׁלֹשׁ רְגָלִים".

noted above, the laws of *appearing* are derived from those of *Assembly.*

[Only עֲבָדִים כְּנַעֲנִים, *non-Jewish slaves,* are exempt; עֲבָדִים עִבְרִים, *Jewish indentured servants,* however, are not diminished in status by their servitude, and are obligated to observe all precepts. If a non-Jewish slave was freed, he is a full-fledged Israelite and becomes responsible for the performance of all precepts.]

The *Gemara* derives from the apparent redundancy of שֶׁאֵינָן מְשֻׁחְרָרִים, *unfreed* — since *slaves,* by definition, are not free — that even if a slave was owned by two partners and freed by one of them, with the result that he is חֲצִי עֶבֶד וַחֲצִי בֶּן חוֹרִי, *half slave and half freedman,* he is nevertheless exempt from *appearing* since he lacks total freedom (4a).

Alternatively, we can derive the exemption of slaves from the precepts of *appearing* and the attendant sacrifices from the Torah's statement, אֶל פְּנֵי הָאָדֹן ה׳, *before the Master, HASHEM;* those who are beholden to HASHEM as their only Master are obligated to appear. Slaves, because they are also subservient to mortal masters, are exempt. Accordingly, one who is half slave and half free would also be exempt from the precept since he is not completely free of subservience to man *(Gem.* 4a).

הַחִגֵּר, וְהַסּוּמָא, וְהַחוֹלֶה, וְהַזָּקֵן, וּמִי שֶׁאֵינוֹ יָכוֹל לַעֲלוֹת בְּרַגְלָיו. — *the lame, the blind, the infirm, the aged and one who is unable to ascend by foot.*

All those who are incapable of making the ascent from Jerusalem to the Temple Mount because of physical infirmities are exempt from the precept of *appearing.* This is derived from the Torah's reference to the pilgrimage festivals as שָׁלֹשׁ רְגָלִים, lit. *three feet* [from רֶגֶל, *foot*], implying that only those capable of making the pilgrimage בְּרֶגֶל, *on foot,* are obligated.

The blind are exempt because the Torah states that Israel makes the pilgrimage לֵרָאוֹת, *to appear* [lit. *to be seen*]. The word can also be vowelized לִרְאוֹת, *to see.* Just as Israel is obligated to *appear* before HASHEM, so is it obligated *to see* the seat of His Glory and Holiness, thus exempting a blind man. Even a person who is blind in one eye is exempt since he cannot see the Temple Mount fully (*Rav; Rambam, Chagigah* 2:1).

In the category of people unable to ascend by foot, the *Gemara* (4b) includes one who is too delicate to walk barefoot as required for entry into the Temple Mount area. One who is not well enough to travel to Jerusalem is included among those exempt from the precept on the grounds of infirmity.

1 have not been freed, the lame, the blind, the infirm,
1 the aged and one who is unable to ascend by foot.

Who is deemed a minor? Whoever cannot ride on his father's shoulders and ascend from Jerusalem to the Temple Mount — [this is the opinion] of Beis Shammai.

Beis Hillel say: Whoever cannot hold his father's hand and ascend from Jerusalem to the Temple Mount, for the verse states: *three pilgrimages* [*Exodus* 23:14].

YAD AVRAHAM

אֵיזֶהוּ קָטָן? — *Who is deemed a minor?*

To whom does the exemption from the precept of *re'eyah* on the grounds of being a minor apply?

[Although minors are never under Scriptural obligation to perform commandments, their parents are Rabbinically obliged to train them from the time they attain sufficient understanding and physical capacity to perform the commandments. Hence this question concerns a minor's eligibility for this stage of his education.]

כָּל שֶׁאֵינוֹ יָכוֹל לִרְכֹּב עַל־כְּתֵפָיו שֶׁל־אָבִיו וְלַעֲלוֹת מִירוּשָׁלַיִם לְהַר הַבַּיִת; דִּבְרֵי בֵית שַׁמַּאי. — *Whoever cannot ride on his father's shoulders and ascend from Jerusalem to the Temple Mount — [this is] the opinion* [lit. *words*] *of Beis Shammai.*

Children must be able to make the ascent while riding on their father's or anyone else's shoulders without protest or ill effects. If they are too delicate to do so, they are deemed too young for training in the precept of *re'eyah* (*Tif. Yis.*).

[Although it is immaterial on whose shoulders the child rides, the mishnah mentions the father because he is the person obligated to train his son in the performance of precepts.]

Although the mishnah mentions the Temple Mount, the precept is to appear in the Temple *court.* The latter is equivalent to the courtyard of the Tabernacle in the wilderness, the מַחֲנֵה שְׁכִינָה, *Camp of the Divine Presence.* The Temple Mount itself is the equivalent of מַחֲנֵה לְוִיָּה, *the camp of the Levites;* an area that cannot be deemed 'before HASHEM'. The mishnah refers to the Temple Mount only as a generality, for if one can ascend to that point, one can surely ascend the stairs that lead from the Temple Mount to the Temple Court (*Tos. Yom Tov*).

וּבֵית הִלֵּל אוֹמְרִים: כָּל־שֶׁאֵינוֹ יָכוֹל לֶאֱחֹז בְּיָדוֹ שֶׁל־אָבִיו וְלַעֲלוֹת מִירוּשָׁלַיִם לְהַר הַבַּיִת, — *Beis Hillel say: Whoever cannot hold his father's hand and ascend from Jerusalem to the Temple Mount,*

Any child incapable of holding his father's hand and ascending the Temple Mount by foot need not be trained in the performance of the precept of *re'eyah,* even though he can ride on his father's shoulders.

שֶׁנֶּאֱמַר ,,שָׁלֹשׁ רְגָלִים״. — *For the verse states: Three pilgrimages* [lit. *feet*] (*Ex.* 23:14).

Since the Torah uses the expression רְגָלִים, plural of רֶגֶל, *foot,* instead of פְּעָמִים, *times,* we deduce that only those who can climb the

א
ב

[ב] **בֵּית** שַׁמַּאי אוֹמְרִים: הָרְאִיָּה שְׁתֵּי כֶסֶף, וַחֲגִיגָה מָעָה כֶסֶף. וּבֵית הִלֵּל אוֹמְרִים: הָרְאִיָּה מָעָה כֶסֶף, וַחֲגִיגָה שְׁתֵּי כֶסֶף.

Temple Mount by foot are required to appear *(Rambam; Tif. Yis.)*.

Since adults who cannot make the ascent by foot are exempt, children who cannot do so are similarly exempt from being trained in the performance of this *mitzvah (Rav)*.

[Beis Shammai, on the other hand, maintain that the deduction from שָׁלֹשׁ רְגָלִים, *three feet*, applies only to adults incapable of making the ascent. Since the Rabbinical obligation to train minors is educational, the only exemption is for children too young to be trained. For this purpose, the standard is whether a child is too delicate or weak to make the ascent even if he is carried on some one's shoulders.]

2.

As noted in the preface to this tractate, each Jew who is obligated to make the pilgrimage is required to offer two sacrifices on the first day of the festival: a burnt offering known as עוֹלַת רְאִיָּה, *olas re'eyah*, and a peace offering known as שַׁלְמֵי חֲגִיגָה, *shalmei chagigah*. Though the Torah did not set minimum values for these sacrifices, the Rabbis did. That minimum is discussed in the mishnah.

בֵּית שַׁמַּאי אוֹמְרִים: הָרְאִיָּה שְׁתֵּי כֶסֶף וַחֲגִיגָה מָעָה כֶסֶף. — *Beis Shammai say: The* [*olas*] *re'eyah* [*must be worth at least*] *two silver* [*maos*], *and the* [*shalmei*] *chagigah* [*at least*] *one silver maah.*

A *maah* is one-sixth of a *dinar*. Beis Shammai maintain that because the *olas re'eyah* is offered completely to God, it must be worth more than the *shalmei chagigah* which is partially consumed by the person offering the sacrifice, along with members of his household and his guests (*Gem.* 6a).

וּבֵית הִלֵּל אוֹמְרִים: הָרְאִיָּה מָעָה כֶסֶף, וַחֲגִיגָה שְׁתֵּי כֶסֶף. — *Beis Hillel say: The* [*olas*] *re'eyah* [*must be worth at least*] *one silver maah and the* [*shalmei*] *chagigah* [*at least*] *two silver maos.*

The *shelamim* is divided into three portions. One portion is consumed by the owner, a second is given to the *kohanim*, and the third is burned on the altar. Since it must be so divided, the *shalmei chagigah* must be of greater value than the *olas re'eyah* which is totally burned on the altar *(Rav)*.

As is the general rule, the *halachah* is in accordance with Beis Hillel *(Meiri)*.

The intent of the Rabbis in instituting a minimum value is to ensure that more meat will be available for consumption. The crux of the dispute is whether we look at the relative importance of the *korban* as do Beis Shammai, or at the amount needed because of the division of the meat, as do Beis Ḥillel *(Sfas Emes)*.

As noted in the preface, in addition to the *olas re'eyah* and *shalmei chagigah*, one is required to offer שַׁלְמֵי שִׂמְחָה, *shalmei simchah*, if the *shalmei chagigah* did not supply adequate meat for his household. For the *shalmei simchah* the Rabbis did not establish a minimum value

1 **2.** **B**eis Shammai say: The [*olas*] *re'eyah* [must be
2 worth at least] two silver [*maos*], and the [*shalmei*] *chagigah* [at least] one silver *maah*.

Beis Hillel say: The [*olas*] *re'eyah* [must be worth at least] one silver *maah*, and the [*shalmei*] *chagigah* [at least] two silver *maos*.

YAD AVRAHAM

[but see mishnah 5] (*Rav*).

Rav, following *Rashi* (6b), comments that women are obligated in the last category, *shalmei simchah*, because women, too, are required to observe the precept of being joyous on festivals. *Tosafos (Kiddushin* 34b) holds that the obligation does not rest on women *per se;* their husbands are required to gladden them by means of the offerings *(Tos. Yom Tov).*

3.

Vow and Gift Offerings

Apart from the required sacrifices discussed above, other *korbanos* were customarily brought on the festival although they are not directly connected with it. Such *korbanos* are נְדָרִים וּנְדָבוֹת, *vow and gift offerings*, which one had undertaken during the year to bring at some unspecified time. Since there is a positive commandment to discharge such obligations by the first festival after the pledge is made (see *Rosh HaShanah* 1:1), it was common for people who had come to Jerusalem for the pilgrimage to bring such offerings.

Maaser Sheni

Another category of offerings commonly brought during the festival are those purchased with funds bearing the sanctity of מַעֲשֵׂר שֵׁנִי, *the second tithe.* During four specified years of the seven-year *Shemitah* cycle [the first, second, fourth and fifth], farmers separate a tenth of their produce as *maaser sheni,* which may only be eaten in Jerusalem under conditions of spiritual purity. If, as is often the case, the owner is unable to transport all his *maaser sheni* to Jerusalem, he is permitted to redeem it for money. The funds, which acquire the restrictions of *maaser sheni,* must be taken to Jerusalem and used only for the purchase of food to be eaten in the Holy City. *Shelamim* could be purchased because portions of these offerings are eaten by the *kohanim* and the owner, but *olos,* because they are consumed on the altar, are not considered food and may not be purchased with *maaser sheni* funds (*Deut.* 14:22-27; *Sifri).*

The Torah placed a further restriction on these funds: They are not to be used to purchase *shelamim* for which one had obligated himself through a vow, for this is tantamount to using *maaser sheni* funds to settle personal accounts. The same restriction was applied to the purchase of *shalmei chagigah;* since they are obligatory, they may not be purchased with funds of *maaser sheni* (see *Menachos* 7:6). *Shalmei simchah,* however, are in a different category. Although such offerings are brought on festivals and it is meritorious to bring them, they are not required of themselves; their purpose is to assure that one enjoys the festival with an abundant supply of meat. A person who has sufficient meat from other sources, is not required to offer *shalmei simchah.*

א
ג

[ג] **עוֹלוֹת** בַּמּוֹעֵד בָּאוֹת מִן־הַחֻלִּין, וְהַשְּׁלָמִים מִן־הַמַּעֲשֵׂר.
יוֹם טוֹב הָרִאשׁוֹן שֶׁל פֶּסַח, בֵּית שַׁמַּאי אוֹמְרִים: מִן־הַחֻלִּין. וּבֵית הִלֵּל אוֹמְרִים: מִן־הַמַּעֲשֵׂר.

יד אברהם

עוֹלוֹת בַּמּוֹעֵד בָּאוֹת מִן הַחֻלִּין — *Olos which are not obligatory may be brought* [during *Chol*] *HaMoed.* [*All olos may be brought only*] *from unconsecrated funds.*

The literal translation of the sentence is, *Burnt offerings during Intermediate Days of the Festival should be brought from unconsecrated funds.* The *Gemara* (7b), however, finds this rendering exceedingly difficult since it would imply that burnt offerings brought on *Yom Tov* (i.e., *olas re'eyah)* — as opposed to *Chol HaMoed* — may be brought even from *maaser sheni* funds. Such, however, is not the case since, as we have seen above, *maaser sheni* funds may never be used for obligatory offerings. Therefore, the *Gemara* interprets the mishnah as an instance of חֲסוּרֵי מִחְסְרָא, *a defective rendering;* when Rabbi Yehudah HaNassi composed the *Mishnah* with his customary brevity, he condensed two laws into this one phrase. Our translation follows the *Gemara;* the laws are explained below.

נְדָרִים וּנְדָבוֹת, *vow and gift offerings,* which are not part of the sacrificial service of the festival, may not be brought on *Yom Tov* when labor is generally forbidden; such offerings should be postponed for *Chol HaMoed.* The *olas re'eyah,* however, should be offered on *Yom Tov* itself since it is part of the festival precept (*Rav; Tif. Yis.; Gem.* 7b).

[Notwithstanding the fact that seven days were allotted to bring the *olas re'eyah,* its primary time of fulfillment is on the first day of the festival.]

The mishnah now proceeds to state that all burnt offerings, whether the obligatory *olas re'eyah* or self-imposed vow or gift-offerings, may come only from חֻלִּין, *unconsecrated funds,* since tithe money [see below] is consecrated and thus may not be used for the fulfillment of any obligation (*Gem.* 7b).

Tiferes Yisrael, in an alternative interpretation, renders that *olos,* even those that may be offered only during *Chol HaMoed,* but not on *Yom Tov* itself, (i.e., since they come to fulfill self-imposed vows and are not required by Scripture) may not be purchased with *maaser sheni* funds. Surely, therefore, the obligatory *olas re'eyah* may not be purchased with such funds.

Sfas Emes notes that *maaser sheni* funds may never be used to purchase *olos,* for these funds may only be spent on food for human consumption, while *olos* are totally consumed by the altar fire. The mishnah does not mention חֻלִּין, *unconsecrated funds,* to exclude *maaser sheni.* Rather this expression excludes animals previously consecrated as vow or gift offerings. Although he designated an animal as an *olah,* that animal cannot be used for the *olas re'eyah* which must come from unconsecrated funds.

3. Olos [which are not obligatory] may be brought during [*Chol*] *HaMoed.* [All *olos* may be brought only] from unconsecrated funds, while *shelamim* [may be purchased] with tithe money.

[Concerning the *chagigah* brought] on the first day of Pesach, Beis Shammai say: [It may be purchased only] with unconsecrated money. Beis Hillel say: [It may be purchased] with tithe money.

YAD AVRAHAM

וְהַשְּׁלָמִים מִן־הַמַּעֲשֵׂר — *While shelamim [may be purchased] with tithe money.*

This refers to *shalmei simchah,* which are not mandatory unless one does not have sufficient meat for the festival without them (see above). Since they are not obligatory, they may be purchased with *maaser sheni* funds *(Rav).*

◆§ The Pesach Chagigah

In addition to the *chagigah* prescribed for every pilgrimage festival, Pesach has an additional *chagigah* known as חֲגִיגַת י״ד, *the chagigah of the fourteenth* [of *Nissan*]. This *korban* is brought only under a particular set of circumstances. The *pesach* offering must be eaten at the end of the *Seder* feast so that, upon its completion, the participants in the *Seder* would no longer be hungry. [Our *afikomen* is eaten last as a reminder of the *pesach* offering.] In the event, as generally occurred, that a large group eats at the *Seder* together, the portion available to each from the *pesach* offering would be insufficient to satisfy his hunger. Such groups would bring *chagigah* offerings along with their *pesach* offering on the fourteenth of *Nissan.* The *chagigah* would be eaten first and provide the main part of the feast, with the *pesach* portion eaten last. This *chagigah* is not obligatory and could therefore be purchased with consecrated money. Concerning the *chagigah* which is required by the Torah on the first day of every pilgrimage festival, consecrated money may not be used, as we have seen above. The mishnah discusses next the case of one who has so many guests at his festival meal that one *chagigah* of minimum value [see mishnah 2] will not suffice to feed them all. The minimum value of two *maos* [Beis Hillel] or one *maah* [Beis Shammai] is obligatory and must come from unconsecrated funds, but what of the additional expense of a larger animal or even a second animal for a *chagigah?*

יוֹם טוֹב הָרִאשׁוֹן שֶׁל פֶּסַח, — *[Concerning the chagigah brought on] the first day of Pesach,*

This discussion includes the *chagigah* that one may bring in addition to the single required *chagigah* on the first day of *any* pilgrimage festival [see preface to tractate]. The Tanna specifies Pesach only to differentiate its *first* day which is the subject of the following dispute, from the *chagigah of the fourteenth* which all agree may be purchased with *maaser sheni* funds [see preface] *(Rav).*

בֵּית שַׁמַּאי אוֹמְרִים: מִן־הַחֻלִּין. — *Beis Shammai say: [It must be purchased only] with unconsecrated money.*

[*Beis Shammai* view the prohibition of using tithe money for sacrifices which are initially obligatory as a blanket prohibition, regardless of whether it is for the first *chagigah* or the supplementary ones.]

[ד] **יִשְׂרָאֵל** יוֹצְאִין יְדֵי חוֹבָתָן בִּנְדָרִים וּבִנְדָבוֹת וּבְמַעְשַׂר בְּהֵמָה, וְהַכֹּהֲנִים — בְּחַטָּאוֹת, וּבַאֲשָׁמוֹת, וּבִבְכוֹר, וּבְחָזֶה וָשׁוֹק, אֲבָל לֹא בְעוֹפוֹת, וְלֹא בִמְנָחוֹת.

[ה] **מִי** שֶׁיֶּשׁ־לוֹ אוֹכְלִים מְרֻבִּים וּנְכָסִים מֻעָטִים, מֵבִיא שְׁלָמִים מְרֻבִּים

יד אברהם

וּבֵית הִלֵּל אוֹמְרִים: מִן־הַמַּעֲשֵׂר. — *Beis Hillel say: [It may be purchased] with tithe money.*

Beis Hillel concur with *Beis Shammai* that the initial *chagigah* must be purchased from unconsecrated money since it is mandatory. *Beis Hillel* maintain, however, that if one purchased an animal from his personal funds, but it was insufficient for all those eating with him, he may purchase additional animals. Although these *shelamim* are *shalmei chagigah,* they may be purchased with tithe money since they are not mandatory, as explained above *(Rav; Tif. Yis.; Gem.* 8a).

4.

⁂ Shalmei Simchah

Shalmei simchah are offered in fulfillment of the Torah's command: וְשָׂמַחְתָּ לִפְנֵי ה׳ אֱלֹהֶיךָ, *you shall be joyful before HASHEM your God (Deut.* 16:11). Relying on the principle אֵין שִׂמְחָה אֶלָּא בְּבָשָׂר, *there is no joy except through* [*eating*] *meat (Pesachim* 109a), the Sages interpret וְשָׂמַחְתָּ, *you shall rejoice,* as a requirement of eating (and being sated from) meat of a sacrifice during festivals. Hence the obligation to offer *shalmei simchah (Rav).*

Unlike the other festival offerings, *shalmei simchah* are not absolutely required unless one lacks adequate meat from other sources *(Rashi).*

The mishnah now proceeds to list the offerings that would suffice to spare one from bringing *shalmei simchah.*

יִשְׂרָאֵל... — *Israelites* [lit. *an Israelite*]...

I.e., as opposed to *kohanim,* who may fulfill their obligation by eating the meat of other sacrifices, as delineated in the latter part of the mishnah *(Tos. Yom Tov; Rashi).*

יוֹצְאִין יְדֵי חוֹבָתָן... — *discharge their obligation...*

... to offer *shalmei simchah* on the festival *(Rav).*

בִּנְדָרִים וּבִנְדָבוֹת... — *with vow offerings, (or with) gift offerings,*

Vow offerings and gift offerings pledged during the year may be brought during the pilgrimage to Jerusalem. As part of the sacrificial laws, the owners eat their portion of the meat after the prescribed parts are placed on the altar *(Rashi).*

וּבְמַעְשַׂר בְּהֵמָה, — *or (with) the animal tithe;*

[One is obligated to tithe his cattle and sheep and bring each tenth one as an offering (see *Lev.* 27:32). The meat of this *korban,* too, is eaten by the owner.]

וְהַכֹּהֲנִים— — *and kohanim* [*fulfill*

4. Israelites discharge their obligation with vow offerings, gift offerings, or the animal tithe; and *kohanim* [fufill their obligation] with sin offerings, guilt offerings, first-born [of animals], and the breast and thigh [of *shelamim*], but not with fowl [offerings] nor with meal offerings.

5. One who has many that eat but few possessions should bring many *shelamim* and few *olos*.

YAD AVRAHAM

their obligation]...

[In addition to the above-mentioned offerings, *kohanim* may fulfill their obligation by eating their allotted portion of the following sacrifices]:

בְּחַטָּאוֹת, וּבַאֲשָׁמוֹת, — *with sin offerings, guilt offerings,*

[I.e., that were offered during the festival by the pilgrims. Since the flesh would be eaten by the *kohanim*, they could thereby fulfill their obligation of being joyous with meat. See *Num.* 18:9.]

וּבִבְכוֹר, — *first-born* [*of animals*],

[I.e., with the meat of a first-born animal which must be given to a *kohen* and offered as a sacrifice (see *Num.* 18:18).]

וּבְחָזֶה וָשׁוֹק, — *and the breast and thigh* [*of shelamim*],

[Although the meat of *shelamim* is eaten by the owners, the Torah prescribes that the breast and thigh be given the *kohanim* as their portion (see *Lev.* 7:31-33).]

אֲבָל לֹא בְעוֹפוֹת וְלֹא בִמְנָחוֹת. — *but not with fowl* [*offerings*] *nor with meal offerings.*

I.e., the *kohen* cannot fulfill his obligation of שִׂמְחָה, *joyfulness*, by eating the meat of fowl or meal offerings. The *Gemara* (8a) derives this from the verse: וְשָׂמַחְתָּ בְּחַגֶּךָ, *and you shall be joyful on your festival (Deut.* 16:14). Since the word בְּחַגֶּךָ may be interpreted as *your chagigah*, it implies that the required festival joy can come only from the meat of species that may be used for the *chagigah*. This excludes fowl and flour, which are ineligible for the *chagigah (Rav).*[1]

5

מִי שֶׁיֶּשׁ־לוֹ אוֹכְלִים מְרֻבִּים... — *One who has many that eat...*

I.e., one who has a large household which will share his festival meals *(Rav; Tif. Yis.).*

וּנְכָסִים מֻעָטִים, — *but few possessions...*

I.e., he has limited means with which to purchase animals for sacrifices *(Tif. Yis.).*

מֵבִיא שְׁלָמִים מְרֻבִּים... — *should bring many shelamim...*

In dividing the limited money at his disposal between *shelamim* from

1. That the *chagigah* cannot be brought from fowl or flour is derived from the verse concerning festival offerings: וְלֹא־יָלִין חֵלֶב־חַגִּי עַד־בֹּקֶר, *and the fat of My chagigah shall not be left until morning* [*Exod.* 23:18]. This is a clear indication that the *chagigah* must contain חֵלֶב, *suet*, which is found in neither fowl nor flour *(Rashi).*

וְעוֹלוֹת מְעָטוֹת; נְכָסִים מְרֻבִּים וְאוֹכְלִין א
מְעָטִין, מֵבִיא עוֹלוֹת מְרֻבּוֹת וּשְׁלָמִים מְעָטִין; ו
זֶה וָזֶה מְעַט, עַל־זֶה נֶאֱמַר: „מָעָה כֶסֶף וּשְׁתֵּי
כֶסֶף"; זֶה וָזֶה מְרֻבִּים, עַל־זֶה נֶאֱמַר: „אִישׁ
כְּמַתְּנַת יָדוֹ כְּבִרְכַּת ה' אֱלֹהֶיךָ אֲשֶׁר נָתַן־לָךְ".

[ו] **מִי** שֶׁלֹּא חַג בְּיוֹם טוֹב הָרִאשׁוֹן שֶׁל חַג, חוֹגֵג אֶת־כָּל־הָרֶגֶל וְיוֹם טוֹב הָאַחֲרוֹן שֶׁל חַג.

which he will receive meat and *olos* which will be totally consumed on the altar, he should offer only the minimum required *olah* and spend the balance to purchase animals for *shelamim* from which he can provide for the needs of his dependents *(Rashi* on *Ran).*

Moreover, he may supplement his limited means by using tithe money (see mishnah 3) to purchase additional animals or a larger animal for *shelamim* to insure that he have enough meat to feed his household *(Tos. Yom Tov; Tif. Yis.; Gem.* 8b).

He may surely purchase *shalmei simchah* from tithe money, as is explained in mishnah 3 *(Tos. Yom Tov).*

וְעוֹלוֹת מְעָטוֹת; — *and few olos.*

I.e., he spends the minimum amount, as prescribed in mishnah 2, for the *olas re'eyah (Tif. Yis.).*

נְכָסִים מְרֻבִּים וְאוֹכְלִין מְעָטִין, — [*One who has*] *many possessions but few that eat...*

[I.e., if he is wealthy but has few dependents.]

מֵבִיא עוֹלוֹת מְרֻבּוֹת וּשְׁלָמִים מְעָטִין; — *should bring many olos and few shelamim.*

He should sacrifice more *olos*, to fulfill the Torah's precept of (*Deut.* 16:17) אִישׁ כְּמַתְּנַת יָדוֹ, *every man according to his hand's giving (Rashi; Tos. Yom Tov).* [He need not bring more *Shelamim* (aside from the minimum requirement) than are needed to provide for his household. Since few people depend on him for meat with which to celebrate the festival, he can allow himself to concentrate his means on sacrifices which are totally consumed on the altar.]

זֶה וָזֶה מְעַט, — *If both* [*possessions and eaters*] *are few —*

[I.e., if one has limited means and few dependents.]

עַל־זֶה נֶאֱמַר: — *concerning this it is said:*

[This sort of situation was the concern of Beis Shammai and Beis Hillel in mishnah 2 when they gave absolute minimum requirements for the festival sacrifices.]

„מָעָה כֶסֶף וּשְׁתֵּי כֶסֶף": — *'One silver maah and two silver* [*maos*].*'*

[I.e. one *maah* for the *olas re'eyah* and two *maos* for the *shalmei chagigah* according to Beis Hillel whom the halachah follows.]

זֶה וָזֶה מְרֻבִּים, — *If both* [*possessions and eaters*] *are many —*

[If one has abundant means as well as a large household.]

עַל־זֶה נֶאֱמַר: „אִישׁ כְּמַתְּנַת יָדוֹ כְּבִרְכַּת ה' אֱלֹהֶיךָ אֲשֶׁר נָתַן־לָךְ". — *concerning this it is said: Every man, according*

1 [One who has] many possessions but few that eat
6 should bring many *olos* and few *shelamim*. If both [possessions and eaters] are few — concerning this it is said: 'One silver *maah* and two silver [*maos*].' If both [possessions and eaters] are many — concerning this it is said: *Every man according to his hand's giving, according to the blessing HASHEM, your God, has given you* [*Deut.* 16:17].

6. One who did not offer the *chagigah* on the first *Yom Tov* of the festival, may offer the *chagigah* throughout the festival or on the last *Yom Tov* of the festival.

YAD AVRAHAM

to his hand's giving, according to the blessing HASHEM, your God, has given you [*Deut.* 16:17].

[The verse clearly refers to one whose giving is limited only by the extent of his generosity. Since he has been blessed with ample means, he should show his recognition of the fact that he has been so blessed by sacrificing many *olos*, which are totally burnt on the altar, *shelamim*, which are partially burnt on the altar and partially fed to his household.]

6.

Time Limit for Festival Offerings

Olas re'eyah and *shalmei chagigah* should optimally be brought on the first day of the festival. One who neglected to do so, however, may offer them for the duration of the festival. This is derived from the verse (*Lev.* 23:41): וְחַגֹּתֶם אֹתוֹ חַג לַה׳ שִׁבְעַת יָמִים בַּשָּׁנָה, *and you shall celebrate it as a festival to HASHEM for seven days*. From this is derived that the offerings may be brought for a *total* of seven days (*Gem.* 9a). On Pesach, this includes every day of the festival. On Shavuos, it means the festival and the six following days (*Moed Katan* 24b). If this rule were to be followed in connection with Succos, then the offerings would be valid during the seven days of Succos, but not during *Shemini Atzeres* which is the eighth day from the beginning of the festival. Therefore, the *Gemara* (9a) requires a specific Scriptural teaching to extend the permissible time for the offerings through *Shemini Atzeres*. [Of course, the verse only speaks of the Scripturally ordained festival days, those celebrated today in *Eretz Yisrael*. The additional day added by the Jews of the Diaspora to each festival are not included.]

מִי שֶׁלֹּא חַג... — *One who did not offer the chagigah...*

I.e., one who neglected to bring either the *olas re'eyah* or the *shalmei chagigah* (*Tos.* 2a; *Rambam; Rav*).

Lechem Mishnah (*Chagigah* 1:2) maintains that this includes one who neglected to bring *shalmei simchah*. *Tosefos Yom Tov*, however, questions this view inasmuch as one is required to offer those *korbanos* each day of the festival. Thus, the *shalmei simchah* of any

א ז

עָבַר הָרֶגֶל וְלֹא חַג, אֵינוֹ חַיָּב בְּאַחֲרָיוּתוֹ. עַל־זֶה נֶאֱמַר: ,,מְעֻוָּת לֹא־יוּכַל לִתְקֹן, וְחֶסְרוֹן לֹא־יוּכַל לְהִמָּנוֹת״.

[ז] **רַבִּי** שִׁמְעוֹן בֶּן־מְנַסְיָא אוֹמֵר: אֵיזֶהוּ מְעֻוָּת שֶׁאֵינוֹ יָכֹל לִתְקֹן? זֶה הַבָּא עַל הָעֶרְוָה וְהוֹלִיד מִמֶּנָּה מַמְזֵר; אִם תֹּאמַר

יד אברהם

On Pesach, one can bring the sacrifice on any of the seven days of the holiday. Although Shavuos is only celebrated for one day, the *chagigah* may be offered six days afterwards as well (*Rav; Moed Katan* 24b). With reference to the precept of *re'eyah,* the Torah compares all three pilgrimage festivals: בְּחַג הַמַּצּוֹת וּבְחַג הַשָּׁבֻעוֹת וּבְחַג הַסֻּכּוֹת, *On the festival of Matzos, on the festival of Shavuos, and on the festival of Succos (Deut.* 16:16); just as during the festival of *Matzos* the offerings may be brought for seven days, so on the festival of Shavuos the offerings may be brought for seven days (*Rav; Gem.* 17a).

R' Yochanan derives from Scripture that the *olas re'eyah* and *shalmei chagigah* of Succos may be brought on the eighth day. The seventh day of Pesach is called עֲצֶרֶת, *Atzeres* [lit. *withholding*] *(Deut.* 16:8) and the eighth day of Succos is called עֲצֶרֶת, *Atzeres, (Lev.* 23:36; *Num.* 29:35); just as the offerings of Pesach may be withheld until its *Atzeres,* i.e., seventh day, so may the offerings of Succos be withheld until its *Atzeres,* i.e., its eighth day (*Gem.* 9a).

עָבַר הָרֶגֶל וְלֹא חַג, — *If the festival passed and he did not offer the chagigah,*

[I.e., if the entire festival passed, and he did not avail himself of the festival day are considered as fulfillment of that day's obligation, not as amends for the previous day's omission.

בְּיוֹם טוֹב הָרִאשׁוֹן שֶׁל חַג, — *on the first Yom Tov* [lit. *festival day*] *of the festival,*

[I.e., if one failed to bring his offerings on the first day of the festival, which is the preferred time for them.]

חוֹגֵג אֶת־כָּל־הָרֶגֶל... — *may offer the chagigah throughout the festival...*

[Having failed to bring his offerings on the first day as he should have done ideally, he may bring them until the festival is over.]

וְיוֹם טוֹב הָאַחֲרוֹן שֶׁל חַג. — *or on the last Yom Tov of the festival.*

[Our mishnah uses two terms: רֶגֶל, *regel* (lit. *foot*) and חַג, *chag.* Both are commonly translated *festival;* however, in Mishnaic usage, the word חַג is used exclusively for Succos whereas רֶגֶל may refer to any of the three pilgrimage festivals.]

I.e., one may offer the overdue *shalmei chagigah* and *olas re'eyah* on the eighth day of Succos, known as *Shemini Atzeres.* The mishnah must specify the acceptability of *Shemini Atzeres* for the overdue Succos sacrifices for, unlike the last day of Pesach, *Shemini Atzeres* is considered an independent festival day, apart from Succos which preceded it *(Rav).*

If the festival passed and he did not offer the *chagigah*, it is no longer his responsibility. Concerning this it is said: *A twisted thing cannot be made straight, and what is not there cannot be numbered* [*Koheles* 1:15].

7. R' Shimon ben Menasya says: What is [referred to as] a twisted thing cannot be made straight? One who has an illicit relationship and begets a *mamzer*. Were you to say that [the

YAD AVRAHAM

opportunity of bringing the festive offerings in the additional time period allowed him.]

אֵינוֹ חַיָּב בְּאַחֲרָיוּתוֹ. — *it is no longer his responsibility.*

[He can no longer make amends for his neglect; hence he has no further obligation to offer these sacrifices. Even were he to voluntarily offer sacrifices, they would not be considered as fulfillment of the obligation.]

עַל־זֶה נֶאֱמַר: ,,מְעֻוָּת לֹא־יוּכַל לִתְקֹן, וְחֶסְרוֹן לֹא־יוּכַל לְהִמָּנוֹת״. — *concerning this it is said: A twisted thing cannot be made straight; and what is not there cannot be numbered* [*Koheles* 1:15].

The lack of the festive offerings cannot be made up since the time allotted for the precept has passed (*Tif. Yis.*).

7.

The verse (*Koheles* 1:15) cited in the previous mishnah speaks of unrectifiable sins of commission — *A twisted thing cannot be made straight* — and of unrecstifiable sins of omission — *what is not there cannot be counted.* The latter was discussed in the preceding mishnah in describing one's failure to perform a *mitzvah*, namely, the festive offerings, at the proper time. Mishnah 7 gives examples of the act of transgression which once committed can never be completely undone (*Tos. Yom Tov*).

רַבִּי שִׁמְעוֹן בֶּן־מְנַסְיָא אוֹמֵר: אֵיזֶהוּ מְעֻוָּת שֶׁאֵינוֹ יָכֹל לִתְקֹן? — *R' Shimon ben Menasya says: What is referred to as] a twisted thing that cannot be made straight?*

זֶה הַבָּא עַל־הָעֶרְוָה... — *One who has an illicit relationship...*

[I.e., one of the forbidden unions delineated in *Leviticus* 18:6-18.]

וְהוֹלִיד מִמֶּנָּה מַמְזֵר: — *and begets a mamzer.*

One who causes a *mamzer* to be born has a constant and permanent reminder of his transgression, for the product of his sin cannot be undone through repentance (*Rashi; Rav*).

[A child is ruled a *mamzer* if it is the product of a forbidden union punishable by כָּרֵת [*kares*], *spiritual excision*, as set forth in *Leviticus*. Such a child is forbidden to marry Jews of untainted parentage and the stigma is irrevocable (see *Kiddushin* 4:1).]

א בְּגוֹנֵב וְגוֹזֵל, יָכֹל הוּא לְהַחֲזִירוֹ וִיתַקֵּן.
ח רַבִּי שִׁמְעוֹן בֶּן־יוֹחַאי אוֹמֵר: אֵין קוֹרִין
מְעֻוָּת אֶלָּא לְמִי שֶׁהָיָה מְתֻקָּן בַּתְּחִלָּה וְנִתְעַוֵּת.
וְאֵיזֶהוּ? זֶה תַּלְמִיד חָכָם הַפּוֹרֵשׁ מִן־הַתּוֹרָה.

[ח] **הֶתֵּר** נְדָרִים פּוֹרְחִין בָּאֲוִיר, וְאֵין לָהֶם עַל־מַה־שֶּׁיִּסְמֹכוּ. הִלְכוֹת שַׁבָּת,

יד אברהם

אִם תֹּאמַר בְּגוֹנֵב וְגוֹזֵל, — *Were you to say that* [*the reference is to*] *one who steals or robs...*

I.e., if you say that one who steals or robs also can not have his sin obliterated since the stolen article remains in existence, even after its return, as a constant reminder of his thievery *(Tif. Yis.)*.

...יָכֹל הוּא לְהַחֲזִירוֹ — [*this could not be the meaning since*] *he can make restitution...*

By returning the stolen article [and also repenting], the thief purges himself of the crime. Since the crime is atoned for, its effects cannot be said to be permanent *(Tif. Yis.)*.

Alternatively, you might think that that verse refers to a case where the stolen article has been used up or destroyed making true restitution impossible. This is not so for he can always return the full monetary value and thus 'straighten what he twisted' *(Rav)*.

וִיתַקֵּן. — *and thus make it straight.*

By means of restitution, he can 'make straight' what had been twisted as a result of his misdeed. The same holds true even of sins of the magnitude of idolatry and murder, for once repentance and atonement have been achieved, no *tangible* evidence of the sin remains. The exception, as the mishnah said, is an illicit union which resulted in the birth of a *mamzer (Tos. Yom Tov; Tif. Yis.)*.

רַבִּי שִׁמְעוֹן בֶּן־יוֹחַאי אוֹמֵר: אֵין קוֹרִין מְעֻוָּת אֶלָּא לְמִי שֶׁהָיָה מְתֻקָּן בַּתְּחִלָּה וְנִתְעַוֵּת. — *R' Shimon ben Yochai says: We do not call one twisted unless he was initially straight and then became twisted.*

The *Baraisa* quotes R' Shimon ben Yochai as saying: We do not say, 'Examine a camel', we say, 'Examine a lamb'. Since a camel, as an unclean animal, is disqualified for a Temple offering in any case, it is pointless to examine it for blemishes. We do, however, examine a lamb — a clean and acceptable animal — to ascertain whether it has become blemished and disqualified for sacrifice. Similarly, we use the term bent for one who was initially straight, but not for one who was never known to have been straight *(Gem.* 9b).

R' Shimon ben Yochai says, that, by definition, the term מְעֻוָּת, *twisted*, refers only to something which was initially straight but then became contorted.

וְאֵיזֶהוּ? זֶה תַּלְמִיד חָכָם הַפּוֹרֵשׁ מִן־הַתּוֹרָה. — *And who is this? This is a scholar who forsakes the Torah.*

R' Shimon ben Yochai does not consider one who had an illicit relationship as having been initially straight; he simply had never before

1
8

reference is to] one who steals or robs [this could not be the meaning since] he can make restitution and [thus] make it straight.

R' Shimon ben Yochai says: We do not call one twisted unless he was initially straight and then became twisted. And who is this? This is a scholar who forsakes the Torah.

8. [The regulations governing] release from vows hover in the air and have no [firm Scriptural] support. [Certain] laws of the Sabbath, *chagigah* and

YAD AVRAHAM

had the opportunity to commit such a sin of immorality. However, one who studied Torah and abided by its laws and precepts, and afterward went astray, can be called מְעֻוָּת, *one who became 'twisted' (Maharsha).*

Such a person *was* straight and then became twisted. Although he can always return to his studies and practices, the time he has lost is irretrievable *(Chiddushin* on *Ein Yaakov).*

The term תַּלְמִיד חָכָם is variously rendered as *wise disciple* or *disciple of the wise. Tishbi* takes it as an expression of humility used by the Sages in preference to חָכָם, *wise man*, which is more assuming. Others take this as a reference to a scholar who was never ordained but remained a student. This expression is used in reference to Ben Azzai and Ben Zoma *(Berachos* 57b) who were outstanding scholars, but were never formally ordained *(Raglei Mevaser).*

8.

⁂ Written and Oral Torah

Only part of the Law revealed to Moses at Sinai was written [תּוֹרָה שֶׁבִּכְתָב, *written Torah*, i.e., Scripture]. The rest was taught orally [תּוֹרָה שֶׁבְּעַל־פֶּה, *oral Torah*] and was subsequently codified in the Talmud.

Some מִצְוֹת דְּאוֹרַיְיתָא, *precepts of the Torah*, such as circumcision and refraining from labor on the Sabbath, are clearly commanded in Scripture, while their detailed laws and applications are left for the Oral Law. Other precepts of the Torah (מִצְוֹת דְּאוֹרַיְיתָא) such as the obligation to bring the חֲגִיגָה, *festival offering* (Mishnah 2), are known *only* through oral tradition, by means of which God conveyed to Moses the detailed implications of Scriptural allusions.

Our Mishnah brings examples of those Torah precepts, which only vaguely alluded to in Scripture, would not be known without the Oral Law.

הֶתֵּר נְדָרִים פּוֹרְחִין בָּאֲוִיר, — *[The regulations governing] release from vows hover in the air...*

One of the precepts of the Torah known only through the oral Torah [see preface] is the right of an outstanding sage (or a court of three knowledgable laymen) to release a person from his vows on the basis of the conditions described in tractate *Nedarim* (chap. 9; see also *Moed Katan* 3:1). The Scriptural basis for this law is tenuous. It is deduced from the verse: לֹא יַחֵל

א חֲגִיגוֹת, וְהַמְּעִילוֹת, הֲרֵי הֵם כַּהֲרָרִים הַתְּלוּיִן
ח בְּשַׂעֲרָה, שֶׁהֵן מִקְרָא מְעַט וַהֲלָכוֹת מְרֻבּוֹת.
הַדִּינִין, וְהָעֲבוֹדוֹת, הַטָּהֳרוֹת, וְהַטֻּמְאוֹת,

יד אברהם

דְּבָרוֹ, *he shall not profane his word* (*Numbers* 30:2); only 'he', i.e., the one who undertook the vow, may not profane his word. This infers that other qualified parties, however, have the power to profane 'his' word by rendering the vow null and void. The precept's Scriptural allusion is far from explicit and is only known through the exegesis of the oral Torah (*Rav; Tos. Yom Tov*).

וְאֵין לָהֶם עַל־מַה־שֶּׁיִּסְמֹכוּ. — *and have no [firm Scriptural] support.*

The deduction upon which the law is based would be insufficient basis for the *halachah* were there no oral tradition that explicated it (*Rashi; Rav*).

Purposeful Work on the Sabbath

While the Torah clearly prohibits labor on the Sabbath, one of the basic principles delineating the quality of forbidden work is derived not from the verses discussing the Sabbath, but from those discussing the construction of the Tabernacle. This principle is that work is not Scripturally forbidden unless it is מְלֶאכֶת מַחְשֶׁבֶת, *purposeful work* (*Gem.* 10b). Any work not needed for its defined purpose is permitted under Torah law, but may be Rabbinically prohibited. The Talmud (*Shabbos*) gives various applications of this principle. Our *Gemara* (10a) discusses the case of הַחוֹפֵר גּוּמָא בְּשַׁבָּת וְאֵין צָרִיךְ אֶלָּא לַעֲפָרָהּ, *one who digs a hole on the Sabbath because he needs the earth* [*rather than the hole*]. The Sages define the purpose of the forbidden act of digging as the creation of a hole or furrow for its own sake. Thus, had one dug a hole in the ground to store goods or water, for example, such digging on the Sabbath would be a capital offense. In our case he had no need for the hole per se, but required only the earth which he removed from the ground, thus he has not performed the sort of purposeful labor forbidden by Scripture. This particular instance is known as מְלָאכָה שֶׁאֵינָהּ צְרִיכָה לְגוּפָהּ, *a labor not needed in and of itself* [i.e., for its defined purpose]. An alternative reason for the lack of Scriptural prohibition for this instance of digging is that forbidden labors must be מְתַקֵּן, *of a beneficial outcome.* This type of digging does not improve the ground; on the contrary, it is מְקַלְקֵל, *damaging,* to the earth upon which the digging is done. That the dirt will be used elsewhere is tangential to the physical act of digging.

הִלְכוֹת שַׁבָּת, — [*Certain*] *laws of the Sabbath,*

The major principle that only purposeful labor is Scripturally forbidden on the Sabbath is not set forth in relation to the Sabbath, but in relation to the construction of the Tabernacle. That it applies to the Sabbath as well is known only because the chapters of the Sabbath and of the Tabernacle are juxtaposed in *Exodus* 35 (*Rashi* 10b).

חֲגִיגוֹת, — *chagigah,*

There is no unambiguous reference to the *shalmei chagigah, in the Torah. The word* חַג, can be interpreted as either a *celebration* or a *festival offering.* Therefore, the injunction וְיָחֹגּוּ לִי בַּמִּדְבָּר, *and they shall make a* חַג [*along*] *for My sake in the wilderness* (*Exodus* 5:1) could be interpreted as a Divine command to celebrate the festivals in a joyful manner. Other mentions of חַג, *chag,* can be similarly interpreted. That they are to be understood as commands to bring *chagigah* offer-

1 *me'ilah* are like mountains suspended by a hair, for
8 there are few Scriptural references and many laws.
[The regulations governing] property law, the [sacrificial] services, purity and contamination, and

ings is derived from *Amos* (5:25) which refers to Israel's pilgrimage to the desert, saying: הַזְּבָחִים וּמִנְחָה הִגַּשְׁתֶּם לִי בַמִּדְבָּר, *Did you bring shelamim and meal offerings to Me in the wilderness?* The implication of this verse is that the celebration mentioned in *Exodus* refers to sacrifices. Thus, the interpretation of the Torah verse is clarified by the verse from Prophets. Since laws of the Torah cannot be derived from the words of Prophets, this is not considered a valid derivation, but a mere supportive allusion (*Gem.* 10b).

וְהַמְּעִילוֹת, — *and me'ilah.*

Me'ilah, which is variously translated as *trespass, abuse,* or *unfaithfulness,* involves the prohibited use of concecrated objects for secular purposes. One who does so unintentionally is required to bring אֲשַׁם מְעִילוֹת, *a me'ilah guilt offering.* The *me'ilah* law described by our mishnah as having little Scriptural basis is this: If someone unintentionally asks an agent to misuse a consecrated object, the *sender,* not the agent, is liable. If, however, the sender were to realize that the object was consecrated, the unwitting agent becomes liable to bring the אָשָׁם, *guilt offering,* since its purpose is to atone only for *unintentional* transgressions. Thus, the messenger, through no fault of his own, became liable. Since there is no obvious reason or derivation for this ruling, it is considered, as the mishnah concludes, like a mountain suspended on a hair (*Gem.* 10b, 11a).

מְעִילָה, *trespass,* is the exception to the rule: אֵין שָׁלִיחַ לִדְבַר עֲבֵירָה, *there is no agency for the performance of a forbidden act;* (see *Kiddushin* 2:1), if one delegates an agent to perform a proscribed act, it is as if the agent acted on his own volition. The reason for this differentiation is that the agent should have chosen not to perform the act since? דִּבְרֵי הָרַב וְדִבְרֵי הַתַּלְמִיד, דִּבְרֵי מִי שׁוֹמְעִין, *If ordered by the teacher* [i.e., Hashem, who proscribed the act] *and ordered by the student* [i.e., the sender, who commissioned the forbidden act], *whose order is obeyed.* Therefore, the sender can claim that he did not expect the agent to commit the transgression.

הֲרֵי הֵם כַּהֲרָרִים הַתְּלוּיִן בְּשַׂעֲרָה, שֶׁהֵן מִקְרָא מְעַט וַהֲלָכוֹת מְרֻבּוֹת. — *are like mountains suspended by a hair for there are few Scriptural references and many regulations.*

In each case, there is little Scriptural foundation for the precepts, which are known only through the oral Torah. The many regulations depend on meager Scriptural reference like mountains suspended by the hair of the head *(Rav).*

הַדִּינִין. — *Property Law,*

I.e., laws involving property damage. Although, generally speaking, the laws governing property damage are explicit, there is one instance that would be unknown were it not expounded. Rabbi [i.e., R' Yehudah HaNassi] rules that if one intended to kill one person and unintentionally killed another, the

ב
א

וַעֲרָיוֹת יֵשׁ לָהֶן עַל־מַה־שֶּׁיִּסְמֹכוּ. הֵן הֵן גּוּפֵי תוֹרָה.

[א] **אֵין** דּוֹרְשִׁין בָּעֲרָיוֹת בִּשְׁלֹשָׁה, וְלֹא בְמַעֲשֵׂה בְרֵאשִׁית בִּשְׁנַיִם, וְלֹא

יד אברהם

murderer is liable to pay the value of the dead person. [He is not liable to the death penalty because there was no premeditation for his actual victim.] Rabbi gives this interpretation to the verse וְנָתַתָּה נֶפֶשׁ תַּחַת נָפֶשׁ, *you shall give [the value of] a soul for a soul* [*Exodus* 21:23]. Although this is clearly not the plain meaning of the verse, Rabbi derives it by means of valid exegesis (*Tos. Yom Tov;* 11a).

וְהָעֲבוֹדוֹת, — *the [sacrificial] services,*

I.e., the various components of the sacrificial service. Although all the other components are explicit, the obligation to physically carry the blood of the slaughtered sacrificial animal to the altar is derived from an unusual expression in the text. The Torah uses the term וְהִקְרִיבוּ, *and they shall draw near (Lev.* 1:5), for the act of *receiving* the blood in a vessel, although this expression normally refers the *carrying* of the blood. This indicates that the carrying of the blood, like the receiving, is considered part of the service (*Tif. Yis.; Gem.* 11a).

הַטָּהֳרוֹת, — *purity...*

The means of returning from a state of contamination to a cleansed state through immersion in a proper *mikvah (Tos. Yom Tov; Tif. Yis.; Gem.* 11a).

וְהַטֻּמְאוֹת, — *And contamination,*

Although the laws of טוּמְאָה, *contamination,* are given in Scripture, the minimum amount (of the carcass of certain rodents and reptiles) that transmits contamination is not specified. The Sages derive that the amount is a part of the carcass the size of a lentil [כַּעֲדָשָׁה] *(Tos. Yom Tov; Gem.* 11a).

וַעֲרָיוֹת, — *and illicit relationships...*

That one may not live with his daughter born out of wedlock is not explicitly stated among those proscribed by the Torah in *Leviticus.* Nevertheless, the prohibition is derived by means of exegesis (*Tos. Yom Tov; Tif. Yis.; Gem.* 11b; see *Rashi, Lev.* 18:10).

יֵשׁ לָהֶן עַל־מַה־שֶּׁיִּסְמֹכוּ. — *have [firm Scriptural] support.*

Although none of these laws is stated explicitly, they all have valid Torah derivations *(Tif. Yis.).*

הֵן הֵן גּוּפֵי תוֹרָה. — *All of these are essentials of the Torah.*

Both those laws that are known only through oral tradition and those written explicitly in the Torah are essentials of the Torah. All are of equal weight and validity (*Rav; Tif. Yis.; Gem.* 11b).

Chapter 2

1.

Chapter 1 concluded with a discussion of laws not explicitly stated in the written Torah, but which are derived through the exegetical principles of the oral Torah. The last subject mentioned there was illicit relationships. The Tanna now cautions

2
1

illicit relationships have [firm Scriptural] support. All of these are essentials of the Torah.

1. We may expound neither on [the subject of] illicit relationships to [a group of] three, nor on the account of the Creation to [a group of] two,

YAD AVRAHAM

teachers of Torah not to expound on this precept publicly lest miscomprehension of the laws result. Other subjects which demand similar precautions are mentioned incidentally.

As mishnah 1 is tangential to the last mishnah of chapter 1, it should actually be the concluding mishnah of that chapter. However, since this mishnah finishes with an unpleasant thought — *it would be better for him had he not come into the world* — R' Yehudah HaNassi [the compiler of the *Mishnah*] did not want to use it to end a chapter *(Tif. Yis.;* see also *comm.* end of *Moed Katan).*

אֵין דּוֹרְשִׁין בָּעֲרָיוֹת... — *We may neither expound on [the subject of] illicit relationships...*

I.e., forbidden sexual unions that are not explicitly stated by the Torah for, as will be explained below, mishaps can result from careless teaching of such laws. Examples of such relationships are the prohibitions against marrying one's own daughter who was born from his union with an unmarried woman, and marrying his wife's grandmother, both of which are derived in *Sanhedrin* 75a through exegesis *(Rashi).*

בִּשְׁלֹשָׁה, — *to [a group of] three,*

A teacher may not expound on this subject in the presence of three or more students. Were he to do so, we fear that he will become involved in a discussion with one of the students while the other students talk among themselves. The inattentive students may misunderstand or fail to hear some of the laws expounded by their teacher with the result that they may permit the forbidden. The danger that students will become engrossed in private discussion to the point of inattentiveness exists particularly regarding this subject, for it involves a matter in which people have powerful urges *(Rav; Tif. Yis.; Gem.* 11b).

Maharsha explains that the prohibition against marrying one's sister can be particularly incomprehensible to students. Since Cain, Abel and Seth necessarily married their own sisters, the world's population is the result of their incestuous unions. Why then should such union be forbidden for later generations? Similarly, since Jacob married two sisters, why did the Torah forbid such union to his descendants? [We may add Amram's marriage to his aunt Yocheved. Although they married before the Torah was given, in future generations such a union would be punishable by כָּרֵת, *spiritual excision,* and any offspring born of it would be *mamzerim,* illegitimate offspring. The children of Amram and Yocheved were Aaron, Moses, and Miriam, who led the Israelites through the desert and established the foundations of the nation.] The students, engrossed in their own discussion, may not hear the explanation given by their

ב א בַּמֶּרְכָּבָה בְּיָחִיד, אֶלָּא אִם כֵּן הָיָה חָכָם וּמֵבִין מִדַּעְתּוֹ.

כָּל־הַמִּסְתַּכֵּל בְּאַרְבָּעָה דְבָרִים, רָאוּי לוֹ כְּאִלּוּ לֹא בָא לָעוֹלָם: מַה־לְּמַעְלָה, מַה־לְּמַטָּה, מַה־לְּפָנִים, וּמַה־לְּאָחוֹר.

teacher and may be tempted to take these prohibitions lightly.

In the presence of only two students, however, we do not fear inattention. Even if the teacher becomes involved in a discussion with one student, the second will listen since he has no one else with whom to talk *(Meiri; Gem.* 11b).

וְלֹא בְמַעֲשֵׂה בְרֵאשִׁית... — *nor on the account of the Creation* [lit. *the beginning*]...

I.e., on the subject of what occurred during the Six Days of Creation *(Rav).*

According to *Rabbeinu Tam,* this refers to the Divine Name composed of forty-two letters, which emanates from the first two verses of *Genesis (Tos.* 11b; see also *Sefer Raziel HaMalach).*

Rambam interprets this as the wisdom of nature and its laws. Since the subject is so complex and unfathomable, and ordinary people cannot hope to understand more than a minute fraction of the orderly functioning of Creation, it should be taught to only one student at a time. When two or more students are taught, one of them is likely to become distracted and err.

According to *Tiferes Yisrael,* this refers to the *Kabbalah* that teaches how God created the world by first creating spiritual worlds of high perfection, until gradually our material universe was created.

בִּשְׁנַיִם, — *to [a group of] two,*

I.e., in the presence of two or more. The profundities of these subjects can be transmitted clearly and comprehensibly only in a one to one relationship *(Rambam).*

The *Gemara* (11b) bases this on the verse: כִּי שְׁאַל־נָא לְיָמִים רִאשֹׁנִים, *for ask now concerning the earliest days (Deut.* 4:32) The singular form of the verse implies that only a single person may inquire into Creation *(Rav).*

וְלֹא בַמֶּרְכָּבָה... — *nor on [the account of] the Merkavah...*

[I.e., the esoteric and supremely mystical account of the heavenly worlds as it is related in *Ezekiel* 1 and *Isaiah* 6. See ArtScroll *Ezekiel* pp. 69-71.]

Rambam explains the *Merkavah* as the study of such matters as the totality of existence, the existence of the Creator, His knowledge, His attributes, the things that derive from Him, the angels, the soul, the mind which is joined to man, and what occurs after death.

Tiferes Yisrael interprets this as the study of the סְפִירוֹת [*sefiros*], *emanations,* through which God makes the world function. This study is called קַבָּלָה אֱלֹהִית, *Divine Kaballah.* Through study of the *sefiros,* one learns to recognize the Creator. Alternatively, it may refer to קַבָּלָה מַעֲשִׂית, *practical Kabbalah,* the knowledge of how to combine God's Holy Names in order to perform supernatural feats (see *Rashi, Exod.* 2:14).

Rav explains that by pronounc-

2 nor on [the account of] the *Merkavah* to an in-
1 dividual unless he is wise and understanding through
his own knowledge.

Whoever speculates on four subjects, it would be better for him had he not come into the world: What is above, what is below, what was before, and what will be after.

YAD AVRAHAM

ing God's Holy Names, one can gain insight into the functioning of the angels, and other such Divine visions, as if one had been given רוּחַ הַקֹּדֶשׁ, *Divine inspiration.*

בְּיָחִיד אֶלָּא אִם כֵּן הָיָה חָכָם וּמֵבִין מִדַּעְתּוֹ — *to an individual unless he is* [lit. *was*] *wise and understanding through his own knowledge.*

The secrets of the *Merkavah* should not be taught even privately unless the student is sufficiently wise and understanding to be taught the broad outline and to comprehend the rest on his own *(Rav).*

This is in keeping with the verse: כְּבֹד אֱלֹהִים הַסְתֵּר דָּבָר, *the honor of God is to conceal a thing* [*Prov.* 25:2] *(Tif. Yis.).*

The *Gemara* (13a) bases this ruling on *Shir HaShirim* (4:11) דְּבַשׁ וְחָלָב תַּחַת לְשׁוֹנֵךְ, *honey and milk lie under your tongue;* words that are sweet as honey and milk [i.e. the mysteries of the *Merkavah*] shall be concealed under your tongue.

כָּל־הַמִּסְתַּכֵּל בְּאַרְבָּעָה דְבָרִים רָאוּי לוֹ כְּאִלּוּ לֹא בָא לָעוֹלָם: — *Whoever speculates* [lit. *looks closely*] *on four things, it would be better for him had he not come into the world:*

Since the four questions listed below are beyond human resolution, one who speculates upon them can fall prey to heresy. Since he cannot find answers within the scope of his faith, he may ח״ו conclude that his faith was mistaken *(Tif. Yis.).*

מַה־לְּמַעְלָה, — *What is above,*

I.e., what is above the confines of the finite universe, and...

מַה־לְּמַטָּה, — *what is below,*

I.e., what is below the finite universe, as by definition the universe as an entity must have boundaries *(Tif. Yis.).*

מַה־לְּפָנִים, — *what was before,*

I.e., what happened before time was created since by definition time can be measured only from a given starting point *(Tif. Yis.).*

וּמַה־לְּאָחוֹר. — *and what will be after.*

I.e. what will be at the end of time for, as a creation, time must have an end.

These four questions are mentioned here because they are related to the *Merkavah* and Creation which were mentioned above.

Alternative interpretations are:

— What is above the heads of חַיּוֹת הַקֹּדֶשׁ, *the Holy Chayos,* mentioned in *Ezekiel* 1:22, and what is below them. What is outside the confines of the heavens in the east, and what is outside its confines in the west [the words פָּנִים and אָחוֹר often mean *east* and *west,* respectively] *(Rashi; Rav).*

— What existed before the universe was created, and what will exist after it ends *(Rav).*

ב
ב

וְכָל־שֶׁלֹּא חָס עַל־כְּבוֹד קוֹנוֹ, רָאוּי לוֹ שֶׁלֹּא בָּא לָעוֹלָם.

[ב] **יוֹסֵי** בֶּן־יוֹעֶזֶר אוֹמֵר שֶׁלֹּא לִסְמֹךְ, יוֹסֵי בֶּן יוֹחָנָן אוֹמֵר לִסְמֹךְ. יְהוֹשֻׁעַ בֶּן־

יד אברהם

Rambam (last chapter of *Sanhedrin*) likens man's attempts at metaphysical speculation to a fish trying to comprehend the nature of fire. Fire cannot exist in the water which the fish cannot leave. Thus the fish can never truly understand the nature of fire. So too, is man's material world so different from the metaphysical one that he cannot possibly completely comprehend it.

Maharal writes that man's dependency on time prevents him from understanding matters that can exist outside of time. Human understanding is dependent on logical truths or perceived facts which are within the limits of man's ability to perceive them; Divine truth exists outside of these confines, for God is not limited by the laws of nature which He created. Thus, speculation is futile and nothing more than an exercise in semantics. On this basis, *Maharal* rejected the philosophical writings common in the Middle Ages.

וְכָל־שֶׁלֹּא חָס אַל־כְּבוֹד קוֹנוֹ, רָאוּי לוֹ שֶׁלֹּא בָּא לָעוֹלָם. — *Similarly, whoever has no regard for the honor of his Maker, it would be better for him had he not come into the world.*

One who sins secretly and says: 'God is not here; who sees me and who knows of me?' (*Rav; Gem.* 16a).

Though such a person is ashamed to sin when people see him, he sins in private although God knows what the person is doing. Thus, he shows that he has no regard for the honor of his Maker. Similarly, if he speculates on the four questions mentioned above, he has no regard for the honor of his Maker, for he does not recognize his own human limitations (*Tif. Yis.*).

Alternatively, *the honor of his Maker* alludes to the human intellect. One who asks questions which he cannot possibly answer drives himself insane, thereby destroying God's most precious gift. Similarly, one who hides from people in order to sin, is submerging his intellect to his desires. The Rabbis stated: No one commits adultery unless a spirit of foolishness enters him (*Sotah* 3a). He acts like a beast and would have been better off had he been created an animal instead of a human (*Rambam*).

2.

Semichah

The Tanna returns to the primary topic of the tractate, the laws surrounding festival offerings. He now discusses the question of whether or not סְמִיכָה [*semichah*], *leaning* [on the head of the offering], is performed on *Yom Tov*. Regarding most animal sacrifices, whether obligatory or voluntary, offered by individuals, the Torah ordained that the owner must place his hands on the living animal's head and lean on it with his full strength (*Gem.* 16b), as the Torah states: וְסָמַךְ יָדוֹ עַל־רֹאשׁ קָרְבָּנוֹ, *He shall lean his hands on the head of his sacrifice* (*Lev.* 3:2). Tradition teaches us that this is required of all individual animal sacrifices

2 Similarly, whoever has no regard for the honor of
2 his Maker, it would be better for him had he not come into the world.

2. Yose ben Yoezer says not to lean [the hands on the head of a sacrificial animal on *Yom Tov*]; Yose ben Yochanan says to lean. Yehoshua ben

YAD AVRAHAM

with the exception of the Pesach lamb, the first-born, and the animal tithe (*Rambam, Maaseh HaKorbanos* 3:6).

Since the *mitzvah* requires one to lean upon the animal with all his might, it is comparable to riding the animal which is forbidden on *Yom Tov (Beitzah* 5:2). Hence the question arises as to whether *semichah* is done in the case of *chagigah* and *olas re'eyah* when they are offered on *Yom Tov*. [If the offerings are brought on *Chol HaMoed, semichah* is not forbidden, indeed, it is required.]

One view is that it is permissible to perform *semichah* the day before a *korban* is sacrificed. This would obviate the need for *semichah* on *Yom Tov*. The other view is תֵּכֶף לִסְמִיכָה, שְׁחִיטָה, *immediately following the semichah, the slaughter* (must be done); therefore, the *semichah* could only be performed on *Yom Tov* itself, just before the slaughter.

This dispute continued through several generations during the period when the *Sanhedrin* was governed by two officials, the נָשִׂיא [*Nassi*; plural, *Nesiim*], *prince* of the nation, and the אַב בֵּית דִּין [*Av Beth Din*], *head of the court*. This combined leadership was known as זוגות [*zugos*; sing, *zug*], *pairs*. The era of the *zugos* ended with Hillel and Shammai. Thereafter, the Tannaitic era began.

During the period of the *zugos* a dispute developed concerning the permissibility of *semichah* on festivals, a dispute that continued through five pairs of leaders. Of these *zugos*, most of the *Nesiim* maintained that *semichah* was not to be performed, whereas the heads of the *Beth Din* maintained that it should be. This was the first halachic dispute that went unresolved for any significant period. Previously, whenever a question arose, the *Sanhedrin* would vote on the matter and establish the *halachah*. As a result, the Torah and its interpretation remained as clear as the day the Law was given at Sinai. The dispute concerning *semichah* began as a result of Syrian-Greek persecution which had two effects: The intensive study of Torah was interfered with, and the *Sanhedrin* could not meet to decide the *halachah*. This tragic situation began long after the death of Yose ben Yochanan, the *Av Beth Din* who ruled that *semichah* should be performed, and toward the end of the lifetime of Yose ben Yoezer, the *Nassi* who came to the conclusion that his late colleague had been mistaken. Due to continuing persecution, the controversy continued until the time of Hillel and Shammai when it was resolved in favor of Hillel that *semichah* should be performed on *Yom Tov*. (See *Temurah* 16a; *Doros HaRishonim* 2:13; *Toldos Am Olam*).

יוֹסֵי בֶן־יוֹעֶזֶר אוֹמֵר שֶׁלֹּא לִסְמוֹךְ, — *Yose ben Yoezer says not to lean [the hands on the head of a sacrificial animal on a Yom Tov];*

Since placing the hands must be done with all one's might, it is considered making use of an animal and is forbidden, as is riding the animal, on *Yom Tov (Rav; Tif. Yis.;* see also *Tos. Yom Tov, Beitzah* 2:4.)

Yose ben Yoezer held that it was not necessary to perform the *semichah* directly before the slaugh-

ב
ב

פְּרַחְיָה אוֹמֵר שֶׁלֹּא לִסְמֹךְ, נִתַּאי הָאַרְבֵּלִי אוֹמֵר לִסְמֹךְ. יְהוּדָה בֶּן־טַבַּאי אוֹמֵר שֶׁלֹּא לִסְמֹךְ, שִׁמְעוֹן בֶּן־שָׁטַח אוֹמֵר לִסְמֹךְ. שְׁמַעְיָה אוֹמֵר לִסְמֹךְ, אַבְטַלְיוֹן אוֹמֵר שֶׁלֹּא לִסְמֹךְ. הִלֵּל וּמְנַחֵם לֹא נֶחֱלָקוּ. יָצָא מְנַחֵם, נִכְנַס שַׁמַּאי. שַׁמַּאי אוֹמֵר שֶׁלֹּא לִסְמֹךְ, הִלֵּל אוֹמֵר לִסְמֹךְ.

הָרִאשׁוֹנִים הָיוּ נְשִׂיאִים, וּשְׁנִיִּים לָהֶם, אֲבוֹת בֵּית דִּין.

ter of an offering. If so, *semichah* could have been done before the festival (*Beitzah* 20a).

יוֹסֵי בֶּן־יוֹחָנָן אוֹמֵר לִסְמֹךְ. — *Yose ben Yochanan says to lean.*

Yose ben Yochanan holds תֵּכֶף לִסְמִיכָה, שְׁחִיטָה, *immediately following semichah, the slaughter* (must be done). If so, the *semichah* could not have been done prior to the festival and it is considered to be an unavoidable part of the *Yom Tov* service (*Beitzah* 20a).

[This was the first *zug* in which the *Nassi* forbade *semichah* on *Yom Tov* whereas the *Av Beth Din* required it.]

יְהוֹשֻׁעַ בֶּן־פְּרַחְיָה אוֹמֵר שֶׁלֹּא לִסְמֹךְ, נִתַּאי הָאַרְבֵּלִי אוֹמֵר לִסְמֹךְ. — *Yehoshua ben Perachiah says not to lean; Nittai the Arbelite says to lean.*

[This was the second *zug* in which the *Nassi* forbade *semichah* on *Yom Tov*, while the *Av Beth Din* required it.]

יְהוּדָה בֶּן־טַבַּאי אוֹמֵר שֶׁלֹּא לִסְמֹךְ, שִׁמְעוֹן בֶּן־שָׁטַח אוֹמֵר לִסְמֹךְ. — *Yehudah ben Tabbai says not to lean; Shimon ben Shatach says to lean.*

[This is the third generation in which the controversy persisted.]

As our mishnah concludes, the first member of each pair is the *Nassi.* In identifying Yehudah ben Tabbai as *Nassi,* our mishnah follows R' Meir's view. The Rabbis, however, hold that Yehudah ben Tabbai was the *Av Beth Din (Gem.* 16b).

שְׁמַעְיָה אוֹמֵר לִסְמֹךְ, אַבְטַלְיוֹן אוֹמֵר שֶׁלֹּא לִסְמֹךְ.— *Shemaiah says to lean; Avtalyon says not to lean.*

In the other four generations of disputants, the *Av Beth Din* was always the one who required *semichah.* In the case of this *zug,* the fourth generation, the roles are reversed: Shemaiah, the *Nassi,* is the one who calls for *semichah.*

The name אַבְטַלְיוֹן, *Avtalyon,* is a composite of two words: אָב [*av*], *father,* and טַלְיָן [*talin*], *youngsters.* As head of the *Beth Din,* Avtalyon was charged with protecting the rights of young orphans. Hence, he was known as the *father of youngsters (Rav, Avos* 1:10).

הִלֵּל וּמְנַחֵם לֹא נֶחֱלָקוּ. — *Hillel and Menachem did not disagree.*

Since Menachem resigned his office, as mentioned further in the mishnah, it was never known whe-

2
2 Perachiah says not to lean; Nittai the Arbelite says to lean. Yehudah ben Tabbai says not to lean; Shimon ben Shatach says to lean. Shemaiah says to lean; Avtalyon says not to lean. Hillel and Menachem did not disagree. Menachem left [office]; Shammai entered. Shammai says not to lean; Hillel says to lean.

The former [of the respective pairs] were *Nesi'im;* the latter were heads of the *Beth Din.*

ther or not he differed with Hillel *(Rav).*

Alternatively, Menachem concurred with Hillel, who required *semichah* on *Yom Tov (Meiri).*

יָצָא מְנַחֵם, — *Menachem left* [*office*];

According to one view, he left the Sanhedrin to enter the service of King Herod (*Gem.* 16b).

When Herod was young, Menachem predicted that he would be a king. Therefore, when Herod assumed the throne, he summoned Menachem to his court and took him into his service *(Tif. Yis.,* quoting *Josephus* 15:13).

Menachem prophesied that Herod would rule for more than thirty years. Indeed he ruled for thirty-seven years. Therefore, Herod bestowed great wealth upon him *(Sefer Yuchasin).*

According to another view in the *Gemara* (16b), Menachem became an apostate. *Tiferes Yisrael* comments that he joined the **בַּיְיתוּסִים,** *Bethusians,* who deny the validity of the oral Torah [see pref. 1:8]. There is, however, no *Talmudic* support for his view.

.נִכְנַס שַׁמַּאי — *Shammai entered.*

Shammai succeeded Menachem as *Av Beth Din (Rav; Tif. Yis.).*

שַׁמַּאי אוֹמֵר שֶׁלֹּא לִסְמֹךְ, הִלֵּל אוֹמֵר לִסְמֹךְ. — *Shammai says not to lean; Hillel says to lean.*

[This was the fifth and final *zug* involved in the long-standing dispute.]

הָרִאשׁוֹנִים הָיוּ נְשִׂיאִים, — *The former* [*of the respective pairs*] *were Nesi'im;*

The first one of each *zug* mentioned in the mishnah was the *Nassi (Rav; Tif. Yis.).*

וּשְׁנִיִּים לָהֶם, אֲבוֹת בֵּית דִּין. — *the latter* [lit., *those second to them*] *were heads of the Beth Din.*

Shammai, who was an *Av Beth Din,* is the exception to this rule since he is mentioned before Hillel. Since Hillel's position as *Nassi* was already established by his having been named before Menachem, the reversal of positions would not cause the reader to erroneously regard Shammai as the *Nassi.* The reason Shammai's view was given first is because it coincides with that of the first three *Nesi'im.* The general pattern of mentioning Shammai before Hillel throughout the *Mishnah* is based on our mishnah (*Tos. Yom Tov; Tos.* 16a).

Following the general rule that disputes between Hillel and Shammai are decided in favor of Hillel, the *halachah* was set down that *semichah* is performed on *Yom Tov (Rambam, Hilchos Chagigah* 1:9).

ב
ג־ד

[ג] **בֵּית** שַׁמַּאי אוֹמְרִים: מְבִיאִין שְׁלָמִים וְאֵין סוֹמְכִין עֲלֵיהֶם, אֲבָל לֹא עוֹלוֹת. וּבֵית הִלֵּל אוֹמְרִים: מְבִיאִין שְׁלָמִים וְעוֹלוֹת וְסוֹמְכִין עֲלֵיהֶם.

[ד] **עֲצֶרֶת** שֶׁחָלָה לִהְיוֹת בְּעֶרֶב שַׁבָּת, בֵּית שַׁמַּאי אוֹמְרִים: יוֹם טְבוֹחַ אַחַר הַשַּׁבָּת. וּבֵית הִלֵּל אוֹמְרִים: אֵין יוֹם טְבוֹחַ

יד אברהם

3.

Continuing the theme of the preceding mishnah, the Tanna informs us that Beis Shammai and Beis Hillel, the respective academies founded by Shammai and Hillel, followed the views of their masters. Also, they disagreed as to whether the *olas re'eyah* is offered on *Yom Tov* or delayed until *Chol HaMoed.*

This mishnah also appears in *Beitzah* 2:4, where the *Gemara* discusses it at length. It is repeated here because it deals with the *chagigah,* the subject of our tractate *(Tos.* 8a).

...בֵּית שַׁמַּאי אוֹמְרִים: מְבִיאִין שְׁלָמִים — *Beis Shammai say: We may bring shelamim* [*on Yom Tov*]...

We are permitted to bring *shalmei chagigah* on *Yom Tov.* Since the meat of these offerings is used for human consumption, the work involved in bringing them is permitted on *Yom Tov* as is any other food preparation *(Rav; Rashi).*

וְאֵין סוֹמְכִין עֲלֵיהֶם, — *without leaning on them,*

Since *semichah* can be performed on the day before the festival, it may not be done on *Yom Tov.* This is in keeping with Shammai's ruling that the sacrifice need not be slaughtered immediately after the *semichah (Rashi; Rav; Tiferes Yisrael;* see mishnah 2).

אֲבָל לֹא עוֹלוֹת. — *but* [*we may*] *not* [*bring*] *olos.*

No private *olos* may be brought on a *Yom Tov* — not even an *olas re'eyah. Beis Shammai* derives this rule from the verse *(Numb.* 29:35): עֲצֶרֶת תִּהְיֶה לָכֶם, *It shall be a festival for you;* by using the word לָכֶם, *for you,* the Torah implies that on *Yom Tov* only that work necessary *for you,* i.e., for human food, may be done, but not work done to feed God's altar. Therefore, *olos* which no human being consumes may not be offered on *Yom Tov.* They are, instead, offered on the following day *(Rav).*

Alternatively, Beis Shammai bases their ruling on *(Exodus* 12:16): אַךְ אֲשֶׁר יֵאָכֵל לְכָל־נֶפֶשׁ הוּא לְבַדּוֹ יֵעָשֶׂה לָכֶם, *But that which will be eaten by any person — that alone may be done for you (Rashi).* [Again, the emphasis is on *for you.*]

וּבֵית הִלֵּל אוֹמְרִים: מְבִיאִין שְׁלָמִים וְעוֹלוֹת, — *Beis Hillel say: We* [*may*] *bring* [*both*] *shelamim and olos...*

Even on *Yom Tov,* we bring both *shalmei chagigah* and *olos re'eyah.* Beis Hillel derive this from *(Deut.*

2
3-4

3. Beis Shammai say: We may bring *shelamim* [on *Yom Tov*] without leaning on them, but [we may] not [bring] *olos*.

Beis Hillel say: We may bring [both] *shelamim* and *olos*, and we may lean on them.

4. If Shavuos fell on the eve of the Sabbath, Beis Shammai say: The day-of-slaughter is after the Sabbath. Beis Hillel say: There is no day-of-slaughter

YAD AVRAHAM

16:8): עֲצֶרֶת לַה׳ אֱלֹהֶיךָ, *A festival for HASHEM, your God,* meaning that not only may work be performed for human consumption, but also for the sake of God's altar. Beis Hillel's decision that sacrifices may be offered on *Yom Tov* applies only to *olos re'eyah* and *shalmei chagigah* which are obligations of the day.

As the *Gemara* explains, Beis Hillel maintain that ordinary offerings, whether voluntary or obligatory, should not be brought on *Yom Tov* since they can just as well be brought on *Chol HaMoed* or after the festival. *Olos re'eyah* and *shalmei chagigah,* however, can only be brought during a seven day period; therefore, they should not be postponed at all (*Beitzah* 20b).

No other sacrifices, not even *shelamim* which yield meat for their owner, may be sacrificed on *Yom Tov (Rav; Beitzah* 19a).

וְסוֹמְכִין עֲלֵיהֶם. — *and we may lean on them.*

[*Semichah* cannot be advanced to the day before the festival because the animal must be slaughtered immediately after it. We are left, therefore, with a Scriptural requirement that *semichah* be done on the *Yom Tov* in opposition to a Rabbinical prohibition against leaning (or riding) on an animal. Therefore, the Rabbis ruled that the precept of *semichah* should supersede their prohibition (see mishnah 2).]

4.

עֲצֶרֶת שֶׁחָלָה לִהְיוֹת בְּעֶרֶב שַׁבָּת, — *If Shavuos falls on the eve of the Sabbath,*

The name עֲצֶרֶת, *Atzeres,* implies the concluding day of a longer time period. Thus the Torah refers to both the eighth day of Succos and the seventh day of Pesach as *Atzeres.* But for Shavuos, which is only a one-day festival, the Torah does not use this name. The Sages, however, almost exclusively refer to Shavuos as *Atzeres.* Implied is that this brief festival is the culmination of a longer season, namely, the forty-nine day *Omer* period which began with Pesach, and so Shavuos is linked to Pesach (*Ramban, Lev.* 23:36).

This linkage demonstrates that the purpose of the Pesach exodus was the acceptance of the Torah on Shavuos. Had Israel not received the Torah, the exodus would have been incomplete *(Sfas Emes).*

בֵּית שַׁמַּאי אוֹמְרִים: יוֹם טְבוֹחַ אַחַר הַשַּׁבָּת. — *Beis Shammai say: The day-of-slaughter is after the Sabbath.*

ב אַחַר הַשַּׁבָּת. וּמוֹדִים שֶׁאִם חָלָה לִהְיוֹת
ד בַּשַּׁבָּת, שֶׁיּוֹם טְבוֹחַ אַחַר הַשַּׁבָּת.
וְאֵין כֹּהֵן גָּדוֹל מִתְלַבֵּשׁ בְּכֵלָיו, וּמֻתָּרִין

יד אברהם

This refers to the *olas re'eyah* which according to Beis Shammai in mishnah 3, could not be offered on *Yom Tov* itself. Since no private offerings may be brought on the Sabbath, the *olas re'eyah* must be delayed until Sunday (fig. 1a). This postponement will not prevent the offering of the *olos re'eyah* since it, like the *chagigah*, can be brought for a total of seven days beginning with Shavuos (see pref. 1:6). This rule also applies when either Pesach or Succos falls on a Friday. The mishnah specifies Shavuos lest one erroneously think that the seven-day rule is only valid for the festivals of Pesach and Succos which are each of seven days duration (*Rav; Gem.* 17a).

[Alternatively, Shavuos is mentioned because the last part of this mishnah refers specifically to that festival.]

וּבֵית הִלֵּל אוֹמְרִים: אֵין יוֹם טְבוֹחַ אַחַר הַשַּׁבָּת. — *Beis Hillel say: There is no day-of-slaughter after the Sabbath,*

An alternate reading is: אֵין־לָהּ יוֹם טְבוֹחַ, *It has no day-of-slaughter (Rashi; Rav).*

There is no *necessity* for a special day-of-slaughter on Sunday, since, according to Beis Hillel (see mishnah 3), the *olas re'eyah* may be offered on the *Yom Tov* of Shavuos itself (fig. 1b). [If one neglected to do so, however, he still has the full seven-day period, of course.] Although our mishnah apparently does no more than draw logical conclusions from previously stated opinions of Beis Shammai and Beis Hillel, it had to be explicated nevertheless. It teaches that Beis Shammai postpones the day-of-slaughter even though a two-day delay will result *(Rav; Gem.* 17b), despite the fear that such a delay might lead to forgetting the *olas re'eyah* entirely (*Rashi* 17b).

The *Gemara* states further that mishnah 3 is needed to clarify the ruling of Beis Hillel. For if we had only our mishnah, we might think that Beis Hillel approved of slaughter on a Friday in order to avoid a *two*-day postponement (fig. 1a). If, however, *Yom Tov* fell on a different weekday (fig. 2), Beis Hillel might concur with Beis Shammai and call for a posponement of only *one* day *(Tos. Yom Tov).*

וּמוֹדִים שֶׁאִם חָלָה לִהְיוֹת בַּשַּׁבָּת, שֶׁיּוֹם טְבוֹחַ אַחַר הַשַּׁבָּת. — *They* [i.e., Beis Hillel] *concur that if it fell on the Sabbath, the day-of-slaughter is after the Sabbath,*

Beis Hillel, too, agree that if the festival falls on a Sabbath, none of the private festival sacrifices is offered until Sunday (fig. 3). The only exception to this rule is the Pesach offering which must be brought on the Sabbath because it cannot be brought at any time other than the eve of Pesach *(Tif. Yis.).*

The Talmud (*Pesachim* 70b) raises the following question: In general, a קָרְבַּן צִבּוּר, *communal sacrifice* (such as the תָּמִיד, *daily morning and evening sacrifice)* supersedes the Sabbath. But since both the *chagigah* and the *olas re'eyah* are offered in an assembly, should they not be considered communal sacrifices and supersede the Sabbath? The Talmud answers that there is a Scriptural source for not

2 after the Sabbath. They concur that if it fell on the
4 Sabbath, the day-of-slaughter is after the Sabbath.

The *kohen gadol* does not don his [special] garments [on that day]; moreover, they are permitted to

YAD AVRAHAM

offering the *chagigah* on the Sabbath. The Torah states: וְחַגֹּתֶם אֹתוֹ חַג לַה׳ שִׁבְעַת יָמִים בַּשָּׁנָה, *And you shall celebrate it as a festival offering to HASHEM, seven days in the year* (*Lev.* 23:41). The verse refers to Succos when, as we saw above in 1:6, the *chagigah* may be brought during an *eight*-day period; nevertheless, the Torah speaks of *seven* days. This implies that the Sabbath is not one of the days on which the *chagigah* may be offered; hence, there are only seven days during the eight-day period when the sacrificial service may be performed. *Olas re'eyah* is governed by the same rules as *shalmei chagigah*. Therefore, it, too, does not supersede the Sabbath (*Tos. Yom Tov; Tos., Pes.* 76b).

According to *Rambam* (*Hilchos Chagigah* 1:8; see also *Megillah* 1:3) since *olas re'eyah* and *shalmei chagigah* may be brought during the entire week, they are deemed sacrifices that have *no set time*, and therefore do not supersede the Sabbath. Clearly, therefore, the fact that they are considered communal offerings is not sufficient to permit them to be brought on the Sabbath.

S	M	T	W	T	F	S
					SHAVUOS	SABBATH
DOS						

Figure 1a. Beis Shammai: day-of-slaughter postponed two days.

S	M	T	W	T	F	S
					SHAVUOS DOS	SABBATH

Figure 1b. Beis Hillel; no postponement.

Figures 1a-b. Shavuos on Friday. (Shaded area indicates days on which *olas re'eyah* may be brought.)

S	M	T	W	T	F	S
		SHAVUOS	DOS			SABBATH

Figure 2. Shavuos on weekday other than Friday according to Beis Shammai; day-of-slaughter postponed one day.

S	M	T	W	T	F	S
						SABBATH SHAVUOS
DOS						

Figure 3. Shavuos on the Sabbath according to both Beis Hillel and Beis Shammai; day-of-slaughter postponed one day.

וְאֵין כֹּהֵן גָּדוֹל מִתְלַבֵּשׁ בְּכֵלָיו, — *the kohen gadol does not don his* [*special*] *garments* [*on that day*];

[On the occasions when the day-of-slaughter occurred on Sunday, the Sages were concerned lest the impression be given that that Sunday was a festival rather than merely an ordinary weekday when the postponed festival offerings were brought. This concern involved only Shavuos, as the mishnah explains below. To avoid this error, the Sages decreed the following rules to make clear that the day was not a festival:] In the event the day-of-slaughter is observed on Sunday, the *kohen gadol* should not wear his

ב ד בְּהֶסְפֵּד וּבְתַעֲנִית, שֶׁלֹּא לְקַיֵּם דִּבְרֵי הָאוֹמְרִין עֲצֶרֶת אַחַר הַשַּׁבָּת.

festival finery. This refers not to the priestly garments which are the same on all days of the year, but to his private clothing *(Rashi; Rav).*

Alternatively, the mishnah refers to the *kohen gadol's* priestly garments. It was customary for him to perform the sacrificial service on Sabbaths and festivals, an act for which he was required to don the eight priestly garments that were used only by him (see *Exod.* 28:4; *Yoma* 7:5). Were he to wear these garments on a Sunday day-of-slaughter, people might think it was a festival. Therefore, he should refrain from performing the sacrificial service on that day in order not to wear his priestly garments *(Tos. Yom Tov; Tos.; Yerushalmi).*

וּמְתָּרִין בְּהֶסְפֵּד וּבְתַעֲנִית, — *moreover, they are permitted to eulogize and fast (*lit. *in eulogy and fasting).*

Whenever people observe a day-of-slaughter by bringing their festival sacrifices, regardless of which day of the week, that day should normally be considered one of personal rejoicing. Nevertheless, they are given permission to eulogize and fast in order to demonstrate that the day has no sanctity. If such practices were forbidden, then when the day fell on a Sunday, people might deem it a holiday *(Tos. Yom Tov; Tif. Yis.).*

Our translation of this phrase follows *Tosefos Yom Tov's* alternate interpretation which views the tacit subject of the plural verb מְתָּרִין, *are permitted,* to be 'the people'. The plural verb cannot refer to the days-of-sacrifice, because, according to Beis Hillel whom the *halachah* follows, there is only *one* possibility of a day-of-sacrifice, namely, when Shavuos falls on the Sabbath.

According to this, there is no reference to a day of slaughter on other days. Hence *Tiferes Yisrael* explains that although eulogies and fasting are prohibited on אִסְרוּ חַג, *the day after a festival,* in other circumstances, if *Shavuos* falls on a Sabbath and the day-of-slaughter is postponed until Sunday, fasting and eulogies are permitted for the reason given below.

Alternatively, this mishnah is in accordance with Beis Shammai's opinion that every *Yom Tov* which falls on a Friday or the Sabbath generates a day-of-sacrifice on the following Sunday. Hence the plural verb refers to the days-of-sacrifice *(Tos. Yom Tov).*

שֶׁלֹּא לְקַיֵּם דִּבְרֵי הָאוֹמְרִין עֲצֶרֶת אַחַר הַשַּׁבָּת. — *in order not to confirm the view of those who say that Shavuos is always* [*the day*] *after the Sabbath,*

The בַּיְיתוּסִים, *Boethusians,* a sister group of the צְדוּקִים, *Sadducees,* insisted that Shavuos always falls on Sunday. They based this on a literal interpretation of the verse that designates the day of Shavuos: וּסְפַרְתֶּם לָכֶם מִמָּחֳרַת הַשַּׁבָּת...עַד מִמָּחֳרַת הַשַּׁבָּת הַשְּׁבִיעִית, *And you shall count for yourselves from the morrow of the Sabbath ... until the morrow of the seventh Sabbath (Lev.* 23:15-16). The word שַׁבָּת, *Sabbath,* literally means rest day and usually refers to the seventh day of the week. By extension the word may also refer to an entire week. The word may also be used to designate a *Yom Tov,* since

2 eulogize and fast, in order not to confirm the view of
4 those who say that Shavuos is always [the day] after
the Sabbath.

YAD AVRAHAM

on that day we must 'rest' from certain types of labor. The traditional interpretation is that first 'Sabbath' of the verse refers to the *Yom Tov* of Pesach, thus, *from the morrow of the festival* you are to begin counting the seven weeks of the *Omer* period. The second 'Sabbath' of the verse means week, thus *until the morrow of the seventh week.* The Boethusians, however, translated שַׁבָּת is its literal application as the *Sabbath.* To their way of thinking, Shavuos always fell *on the morrow of the Sabbath,* i.e., Sunday (*Rav; Menachos* 65a).

Alternatively, these practices were abolished only on a Sunday day-of-slaughter, lest the *kohen gadol* be suspected of sympathizing with the Boethusians (see above). When the day of slaughter fell during the week, however, it was observed with festive attire and abstention from eulogies and fasting *(Meiri).*

5.

◆§ Tumah and Taharah

With this mishnah the concluding portion of the tractate, an exposition of various laws of טֻמְאָה, [*tumah*] *contamination,* and טָהֳרָה [*taharah*] *purity,* begins. Although it would have been appropriate to begin a new chapter with this subject, the Tanna refrained from doing so in order not to conclude chapter 2 with a reference to the heretical beliefs of the Boethusians and Sadducees. These laws of *tumah* and *taharah* are especially relevant to our tractate's discussion of festival offerings, since spiritual purity was a prerequisite for appearance in the Temple and eating sanctified food such as sacrificial meat and *maaser sheni.* During the course of the discussion, many other laws relating to the general subject of *tumah* and *taharah* are included *(Meiri).*

Alternatively, these laws follow those of *chagigah* because they conclude by teaching that even עַמֵּי הָאָרֶץ, *ignorant people,* who are generally unversed in and unconcerned with the intricate laws of purity, were given the status of the ritually pure during festivals. This was in contrast to their halachic status all year round when, as a result of their careless behavior and ignorance, they had to be regarded as *tamei* [spiritually contaminated] as a precautionary measure. Introductory to this rule, the Tanna outlines the many stringencies that surround the laws of *Tumah* and *Taharah (Rashi; Rav).*

The Sages instituted many decrees to safeguard the *taharah* of the respective levels of sanctity from being contaminated by *tumah.* The next mishnayos discuss Rabbinic decrees concerning five ascending levels of sanctity which must be protected from *tumah:*

(1) חֻלִּין [*chullin*], *unsanctified food;*
(2) מַעֲשֵׂר שֵׁנִי [*maaser sheni*], *second tithe* (see 1:3);
(3) תְּרוּמָה [*terumah*], *kohen's share;*
(4) קֹדֶשׁ [*kodesh*], *sanctity,* i.e., sacrificial meat or flour; and
(5) מֵי חַטָּאת, *cleansing water.*

Each of these five levels has more stringent *tumah* and *taharah* regulations than those preceding it.

ב
ה־ו

[ה] **נוֹטְלִין** לְיָדַיִם לְחֻלִּין, וּלְמַעֲשֵׂר, וְלִתְרוּמָה; וּלְקֹדֶשׁ מַטְבִּילִין; וּלְחַטָּאת, אִם נִטְמְאוּ יָדָיו נִטְמָא גוּפוֹ.

[ו] **הַטּוֹבֵל** לְחֻלִּין וְהֻחְזַק לְחֻלִּין, אָסוּר לְמַעֲשֵׂר. טָבַל לְמַעֲשֵׂר וְהֻחְזַק

יד אברהם

נוֹטְלִין לְיָדַיִם לְחֻלִּין, — *We must wash the hands for unsanctified food,*

The Rabbis decreed that before eating bread, one must rinse his hands from a vessel containing at least a fourth of a *log* of water even though he had not knowingly touched any ritually unclean object *(Rambam, Hilchos Berachos* 6:1).

The rinsing is required only before *eating bread.* Such rinsing is not required before *touching* bread or before eating fruit or any other food *(Tos. Yom Tov; Gem.* 18b).

וּלְמַעֲשֵׂר, — *and for maaser,*

I.e., before eating מַעֲשֵׂר שֵׁנִי, *the second tithe.* One need not rinse his hands before merely touching such food, however *(Tos. Yom Tov; Gem., 18b).*

וְלִתְרוּמָה; — *and for terumah,*

Terumah possesses a higher degree of sanctity and must, therefore, be more scrupulously guarded from contact with any type of contamination. The Rabbis decreed therefore, that hands must be washed before even *touching* any *terumah (Tos. Yom Tov; Gem., 18b).*

In this sense, the regulations of *terumah* are more stringent than those of *maaser.* These three types of food, however, require no purification other than נְטִילַת יָדַיִם, *rinsing the hands.* Immersion of the hands in a *mikvah* is not necessary *(Rav).* This is true even in the case of Rabbinically decreed contamination, such as hands that touched Books of Scripture, or hands that touched contaminated food. In both cases, the person does not become contaminated, but by Rabbinic decree his hands require rinsing *(Meiri,* see *Yadaim* 3:2; see *Rav, Shabbos* 1:4).

וּלְקֹדֶשׁ מַטְבִּילִין; — *but for sanctified foods we must immerse* [*the hands*].

The food in question is the meat of sacrifices. For an Israelite it involves the meat of שְׁלָמִים, *peace offerings,* which are permitted him; for a *kohen* it includes the meat of חַטָּאוֹת וַאֲשָׁמוֹת, *sin offerings and guilt offerings* [and also מְנָחוֹת, *meal offerings*] *(Rav).*

Before eating such foods, one must immerse his hands in a *mikvah* [*ritual pool*]; even though there is no evidence that the hands had come in contact with any contaminated object *(Rashi; Rav).*

Others maintain that this stringent ruling applies only if the hands definitely touched an unclean object. Otherwise, ordinary rinsing is sufficient *(Meiri).*

That hands are decreed contaminated as regards sanctified foods was promulgated by King Solomon. That they are so considered regarding unsanctified food was decreed by the Rabbis of the later generations *(Shabbos* 14b).

וּלְחַטָּאת, — *Regarding the water of cleansing,*

5. We must wash the hands for unsanctified food, for *maaser*, and for *terumah;* but for *kodesh* we must immerse [the hands].

Regarding the [water of] cleansing, if one's hands became contaminated, his [entire] body is [considered] contaminated.

6. If one immersed himself for unsanctified food and [only] intended [to cleanse himself] for unsanctified food, he is prohibited from [eating] *maaser*. If he immersed himself for *maaser* and [only] intended [to cleanse himself] for *maaser*, he is

Water containing the ashes of the פָּרָה אֲדֻמָּה, *Red Cow*, was sprinkled on persons or objects who were contaminated by contact with a corpse. By means of the procedure given in *Numbers* 19, they became cleansed. Due to the more stringent nature of the water of cleansing, the Rabbis decreed the following regulation which they did not apply to the foods mentioned earlier *(Rashi; Rav).*

אִם נִטְמְאוּ יָדָיו נִטְמָא גוּפוֹ. — *if one's hands became contaminated, his* [*entire*] *body is* [*considered*] *contaminated.*

A person contaminated through a type of *tumah* which affects only the hands (as in the above cases), has a more stringent status as regards water of cleansing. Due to its greater sanctity, he is required to immerse his entire body before touching such water *(Rashi; Rav).*

6.

Purposeful Immersion

The Tanna continues his discussion of the five levels of sanctity. He now teaches that the Rabbis promulgated that in order to achieve a state of *taharah* through immersion in a *mikvah*, one must bear in mind the particular degree of sanctified food which he intends to involve himself with. If he were to lack such intended purpose, his immersion would not avail him.

הַטּוֹבֵל לְחֻלִּין וְהֻחְזַק לְחֻלִּין, — *If one immersed himself for unsanctified food and* [*only*] *intended* [*to cleanse himself*] *for unsanctified food,*

I.e., if one immersed himself before eating unsanctified food. Although this cleansing process is not required, some very pious people refrain from eating even such food unless they are in a state of *taharah (Tif. Yis.).*

Rambam's reading omits the conjunctive *vav*. The reading is הַטּוֹבֵל לְחֻלִּין, *one who immersed himself for unsanctified food,* הֻחְזַק לְחֻלִּין, *he is certified* [*as cleansed*] *for the purpose of* [*eating*] *unsanctified food.* According to this reading, the second phrase does not describe his intention; rather it gives the

ב ו

לְמַעֲשֵׂר, אָסוּר לִתְרוּמָה. טָבַל לִתְרוּמָה וְהֻחְזַק לִתְרוּמָה, אָסוּר לְקֹדֶשׁ. טָבַל לְקֹדֶשׁ וְהֻחְזַק לְקֹדֶשׁ, אָסוּר לְחַטָּאת. טָבַל לְחָמוּר, מֻתָּר לְקַל.

טָבַל וְלֹא הֻחְזַק, כְּאִלּוּ לֹא טָבַל.

יד אברהם

law that one is certified as cleansed only to the degree of his intention *(Avos HaTumah* 13:2).

אָסוּר לְמַעֲשֵׂר. — *he is prohibited from [eating] maaser.*

Despite his intention of attaining a state of *taharah,* he may not eat *maaser* or higher forms of sacred food because he must immerse expressly to cleanse himself for that high a degree of sanctity. For ordinary food, no intention is required during immersion, even though he had accepted upon himself the personal restriction of eating all food only in a state of *taharah (Tif. Yis.; Gem.* 19a).

טָבַל לְמַעֲשֵׂר וְהֻחְזַק לְמַעֲשֵׂר, — *If he immersed himself for maaser and [only] intended [to cleanse himself] for maaser,*

A person immersed himself with the intention of eating *maaser sheni* (see 1:3) in a state of *taharah* in Jerusalem *(Rav).*

אָסוּר לִתְרוּמָה. — *he is prohibited from [eating] terumah.*

If he is a *kohen,* he may not eat *terumah* since he had no intention of cleansing himself for the eating of *terumah.* [Levites and Israelites are forbidden to eat *terumah* in any case.]

He does not, however, contaminate *terumah* on contact *(Tif. Yis.).*

טָבַל לִתְרוּמָה וְהֻחְזַק לִתְרוּמָה, — *if he immersed himself for terumah and [only] intended [to cleanse himself] for terumah,*

[The *kohen* who immersed himself had no intention of eating *kodesh,* only *terumah.*]

אָסוּר לְקֹדֶשׁ. — *he is prohibited from [eating] kodesh.*

[He may not partake of sacrificial meat or flour, which have a higher level of sanctity. See preface and preceding mishnah.]

טָבַל לְקֹדֶשׁ וְהֻחְזַק לְקֹדֶשׁ, — *If he immersed himself for kodesh and [only] intended [to cleanse himself] for kodesh,*

The *kohen's* intention was to cleanse himself for the purpose of eating sacrificial meat.

אָסוּר לְחַטָּאת. — *he is prohibited from [touching] water of cleansing.*

He is not permitted to touch water containing the ashes of the Red Cow, used to cleanse those who came in contact with a corpse *(Rav).*

טָבַל לְחָמוּר, מֻתָּר לְקַל. — *If he immersed himself for a more stringent matter he is permitted [to occupy himself with] a less stringent matter.*

[One who immersed himself with the intention of cleansing, is considered ritually pure regarding all the lesser degrees. For example, if he immersed himself for consecrated food, he may eat *terumah, maaser,* and unsanctified food; and so on.]

2
6 prohibited from [eating] *terumah.* If he immersed himself for *terumah* and [only] intended [to cleanse himself] for *terumah,* he is prohibited from [eating] *kodesh.* If he immersed himself fo *kodesh,* and [only] intended [to cleanse himself] for *kodesh,* he is prohibited [from touching] water of cleansing.

If he immersed himself for a more stringent matter, he is permitted [to occupy himself with] a less stringent matter.

If he immersed himself without any intention, it is deemed as if he had not immersed himself.

YAD AVRAHAM

טָבַל וְלֹא הֶחְזֵק, — *If he immersed himself without any intention,*

His intention was to bathe rather than to bring himself to a state of *taharah (Rav).*

כְּאִלּוּ לֹא טָבַל. — *is deemed as if he had not immersed himself (Rav).*

He is not cleansed regarding *maaser, terumah kodesh,* and water of purification. Regarding unsanctified food, however, he is considered cleansed since no intention is required for unsanctified food (*Rav; Gem.* 19a).

7.

◆§ Midras Contamination

Consistent with the principles noted in the preceding mishnayos concerning the five degrees of *taharah,* the Rabbis promulgated a decree that those who are conscientious in their observance of only one level of *taharah* are considered lax as regards higher levels. Moreover, because their 'laxity' casts a doubt on their *taharah,* they are deemed contaminated with the most stringent degree of *tumah,* i.e., אַב הַטֻּמְאָה, *the primary cause of contamination.* Specifically in the case of our mishnah. we assign to them the contamination of מִדְרָס, *an article which supported the weight of a zav or a niddah* [*menstruant*]. [The word מִדְרָס, from דרס, *to step,* means *something stepped on.*]

In delineating the *tumah* of a *zav,* the Torah states: וְאִישׁ אֲשֶׁר יִגַּע בְּמִשְׁכָּבוֹ... וְהַיֹּשֵׁב עַל־הַכְּלִי אֲשֶׁר־יֵשֵׁב עָלָיו הַזָּב יְכַבֵּס בְּגָדָיו, *and a person who touches his bed... or who sits on the seat* [lit. *utensil*] *upon which the zav sits shall wash his clothes (Lev.* 15:5-6). The wording used in the case of the *niddah* is almost identical (*Lev.* 15:20-22). From these verses we see that such articles as the bed, couch, or chair of the *zav* or *niddah* acquire the same level of contamination as the person from whom the *tumah* emanates. One who touches any of these articles must immerse not only himself, but also his garments. The mishnah calls the contamination of objects upon which one of these people rests or leans by the term *midras.* One may contaminate through *midras* in any of five ways: by standing, sitting, or lying on an object, using leverage to move it (for example a seesaw or balance scale), or leaning against it (*Zavim* 2:4). [By specifying bed and seat, Scripture implies that *midras,* contamination, only applies to articles which are intended as chairs or similar supports for people. A makeshift seat, such as an inverted pot (about which a worker

ב
ז

[ז] **בִּגְדֵי** עַם הָאָרֶץ מִדְרָס לִפְרוּשִׁין. בִּגְדֵי פְרוּשִׁין מִדְרָס לְאוֹכְלֵי תְרוּמָה. בִּגְדֵי אוֹכְלֵי תְרוּמָה מִדְרָס לְקֹדֶשׁ. בִּגְדֵי קֹדֶשׁ מִדְרָס לְחַטָּאת.
יוֹסֵף בֶּן־יוֹעֶזֶר הָיָה חָסִיד שֶׁבַּכְּהֻנָּה, וְהָיְתָה

יד אברהם

may say, 'Arise! Let us do our job!') does not acquire midras-contamination (*Shabbos* 59a).]

Our mishnah lists categories of people according to their scrupulousness in observing the requirements of *taharah*. The more scrupulous must regard the belongings of the less scrupulous as if they had *midras*-contamination. This rule is a Rabbinic decree designed to safeguard the integrity of *taharah*. Under Scriptural law, such *tumah* could not be assumed; there would have to be clear knowledge that a *tumah* existed for articles to be deemed *midras*-contaminated.

◆§ Ammei HaAretz and Perushim

The mishnah begins with עַם הָאָרֶץ [*am haaretz*, plural, *ammei haaretz*], *ignorant people* [lit. *people of the land*]. This designation is used for those who sincerely seek to benefit the world by their behavior, but are ignorant of what is required of them in the accomplishment of their goal (*Rav, Avos* 5:10). In our case, the *am haaretz* thinks he is familiar with laws of *tumah* and *taharah*, but is not. Because he could not be relied upon to maintain *taharah*, the Sages decreed that his belongings be considered by *Perushim* as *midras*-contaminated.

Perushim [singular, *parush*] means *those who will withdraw*. The usual English rendering is Pharisees; but because the word Pharisees has often been used pejoratively, we prefer transliterating the term. The *perushim* were devout people, well versed in the laws of *tumah* and *taharah* who carefully withdrew from the company of the *am haaretz* whose care in avoidance of *tumah* was suspect.

בִּגְדֵי עַם הָאָרֶץ... — *The garments of an am haaretz.*

[I.e., the garments of an ignorant person who is not scrupulous in his observance of the laws of ritual purity (see preface).]

מִדְרָס... — *have midras [contamination]*

We fear that his wife may have sat on them during her *niddah* state, thus contaminating them for having supported her weight (*Tos. Yom Tov; Chulin* 35a).

Therefore, should one touch these garments, he and his clothing become contaminated and require ritual immersion (*Rav;* see preface).

The Sages, however, did *not* decree that the *am haaretz* himself should be considered a *zav*. Such a decree would have been too severe for most people to observe without great hardship, for instance, it would have become virtually impossible to find workers who could move barrels of wine from place to place without contaminating their contents because most laborers were unlearned. Thus, the mishnah's expression בִּגְדֵי עַם הָאָרֶץ, *the 'garments' of an am haaretz*, is carefully chosen; only the garments are contaminated, not the *am-haaretz* himself (*Tos. Yom Tov; Tos. Chulin* 35a, *Niddah* 34a).

Rambam, however, considers the *am-haaretz* himself to be a *zav*

2
7

7. The garments of an *am haaretz* have *midras*-[contamination] for *perushim*. Garments of *perushim* have *midras*-[contamination] for those who eat *terumah*. Garments of those who eat *terumah* have *midras*-[contamination] for [those who eat] *kodesh*. Garments of [those who eat] *kodesh* have *midras*-[contamination] for [those who handle] water of cleansing.

Yosef ben Yoezer was the most devout of the *kohanim*; yet his napkin was [deemed to have]

YAD AVRAHAM

(Avos Hatumah 13:1). Both views are discussed in *Yerushalmi*.

.לִפְרוּשִׁין — *for perushim.*

The *perushim* keep apart from *ammei haaretz* to avoid contamination. They were conscientious in their observance of *taharah* and were careful to eat even ordinary food in a state of *taharah (Tif. Yis.; Aruch).*

בִּגְדֵי פְרוּשִׁין מִדְרָס לְאוֹכְלֵי תְרוּמָה — *Garments of perushim have midras-[contamination] for those who eat terumah.*

The *Gemara* (19b) notes the absence in our mishnah of any reference to *maaser sheni*, which should have been mentioned here as it was in the previous mishnah. The *Gemara* concludes, therefore, that the text of our mishnah is defective. It should read: *Garments of perushim have midras-[contamination] for those who eat maaser [sheni]. Garments of those who eat maaser sheni have midras-[contamination] for those who eat terumah (Rav; Gem.* 19b).

.בִּגְדֵי אוֹכְלֵי תְרוּמָה מִדְרָס לְקֹדֶשׁ — *Garments of those who eat terumah have midras-[contamination] for [those who eat] kodesh.*

See preface to mishnah 5.

.בִּגְדֵי קֹדֶשׁ מִדְרָס לְחַטָּאת — *Garments of [those who eat] kodesh have midras-[contamination] for [those who have contact with] purification water.*

[Although they must maintain their *taharah* in order to eat *kodesh*, their garments are still regarded as *midras* for those who prepare the purification water of the פָּרָה אֲדֻמָּה, *Red Cow.*]

[As explained above, all these stringent rulings are Rabbinic decrees enacted for fear that those who observe *taharah* on lower levels may not be conscientious enough in their observance and perhaps a *niddah* sat on her husband's clothing.]

,יוֹסֵף בֶּן־יוֹעֶזֶר הָיָה חָסִיד שֶׁבַּכְּהֻנָּה — *Yosef ben Yoezer was the most devout of the kohanim;*

[He was the first *Nassi* of the *zugos* enumerated above in mishnah 2. The names יוֹסֵף, *Yosef*, and יוֹסֵי, *Yose*, are interchangeable. In fact, some texts have *Yosef* in mishnah 2, others have *Yose* in our mishnah.]

As the most devout of the *kohanim*, he obviously ate *terumah* with the required purity *(Meiri).*

...וְהָיְתָה מִטְפַּחְתּוֹ — *yet his napkin* [lit. *cloth*]...

I.e., the napkin with which he

ג א מִטְפַּחְתּוֹ מִדְרָס לְקֹדֶשׁ. יוֹחָנָן בֶּן־גֻּדְגְּדָא הָיָה אוֹכֵל עַל־טָהֳרַת הַקֹּדֶשׁ כָּל יָמָיו, וְהָיְתָה מִטְפַּחְתּוֹ מִדְרָס לְחַטָּאת.

[א] **חֹמֶר** בְּקֹדֶשׁ מִבִּתְרוּמָה, שֶׁמַּטְבִּילִין כֵּלִים בְּתוֹךְ כֵּלִים לִתְרוּמָה, אֲבָל לֹא לְקֹדֶשׁ.

יד אברהם

wiped his hands during meals *(Tif. Yis.).*

מִדְרָס לְקֹדֶשׁ. — *was* [*deemed to have*] *midras*-[*contamination*] *for those who eat kodesh.*

The mishnah cites the fact that the *midras* decrees apply even to as great a person as Yosef ben Yoezer. This is true for two reasons:

— Lest we think that these decrees were promulgated only because members of the lower groups were regarded as careless or not conscientious enough, the *mishnah* informs us that the ruling applied even to Yose ben Yoezer, the most devout of all the *kohanim* and the *Nassi* (*-Tif. Yis.).*

— No favoritism was shown even for great scholars and pious men *(Meiri).*

יוֹחָנָן בֶּן־גֻּדְגְּדָא הָיָה אוֹכֵל עַל־טָהֳרַת הַקֹּדֶשׁ כָּל יָמָיו, — *Yochanan ben Gudgada used to eat according to the purity of kodesh all his life;*

He guarded even ordinary food, as if it were sacrificial food. He protected it even from types of contamination that defile *kodesh.* The stringency of sacrificial meat is such that some orders of *tumah* contaminate it even though these same forms of *tumah* would not affect ordinary food. Nevertheless, Yochanan carefully kept such forms of *tumah* from touching even his ordinary food *(Rav).*

וְהָיְתָה מִטְפַּחְתּוֹ מִדְרָס לְחַטָּאת. — *yet his napkin* [lit. *cloth*] *was* [*deemed to have*] *midras*-[*contamination*] *for* [*those who handle*] *purification water.*

His napkin was considered a *midras* only as regards purification water. For sacrificial meat, however, it was considered ritually pure. This Tanna maintains that ordinary food, if prepared with the *tumah* and *taharah* stringencies required of *kodesh,* acquires the pure status of sanctified food. Therefore, the care taken for this ordinary food is adequate to prevent the *midras* decree from applying to *kodesh.* The *halachah,* however, follows the view expressed in *Niddah* 71b and *Chullin* 3b, that it is *not* like sanctified food *(Rav).*

Chapter 3

1.

⤙§ Standards of Taharah

As we saw earlier in 2:5-7, the Rabbis imposed stringent safeguards to protect the purity of items with varying degrees of sanctity. With the exception of water of cleansing, the highest degree of sanctity is קֹדֶשׁ, *kodesh* [lit. *holy*], which includes

midras-[contamination] for [those who eat] *kodesh.*

Yochanan ben Gudgada used to eat according to the purity [regulations] of *kodesh* all his life; yet his napkin was [deemed to have] *midras*-[contamination] for [those who handle] water of cleansing.

1. The stringency of *kodesh* compared to *terumah* is [as follows]:

(a) We may immerse vessels within [other] vessels for *terumah* but not for *kodesh.*

YAD AVRAHAM

the sanctified meat and flour of sacrificial offerings which are eaten, each according to its own *halachah.* The degree of sanctity just below *kodesh* is that of *terumah.* The first three mishnayos of this chapter list the eleven instances in which the Rabbis decreed that *kodesh* has a higher standard of *taharah* than *terumah.* Such standards are known as מַעֲלוֹת, *steps.*

חֹמֶר בְּקֹדֶשׁ מִבִּתְרוּמָה, — *The stringency of kodesh compared to terumah is [as follows:]*

With regard to the Rabbinically imposed safeguards of purity, *kodesh* has eleven stringent rules that do not apply to *terumah.* They are listed below *(Tif. Yis.).*

שֶׁמַּטְבִּילִין כֵּלִים בְּתוֹךְ כֵּלִים לִתְרוּמָה, — (a) *We may immerse vessels within [other] vessels for terumah...*

If two contaminated vessels are being immersed in a *mikvah* to cleanse them, the smaller may be within the larger one during the immersion *(Rav).*

[Although the two vessels rest one upon the other, the *mikvah* water can still circulate freely enough to touch all parts of both vessels, thus making the immersion valid.]

אֲבָל לֹא לְקֹדֶשׁ. — *but not for kodesh.*

Such an immersion was decreed to be invalid if the vessels are to be used for *kodesh.* In view of the great holiness of *kodesh,* the Rabbis forbid such immersion because it is possible that the inner vessel would weigh so heavily upon the outer one that the *mikvah* water could not circulate freely. Were this to happen, the immersion could not be valid since parts of the vessels would not have been touched by the water. In order to avoid the possibility of such a thing ever happening, they forbade such immersions even if the inner vessel was very small or light *(Rashi; Rav; Gem.* 22a).

The *Gemara* (22a) offers an alternative version of the danger which caused the Rabbis to promulgate the decree. There is a case where a vessel cannot be immersed within a larger one even for use with ordinary food: if the outer vessel is completely closed except for an opening smaller than שְׁפוֹפֶרֶת הַנּוֹד, *the tube of a leather bottle.* (That opening is defined as one too narrow to permit an average-sized person to insert two fingers in the opening and move them freely in all directions.) If such is the case, the water inside the vessel is considered to be separate from the rest of the *mikvah* and thus unsuitable for the immersion of needles or other small objects that can be placed inside the narrow-necked container. Since a

ג א אֲחוֹרַיִם, וְתוֹךְ, וּבֵית הַצְּבִיטָה בִּתְרוּמָה, אֲבָל לֹא בְקֹדֶשׁ.

הַנּוֹשֵׂא אֶת־הַמִּדְרָס, נוֹשֵׂא אֶת־הַתְּרוּמָה, אֲבָל לֹא אֶת־הַקֹּדֶשׁ.

case where a vessel cannot be halachically immersed within a larger one does exist, the Rabbis decreed that, for *kodesh*, no vessel should ever be immersed within another one lest people gain the erroneous impression that they may immerse contaminated needles within narrow-necked jars. This prohibition applies even if the smaller vessel is too light to weigh upon the larger one and thus impede the flow of water. However, if *both* vessels are contaminated, the immersion is valid since it would be incongruous for the outer one to become purified, but not the inner one *(Tif. Yis.; Rambam, Avos Hatumah* 12:1; see *Gem.* 22a).

Compound Vessels

[In all cases of טְמְאָה דְאוֹרַיְתָא, *contamination acquired according to Torah law,* all parts of the affected person or object become contaminated. Thus, if a man's finger touched a corpse, his entire body acquires a state of *tumah*; if one pocket of a garment touched a carcass, the entire garment is contaminated. In cases of *tumah* that are imposed by rabbinic decree, however, the Rabbis made an exception where separate parts of an article can function as independent vessels. For example, if the bottom of a vessel has a depression that can serve as a receptacle without the aid of the vessel's outer walls, the bottom is treated as an independent vessel. If that bottom were to be touched by something which by rabbinic decree contaminates, then the bottom, but *not* the rest of the vessel, becomes contaminated. Concerning this rule, the mishnah now makes a distinction between *kodesh* and *terumah*.

אֲחוֹרַיִם, — (b) *The bottom,*

If the bottom of the vessel can be used as an independent receptacle, it may be deemed a separate vessel insofar as its contamination will not carry over to the rest of the vessel. This is so if it touched contaminated liquids. By Torah law, such liquids cannot convey their contamination to vessels. The Rabbis, however, decreed that the vessel should be considered as contaminated. [The reason for this decree that all contaminated liquids should affect vessels is that people may become lax regarding those liquids which according to Torah law are contaminated. Examples of this are liquids exuding from a *zav* or *zavah (Tif. Yis.).*] However, the Rabbis softened the stringency of the decree by ruling that separate parts of the vessel would not transmit contamination to one another *(Rav).*

וְתוֹךְ, — *the inside,*

The inside, too, is deemed a separate vessel. Therefore, if it receives rabbinically ordained *tumah* the rest of the vessel remains ritually pure *(Rav).*

וּבֵית הַצְּבִיטָה... — *and the handle...*

The use of this word for *handle* is derived from וַיִּצְבָּט, *and he handed (Ruth* 2:14), thus the part of a vessel by means of which it is 'handed' is called בֵּית הַצְּבִיטָה. Other versions read בֵּית־הַצְּבִיעָה, *the place for the finger*, from the word אֶצְבַּע, *finger*, i.e., the handle into which one in-

3
1

(b) The bottom, the inside, and the handle [are considered separate vessels] as regards *terumah*, but not as regards *kodesh*.

(c) Someone carrying a *midras* may [simultaneously] carry *terumah*, but not *kodesh*.

serts his finger in order to pick up the vessel *(Rav)*.

בִּתְרוּמָה, — [*are considered separate vessels*] *as regards terumah,*

If any one of the three parts becomes rabbinically contaminated, the other two may still be used for *terumah (Rav)*.

אֲבָל לֹא בְקֹדֶשׁ. — *but not as regards kodesh.*

In the same case, no part of the vessel may be used for *kodesh*. Due to the greater sanctity of *kodesh*, the Rabbis ruled that the entire vessel should be considered contaminated *(Rav)*.

הַנּוֹשֵׂא אֶת־הַמִּדְרָס, — (c) *Someone carrying a midras...*

[For an explanation of *midras*, see 2:7.]

This refers to one who carries a shoe that had been worn by a *zav (Rashi; Rav)*, or any other garment or vessel that had borne the weight of a *zav*, through sitting, leaning or treading *(Tif. Yis.; Rambam)*.

נוֹשֵׂא אֶת־הַתְּרוּמָה, — *may* [*simultaneously*] *carry terumah,*

Although he is holding a *midras* he may simultaneously carry wine of *terumah* in an earthenware barrel since vessels of חֶרֶס, *clay*, or *earthenware*, contract *tumah* only through the inside. Therefore, even if the *midras* were to touch the outside of the barrel, the wine within would not become defiled *(Rashi; Rav)*.

We need not fear that he will insert the *midras* into the barrel thereby contaminating the wine. It is forbidden, however, to carry a *midras* and a *wooden* barrel of wine; since wooden vessels contract *tumah* from the outside, we fear that the *midras* may touch the barrel, contaminating it and the wine within. Moreover, if he were to carry loose *terumah*, since the *midras* is an אַב הַטֻּמְאָה [*av hatumah*], *original source of contamination*, the person carrying it becomes a רִאשׁוֹן לְטֻמְאָה, *first degree of tumah*, who in turn renders the *terumah* a שֵׁנִי לְטֻמְאָה, *second degree of tumah (Meiri*; see introduction to *Degrees of Tumah*, mishnah 2).

Others permit such carrying as long as neither the carrier nor the *midras* touch the *terumah (Rambam, Avos Hatumah* 12:3).

This is possible if he carries the *midras* on one shoulder and the *terumah* on the other, or both are strapped far apart from one another on a board *(Rambam* on *Mishnah)*.

אֲבָל לֹא אֶת־הַקֹּדֶשׁ. — *but not kodesh.*

[While one carries a *midras*, he may not simultaneously carry *kodesh*.]

This decree was promulgated because of an actual occurrence. Someone carrying wine of *kodesh* was wearing a shoe that was a *midras*. When his shoelace tore, he removed it and placed it atop the barrel of wine. Accidentally, it fell into the barrel contaminating the wine. Since the incident took place with *kodesh*, the precautionary decree was enacted only as regards *kodesh (Rav; Gem.* 23a).

ג בִּגְדֵי אוֹכְלֵי תְרוּמָה מִדְרָס לְקֹדֶשׁ.
ב לֹא כְמִדַּת הַקֹּדֶשׁ מִדַּת הַתְּרוּמָה: שֶׁבְּקֹדֶשׁ
מַתִּיר, וּמְנַגֵּב, וּמַטְבִּיל, וְאַחַר־כָּךְ קוֹשֵׁר:
וּבִתְרוּמָה קוֹשֵׁר וְאַחַר־כָּךְ מַטְבִּיל.

[ב] **כֵּלִים** הַנִּגְמָרִין בְּטָהֳרָה, צְרִיכִין טְבִילָה לְקֹדֶשׁ, אֲבָל לֹא לִתְרוּמָה.

יד אברהם

בִּגְדֵי אוֹכְלֵי תְרוּמָה... — *(d) The garments of those who eat terumah...*

[I.e., the garments of *kohanim* who eat *terumah* and are scrupulous in their observance of *taharah.*]

מִדְרָס לְקֹדֶשׁ. — *have midras-contamination for* [*those who eat*] *kodesh.*

[Since the care taken to maintain the purity necessary to *terumah* is inadequate for the purity of *kodesh,* those who eat *kodesh* must regard the garments of *terumah* eaters as if they were a *midras.* See *comm.* 2:7.]

לֹא כְמִדַּת הַקֹּדֶשׁ מִדַּת הַתְּרוּמָה: — *(e) Unlike the rule of* kodesh *is the rule of terumah;*

[This portion of the mishnah deals with חֲצִיצָה, [*chatzizah*], *interposition.* In order for immersion to be valid, there may be no interposition of any foreign substance that prevents the water of the *mikvah* from reaching all surfaces of the person or object being immersed.]

The laws of *chatzitzah* regarding vessels to be used with *terumah* are not as stringent as the laws dealing with vessels to be used for *kodesh (Rashi; Rav).*

[The introductory expression: *Unlike the rule of kodesh is the rule of terumah,* is apparently redundant since it seems to echo the first clause of our mishnah: *The stringency of kodesh compared to terumah.*] *Tosafos* (20b) explains that both the first *halachah* of the mishnah and this one deal with laws of *chatzitzah.* Since other laws intervened between these two similar rules, the mishnah repeats the essence of the first introduction *(Tos. Yom Tov).*

But why must stringency regarding the rule of *chatzitzah* be stated twice? The first instance, immersing vessels within other vessels, refers to *chatzitzah* caused by the pressure exerted by one vessel on the other. The latter case refers to *chatzitzah* as a result of a garment being knotted. Since the circumstance of the two cases are different, both must be clearly stated (*Tos. Yom Tov; Gem.* 21a).

Alternatively, the Tanna tells us that in the following matters *terumah* has a more lenient ruling in *two* respects. Hence the wording of the mishnah means: *Entirely different from the rule governing consecrated items is the rule governing terumah.* This will be explained in each case as we go along *(Tif. Yis.).*

שֶׁבְּקֹדֶשׁ מַתִּיר, — *for in the case of* [*immersing garments to be worn while handling*] *kodesh, one must untie* [*the knots*],

In the case of a contaminated *kodesh* garment in which there are knots [for example, a garment which is laced together], one must untie the knots prior to immersion. Should he fail to do so, the knots would be a form of *chatzitzah* in-

3 (d) The garments of those who eat *terumah* have
2 *midras*-[contamination] for [those who eat] *kodesh*.

(e) Unlike the rule of *kodesh* is the rule of *terumah*; for in the case of [immersing garments to be worn while handling] *kodesh*, one must untie [the knots], dry, immerse, and then retie [them]; but in [the case of] *terumah*, he may tie and then immerse.

2. (f) Vessels that were completed in a state of *taharah* require immersion for [use with] *kodesh*, but not for [use with] *terumah*.

YAD AVRAHAM

validating the immersion *(Rashi; Rav)*.

וּמְנַגֵּב, — *dry,*

[Any foreign substance is deemed a *chatzitzah* and must be removed from the surface of the garment of the vessel being immersed. Therefore,] if the article is wet, it must be dried before it is immersed, since the liquid [although not an actual *chatzitzah* for it will be washed away by the *mikvah* water] resembles a *chatzitzah (Rav)*.

Alternatively, wetness causes a garment to expand and its surface to become wrinkled. Since it is conceivable that the *mikvah* water will not get into the wrinkles, this condition creates a possible *chatzitzah (Meiri)*.

Alternatively, after untying the knots, he must cleanse the garment of any dirt or mud trapped in the knot *(Meiri)*.

According to *Rambam*, the mishnah deals with vessels constructed of several parts. They must be dismantled and cleansed to insure that no grease or dirt was stuck between the parts *(Avos HaTumah* 12:5).

וּמַטְבִּיל, — *immerse,*

[Only after the garment or vessel has been untied and dried or cleaned may it be immersed.]

וְאַחַר־כָּךְ קוֹשֵׁר: — *and then retie [them];*

[Once the immersion has been completed, the knots may be retied.]

וּבִתְרוּמָה קוֹשֵׁר וְאַחַר־כָּךְ מַטְבִּיל. — *but [in the case of] terumah, one may tie and then immerse.*

Not only is it unnecessary to untie knots already in the garment, one may even tie such knots before immersion. Hence, compared to *kodesh, terumah* has two leniencies *(Tif. Yis.)*.

2.

כֵּלִים הַנִּגְמָרִים בְּטָהֳרָה, — *(f) Vessels that were completed in a state of taharah...*

Before a vessel is completed and ready for use, it cannot become *tamei* even if it is touched by a corpse or a *zav*. Therefore, no matter what may have been done with it earlier, as long as the completion of the vessel took place in a state of *taharah* and it was safeguarded from then on, it cannot have become contaminated.

If the finishing touches of the

ג ב

הַכְּלִי מְצָרֵף מַה־שֶּׁבְּתוֹכוֹ לְקֹדֶשׁ, אֲבָל לֹא לִתְרוּמָה.
הָרְבִיעִי בְקֹדֶשׁ פָּסוּל, וְהַשְּׁלִישִׁי בִתְרוּמָה.

יד אברהם

vessel were made by a חָבֵר, *chaver* [lit., *colleague* (of the Sages)], i.e., one who is scrupulous in his observance of *taharah*, there is no possibility that the vessel is contaminated. Such a person is equivalent in reliability to a *parush* (see 2:7; *Rav; Gem.* 23a).

צְרִיכִין טְבִילָה לְקֹדֶשׁ, — *require immersion for* [*use with*] *kodesh,*

This regulation was promulgated because of fear that the saliva of an *am haaretz* (see 2:7) may have fallen upon the vessel just before its completion. If the saliva had not yet evaporated by the time the vessel was completed, the newly completed article would be contaminated. This is based on the principle that a person unlearned in the laws of *tumah* must as a precautionary measure be considered contaminated *(Rav; Gem.* 23a).

Tiferes Yisrael adds another possible fear: perhaps the *chaver* who completed the vessel may have spit on it or moistened it in some other way. If so, his hands which were not immersed, would contaminate the moisture and, through it, the vessel.

אֲבָל לֹא לִתְרוּמָה. — *but not* [*for use*] *with terumah.*

Such vessels may be used for *terumah*. Besides having no fear that an *am haaretz* spat on the vessel before its completion, we also have no fear that a *chaver* spat on the vessel and touched it with unwashed hands thereby contaminating the vessel through the saliva. Thus *terumah* has two leniencies as compared to *kodesh* *(Tif. Yis.)*.

הַכְּלִי מְצָרֵף מַה־שֶּׁבְּתוֹכוֹ לְקֹדֶשׁ, — *(g) A vessel combines whatever is in it with regard to kodesh,*

If many separate pieces of food were in one vessel and a contaminated person touched one of them, all the pieces become contaminated. They are not regarded as separate and unrelated items because the vessel that contains them all gives them the status of one piece, causing them all to be contaminated just as a single loaf of bread is contaminated in its entirety even if only a small part of it is touched by *tumah*. This is based on the phrase: כַּף אַחַת, *one spoon* *Num.* 7:14) which implies that the spoon renders all of its contents as one *(Rav, Tif. Yis.; Gem.* 23b).

Even if the pieces do not touch one another, they are nevertheless considered one *(Rambam, Avos HaTumah* 12:7).

Tosefos Yom Tov cites *Rambam* and *Rav (Eiduyos* 8:1) that the verse is only a Scriptural support [אַסְמַכְתָּא] for a Rabbinic decree. In our *Gemara* (23b), however, whether the Rabbinic decree is supported by this verse or not is in dispute.

Tiferes Yisrael comments that the vessel combines all its contents with regard to *kodesh* even if the vessel is flat, having no walls which contain and thus unify all its contents. [See *Rav, Eiduyos* 8:1.]

אֲבָל לֹא לִתְרוּמָה. — *but not with regard to terumah.*

I.e., if a defiled person touches

3
2 (g) A vessel combines what is in it with regard to *kodesh,* but not with regard to *terumah.*

(h) The fourth degree [of contamination] in the case of *kodesh* is *invalid,* but [only] a third degree [is invalid] in the case of *terumah.*

one of many pieces of *terumah* within a vessel, only that piece becomes contaminated. The other pieces in the same vessel, however, retain their *taharah (Rav).*

In keeping with his postulate that the mishnah lists cases where *terumah* has double leniency, *Tiferes Yisrael* comments that this leniency of *terumah* applies not only to a flat vessel which has no sides but even to a deep vessel.

Degrees of Tumah

The severity of *tumah* and the ability of one contaminated person or object to convey *tumah* to another are not uniform, but vary according to the degree of *tumah* and the class of object which has become contaminated.

The strictest level of *tumah,* אֲבִי אֲבוֹת הַטֻּמְאָה, *the most severe origin* [lit., *father of fathers*] *of contamination,* is a corpse. The next, and far more common, level is known as אַב הַטֻּמְאָה [*av*], *the origin* [lit. *father*] *of contamination.* This category includes: one who touched the carcass of a שֶׁרֶץ, one of eight species of *rodent or reptile,* or of a נְבֵלָה, *the carcass* of an animal that died by means other than a valid ritual slaughter; also a *zav, zavah,* or *niddah* discussed above in 2:7. (The various forms of this category are listed in *Keilim,* ch. 1, and elucidated by *Rambam* in his introduction to *Seder Toharos*).

A vessel or food that is contaminated by an *av* is a ראשון לְטֻמְאָה [*rishon*], *first degree of contamination.* An object contracting *tumah* from a *rishon* is a שֵׁנִי לְטֻמְאָה [*sheni*], *second degree of contamination.* In the case of חֻלִּין, *unsanctified food,* contamination can go no further than a *sheni;* thus, if a *sheni* touches another unsanctified food, the latter food acquires no degree of contamination whatever.

Due to the respectively greater degrees of stringency associated with *terumah, kodesh,* and cleansing water, their levels of contamination can go beyond that of *sheni.* Thus, if a *sheni* touches *terumah,* it becomes a שְׁלִישִׁי לְטֻמְאָה [*shelishi*], *third degree of contamination* — but the *tumah* of *terumah* goes no further than this third degree. *Kodesh* can go a step further, to רְבִיעִי לְטֻמְאָה [*revi'i*], *fourth degree of contamination,* while purification water can go as far as חֲמִישִׁי לְטֻמְאָה [*chamishi*], *fifth degree of contamination.*

As a general rule, the word טָמֵא [*tamei*], *contaminated,* is applied only to an object which can convey its *tumah* to another object. An object which cannot convey its *tumah* is called פָּסוּל [*pasul*], *invalid,* rather than *tamei.* Thus a second degree of *tumah* in the case of ordinary food, a third degree in the case of *terumah,* a fourth degree in the case of *kodesh,* and a fifth degree in the case of cleansing water are all known as *pasul* since they cannot convey their contamination to another object.

הָרְבִיעִי בְקֹדֶשׁ פָּסוּל, — *(h) The fourth degree [of contamination] in the case of kodesh is invalid,*

If the fourth consecutive recipient of *tumah* from an *av* is *kodesh,* it is rendered invalid for the Temple service or for eating, but it is only *pasul* in the sense that it cannot contaminate other *kodesh (Rav).*

וְהַשְּׁלִישִׁי בִתְרוּמָה. — *but [only] a third degree [is invalid] in the case of terumah.*

ג ג ובִתְרוּמָה, אִם נִטְמֵאת אַחַת מִיָּדָיו, חֲבֶרְתָּהּ טְהוֹרָה. וּבְקֹדֶשׁ מַטְבִּיל שְׁתֵּיהֶן, שֶׁהַיָּד מְטַמָּא אֶת־חֲבֶרְתָּהּ בְּקֹדֶשׁ, אֲבָל לֹא בִתְרוּמָה.

[ג] **אוֹכְלִין** אֳכָלִים נְגוּבִין בְּיָדַיִם מְסֹאָבוֹת בִּתְרוּמָה, אֲבָל לֹא בְקֹדֶשׁ.

יד אברהם

[In the case of *terumah*, the final degree of contamination, beyond which it cannot be conveyed, is the third.]

וּבִתְרוּמָה, אִם נִטְמֵאת אַחַת מִיָּדָיו, חֲבֶרְתָּהּ טְהוֹרָה. — *(i) In the case of terumah, if one of a person's hands became contaminated, the other one is [still] pure;*

If someone touched objects that are considered contaminated only by Rabbinic decree, only the hand that was in contact with the *tumah*, but not the rest of his body, becomes *tamei*. An example of such objects is contaminated food which cannot render a person *tamei (Rav)*. [Since only the offending hand is *tamei*, he may touch *terumah* with the other hand.]

Moreover, the contaminated hand does not require immersion: Rinsing is sufficient *(Rambam;* see above 2:5).

וּבְקֹדֶשׁ מַטְבִּיל שְׁתֵּיהֶן, — *but in the case of kodesh, he must immerse them both,*

If the contaminated hand was wet at the time it became *tamei*, the Rabbis decreed that the other hand is automatically *tamei*. If, however, the affected hand did not become wet, the other hand would not become *tamei* unless it were to touch the contaminated hand *(Rav; Rambam, Avos HaTumah* 12:12).

Raavad argues that even in the case of a wet hand, there is no logical reason to impose *tumah* on the other hand if it did not touch the contaminated hand.

Kesef Mishneh, however, defends *Rambam* on the ground that the Sages decreed higher standards of purity for *kodesh (Tos. Yom Tov).*

שֶׁהַיָּד מְטַמָּא אֶת־חֲבֶרְתָּהּ בְּקֹדֶשׁ, — *for one hand contaminates the other one as regards kodesh,*

Before touching *kodesh*, he must immerse both hands as explained above. This apparently redundant clause was included in the mishnah to allude to the case where he touched the hand of someone else with his contaminated hand. The second person is thereby rendered *tamei* and may not touch *kodesh (Tos. Yom Tov; Gem.* 24b).

אֲבָל לֹא בִתְרוּמָה. — *but not as regards terumah.*

Not only may he touch *terumah* with his clean hand if it did not touch the contaminated one, but even if his hands did touch, he may eat *terumah* with the clean one as long as the contaminated hand was not wet when they touched. Thus, *terumah* has two leniencies compared to *kodesh (Tif. Yis.).*

3.

The final decrees promulgated by the Rabbis for *kodesh* involve the following fundamentals:

(1) Scripture provides that food cannot contract *tumah* unless it has become

3
3 (i) In the case of *terumah*, if one of a person's hands became contaminated, the other one is [still] pure; but in the case of *kodesh*, he must immerse them both, for one hand contaminates the other as regards *kodesh*, but not as regards *terumah*.

3. (j) We may eat dry foods with contaminated hands if [the foods are] *terumah*, but not if they are *kodesh*.

YAD AVRAHAM

מֻכְשָׁר [*muchshar*], *prepared* or *made fit*, through being moistened by water or one of the other liquids [dew, wine, oil, blood, milk, honey] listed in *Machshirin* 6:4-8. Once the food has become *muchshar* through wetness, it retains its status even after becoming dry.

(2) *Kodesh*, however, can contract *tumah* even though it *never* became wet. This is the principle of חִבַּת הַקֹּדֶשׁ מַכְשַׁרְתָּן, *the higher esteem of kodesh makes it fit for contamination*, even without prior contact with liquids (*Chullin* 33a).

(3) Unwashed hands are given the status of a *sheni* for *terumah* even though they are not known to have come in contact with *tumah*. See previous mishnah and 2:5.

(4) Liquids, when touched by contaminated objects, always receive the status of *rishon*, even though the contaminator may be only a *sheni*. [The last two of these principles are Rabbinic in origin. See *Shabbos* 1:4.]

אוֹכְלִין אֳכָלִים נְגוּבִין בְּיָדַיִם מְסֹאָבוֹת, בִּתְרוּמָה, — *We may eat dry foods with contaminated hands if [the foods are] terumah,*

Food that never came in contact with liquid from the time it was harvested never became *muchshar* [*prepared*] to receive *tumah*. Therefore, it is not affected by contaminated hands. In the case of *terumah* [or a lesser sanctity] the food may be eaten even if held by such hands (*Rambam*).

.אֲבָל לֹא בְקֹדֶשׁ — *but not if they are kodesh.*

Since *kodesh* does not require הֶכְשֵׁר, *preparation* [see principle 2 in preface], the food can contract *tumah* even if it never came into contact with liquids. Therefore, if one were to eat *kodesh* with such hands, he would contaminate it. Even if he were to eat it with a fork or if a second person were to place the *kodesh* directly into his mouth so that his hands would not come in contact with it, it is nevertheless forbidden. The Rabbis feared that he might rinse a radish or an onion of *chullin* [*unsanctified food*] and put it into his mouth together with the *kodesh*. The *chullin*, having been moistened, would be *muchshar* and become contaminated by his hands. They would in turn render the *kodesh* in his mouth *tamei* (*Rambam*).

Others interpret the mishnah differently. *They may eat* [ordinary] dry *foods with contaminated hands,* [even] *with terumah.*

One may eat dry *chullin* together with *terumah* even though his hands are *tamei*, provided he eat the *terumah* with a fork or someone else puts it directly into his mouth. Since his hands have the status of *sheni*, they cannot convey *tumah* to the dry *chullin* since there is no

ג
ד

הָאוֹנֵן וּמְחֻסַּר כִּפּוּרִים צְרִיכִין טְבִילָה לְקֹדֶשׁ, אֲבָל לֹא לִתְרוּמָה.

[ד] **חֹמֶר** בִּתְרוּמָה שֶׁבִּיהוּדָה נֶאֱמָנִים עַל־טָהֳרַת יַיִן וָשֶׁמֶן כָּל־יְמוֹת הַשָּׁנָה,

יד אברהם

shelishi in *chullin* (see mishnah 2).

If the *chullin* were wet, however, the contaminated hands would render the liquid a *rishon*, (see preface). In turn, the *chullin*, would then become a *sheni*, could make the *terumah* a *shelishi* (mishnah 2).

[This may not be done] with *kodesh*.

If one is eating *kodesh* he may not partake of dry *chullin* along with it since there is a possibility that he will raise his contaminated hand to his mouth, thereby touching the *kodesh* and making it *tamei*. Although, theoretically, the same fear exists in the case of *terumah* as well, the Rabbis did not decree any precautionary measures because they relied on the acknowledged cautionary zeal of *kohanim* while eating *terumah*. As regards *kodesh*, however, the Rabbis were consistently more stringent in their decrees *(Rashi* 24b; *Rav)*.

הָאוֹנֵן... — *(h) The onein*...

Each immediate relative of a newly deceased person acquires a status of אוֹנֵן, *onein*. This status is in effect by Scriptural law until the deceased has been buried *(Tif. Yis.* citing *Shach, Yoreh Deah* 341:2; *Smag; Bach)*.

[*Tiferes Yisrael's* proof seems difficult since, as *Rambam (Bias Mikdash* 2:9) rules, that regarding the prohibition against eating *kodesh* the *onein* status extends until the day's end. *Yoreh Deah* 341:2 refers only to other laws of *onein*.]

Our mishnah refers to an *onein* who has not become contaminated by having touched or been under the same roof with the dead person. The law given by our mishnah is based on the regulations of mourning, rather than those of contamination *(Rav)*.

וּמְחֻסַּר כִּפּוּרִים... — *and one who needs to bring* [lit., *lacks*] *an atonement offering*...

[A *zav, zavah*, woman after childbirth, and *metzora*, who have immersed themselves as required by Scripture, are still prohibited from eating *kodesh* until they bring their respective atonement offerings as delineated in *Leviticus* (12; 13:1-32; 15:14-15,29-30). They may, however, eat *terumah* (where permitted) upon the nightfall after their immersion.]

צְרִיכִין טְבִילָה לְקֹדֶשׁ, — *require immersion for* [*eating*] *kodesh*,

Both an *onein* and one who had not been permitted to eat *kodesh* for lack of his atonement offering are required to immerse themselves before they are permitted to eat *kodesh*. This immersion is not to remove contamination, for, in the case of an *onein*, he had not been contaminated, and in the case of the bringer of an atonement offering, he had already purified himself by means of a prior immersion. Rather, the Rabbis decreed that one immerse himself whenever he leaves a state during which he had been forbidden to eat *kodesh*. Prior to this immersion, an *onein* who touched *kodesh* would not have con-

(k) The *onein* and one who needs to bring an atonement offering require immersion for [eating] *kodesh,* but not for [eating] *terumah.*

4. The stringency of *terumah* is [as follows]:

(a) In Judea [the *ammei haaretz*] are believed concerning the *taharah* of wine and oil throughout the

taminated it, but one who lacked an atonement offering would have contaminated *kodesh* merely by touching it *(Rav).*

Concerning the latter question of whether either of these people would contaminate *kodesh* by touch, *Tosefos Yom Tov* brings differing opinions including those of *Rav* and *Rambam.*

אֲבָל לֹא לִתְרוּמָה. — *but not for [eating] terumah.*

Since both the *onein* and the bringer of an atonement offering were permitted to eat *terumah,* even during periods when they were not permitted to eat *kodesh,* there is no basis for requiring their immersion before eating *terumah (Rav).*

4.

◆§ Stringencies of Terumah

After delineating the areas in which the laws of *kodesh* are more stringent than those of *terumah,* the Tanna delineates areas in which the laws of *terumah* are more stringent than those of *kodesh.*

The laws of our mishnah are based primarily on the fact that עַמֵּי הָאָרֶץ [*ammei haaretz;* sing., *am haaretz*], *ignorant people,* in *Eretz Yisrael* were very scrupulous concerning the purity of *kodesh,* but they tended to be lax with *terumah* for they did not acknowledge its stringency. If they claimed, therefore, that *kodesh* had not become contaminated, more credence could be given them than if they made a similar claim concerning *terumah.*

...חֹמֶר בִּתְרוּמָה — *The stringency of terumah* is [as follows]:

[Regarding the following areas, the laws of *terumah* are more stringent than those of *kodesh.*]

...שֶׁבִּיהוּדָה — *(a) In Judea...*

The Temple was situated in Judea, the southern sector of *Eretz Yisrael,* from which wine and oil could be transported directly to Jerusalem for use in the sacrificial service. However, between the northern province of Galilee and Jerusalem, there was a strip of foreign owned land. Since the Rabbis had decreed that all foreign land should be regarded as *tamei,* no wine or oil could be transported from Galilee to the Temple without becoming contaminated. Therefore, the following law is relevant only in Judea (*Rav; Gem.* 25a).

...נֶאֱמָנִים עַל־טָהֳרַת יַיִן וָשֶׁמֶן — *the [ammei haaretz] are believed concerning the taharah of wine and oil...*

If *ammei haaretz* bring wine for נְסָכִים, [*nesachim*] *wine offerings,* or if they bring oil for מְנָחוֹת, *meal offerings,* and claim that the wine or oil has been pressed and transported with the required *taharah,* they can be trusted. Even people who cannot be considered reliable with regard to

ג ובִשְׁעַת הַגִּתּוֹת וְהַבַּדִּים אַף עַל־הַתְּרוּמָה.
ד עָבְרוּ הַגִּתּוֹת וְהַבַּדִּים וְהֵבִיאוּ לוֹ חָבִית שֶׁל־יַיִן שֶׁל־תְּרוּמָה, לֹא יְקַבְּלֶנָּה מִמֶּנּוּ; אֲבָל מַנִּיחָהּ לַגַּת הַבָּאָה. וְאִם אָמַר לוֹ: הִפְרַשְׁתִּי לְתוֹכָהּ רְבִיעִית קֹדֶשׁ, נֶאֱמָן.

יד אברהם

terumah do not take lightly the stringency of *kodesh*. Although their testimony would be suspect regarding *terumah*, their claims concerning *kodesh* are believed *(Rav)*.

כָּל־יְמוֹת הַשָּׁנָה, — *throughout the year* [lit. *all the days of the year*];

The *am haaretz* is believed at any time if he claims that he guarded wine or oil for use as offerings *(Rav)*.

[As the mishnah continues, however, they can be trusted for *terumah* only at certain times of the year.]

וּבִשְׁעַת הַגִּתּוֹת וְהַבַּדִּים אַף עַל־הַתְּרוּמָה. — *and during the wine pressing and olive pressing seasons* [*the ammei haaretz are believed*] *even concerning terumah.*

During the seasons when grapes and olives are pressed, all people customarily purify their vessels and their utensils in order to set aside their *terumah* in *taharah*. Since it is a reasonable assumption that wine and olive oil were pure during those times, even an *am haaretz* is considered trustworthy if he testifies to that effect *(Rav)*.

עָבְרוּ הַגִּתּוֹת וְהַבַּדִּים... — [*If*] *the wine pressing and olive pressing* [*seasons*] *have passed...*

I.e., after the vintage season or after the season when most people press their olives *(Rav;* see also *Tos. Yom Tov, Bava Basra* 3:1).

וְהֵבִיאוּ לוֹ חָבִית שֶׁל־יַיִן שֶׁל־תְּרוּמָה — *and they then brought him a barrel of wine of terumah.*

After the vintage season, an *am haaretz* brought a *kohen*, who was a *chaver* [one scrupulous concerning matters of purity] a barrel of *terumah* wine, claiming it was ritually pure *(Rav)*.

The mishnah uses the plural form וְהֵבִיאוּ, *and 'they' brought,* to indicate that even though several *ammei haaretz* testified that the wine was uncontaminated, their testimony is not accepted since they are suspected of being lax in their observance of *taharah (Tif. Yis.)* [It is a general principle that we must doubt the testimony of otherwise honest people if they testify concerning something toward which they are habitually lax or which they regard as trivial or with contempt.]

לֹא יְקַבְּלֶנָּה מִמֶּנּוּ; — *he should not accept it from them;*

The *kohen* may not accept it on the basis of the *am haaretz's* claim that it is ritually pure *(Rav)*.

אֲבָל מַנִּיחָהּ לַגַּת הַבָּאָה. — *but he may set it aside for the next wine pressing season.*

Ammei haaretz are regarded as dependable during the pressing season. Therefore, should one of them wish to fulfill his *mitzvah* of giving *terumah* wine to the *kohen*, the *am haaretz* may store the barrel until the following vintage season,

3
4 year; and during the wine pressing and olive pressing [seasons the *ammei haaretz* are believed] even concerning *terumah.*

[If] the wine pressing and olive pressing [seasons] have passed, and they then brought him a barrel of wine of *terumah,* he should not accept it from them; but he may set it aside for the next wine pressing season. However, if he told him: 'Within I have separated a fourth [of a *log*] as *kodesh,*' he is believed.

YAD AVRAHAM

when his claim of *taharah* will be accepted, and then bring it to the *kohen (Rashi; Rav).*

Although the *kohen* knows that the wine was produced before the current vintage, he may, nevertheless, accept it because the Rabbis did not decree *tumah* on the *terumah* of *ammei haaretz* during this season *(Tos. Yom Tov; Rambam, Mishkav U'Moshav* 11:2; *Tosefta* 3:11).

וְאִם אָמַר לוֹ: הִפְרַשְׁתִּי לְתוֹכָהּ רְבִיעִית קֹדֶשׁ, — *However, if he told him: 'Within it I have separated a fourth [of a log] as kodesh,'*

If the *am haaretz* tells the *kohen* that in the barrel of *terumah* wine he has also placed the amount of wine he will require for the *nesachim* [wine offering] of his sacrifice, such wine is regarded as *kodesh* and the *am haaretz* may testify to its *taharah* status *(Meiri).*

Ordinarily, it is not permissible to mix *terumah* with *kodesh* since *terumah* is meant for the *kohen's* personal use while *kodesh* wine may not be used for human consumption.

Tosafos (Chullin 35b) explains that the *am haaretz* would have been permitted to mingle *terumah* with *kodesh* by making the following pronouncement: 'The quarter of a *log* that I will later set aside from this barrel to use as *nesachim,* shall now become *kodesh;* and all other wine in the barrel shall be *terumah.'* Although at the time of his declaration, it cannot be known exactly which wine will later be drawn off for *nesachim,* the formula is nevertheless valid. This is known as בְּרֵירָה, *retroactive clarification;* it provides that under certain conditions, one may assume that a later event falls under the halachic classification he had set forth earlier.

[A fourth of a *log* (approximately 3-4 fluid ounces) is the quantity used for Sabbath Eve *kiddush.* For the exact amount, see *Haggadah Kol Dodi,* by *R' David Feinstein.* This quantity is insufficient for even the smallest wine offering which must contain three *logim.* The mishnah means that the *am haaretz* claims this wine is to be used to supplement other wine for use as *nesachim.*]

נֶאֱמָן. — *he is believed.*

The *am haaretz's* claim concerning the entire barrel's *taharah* is accepted. Since he is trusted concerning the *kodesh,* he is also trusted concerning the *terumah* from the same barrel (*Rav; Gem.* 25b).

It would be a disgrace for the altar were we to consider the

ג
ה

כַּדֵּי יַיִן וְכַדֵּי שֶׁמֶן הַמְדֻמָּעוֹת נֶאֱמָנִין עֲלֵיהֶם בִּשְׁעַת הַגִּתּוֹת וְהַבַּדִּים, וְקֹדֶם לַגִּתּוֹת שִׁבְעִים יוֹם.

[ה] **מִן־הַמּוֹדִיעִית** וְלִפְנִים נֶאֱמָנִין עַל־כְּלֵי חֶרֶס. מִן־הַמּוֹדִיעִית וְלַחוּץ, אֵין נֶאֱמָנִים. כֵּיצַד? הַקַּדָּר

יד אברהם

terumah to be *tamei* while wine from the very same barrel is poured on the altar as a libation *(Rashi; Gem.* 25b).

(b) — כַּדֵּי יַיִן וְכַדֵּי שֶׁמֶן הַמְדֻמָּעוֹת... *[Concerning] jugs of wine or jugs of oil that are [still] mingled,*

The produce discussed here is *mingled* in the sense that tithes had not yet been separated from it. Thus, it is as if *terumah, maaser,* and *chullin,* which would later be separate entities, were intermingled. Produce in this state is known as טֶבֶל, *tevel.* The *am haaretz* who owned the produce intended to guard it from contamination so that he could later use part of it for *kodesh (Rav; Gem.* and *Rashi* 25b).

נֶאֱמָנִין עֲלֵיהֶם בִּשְׁעַת הַגִּתּוֹת וְהַבַּדִּים, — *they are believed about them during the wine pressing and the olive pressing seasons.*

Since it is the stated intention of the *am haaretz* to use part of the wine for *nesachim* and part of the oil for a meal offering, he is trusted not only concerning the *taharah* of the wine and oil, but even regarding the purity of the jugs in which he keeps them. Ordinarily, the *am haaretz* could not be relied upon to safeguard his vessels from *tumah.* In our case, however, since he is believed concerning the wine to be poured on the altar, it would be a disgrace to consider the jugs from which the wine had been poured as contaminated *(Rav; Rashi* 25b).

וְקֹדֶם לַגִּתּוֹת שִׁבְעִים יוֹם. — *and [even for] seventy days prior to the wine pressing [season].*

It was customary to begin preparing and cleansing the vessels seventy days before the wine pressing season. Therefore, an *am haaretz* is believed concerning their *taharah* from that time onward *(Rav; Rashi).*

The mishnah apparently contradicts itself. Earlier, an *am haaretz* who claims that a barrel contains *kodesh* is trusted also concerning the *terumah* contents of the same barrel. Here, however, where the wine is 'mingled' — i.e., a combination of intended *terumah* and *kodesh* — the *am haaretz* is believed only during the vintage season.

Tosafos (26b) answers that the above *halachah* deals with one who has actually consecrated the wine for *nesachim;* where he deals with actual, rather than anticipated, *kodesh,* even an *am haaretz* may be trusted at all times. The last part of the mishnah refers to one who has prepared or purchased a barrel of wine merely with the intention of using part of it for *nesachim.* Since we deal here with intentions rather than realities, the mishnah rules that he can be trusted only in season, or during the seventy-day

(b) [Concerning] jugs of wine or jugs of oil that are [still] mingled, they are believed about them during the wine pressing and olive pressing [season,] and [even for] seventy days prior to the wine pressing [season].

5. (c) From Modin inward, they are believed concerning earthenware vessels. From Modin outward, they are not believed. How so? If the potter

YAD AVRAHAM

preparation period.

Tiferes Yisrael comments that the seventy-day limitation refers to the vessels in which the future *nesachim* are stored. The *am haaretz's* credibility concerning vessels which do not contain actual *kodesh* is limited to the period when vessels are cleansed for use during the vintage season.

5.

The next two mishnayos continue to delineate areas in which the stringencies applied to *terumah* are greater than those applied to *kodesh.*

מִן־הַמּוֹדִיעִית וְלִפְנִים... — *(c) From Modin inward,*

Modin was a city fifteen *mil* from Jerusalem. The law about to be given applies from Modin *inward* all the way to Jerusalem (*Rav; Rashi; Meiri, Pesachim* 93b).

נֶאֱמָנִין עַל־כְּלֵי חֶרֶס. — *they are believed concerning earthenware vessels.*

Within the fifteen-*mil* range from Modin to Jerusalem, potters are trusted if they claim that their pottery was manufactured without becoming *tamei.* This trustworthiness extends even to *ammei haaretz* who are ordinarily suspect in matters of *taharah (Rashi; Rav).*

Such pottery was constantly needed for the preparation of sacrificial meat. Once used for *kodesh*, earthenware utensils could not be reused, as the Torah states: וּכְלִי־חֶרֶשׂ אֲשֶׁר תְּבֻשַּׁל־בּוֹ יִשָּׁבֵר, *and an earthenware vessel in which it is cooked shall be broken (Lev.* 6:21). Had the potters of Modin and elsewhere been unacceptable because of the decree of *tumah* imposed upon *ammei haaretz,* those people wishing to bring offerings would have suffered excessive hardship. Since this would have constituted גְּזֵרָה שֶׁאֵין רוֹב הַצִּבּוּר יְכוֹלִים לַעֲמוֹד בָּהּ, *a decree that the majority of the people could not endure,* the Rabbis exempted these potters from the effect of the decree *(Rav; Meiri; Rashi).*

Pottery kilns were prohibited in Jerusalem itself because their excessive smoke would blacken the walls and mar the beauty of the Holy City (*Rashi; Bava Kama* 82b).

The fifteen-*mil* radius would include other cities as well as Modin, but the mishnah specifies Modin because it was the main pottery center. It was unnecessary, therefore, to permit the purchase of pottery in other places *(Tos. Yom Tov).*

The trustworthiness of *ammei haaretz* extends only to pottery for

שֶׁהוּא מוֹכֵר הַקְּדֵרוֹת, נִכְנַס לִפְנִים מִן ג
הַמּוֹדִיעִית — הוּא הַקַּדָּר וְהֵן הַקְּדֵרוֹת וְהֵן ו
הַלּוֹקְחִים — נֶאֱמָן. יָצָא, אֵינוֹ נֶאֱמָן.

[ו] **הַגַּבָּאִין** שֶׁנִּכְנְסוּ לְתוֹךְ הַבַּיִת, וְכֵן הַגַּנָּבִים שֶׁהֶחֱזִירוּ אֶת־הַכֵּלִים, נֶאֱמָנִין לוֹמַר „לֹא נָגַעְנוּ".

וּבִירוּשָׁלַיִם נֶאֱמָנִין עַל־הַקֹּדֶשׁ; וּבִשְׁעַת הָרֶגֶל אַף עַל־הַתְּרוּמָה.

יד אברהם

use with sacrifices since it was impossible to rely solely on *chaverim* to supply enough small earthenware vessels for the Temple. As regards pottery for use with *terumah,* however, they are not trusted (*Gem.* 26a).

מִן הַמּוֹדִיעִית וְלַחוּץ, אֵין נֶאֱמָנִים. — *From Modin they are not believed.*

[Being *ammei haaretz,* the potters were lax in their observance of *taharah* and could not be trusted concerning the status of their products.]

כֵּיצַד? הַקַּדָּר שֶׁהוּא מוֹכֵר הַקְּדֵרוֹת, נִכְנַס לִפְנִים מִן הַמּוֹדִיעִית—הוּא הַקַּדָּר וְהֵן הַקְּדֵרוֹת וְהֵן הַלּוֹקְחִים—נֶאֱמָן. — *How so? If the potter selling the pots came inward of Modin — regarding the very potter, the very pots, and the very purchasers — he is believed;*

If a potter entered the area between Modin and Jerusalem with his wares, he is believed in his claim about their *taharah.* This credibility, however, applies only to the potter who brought in the pots. If he gives them to another potter in this area, however, the second potter is not believed. Also, the importing potter is believed only as regarding his own pots. If he buys pots from another potter, however, he is not believed concerning them. Another condition is that only purchasers who saw the potter enter may believe him. Others, who did not see him enter, may not rely upon him *(Rav; Rashi).*

Alternatively, even though he is the very same potter and the pots are the very same pots and the purchasers are the very same purchasers who would not be allowed to purchase these pots for use with *kodesh* had they met him outside of Modin, yet, since they met him inwards from Modin, he is believed concerning the pots. The Rabbis instituted the rule that only in this location the *ammei haaretz* are believed concerning their pots *(Meiri).*

יָצָא, — *[but] if he left,*

I.e., if the potter left Modin in a direction away from Jerusalem, thus leaving the area in which he is believed *(Rav).*

אֵינוֹ נֶאֱמָן. — *he is not believed.*

The same potter who would be believed if he sold his pots on one side of Modin cannot be relied upon if he sells them on the other side of Modin *(Meiri).*

selling the pots came inward of Modin — regarding the very potter, the very pots, and the very purchasers — he is believed; [but] if he left, he is not believed.

6. (d) Tax collectors who entered a house, and likewise thieves who returned utensils [they had stolen], are believed to say: 'We did not touch [them].'

(e) In Jerusalem they are believed concerning *kodesh* [the entire year], and during the festival season [they are believed] even concerning *terumah.*

YAD AVRAHAM

6.

הַגַּבָּאִין שֶׁנִּכְנְסוּ לְתוֹךְ הַבַּיִת, — *(d) Tax collectors who entered a house,*

Jews appointed by a gentile king to collect taxes entered a home to seize collateral until the householder paid his assessment *(Rashi; Rav).*

The Jewish tax-collectors and thieves are believed only if no gentile was overseeing them. Otherwise, we would assume that they inspected everything in their zeal to please him *(Tif. Yis.).*

וְכֵן הַגַּנָּבִים שֶׁהֶחֱזִירוּ אֶת־הַכֵּלִים, — *and likewise thieves who returned utensils [they had stolen],*

I.e., thieves who stole earthenware utensils and returned them out of remorse, not out of fear of being caught *(Rav; Gem.* 26a).

נֶאֱמָנִין לוֹמַר „לֹא נָגַעְנוּ". — *are believed to say: 'We did not touch them.'*

Even though they may be *ammei haaretz,* the tax agents are trusted if they claim they did not touch any utensils other than those that they took as security. Similarly, thieves are believed to say that they did not touch the inside of stolen earthenware utensils. Since earthenware utensils contract *tumah* from the inside only, it is possible that the thieves touched only the outside and did not contaminate the vessels *(Meiri).*

We already stated that this ruling applies only to *kodesh,* but not to *terumah,* since the Rabbis were motivated by the scarcity of earthenware vessels needed for use with sacrificial meat and wine *(Rambam; Rashi; Tosefta; Meiri).*

וּבִירוּשָׁלַיִם נֶאֱמָנִין עַל־הַקֹּדֶשׁ; — *(e) In Jerusalem they are believed concerning kodesh [the entire year],*

I.e., in Jerusalem itself, *ammei haaretz* are believed concerning all shapes and sizes of earthenware vessels since there was a shortage of such pottery. Large earthenware vessels, such as barrels from which to distribute the wine for *nesachim* were needed only by the Temple officials, but no others. Therefore, it was sufficient to permit only those available in Jerusalem itself. Small vessels, however, such as pots and cups, were needed by each individual who brought a sacrifice. In order to assure them an adequate supply, the Rabbis found it neces-

ג
ז

[ז] **הַפּוֹתֵחַ** אֶת־חָבִיתוֹ וְהַמַּתְחִיל בְּעִסָּתוֹ עַל־גַּב הָרֶגֶל, רַבִּי יְהוּדָה אוֹמֵר: יִגְמֹר. וַחֲכָמִים אוֹמְרִים: לֹא יִגְמֹר. מִשֶּׁעָבַר הָרֶגֶל הָיוּ מַעֲבִירִין עַל־טָהֳרַת

sary to permit all such small vessels that were found between Jerusalem and Modin (*Tos. Yom Tov; Gem.* and *Rashi* 26a).

וּבִשְׁעַת הָרֶגֶל אַף עַל־הַתְּרוּמָה. — *and during the festival season,* [*they are believed*] *even concerning terumah.*

Although *ammei haaretz* are not believed concerning the *taharah* of *terumah* (see mishnah 4) or earthenware vessels for use with *terumah* (see mishnah 5), on festivals, when all Jews are gathered in Jerusalem, they are trusted. This leniency is based on the verse: וַיֵּאָסֵף כָּל־אִישׁ יִשְׂרָאֵל אֶל־הָעִיר כְּאִישׁ אֶחָד חֲבֵרִים, *And all the men of Israel assembled to the city like one man, chaverim (Judges* 20:11). When all Jews are assembled as one, they are regarded as *chaverim*, scrupulous, and therefore, trustworthy, regarding the laws of *taharah* (see preface 2:7; *Rav; Gem.* 26a).

Rashi adds: The festival is a time of assembly.

Rambam explains this ruling in the following manner: The assumption of contamination regarding the *am haaretz* does not apply on the festival for all Jews are *chaverim* on the festivals. Their utensils, foods, and beverages are uncontaminated on the festival because they all cleanse themselves before the pilgrimage. Therefore, all are trusted during the festival concerning both *kodesh* and *terumah* (*Hilchos Mishkav U'Moshav* 11:10).

7.

◆§ After the Festival

Having taught in the previous mishnah that on festivals all Jews are regarded as *chaverim*, and that even the foods and vessels of *ammei haaretz* are considered ritually pure, the mishnah proceeds to discuss the case of a *chaver* merchant who allowed his food to be touched by *ammei haaretz* during the festival. What may he do with it after the festival, when the *ammei haaretz* revert to their status of *tumah*? *(Meiri).*

הַפּוֹתֵחַ אֶת־חָבִיתוֹ, — *If one opens his barrel...*

A *chaver* opened his barrel to sell wine in Jerusalem during the festival, with the result that many prospective customers, including *ammei haaretz*, touched it *(Rashi; Rav; Tif. Yis.).*

וְהַמַּתְחִיל בְּעִסָּתוֹ עַל־גַּב הָרֶגֶל; — *or begins using his dough for festival needs,*

A *chaver* began selling his pastries for the festival and his customers, among them *ammei haaretz*, touched them *(Meiri; Tif. Yis.).*

רַבִּי יְהוּדָה אוֹמֵר: יִגְמֹר. — *R' Yehudah says: He may finish* [*selling after the festival*].

If any wine or dough is left after the festival, R' Yehudah maintains that he may continue to sell them as

7. **I**f one opens his barrel or begins using his dough for festival needs, R' Yehudah says: He may finish [selling after the festival]. The Sages say: He may not finish.

Once the festival was over, they would remove [everything] to facilitate the cleansing of the Temple

pure despite the fact that they had been touched by *ammei haaretz.* Since the Rabbis removed the decreed status of contamination from the *ammei haaretz,* anything touched by them acquires no *tumah.* R' Yehudah argues that if a merchant were not permitted to finish selling his wine and cake after the festival, he would be reluctant to stock sufficient merchandise, with the result that pilgrims would find it difficult to purchase food *(Rav).*

וַחֲכָמִים אוֹמְרִים: לֹא יִגְמֹר. — *The Sages say: He may not finish.*

He may not continue to sell the remaining wine and dough after the festival. The Sages reason that actually the *ammei haaretz* are suspected of laxness in their observance of *taharah* and they must therefore be considered as *tamei.* On the festival, however, only a special dispensation allows us to rely upon them. After the festival we must again consider them as contaminated retroactively. Hence, the storekeeper may not continue to sell any wares that were touched by *ammei haaretz.* For this reason, we cleanse the Temple Courtyard immediately after the conclusion of the festival. Even R' Yehudah concurs that the Temple must be cleansed, as will be seen later in our mishnah. Regarding the purity of food, however, he disagrees, as explained above *(Rav; Rashi, Beitzah* 11b).

The *halachah* is in accordance with the Sages *(Rav).*

מִשֶּׁעָבַר הָרֶגֶל הָיוּ מַעֲבִירִין עַל־טָהֳרַת הָעֲזָרָה. — *Once the festival was over, they would remove [everything] to facilitate the purification of the Temple Courtyard.*

Although the Tanna uses the word עֲזָרָה, *(Temple) Courtyard,* the reference is to the vessels of the Sanctuary itself which were brought out to the Courtyard to be cleansed. The Courtyard itself cannot become contaminated *(Meiri).*

All vessels would be removed in order to immerse those that were touched by *ammei haaretz* during the festival and to enable the *kohanim* to cleanse the Temple Courtyard of all *tumah (Rashi; Rav).*

As explained previously, the vessels that came in contact with *ammei haaretz* during the festival are considered *tamei* retroactively.

There are various other interpretations of the word מַעֲבִירִין. Some render: *They would announce [the necessity] of cleansing the Temple Court.* This usage is based on the verse (*Exodus* 36:6): וַיַּעֲבִירוּ קוֹל בַּמַּחֲנֶה, *And they caused a voice to pass in the camp (Tos.; Rid; Meiri).*

Others explain: *They would leave over everything for the sake of cleansing the Temple Courtyard (Meiri).*

Alternatively, *they give precedence to the cleansing of the*

ג ח הָעֲזָרָה. עָבַר הָרֶגֶל בְּיוֹם שִׁשִּׁי, לֹא הָיוּ מַעֲבִירִין, מִפְּנֵי כְבוֹד הַשַּׁבָּת.

רַבִּי יְהוּדָה אוֹמֵר: אַף לֹא בְיוֹם חֲמִישִׁי, שֶׁאֵין הַכֹּהֲנִים פְּנוּיִין.

[ח] **כֵּיצַד** מַעֲבִירִים עַל־טָהֳרַת הָעֲזָרָה? מַטְבִּילִין אֶת־הַכֵּלִים שֶׁהָיוּ בַמִּקְדָּשׁ, וְאוֹמְרִין לָהֶם: „הִזָּהֲרוּ שֶׁלֹּא תִגְּעוּ בַשֻּׁלְחָן (וּבַמְּנוֹרָה) וּתְטַמְּאוּהוּ״.

כָּל־הַכֵּלִים שֶׁהָיוּ בַמִּקְדָּשׁ, יֵשׁ לָהֶם שְׁנִיִּים וּשְׁלִישִׁים, שֶׁאִם נִטְמְאוּ הָרִאשׁוֹנִים יָבִיאוּ שְׁנִיִּים תַּחְתֵּיהֶן.

יד אברהם

Temple Courtyard (Meiri).

עָבַר הָרֶגֶל בְּיוֹם שִׁשִּׁי, לֹא הָיוּ מַעֲבִירִין, מִפְּנֵי כְבוֹד הַשַּׁבָּת. — *If the day after the festival was* [lit., *if the festival passed on*] *Friday, they would not remove* [*the vessels*], *in deference to the honor of the Sabbath.*

[If the last day of the festival was Thursday, making Friday the first free day] they would not commence with the cleansing of the Temple Courtyard until Sunday since the *kohanim* were busy at home preparing for the Sabbath *(Rav).*

רַבִּי יְהוּדָה אוֹמֵר: אַף לֹא בְיוֹם חֲמִישִׁי, — *R' Yehudah says: Not even* [*if the day after the festival was*] *Thursday,*

If the last day of the festival was Wednesday, making Thursday the first free day, they would not immerse the vessels until Sunday *(Rav).*

שֶׁאֵין הַכֹּהֲנִים פְּנוּיִין. — *because the kohanim were not free.*

On the day after the festival, the *kohanim* were occupied with removing the ashes that had accumulated on the altar from the numerous offerings that were sacrificed during the festival (Rav).

8.

כֵּיצַד מַעֲבִירִים עַל טָהֳרַת הָעֲזָרָה? מַטְבִּילִין אֶת־הַכֵּלִים שֶׁהָיוּ בַמִּקְדָּשׁ, — *How did they go about removing* [*everything*] *for the cleansing of the Temple Courtyard? They immersed the vessels that were in the Temple,*

[They immersed the vessels because they were touched by *ammei haaretz* during the festival, thus contaminating them. (See preceding mishnah.)]

וְאוֹמְרִין לָהֶם: „הִזָּהֲרוּ שֶׁלֹּא תִגְּעוּ בַשֻּׁלְחָן (וּבַמְּנוֹרָה) וּתְטַמְּאוּהוּ״. — *After they had said to them: 'Be careful not to touch the Table (and the Menorah)* [*lest you*] *contaminate it.'*

This admonition was given throughout the festival. Since the שֻׁלְחָן, *Table,* upon which the לֶחֶם הַפָּנִים, *showbread,* was placed had to remain in place, it could not be immersed in a *mikvah* if it became

Courtyard. If the day after the festival was Friday, they would not remove [the vessels], in deference to the honor of the Sabbath.

R' Yehudah says: Not even [if the day after the festival was] Thursday, because the *kohanim* were not free.

8. How did they go about removing [everything] for the cleansing of the Temple Courtyard? They immersed the vessels that were in the Temple, after they had said to them: 'Be careful not to touch the Table (and the *Menorah*) [lest you] contaminate it.'

All the vessels that were [used] in the Temple had second and third [replacement] sets so that if the first one became contaminated, they would bring the second ones to replace them.

YAD AVRAHAM

tamei. Therefore, precautions were taken to maintain its uninterrupted *taharah (Rav).*

Tosafos (28b) comments that this warning was directed at unlearned *kohanim* rather than Israelites. Since the Table was located inside the הֵיכָל, *Temple building,* where Israelites were not permitted to enter, there was no fear of contamination by them. An ignorant *kohen,* however, in his zeal to prostrate himself within, might touch the Table.

The Table had to remain in place for the Torah declares *(Exod.* 25:30): לֶחֶם פָּנִים לְפָנַי תָּמִיד, *showbread before Me continuously,* which the *Gemara* (26b) interprets as a command that the Table not be moved *(Rav).*

The *Gemara* (26b) implies clearly that the *Menorah* may be moved if necessary. Therefore, were it ever to become *tamei,* it could be removed for immersion. Although the Torah uses the word תָּמִיד with reference to the *Menorah (Exod.* 27:20), the word there means *continually,* i.e., the flames should be lit uninterruptedly, night after night, not that they must continuously remain in place *(Rashi).* Therefore, the word וּבַמְּנוֹרָה, *and the Menorah,* should be deleted from the mishnah. There was no reason for such a special warning *(Tos. Yom Tov; Tif. Yis.).*

כָּל־הַכֵּלִים שֶׁהָיוּ בַמִּקְדָּשׁ, יֵשׁ לָהֶם שְׁנִיִּים וּשְׁלִישִׁים, — *All the vessels that were [used] in the Temple had second and third [replacement] sets...*

Concerning the Table, *Meiri* quotes commentaries who hold that there was but one. *Tiferes Yisrael,* however, contends that there were two, since it was possible for it to become contaminated despite all precautions.

שֶׁאִם נִטְמְאוּ הָרִאשׁוֹנִים יָבִיאוּ שְׁנִיִּים תַּחְתֵּיהֶן. — *so that if the first ones became contaminated, they would*

ג כָּל־הַכֵּלִים שֶׁהָיוּ בַמִּקְדָּשׁ טְעוּנִין טְבִילָה,
ח חוּץ מִמִּזְבַּח הַזָּהָב וּמִזְבַּח הַנְּחֹשֶׁת, מִפְּנֵי שֶׁהֵן
כְּקַרְקַע; דִּבְרֵי רַבִּי אֱלִיעֶזֶר. וַחֲכָמִים אוֹמְרִים:
מִפְּנֵי שֶׁהֵן מְצֻפִּין.

יד אברהם

bring the second ones to replace them.

[Compare *Yoma* 1:1 — They would prepare a substitute *kohen gadol* before *Yom Kippur*, that he may immediately be ready to perform the services of the day if the first *kohen gadol* became contaminated.]

כָּל־הַכֵּלִים שֶׁהָיוּ בַמִּקְדָּשׁ טְעוּנִין טְבִילָה, — *All the vessels that were [used] in the Temple require immersion...*

All required immersion because of the *tumah* that they may have contracted during the festival *(Rashi; Rav).*

The same ruling pertains if they became *tamei* at any time during the year *(Meiri).*

חוּץ מִמִּזְבַּח הַזָּהָב וּמִזְבַּח הַנְּחֹשֶׁת, — *except for the Golden Altar and the Copper Altar,*

[Each of these altars is called by three names which respectively represent its composition, purpose and location:

Built of *shittim*-wood plated with זָהָב, *gold (Exod.* 30:1-3), one altar was used primarily for the daily burning of קְטֹרֶת, *incense (Exod.* 30:1), and was located within the Temple building itself. This altar was called: מִזְבַּח הַזָּהָב, *the Golden Altar (Exod.* 39:38; *I Kings* 7:48); מִזְבַּח הַקְּטֹרֶת, *the Incense Altar (Exod.* 30:27; *I Chron.* 6:34); and מִזְבֵּחַ הַפְּנִימִי, *the Inner Altar* (a name not found in Scripture).

The other altar was originally built of *shittim*-wood plated with נְחֹשֶׁת, *copper (Exod.* 27:1-2). After the nation entered *Eretz Yisrael* the Tabernacle was erected in Shiloh. There the altar was built of stone, in fulfillment of the verse: *When you make a stone altar for me... (Exod.* 20:22). Whether this altar was plated with copper or not is the subject of a dispute (see *Zevachim* 61b). When King Solomon built the First Temple, he erected a copper altar (*II Chron.* 4:1) but Scripture does not specify whether it contained wood, stone or any material other than copper. The altar of the Second Temple is not described in Scripture but is described in the *Mishnah (Middos* 3) as being of stone.

This altar was used primarily for animal sacrifices. Of all animal sacrifices only the עוֹלָה [*Olah*], *burnt offering*, is entirely consumed by the altar fire. The meat of other sacrifices is also eaten by either the owner, the *kohen*, or both.

Finally, this altar stood out-of-doors in the Temple Courtyard. The three names of this altar are: מִזְבַּח הַנְּחֹשֶׁת, *the Copper Altar (Exod.* 38:30; *I Kings* 8:64); מִזְבַּח הָעֹלָה, *the Olah Altar (Exod.* 38:1; *Lev.* 4:7; *II Chron.* 29:18); and מִזְבֵּחַ הַחִיצוֹן, *the Outer Altar* (a name not found in Scripture).]

Since mishnah 4, the Tanna has been discussing laws pertaining to the status of *tumah* which the Sages

3
8 All the vessels that were [used] in the Temple require immersion except for the Golden Altar and the Copper Altar, because they are like earth — these are the words of R' Eliezer. The Sages say: Because they are plated.

YAD AVRAHAM

conferred upon *ammei haaretz*. At the time this decree was promulgated, the Copper Altar had already been replaced by one of stone. Inclusion of the Copper Altar in the mishnah is therefore either academic, or refers to some future time when the altar will, perhaps, once again be copper plated *(Tos. Yom Tov)*.

Alternatively, the mishnah may refer to contamination from sources other than an *am haaretz;* for example, contact with a dead שֶׁרֶץ, *rodent*, from those listed in *Leviticus* 11:29,30 *(R' David Feinstein)*.

מִפְּנֵי שֶׁהֵן כְּקַרְקַע; דִּבְרֵי רַבִּי אֱלִיעֶזֶר. — *because they are like earth — these are the words of R' Eliezer.*

Only movable objects can become *tamei*, but not the earth itself or anything regarded as part of it. The Torah refers to the Copper Altar as מִזְבַּח אֲדָמָה, *Earthen Altar (Exod.* 20:21), thus likening it to earth which cannot become *tamei*. Furthermore, since the Torah describes the two altars collectively with the word מִזְבְּחוֹת, *altars (Num.* 3:31), we infer that both share the same status. Therefore, since the Copper Altar does not acquire *tumah*, neither does the Golden Altar *(Rav; Rashi)*.

Although the Table would have required immersion in the event it became contaminated. Actually it was never immersed because the *ammei haaretz* were warned not to touch it [see above] *(Rav; Rashi)*.

וַחֲכָמִים אוֹמְרִים: מִפְּנֵי שֶׁהֵן מְצֻפִּין. — *The sages say: Because they are plated.*

The Sages maintain that the altars do require immersion because they are plated, respectively, with gold and copper; the metal covering removes them from the category of wooden vessels. Had they not been plated, they would be considered as wooden vessels designed to remain permanently at rest which Scripture excludes from contracting contamination *(Rav)*.

Alternatively, the Sages concur with R' Eliezer that the altars are not susceptible to *tumah*; they disagree only with his reason why. They maintain that the altars are indeed considered as wooden vessels made to rest, since their gold and copper are merely covering plates rather than primary components of the altars *(Rav* citing *Rambam)*.

סליק מסכת חגיגה
הדרן עלך סדר מועד

Hadran – הַדְרָן

Upon the סיום, *completion*, of the study of the entire *Seder Moed*, a festive meal, preferably with a *minyan* should be arranged. It has the status of a *Seudas Mitzvah*. The following prayers of thanksgiving are recited by one who has completed the learning.

הַדְרָן עֲלָךְ סֵדֶר מוֹעֵד וַהֲדָרָךְ עֲלָן, דַּעְתָּן עֲלָךְ סֵדֶר מוֹעֵד וְדַעְתָּךְ עֲלָן, לָא נִתְנְשֵׁי מִינָךְ סֵדֶר מוֹעֵד וְלָא תִתְנְשֵׁי מִינָן לָא בְּעָלְמָא הָדֵין וְלָא בְּעָלְמָא דְּאָתֵי. (Recite three times)

יְהִי רָצוֹן מִלְּפָנֶיךָ יהוה אֱלֹהֵינוּ וֵאלֹהֵי אֲבוֹתֵינוּ שֶׁתְּהֵא תוֹרָתְךָ אוּמָנוּתֵינוּ בָּעוֹלָם הַזֶּה, וּתְהֵא עִמָּנוּ לָעוֹלָם הַבָּא. חֲנִינָא בַּר פַּפָּא, רָמִי בַּר פַּפָּא, נַחְמָן בַּר פַּפָּא, אַחַאי בַּר פַּפָּא, אַבִּי מָרִי בַּר פַּפָּא, רַפְרָם בַּר פַּפָּא, רָכִישׁ בַּר פַּפָּא, סוּרְחָב בַּר פַּפָּא, אָדָא בַּר פַּפָּא, דָּרוּ בַּר פַּפָּא:

הַעֲרֶב נָא יהוה אֱלֹהֵינוּ אֶת־דִּבְרֵי תוֹרָתְךָ בְּפִינוּ וּבְפִי עַמְּךָ בֵּית יִשְׂרָאֵל, וְנִהְיֶה כּוּלָּנוּ אֲנַחְנוּ וְצֶאֱצָאֵינוּ וְצֶאֱצָאֵי עַמְּךָ בֵּית יִשְׂרָאֵל כֻּלָּנוּ יוֹדְעֵי שְׁמֶךָ וְלוֹמְדֵי תוֹרָתֶךָ. מֵאוֹיְבַי תְּחַכְּמֵנִי מִצְוֹתֶיךָ כִּי לְעוֹלָם הִיא לִי. יְהִי לִבִּי תָמִים בְּחֻקֶּיךָ לְמַעַן לֹא אֵבוֹשׁ. לְעוֹלָם לֹא אֶשְׁכַּח פִּקּוּדֶיךָ כִּי בָם חִיִּיתָנִי. בָּרוּךְ אַתָּה יהוה לַמְּדֵנִי חֻקֶּיךָ. אָמֵן אָמֵן אָמֵן סֶלָה וָעֶד:

מוֹדֶה אֲנִי לְפָנֶיךָ ה׳ אֱלֹהֵינוּ וֵאלֹהֵי אֲבוֹתֵינוּ, שֶׁשַּׂמְתָּ חֶלְקִי מִיּוֹשְׁבֵי בֵּית הַמִּדְרָשׁ וְלֹא שַׂמְתָּ חֶלְקִי מִיּוֹשְׁבֵי קְרָנוֹת, שֶׁאֲנִי מַשְׁכִּים וְהֵם מַשְׁכִּימִים. אֲנִי מַשְׁכִּים לְדִבְרֵי תוֹרָה וְהֵם מַשְׁכִּימִים לִדְבָרִים בְּטֵלִים. אֲנִי עָמֵל וְהֵם עֲמֵלִים. אֲנִי עָמֵל וּמְקַבֵּל שָׂכָר וְהֵם עֲמֵלִים וְאֵינָם מְקַבְּלִים שָׂכָר. אֲנִי רָץ וְהֵם רָצִים. הֵם רָצִים לִבְאֵר שַׁחַת וַאֲנִי רָץ לְחַיֵּי הָעוֹלָם הַבָּא, שֶׁנֶּאֱמַר: וְאַתָּה אֱלֹהִים, תּוֹרִדֵם לִבְאֵר שַׁחַת, אַנְשֵׁי דָמִים וּמִרְמָה לֹא יֶחֱצוּ יְמֵיהֶם, וַאֲנִי אֶבְטַח בָּךְ:

יְהִי רָצוֹן מִלְּפָנֶיךָ יהוה אֱלֹהַי וֵאלֹהֵי אֲבוֹתַי כְּשֵׁם שֶׁעֲזַרְתַּנִי לְסַיֵּים סֵדֶר מוֹעֵד כֵּן תְּעַזְרֵנִי לְהַתְחִיל מַסֶּכְתּוֹת וּסְפָרִים אֲחֵרִים וּלְסַיְּימָם, לִלְמוֹד וּלְלַמֵּד, לִשְׁמוֹר וְלַעֲשׂוֹת וּלְקַיֵּים אֶת־כָּל־דִּבְרֵי תַלְמוּד תּוֹרָתְךָ בְּאַהֲבָה, וּזְכוּת כָּל־הַתַּנָּאִים וַאֲמוֹרָאִים וְתַלְמִידֵי חֲכָמִים יַעֲמוֹד לִי וּלְזַרְעִי שֶׁלֹּא תָמוּשׁ הַתּוֹרָה מִפִּי וּמִפִּי זַרְעִי וְזֶרַע זַרְעִי עַד עוֹלָם. וְתִתְקַיֵּים בִּי, בְּהִתְהַלֶּכְךָ תַּנְחֶה אוֹתָךְ בְּשָׁכְבְּךָ תִּשְׁמוֹר עָלֶיךָ וַהֲקִיצוֹתָ הִיא תְשִׂיחֶךָ; כִּי בִי יִרְבּוּ יָמֶיךָ וְיוֹסִיפוּ לְךָ שְׁנוֹת חַיִּים; אוֹרֶךְ יָמִים בִּימִינָהּ עוֹשֶׁר וְכָבוֹד בִּשְׂמֹאלָהּ; יהוה עֹז לְעַמּוֹ יִתֵּן יהוה יְבָרֵךְ אֶת־עַמּוֹ בַשָּׁלוֹם:

If a *minyan* is present, the following *Kaddish* is recited.

יִתְגַּדַּל וְיִתְקַדַּשׁ שְׁמֵהּ רַבָּא. בְּעָלְמָא דִּי הוּא עָתִיד לְאִתְחַדָּתָא, וּלְאַחֲיָאָה מֵתַיָּא, וּלְאַסָּקָא (יָתְהוֹן) לְחַיֵּי עָלְמָא, וּלְמִבְנֵא קַרְתָּא דִּי יְרוּשְׁלֵם, וּלְשַׁכְלָלָא הֵיכְלֵהּ בְּגַוַּהּ, וּלְמֶעְקַר פָּלְחָנָא נֻכְרָאָה מִן אַרְעָא, וְלַאֲתָבָא פָּלְחָנָא דִּי שְׁמַיָּא לְאַתְרֵהּ, וְיַמְלִיךְ קֻדְשָׁא בְּרִיךְ הוּא בְּמַלְכוּתֵהּ וִיקָרֵהּ, בְּחַיֵּיכוֹן וּבְיוֹמֵיכוֹן וּבְחַיֵּי דְכָל בֵּית יִשְׂרָאֵל, בַּעֲגָלָא וּבִזְמַן קָרִיב. וְאִמְרוּ: אָמֵן. יְהֵא שְׁמֵהּ רַבָּא מְבָרַךְ לְעָלַם וּלְעָלְמֵי עָלְמַיָּא יִתְבָּרַךְ וְיִשְׁתַּבַּח וְיִתְפָּאַר וְיִתְרוֹמַם וְיִתְנַשֵּׂא וְיִתְהַדָּר וְיִתְעַלֶּה וְיִתְהַלָּל שְׁמֵהּ דְּקֻדְשָׁא בְּרִיךְ הוּא; לְעֵלָּא מִן כָּל בִּרְכָתָא וְשִׁירָתָא תֻּשְׁבְּחָתָא וְנֶחֱמָתָא, דַּאֲמִירָן בְּעָלְמָא. וְאִמְרוּ: אָמֵן.

עַל יִשְׂרָאֵל וְעַל רַבָּנָן, וְעַל תַּלְמִידֵיהוֹן וְעַל כָּל תַּלְמִידֵי תַלְמִידֵיהוֹן, וְעַל כָּל מָאן דְּעָסְקִין בְּאוֹרַיְתָא, דִּי בְּאַתְרָא הָדֵין וְדִי בְּכָל אֲתַר וַאֲתַר. יְהֵא לְהוֹן וּלְכוֹן שְׁלָמָא רַבָּא, חִנָּא וְחִסְדָּא וְרַחֲמִין, וְחַיִּין אֲרִיכִין, וּמְזוֹנֵי רְוִיחֵי, וּפֻרְקָנָא מִן קֳדָם אֲבוּהוֹן דִּי בִשְׁמַיָּא (וְאַרְעָא). וְאִמְרוּ: אָמֵן. יְהֵא שְׁלָמָא רַבָּא מִן שְׁמַיָּא, וְחַיִּים (טוֹבִים) עָלֵינוּ וְעַל כָּל יִשְׂרָאֵל. וְאִמְרוּ: אָמֵן.

עֹשֶׂה שָׁלוֹם בִּמְרוֹמָיו, הוּא בְּרַחֲמָיו יַעֲשֶׂה שָׁלוֹם עָלֵינוּ, וְעַל כָּל יִשְׂרָאֵל. וְאִמְרוּ: אָמֵן.